Legislatures

Legislatures
Comparative Perspectives on Representative Assemblies

Edited by
Gerhard Loewenberg,
Peverill Squire, and
D. Roderick Kiewiet

Ann Arbor
THE UNIVERSITY OF MICHIGAN PRESS

Copyright © by the University of Michigan 2002
All rights reserved
Published in the United States of America by
The University of Michigan Press
Manufactured in the United States of America
⊚ Printed on acid-free paper

2005   2004   2003   2002   4   3   2   1

No part of this publication may be reproduced, stored in a
retrieval system, or transmitted in any form or by any means,
electronic, mechanical, or otherwise, without the written
permission of the publisher.

A CIP catalog record for this book is available from the British Library.

Library of Congress Cataloging-in-Publication Data

Legislatures : comparative perspectives on representative assemblies / edited by Gerhard
   Loewenberg, Peverill Squire, and D. Roderick Kiewiet.
      p.   cm.
   Includes bibliographical references and index.
   ISBN 0-472-09790-3 (cloth) — ISBN 0-472-06790-7 (paper)
      1. Legislative bodies.   2. Comparative government.   I. Loewenberg, Gerhard.
II. Squire, Peverill.   III. Kiewiet, D. Roderick.

JF511 .L386   2002
328—dc21   2002023603

Contents

Preface vii

Part 1. Introduction

The Implications of the Study of the U.S. Congress for Comparative
Legislative Research 3
    D. Roderick Kiewiet, Gerhard Loewenberg, and Peverill Squire

Part 2. Legislative Recruitment and Legislative Careers

Legislative Careers: Why and How We Should Study Them 25
    John R. Hibbing
Recruitment and Retention in U.S. Legislatures 46
    Gary F. Moncrief
Recruitment and Retention in Western European Parliaments 80
    Werner J. Patzelt
Recruitment and Retention of Legislators in Brazil 119
    Fabiano Santos

Part 3. Legislative Representation

Electoral Systems and the Representation of Minority Interests in
Legislatures 149
    David T. Canon
The Study of Japan's Medium-Sized District System 178
    Sadafumi Kawato

Part 4. Party Structures in Legislatures

Divided Parties, Divided Government 201
    Michael Laver
Positive Theories of Congressional Parties 224
    Steven S. Smith

Part 5. Rules and Procedures in Legislatures

On the Effects of Legislative Rules 247
    Gary W. Cox
Parliamentary Floor Voting Procedures and Agenda Setting in Europe 269
    Bjørn Erik Rasch

Part 6. The Evolution of Legislatures

Transitional Governance in the United States: Lessons from the First Federal Congress 291
  Rick K. Wilson

Politicians, Bureaucrats, and Interest Groups in Japan: Transformation from One-Party Predominance or Not? 314
  Junko Kato

Change Is Short but Continuity Is Long: Policy Influence of the National Assembly in Newly Democratized Korea 329
  Chan Wook Park

Legislative Autonomy in New Regimes: The Czech and Polish Cases 352
  John M. Carey, Frantisek Formanek, and Ewa Karpowicz

Part 7. Conclusions

Assessing Comparative Legislative Research 387
  Kenneth A. Shepsle

Contributors 399

Index 401

Preface

The purpose of this book is to bridge the gap between the large, systematic body of scholarship on the U.S. Congress and the significant though more scattered scholarship on legislatures outside the United States. Although there is no single paradigm that guides research on Congress, there has been a succession of dominant methodologies. Among these the rational choice approach is the most recent. Furthermore, the sustained work on Congress has produced an accepted body of knowledge on many aspects of the institution, and considerable agreement on the current research agenda. By comparison, research on legislatures outside the United States employs a greater variety of methodologies and substantive emphases, influenced by the different contexts in which these legislatures exist and by differences in national scholarly traditions. The theories, concepts, and measures that guide this research have varied considerably. It is therefore difficult to relate the contributions of research on legislatures outside the United States to our general understanding of the legislative institution. The premise underlying this book is that students of the U.S. Congress and students of other legislatures have a great deal to learn from each other.

The political science literature on Congress is impressive but its findings are parochial in the sense that they are seldom tested in other legislative settings. Legislative specialists seem to be comfortable with the implicit but improbable conclusion that the U.S. Congress is unique. Overall, to the extent that legislative research is confined within national compartments, few generalizations can be made about legislatures as such.

In the introduction to this volume, we set out what we regard as the implications of research on Congress for the field of comparative legislative research. The subsequent essays—on legislative recruitment and careers; on legislative representation; on party structures in legislatures; on rules and procedures; and on the evolution of legislatures—demonstrate that there is by now considerable convergence in methods and substantive interests among all legislative scholars. The final essay draws some conclusions about past obstacles to that convergence and about present prospects for its further development.

Many of the essays in this volume were originally presented at an international legislative research conference at the University of Iowa in 1998. We are grateful to the National Science Foundation, the Benjamin F. Shambaugh Memorial Fund, the Charles Stewart Mott Foundation, and the University of Iowa for their support of this conference. We appreciate the work of Karen Stewart, Administrative Assistant in the Department of Political Science at the University of Iowa, for her work in organizing the conference.

The papers presented at the conference were the subject of discussion and of written critiques by a group of distinguished commentators: Richard Calland (Cape Town Democracy Center), Herbert Döring (University of Potsdam), Heinz Eulau (Stanford University), C. Lawrence Evans (College of William and Mary), Malcolm E. Jewell (University of Kentucky), Keith Krehbiel (Stanford University), David R. Mayhew (Yale University), Michael L. Mezey (DePaul University), Njuguna Ng'ethe (University of Nairobi), Lia Nijzink (University of Leiden), Samuel C. Patterson (Ohio State University), Suzanne Schüttemeyer (University of Halle), Käare Strøm (University of California at San Diego), and John R. Wright (Ohio State University). On the basis of that discussion, all of the papers were substantially revised.

The essays in this volume by John R. Hibbing, Gary F. Moncrief, Werner J. Patzelt, Fabiano Santos, David T. Canon, Michael Laver, Steven S. Smith, Gary W. Cox, Bjørn Erik Rasch, Rick K. Wilson, and John M. Carey, Frantisek Formanek, and Ewa Karpowicz were first published in the *Legislative Studies Quarterly*. We thank the Comparative Legislative Research Center of the University of Iowa, which publishes this journal, for permission to reprint these essays here. Finally, we are grateful to Michelle L. Wiegand, Managing Editor of the *Quarterly,* for supervising all aspects of the publication of these essays.

We intend this volume, and the substantial references to the literature that accompany each essay, to be both a reflection of and a contribution to cross-national collaboration in the field of legislative studies. We hope it will strengthen comparative legislative research.

                                        Gerhard Loewenberg
                                        Peverill Squire
                                        D. Roderick Kiewiet

                                        Iowa City, Iowa,
                                        Pasadena, California,
                                        May 1, 2001

Part 1
Introduction

The Implications of the Study of the U.S. Congress for Comparative Legislative Research

D. Roderick Kiewiet, Gerhard Loewenberg, and Peverill Squire

Introduction

Comparative research is at the heart of the social scientific enterprise, but too little of it ever gets done. In the prodigious amount of research that has been devoted to the U.S. Congress, scholars have rarely investigated whether their findings were generalizable to legislative institutions outside the United States or, conversely, whether research on other legislatures had implications for the understanding of Congress. Our theories have rarely sought to identify the equivalences among structures, procedures, and behaviors in legislative institutions in diverse national settings.

There are many reasons why not enough has been done to place studies of Congress in a comparative context. There is the simple matter of numbers: far more scholars have been engaged in research on Congress than on legislatures in other countries. With its complicated, interlaced system of party caucuses and committees and other unusual and seemingly idiosyncratic characteristics, it is also understandable that many scholars have regarded Congress as sui generis and do not believe that our understanding of it is aided by comparisons with other institutions. Furthermore, the data and methodologies employed in the study of Congress are so closely tied to its distinctive characteristics that they seem to have very limited applicability to the study of other legislatures.

However, for two major reasons this is a good time to undertake a strong, new initiative in comparative legislative research. First, students of the U.S. Congress in the last two decades have developed new theoretical models of legislative behavior and brought to bear new streams of data. These provide new perspectives and techniques for legislative research that have influenced some analyses of legislatures outside of the United States; prominent examples include studies by Cain, Ferejohn, and Fiorina (1987), Huber (1992), Heller (1994), and Laver and Shepsle (1996). Second, during the past decade new (or newly reestablished) legislatures have come into being in many countries throughout the world—in the former Soviet-bloc countries of Central and Eastern Europe, in Latin America, and in many parts of Africa and Asia. Several scholars have applied some of the key models and analytical techniques developed to investigate the U.S. Congress to these new legislatures (e.g., Hibbing and Patterson 1992; Myagkov and Kiewiet 1996; Remington and Smith 1995, 1996; Londregan 1996), but they have just begun to scratch the surface. As Patzelt (1994) explains, "empirical political science, for well-known reasons, has had no strong tradition in the former communist states, and research on parliamentary democracy has had no object on which to focus. Experience, skills, and infrastructure for such studies are still generally lacking in Central and Eastern Europe, which should make cooperation with Western scholars highly attractive" (442).

What is particularly exciting about the establishment of new legislatures for scholars is that they are able to witness contemporaneously the choices made in designing these new institutions. The long history of the U.S. Congress reveals that many of its key features are the unintended and unanticipated consequences of early choices. Today constitutional engineering and the actual design of legislative organizations are proceeding more quickly than is our scientific understanding of these institutions. Hopefully, by observing in new legislative settings the consequences of institutional choice, particularly for policy outcomes, our science will catch up to the engineering. We hope that as these legislatures evolve to meet new and different demands placed upon them, our understanding of them will grow as well.

A final and perhaps most important reason for pursuing comparative legislative research is that so much of the recent research on the U.S. Congress has been inconclusive. There is a strong sense among congressional scholars that the theoretical insights that have driven research over the past few decades, derived primarily from various manifestations of the rational choice approach, have raised many issues but resolved few of them. One set of controversies has superseded another. Rival theories of congressional organization and policymaking have emerged that, instead of yielding different empirical predictions, "have virtually identical observational implications for a wide range of legislative phenomena" (Ferejohn 1995, ix). The analytical problem this presents is that of "observational equivalence": what are commonly regarded as the major empirical properties of Congress and congressional policy-making are consistent with quite different and competing theoretical perspectives.

It is possible that increasingly sophisticated analyses of data on the U.S. Congress, such as roll call votes, amendment activity, and committee membership lists, may provide ways of disentangling the predictions of one theory from those of another. But it seems to us more likely that renewed progress in our understanding of legislatures will come from comparative research involving the U.S. Congress and other national legislatures. Although formal theories of legislative organization and behavior have been derived primarily from the particular environment of Congress, their abstractness may make it possible to test these theories in the diverse settings of other national and subnational legislatures. For this to happen, congressional scholars need to become more aware of the state of research on other legislatures. That is the purpose of this volume.

In this introductory essay we will summarize the principal lines of research that have been pursued recently by scholars studying the U.S. Congress and enumerate some of the questions raised by this research that might be explored by the comparative study of legislatures.

Recent Research on the U.S. Congress:
A Brief Overview

In the last two decades most of the major innovations in the field of U.S. congressional research result from a shift in the field's theoretical center of gravity from a generally sociological, systems-theory approach to that of rational choice. As most scholars both within and outside the rational choice camp would agree, "instrumental rationality has been the theoretical engine" driving the field (Shepsle and Weingast 1995, 5), especially when coupled with the assumption that the primary goal of the individual member is reelection.

The impact of the rational choice approach upon the field of congressional research has been evolutionary rather than revolutionary. It has not caused the severe methodological disputes that have occurred elsewhere in the discipline of political science. There are many reasons why this has been the case, but the major one may simply be the members of the U.S. Congress themselves. The assumption that these actors, existing as they do in an intensely competitive political environment, are engaged primarily in purposive behavior intended to further their reelection goals seems eminently plausible. Some of the first major studies of Congress that were explicitly informed by a rational choice perspective stressed the extent to which the everyday activities of members of Congress—advertising, credit-claiming, position-taking, and problem-fixing—could be understood as an ongoing campaign for reelection (Mayhew 1974; Fiorina 1977). Other scholars have employed the calculus of expected utility maximization in analyzing congressional career decisions—whether or not to run for office, whether to seek reelection to the House or to run for higher office, and whether and when to retire (Rohde 1979; Jacobson and Kernell 1981; Hibbing 1982; Kiewiet and Zeng 1993; Francis et al. 1994).

In their research, Mayhew and Fiorina show how the nature of the "electoral connection" between members of Congress and their constituencies is a function of the particular constitutional and historical context in which they operate. Elected from single-member districts, they can serve as monopoly suppliers of "bureaucratic unsticking services" (Fiorina 1977, 47) to their constituents. They are able to build individual bases of political support distinct from and independent of the party to which they belong. If they are incumbents, they possess formidable resources of money, staff, and access to the media. Cain, Ferejohn, and Fiorina (1987) found that by the 1980s some members of the British Parliament were also seeking to build their own personal constituency base but lacked the resources available to their U.S. counterparts. Members of parliament in other countries may have more resources than British MPs have, but nothing close to the resources available to members of the U.S. Congress.

The previous generation of scholarship on Congress, using the framework of sociological systems theory and structural functionalism, employed data on the attitudes and behavior of individual members to support its generalizations. The major empirical questions that motivated researchers in this tradition included such things as how legislators viewed their roles, the degree to which they felt constrained by their constituents or by party and committee leaders, the ways in which they were socialized into the ongoing norms and folkways of the institution, and the informational cues they used to navigate a complex and highly uncertain environment (Matthews 1960; Wahlke et al. 1962; Fenno 1966; Kingdon 1973). Such questions remain interesting to many scholars within the rational choice camp, particularly to those concerned with the role of reputation (Kreps and Wilson 1982), signaling and information revelation (Spence 1974; Ferejohn and Shipan 1989) and culture (Kreps 1990; Milgrom and Roberts 1992). Moreover, data on the behavior of individual members remain of central concern to congressional scholars. There is, for instance, currently a lively debate over how best to scale the data on individual roll call votes (Poole and Rosenthal 1997; Heckman and Snyder 1997).

Paradoxically, while attempts to support systems-theoretical explanations of legislative behavior primarily employed individual-level data, attempts to support rational choice explanations have generally made *assumptions* about individual choice and behavior, and have used macrolevel data on collective results to support their theories. We will return below to the problems of evidence and inference in the study of legislatures.

Once the rational choice approach took hold, social choice theory, game theory, spatial modeling, and the "New Institutionalism" (North 1990) broadly influenced the study of Congress. Shepsle and Weingast (1995) identify the most important theoretical and empirical developments that emerged from this line of inquiry. As they see it, a first generation of studies sought to explain why congressional policy-making seemed to exhibit so much stability and incrementalism when social choice theory predicted that a succession of votes would produce a cycling of majorities, that there was pervasive opportunity for agenda manipulation, and that equilibrium outcomes would not occur (Ferejohn and Fiorina 1975; Tullock 1981).

A second generation of studies sought to show that stable, conclusive outcomes of legislative deliberations were the result of institutional and procedural restrictions on the way in which a legislature made its choices. Shepsle (1979) showed that if each dimension of policy choice is placed under the jurisdiction of a single committee, and if committees possessed a monopoly over the making of proposals in that jurisdiction, a "structure-induced" equilibrium would emerge. Similar models have been developed and applied to the interaction between chambers in bicameral regimes (Tsebelis and Money 1997) and to the three-way interplay between the House, the Senate, and the president (Krehbiel 1998). A related line of research concerned the role of committees in fixing the distribution of government benefits to the districts and states of individual congressmen and senators. The generic theoretical problem faced here is illustrated by the simple game in which three people must decide on how to divide a dollar by means of majority rule: for any proposal that might be made there always exists a counterproposal that will defeat it. Ferejohn (1986) and others have argued that committees endowed with significant parliamentary prerogatives could serve as the crucial mechanism for ensuring that once an agreement on the distribution of benefits was struck—a "logroll," in the parlance of the trade—it would not subsequently be overturned.

A major contribution of this body of research was to offer a theoretically consistent explanation of major aspects of the behavior of the U.S. Congress. It emphasized the crucial role of the agenda-setting process in legislatures. Every legislature confronts an infinity of potential issues and policy choices but, given the limits of time and labor, it can consider only a small number of proposals in a given session. "Sequential" choice theory, which has been posed as an alternative to the structure-induced equilibrium approach, underscores how important it is simply to have the right to present a proposal to the legislature. According to its proponents, the fact that proposals must necessarily be taken up in sequence, coupled with the perfectly reasonable assumption that members are at least slightly risk averse, implies that choices made by a legislature can be stable without further institutionally imposed restrictions on the consideration of legislation (Enelow 1986; Baron and Ferejohn 1989). In short, to understand the process by which policy choices are proposed, filtered, and ultimately considered is to understand a great deal about how the institution works.

Just as the ideas of structure-induced equilibria and committee-based logrolling arose in response to the questions raised by earlier studies, these in turn have provoked a third generation of theorizing and empirical analysis. Riker (1980), Shepsle (1986), and others argued that while it is important to understand how particular institutional arrangements can yield stable, equilibrium outcomes, it is also necessary to understand how these arrangements are themselves chosen by the legislature. Or, as Gilligan and Krehbiel (1995) put it, "[a] theory of legislative organization should not merely identify desirable properties associated with an organizational form and then assume (usually implicitly) that because the form possesses desirable aggregate properties it will therefore be chosen by self-interested individuals" (57).

The third generation of research that is currently emerging has come up with a number of different explanations for the way in which Congress organizes itself. The first explanation, the "distributional" or "gains from exchange" hypothesis, holds that legislators with diverse policy preferences and priorities find it in their interest to surrender parliamentary prerogatives, and thus policy influence, in areas which they do not care about, in return for greater authority and influence in policy domains which are more important to them (Weingast and Marshall 1988). Doing so is "in their interest," of course, because it enables them to achieve more favorable outcomes in areas that are salient to their constituents and thus furthers their reelection prospects. These considerations thus lead members to adopt an organizational arrangement that assigns agenda-setting authority to jurisdictionally distinct committees while simultaneously allowing members to serve on the committees of their choice.

Krehbiel (1991) offers a different organizational rationale. He asserts that the basic principle of congressional organization is not distributional but rather informational: individual members must be given sufficient incentive both to engage in the hard work of obtaining information concerning the probable consequences of different policy choices and then to reveal this valuable information to the rest of the legislature rather than to extract the advantages that inhere in having private information. As he puts it, "the challenge of legislative organization . . . is to capture gains from specialization while minimizing the degree to which enacted policies deviate from majority-preferred outcomes" (5).

Finally, a number of scholars, including Rohde (1991), Kiewiet and McCubbins (1991), Cox and McCubbins (1993), and Dion (1997), regard the majority party within Congress as a coherent actor that has the prerogative to organize or to reorganize the institution. The structure of Congress and the procedures it follows in making policy are thus products of the way in which the majority party has chosen to delegate authority.

There are many assumptions about the U.S. Congress that scholars share, most notably the centrality of the reelection motive, the rational basis of congressional career decisions, and the crucial importance of agenda setting. Moreover, the rational choice approach has identified a key set of questions that can be fruitfully posed in almost any imaginable legislative setting. Such questions include the following:

1. What are the major features of the electoral connection between members of the legislature and the voters, and how do they affect the behavior, strategies, and career choices of individual legislators?

2. What is the underlying rationale for the organizational structure of the legislature?
3. To what extent can we usefully regard the political party within the legislature to be a unitary actor?
4. How do the rules and procedures under which the decisions of the legislature are made determine the opportunities for agenda setting? For instance, does procedure tend to favor those who move first (i.e., those who propose a motion) or those, armed with veto power, who move last? How does procedure take account of party interests in agenda setting?
5. Does the way in which the legislature is organized disproportionately favor "preference outliers," that is, members with relatively extreme views with respect to a particular policy, or more moderate, centrist members?

When thinking of the U.S. Congress, the unit of observation is usually the individual member. In other legislatures, it may well be parliamentary parties or parliamentary coalitions.

Observational Equivalence, Stylized Facts, and Institutional Change

While the rational choice approach has produced a consensus on a set of central research questions, it has not reached a consensus on the theoretical explanations for the observations of Congress that it has generated. In fact, the field of congressional studies currently finds itself at something of a theoretical impasse. One of the major symptoms (if not the cause) of this impasse, as indicated earlier, is that different theories about the basic nature of the U.S. Congress tend to yield highly similar empirical predictions. Put another way, it has proven difficult to devise critical tests based on the observations of the U.S. Congress in which the relative merits of various theories can be clearly distinguished. Let us turn to a few examples of the problem of "observational equivalence," some of which we have already mentioned.

Stability in policy choices. Many scholars have concluded that the policy outcomes that emerge from Congress are not marked by the majority-rule cycling and otherwise chaotic behavior that social choice theory would suggest, but are instead highly stable. But why? Is it because equilibrium outcomes are "structurally induced" by the organization of Congress and the rules under which it considers legislation? Is it because most policy conflict in Congress occurs along a simple, underlying liberal versus conservative dimension—a condition under which we would expect equilibria to exist? Or is the mere fact that proposals must be considered sequentially sufficient to ensure stable policy choices (Baron and Ferejohn 1989)?

Other explanations for policy stability are implied by more general accounts of congressional policy-making. One derives from the long-standing critique that the decentralized, committee-based nature of Congress gives way to policy-making by "subgovernments," that is, collusive arrangements of powerful interest groups, administrative agencies, and congressional committees. Policy changes little because the preferences of relevant interest groups (for government contracts, protection from competitors, and tax breaks), the preferences of committee members (for campaign contributions), and the preferences of bureaucrats (for friendly treatment by oversight committees now and a job in the private sector later) change little. Yet another possibility is that the policy positions and priorities of the major parties, selected out in the vigorous, Downsian competition of the electoral arena, do not differ enough to produce dramatic policy change even when there is a shift in party control in Congress.

Deference to committees. Many scholars have found it remarkable that individual members of Congress apparently "defer" to committees and thus refrain from offering amendments to committee proposals when they come to the floor. Likewise, large majorities in Congress routinely approve rules that dramatically restrict (sometimes completely) the ability of individual members to offer floor amendments (Bach and Smith 1988). This pattern of reciprocal deference was conventionally viewed as a cooperative arrangement in which members yield their right to amend the bills produced by other committees in the expectation that other members would in turn defer to proposals coming out of their committee.

However, Shepsle and Weingast (1987) offer a different explanation. They have shown that members rarely propose amendments to committee proposals because the committee is able subsequently to ignore such changes for the following reason. The Senate and House rarely pass identical versions of a bill; the two chambers send members to a conference committee to reconcile differences. Customary practice is to send members of the original committees of jurisdiction. The resultant legislative product, the conference report, is then sent back to each chamber where it is considered for final approval *without* the floor amendments that the committee found objectionable. Seeking to amend bills sponsored by committees with this sort of "ex post veto" authority is thus an exercise in futility.

Legislative lassitude. A long-standing theme in the scholarly literature on U.S. politics is that Congress has ceded much of its authority to nonelected officials in the executive branch: Congress relies heavily upon the president, the Office of Management and Budget, and other executive agencies for legislative initiative and, once it has enacted legislation, pays little heed to the manner in which agencies charged with carrying out policy actually implement it. The consequence is a loss of electoral accountability, the ascendancy of subgovernments, and the replacement of representative democracy by an administrative state. Alternative explanations can be given for these observations. Beginning with Weingast and Moran (1983), many scholars have argued that if Congress has delegated effectively and created the proper incentives, agencies will carry out their missions so as to not provoke congressional sanctions, thus assuring agency responsiveness without continual congressional scrutiny. McCubbins, Noll, and Weingast (1989) place particular emphasis upon the ways in which congressionally mandated rules and procedures constrain the choices made by administrative agencies.

As students of comparative politics are well aware, legislatures in many other countries have been similarly characterized as ineffectual. Indeed, Bryce (1921) made this observation about legislatures throughout the Western world over seventy-five years ago. In recent decades some scholars have asserted that the Japanese Diet is irrelevant to the policy-making process, serving primarily to rubber-stamp decisions made in the inner circles of the country's powerful ministries (Johnson 1982). McCubbins and Noble (1995) challenge this view with much the same reasoning employed by Weingast and Moran. They point out that the fact that the Diet routinely approves ministerial proposals does not preclude the possibility that the need for the approval of the Diet imposes real constraints on the ministries and that in formulating their proposals they take this into account ex ante.

Party and preferences. Roll call votes cast by members of one party caucus in Congress differ reliably from the roll call votes cast by members of the other party. The strength of this correlation between roll call voting behavior and party varies over time, but during the past quarter century or so it has been quite strong. About this fact there is little disagreement. But congressional scholars disagree sharply about what these observed party differences mean. In one view, congressional parties, while not capable of imposing the lockstep party discipline characteristic of parliamentary regimes, can achieve a reasonable approximation of it known as "conditional party government" (Rohde 1991). Proponents of this view reason that as policy preferences within a congressional party become more homogenous, members find it in their interests to delegate more authority to party leaders, who in turn are able to induce more uniformity on roll call votes. In a conditional party government regime, some members choose to support their party when a calculation based solely upon personal preferences (and/or constituency interests) would lead them to do otherwise. Conditional party government thus posits a positive feedback loop between preference homogeneity and party discipline on roll call votes.

A contrary view, championed primarily by Krehbiel (1993), is that congressional parties are indeed collections of like-minded people, but parties *as legislative organizations* may exercise no significant influence over legislation. Democrats in Congress tend to vote like other Democrats, and Republicans like other Republicans, but this may be simply because they hold similar policy preferences. When their preferences are at odds with those held by most other party members, they can (and do) defect and vote with the other party. As Krehbiel puts it:

> In casting apparently partisan votes, do individual legislators vote with fellow party members *in spite of their disagreement* about the policy in question, or do they vote with party members *because of their agreement* about the policy in question? . . . The temptation—as well as the tendency in the literature—is to infer that, since party members vote cohesively over the policies under consideration, parties are strong in a policy-relevant way. However, a comparably plausible inference is that, since individuals vote perfectly consistently with their preferences, parties are not policy-relevant. . . . the data cannot discriminate between a party hypothesis and a preference hypothesis. (238)

Krehbiel is open to the possibility that the party organizations in Congress may constrain the behavior of their members and so exercise an important policy-making role, and that the conditional party government scenario may account for when this does or does not occur. What he rejects is the idea that a positive feedback loop between preference homogeneity and party discipline can be inferred from the strength of the correlation between party label and roll call voting behavior.

In seeking to isolate what Krehbiel calls "significant party effects," researchers have pursued a number of strategies. Snyder and Groseclose (1997) proceed by first deriving an estimate of members' locations on a liberal—conservative continuum that is based solely upon lopsided votes. They assume that members encounter no pressure from their party on such votes (the outcome is a foregone conclusion) and so take this to be a measure of members' true policy preferences. They then examine close votes and seek to determine if knowing a member's party improves predictions based solely upon the original measure of preferences. They find it does and attribute this to the effect of party. McCarty, Poole, and Rosenthal (1999), however, conclude that the Snyder-Groseclose method may erroneously identify party effects when none are actually present.

Following another lead, Sinclair (1998) documents instances in which majority party members vote in favor of a restrictive rule in bringing a bill to the floor, but end up opposing the bill on final passage. She explains this inconsistency as members showing that they may support their party's position on legislation even though they themselves do not favor it. Nokken (1998) gives another example; he finds that the twenty members of Congress who from 1947 through 1997 changed their party affiliations altered their voting behavior dramatically at the time of the switch. Assuming that underlying preferences change only gradually, he attributes these sharp discontinuities in behavior to the replacement of one set of party pressures by another set pushing in the opposite direction.

A particularly promising new approach to this problem is that of Ansolabehere, Snyder, and Stewart (1999). They use the responses of congressional incumbents and other candidates to issue position questions posed in a survey (the National Political Aptitude Test) to derive measures of preferences that are independent of the roll call voting behavior. They report that on many (though not all) roll calls, knowledge of a member's party membership does significantly augment the accuracy of predictions based only upon this preference measure. Another strategy is pursued by Cox and McCubbins (1999), who argue that the majority party leadership does not act so much to constrain the roll call votes of their members as it does to determine just what it is they vote on. The majority party, in other words, controls the agenda, as evidenced by data indicating that the House almost never passes bills that are opposed by a majority of the majority party.

Evidence and Inference

There are many reasons why the same facts may be consistent with very different competing theories. The major ones are as follows.

The problem of expectations. We can assume that members of legislatures are rational players who base their actions upon their forecasts of the choices others will make, either contemporaneously or at later stages of the process. This anticipation of what other actors will do informs all of the instances of observational equivalence discussed previously. Congress may make no effort to effect policy change because of the high probability the president would veto the legislation. A committee that is seemingly powerful because the bill it reported was not amended on the floor may have simply done a very good job of gauging sentiment in the parent chamber. An agency deemed to be largely autonomous because its congressional overseers never take corrective or punitive measures may have been effectively constrained by the terms of Congress's delegation of authority. Party organizations, finally, may achieve high levels of loyalty on roll call votes by choosing not to advance bills that would be difficult for many of their members to support.

Stylized facts. The empirical records used to test rational choice explanations of legislative behavior often consist of "stylized facts"—admittedly rough approximations of reality, but, the argument goes, realistic enough to describe the phenomena that theory needs to explain. A simplification of complex reality is always a necessary aspect of empirical testing of theory, but in recent research it may have gone too far. Instead of seeking to explain general deference to committees, perhaps we should try to explain variation, either temporal or cross-sectional, in the extent to which committee bills are challenged by floor amendments (Bach and Smith 1988). Similarly, instead of seeking to explain why congressional policy choices are so stable, it may be better to try to explain the conditions under which major policy changes are likely to occur (Mayhew 1991; Krehbiel 1998).

Change in the object of study. There is still another reason why it is difficult to choose among competing theories on the basis of stylized facts gathered from observations of a single legislature. A legislative institution does not hold still: it changes. Many of the stylized facts discussed above were associated with a "textbook Congress" (Shepsle 1989) that existed before the mid-1970s and that has changed rapidly since then even as congressional scholars were seeking to provide theoretically compelling accounts for it. First, there was the withering away of committee deference. Beginning in the 1970s, under the auspices of new rules and new technology, members began challenging many more committee-sponsored bills by offering more and more floor amendments (Smith 1989). A series of reforms undertaken in the 1970s significantly enhanced the role of both subcommittees and the leadership of the majority party. In 1994 Republicans in the 104th Congress, attaining majority status for the first time in forty years, ignored seniority in selecting many committee chairmen, abolished some committees entirely, and circumvented the entire committee structure by developing proposed legislation under the auspices of party-based task forces (Fenno 1997).

The arrival of relatively large numbers of newcomers in Congress—seventy-five Democrats in 1974 and seventy-three Republicans in 1994—was the proximate cause for much of this change. Many of the new members in these sessions insisted on changing the rules by which policy was made in order to move policy in the direction that they preferred (Loomis 1988; Fenno 1997). Furthermore, Diermeier (1995) demonstrates that "norms of deference may collapse due to a large influx of new legislators even if the new legislators have exactly the same preferences as the senior members they replace" (345).

The view that congressional policy outcomes are stable has also become more problematic as successive Congresses in the 1980s and 1990s have adopted major policy changes. As the facts about Congress have changed, scholars face the difficulty of determining whether their theories should be tested with the observations of the "textbook Congress" that existed before 1974 or the Congress that has evolved since that time.

We have suggested that the field of congressional research finds itself at something of a theoretical impasse because observations of Congress are consistent with very different theoretical perspectives. However, this research has generated a series of fundamental questions about legislative institutions and institutional change that can usefully guide the study of other legislatures.

1. What institutional features of the legislature contribute to stability in policy outcomes?
2. Do there appear to be patterns of deference within the legislature or within legislative party organizations? If so, under what conditions does this deference occur? Is observed deference more apparent than real?
3. Does the legislature appear to be weak and ineffectual, especially in comparison with the bureaucracy? If so, is this actually the case?
4. Does the entry of a large number of new members or new party alignments lead to significant changes in the organization of the legislature and in the way in which it considers legislation?
5. Is the degree of congruence between party membership and roll call voting behavior greater than what would result from the congruence in members' policy preferences?

Observations of legislatures outside the United States might well help us to choose among alternative theoretical explanations of behavior observed in the U.S. Congress.

Historical Studies of Congress and the Design of New Legislatures

Some of the most important contributions to the study of the U.S. Congress are those that have documented and sought to explain its historical evolution. Polsby (1968) charted several important trends in the history of the House of Representatives, most notably the increasing professionalization (or at least careerism) of its membership, indicated by the decline in the percentage of first-term members and the concomitant increase in the average number of terms served. Among other important examples of historical congressional scholarship are Cooper's (1970) study of the origins and development of the committee system, Brady's (1988) analysis of critical elections and congressional policy-making, Stewart's (1989) study of the appropriations process, and Poole and Rosenthal's (1997) history of roll call voting.

These and other historical studies add an important dimension to our scientific understanding of the institution. They also speak most directly and concretely to the issues confronting contemporary political engineers—the politicians in countries throughout the world who are seeking to establish and nurture new national legislatures. They face the same formidable challenges encountered by those who gathered in Philadelphia over two hundred years ago and must see their way through a series of difficult choices. As Reynolds (1995) puts it, "the task of the constitutional engineer is to find the least imperfect system and then adapt it to the needs of the emerging democracy" (97).

The history of the U.S. Congress holds a number of lessons. First, it is likely that new legislatures will evolve in ways that their founders never anticipated. As detailed in Cooper's (1970) study of the early Congress, the Jeffersonian vision of Congress was of an extremely egalitarian assembly, "a forum where every member was a peer and no man led" (14). Bills were to be taken up initially by the full membership of the House, which, after determining the "general principles" of the legislation, would assign to a small committee the narrow task of formulating the details. Congress might call upon executive officers to provide purely factual testimony regarding pending legislation, but they were to be given no role in initiating policy and no discretion in implementing it. Within a short time, however, the original vision repeatedly gave way to practical necessity. By the early nineteenth century the House considered legislation only after the standing committees to which it had been initially referred reported it out to the floor. Executive departments were increasingly the source of legislative proposals within their jurisdictions, and the principle that appointed officers of the government could (and should) exercise considerable discretion in carrying out policy had been firmly established.

A second lesson is that changes in electoral laws may have unintended and unanticipated consequences for the structure and operation of the legislature. In the 1890s, for example, individual states enacted a series of election law reforms, most notably the replacement of party-strip ballots, supplied by the parties and already completed, with ballots supplied by the government that the voter marked in the secrecy of the voting booth. These reforms were directed primarily at the corrupt practices of large, urban, and usually Democratic "machines," but they also increased both the ability and the need of congressional candidates to build individual reputations over and above their party affiliation. According to the analysis by Katz and Sala (1996), the unintended consequence of these reforms was thus the rapid growth in Congress of the "property right" norm of reappointment, by which returning members of Congress automatically retained their previous committee assignments. This study obviously incorporates the third-generation perspective (referred to above) that the way in which Congress is organized is itself the product of other choices. Institutional arrangements must be consistent with the electoral motivations of the members.

Third, it is a critical stage in the life of a legislature when its members come to view their service in it as a long-term career. During the nineteenth century the extent of membership turnover in Congress from election to election declined dramatically. Indeed, in many early Congresses it was not uncommon for members to leave, never to return, before serving even one full term. As shown by Kernell (1977), the trend toward longer congressional careers was partly due to higher reelection rates, but its primary cause was the growing tendency of incumbents to seek reelection. Once elected to the House, more and more members desired to remain there for an extended period of time. According to Price (1975), it was the long-run perspective of congressional careerists that led them to increasingly support the norms that underlay the classic committee system—the automatic reassignment of incumbents to the committees on which they had served previously, and advancement to the chairmanship on the basis of seniority. Price's conclusions are bolstered by the findings of Squire's (1992) analysis of the evolution of the California Assembly in the decades following World War II. He observed many of the same trends as had Polsby—particularly, growing professionalization—but no evidence that seniority had come to matter much in naming members to positions of leadership. He attributes this to a crucial difference in electoral motivation. Because so many members of the California Assembly see their current position as only a stepping-stone to higher office, they lack the long-term career perspective that fosters adherence to seniority and property-rights norms.

To a considerable extent the structural and procedural development of legislatures is path dependent. Decisions about committee prerogatives taken in the 1990s reflect decisions made in the same legislature in prior decades. A particular institutional arrangement reflects the interests of members, and change depends on a change in these interests. Because of this dependency of present upon past arrangements, we cannot really understand institutional change in legislatures without observing a variety of examples of this institution.

The development of new or fundamentally reorganized legislatures in many countries outside the United States and Western Europe provides us with an exceptional opportunity to observe institutional change. Our discussion of historical research on the U.S. Congress suggests a number of questions that might be useful to consider in undertaking comparative studies of these rapidly developing institutions.

1. What are the motives that guide formative choices about organization and procedure of legislatures?
2. What factors influence the institutional autonomy of legislatures?
3. Is the equilibrium in which existing institutional arrangements are embedded stable, or is it the product of conditions that could change suddenly or unexpectedly?
4. What is the institutional consequence of whether members of the legislature view service in it as a long-term career or as a short-term avocation?

Prospects for Comparative Legislative Research

This overview of recent research on the U.S. Congress and of the unresolved theoretical issues that this research has raised underscores the value of broadening the study of legislatures to include the many other instances of the institution that exist in the world. A truly comparative study of legislatures can help us to answer questions that even the intensive study of one legislature must necessarily leave unresolved. But comparative study requires some agreement on the basic concepts to be employed, the most promising theories to be tested, and the equivalence of the measures to be used. This is no simple matter in a field that has been marked by a relatively parochial approach in which each country's legislative scholars have tended to regard their country's legislature as the unique product of its history and society.

In the essays that follow, there are some recurrent themes that encourage us to believe that there are indeed key concepts that can serve in the observation of a wide variety of examples of legislatures. Four of the following essays employ the concepts of recruitment, membership turnover, professionalization, and careerism. They discuss the impact of members' career incentives on institutional stability. Two essays deal with the "electoral connection" and particularly with the relationship between the electoral system and the composition of legislatures. Two deal with party structures and suggest the importance of recognizing the varieties of party organization of legislatures. Two further essays relate the effect of variation in the rules of procedure on legislative outcomes. Finally, four essays consider the continuities and discontinuities that exist in the evolution of legislatures in different historical settings.

These essays, written by students of the U.S. Congress, of U.S. state legislatures, and of the legislatures of an array of Asian, European, and Latin American legislatures, also suggest that the study of varieties of legislatures can expand the empirical record of legislative behavior that we now have. They provide evidence of the variance of institutional attributes that we miss by a single-minded attention to just one legislature at a time. In a concluding essay, one of the pioneers of the rational choice approach to the study of legislatures, Kenneth Shepsle, assesses the extent to which the essays comprising this volume suggest answers to the questions we have raised in this introduction.

REFERENCES

Ansolabehere, Stephen, James Snyder, and Charles Stewart. 1999. "The Effects of Party and Preferences on Congressional Roll Call Voting." Manuscript, Massachusetts Institute of Technology.
Bach, Stanley, and Steven Smith. 1988. *Managing Uncertainty in the House of Representatives: Adaptation and Innovation in Special Rules*. Washington, DC: Brookings Institution.
Baron, David, and John Ferejohn. 1989. "Bargaining in Legislatures." *American Political Science Review* 83:1181–1206.
Brady, David. 1988. *Critical Elections and Congressional Policy Making*. Stanford: Stanford University Press.

Bryce, James. 1921. "The Decline of Legislatures." Reprinted in Gerhard Loewenberg, ed., *Modern Parliaments: Change or Decline?* Chicago: Aldine Atherton, 1970.

Cain, Bruce, John Ferejohn, and Morris Fiorina. 1987. *The Personal Vote.* Cambridge: Harvard University Press.

Cooper, Joseph. 1970. *The Origins of the Standing Committees and the Development of the Modern House.* Houston: Rice University.

Cox, Gary, and Mathew McCubbins. 1993. *Legislative Leviathan.* Berkeley: University of California Press.

Cox, Gary, and Mathew McCubbins. 1999. "Agenda Power in the U.S. House of Representatives." Presented at the Conference on the History of Congress, Stanford University.

Diermeier, Daniel. 1995. "Commitment, Deference, and Legislative Institutions." *American Political Science Review* 89:344–55.

Dion, Douglas. 1997. *Turning the Legislative Thumbscrew: Minority Rights and Procedural Change in Legislative Politics.* Ann Arbor: University of Michigan Press.

Enelow, James. 1986. "The Stability of Logrolling: An Expectations Approach." *Public Choice* 51:285–94.

Fenno, Richard. 1966. *The Power of the Purse.* Boston: Little, Brown.

Fenno, Richard. 1997. *Learning to Govern.* Washington, DC: Brookings Institution.

Ferejohn, John. 1986. "Logrolling in an Institutional Context: A Case Study of Food Stamp Legislation." In *Congress and Policy Change,* ed. Gerald Wright, Leroy Rieselbach, and Lawrence Dodd. New York: Agathon.

Ferejohn, John. 1995. "Foreword." In *Positive Theories of Congressional Institutions,* ed. Kenneth Shepsle and Barry Weingast. Ann Arbor: University of Michigan Press.

Ferejohn, John, and Morris Fiorina. 1975. "Purposive Models of Legislative Behavior." *American Economic Review, Papers and Proceedings* 65:407–15.

Ferejohn, John, and Charles Shipan. 1989. "Congressional Influence on Administrative Agencies: A Case Study of Telecommunications Policy." In *Congress Reconsidered,* 4th ed., ed. Lawrence Dodd and Bruce Oppenheimer. Washington, DC: Congressional Quarterly Press.

Fiorina, Morris. 1977. *Congress: Keystone of the Washington Establishment.* New Haven: Yale University Press.

Francis, Wayne, Lawrence Kenny, Rebecca Morton, and Amy Schmidt. 1994. "Retrospective Voting and Political Mobility." *American Journal of Political Science* 38:999–1024.

Gilligan, Thomas, and Keith Krehbiel. 1995. "The Gains from Exchange Hypothesis of Legislative Organization." In *Positive Theories of Congressional Institutions,* ed. Kenneth Shepsle and Barry Weingast. Ann Arbor: University of Michigan Press.

Heckman, James, and James Snyder. 1997. "Linear Probability Models of the Demand for Attributes with an Empirical Application to Estimating the Preferences of Legislators." *Rand Journal of Economics* 28:142–89.

Heller, William B. 1994. "Holding the Line on Policy: Amendments and Government Legislation in Italy." Presented at the Annual Meeting of the Public Choice Society, Austin, TX.

Hibbing, John. 1982. *Choosing to Leave: Voluntary Retirement from the U.S. House of Representatives.* Washington, DC: University Presses of America.

Hibbing, John, and Samuel Patterson. 1992. "A Democratic Legislature in the Making: The Historic Hungarian Elections of 1990." *Comparative Political Studies* 24:430–54.

Huber, John. 1992. "Restrictive Legislative Procedures in France and the United States." *American Political Science Review* 86:675–87.

Jacobson, Gary, and Sam Kernell. 1981. *Strategy and Choice in Congressional Elections.* New Haven: Yale University Press.

Johnson, Chalmers. 1982. *MITI and the Japanese Miracle: The Growth of Industrial Policy, 1925–1975.* Stanford: Stanford University Press.

Katz, Jonathan, and Brian Sala. 1996. "Careerism, Committee Assignments, and the Electoral Connection." *American Political Science Review* 90:21–33.

Kernell, Samuel. 1977. "Toward Understanding Nineteenth Century Congressional Careers: Ambition, Competition, and Rotation." *American Journal of Political Science* 21:669–94.

Kiewiet, D. Roderick, and Mathew McCubbins. 1991. *The Logic of Delegation.* Chicago: University of Chicago Press.

Kiewiet, D. Roderick, and Langche Zeng. 1993. "An Analysis of Congressional Career Decisions, 1947–86." *American Political Science Review* 87:928–41.

Kingdon, John. 1973. *Congressmen's Voting Decisions.* New York: Harper and Row.

Krehbiel, Keith. 1991. *Information and Legislative Organization.* Ann Arbor: University of Michigan Press.

Krehbiel, Keith. 1993. "Where's the Party?" *British Journal of Political Science* 23:235–66.

Krehbiel, Keith. 1998. *Pivotal Politics: A Theory of U.S. Lawmaking.* Chicago: University of Chicago Press.

Kreps, David. 1990. "Corporate Culture and Economic Theory." In *Perspectives on Positive Political Economy,* ed. James E. Alt and Kenneth A. Shepsle. New York: Cambridge University Press.

Kreps, David, and Robert Wilson. 1982. "Reputation and Imperfect Information." *Journal of Economic Theory* 27:253–79.

Laver, Michael, and Kenneth Shepsle. 1996. *Making and Breaking Governments.* Cambridge: Cambridge University Press.

Loewenberg, Gerhard. 1967. *Parliament in the German Political System.* Ithaca: Cornell University Press.

Loewenberg, Gerhard, Samuel Patterson, and Malcolm Jewell. 1985. *Handbook of Legislative Research.* Cambridge: Harvard University Press.

Londregan, John. 1996. "Estimating Ideal Points in Small Legislatures." Presented at the Annual Meeting of the Midwest Political Science Association, Chicago.

Loomis, Burdett. 1988. *The New American Politician.* New York: Basic Books.

Matthews, Donald R. 1960. *U.S. Senators and Their World.* Chapel Hill: University of North Carolina Press.

Mayhew, David R. 1974. *Congress: The Electoral Connection.* New Haven: Yale University Press.

Mayhew, David R. 1991. *Divided We Govern.* New Haven: Yale University Press.

McCarty, Nolan, Keith Poole, and Howard Rosenthal. 1999. "The Hunt for Party Discipline in Congress." Manuscript, Columbia University.

McCubbins, Mathew, Roger Noll, and Barry Weingast. 1989. "Structure and Process, Politics and Policy: Administrative Arrangements and the Political Control of Agencies." *Virginia Law Review* 75:431–82.

McCubbins, Mathew, and Gregory Noble. 1995. "Equilibrium Behavior and the Appearance of Power: Legislators, Bureaucrats and the Budget Process in the U.S. and Japan." In *Structure and Policy in Japan and the United States,* ed. P. Cowhey and M. McCubbins. New York: Cambridge University Press.

Milgrom, Paul, and John Roberts. 1992. *Economics, Organization, and Management.* Englewood Cliffs, NJ: Prentice-Hall.

Myagkov, Mikhail G., and D. Roderick Kiewiet. 1996. "Czar Rule in the Russian Congress of People's Deputies?" *Legislative Studies Quarterly* 21:5–40.

Nokken, Timothy. 1998. "Dynamics of Congressional Loyalty: Party Defection and Roll Call Behavior, 1947–1997." Presented at the Annual Meeting of the Midwest Political Science Association, Chicago.

North, Douglass. 1990. *Institutions, Institutional Change and Economic Performance.* Cambridge: Cambridge University Press.

Patzelt, Werner. 1994. "A Framework for Comparative Parliamentary Research in Central and Eastern Europe." In *Working Papers on Comparative Legislative Studies,* ed. Lawrence Longley. Appleton, WI: Research Committee of Legislative Specialists of the International Political Science Association.

Polsby, Nelson. 1968. "The Institutionalization of the House of Representatives." *American Political Science Review* 62:144–68.

Poole, Keith T., and Howard Rosenthal. 1997. *Congress: A Political-Economic History of Roll Call Voting.* Oxford: Oxford University Press.

Price, H. Douglas. 1975. "Congress and the Evolution of Legislative 'Professionalism.'" In *Congress in Change,* ed. Norman Ornstein. New York: Praeger.

Remington, Thomas, and Steven Smith. 1995. "The Development of Parliamentary Parties in Russia." *Legislative Studies Quarterly* 20:457–89.

Remington, Thomas, and Steven Smith. 1996. "Political Goals, Institutional Context, and the Choice of an Electoral System: The Russian Parliamentary Election Law." *American Journal of Political Science* 40:1253–79.

Reynolds, Andrew. 1995. "Constitutional Engineering in South Africa." *Journal of Democracy* 6:86–100.

Riker, William. 1980. "Implications from the Disequilibrium of Majority Rule for the Study of Institutions." *American Political Science Review* 74:432–46.

Rohde, David W. 1979. "Risk-Bearing and Progressive Ambition: The Case of Members of the United States House of Representatives." *American Journal of Political Science* 23:1–26.

Rohde, David W. 1991. *Parties and Leaders in the Postreform House.* Chicago: University of Chicago Press.

Shepsle, Kenneth. 1979. "Institutional Arrangements and Equilibrium in Multidimensional Voting Models." *American Journal of Political Science* 23:27–59.

Shepsle, Kenneth. 1986. "Institutional Equilibrium and Equilibrium Institutions." In *The Science of Politics: Political Science,* ed. Herbert Weisberg. New York: Agathon.

Shepsle, Kenneth. 1989. "The Changing Textbook Congress." In *Can the Government Govern?* ed. John Chubb and Paul Peterson. Washington, DC: Brookings Institution.

Shepsle, Kenneth, and Barry Weingast. 1987. "The Institutional Foundations of Committee Power." *American Political Science Review* 81:85–104.

Shepsle, Kenneth, and Barry Weingast. 1995. "Positive Theories of Congressional Institutions." In *Positive Theories of Congressional Institutions*, ed. Kenneth Shepsle and Barry Weingast. Ann Arbor: University of Michigan Press.

Sinclair, Barbara. 1998. "Do Parties Matter?" Presented at the Annual Meeting of the Midwest Political Science Association, Chicago.

Smith, Steven. 1989. *Call to Order: Floor Politics in the House and Senate.* Washington, DC: Brookings Institution.

Snyder, James, and Tim Groseclose. 1997. "Party Pressure in Congressional Roll-Call Voting." Manuscript, Massachusetts Institute of Technology.

Spence, Michael. 1974. *Market Signaling.* Cambridge: Harvard University Press.

Squire, Peverill. 1992. "The Theory of Legislative Institutionalization and the California Assembly." *Journal of Politics* 54:1026–54.

Stewart, Charles. 1989. *Budget Reform Politics: The Design of the Appropriations Process in the House of Representatives, 1865–1921.* Cambridge: Cambridge University Press.

Tsebelis, George, and Jeannette Money. 1997. *Bicameralism: The Political Economy of Institutions and Decisions.* Cambridge: Cambridge University Press.

Tullock, Gordon. 1981. "Why So Much Stability?" *Public Choice* 37:189–202.

Wahlke, John, et al. 1962. *The Legislative System: Explorations in Legislative Behavior.* New York: John Wiley and Sons.

Weingast, Barry, and William Marshall. 1988. "The Industrial Organization of Congress." *Journal of Political Economy* 96:132–63.

Weingast, Barry, and Mark Moran. 1983. "Bureaucratic Discretion or Congressional Control? Regulatory Policy-Making by the Federal Trade Commission." *Journal of Political Economy* 91:765–800.

Part 2
Legislative Recruitment and Legislative Careers

Legislative Careers: Why and How We Should Study Them

John R. Hibbing

If suggestions about the appropriate future direction for a stream of research are to have any value, they must be based on an appreciation of the current status of that research. Accordingly, I begin this essay on legislative careers by proposing a means of organizing extant research on the topic. For two reasons, however, this "literature review" section is relatively brief. First, accompanying essays by Gary Moncrief and Werner Patzelt do an impressively thorough job of cataloguing previous research and, second, my main goal is to offer ideas about the topic of legislative careers that might be useful for future research. Thus, my review of the literature will be illustrative, not comprehensive.

Classifying Research on Legislative Careers

An obvious way of organizing previous research on legislative careers is to identify the scholarly purpose or justification for studying the topic in the first place. While each researcher is likely to have multiple motivations, four overarching goals can be discerned. These goals are to investigate (1) legislators, (2) a certain legislative body, (3) the larger sociopolitical system of which a legislature is a part, and (4) generalizable patterns across sociopolitical systems.

Understanding Legislator Motivation

For many scholars, a major reason to study legislative careers is to understand the motivation of legislators and humans more generally. Why do certain people run for legislative office? This question has proven surprisingly difficult to answer since it implies comparison with a group of people who did *not* run for legislative office. But who should be included in this group? All adults who

---

Reprinted with permission from *Legislative Studies Quarterly* 24, no. 2 (May 1999): 149–71.

have never sought a legislative office? Only those who are in occupations frequently leading to legislative careers? Only those who actually considered running? In many parts of the world, the central role of political parties structures recruitment, but such matters are largely unresolved in the case of United States legislatures, despite imaginative efforts by Tobin and Keynes (1975), Rosenthal (1981), Maisel (1986, 1987), Fowler and McClure (1989), Canon (1990), Moncrief and Thompson (1992), and Kazee (1994).

Outside the United States, recruitment of legislators is usually more structured, thanks to the intrusive role of political parties. Thus, research on legislative recruitment is likely to be seen as research on institutions rather than as research on individual motivation. For examples, see Byrd (1963) on post-colonial Uganda, Ranney (1965) on the U.K., Czudnowski (1970) on Israel, Agor (1971) on Chile, Pedersen (1977) on Denmark, Mishler (1978) on Canada, and Irwin, Budge, and Farlie (1979) on the Netherlands.

Once the legislative career enters the phase of actual legislative service, analysis in some ways becomes infinitely more complicated. Rather than simply studying the single decision of whether or not to try to enter a legislature, decision points involved with the internal legislative career multiply quickly. We may want to know why some members decide to run for one of many higher offices (for examples, see Abramson, Aldrich, and Rohde 1987; Brace 1984; Copeland 1989; Rohde 1979; Squire 1988a). Or we may want to know why members seek the career track they do *within* a single legislative body (Fenno 1996, 21; Hibbing 1993; Loomis 1988; Simon 1987; Squire 1988b). But the myriad combinations and moves make it impossible to cover all eventualities.

The end of legislative careers has been of as much interest to scholars as the beginning. Just as they have asked why some people run for legislative office while most do not, researchers have also asked why some legislators leave office when they are not under the legal obligation to do so. Are most legislators driven by a desire for power, fame, policy, promotion, or money? Are they motivated by a desire to "have fun" in their legislative body? Or are most retirement decisions made simply to avoid the ignominy of an impending scandal or electoral defeat? Questions such as these have been addressed by Smith and Miller (1977), Frantzich (1978), Cooper and West (1981), Jacobson and Kernell (1981), Hibbing (1982), Brace (1984), Francis and Baker (1986), Lascher (1993), Kiewiet and Zeng (1993), Jacobson and Dimock (1994), Moore and Hibbing (1998), and Theriault (1998).

Understanding a Certain Legislative Body

Another collection of studies on legislative careers has been undertaken with the hope of discovering something about a given legislative body rather than something about the human condition. Usually, the specific goal is to determine a legislature's stage of institutionalization, a concept referring to the complexity, boundedness, and stable structure of a body (for general treatments of institutionalization, see Eisenstadt 1964; Huntington 1965; Sisson 1973).

Thus, Cohen (1980) has used career information to evaluate the institutionalization of the Yugoslav Assembly, King (1981) and Hibbing (1988) have done the same for the British House of Commons; Opello (1986) for the Portuguese Parliament; and most famously Polsby (1968) for the U.S. House of Representatives. State legislatures in the United States have attracted special interest along these lines as they present a wonderful array of stages of institutionalization (see Rosenthal 1996; Squire 1992).

Following Polsby, the general idea is that the longer the median career in a legislature, the more lateral entry for leadership positions is discouraged, and the more careers follow unbending and internally imposed institutional norms, the more institutionalized that legislature can be said to be. For a legislature to be institutionalized it must have clear boundaries, and for a legislature to have boundaries, it is thought that members must not be assuming leadership positions without paying dues *in* the body, must not be moving in and out of the chamber at a breakneck pace, and must not be making up norms as they go along. In this sense, features of the legislative career become central indicators of the nature and developmental stage of legislatures themselves.

Understanding a Certain Sociopolitical System

A great deal of previous research has attempted to identify sociodemographic characteristics and prelegislative-service activities that increase the likelihood of subsequent legislative service. This may seem identical to research described earlier dealing with the activities in which people would engage in order to be able to enter a legislature, but there is an important difference. Now, the focus of attention has shifted to studies attempting to determine the biases existing in a society; and away from those attempting to determine the factors driving legislators and potential legislators. If we observe that only elderly, well-to-do businessmen of the polity's majority ethnic and religious group find their way to a legislative career, we have learned something about the nature of power in that society. Since legislative bodies tend to be sizable and visible, they often become the main stage on which the public can observe political actors. Thus, if scholarly interest comes to rest on a society's "circulation of elites," this interest is likely at some point to be directed at major legislative bodies in that society.

The traits and life-experiences of legislators have attracted substantial interest from scholars. This is not surprising given the centrality of the question, "who governs?" to an understanding of a sociopolitical system (see Dahl 1961; Michels 1959; Mosca 1939). Just about every national legislature (and many subnational legislatures as well) has at one time or another been subjected to an analysis of how representative it is of the country's people (see Matthews 1984 for a good listing).

For some scholars the goal is not to set a legislative body in the context of the people of that society, but rather in the context of other political offices in that society. Placing legislatures in the larger political opportunity structure of a polity is made easier by paying attention to legislative careers. Determining the nature of membership flows into and out of legislative bodies makes it possible to draw inferences about the bodies in which legislators most prefer to serve. Schlesinger (1966) has done more than anyone to map out the opportunity structure of a political system (see also Strøm 1997). Do U.S. senators leave in order to run for the U.S. House, or do U.S. representatives happily seek a Senate seat whenever they think they have the chance to win one? Has the European Parliament finally become a desirable legislature in which to serve? Are people leaving good positions to go to Strasbourg (Kirchner 1983)? Once there, are they staying? Do leadership positions only go to those with long service in the body itself, or is experience in other institutions viewed as an adequate substitute? Data on legislative careers are needed for answering questions such as these.

Tracing the career activities of legislators *after* they have ceased being legislators is particularly useful in understanding the larger society and a given legislature's place in it. Is legislative service a stepping-stone to private sector positions or are ex-legislators ostracized? What kinds of skills are valued, and what skills are perceived to be honed by way of legislative service? Is service in a given legislature so desirable that members will leave it only for high quality, nonlegislative positions? Scholars have used legislative career information to plumb these questions (see, for example, Borders and Dockery 1995; Herrick and Nixon 1996).

Generalizing across Sociopolitical Systems

In some ways the most ambitious research is that which seeks to work across many legislatures in a variety of systems in the hopes of drawing general conclusions. Does proportional representation increase the percentage of legislators who are not members of the dominant ethnic, racial, or economic group? Is legislator salary related (presumably inversely) to the percentage of legislators who depart voluntarily? This, of course, is real comparative research with all the possibilities and all the difficulties that come along with it. Comparable data across polities have always proven elusive. For this reason and others, there is less of this kind of research on legislative careers than there should be.

But there *is* some truly comparative research on legislative careers. Consider for example the question of why the percentage of female legislators varies so much from country to country. Norris (1985), Rule (1987), and Matland

(1998) have addressed the matter straight on and have specified a clear set of factors that seem to encourage women to engage in a legislative career at the national level. Kim and Patterson (1987) compare a broader range of traits in several diverse countries. Loewenberg and Patterson analyze the relationship between legislative salary and membership turnover in countries as diverse as Germany, the United States, Japan, and Kenya (1979, 105–12). Welsh (1980) has provided general but useful information about variation in careers within Central and Eastern European systems prior to the breakup of the USSR. And Schultz (1973) is eager to examine legislators in a cross-national fashion. Still, the overall conclusion has to be that research rigorously comparing two or more national legislative bodies is rare. Comparison of careers in subnational legislatures, particularly U.S. state legislatures, is somewhat more common (see Rosenthal 1981 and Squire 1993, for overviews).

Suggestions for Future Research on Legislative Careers

As is apparent from the foregoing sample, the theoretical bases for studying legislative careers are wonderfully diverse. In the interest of brevity and cohesion, I will direct my suggestions for reorienting career research to the goals of understanding the nature of legislatures and the patterns of legislative change across legislative bodies. In other words, from this point on, I will have little to say about why individual legislators might behave as they do or why certain genders, races, or occupational backgrounds might be over- or underrepresented in certain legislatures. This selected focus seems appropriate given the need to chart directions for truly comparative legislative research, and since a great deal of recent interest within the community of legislative scholars has centered on the sources of change in legislatures, particularly when seen from a neo-institutionalist perspective.

Why do legislatures look the way they do? Why have they evolved the way they have? Are they subject to the same forces that affect the shape and evolution of other institutions? To what extent can the shape and evolution be manipulated? These are basic questions. For the most part, information on legislative careers has not been as useful in answering these questions as it should be. My hope in the final half of this paper is to offer suggestions that might allow legislative career information to be of more assistance in this regard. But before analyzing how legislative career data might be useful, it is necessary to provide some background on theories of institutions and, particularly, institutional change.

Are Institutions Shaped by Outside or Inside Forces?

Scholars disagree about the primary source of institutional, and therefore legislative, change. At the risk of oversimplification, some see the shape of legislatures as being determined primarily by the desires and preferences of the people inside the body; that is, by the legislators themselves. Others see the shape of legislatures as being determined primarily by external forces—technological changes, alterations in the public mood, the activities of other institutions, etc.

The view that inside players shape institutions is usually, though certainly not always, associated with the rational-choice school of thought (but see Epstein et al. 1997). This is fitting. If people are thought to be preference maximizers, then people in a legislature will set to work creating a body that allows them to maximize their preferences. In other words, they will shape the institution to their own ends, whatever these ends may be. Of course, even within the rational-choice community, serious disagreement persists on what it is that legislators desire. Mayhew takes the goal of (U.S.) legislators to be electoral success, and when he looked at the U.S. Congress in the early 1970s he concluded that anyone would be "hard pressed" to design an institution better suited to "members' electoral needs" (1974, 82). He was thinking especially of the weak parties, strong committees, and large staffs that afforded members flexibility in roll-call decisions, authoritative platforms for position-taking, and resources for servicing constituents—all, presumably, useful at attracting votes. Structure induced equilibrium notions, on the other hand, emphasize distributive policies and describe a Congress adept (largely due to its committee system) at getting the right kind of pork to the most appreciative districts (see Shepsle 1979; Shepsle and Weingast 1987). Still other observers stress the need members feel for accurate information on the long-term policy ramifications of various proposals being considered, and conclude that this need dictates quite a different set of institutional features, notably committee arrangements (Gilligan and Krehbiel 1987, 1990; Krehbiel 1991).

In effect, we are left to decide whether legislators want to look good (Mayhew), do good (Krehbiel), or ladle pork (Shepsle), with each school claiming Congress has been particularly shaped to meet that objective. The disagreement is disconcerting. If the same feature of the same body (say, standing committees in the U.S. House) can be described as maximizing very different and occasionally incompatible member goals, can we be confident in the original assumption that the institution looks the way it does primarily because of member actions? Relatedly, if weak parties and strong committees were so useful in maximizing members' preferences in the early 1970s United States, why have parties since become stronger (see Cox and McCubbins 1993; Rohde 1991) and committees weaker (Cohen 1990; Ehrenhalt 1986)? Maybe the environment changed such that in order for members to achieve their preferences, certain alterations in the institution had to be made. If this is true, however, legislators become mere automatons and the real variable of interest becomes the environment.

This is exactly the conclusion reached by those eager to apply organizational theory concepts to legislative evolution, most notably Joseph Cooper (1981; see also Cooper and Brady 1981). The basic idea is that an organization (in this case, a legislature) is to a great extent a product of the environment in which it operates; thus, rather than tracing the connection between member goals and institutional shape, time is better spent tracing the connection between "facets of [legislative] structure and external determinants" (Cooper and Brady 1981, 997). But there are problems here as well. Most importantly, the concept of "the environment" or "external determinant" is so amorphous that practically anything could be made to fit. Rather than well-operationalized environmental variables, research of this ilk tends to offer post-hoc and analytically casual, environmental explanations for selected legislative features or trends (for more on this point, see Patterson, 1981). Often, there is another environmental explanation that would have led us to expect a different legislative feature or trend. In effect, the breadth of the concept of "environment" makes it practically worthless as a predictor.

Institutionalization enters at this point. As it is usually conceived, institutionalization is actually a subspecies of organization theory. For reasons not always specified, institutionalization assumes environmental factors tend to push organizations in a certain direction; specifically, toward greater complexity, boundedness, and standardization. So, in the tradition of organization theory, environmental changes lead to institutional changes. What makes institutionalization distinctive, however, is that it specifies a directionality that is lacking in organization theory. Whereas with basic organization theory the institution in question could move in any direction depending upon changes in the environment, institutionalization implies a process in which the environment is moving in a particular direction. This, in turn, moves organizations in a particular direction—i.e., toward more institutionalization. As a result, institutionalization generates talk of unidirectionality or perhaps even monotonicity (Mishler, Lee, and Tharpe 1973, 363) as well as visions of a linear rather than cyclical historical pattern. Institutionalization allows assumptions to be made about environmental movement. But this directionality is also a curse. Does it mean that bodies can never de-institutionalize? Indicators suggest that some legislatures have done just that—at least in certain time periods (see Baldino 1983; Cavanaugh 1982–83; Rosenthal 1996). If institutionalization is an on-again, off-again process, what turns it on and what turns it off? More importantly, what then would separate institutionalization from straight-up organization theory?

Legislative Careers and Institutional Change

Can information on legislative careers tell us anything about the nature of institutional change? Such information has been used by proponents of both the internally- and externally-driven change schools of thought. Some see lengthening careers as indicative that members have been able to carve out a situation in which the benefits of serving outweigh the costs (see Black 1972). Others see varying legislative career length as a response to oscillating environmental forces (see Cooper and West 1981). And still others see the generally increasing career length (in the U.S. case, at least) as a sign of an institutionalizing body (Polsby 1968).

Legislative career information should not be expected to identify a winner from among these various theories of legislative change, but, used properly, it may be able to shed some light on a few of the merits and demerits of each. I will illustrate this point by concentrating on institutionalization, as this is the theory that has been used most widely in the study of comparative legislatures (see, for example, the contributors in Kornberg 1973, as well as several of the essays in Copeland and Patterson 1994).

As mentioned earlier, generalizing about trends, patterns, and relationships across legislatures is done all too rarely, so it ill-behooves us to be critical of a concept like institutionalization that has at least been the basis for attempts at generalization. But measurement of the concept of institutionalization needs to be subjected to serious adjustment and qualification if meaningful generalization is to occur. My initial contention is not particularly bold but is worth making nonetheless: Using legislative career information to make inferences about the status and evolution of legislative bodies is not as straightforward as is sometimes assumed. The most commonly employed measure of legislative careers (average length), for example, means quite different things in different contexts. More importantly, in some legislatures—indeed in most of the world's legislatures—legislative career length (or, conversely, turnover rates) may not even be a valid indicator of institutionalization at all. This assertion goes against conventional wisdom holding that increasing career length is central to the institutionalization process, so an explanation is necessary.

Institutions Can Have High Membership Turnover and Still Be Institutionalized. The perfectly sensible assumption popularized by Polsby and employed by most students of legislative institutionalization is that the longer the typical legislative career the more institutionalized the legislature, other things being equal. But there is another way of thinking about the connection between membership turnover and institutionalization. This alternative comes to us by way of the organizational theory literature. Here, institutionalization is achieved not by minimizing membership turnover but by minimizing the *relevance* of that turnover. The goal of many private-sector entities, for example, is not so much to minimize turnover but to make sure that whatever turnover *does* occur has minimal impact on the institution. The phrase "company man" from the pre-gender-neutral 1950s illustrates these points nicely. When replacing outgoing members, the goal of GM or IBM was then (and probably still is) to recruit people who were roughly similar to the outgoing parties and then to train and socialize the new recruits until the replacements were virtual clones of the departing members, thus producing minimal disruption to the organization. In this way, institutions were able to reduce one area of potential uncertainty—and this outcome is generally pleasing to institutions since they already have enough uncertainty in their environments.

The indoctrination of the company man into the dress, mannerisms, comportment, orientation, and behavior desired at the workplace has a ready parallel in many legislative settings, and institutionalization could just as effectively occur via this method as via discouraging turnover at all. In fact, the concept, "minimize the effects of turnover," is probably more consistent with institutionalization since in it the individual is rendered irrelevant by the force of the institution. The real measure of institutionalization is not the level of membership turnover but the net impact of turnover. If the impact is minimal, regardless of the absolute number of new members, a body should be thought of as relatively institutionalized—at least with regard to this particular aspect of institutionalization. Ironically, if this formulation has merit, then long, influential, and memorable careers, far from being the indicators of institutionalization Polsby takes them to be, actually could be seen as indicators of an *absence* of institutionalization—an inability of the institution to quash variance in individual members.

The seniority rule, the apprenticeship norm, and Sam Rayburn's oft-repeated exhortation to new members that they "get along by going along" are all mores of the modern U.S. Congress that contribute to member socialization and, relatedly, to a muffling of individual variation. Of course, the occasional renegade will still be in evidence, but the great majority of members learn how they are supposed to behave and then behave that way. Even a quick read of those studies that have followed the evolution of legislators (see especially, Fenno 1996; Killian 1998; Loomis 1988) indicates how members typically learn what it means to be a member of Congress. Many become less caustic and more compromising during their stays in Congress. For examples, contrast the early and late stages of the congressional careers of Newt Gingrich and Ron Dellums, of David Dreier and Steve Largent, to see how the institution shapes member behavior. In a variety of ways, most of them subtle but some not, legislatures, like most organizations, are able to minimize the consequences of membership turnover.

Legislative scholars in many countries outside the U.S. do not see why their U.S. colleagues are so concerned with incumbency advantage, membership turnover rates, typical career lengths, and arguments for and against legislative term limits. And for their part, U.S. scholars may sometimes be miffed by foreign scholars' apparent indifference to these same variables in their own country's legislative bodies. But in most countries outside the U.S., individual legislative career information is of less moment because new members are likely to be similar to those they replaced. As such, in most legislatures of the world, raw turnover levels and mean length of stay are inadequate measures of institutionalization. Other career information—for example, mean length of service in the body *before* leadership positions become a real possibility, or the percent of members who wish to stay in the body (regardless of whether or not they *do* stay)—may well prove to be more useful measures (Epstein et al. 1997, for example, wisely measure the "regularity" of careers).

Institutionalized Parties, Not Legislatures. If this were the end of the story, a valid conclusion could be that the level of legislative institutionalization around the world has been underestimated due to the heavy reliance of scholars on the length of careers and level of membership turnover. Recruitment and socialization may be achieving a level of legislative institutionalization far beyond that indicated by turnover levels. For this to be true would merely require that members, new or old, play by a set of rules that compromises their individuality. It seems quite indisputable that this is exactly the situation confronting most legislators. But the trick is that this set of rules emanates from the party and not the legislature (see also, Epstein et al. 1997, 966).

Oh, legislative norms exist and sometimes mold behavior for members in certain ways. But we must keep a sense of perspective, and this purely legislative shaping pales next to that effected by political parties. In the British House of Commons, for example, the withholding and dispensing of rewards is done less by a legislative establishment and more by a party establishment. The result is that the behavior of MPs is substantially more consistent within parties than within the entire body. (In this sense, prevailing norms within the institution are more heavily dependent (than in the U.S. Congress) on the outcome of elections and the resultant party split, making full institutionalization impossible.) Though slightly less true today than yesterday, it is still fairly easy to distinguish Tory and Labour MPs on the basis of their attire, speech, preferred drink, general demeanor, prelegislative experiences, and so on. Most importantly, of course, the party is able to dictate nearly all policy-relevant actions such as roll-call votes (though see Norton 1980). And in these respects, of course, the British House of Commons is far more typical than Congress.

Once we move outside the U.S., it becomes virtually impossible to consider legislative institutionalization without considering political parties. What we find is that individual members have been rendered relatively inconsequential by an institutionalizing process, but it is the parties and not the legislatures that are primarily responsible for this effect. The parties are very good at obtaining the kind of behavior they want, effectively reducing legislators in many systems to little more than drones (see Rose 1986). Thus, we are subjected to persistent hand wringing over "the crisis of the backbencher," and to repeated efforts to make these backbenchers something more than "lobby fodder."

Of course, I am overstating the case. MPs in most legislatures are not totally devoid of autonomy. Even in the U.K., certain members may hold more surgeries, deal more effectively with the media, be more inclined to vote against the party whip, and even garner small "personal" votes (see Cain, Ferejohn, and Fiorina 1987; although this claim has been challenged recently by Gaines 1998). MPs do face certain norms set down by the body and not by the party. But most objective observers would concede that party norms usually trump legislative norms—in the U.K. and in most other countries. When this is the case, a legislature will be limited in the extent to which it can institutionalize.

Varying Potential for Legislatures to Institutionalize. The reason parties limit legislative institutionalization in many political systems is, of course, constitutional design. Parliamentary systems are more common than true separation of powers systems, and parliamentary systems, for obvious reasons, encourage strong parties that then intrude into the legislature, thereby diminishing the maximum boundedness and autonomy possible in a legislative body. In effect, the systemic designs of most polities make it impossible for legislatures to fully institutionalize. Perhaps a simple figure will help to illustrate this point.

Polsby believes it to be "most implausible that there should be one set of laws governing human behavior in business corporations, another set for legislatures, still another set for institutions of higher education. . . . Underlying all sectors there should be, if not uniformity, at least kinship in the propositions that purport to explain growth and change" (1975, 291). It may well be that institutionalization is a base process that can be seen in virtually all organizations, but, as Polsby was wise to suggest, this does not require there to be perfect uniformity. In fact, in light of the constitutional differences just discussed, such uniformity seems quite unlikely. Consistent with these remarks, Figure 1 indicates that legislatures in parliamentary systems, with executives and parties blurring the boundaries, will probably never be as institutionalized as the U.S. Congress. The distinct tracks suggest it is wrong to believe some legislatures just need more time to develop. Many legislatures are unlikely to take on the accouterments of an institutionalized legislative body. Constitutional designs often go so far as to make this highly unlikely.

To add perspective, I include in Figure 1 the hypothetical trajectory of a traditional private-sector hierarchical organization. Just as some legislatures cannot institutionalize as much as others, legislatures, for the most part, cannot institutionalize as much as more common hierarchical organizational forms. Polsby was proud to have demonstrated that "organizations other than bureaucracies" appear to institutionalize (1968, 168). What remains to be stressed is that vast differences may persist in the degree to which organizations of different types institutionalize.

The reason legislative institutionalization will usually be truncated is not, as Polsby seems to suspect, the collegial organizational structure of legislatures

FIGURE 1
Hypothesized Rates of Institutionalization

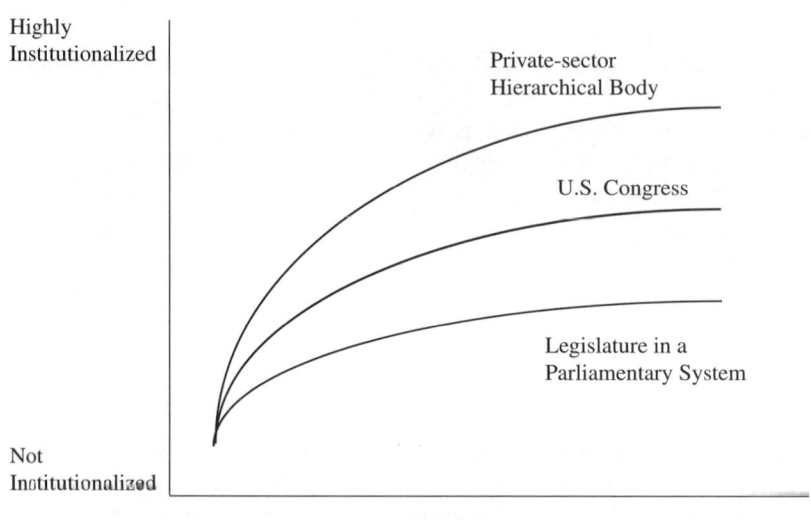

but rather their other main identifying trait (Loewenberg 1971, 4): their grounding in a constituency, that is, their representational role. Legislatures are designed to be in tune with their environment, not to develop boundaries cordoning off that environment. If institutionalization is the process of an organization isolating itself from its environment by developing distinctive norms, idiosyncratic inside lingo, magnificent infrastructures, and unique career tracks, legislatures are simply unable to go very far down the road of institutionalization. This is why the curve for nonlegislative organizations flattens out at a higher level of institutionalization than legislatures, whether in parliamentary or presidential political systems. But it nevertheless seems likely that institutionalization even for business organizations must level out at some point. In other words, the process of institutionalization cannot continue without an organization—any organization—becoming too complex, too rigid, and too isolated from its environment.

The essential point is that various organizational arrangements are associated with widely different institutionalizing possibilities. All bodies may institutionalize, but they clearly do not do so in the same fashion or to the same degree. Our understanding of legislative institutionalization would be greatly assisted if, instead of being smitten with vague similarities, we would begin to explore obvious differences. Thus, the verdict is somewhat depressing. Not only is it the case that legislative career length cannot accurately be viewed as a constant (across legislatures) indicator of institutionalization, but legislative institutionalization itself should not be expected to be identical across legislatures in different political systems.

Professionalization as Artificial Institutionalization. To this point I have escaped the need to distinguish between two terms that are sometimes used nearly interchangeably: institutionalization and professionalization. Legislative professionalization is certainly similar to what I have been calling legislative institutionalization, though the former is the phrase of choice for students of state legislatures (see Kurtz 1990; and many others), and the latter for students of Congress (Polsby 1968). But Squire (1992, 1027) and Rosenthal (1996, 175–85) suggest an important difference between the two terms that will be useful here. Professionalization can be thought of as involving changes that deal with the body itself and that can be accomplished by statute or by legislative edict. Included would be session length, member compensation, number of staff, other perquisites, general legislative resources, and committee structures. If money is available, these traits can simply be manufactured. Institutionalization, on the other hand, can be thought of as involving more amorphous legislative traits that are not capable of being directly manufactured: norms and standard operating procedures, institutional autonomy, leadership positions that require extensive service in the body itself, and extended careers in the body. Though certain of these features could in theory be decreed (term minimums instead of term maximums?), this is not usually the case.

Theoretically, this distinction affords the opportunity to determine the extent to which professionalization can induce institutionalization. Perhaps (referring back to Figure 1) a legislature in a parliamentary system could buy its way to a higher plane of institutionalization than is otherwise possible. (After all, mean length of service in a legislative body *will* go up with reimbursement levels.) Assuming all measurement problems could be solved (a particularly heroic assumption), a composite measure of institutionalization for each of several legislatures could be regressed on a measure of professionalization and the resulting residual could arguably be viewed as an indication of authentic institutionalization. How closely related would these residuals be to the length of time the body has been in existence? With other possible independent variables? How highly correlated are professionalization and institutionalization in the first place? Is the relationship spurious? Answering questions such as these would be valuable for understanding institutional change and the manipulability of that change.

Regardless of what the results of such studies would show, the larger point is that many variables besides constitutional arrangements will affect legislative institutionalization. Some of these variables could be quite self-consciously altered, possibly resulting in higher levels of institutionalization. The curves in Figure 1 might be thought of as means for different types of institutions. Variance around these mean patterns may be produced by varying levels of professionalization as well as by chance and other variables not considered here (a conclusion consistent with Squire's [1992] notion that professionalization often, but not always, leads to institutionalization).

The Timing and Causes of Institutionalization. Confusion exists regarding the causes of institutionalization and, obviously, a measure of institutionalization (whether corrected for professionalization or not) that could then be applied to the histories of several legislatures would be useful for furthering understanding of these causes. It seems likely that some movement in an institutionalizing direction is the norm for most organizations, and it also seems likely (though certainly this is arguable and largely untested) that the pace of institutionalization decreases with time, perhaps as institutions approach a ceiling. But beyond this, what governs the process and its pace? No one is confident of an answer. Polsby, for example, only speculates. Perhaps, he says citing Durkheim, institutionalization is connected to the increasing complexity and division of labor within the larger society (1968, 164). Others (see Sisson 1973) imply that institutionalization would occur without increasing complexity. It simply results from the process by which a new institution settles into a niche in the environment. Krehbiel suggests that over time the "abstract egalitarian principles" of "legislatures in their primitive states" give way to "the emergence of asymmetries" necessary for a legislature to do its job (1991, 248). This concept of the nature and reasons for institutionalization flies in the face of Polsby's conclusion that "increasing hierarchical structure is not a necessary feature of the institutionalization process" (1968, 168).

Substantial insight into the causes of legislative institutionalization would be obtained if we could determine whether the process has been similar in various historical eras or whether institutionalization in any era is simply institutionalization. Should a legislature born, like the U.S. Congress around 1790 before the industrial revolution and other changes that led to remarkable societal differentiation, be expected to change in the same fashion as a legislature, like the Hungarian National Assembly, born (or at least reborn) around 1990 after differentiation had (arguably) progressed almost as far as it could? Is a lengthy institutionalization process avoidable? If so, how? Has the process changed over the years? If so, how? Can a legislature be made more institutionalized by granting it a full complement of professional bells and whistles? Compared to previous centuries, do modern legislatures have a better chance of becoming fully institutionalized? Not only are these questions difficult to answer, they imply that institutionalization is universally admired, and this is far from the case.

Conclusion: Is Legislative Institutionalization Desirable?

For Polsby, legislative institutionalization is a good thing. Consistent with structural-functional notions, he believes the institutionalizing process increases legislatures' "viability in the modern world" (1968, 168). The implication seems to be that those wishing to imbue their polities with workable legislatures should strive to institutionalize those legislatures as quickly as possible. Assuming the studies proposed above showed a strong, nonspurious relationship between professionalized and institutionalized legislatures, we might conclude that if legislators are lavished with money, perquisites, information, and staffers, they should then stay in the legislature (to the extent this decision is theirs and not their party's or their electorate's) and endeavor to create an institutionalized and therefore viable parliamentary body. In this fashion, the legislative body will have been taken on a forced march to institutionalization—and the polity will be the better for it.

Even if research indicates institutionalization can be achieved in such a fashion, caution is in order. As much as it might give social engineers a feeling of accomplishment, the evidence for legislative institutionalization being desirable is hardly unequivocal. A provocative recent article by Charles Mahtesian (1997) posits persuasive anecdotal evidence that the most professionalized of the U.S. state legislatures are also among the "sickest." Focusing particularly on California and Minnesota (two of the most professionalized) and contrasting them with Tennessee (one of the least), Mahtesian hypothesizes (in direct contrast to Polsby) that professionalization can be pathological—or can at least produce some deleterious consequences such as a lack of comity, extreme partisanship, unwillingness to compromise, a paucity of political courage, haughtiness, ineffectiveness, and irrelevance, just to provide a partial list. These concerns can also be found occasionally in the writings of Ehrenhalt (1991), Rosenthal (1993), and others. In addition, Fiorina worries about the unintended consequences of professionalization for the partisan mix of legislators (1994).

Speaking more broadly, there is the well-known popular desire in many parts of the world, and especially in the United States, for more citizen-based and less institutionalized legislatures. The popular yearning for term limits, staff reductions, salary cuts, easy methods for demanding recall votes, and more referenda and initiatives all bespeak a public turned off by any sort of developed legislative structure (see Hibbing and Theiss-Morse 1995). Many citizens in the United States wonder what they are getting for their investment in an institutionalized legislature. They see only entourages, boondoggles, and unbecoming subservience to special interests and political parties. One serious problem with legislative institutionalization is that ordinary people do not like it one bit.

So, on the whole, legislative institutionalization is not an unmitigated asset. Reasonable people can certainly differ on the degree to which it is salutary. For the sake of argument, let us assume institutionalization *is* desirable. Further, and again for the sake of argument, let us assume the research agenda described above makes it possible for us to understand the institutionalizing process to the point of being able to manipulate it. Even at this, we still need to proceed cautiously. A common complaint with the legislative term-limit movement in the U.S. is that partially de-institutionalizing a single institution in a system that is otherwise universally institutionalized could lead to bigger problems. This is why opponents have worried that term limits for legislators would only increase the relative power of other institutionalized actors (interest groups and the executive branch, most obviously). Deinstitutionalizing just one organization in a heavily institutionalized system is likely to accomplish little at best and may evoke serious imbalances.

Similar sorts of dangers could accompany efforts to consciously increase the level of institutionalization of any legislature around the world without a deep understanding of the social and political context in which that legislature is operating. A legislature may have followed the particular developmental path it did for a reason, and artificially priming that process without corresponding adjustments to the rest of the polity may do more harm than good. If the constitutional arrangements and general tenor of a society are not conducive to legislative institutionalization, it should not be forced onto a system, even if we could all magically agree that institutionalization were generally desirable. An overly "viable" legislature in a system not equipped to handle one may be a bad prescription.

But this does not mean we should not do all we can to understand the process of institutional change. Institutions are such a central aspect of modern life that understanding the forces to which they are responding becomes a primary responsibility of social scientists. And because of their importance and openness, *legislative* institutions are especially inviting targets for analysis. But the research agenda described here has data demands that may be too extreme. Systematic data on norms, standard operating procedures, autonomy, and boundedness, are unlikely to be readily available in the near future. As a result, the best that can be hoped for is likely to be data on legislative careers.

And if we are going to use career information to indicate the level of institutionalization, we are going to have to be more discerning and inventive. We must begin by acknowledging that the potential for institutionalization is not the same for all legislative bodies. We must then admit that raw levels of membership turnover or mean length of stay (the easiest and most available measures) are poor substitutes for the real variable of interest, which is the institution's ability to steel itself from the effects of membership turnover. Career data *can* permit useful generalizations about legislative evolution, but in order for this to happen we need to be willing to conceptualize and operationalize more subtle career features and to be more sensitive to the idiosyncrasies of the polities in which careers are unfolding. Used properly, such information should be able to help us discover the reasons institutionalized legislatures come to be and what if anything can be done to stimulate the institutionalization process, should anyone want to do so.

NOTE

An earlier version of this paper was presented at the Shambaugh Conference on Comparative Legislative Research, April 16–18, 1998, University of Iowa, Iowa City, Iowa. Pev Squire provided valuable suggestions along the way.

REFERENCES

Abramson, Paul R., John H. Aldrich, and David W. Rohde. 1987. "Progressive Ambition among United States Senators." *Journal of Politics* 49:3–35.
Agor, Weston. 1971. *The Chilean Senate*. Austin, TX: University of Texas Press.
Baldino, Thomas J. 1983. "The House Is no Longer a Home: Aspects of Deinstitutionalization in the U.S. House of Representatives, 1970–82." Presented at the annual meeting of the Midwest Political Science Association, Chicago.
Black, Gordon. 1972. "A Theory of Political Ambition: Career Choice and the Role of Structural Incentives." *American Political Science Review* 66:144–59.
Borders, Rebecca, and C.C. Dockery. 1995. *Beyond the Hill: A Directory of Congress*. Lanham, MD: University Press of America.
Brace, Paul. 1984. "Progressive Ambition in the House." *Journal of Politics* 46:556–71.
Byrd, Robert O. 1963. "Characteristics of Candidates for Election in a Country Approaching Independence: The Case of Uganda." *Midwest Journal of Political Science* 7:1–27.
Cain, Bruce, John Ferejohn, and Morris Fiorina. 1987. *The Personal Vote*. Cambridge, MA: Harvard University Press.
Canon, David. 1990. *Actors, Astronauts, and Athletes*. Chicago: University of Chicago Press.
Cavanaugh, Thomas E. 1980. "The Dispersion of Authority in the House of Representatives." *Political Science Quarterly* 97:623–37.
Cohen, Lenard. 1980. "Politics as an Avocation: Legislative Professionalization and Participation in Yugoslavia." *Legislative Studies Quarterly* 5:175–209.
Cohen, Richard E. 1990. "Crumbling Committees." *National Journal* (4 August 1990): 1876–1881.
Cooper, Joseph. 1981. "Organization and Innovation in the House of Representatives." In *The House at Work*, ed. Joseph Cooper and G. Calvin Mackenzie. Austin, TX: University of Texas Press.
Cooper, Joseph, and David W. Brady. 1981. "Toward a Diachronic Analysis of Congress." *American Political Science Review* 75:988–1006.

Cooper, Joseph, and William West. 1981. "Voluntary Retirement, Incumbency, and the Modern House." *Political Science Quarterly* 96:279–300.
Copeland, Gary W. 1989. "Choosing to Run: Why House Members Seek Election to the Senate." *Legislative Studies Quarterly* 14:549–66.
Copeland, Gary W., and Samuel C. Patterson. 1994. *Parliaments in the Modern World.* Ann Arbor, MI: University of Michigan Press.
Cox, Gary W., and Mathew McCubbins. 1993. *Legislative Leviathan: Party Government in the House.* Berkeley, CA: University of California Press.
Czudnowski, Moshe M. 1970. "Legislative Recruitment under Proportional Representation in Israel." *Midwest Journal of Political Science* 14:216–48.
Dahl, Robert A. 1961. *Who Governs?* New Haven, CT: Yale University Press.
Ehrenhalt, Alan. 1986. "Media, Power Shifts Dominate O'Neill's House." *Congressional Quarterly Weekly Report* 44:2131–38.
Ehrenhalt, Alan. 1991. *The United States of Ambition.* New York: Random House.
Eisenstadt, S. N. 1964. "Institutionalization and Change." *American Sociology Review* 29:235–47.
Epstein, David; David Brady; Sadafumi Kawato, and Sharyn O'Halloran. 1997. "A Comparative Approach to Legislative Organization: Careers and Seniority in the United States and Japan." *American Journal of Political Science* 41:965–88.
Fenno, Richard F., Jr. 1996. *Senators on the Campaign Trail.* Norman, OK: University of Oklahoma Press.
Fiorina, Morris. 1994. "Divided Government in the American States: A Byproduct of Legislative Professionalism?" *American Political Science Review* 88:304–16.
Fowler, Linda L., and Robert D. McClure. 1989. *Political Ambition: Who Decides to Run for Congress?* New Haven, CT: Yale University Press.
Francis, Wayne L., and John R. Baker. 1986. "Why Do U.S. State Legislators Vacate their Seats?" *Legislative Studies Quarterly* 11:119–26.
Frantzich, Stephen E. 1978. "Opting Out: Retirement from the House of Representatives." *American Politics Quarterly* 6:251–73.
Gaines, Brian. 1998. "The Impersonal Vote? Constituency Service and Incumbency Advantage in Elections to the British House of Commons, 1950–92." *Legislative Studies Quarterly* 23:167–96.
Gilligan, Thomas W., and Keith Krehbiel. 1987. "Collective Decision-Making and Standing Committees." *Journal of Law, Economics, and Organization* 3:287–335.
Gilligan, Thomas W., and Keith Krehbiel. 1990. "Organization of Informative Committees by a Rational Legislature." *American Journal of Political Science* 34:531–64.
Herrick, Rebekah, and David Nixon. 1996. "Is There Life after Congress? An Exploration of Post-Congressional Careers." *Legislative Studies Quarterly* 22:223–39.
Hibbing, John R. 1982. "Voluntary Retirement from the U.S. House of Representatives: Who Quits?" *American Journal of Political Science* 26:467–84.
Hibbing, John R. 1988. "Legislative Institutionalization with Illustrations from the British House of Commons." *American Journal of Political Science* 32:681–712.
Hibbing, John R. 1993. "The Career Paths of Members of Congress." In *Ambition and Beyond,* ed. Shirley Williams and Edward L. Lascher, Jr. Berkeley, CA: Institute of Governmental Studies Press.

Hibbing, John R., and Elizabeth Theiss-Morse. 1995. *Congress as Public Enemy.* Cambridge, UK: Cambridge University Press.
Huntington, Samuel P. 1965. "Political Development and Political Decay." *World Politics* 17:386–430.
Irwin, Galen, Ian Budge, and Dennis Farlie. 1979. "Social Background vs. Motivational Determinants of Legislative Careers in the Netherlands." *Legislative Studies Quarterly* 4:447–65.
Jacobson, Gary C., and Michael Dimock. 1994. "Checking Out: The Effects of Bank Overdrafts on the 1992 House Elections." *American Journal of Political Science* 38:601–24.
Jacobson, Gary C., and Samuel Kernell. 1981. *Strategy and Choice in Congressional Elections.* New Haven, CT: Yale University Press.
Kazee, Thomas A. 1994. *Who Runs for Congress?* Washington, DC: Congressional Quarterly Press.
Kiewiet, D. Roderick, and Langche Zeng. 1993. "An Analysis of Congressional Career Decisions, 1947–1986." *American Political Science Review* 87:928–41.
Killian, Linda. 1998. *The Freshmen: What Happened to the Republican Revolution?* Boulder, CO: Westview Press.
Kim, Chong Lim, and Samuel C. Patterson. 1987. "Parliamentary Elites in Six Nations." *Comparative Politics* 20:379–99.
King, Anthony. 1981. "The Rise of the Career Politicians–and Its Consequences." *British Journal of Political Science* 11:249–85.
Kirchner, Emile. 1983. "Background and Activities of Members of the European Parliament." *Res Publica* 25:21–38.
Kornberg, Alan. 1973. *Legislatures in Comparative Perspective.* New York: David McKay.
Krehbiel, Keith. 1991. *Information and Legislative Organization.* Ann Arbor, MI: University of Michigan Press.
Kurtz, Karl T. 1990. "The Changing State Legislatures." In *Leveraging State Government Relations*, ed. Wesley Pedersen. Washington, DC: Public Affairs Council.
Lascher, Edward L., Jr. 1993. "The Impact of Job Satisfaction on the Career Decisions of Local Lawmakers." In *Ambition and Beyond*, ed. Shirley Williams and Edward L. Lascher, Jr. Berkeley, CA: Institute of Governmental Studies Press.
Loomis, Burdett A. 1988. *The New American Politician.* New York: Basic Books.
Loewenberg, Gerhard. 1971. *Modern Parliaments: Change or Decline.* Chicago: Aldine.
Loewenberg, Gerhard, and Samuel C. Patterson. 1979. *Comparing Legislatures.* Boston: Little, Brown.
Mahtesian, Charles. 1997. "The Sick Legislature Syndrome and How to Avoid It." *Governing* (February 1997):16–20.
Maisel, L. Sandy. 1986. *From Obscurity to Oblivion: Running in the Congressional Primary*, 2d ed. Knoxville, TN: University of Tennessee Press.
Maisel, L. Sandy. 1987. "Candidates and Non-Candidates in the 1986 Congressional Elections." Presented at the annual meeting of the Midwest Political Science Association, Chicago.
Matland, Richard E. 1998. "Women's Representation in National Legislatures: Developed and Developing Countries." *Legislative Studies Quarterly* 23:109–26.

Matthews, Donald R. 1984. "Legislative Recruitment and Legislative Careers." *Legislative Studies Quarterly* 9:547–85.

Mayhew, David R. 1974. *Congress: The Electoral Connection*. New Haven, CT: Yale University Press.

Michels, Roberto. 1959. *Political Parties*. New York: Dover.

Mishler, William. 1978. "Nominating Attractive Candidates for Parliament: Recruitment to the Canadian House of Commons." *Legislative Studies Quarterly* 3:581–99.

Mishler, William, James Lee, and Alan Tharpe. 1973. "Determinants of Institutional Continuity: Freshman Cue-taking in the U.S. House of Representatives." In *Legislatures in Comparative Perspective*, ed. Alan Kornberg. New York: David McKay.

Moncrief, Gary, and Joel A. Thompson. 1992. *Changing Patterns in State Legislative Careers*. Ann Arbor, MI: University of Michigan Press.

Moore, Michael, and John R. Hibbing. 1998. "Situational Dissatisfaction in Congress: Explaining Voluntary Departures." *Journal of Politics* 60:1088–1107.

Mosca, Gaetano. 1939. *The Ruling Class*. New York: McGraw-Hill.

Norris, Pippa. 1985. "Women's Legislative Participation in Western Europe." *Western European Politics* 8:90–101.

Norton, Philip. 1980. *Dissension in the House of Commons, 1974–79*. Oxford: Oxford University Press.

Opello, Walter C. 1986. "Portugal's Parliament: An Organizational Analysis of Legislative Performance." *Legislative Studies Quarterly* 11:291–320.

Patterson, Samuel C. 1981. "Understanding Congress in the Long Run." *American Political Science Review* 75:1007–09.

Pedersen, Mogens N. 1977. "The Personal Circulation of a Legislature: The Danish Folketing, 1849–1968." In *The History of Parliamentary Behavior*, ed. William O. Aydelotte. Princeton, NJ: Princeton University Press.

Polsby, Nelson W. 1968. "The Institutionalization of the U.S. House of Representatives." *American Political Science Review* 62:144–68.

Polsby, Nelson W. 1975. "Legislatures." In *Handbook of Political Science*, ed. Fred I. Greenstein and Nelson W. Polsby. Volume V. Reading, MA: Addison-Wesley.

Ranney, Austin. 1965. *Pathways to Parliament: Candidate Selection in Britain*. Madison: University of Wisconsin Press.

Rohde, David W. 1979. "Risk-Bearing and Progressive Ambition: The Case of the United States House of Representatives." *American Journal of Political Science* 23:1–26.

Rohde, David W. 1991. *Parties and Leaders in the Post-reform House*. Chicago: University of Chicago Press.

Rose, Richard. 1986. "British MPs: More Bark than Bite?" In *Parliaments and Parliamentarians in Democratic Politics*, ed. Ezra N. Suleiman. New York: Holmes and Meier.

Rosenthal, Alan. 1981. *Legislative Life*. New York: Harper and Row.

Rosenthal, Alan. 1993. "The Legislative Institution—In Transition and at Risk." In *The State of the States*, 2d ed., ed. Carl E. Van Horn. Washington, DC: Congressional Quarterly Press.

Rosenthal, Alan. 1996. "State Legislative Development: Observations from Three Perspectives." *Legislative Studies Quarterly* 21:169–97.

Rule, Wilma. 1987. "Electoral Systems, Contextual Factors, and Women's Opportunity for Election to Parliament in Twenty-Three Democracies." *Western Political Quarterly* 40:477–98.

Schlesinger, Joseph A. 1966. *Ambition and Politics*. Chicago: Rand McNally.

Schultz, Ann T. 1973. "A Cross-National Examination of Legislators." *The Journal of Developing Areas* 7:571–90.

Shepsle, Kenneth A. 1979. "Institutional Arrangements and Equilibrium in Multi-dimensional Voting Models." *American Journal of Political Science* 23:27–59.

Shepsle, Kenneth A., and Barry R. Weingast. 1987. "The Institutional Foundations of Committee Power." *American Political Science Review* 81:935–45.

Simon, Lucinda. 1987. "The Climb to Leadership: Career Paths and Personal Choices." *The Journal of State Government* 60:245–51.

Sisson, Richard. 1973. "Comparative Legislative Institutionalization: A Theoretical Explanation." In *Legislatures in Comparative Perspective*, ed. Alan Kornberg. New York: McKay.

Smith, Roland E., and Lawrence W. Miller. 1977. "Leaving the Legislature: Why Do They Go?" *Public Service* 4:6–8.

Squire, Peverill. 1988a. "Career Opportunities and Membership Stability in Legislatures." *Legislative Studies Quarterly* 13:65–82.

Squire, Peverill. 1988b. "Member Career Opportunities and the Internal Organization of Legislatures." *Journal of Politics* 50:726–44.

Squire, Peverill. 1992. "The Theory of Legislative Institutionalization and the California Assembly." *Journal of Politics* 54:1026–54.

Squire, Peverill. 1993. "State Legislative Careers." In *Ambition and Beyond*, ed. Shirley Williams and Edward L. Lascher, Jr. Berkeley, CA: Institute of Governmental Studies Press.

Strøm, Kaare. 1997. "Rules, Reasons and Routines: Legislative Roles in Parliamentary Democracies." *Journal of Legislative Studies* 3:155–73.

Theriault, Sean M. 1998. "The Thrill Is Gone: Making Sense of Congressional Retirement." *Legislative Studies Quarterly* 23:419–34.

Tobin, Richard J., and Edward Keynes. 1975. "Institutional Differences in the Recruitment Process: A Four-State Study." *American Journal of Political Science* 19:667–82.

Welsh, William A. 1980. "The Status of Research on Representative Institutions in Eastern Europe." *Legislative Studies Quarterly* 5:275–308.

Recruitment and Retention in U.S. Legislatures

Gary F. Moncrief

Introduction

Institutions are defined and refined by individuals. And individual behavior is constrained and channeled by institutions. At the level of generalization, these are basic, obvious statements. At the legislative level, they signal the importance of the study of recruitment and retention of legislators.

From the standpoint of democratic theory, we assume that it matters who runs and who is elected.[1] We assume it matters for both policy-making and symbolic reasons. Ultimately, questions of recruitment and retention—of candidacy and careers, as it were—are central to our understanding of the nature of representative democracy, the role of elections in translating public mood into public policy, and the processes of system change and system maintenance (Fowler 1993, vii). The debate in the U.S. over term limits is an excellent example of the presumed importance of candidacies, careers, and change.

For years, the subfield of congressional study and the subfield of state legislative study have each proceeded almost as if the other did not exist. They have often asked different questions; when they do ask the same question it is often at different times. Part of the difference in approach between congressional and state legislative students is, I believe, a difference in the "natural" units of analysis. For state legislative students, with an N of ninety-nine legislative chambers, the inclination is toward comparing institutions. For congressional scholars, since the focus is on a single legislature (albeit one with two distinctly different chambers), the unit of analysis is often the individual within the institution.

This distinction between the inclinations of congressional and legislative scholars can be overdrawn of course; there is certainly more than a modicum of single-state legislative studies. Nonetheless, it is clear that each subfield has tended to ignore the other. Recently, however, some political scientists have

---

Reprinted with permission from *Legislative Studies Quarterly* 24, no. 2 (May 1999): 173–208.

begun to attend to the career linkages between Congress and the state legislatures (e.g., Berkman 1993, 1994; Fowler and McClure 1989; Squire 1988a). American legislatures certainly do not present a seamless whole, but there is a closer connection between Congress and the state legislatures than many people realize. And as the opportunity structure changes in many state legislatures this connection will become an increasingly important arena for both congressional and state legislative scholars. Change has rapidly occurred at the state legislative level in the past several decades, and the implications of these changes have not been adequately explored. Indeed, important change continues apace at the state level, and the situation invites study and reflection by legislative scholars. In particular, the issues of state legislative professionalization and careerism are very much in the air. Closely related to these factors, of course, is the term-limit phenomenon. With almost 40% of the state legislatures now or soon to be operating under some type of term limit, we have about the closest thing we, as political scientists, can hope to find to a "natural experiment." And the term-limit issue goes to the heart of questions of recruitment and retention.

Similarly, change is quite evident in Congress, especially in the U.S. House in the past few years. And these changes provide an opportunity to test the prevailing theories about recruitment and retention at the national level.

While I seek to review the general contours of the congressional landscape, I make no claim that this review is exhaustive of that literature. I seek to illustrate the major trends in congressional research, making reference to selected (and what I think are representative) studies and trends. I come closer to making a claim of a thorough review of the state legislative field.

Recruitment

Legislatures purport to be representative institutions. At the heart of the concept of representation are the questions of who runs for the legislature and why, who wins and how, and what are the consequences for both the institution of the legislature and the polity itself. In the broadest meaning of the concept, these are questions of recruitment. Although "recruitment" the *term,* has fallen out of favor in contemporary studies of American legislatures, recruitment the *issue,* is very much in evidence in such studies.

Recruitment is just one component of the career.[2] And either term can be used in reference to a specific institution (e.g., recruitment to the California Assembly; the U.S. House career) or, more broadly, to politics generally (e.g., the political career of Mike Crapo, who served first in the Idaho State Legislature, then the U.S. House of Representatives, and later the U.S. Senate—a standard example of progressive ambition). It is sometimes difficult to separate the ways in which the terms are being used, because the relatively open system of candidacy in the U.S., coupled with a federal political structure, often means that recruitment to one level is preceded by recruitment to another (lower) level. This is clearly not the case in all political systems—not even all federal political systems. For example, fewer than 10% of the members of the Canadian House of Commons have served in a provincial legislature (Docherty 1997). The recruitment (and career) tracks are distinctly different, therefore, for national and subnational legislative office (Moncrief 1998). In the United States, however, the notion of "careerism" has become so intertwined with the idea of "progressive ambition" that some ambiguity is often introduced.

Matthews (1984, 547) defines legislative recruitment as the study of "Who belongs to legislative assemblies and how they got there."[3] This definition covers a lot of territory. It includes at least all of the following types of studies: (1) the backgrounds of legislators, (2) the role of gatekeepers or sponsors such as political parties and interest groups, (3) the nature of the nominating system and the electoral rules, (4) the decision-making calculus of potential aspirants to public office, and, ultimately, (5) the consequences of the particular recruitment patterns.

Depending on who is doing the slicing (e.g., Canon 1994; Czudnowski 1975; Fowler 1993; Kazee 1994a; Matthews 1984), recruitment studies in the U.S. are generally divided into at least three or four "schools" or "approaches." Often these approaches are distinguishable by which primary question they seek to address: Who is recruited? How are they recruited? Why do they run? Roughly, these questions correspond to approaches usually described as the *sociological*, the *process*, and the *rational-actor* models.

Sociological Approach

One of the earliest approaches to studying recruitment was sociological, asking questions about what types of people were elected to office (Eulau and Sprague 1964; Matthews 1954; Prewitt and Eulau 1971). The focus of these studies was on those who had already obtained office—by definition, *elite recruitment*. Much of the work described the social backgrounds—educational attainment, occupation, age, etc.—of those who had achieved office. Most of the very earliest work was primarily descriptive, but some of these early studies (e.g., Derge 1959; Eulau and Sprague 1964; Matthews 1960) were trying to make an important link between background characteristics and legislative behavior.

The ability to tie specific background characteristics to behavior, however, has been difficult. While Matthews (1984, 554) states that "the social and political backgrounds of legislators have been linked to their behavior in office," ultimately he determines that the results are "inconclusive." For this reason, studies of social backgrounds have all but disappeared as part of the recruitment literature on Congress. But, as Canon (1994, 324) points out, there are other legitimate reasons to study the backgrounds of legislators ". . . whether sanctioned by political scientists or not, practitioners of politics care about descriptive or symbolic representation."

The Process of Recruitment

A second line of inquiry concentrates on the *process* of recruitment as "several selective phases" (Matthews 1984, 563), and emphasizes the political role of gatekeepers such as political parties and interest groups, as well as the mechanisms of selection (nomination and election). Two of the best-known early studies in this regard are Sorauf's (1965) study of the role of political parties in recruitment in Pennsylvania and the work by Seligman et al. (1974) on Oregon. Others include Patterson and Boynton (1969) and an often-overlooked study by Kim et al. (1976) which studies the extent of party recruitment in Iowa and the level of party roll-call voting. Tobin and Keynes (1975) examined the nature of nominating systems in four states and concluded that such systems had an important effect on the parties' ability to control the recruitment process. All of these studies were of state legislatures. There were, however, a number of studies of congressional candidates, often focusing on the role of party in recruitment (e.g., Fishel 1973; Snowiss 1966; and later, Kazee and Thornberry 1990).

The most ambitious of the early works was the four-state study (Wahlke et al. 1962). It was noteworthy for two reasons. First, a defining characteristic of the study was its meticulous effort to tie social factors (socialization, backgrounds), systemic variables (party strength, legislative professionalization), and legislative behavior together through the intermediate concept of role. While this effort was not entirely successful, it represents the earliest effort toward building a comprehensive theory of recruitment and, to some extent careers.

Second, it was one of the earliest truly comparative studies of recruitment to American legislatures. The other seminal works from this time period each focused on a single institution: Matthews (1960) on the U.S. Senate; Sorauf (1963) on the Pennsylvania legislature; and Barber (1965) on the Connecticut House of Representatives.

But the four-state study undertaken by Wahlke and his associates permitted a broader view of recruitment, allowing for the interaction between individual backgrounds and inclinations and institutional arrangements. Theirs was a far more comprehensive view than was the norm for the time, and the focus was on how certain institutional arrangements could affect the recruitment patterns, and how those who are recruited then "behave" in the legislative institution. By widening the scope to several state legislatures, Wahlke and his associates were able to observe and speculate on how systemic differences (e.g., party strength, legislative professionalism) affected recruitment. In this sense, recruitment could be viewed as both a dependent and independent variable.

This remains the potential strength of studies at the state legislative level—the ability to consider the effect of institutional (both social and political) arrangements on the patterns of candidate and elite recruitment. It is a strength that state legislative scholars have not exploited fully, and it is a strength which congressional scholars have not often recognized.

Almost all of these studies are based on interviews or surveys. Moreover, they tended to be surveys of legislators *after* they achieved office, not as candidates per se. An exception is the study by Seligman et al. (1974), in which the authors interviewed almost all candidates who ran for the Oregon state legislature. They found that recruitment patterns were varied, and often included friends, families, local organizations and interest groups, as well as political parties. Of particular importance, they found that the party was most important as a recruiting agent in districts in which the party had little chance of winning, and was seeking to draft someone onto the ballot. But in other types of races (i.e., marginal districts, or when the party was the dominant party in a safe district), a different recruitment process was under way. Self-starters were more likely to emerge in both parties in marginal districts and within the majority party in safe districts.

The study by Seligman and associates exemplifies the process-oriented view of recruitment: "As a selective flow of individuals, the political recruitment process unfolds in three phases" and involves "the sequential phases of interaction" (1974, 14). This is reminiscent of Prewitt's and Eulau's (1969, reprinted 1978, 138) definition of recruitment as "the process or set of processes by which . . . the population is narrowed" to those who are elected, or of Norris's (1997, 1) "funnel of causality."

This view more fully represents the totality of influences that come into play as a potential candidate moves toward candidacy, nomination, and election. It also provides a more precise accounting of the *variations* that may exist between different political systems in one or another of the recruitment stages. In this sense, the process school was particularly interested in political institutions—political parties, electoral systems, and interest groups.

Rational Actor

The earliest explanations seeking to answer the question "why they run" were psychologically based. Lasswell (1948) contended that politicians had a specific personality driven by an ego-need for power, which political office could help satisfy. Barber's (1965) study of Connecticut legislators is basically a psychological approach—he builds a categorization based on the active-passive nature of legislators, coupled with their short- or long-term commitment to the legislative institution. There were few efforts to test these theories in terms of legislative behavior and numerous critics claim that the psychological approach has been unproductive (Fowler 1993, 53; Loomis 1994, 345; Matthews 1984, 559).

While this may be true, the focus on "why they run" has become the preeminent focus in studies of recruitment and careers in the U.S. But rather than concentrating on the psychological dimension, the image has shifted to the simple assumption that office-seekers are driven by a specific motivation: ambition.

The fountainhead of this perspective is Schlesinger's (1965) study. His book is not actually a study of legislative recruitment but of political careers. Nonetheless, the concept of ambition as a motivation for candidacy has become so widely applied that its role in recruitment theory must be acknowledged. Schlesinger explicitly recognizes ambition as the motivation for office seeking: "The central assumption of ambition theory is that a politician's behavior is a response to his office goals. Or, to put it another way, the politician as office seeker engages in political acts and makes decisions appropriate to gaining office" (1965, 6).

The advantage of this perspective is that it permits us to make an important link between ambition and behavior—behavior is purposive in the sense that it is designed to serve the politician's ambition. And the notion of purposive behavior, implying rationality, lends itself to a type of analysis that borrows heavily from economics, as Black (1972) demonstrated. It also allows us to trace the effect of a particular motive from candidacy through the institutional career, helping to make the link between the nature of the recruitment process (including self-selection) and behavior in the institution.

Schlesinger posited three types of ambition, *discrete*: an ambition to hold a specific office for a specified period, after which the individual will "withdraw from public life" (10); *static*: an ambition to hold the same office for a long period of time; and *progressive*: a desire to "attain an office more important than the one he now seeks or is holding" (10).

While much of Schlesinger's work was actually aimed at pointing out the institutional framework—the "opportunity structure" of elective offices and relative party strength in various states—the focus was on how the opportunity structure encouraged or constrained the individual's ambition. According to Fowler (1993, 60), this focus on individual ambition

> turned scholars' attention to individual calculation and focused their attention exclusively on the unfolding of political careers. . . . (T)he stage was set for the purposive actor—the self-starter, the freebooting entrepreneur, the strategic politician—so familiar to congressional scholars today. This autonomous individual is now at the core of theoretical and empirical work on candidacy, which appropriately bears the name ambition theory.

From the perspective of recruitment to candidacy, the focus became the conditions under which politically ambitious people will seek an office they do not presently hold. Thus, Rohde's (1978) premise that all legislators are progressively ambitious but risk-averse, and Jacobson's and Kernell's (1981) theory of strategic politicians, who carefully choose when to run, are now the dominant assumptions for studies of congressional elections. The past fifteen years have witnessed a multitude of such studies (for example, Adams and Squire 1997; Banks and Kiewiet 1989; Bianco 1984; Bond et al. 1997; Bond et al. 1985; Brace 1984; Krasno and Green 1988; Lublin 1994; Payne 1982; Squire 1989; Squire and Smith 1996; Stewart 1989). They have clarified our understanding of candidacies and elections at both the House and Senate level. Most such studies focus on the presence or absence of an incumbent in the race. If an incumbent is present, the focus is on specifying the conditions under which that incumbent is potentially vulnerable (e.g., a slim margin of victory in the previous election; a poor standing in public opinion polls; the presence of national conditions which the incumbent may not be able to overcome) and which may induce a "quality" candidate to run. What is important here is that recruitment (candidacy) is viewed as the product of an *individual*'s calculation about the chances of winning, and there is little attention to the role of potential recruiting agents, such as political parties. As Kazee (1994a, 8) notes, "This research stream dovetailed nicely with the candidate-centered paradigm of American congressional elections."

The methods used in the rational-actor approach are based on formulating deductive models of the variables important in making decisions about candidacy, then devising objective measures of those variables (e.g., vote in previous election). In studies focusing on the "quality" of the candidate, a good deal of effort has been devoted to how best to measure quality (e.g., what value should be assigned to different state or local offices). The methodology is distinctly different from almost all other approaches to recruitment because it is based on objective measures of candidacy, rather than on survey or interview data with the candidates.

In his critique of the literature in 1984, Matthews argued that students of legislative recruitment and careers "must do a better job of demonstrating how recruitment matters. . . . In what ways, if at all, do different patterns of legislative recruitment and careers affect the behavior of legislators?" (548). In some ways, the rational-actor model has done just that. This approach has not only crystallized the conditions under which certain candidates will run, or the conditions under which incumbents will act on progressive career ambition, but it has explained a good deal of the behavior of legislators within the institution by focusing on the reelection incentive of incumbents (e.g., Cain et al. 1987; Fiorina 1977; Mayhew 1974).

While the rational-actor approach has much to offer, it is not immune to criticism (see Canon 1990, 1994; Fowler 1993; Kazee 1994a). In particular, ambition theory, because of its focus on static ambition (reelection) or progressive ambition has largely concentrated on incumbent office-holders. But Canon

(1990) has shown that amateurs (contestants with little or no previous experience) constitute a significant portion (averaging around 25%) of the members of the Congress. Moreover, he argues that these amateurs play an important part in bringing change to the congressional institution.

Another criticism is that the excessive focus on individual calculations retards our comprehension of gradual but important changes in the political system itself, such as the changing relative attractiveness of different political offices (Canon 1990, 15; Fowler 1993, 9), or the growth in the role of political parties (Herrnson 1988). Furthermore, since almost all such studies have concentrated on Congress, there has been little reason or inclination to think about the effect of potential systemic differences beyond the obvious difference between house and senate races. But this is an important consideration if the rational-actor approach is to have application in political systems other than at the U.S. national level.

The Context of Candidate Emergence in Congressional Studies

In part because of the perceived limitations of the rational-actor model, some scholars recently have sought to expand the predominant view of candidacy (Fowler 1991, 1993; Fowler and McClure 1989; Kazee 1994a, 1994b; Maisel and Stone 1997; Maisel et al. 1990). This approach seeks to combine the framework of the "process" school with the focus on motivation and rationality from the "ambition" school, to give broader context to the decision to stand for office.

More importantly, it pushes the definition of "recruitment" back a stage, from candidacy to potential candidacy. It seeks to identify the potential candidate pool, and then to assess the structural and personal factors that lead some potential candidates to get out of the pool and into the race, while leading other potential candidates to decline. In other words, it does not assume ambition as a given, but seeks to understand the context in which ambition occurs. In particular, it allows for a fuller understanding of the subjective costs and benefits of candidacy, as perceived by the potential candidates themselves.

This approach requires two things. First, one must identify the potential pool of candidates. Second, one must return to the survey and interview instruments as primary data sources. As Kazee (1994a, 11) says, "Ambition is best measured by asking candidates about their past experiences, career goals, and perceptions of the accommodations political candidacy requires."

While not strictly from the candidate emergence school, Canon's work (1990; Canon and Sousa 1992; Canon et al. 1996) is similar in that it shares an interest in how structural change affects the candidate pool. His work points out that changes in electoral structures (such as redistricting or the rise of the GOP in the South) alter the opportunity structure and consequently will change the nature of the candidate supply.

State Research Today

The rational-actor approach, so prevalent at the congressional level, has had little impact at the state level in terms of empirical studies of *candidates* for legislative office. The exceptions are Francis's (1993) study of the conditions under which state house members run for state senate seats (e.g., exercising progressive ambition), Pritchard's (1992) study of strategic challengers in elections to the Florida House, and a recent study by Van Dunk (1997) which uses previously held elected office at the local level as a measure of candidate quality in state legislative elections. Since ambition and careerism are now viewed as major factors at the state legislative level, more such studies will surely follow.

Except for the rather substantial literature on women in state legislatures, there have been very few recruitment studies of any type at the state level in at least twenty years. It is unclear why this is the case. The decline in interest in recruitment as a topic coincides with the rise of the rational-actor perspective among congressional scholars, but this may be coincidental. Whatever the cause of this apparent disinterest, it is an unfortunate circumstance. The few early comparative studies of recruitment that focused on the state level (e.g., Tobin and Keynes 1975; Wahlke et al. 1962) had uncovered differences in recruitment patterns associated with system-level variables at the state level.

Even today, there is reason to believe there are state differences in the recruitment process, although such differences may be somewhat muted compared to earlier times. For example, the scant evidence that does exist suggests that there are still significant variations from state to state in terms of the recruitment role of the party (Breaux and Jewell 1992, 100-01). There are two recent studies that show a definite recruitment role being played by state Republican Party officials in some southern states (Bullock and Shafer 1997; Cassie 1994).

The emergence of legislative campaign committees (Gierzynski 1992; Jewell and Whicker 1994; C. Rosenthal 1995; Shea 1995) is a relatively recent phenomenon. They are generally characterized as campaign service organizations, providing campaign money, expertise, and training for self-recruited candidates. But there is also evidence that in some instances they actively recruit candidates to run. Moreover, there is anecdotal evidence that some interest groups, most notably conservative Christian groups, are actively seeking to persuade certain individuals to run for state legislative office (Rozell and Wilcox 1996, 61).

There is a definite need for studies of recruitment and candidacy at the state legislative level. It is clear that the conditions have changed considerably since the studies conducted in the 1960s and 1970s. There is a general view that self-starters are more prevalent at the state level today (Ehrenhalt 1991; A. Rosenthal 1998), but there is also evidence that parties and perhaps other organizations are actively seeking candidates in some instances. We simply have very little empirical evidence of the extent to which candidates are recruited or the extent to which they self-select, and whether these patterns are the same everywhere or not.

Women in State Legislatures

The one area in which there has been a good deal of research is the recruitment of women.[4] Because women have comprised a larger proportion of state legislative chambers for a longer period of time than is true at the congressional level, there has been a substantial interest in the conditions under which women become state legislators. For example, there are numerous studies assessing the effect of the electoral structures on women (e.g., Darcy et al. 1994; Matland and Brown 1992; Moncrief and Thompson 1992; Rule 1990; Rule and Zimmerman 1992; Welch and Studlar 1990). Nechemias has shown that the proportion of female state legislators is tied to the political culture of the state (Nechemias 1985, 1987) and that women are more likely to represent districts in closer geographic proximity to the capitol (1985). Both Nechemias (1987) and Squire (1992a) find that women are less likely to serve in the more professional state legislatures. All of these findings are related to differences in the opportunity structure (broadly defined) between states.[5]

But a recent study by Dolan and Ford (1997) finds that, generally, the opportunity structure for women has changed in other ways as well. In particular, the occupational background of female state legislators has changed dramatically over the past three decades (also see Williams 1990). They conclude "The typical profile of women state legislators has changed. . . . Women serving in the 1990s are younger, better educated, and come to the legislature from more professional occupations and more varied political backgrounds" (147). On the other hand, Niven (1998) argues there is still a bias against female candidates among many party elites.

The inclusion of more women in the legislature is important in terms of symbolic representation (Canon 1994, 324). But for our purposes here, the essential question is behavioral: does the recruitment of women into the legislature bring different patterns of behavior? Kathlene (1995), Saint Germain (1989), Thomas (1994), and Thomas and Welch (1991) all find that women have different policy priorities or policy solutions than men. Richardson and Freeman (1995) find that female state legislators attract more casework than men. On the other hand, Reingold (1996) finds that there is no difference between men and women in their adherence to norms of collegiality and cooperation.

There has been very little written about the recruitment of others. The question of minority recruitment to the state legislature has been dominated by attention to the relationship to electoral factors such as district magnitude and especially redistricting (see for example, Grofman and Handley 1989). The question of the behavioral consequences of the recruitment of minorities into legislatures is considerably less studied (but see Barrett 1995; Hedge et al. 1996).

The Retention of Legislators:
Legislative Professionalization and Careerism

Congressional Studies

"Some say careers shape the institution; some say the institution shapes careers. But regardless of the causal order of the career-institution relationship . . . individual congressional careers simply cannot be separated from the study of the institution. Careers are shaped by the institutional context just as they in turn feed back into that context" (Hibbing 1991, 22).

Compared to figures in other countries, turnover rates in American legislatures are low. The average turnover in the U.S. House of Representatives over the past fifty years is 16.5%. To state the obvious, turnover rates are composed of two factors: voluntary exit and electoral defeat. In the U.S. House, turnover is largely a product of voluntary retirement since, on average, over 90% of incumbent house members who run for reelection win, although rates are somewhat lower in the U.S. Senate.[6]

At what point does legislative service become a career? And what are the institutional implications of the development of careerism? What is the causal relationship between institutional development and careerism? At the congressional level, numerous scholars have pegged the development of careerism in the House to a period about a century ago. Fiorina et al. (1975, 32) have shown that turnover dropped substantially in the last half of the nineteenth century (also see Polsby 1968). The causes of the decline in turnover are attributed to various factors: the increased attractiveness of the job of congressman as the role of the federal government became more important and the stabilization of the party system after the 1896 realignment (Price 1975), for example. But whatever the cause of the reduction in turnover and the increasing tenure, most congressional scholars are in agreement that once membership stabilizes and a careerist-orientation develops, the members are likely to try to mold the organization to their own purposes (Swenson 1982).

In fact, considerable congressional research has been devoted to an explanation of how career-minded legislators seek to adapt organizational rules and structures to their needs. Such factors as the development of seniority as the primary decision-rule for the selection of committee chairs (Epstein et al. 1997; Polsby 1968; Polsby et al. 1969), continual assignment to the same committees as a "property right claim" among rank-and-file committee members (Katz and Sala 1996), and the growth in legislative staff (Fiorina 1978) can be viewed in this way. They are the types of institutional change which Davidson and Oleszek (1976) call "consolidative." But not every structural change in Congress is aimed at furthering individual goals; some changes come about as institutional responses to external factors (Cooper and Brady 1981; Davidson and Oleszek 1976; Dodd 1986). At times such changes as the centralization of leadership power may hamper the pursuit of individual goals, while at other times it may serve to further the interests of both the institution and the individual.

State Legislative Studies

The question of ambition, long a mainstay in the congressional literature, is increasingly a focal point in state legislative studies (e.g., Ehrenhalt 1991; Loomis 1990; A. Rosenthal 1998; Squire 1988a, 1988b, 1992a). Ehrenhalt (1991) argues that political ambition today is unfettered in ways not possible previously. His argument is based on two observations. First, the constraints on ambition that previously were imposed by strong political parties (both as recruitment agents and organizing forces within the legislature) are now considerably weaker. Second, the structure of incentives and disincentives for serving is now such that only a particular type of person is willing to undertake the job. It requires a person who is willing to invest substantial time in the job, but for limited financial compensation. As Ehrenhalt (1991, 14) says, "There is no reason to suppose that this is the same set of people who would want to do politics in their spare time." His argument, then, is that both the *process* of recruitment and the changes in the utility structure have led to a "new breed" of ambitious state legislative office-seeker.

Alan Rosenthal (1998, 62) argues that the incentives have improved as a result of institutional capacity-building: "The improvement of facilities, the provision of services, the employment of staff, and the growing power of the legislative branch all appealed to men and women who might have been interested in political careers anyway."

At issue here is the causal connection between the increase in legislative professionalization, ambition, and careerism. It is a relationship which is much discussed (Clucas 1997; Ehrenhalt 1991; Fiorina 1994; Hamm and Hedlund 1990; Loomis 1990; Moncrief et al. 1996; A. Rosenthal 1998; Sollars 1994; Squire 1988a, 1988b, 1992a, 1997; Stonecash 1993; Thompson and Moncrief 1992; Thompson et al. 1996), but not entirely understood.

The Decline in Turnover. In his review essay on the history of legislative careers, Clubb (1994, 484) noted, "It is risky, indeed, to generalize about state legislatures. The terrain is vast and its contours varied." He is quite correct; the tricky thing is that state legislatures and legislative careers changed, but they did not all change at the same rate. Thus, we are forced to think both comparatively and longitudinally, and to do so concurrently.

At the state level, turnover declined gradually over the course of the past fifty years (Hyneman 1938; Niemi and Winsky 1987; Ray 1974; A. Rosenthal 1974; Shin and Jackson 1979). But because the rates were so high earlier in this century, even a steady decline did not lead to anything approaching a stable membership until the past few decades. Turnover in state legislatures averaged over 40% in lower chambers and over 35% in senates until the decade of the 1970s. By the mid-1980s, however, the mean turnover in both chambers had dropped to about 20% (Loomis 1990).[7] Thus, the concept of careerism in state legislatures is a fairly recent notion.

While turnover rates have dropped in virtually all states over the past few decades, there is still variation in membership stability from one state to another (Loomis 1990, 5). Several studies have shown a link between the level of legislative professionalization and retention rates (Luttbeg 1992; Moncrief et al. 1992; Opheim 1994).[8] In a slightly different vein, Squire (1988a) has shown that the mean years served in lower chambers is associated with the salary level (one measure of professionalism) but is also affected by the opportunity structure present in a particular state. Both the longitudinal decline in turnover and the remaining cross-state variation in membership stability raise questions about the relationship between legislative reform and the increase in careerism.

The Increase in Professionalization. As Mooney (1995, 47) notes, "In the past thirty years, state legislatures have undergone what is perhaps the most dramatic metamorphosis of any set of U.S. political institutions in living memory." Some of these changes came about through an explicit and concerted effort to transform state legislatures, which were viewed as decidedly inadequate institutions by mid-century. Alan Rosenthal (1998, 50–54) says that the primary goal of this movement was to build legislative capacity—in other words, to create institutions which would be better able to cope with the demands and needs of the states. Thus, such changes as increased session length and the development of professional staff were advocated. At the same time, reforms were advanced which were designed to attract competent individuals to serve in the legislature. Increased salary and better working conditions (e.g., office space) were such inducements.

Some scholars now attribute the development of legislative careerism to the institutional engineering of the state legislative reform movement. As Alan Rosenthal (1998, 50) recently commented, "The current dissatisfactions may have their roots in the reforms adopted years ago. Many believe, for instance, that the institutional development of legislatures and legislator's professionalism went too far."

Consequently, much attention recently has focused on the issue of professionalization and careerism. Some imprecision exists about the meaning of the two terms, but generally, "professionalization" is viewed as an institutional characteristic, while "careerism" is best seen as an individual characteristic (Squire 1988a). While professionalization and careerism have tended to occur together in the U.S., they are distinct and separate concepts, a point which may be particularly relevant to studies of institutional evolution in non-American settings (Moncrief 1994).

Measuring Professionalization. Measures of state legislative professionalization usually are derived from three variables: length of legislative session, staff support services, and legislative salary (see e.g., Carey et al. 1998; Kurtz 1992; Moncrief 1988; Squire 1988a, 1988b, 1992a, 1997). These variables are often combined to create either an interval (Carey et al. 1998), ratio (Squire 1992a), or ordinal (Kurtz 1992) categorization of state legislative professionalization.

Legislative professionalization can be conceived as either a dependent or an independent variable (Brace and Ward 1989; Moncrief 1988; Mooney 1995; Squire 1993). As an independent variable, the focus is often on explaining personnel patterns. For example, several studies have demonstrated a relationship between legislative professionalization and retention rates (Moncrief et al. 1992; Opheim 1994), while another has shown that more professional legislatures are less diverse in terms of gender, occupation, and racial/ethnic diversity (Squire 1992a).

From the standpoint of the individual, state legislative professionalization alters the cost-benefit equation for serving in the legislature (Francis 1985; Loomis 1990). While benefits are greater (higher salaries, better working conditions), the costs are also higher. Longer sessions not only mean greater demands from the legislative job (and, often, more time away from family) but also greater opportunity costs (in terms of the loss of income from one's outside job). Both of these factors have been found to be important reasons for people leaving the legislature (see Blair and Henry 1981; Francis and Baker 1986).

Legislatures and Types of Ambition

Yet, the concept of legislative professionalization remains a somewhat difficult one to measure precisely. For one thing, the three indicators do not necessarily tap the same dimension (A. Rosenthal 1998, 55). Squire, in particular, has recognized this distinction between the components that are directly related to the institution and those that are more related to the incentive structure of the individual. He has shown (1988a) that session length and staff size are decidedly less important than compensation and the opportunity structure in determining membership stability in lower chambers of state legislatures. Based on these two variables, Squire develops a typology of state legislatures (career, springboard, and dead-end) which closely corresponds to Schlesinger's static, progressive, and discrete ambitions. Arguing that these three types of legislatures offer different sets of career incentives, and therefore will attract "different sorts of people as members" (67), he goes on to demonstrate (1988b, 1992) how institutional arrangements such as leadership ladders and seniority rules will be adapted by members to meet their career goals.

In this way, Squire contends that the professionalization of state legislatures led to increased careerism, which in turn led to changes in the internal operation of the legislature (a component of institutionalization). Taken as a whole, Squire's work shows how ambition is constrained and channeled through the institutional context, and at the same time how ambition can mold some institutional practices to further those channeled ambitions. In this sense, his work is an example of the new institutionalism (March and Olsen 1984).

Recently, Berkman (1994) builds on Squire's work in a way that may be particularly useful for both congressional and state legislative scholars. In a rich and detailed study, Berkman seeks to investigate four factors at the same time: the differences between state legislatures, the changes in state legislatures over time, the career opportunity patterns for majority and minority parties, and the incidence of state legislators moving to the U.S. House. In a nutshell, his argument is that the increase in the number of former state legislators in the U.S. House is attributable to the professionalization of state legislatures. But it is not a simple relationship, Berkman contends. Not all state legislatures have professionalized at the same rate or to the same level. Some state legislatures offer incentives to stay which exceed the benefits of "moving up" (when informed by the risk involved). And this cost-benefit calculus is decidedly different for members of the minority party than for members in the majority (the majority-minority status in both the state legislative chamber and the U.S. House are relevant considerations here).

Berkman's work also builds on that of Fowler and McClure (1989) and Squire (1988a, 1988b) to provide a detailed study of how state legislative professionalization, coupled with the opportunity structure, interacts with congressional conditions to provide a supply of members to Congress with previous legislative experience. And elsewhere, Berkman (1993) has shown how former state legislators in Congress have advantages in some congressional activities by virtue of their prior experience. Together, these two studies show how state legislative and congressional studies can be bridged. Further, they serve to remind us that to the extent that state legislative professionalization changes the patterns of static and progressive ambition, it has implications for *both* state legislatures and Congress.

Is There a Partisan Bias to Legislative Professionalization? Another question revolving around the issue of state legislative professionalization is the potential for its differential effect on the two political parties. This argument has been most clearly articulated by Ehrenhalt (1991) and Fiorina (1992, 1994). The reasoning is as follows: the benefits (prestige, power, and especially salary) of legislative service today in many states, and the costs (time in session, opportunity costs of income foregone in other occupations) are such that the calculus works in favor of Democrats but not Republicans. Specifically, Democrats' commitment to government as a positive force (Ehrenhalt 1991, 23) and the fact that many Democrats have lower wage-earning potential in non-legislative posts leads to a sizeable pool of ambitious and qualified Democratic candidates willing to serve in many state legislatures. On the other hand, Republicans, who are generally less committed to a full-time government role anyway, are particularly averse to absorbing the opportunity cost of income foregone by serving in the legislature for less money than they could earn on the "outside." It is an intriguing argument, and one with important implications for institutional engineering and policy consequences. However, both Squire (1997) and especially Stonecash and Agathangelou (1997) have challenged the assumptions and data on which the argument is based.

Careers in the Chamber

The vigor with which scholars have pursued the electoral connection as the primary motivation for congressional behavior has tended to crowd out interest in other important aspects of careers. There simply has not been much attention devoted to how careers develop within the institution, other than to explain such things as committee assignments and casework as electorally-motivated.

There are a few exceptions, of course (e.g., Loomis 1988). The most important efforts at explaining how congressional careers unfold within the institution are those of Fenno (1978) and Hibbing (1991). Fenno is a tireless and conscientious tiller of this field. His work has enriched our understanding of the various motivations (reelection and otherwise) which compel congressmen through their careers. His method is distinctly different from the sophisticated modeling and statistical techniques used by the rational-choice camp; Fenno is the preeminent practitioner of what he calls "soaking and poking." Essentially, it is a participant-observer method.

It is a difficult technique to use effectively. For one thing, it requires the accommodation of those being observed—the congressmen and senators themselves. Not many political scientists have this sort of access to busy legislators. For another thing, the technique relies on the observer's ability to recognize meaningful patterns of behavior and to conceptualize these patterns in a way imbued with relevance to our understanding of both individual actions and institutional significance. It is a measure of Fenno's skill that legislators respect his work enough to let him look over their shoulder, and that political scientists respect his work enough to listen to what he says.

Hibbing's work (e.g., 1991; Herrick, Moore, and Hibbing 1994) has carefully plotted the constants and changes in the congressional career, using an imaginative procedure which helps control for period effects as both the institution and the cohorts changed over time. His finding that indeed longevity still matters is an important one. In tracking different types of activities he finds that newcomers and veterans may not differ much in terms of electoral margins or casework, but that the more senior members still carry the burden of the actual lawmaking activity.[9]

At the state level, there has been almost no attention paid to the career in the chamber. The exceptions are a few studies of leadership patterns (Freeman 1995; Jewell and Whicker 1994; Squire 1992b). This is an area in which we certainly need more research for two reasons. If, indeed, careers in many state legislatures are becoming longer, we need to know more about how these patterns unfold. Squire has alerted us to the differences in membership stability between "career" institutions and "springboard" institutions (as well as "dead end" ones). And he has shown how some structural patterns (e.g., seniority) may differ from one legislative type to another. Except for recent work by Hamm and Hedlund (see, e.g., 1995) we know little about how careers play out in terms of specialization within committees. Nor do we know much about how careerism affects leadership ladders, or the relative weight that careerists assign to policy influence versus other dimensions of representation.

Second, if discernible patterns do exist in regard to intra-institutional careers, how will these be affected by term limits? Obviously, career patterns within the institution will change but how? And how will this pattern be different under different term-limit conditions?

Leaving the Institution

Obviously, there are two ways by which one can leave the legislative institution: voluntarily and involuntarily. Voluntarily includes retirement from public service and retirement from the specific legislature in order to seek another office. Involuntarily includes electoral defeat. At the congressional level, again because of the rational-actor model's emphasis on choice and individual decision making, the focus is primarily on voluntary exit (since there is no choice to involuntary exit!).

As Kiewiet and Zeng (1993) note, the decision to leave has generally been framed as two binary choices: retiring or running for reelection, versus running for reelection or seeking higher office. Most of the rational choice literature focuses on just one or the other of these binary choices. Here we concentrate on the question of retirement from public office.

Some years ago, a number of studies sought to explain the increase in retirement rates which occurred during the decade of the 1970s (Brace 1985; Cooper and West 1981; Frantzich 1978; Hibbing 1982a, 1982b). The general conclusion was that some "veterans" were dissatisfied with the changes wrought by the post-Watergate reforms that had the effect of fragmenting power to more (and more junior) members. A second effect seemed to be that the nature of the job had become so demanding that some members concluded that the costs outweighed the benefits of continuing to serve. Others perceived their reelection chances were diminished, often due to redistricting. But it is well documented that retirement rates, which had increased in the 1970s, were again on the decline in the 1980s (Hibbing 1991; Livingston and Friedman 1993; Moore and Hibbing 1992), indicating that some of the earlier findings were time-specific.

As retirements again surged upward in the early 1990s, a series of articles investigated the causes. In particular, scholars were interested in the effect of changes in the law regarding pension benefits (Groseclose and Krehbiel 1994) and the effect of the check-kiting scandal (Alford et al. 1994; Jacobson and Dimock 1994). While both these events are interesting in explaining the short-term decision to retire, they have limited value toward the development of a more general theory of retirement; certainly this is true in a comparative sense.

However, Hall and Van Houweling (1995, 126; also see Theriault 1998) place the decision in the larger context of the institution: . . . the premise here is that members serve with a post-election purpose, some purpose independent of achieving yet another reelection." In particular, they find that the decision to retire or stay is in part a function of the power that the individual can expect to exercise in the future. Thus, whether or not the individual is a member of the majority party is an important part of his or her decision to stay or retire (on this point also see Gilmour and Rothstein 1993). This, of course, is not a new finding. But they also find that the decision is based on the individual's standing in the committee queue. Specifically, knowing the age differential between the committee chair and the second-ranking member is an important predictor of whether the latter was likely to retire or run for reelection. In other words, those who were within "striking distance" of committee power were less likely to take the pension windfall and leave. By considering the long-term utility calculations as well as the short-term (reelection) utility calculations, Hall and Van Houweling take a step toward placing the legislator as rational actor "in the context of a larger theory of intra-institutional ambition" (122). Herrick and Moore (1993), defining intra-institutional ambition as desire for party leadership positions, also find behavioral differences between legislators exhibiting this type of ambition compared to those with progressive or static (simple re-election) ambition.

One of the more interesting questions about those who choose to leave is whether or not this decision affects their behavior in the last term. In particular, the question of "shirking" of one's office duties in the last term is a topic of research in some of the public choice literature (e.g., Bender and Lott 1996; Lott 1990; Van Beek 1991; Zupan 1990). There is some evidence that, among those who are retiring, roll-call participation declines (Herrick et al. 1994; Lott 1990), as does constituent attention (as measured by trips home and staff allocations). But there is counterevidence as well, and the question of whether shirking is a genuine last-term problem has not yet been definitively answered (Carey 1996, 65). And last-term behavior associated with voluntary retirement may not be the same as last-term behavior associated with involuntary retirement. But it does raise questions directly relevant to the issue of term limits.

Term Limits

With the existence of state legislative term limits in eighteen states,[10] political scientists are increasingly drawn to the topic. There have been a few efforts to model the effect of term limits on Congress (see, e.g., Gilmour and Rothstein 1994; Mondak 1995; Reed and Schansberg 1995), but most studies focus on the more immediate impact on state legislatures.

If ever there was a "Political Scientists' Full-Employment Act," it surely would be tied to the myriad of term-limit laws which now exist in the states. The differences in the term-limit laws passed, the differences in the state legislatures now subject to term limits, and the magnitude of the potential changes they can cause makes for a remarkable research opportunity.

Since political scientists (especially American legislative scholars) have invested so much time and energy in the study of political ambition, we should be well positioned to contribute sound research to this field. After all, the term-limit movement is premised on the belief that political ambition and careerism are the dysfunctional cells in the American body politic.

There is a multitude of normative works on term limits, arguing why they should or should not be established. Likewise, there is a substantial body of work that investigates the history of the term-limit movement, or analyzes the vote on term-limit initiatives/referenda in a particular state. Neither of these types of study is reviewed here. Empirical work on the projected consequences of the term limits in the states is somewhat limited (but see Daniel and Lott 1997; some of the chapters included in Benjamin and Malbin 1992; Grofman 1996). This is understandable, given that legislative term limitations are a recent innovation in many American jurisdictions—and that they are not yet in full effect in most of the states that have passed term-limit laws.

Early efforts to assess the potential impact of term limits were based on extrapolations of retention rates among previous cohorts (Everson 1992; Moncrief et al. 1992; Opheim 1994; Thompson and Moncrief 1993). To students of state legislatures, the findings were obvious (but nontrivial): since incumbent retention rates varied by the professionalization of the legislature and the advancement opportunities within the state, term limits would likely have different impacts in different states.

Recent work by Francis and Kenney (1997) improves on these early studies. Beginning with an estimation of expected tenure (i.e., retention) in lower chambers over a specified time period, they then consider the changes wrought by term limits in upper chambers. The fact that such seats will become available as open seats will lead some house members to run for the state senate before they are term-limited out of the lower chamber. As Francis and Kenney (1997, 241) point out, "Term limits not only increase the number of open seats; they also alter the preference structure. Legislators will be faced with a new kind of option." Since it is less risky for an incumbent house member to run for an open senate seat rather than to challenge an incumbent senator, the strategic house member may forego his remaining time in the lower chamber to run for the open senate seat when it becomes available. Francis and Kenney develop estimates of house turnover which are higher—in some cases much higher—than we might otherwise expect.

The most comprehensive work on term limits to date is Carey's (1996). This research is significant for two reasons. First, it demonstrates how a rational-choice approach can yield precise and testable hypotheses about the potential impact of term limits. Second, it is an excellent example of the use of comparative research. As Carey notes (1996, 8), "there is frequently an underlying faith in the idea of American exceptionalism; that politics in the United States is driven by a fundamentally different kind of motor from politics elsewhere."

But in the case of term limits, there are a few other countries that impose them, and Carey sets out to show ways in which that experience can inform us. In particular, he focuses on the Costa Rican experience with term limits, conscientiously drawing out the ways in which the system there is similar and the ways in which it is different from the system in the U.S. In so doing, he is able to show how term limits in Costa Rica have not hampered particularism, and how pension-seeking (post-legislative appointive positions) affects legislative behavior.

His conclusion that "legislators are responsive to those who control their future careers" raises interesting research questions for American scholars. Will we see more position-shifting as legislators prime themselves for runs up the career ladder (to state senate or the U.S. House)? Will they become more responsive to specific interest groups that might provide employment after the legislative career is terminated? Will the career ladder change to include more local elective positions, some of which (e.g., county supervisors or commissioners) offer more pay and potentially longer tenure than many state legislative positions? If so, will state legislators engage in even more particularistic behavior (e.g., pork) for credit-claiming purposes?

Recently, Carey and his associates (Carey, Niemi, and Powell 1998) initiated a more direct analysis of the impact of term limits in the states. They seek to answer three sets of questions about the effect of term limits: (1) Do they change the composition of state legislatures in terms of the backgrounds and motivations of the legislators? (2) Do they change the types of behavior in which legislators engage? (3) Do they alter the influence patterns within the legislature and/or the influence of the legislature vis-à-vis other political actors? The data are based on survey responses from over 2,000 state legislators. Their method approaches that of a "natural experiment": by comparing respondents elected before and after term limits were passed, and by comparing them also to respondents from non-term-limited states, Carey et al. hope to isolate the effects of term limits. Clearly, the results are preliminary, since the full effect of term limits are still several years away in some states. And at this point the analysis is based on respondents' perceptions of changes, not on more objective measures. Thus far, they find no dramatic compositional effects, but some evidence of both behavioral and institutional effects. Specifically, it appears that efforts to secure particularistic benefits for the home district are diminished in term-limited states, that the influence of party leadership has diminished, and that governors are perceived as having gained influence relative to the legislature (Carey et al. 1998).

Uncovering the effects of term limits will be a long and difficult task. The structure of incentives and disincentives vary by the professionalized nature of the legislature. The opportunity structure varies as well. And certainly the nature of the term-limit law (what I call the "terms of the term limit") vary from state to state. The restrictions range from a six-year, lifetime limit (the California, Michigan, and Oregon lower chambers) to a twelve-year limit which allows reentry after sitting out one term (Utah). In the latter case, one could actually serve 24 years in a 26-year period!

Is Any of This Exportable?

What can research on American legislatures lend to the study of legislatures elsewhere? The American electoral system is often characterized as candidate-centered. The role of parties as recruiting and nominating agents is clearly constrained (although perhaps not as irrelevant as we sometimes believe). It is largely due to this self-starter image that the phrase, "candidate emergence," rather than "candidate recruitment," has taken hold in the U.S. literature. It is likewise a primary reason for the dominance of the rational-actor model in studies of the

U.S. Congress and, to a lesser (but growing) extent, in studies of American legislatures.

Comparative studies can be particularly informative in explaining how political recruitment patterns are affected by the variety of institutional arrangements that exist in different political systems, and how those recruitment patterns affect political behavior. Norris's (1997) edited volume on recruitment in nine developed nations is a recent example (also see Gallagher 1988). Numerous researchers have demonstrated that the motivation of individual legislators is an extremely useful approach to explaining specific behavior in different legislative settings, e.g., the seeking of particularistic benefits in Brazil (Ames 1997) and Costa Rica (Carey 1996), and to casework in the British House of Commons (Cain et al. 1989; King 1981) and the Canadian House of Commons (Docherty 1997). Moreover, Epstein et al. (1997) show how the development of careerism in Japan has led to the development of a seniority system. And Carey's (1996) work comparing legislative behavior in Costa Rica and Venezuela, under different electoral and party conditions, can yield useful insights into the potential effects of term limits in the U.S. Clearly, there is the potential for a valuable exchange.

Conclusion

At the outset, I noted that congressional and state legislative students have tended to till their own row, paying little attention to what was going on elsewhere in the field. But there are at least two developments, both presently in the state legislative arena, that have the potential to lead to linkages between congressional and state legislative studies. The first is the increase in careerism among state legislators. This is not a new situation to congressional scholars, and students of state legislatures can profit by looking at what congressional research can tell us about the impact of careerism, especially intra-institutional ambition. At the same time, congressional scholars may need to look more closely at the effect of state legislative professionalization on the candidate pool for congressional office. Fowler and McClure (1989) argue convincingly that the incentive structure in the highly professionalized New York legislature is now such that fewer members are willing to leave for a seat in Congress. But this may depend on one's status as a member of the majority or minority party in the state legislature, compared to one's party's status in Congress (Berkman 1994; Canon 1990).

The second development which both congressional and state legislative students must consider is the effect of term limits in the states. We do not yet have an adequate conceptualization of how the different term-limit laws will affect state legislatures, or how the same term-limit law will affect state legislatures at different stages of professionalization, or how state legislative term limits will affect the candidate pool and the competitiveness of congressional elections. For example, term limits should lead to a higher tolerance of risk for progressively ambitious state legislators: since they will no longer have the option of retaining their present position, challenges to incumbent congressmen become more likely. Presumably this will increase the quality of the candidate pool in congressional elections, which may in turn ratchet up efforts on the part of congressional incumbents to engage in behaviors to increase their personal vote. It may also lead to an increase in "scare-off tactics," such as the accumulation of campaign war chests. It is also possible that these will be short-term effects. Proponents of term limits often argue that such limits will lead to a different kind of person being recruited into the state legislature, i.e., those with discrete ambitions. If indeed this turns out to be the case, then state legislatures with term limits would be less likely to produce candidates to run for Congress. It is problematic whether this is indeed what will happen, but only time will tell.

NOTES

1. In addition to Matthews's (1984) milestone article, there are a number of other fine treatises on recruitment and why it matters. One of the best earlier essays is Marvick's (1976). The best recent work is Fowler's (1993) excellent book, from which I have borrowed shamelessly.

2. Thus, in his essay on modern legislative careers, Hibbing (1994, 497) discusses three phases of the career: entry (recruitment), service (the institutional career), and exit. In this instance, Hibbing's use of the term "career" is institution-specific. But the term "careerism" often is used to mean the entire political career, which may span one or more institutions.

3. Pippa Norris gives a similar definition: "The concept of *legislative recruitment* refers to the critical step as individuals move from lower levels into parliamentary careers" (1997, 1).

4. This is not to say there have been no such recent studies at the congressional level. See, for example, Barbara Burrell (1994), Gertzog, (1995), and Whicker et al. (1996). Also see Dabelko and Herrnson (1997), and Green (1998). On the specifics of the election of women to Congress in 1992, the "year of the woman," see Gaddie and Bullock (1995), and Berch (1996).

5. For a discussion of the opportunity structure for women at the congressional level, see Welch and Studlar (1996).

6. These figures are calculated from Table 3.1 in Davidson and Oleszek (1998).

7. Turnover in recent elections has increased slightly. This is certainly due, in part, to the early effect of term limits, although it is probably not the only cause. The success of the Republican party in 1994 also contributed to somewhat higher turnover. In lower chambers in those states in which elections were held, the mean turnover rate in 1994 was almost 25%; in 1996 it was 22.5%. In 1996, the turnover rate in lower chambers was at least 30% in twelve states.

8. It is worth pointing out that in this review we are talking specifically about retention rates, not incumbency advantage (although obviously the latter is a factor in determining the former). There is a fairly extensive body of literature at both the congressional and state legislative level which attempts to determine the precise electoral advantage that incumbents enjoy. We do not review that literature in this essay, but see Cox and Morgenstern (1993) and Cox and Katz (1996) for examples.

9. See Gerber (1996) for a discussion of African-American congressional careers.

10. Term-limit laws affecting state legislatures have actually passed in twenty-one states, but have been invalidated by state supreme courts in Nebraska, Massachusetts, and Washington. It is quite likely that term-limit initiatives will reappear in these states, rewritten to avoid the specific objections voiced by the courts.

REFERENCES

Adams, Greg, and Peverill Squire. 1997. "Incumbent Vulnerability and Challenger Emergence in Senate Elections." *Political Behavior* 19:97–111.

Alford, John, Holly Teeters, Daniel Ward, and Rick Wilson. 1994. "Overdraft: The Political Cost of Congressional Malfeasance." *Journal of Politics* 56:788–801.

Ames, Barry. 1995. "Electoral Rules, Constituency Pressures, and Pork Barrel: Bases of Voting in the Brazilian Congress." *Journal of Politics* 57:324–43.

Banks, Jeffrey, and D. Roderick Kiewiet. 1989. "Explaining Patterns of Candidate Competition in Congressional Elections." *American Journal of Political Science* 33:997–1015.

Barber, James David. 1965. *The Lawmakers: Recruitment and Adaptation to Legislative Life*. Westport, CT: Greenwood Press.

Barrett, Edith. 1995. "The Policy Priorities of African American Women in State Legislatures." *Legislative Studies Quarterly* 20:223–47.

Bender, Bruce, and John Lott. 1996. "Legislator Voting and Shirking: A Critical Review of the Literature." *Public Choice* 87:67–100.

Benjamin, Gerald, and Michael Malbin. 1992. *Limiting Legislative Terms*. Washington, DC: CQ Press.

Berch, Neil. 1996. "'The Year of the Woman' in Context." *American Politics Quarterly* 24:169–93.

Berkman, Michael. 1993. "Former State Legislators in the U.S. House of Representatives: Institutional and Policy Mastery." *Legislative Studies Quarterly* 18:77–104.

Berkman, Michael. 1994. "State Legislators in Congress: Strategic Politicians, Professional Legislatures, and the Party Nexus." *American Journal of Political Science* 38:1025–55.

Berkman, Michael, and R. O'Connor. 1993. "Do Women Legislators Matter? Female Legislators and State Abortion Policy." *American Politics Quarterly* 21:102–24.

Bianco, William T. 1984. "Strategic Decisions on Candidacy in U.S. Congressional Districts." *Legislative Studies Quarterly* 9:351–64.

Black, Gordon. 1972. "A Theory of Political Ambition: Career Choices and the Role of Structural Incentives." *American Political Science Review* 72:144–59.

Blair, Diane, and Jeanie Stanley. 1991. "Personal Relations and Legislative Power: Male and Female Perceptions." *Legislative Studies Quarterly* 16:495–507.

Bond, Jon, Cary Covington, and Richard Fleischer. 1985. "Explaining Challenger Quality in Congressional Elections." *Journal of Politics* 47:510–29.

Bond, Jon, Richard Fleisher, and Jeffery Talbert. 1997. "Partisan Differences in Candidate Quality in Open Seat House Races." *Political Research Quarterly* 50:281–99.

Brace, Paul. 1984. "Progressive Ambition and the House: A Probabilistic Approach." *Journal of Politics* 46:556–71.

Brace, Paul. 1985. "A Probabilistic Approach to Retirement to Retirement from the U.S. Congress." *Legislative Studies Quarterly* 10:107–23.

Brace, Paul, and Daniel Ward. 1989. "The Transformation of the American Statehouse: A Study of Legislative Institutionalization." Presented at the annual meeting of the Midwest Political Science Association, Chicago.

Breaux, David, and Malcolm Jewell. 1992. "Winning Big: The Incumbency Advantage in State Legislative Races." In *Changing Patterns in State Legislative Careers*, ed. Gary Moncrief and Joel Thompson. Ann Arbor: University of Michigan Press.

Bullock, Charles III, and David Shafer. 1997. "Party Targeting and Electoral Success." *Legislative Studies Quarterly* 22:573–84.

Burrell, Barbara. 1994. *A Woman's Place Is in the House: Campaigning for Congress in the Feminist Era.* Ann Arbor: University of Michigan Press.

Cain, Bruce, John Ferejohn, and Morris Fiorina. 1987. *The Personal Vote: Constituency Service and Electoral Independence.* Cambridge: Harvard University Press.

Canon, David T. 1990. *Actors, Athletes, and Astronauts.* Chicago: University of Chicago Press.

Canon. David T. 1994. "The Social Bases of Legislative Recruitment." In *Encyclopedia of the American Legislative System*, ed. Joel H. Silbey. New York: Scribner's Sons.

Canon, David, and David Sousa. 1992. "Party System Change and Political Career Structures in the U.S. Congress." *Legislative Studies Quarterly* 17:347–63.

Canon, David, Matthew Schousen, Patrick Sellers. 1996. "The Supply Side of Congressional Redistricting: Race and Strategic Politicians, 1972–1992." *Journal of Politics* 58:846–62.

Carey, John. 1996. *Term Limits and Legislative Representation.* New York: Cambridge University Press.

Carey, John, and Matthew Shugart. 1995. "Incentives to Cultivate a Personal Vote: A Rank Ordering of Electoral Formulas." *Electoral Studies* 14:417–39.

Carey, John, Richard Niemi, and Lynda Powell. 1998. "The Effects of Term Limits on State Legislatures." *Legislative Studies Quarterly* 23:271–300.

Cassie, William. 1994. "More May Not Always Be Better: Republican Recruiting Strategies in Southern Legislative Elections." *The American Review of Politics* 15:141–55.

Clubb, Jerome. 1994. "The Historical Legislative Career." In *Encyclopedia of the American Legislative System*, ed. Joel H. Silbey. New York: Scribner's Sons.

Clucas, Richard. 1997. "Legislative Professionalism and Careerism: Determining the Causal Order." Portland State University. Typescript.

Cooper, Joseph, and William West. 1981. "The Congressional Career in the 1970s." In *Congress Reconsidered*, ed. Lawrence Dodd and Bruce Oppenheimer. Washington, DC: CQ Press.

Cooper, Joseph, and David Brady. 1981. "Toward a Diachronic Analysis of Congress." *American Political Science Review* 75:988–1006.
Cox, Gary, and Scott Morgenstern. 1993. "The Increasing Advantage of Incumbency in the U.S. States." *Legislative Studies Quarterly* 18:495–514.
Cox, Gary, and Jonathan Katz. 1996. "Why Did the Incumbency Advantage in U.S. House Elections Grow?" *American Journal of Political Science* 40:478–97.
Czudnowski, Moshe. 1975. "Political Recruitment." In *Handbook of Political Science, Vol. 2*, ed. Fred Greenstein and Nelson Polsby. Reading, MA: Addison-Wesley.
Dabelko, Kirsten la Cour, and Paul Herrnson. 1997. "Women's and Men's Campaigns for the U.S. House of Representatives." *Political Research Quarterly* 50:121–36.
Daniel, Kermit, and J. R. Lott, Jr. 1997. "Term Limits and Electoral Competitiveness: Evidence from California's State Legislative Races." *Public Choice* 90:165–84.
Darcy, Robert, Susan Welch, and Janet Clark. 1994. *Women, Elections, and Representation*, 2d ed. Lincoln: University of Nebraska Press.
Davidson, Roger, and Walter Oleszek. 1976. "Adaptation and Consolidation: Structural Innovation in the U.S. House of Representatives." *Legislative Studies Quarterly* 1:37–66.
Davidson, Roger, and Walter Oleszek. 1998. *Congress and Its Members*. Washington, DC: CQ Press.
Derge, David. 1959. "The Lawyer as Decision-Maker in the American State Legislature." *Journal of Politics* 21:408–33.
Docherty, David. 1997. *Mr. Smith Goes to Ottawa: Life in the House of Commons*. Vancouver: UBC Press.
Dodd, Lawrence. 1986. "A Theory of Congressional Cycles: Solving the Problem of Change." In *Congress and Policy Change*, ed. Gerald Wright, Leroy Rieselbach, and Lawrence Dodd. New York: Agathon Press.
Dolan, Kathleen, and Lynne Ford. 1997. "Change and Continuity Among Women State Legislators: Evidence From Three Decades." *Political Research Quarterly* 50:137–51.
Ehrenhalt, Alan. 1991. *The United States of Ambition*. New York: Random House.
Epstein, David, David Brady, Sadafumi Kawato, and Sharyn O'Halloran. 1997. "A Comparative Approach to Legislative Organization: Careerism and Seniority in the United States and Japan." *American Journal of Political Science* 41:965–88.
Eulau, Heinz, and John D. Sprague. 1964. *Lawyers in Politics*. Indianapolis: Bobbs-Merrill.
Everson, David. 1992. "The Impact of Term Limitations of the States: Cutting the Underbrush or Chopping Down the Tall Timber?" In *Limiting Legislative Terms*, ed. Gerald Benjamin and Michael Malbin. Washington, DC: CQ Press.
Fenno, Richard, F. 1978. *Home Style: House Members in Their Districts*. Boston: Little, Brown.
Fiorina, Morris. 1977. *Congress: Keystone to the Washington Establishment*. New Haven, CT: Yale University Press.
Fiorina, Morris. 1992. *Divided Government*. Boston: Allyn and Bacon.
Fiorina, Morris. 1994. "Divided Government in the American States: A Byproduct of Legislative Professionalism?" *American Political Science Review* 88:304–16.

Fiorina, Morris, and T. Prinz. 1994. "Legislative Incumbency and Insulation." In *Encyclopedia of the American Legislative System*, ed. Joel H. Silbey. New York: Scribner's Sons.

Fiorina, Morris, David Rohde, and Peter Wissel. 1975. "Historical Change in House Turnover." In *Congress in Change*, ed. Norman Ornstein. New York: Praeger.

Fishel, Jeff. 1973. *Party and Opposition: Congressional Challengers in American Politics*. New York: David McKay.

Fowler, Linda. 1991. "Congressional Recruitment and Political Context." In *Home Style and Washington Work*, ed. Morris Fiorina and David Rohde. Ann Arbor: University of Michigan Press.

Fowler, Linda. 1993. *Candidates, Congress, and the American Democracy*. Ann Arbor: University of Michigan Press.

Fowler, Linda, and Robert McClure. 1989. *Political Ambition*. New Haven, CT: Yale University Press.

Francis, Wayne. 1985. "Costs and Benefits of Legislative Service in the American States." *American Journal of Political Science* 29:626–42.

Francis, Wayne. 1993. "House to Senate Career Movement in the U.S. States: The Significance of Selectivity." *Legislative Studies Quarterly* 18:309–20.

Francis, Wayne, and John Baker. 1986. "Why Do U.S. State Legislators Vacate Their Seats?" *Legislative Studies Quarterly* 11:119–26.

Francis, Wayne, and Lawrence Kenney. 1997. "Equilibrium Projections of the Consequences of Term Limits Upon Expected Tenure, Institutional Turnover, and Membership Experience." *Journal of Politics* 59:240–52.

Frantzich, Stephen. 1978. "Opting Out: Retirement From the U.S. House of Representatives." *American Politics Quarterly* 6:251–73.

Freeman, Patricia. 1995. "A Comparative Analysis of Speaker Career Patterns in U.S. State Legislatures." *Legislative Studies Quarterly* 20:365–76.

Freeman, Patricia, and Lilliard Richardson. 1996. "Explaining Variation in Casework among State Legislatures." *Legislative Studies Quarterly* 21:41–56.

Gaddie, Ronald, and Charles Bullock III. 1995. "Congressional Elections and the Year of the Woman: Structural and Elite Influences on Female Candidates." *Social Science Quarterly* 76:749–62.

Gallagher, Michael, and Michael Marsh, eds. 1988. *Candidate Selection in Comparative Perspective*. Beverly Hills: Sage Publications.

Garand, James. 1991. "Electoral Marginality in the States." *Legislative Studies Quarterly* 16:7–28.

Gerber, Alan. 1996. "African Americans' Congressional Careers and the Democratic House Delegation." *Journal of Politics* 58:831–45.

Gertzog, Irwin. 1995. *Congressional Women: Their Recruitment, Integration and Behavior*, 2d ed. Westport, CT: Praeger.

Gierzynski, Anthony. 1992. *Legislative Party Campaign Committees in the American States*. Lexington, KY: University Press of Kentucky.

Gilmour, John, and Paul Rothstein. 1993. "Early Republican Retirement: A Cause of Democratic Dominance in the House of Representatives." *Legislative Studies Quarterly* 18:345–65.

Gilmour, John, and Paul Rothstein. 1994. "Term Limitations in a Dynamic Model of Partisan Balance." *American Journal of Political Science* 38:770–96.

Green, Joanne Connor. 1998. "The Role of Gender in Open-Seat Elections for the U.S. House of Representatives." *Women & Politics* 19:33–55.

Grofman, Bernard, ed. 1996. *Legislative Term Limits: Public Choice Perspectives*. Boston: Kluwer Academic Publishers.

Grofman, Bernard, and Lisa Handley. 1989. "Black Representation: Making Sense of Electoral Geography at Different Levels of Government." *Legislative Studies Quarterly* 14:265–80.

Groseclose, Timothy, and Keith Krehbiel. 1994. "Golden Parachutes, Rubber Checks, and Strategic Retirements from the 102nd House." *American Journal of Political Science* 38:75–99.

Hain, Paul, P.G. Roeder, and M. Avalos. 1981. "Risk and Progressive Candidacies: An Extension of Rohde's Model." *American Journal of Political Science* 25:188–92.

Hall, Richard, and Robert Van Houweling. 1995. "Avarice and Ambition in Congress: Representatives' Decisions to Run or Retire from the U.S. House." *American Political Science Review* 89:121–36.

Hamm, Keith, and Ronald Hedlund. 1990. "Legislative Professionalization and the State Policymaking Process." Presented at the annual meeting of the American Political Science Association, San Francisco.

Hamm, Keith, and Ronald Hedlund. 1995. "The Development of Committee Specialization in State Legislatures." Presented at the annual meeting of the American Political Science Association, Chicago.

Hedge, David, James Button, and Mary Spear. 1996. "Accounting for the Quality of Black Legislative Life: The View from the States." *American Journal of Political Science* 40:82–98.

Hedlund, Ronald, and Samuel Patterson. 1992. "The Electoral Antecedents of State Legislative Committee Assignment." *Legislative Studies Quarterly* 17:539–59.

Herrick, Rebekah, and Michael Moore. 1993. "Political Ambition's Effect on Legislative Behavior: Schlesinger's Typology Reconsidered and Revised." *Journal of Politics* 55:765–76.

Herrick, Rebekah, Michael Moore, and John Hibbing. 1994. "Unfastening the Electoral Connection: The Behavior of U.S. Representatives when Reelection Is No Longer a Factor." *Journal of Politics* 56:214–27.

Herrnson, Paul. 1988. *Party Campaigning in the 1980s*. Cambridge: Harvard University Press.

Herrnson, Paul. 1990. "Reemergent National Party Organizations." In *The Parties Respond*, ed. L. Sandy Maisel. Boulder, CO: Westview Press.

Hibbing, John. 1982a. "Voluntary Retirement from the U.S. House of Representatives: Who Quits?" *American Journal of Political Science* 30:651–65.

Hibbing, John. 1982b. "Voluntary Retirement from the U.S. House: The Costs of Congressional Service." *Legislative Studies Quarterly* 7:57–74.

Hibbing, John. 1991. *Congressional Careers*. Chapel Hill: University of North Carolina Press.

Hibbing, John. 1994. "Modern Legislative Careers." In *Encyclopedia of the American Legislative System*, ed. Joel H. Silbey. New York: Scribner's Sons.

Hyneman, Charles. 1938. "Tenure and Turnover of Legislative Personnel." *Annals of the American Academy of Political and Social Science* 23:21–31.

Jacobson, Gary, and Samuel Kernell. 1981. *Strategy and Choice in Congressional Elections*. New Haven, CT: Yale University Press.

Jacobson, Gary, and Michael Dimock. 1994. "Checking Out: The Effects of Overdrafts on the 1992 House Election." *American Journal of Political Science* 38:601–24.

Jewell, Malcolm, and Marcia Whicker. 1994. *Legislative Leadership in the American States*. Ann Arbor: University of Michigan Press.

Kathlene, Lyn. 1995. "Alternative Views of Crime: Legislative Policymaking in Gendered Terms." *Journal of Politics* 57:696–723.

Katz, Jonathan, and Brian Sala. "Careerism, Committee Assignments, and the Electoral Connection." *American Political Science Review* 90:21–33.

Kazee, Thomas. 1994a."The Emergence of Congressional Candidates." In *Who Runs for Congress?* ed. Thomas Kazee. Washington, DC: CQ Press.

Kazee, Thomas. 1994b. "Ambition and Candidacy: Running as a Strategic Calculation." In *Who Runs for Congress?* ed. Thomas Kazee. Washington, DC: CQ Press.

Kazee, Thomas, and Mary Thornberry. 1990. "Where's the Party? Congressional Candidate Recruitment and American Party Organizations." *Western Political Quarterly* 43:61–80.

Kernell, Samuel. 1977. "Toward Understanding Nineteenth-Century Congressional Careers: Ambition, Competition and Rotation." *American Journal of Political Science* 21:669–93.

Kiewiet, D. Roderick, and Langche Zeng. 1993. "An Analysis of Congressional Career Decisions, 1947–1986." *American Political Science Review* 87:928–41.

Kim, Chong Lim, Justin Green, and Samuel Patterson. 1976. "Partisanship in the Recruitment and Performance of American State Legislatures." In *Elite Recruitment in Democratic Polities*, ed. Heinz Eulau and Moshe Czudnowski. New York: Sage Publishing.

King, Anthony. 1981. "The Rise of the Career Politician in Britain—And Its Consequences." *British Journal of Political Science* 11:249–85.

Krasno, Jonathon, and Donald Green. 1988. "Preempting Quality Challengers in House Elections." *Journal of Politics* 50:920–36.

Kurtz, Karl. 1992. "Understanding the Diversity of American State Legislatures." *Legislative Studies Section Newsletter*. Washington, DC: American Political Science Association.

Lasswell, Harold. 1948. *Power and Personality*. New York: Norton.

Livingston, Steven, and Sally Friedman. 1993. "Reexamining Theories of Congressional Retirement: Evidence from the 1980s." *Legislative Studies Quarterly* 18:231–54.

Loomis, Burdett. 1988. *The New American Politician: Ambition, Entrepreneurship, and the Changing Face of Political Life*. New York: Basic Books.

Loomis, Burdett. 1990. "Political Careers and American State Legislatures." Presented at the Eagleton Institute of Politics Symposium on the Legislature in the Twenty-First Century, Williamsburg, VA.

Loomis, Burdett. 1994. "The Motivations of Legislators." In *The Encyclopedia of the American Legislative System*, ed. Joel H. Silbey. New York: Scribner's Sons.

Lott, John R., Jr. 1990. "Attendance Rates, Political Shirking, and the Effect of Post-Election Office Employment." *Journal of Economic Inquiry* 28:133–50.

Lublin, David. 1994. "Quality, not Quantity: Strategic Politicians in U.S. Senate Elections, 1952–1990." *Journal of Politics* 56:228–41.

Luttbeg, Norman. 1992. "Legislative Careers in Six States: Are Some Legislatures More Likely to Be Responsive?" *Legislative Studies Quarterly* 17:49–68.

Maisel, L. Sandy, and Walter Stone. 1997. "Determinants of Candidate Emergence in U.S. House Elections: An Exploratory Study." *Legislative Studies Quarterly* 22:79–96.

Maisel, L. Sandy, Linda Fowler, Ruth Jones, and Walter Stone. 1990. "The Naming of Candidates: Recruitment or Emergence?" In *The Parties Respond*, ed. L. Sandy Maisel. Boulder, CO: Westview Press.

March, James, and Johan Olsen. 1984. "The New Institutionalism: Organizational Factors in Political Life." *American Political Science Review* 78:734–49.

Marvick, Dwaine. 1976. "Continuities in Recruitment Theory and Research: Toward a New Model." In *Elite Recruitment in Democratic Polities*, ed. Heinz Eulau and Moshe Czudnowski. New York: Sage Press.

Matland, Richard, and Deborah Brown. 1992. "District Magnitude's Effect on Female Representation in U.S. State Legislatures." *Legislative Studies Quarterly* 17:469–92.

Matthews, Donald. 1954. *The Social Background of Political Decision-Makers*. New York: Random House.

Matthews, Donald. 1960. *U.S. Senators and Their World*. New York: Vintage Press.

Matthews, Donald. 1984. "Legislative Recruitment and Legislative Careers." *Legislative Studies Quarterly* 9:547–85.

Mayhew, David. 1974. *The Electoral Connection*. New Haven: Yale University Press.

Moore, Michael, and John Hibbing. 1992. "Is Serving in Congress Fun Again? Voluntary Retirements from the House Since the 1970s." *American Journal of Political Science* 36:824–28.

Moncrief, Gary. 1988. "Dimensions of the Concept of Professionalism in State Legislatures: A Research Note." *State and Local Government Review* 20:128–32.

Moncrief, Gary. 1994. "Professionalism and Careerism in Canadian Provincial Assemblies: A Comparison to U.S. State Legislatures." *Legislative Studies Quarterly* 19:33–48.

Moncrief, Gary. 1998. "Terminating the Provincial Career: Retirement and Electoral Defeat in Canadian Provincial Legislatures, 1960–1997." *Canadian Journal of Political Science* 31:359–72.

Moncrief, Gary, and Joel Thompson. 1992a. *Changing Patterns in State Legislative Careers*. Ann Arbor: University of Michigan Press.

Moncrief, Gary, and Joel Thompson. 1992b. "Electoral Structure and State Legislative Representation." *Journal of Politics* 52:246–57.

Moncrief, Gary, Joel Thompson, and Karl Kurtz. 1996. "The Old Statehouse: It Ain't What It Used To Be." *Legislative Studies Quarterly* 21:57–72.

Moncrief, Gary, Joel Thompson, Michael Haddon, and Robert Hoyer. 1992. "For Whom the Bell Tolls: Term Limits and State Legislatures." *Legislative Studies Quarterly* 17:37–47.

Mondak, Jeffrey. 1995. "Elections as Filters: Term Limits and the Composition of the U.S. House." *Political Research Quarterly* 48:701–28.

Mooney, Christopher. 1995. "Citizens, Structures, and Sister States: Influences on State Legislative Professionalism." *Legislative Studies Quarterly* 20:47–67.

Nechemias, Carol. 1985. "Geographic Mobility and Women's Access to State Legislatures." *Western Political Quarterly* 38:119–31.

Nechemias, Carol. 1987. "Changes in the Election of Women to U.S. State Legislative Seats." *Legislative Studies Quarterly* 12:125–41.

Niemi, Richard, and Laura R. Winsky. 1987. "Membership Turnover in U.S. State Legislatures: Trends and Effects of Districting." *Legislative Studies Quarterly* 12:115–23.

Niven, David. 1998. "Party Elites and Women Candidates: The Shape of Bias." *Women & Politics* 19:57–80.

Norris, Pippa, ed. 1997. *Passages to Power: Legislative Recruitment in Advanced Democracies.* New York: Cambridge University Press.

Opheim, Cynthia. 1994. "The Effect of U.S. State Legislative Term Limits Revisited." *Legislative Studies Quarterly* 19:49–60.

Patterson, Samuel, and Robert Boynton. 1969. "Legislative Recruitment in a Civic Culture." *Social Science Quarterly* 50:243–63.

Payne, James. 1982. "Career Intentions and Electoral Performance of Members of the U.S. House." *Legislative Studies Quarterly* 7:93–99.

Polsby, Nelson. 1968. "The Institutionalization of the House of Representatives." *American Political Science Association* 62:144–68.

Polsby, Nelson, William Gallagher, and Barry Rundquist. 1969. "The Growth of the Seniority System in the U.S. House of Representatives." *American Political Science Review* 63:787–807.

Prewitt, Kenneth, and Heinz Eulau. 1971. "Social Bias in Leadership Selection: Political Recruitment and Electoral Context." *Journal of Politics* 33:293–315.

Prewitt, Kenneth, and Heinz Eulau. 1978. "Political Matrix and Political Representation" In *The Politics of Representation*, ed. Heinz Eulau and John Wahlke. Beverly Hills: Sage Publications.

Price, H. Douglas. 1975. "Congress and the Evolution of Legislative 'Professionalism'." In *Congress in Change*, ed. Norman Ornstein. New York: Praeger.

Pritchard, Anita. 1992. "Strategic Considerations in the Decision to Challenge a State Legislative Incumbent." *Legislative Studies Quarterly* 17:381–94.

Ray, David. 1974. "Membership Stability in Three State Legislatures: 1893–1969." *American Political Science Review* 68:106–12.

Ray, David. 1976. "Voluntary Retirement and Electoral Defeat in Eight State Legislatures." *Journal of Politics* 38:426–33.

Reed, W. Robert and D. Eric Schansberg. 1995. "The House Under Term Limits: What Would It Look Like?" *Social Science Quarterly* 76:699–716.

Reingold, Beth. 1996. "Conflict and Cooperation: Legislative Strategies and Concepts of Power Among Female and Male State Legislators." *Journal of Politics* 58:464–85.

Richardson, Lilliard, and Patricia Freeman. 1995. "Gender Differences in Constituency Service Among State Legislatures." *Political Research Quarterly* 48:169–79.
Rohde, David. 1979. "Risk-Bearing and Progressive Ambition: The Case of Members of the United States House of Representatives." *American Journal of Political Science* 23:1–26.
Rosenthal, Alan. 1974. "Turnover in State Legislatures." *American Journal of Political Science* 18:609–16.
Rosenthal, Alan. 1998. *The Decline of Representative Democracy*. Washington, DC: CQ Press.
Rosenthal, Cindy S. 1995. "New Party or Campaign Bank Account? Explaining the Rise of State Legislative Campaign Committees." *Legislative Studies Quarterly* 20:249–68.
Rule, Wilma. 1990. "Why More Women Are State Legislators: A Research Note." *Western Political Quarterly* 43:437–48.
Rule, Wilma, and Joseph Zimmerman, eds. 1992. *U.S. Electoral Systems: Their Impact on Women and Minorities*. Westport, CT: Greenwood Press.
Saint-Germain, Michelle. 1989. "Does Their Difference Make a Difference?" *Social Science Quarterly* 70:956–68.
Schlesinger, Joseph A. 1966. *Ambition and Politics: Political Careers in the United States*. Chicago: Rand McNally.
Searing, Donald. 1991. "Roles, Rules, and Rationality." *American Political Science Review* 85:1239–59.
Seligman, Lester, M. King, C. Kim, and R. Smith. 1974. *Patterns of Recruitment: A State Chooses Its Lawmakers*. Chicago: Rand McNally.
Shea, Daniel. 1995. *Transforming Democracy: Legislative Campaign Committees and Political Parties*. Albany: State University of New York Press.
Shin, Kwang, and John Jackson. 1979. "Membership Turnover in U.S. State Legislatures, 1931–76." *Legislative Studies Quarterly* 4:95–114.
Snowiss, Leo. 1966. "Congressional Recruitment and Representation." *American Political Science Review* 60:627–39.
Sollars, David. 1994. "Institutional Rules and State Legislative Compensation: Success for the Reform Movement?" *Legislative Studies Quarterly* 19:507–20.
Sorauf, Frank. 1963. *Party and Representation*. New York: Atherton Press.
Squire, Peverill. 1988a. "Career Opportunities and Membership Stability in Legislatures." *Legislative Studies Quarterly* 13:65–81.
Squire, Peverill. 1988b. "Career Opportunities and the Internal Organization of Legislatures." *Journal of Politics* 50:726–44.
Squire, Peverill. 1989. "Challengers in U.S. Senate Elections." *Legislative Studies Quarterly* 14:531–47.
Squire, Peverill. 1992a. "Legislative Professionalization and Membership Diversity in State Legislatures." *Legislative Studies Quarterly* 17:69–79.
Squire, Peverill. 1992b. "The Theory of Legislative Institutionalization and the California Assembly." *Journal of Politics* 54:1026–53.
Squire, Peverill. 1993. "Professionalization and Public Opinion of State Legislatures." *Journal of Politics* 55:479–91.

Squire, Peverill. 1997. "Another Look at Legislative Professionalization and Divided Government in the States." *Legislative Studies Quarterly* 22:417–32.

Squire, Peverill, and Eric R.A.N. Smith. 1996. "A Further Examination of Challenger Quality in Senate Elections." *Legislative Studies Quarterly* 21:235–48.

Stewart, Charles III. 1989. "A Sequential Model of U.S. Senate Elections." *Legislative Studies Quarterly* 14:567–601.

Stonecash, Jeffrey. 1993. "The Pursuit and Retention of Legislative Office in New York, 1870–1990: Reconsidering Sources of Change." *Polity* 26:301–15.

Stonecash, Jeffrey, and Anna Agathangelou. 1997. "Trends in the Partisan Composition of State Legislatures: A Response to Fiorina." *American Political Science Review* 91:148–55.

Swenson, Peter. 1982. "The Influence of Recruitment on the Structure of Power in the U.S. House, 1870–1940." *Legislative Studies Quarterly* 7:7–36.

Theriault, Sean. 1998. "Moving Up or Moving Out: Career Ceilings and Congressional Retirement." *Legislative Studies Quarterly* 23:419–33.

Thomas, Sue. 1994. *How Women Legislate*. New York: Oxford University Press.

Thomas, Sue, and Susan Welch. 1991. "The Impact of Gender in Activities and Priorities of State Legislators." *Western Political Quarterly* 44:445–56.

Thompson, Joel, and Gary Moncrief. 1992. "The Evolution of the State Legislature: Institutional Change and Legislative Careers." In *Changing Patterns in State Legislative Careers*, ed. Gary Moncrief and Joel Thompson. Ann Arbor: University of Michigan Press.

Thompson, Joel, and Gary Moncrief. 1993. "The Implications of Term Limits for Women and Minorities: Some Evidence from the States." *Social Science Quarterly* 74:300–09.

Thompson, Joel, Karl Kurtz, and Gary Moncrief. 1996. "We've Lost That Family Feeling: The Changing Norms of the New Breed of Legislators." *Social Science Quarterly* 77:344–62.

Tobin, Richard, and E. Keynes. 1975. "Institutional Differences in the Recruitment Process: A Four-State Study." *American Journal of Political Science* 19:667–82.

Van Beek, James. 1991. "Does the Decision to Retire Increase the Amount of Political Shirking?" *Public Finance Quarterly* 19:444–56.

Van Dunk, Emily, and Ronald Weber. 1997. "Constituency-Level Competition in the U.S. States, 1858–1988: A Pooled Analysis." *Legislative Studies Quarterly* 22:141–59.

Wahlke, John, Heinz Eulau, William Buchanan, and Leroy Ferguson. 1962. *The Legislative System*. New York: John Wiley & Sons.

Weber, Ronald, Harvey Tucker, and Paul Brace. 1991. "Vanishing Marginals in State Legislative Elections." *Legislative Studies Quarterly* 16:29–48.

Welch, Susan, and Donley T. Studlar. 1990. "Multi-Member Districts and the Representation of Women: Evidence from Britain and the United States." *Journal of Politics* 52:391–412.

Welch, Susan, and Donley T. Studlar. 1996. "The Opportunity Structure for Women's Candidacies and Electability in Britain and the United States." *Political Research Quarterly* 49:861–74.

Whicker, Marcia, Malcolm Jewell, and Lois Duke. 1996. "Women in Congress." In *Women in Politics*, 2d ed., ed. Lois L. Duke. Upper Saddle River, NJ: Prentice-Hall.
Williams, Christine. 1990. "Women, Law and Politics: Recruitment Patterns in the Fifty States." *Women and Politics* 10:103–23.
Zupan, Mark. 1990. "The Last Period Problem in Politics: Do Congressional Representatives Not Subject to a Reelection Constraint Alter Their Voting Behavior?" *Public Choice* 65:167–80.

Recruitment and Retention in Western European Parliaments

Werner J. Patzelt

Since politics is made by individuals selected for the positions they hold, the study of the process of selecting, or recruiting, political leaders has always been important. Where parliaments play more than a symbolic role, legislative recruitment is important as well, because in parliamentary democracies, even the top executive positions are filled with politicians once recruited for parliament. Hence, we should study who enters politics, when, and how. We should also know who will *not* enter politics because of small chances of getting elected, or because of more attractive alternatives. The purpose of this paper is to take a look at the research carried out on this subject and to review the "state of the art." I start with a discussion of the particular difficulties faced by recruitment research in Europe. Then I will give a brief overview of the body of such research on Western European countries. Instead of presenting a *bibliographie raisonnée*, it is my main objective to examine the questions raised, the concepts used, and the methods applied. Next, I will offer an assessment of what we know about legislative recruitment in Western Europe, and what we should try to investigate in the future. Finally, I discuss what methods, theories, and basic approaches we have not yet sufficiently developed or used. Of course, we should also have similar reviews of the research on legislative recruitment and retention in Central and Eastern Europe (compare Higley and Pakulski 1992).

Difficulties of Comparative Legislative Research in Europe

Although Rokkan (1967) developed an influential theoretical framework for the comparative study of political elites over 30 years ago, "no attempt was made to coordinate these efforts and establish an integrated database for comparative elite research until recently" (Best and Cotta 1997, 1). Instead, differ-

---

Reprinted with permission from *Legislative Studies Quarterly* 24, no. 2 (May 1999): 239–79.

ent national traditions of research on political and parliamentary elites maintained their distinctive features. On the one hand, this is because this field of study, like many others, remained under the divergent influences of different intellectual traditions in European countries. These traditions differ in the value assigned to empirical research and to quantitative analysis, but they also differ in their willingness to join the predominantly "Americanized" paradigm of international comparative research. On the other hand, the absence of institutional integration in European political science makes it difficult to overcome such divergent influences.

But there are also other reasons why it is difficult to conduct comparative legislative research in Europe. Western Europe comprises some 18 major political systems and parliaments. If we add the legislatures of 16 German and 9 Austrian *länder* and Switzerland's 26 cantons, and if we include the European Parliament, then a total of 70 legislatures on national, subnational, and supranational levels could be studied comparatively. And, because Europe is no longer divided, at least another 12 Central and Eastern European legislative systems need to be included. With almost 30 languages spoken in widely differing political and parliamentary cultures, a comparative analysis of these legislatures is far beyond any individual scholar's capacity. Thus, language barriers play out as research barriers. To make matters worse, language barriers are often linked to significant differences in political cultures and institutional designs. In addition, few European political scientists specialize in the study of legislatures, and scholars with an interest for legislative research in most countries tend to concentrate on their own political systems as such rather than allocating much energy to comparative research of particular institutions. As a consequence, parliamentary research in Europe is fragmented and so is research on legislative recruitment and retention.

With English becoming the dominant language of contemporary political science, the situation has both improved and worsened. It has improved because multinational cooperation in comparative research became possible by using English as the common working language. Conferences organized by the European Consortium for Political Research have produced the most important vehicles for truly European comparative analyses. But it has worsened as well, because publications on national political systems written in English—often by scholars not from the country under study—have tended to become nearly unquestioned "primary sources" for comparative research on political systems with languages other than English. Such publications are often only the tip of the iceberg of relevant information, and this tip is not necessarily representative of the rest of the iceberg.

There is an additional problem connected with this situation. For linguistic reasons, Anglo-American scholars have gained comfortable access to comparative research on European political systems. As a consequence, and because of the large number of American political scientists, American research perspectives and theoretical concepts have attained a privileged position even in genuinely European comparative research. However, conceptual approaches that are fruitful, for example, in congressional research, may not be equally useful when applied to European legislatures. And data bases limited to texts in English, or assembled by scholars not really rooted in the political cultures of the countries under comparison, may be simply too small or too biased to cover the rich variety of highly differentiated European political systems.

Research on Legislative Recruitment and Retention in Western Europe: A Brief Summary

Most European research on legislative recruitment and retention follows the single-country approach. Although many common questions are asked, comparative secondary analyses are hindered by the language barriers mentioned above. As a consequence, genuinely comparative research is relatively rare and most of it took the form of case-oriented, parallel case studies; variable-oriented quantitative research has been undertaken only recently.

Recent Comparative Research

Only a few articles compare legislative recruitment or retention in pairs of Western European nations. The social background, recruitment, and career patterns of postwar French and German political and parliamentary elites have been compared in a series of papers, as in the volume by Dupeux, Hudemann, and Knipping (1996). Their essayistic approach is predominantly historical, without any concern for systematic theory building. Efforts to improve the chances of women to be (s)elected in British and German parties were examined by Hoecker (1996). Eliassen and Pedersen (1978) did a comparative study on parliamentary recruitment in Denmark and Norway and focused on legislative professionalization of the parliamentary elite, conceptualized as both intellectual and political professionalization. They cover the period since 1814 for Norway and 1849 for Denmark, using quantitative methods and a "most similar system-strategy," but they offer only a general picture calling for further research. Candidate selection and the resulting relations between a deputy and his party were studied for Germany and Austria by Nick (1992), and the advantages of incumbents in Britain, Denmark, France, and Germany (as well as in Canada, New Zealand, the USA, Japan, and Israel) were the focus of work by Boll and Römmele (1994). The effect of changes in the composition of leadership groups in the process of redemocratization has been analyzed for Spain and Portugal by Bermeo (1987), with Italy and Greece also included in papers by Higley and Gunther (1992), and Liebert and Cotta (1990).

Three further European countries—Belgium, Italy, and Switzerland—were included along with Turkey, Kenya, and Korea in a comparative analysis of parliamentary elite integration by Kim and Patterson (1987). In that study, social background variables and career paths, together with sponsorship and ambition as factors for legislative careers, were analyzed with regard to elite consensus on key political values. Social background data and their impact on social representation and political attitudes has also been comparatively studied for the Nordic countries by Narud and Valen (1999). An article by Patzelt (1993) gives an overview of recruitment practices in Germany, Austria, France, Britain, and the USA, with a look at the normative question of whether these practices ensure that parliaments really get the personnel required for the effective functioning of modern legislatures. Strøm (1997) considers the utility of legislative role analysis for comparative recruitment research, focusing on candidate selection and election, and the incentive of legislative office.

Some comparisons include one European and one non-European case. Gretz (1993), in a doctoral dissertation, offers a comparison of parliamentarians on the subnational level; his cases are the state legislatures of Baden-Wuerttemberg in southwest Germany and South Carolina. His questions include social background variables and career patterns. Unfortunately, his analysis is largely descriptive. Further comparisons with the USA include the Netherlands (Fairlie, Budge, and Irwin 1977 on elite background and political preferences), France (Graham 1982 on legislative careers between 1871 and 1940), and Britain (Welch and Studlar 1990 on the representation of women). Britain has also been compared with Australia by Bean and Mughan (1989) with regard to the effects of leadership in parliamentary elections.

Most Western European and some non-European countries are included in the studies by Norris (1993; 1997a) and Norris and Lovenduski (1995). Although this research took an analysis of political recruitment in Britain as its point of departure, its approach, and to a certain extent its data base, is comprehensive. First, the traditional interest in the social composition of Parliament is integrated with research on how party organizations work as the central selectorate. This leads to three sets of research questions, which should be addressed for all other European countries as well: (1) who selects and how? (2) who gets selected, and why? and (3) does social bias matter? Second, Norris (1997a) and Norris and Lovenduski (1995) work with a well-elaborated "supply and demand"-model of political recruitment processes and, hence, within a theoretical framework of considerable integrative power. It may well become the main paradigm for recruitment research (compare Best and Cotta 1997, 9–15; Weßels 1997). Third, they offer an even more comprehensive "total model" of the recruitment process linking the variables of this process to the contexts provided by party competition and the political system as a whole. Being both conceptually rich and relatively clear-cut, it is a model well suited for encompassing comparative research (see Figure 1). Norris (1993, 309–30; 1997a, 209–31) provides comparable data on the variables in this model from a great variety of Western European (and some non-European) countries, although her data for Great Britain are more detailed. These include data on occupational background and age, on legal rules for the eligibility of candidates, on party system structure, on candidate competition, and on the structure of alternative professional opportunities.

Another important contribution to comparative recruitment research on Western European parliaments is the book *Candidate Selection in Comparative Perspective* edited by Gallagher and Marsh (1988). It follows a case-oriented country-by-country approach. However, the chapters on eight European states (Lieven De Winter on Belgium, David Denver on Britain, Jean-Louis Thiébault

FIGURE 1
Factors in the Political Recruitment Process

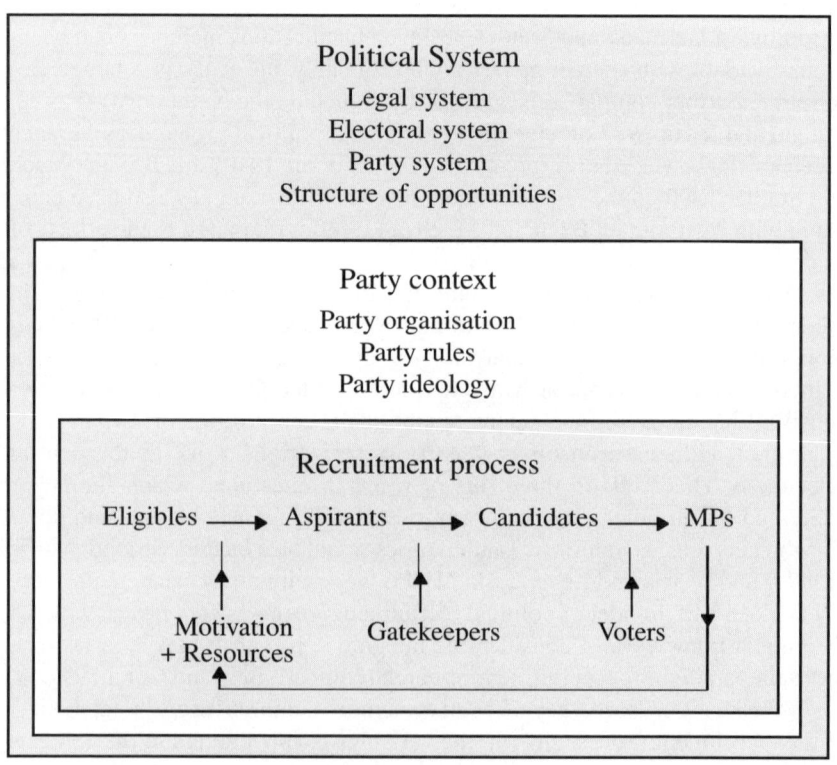

Source: Adapted from Norris and Lovenduski 1995, 184.

on France, Geoffrey Roberts on (West) Germany, Michael Gallagher on Ireland, Douglas A. Wertman on Italy, Ruud Koole and Monique Leijenaar on the Netherlands, and Henry Valen on Norway) as well as the chapter on Japan (by Rei Shiratori) are organized around the same questions and categories. They include the degree of centralization of the candidate selection process, the extent of participation in it, and the qualities of those aspiring to be selected. The book offers valuable findings on the impact that electoral and party systems have on the recruitment process; on intraparty rules and practices of candidate selection; on selectors' preferences (and on the consequences they entail for the candidates' social background and for the elected parliamentarians' behavior); on the position of incumbents; on the role of constituency or local activists; on concerns for group representation among the ranks of candidates; and on the effects of national political culture and political style. The focus of analysis is generally the intraparty selectorate, and the time-span covered is usually the postwar period. Career patterns of candidates prior to nomination are neglected. The country data are drawn from secondary analyses of research published in the languages of the countries under study.

Based on country-specific data, Gallagher (1988b) draws conclusions on the similarities and differences of Western European candidate selection and is able to place his results within an even broader cross-national framework. He discusses differing degrees of centralization in candidate selection (in a small majority of Western European countries it is low); the extent of participation in candidate selection (normally very limited); and what selectors are looking for (mostly incumbents, persons popular within the party who have grassroots ties and characteristics advantageous for "ticket-balancing"). Gallagher examines hypotheses on the influences of five major factors: legal provisions (seldom playing a significant role); the structure of government (federal vs. unitary; unclear effects); the electoral system (most deterministic hypotheses are wrong, but the electoral system itself is extremely consequential); the nature of the selecting party (no clear picture); and the political culture as a category for residual explanations. Gallagher finds that none of these factors can be disregarded; that quantitative analyses might provide further insights, but that there continues to be a great deal of unexplained variance across countries.

It is not easy to establish causal relationships between candidate selection on the one side and the composition of parliaments, the behavior of parliamentarians, and party cohesion on the other. Generally, candidates and MPs have a higher socioeconomic status and more education than the population at large, which seems to be a supply-side phenomenon. Efforts at ticket-balancing bring demand-side factors into play, as exemplified by the growing percentage of women among MPs. Parliamentarians' behavior seems to be shaped more significantly by the political structures in which they work than by recruitment patterns (compare Patzelt and Schirmer 1996). Party cohesion is reduced when there are primaries, since these empower mass media and nonparty organizations with significant influence on selection processes and make candidates much less dependent on their parties. On balance, Gallagher and Marsh 1988 remains one of the best pieces of comparative research on recruitment. However, it is a case-oriented approach, not strongly based on theory, and does not lend itself to quantitative testing of cross-national hypotheses. The same is true for the valuable volumes by Neisser and Plasser (1992) on primaries and candidate nomination, and by Somit et al. (1997) on incumbency effects. Conversely, more concept- or theory-oriented studies, like Peabody (1984) on leadership in legislatures, or Wood and Norton (1992) on incumbents' advantages, are less rich in empirical detail.

One of the ways to go is demonstrated by a research project directed by Heinrich Best and Maurizio Cotta. Made possible by preceding case studies, it takes a clearly variable-oriented approach. Its topic is "Elite Transformation and Parliamentary Representation in Europe," and its results will be published as *The European Representative* (Best 1999; Best and Cotta 1999). In this project, data were collected for 12 Western and Central European countries (Germany, Austria, and Hungary; the Netherlands, Denmark, Norway, and Finland; France and Britain; Italy, Spain, and Portugal), covering a 150-year period from 1848—a symbolic year marking the birth of representative democracy in many parts of Western and Central Europe—to 1998. Among the variables included are social and political background and career data. These include year of election, party affiliation, academic and nonacademic educational background, social background (especially occupation), political background (such as local or regional elective positions or positions in party or cabinet), regional background, gender, age, seniority, and number of successful reelections. Measures for all variables are aggregated as means or percentages for each parliamentary party included in the analysis.

Building such an unprecedented three-dimensional "data cube" (variables, countries, time), Best and Cotta follow a theory-driven, variable-based approach inspired by Stein Rokkan's framework for comparative research formulated over 30 years ago (Rokkan 1967). Their most general concern is the process of modernization and democratization in Western and Central Europe, their focus of research is parliamentary representation on the national level, their central unit of analysis is the parliamentary party, and their starting point for data collection is the individual elected member of parliament. The recruitment of legislators is analyzed both as a dependent and an independent variable.

As a *dependent* variable, Best and Cotta consider actual recruitment as a highly improbable event and the given makeup of a parliament "as the final balance of advantageous and disadvantageous features working in the (self-)selective process preceding the act of recruitment" (Best and Cotta 1997, 9). They distinguish—very much like Norris and Lovenduski—four basic elements in the recruitment process: the contenders, stimulated by different incentives and representing the "offer" on the recruitment market; the selectorates (parties, personal cliques, groups of dignitaries, etc.) in their double role as "demanders" and providers of incentives for supply; the electorate as the (end) consumer, making decisions based on perceptions and changing preferences; and the formal structure of opportunity for parliamentary representation, including all "rules of the game" that have an impact on contenders, selectorates, and electorate. The goal is to relate, by means of cross-national and cross-temporal comparison, the given composition of parliaments as an observable outcome of the recruitment process mirroring the underlying patterns of social power.

Analyzing legislative recruitment as an *independent* variable, Best and Cotta intend to relate the social background of parliamentarians both to systemic features like integration, stability, or performance of the institutions of parliamentary democracy, and to its legislative and policy output. Robert D. Putnam's question "Does social background matter?" is, thus, answered in the affirmative, but no *direct* links between it and policy outcome are established. Rather, social and political background variables are used "as 'structural parameters' establishing or weakening links between factions of political elites or between elites and constituencies, pressure groups or mass organizations" (Best and Cotta 1999, 16). Since establishing or weakening such links has to do with building up, using, or neglecting politically relevant networks, this is an important finding on the structural prerequisites of political representation.

Thus far, some interesting findings of this project relate to changes in legislative recruitment results over time (Best 1997). On the whole, traditional elites lose their position in parliaments, changes in socioeconomic structure are mirrored by changes in immediate parliamentary interest representation, and formerly disadvantaged groups get access to parliament. But there is no rapid synchronization of changes in society and changes in the composition of legislatures. At first, not the "threatening," but the "threatened" social classes increase their percentage of seats in parliament. Only later is societal change followed by a change in the composition of parliaments. Thus, there is a gap in interest representation. On balance, an amazing resistance and an adaptive inertia of recruitment patterns can be observed, including cyclical processes and significant differences between the European countries. Based on these results it might be hypothesized that the rather "conservative" structure of parliamentary representation provides for the stability of representative institutions under pressure for social change (Best 1997). Quite contrary to normative assumptions of the benefits of "descriptive representation" (compare Pitkin 1967), the very *lack* of synchronization between socioeconomic and political development seems to provide parliamentary elites with the necessary political maneuvering space for establishing and stabilizing parliamentary democracy.

Country Studies

Most European research on legislative recruitment and retention is still dominantly or exclusively interested in country studies. Therefore, language barriers play a major role in any attempt to review it. In the subsequent sections, I concentrate on recent books and articles that deal explicitly with candidate selection and legislative recruitment, and I restrict my account to exemplary research. Data found in more general research on parliamentarians and their roles (like Bogdanor 1985), or on parties and elections, are mostly omitted.

Mediterranean Countries. All studies of legislative recruitment in *Italy* must take into account the comprehensive changes of party structure and top political personnel that occurred between 1992 and 1994 as a result of bribery scandals and prosecutions of leading members of Italy's political class. Because of these changes, articles published prior to 1992 can no longer sufficiently explain the present situation. There are, however, useful recent analyses of the transformation of the Italian political and parliamentary class. A general overview can be found in Sidoti (1993), where the structural backwardness of the Italian political elite, the problems of political financing, and the legal prosecution of the old political class are discussed. The consequences of the 1994 elections for party realignment and the composition of Parliament are described and discussed in Bartolini and D'Alimonte (1996) and Mastropaolo (1994). Cotta and Verzichelli (1994) and Verzichelli (1994; 1996) detail the breakdown of the established elite and the rise of new politicians. These articles compare the landslide elections of 1994 to other instances of Italian elite circulation in the twentieth century (1919; 1924; 1969; 1994), and analyze the composition and background of the new parliamentary class. Only a minority of the new legislators have prior parliamentary experience; new party affiliations have emerged; even the social background of MPs has changed significantly; and, on balance, a long period of elite continuity came to an end. Recchi (1996) undertakes a systematic comparison of the recruitment patterns of the parliamentary elites of Italy's First and Second Republics in terms of their prior political activity. He links his analyses to the concept of opportunity structure, which has become increasingly popular within recruitment research. On the whole, these studies rely on publicly accessible data rather than on interviews or questionnaire surveys. Hence, the "subjective side" of the recruitment and selection process is out of analytic reach.

In *Spain*, the interest in legislative recruitment still seems to be focused on questions of permanency and change since the end of the Franco regime. An analysis of the political, social, and regional background of the members of the first democratically elected Parliament after Franco was presented by del Campo, Tezanos, and Santin (1982), and an assessment of the stabilization of the new parliamentary class was made by Morán (1989). Such analyses are closely linked to the analysis of democratic consolidation found in Giol, Cotarelo, Garrido, and Subirats (1990), Gunther (1992), Santamaria (1994), Higley and Gunther (1992), and Cotarelo (1992). Apart from that, processes of candidate selection and legislative recruitment seem to be studied primarily in the context of research on elections and parties.

For *Portugal*, legislative recruitment has also mostly been studied in the context of regime transition and democratic consolidation, more recently in Cruz and Antunes (1990). Data on legislative recruitment in *Greece* appear to be as rare as for Portugal. An older article by Legg (1982) covered the elite changes that came with the dictatorships between 1936 and 1941, between 1967 and 1974, and during the subsequent periods of democratic restoration. It also analyzed the social and political background of the newly elected MPs after 1974. More recently, Kourvetaris (1989) discussed the interplay of political elites and party organization in Greece, with his "entrepreneurial model" coming close to demand and supply-oriented analyses of recruitment processes.

France. In the case of France, as with most European countries, we know much more about the social background of legislators than about the recruitment mechanisms leading to the composition of the French houses of Parliament. Likewise we know more about the French political elite as a whole and about the recruitment and career patterns of French ministers (like Dogan 1989) than about the parliamentary elite as a special subgroup. There are some articles on candidates for national elections (such as Guédé and Rozenblum 1981), and there is also more comprehensive research on the recruitment and selection processes (such as Cayrol and Perrineau 1982; Gaxie 1980; and Thiébault 1988). But the data presented focuses mostly on social or occupational background and local roots. This approach is also used by Gaxie to compare the parliamentary composition in the Fourth and Fifth Republics, whereas Thiébault examines the different recruitment patterns of French parties. Recently, Ysmal (1994) has studied the role of French incumbents and the effect of electoral instability on legislative turnover. Additional evidence may be gained from studies of the role of French deputies (e.g., Acquaviva 1997; Garrigue 1992; Masclet 1979). On balance, French research on legislative recruitment is insufficiently linked to the theoretical frameworks of international comparative parliamentary research.

United Kingdom and Ireland. Britain ranks first among Western European countries in information available about candidate selection and legislative recruitment. There are general assessments of the British political elite (such as Kavanagh 1992 or Setzer 1991) and of British MPs (e.g., Norton 1980; Rush 1979, 1988; or Searing 1994) that include information on social, occupational, or educational background and on previous careers. There are also excellent analyses on selected topics, including the rise of career politicians (King 1981) and their career patterns (Rush 1994); intraparty candidate selection (Bochel and Denver 1983; Conley and Smith 1983; Denver 1988; Norris and Lovenduski 1993b; Rush 1986); role and campaigning activity of candidates (Criddle 1988; Pattie et al. 1994; Radice et al. 1990); incumbency effects (Norton 1994); and parliamentary drop-out (Budge and Fairlie 1975). The last two decades has seen special attention given to gender effects in legislative recruitment and careers (Lovenduski and Norris 1989; Norris and Lovenduski 1995; Rasmussen 1981; Studlar, McAllister, and Ascui 1988; and Studlar and Welch 1987).

These articles and books consider many factors: the effects of incumbency and the special problems of new entrants; the qualifications and disqualifications of candidates; the types of career paths leading into Parliament; the selection procedures and their guiding norms in the British parties; the preferences of the selectors; and the consequences of factors such as MPs' constituency ties for both parliamentary careers and retirement. The important study by Norris and Lovenduski (1995), a full account of legislative recruitment in Britain, is based on a body of research unmatched for any other European country, with the possible exception of Germany. Some of this research is based on interviews or questionnaire responses from candidates or parliamentarians themselves and is not limited to "official" data derived from biographical handbooks. Moreover, recent research (e.g., Norris and Lovenduski 1993a; Norris 1997a, 1–14) develops a theoretical framework truly suitable for cross-national comparison.

The state of research is not nearly so good for *Ireland*. Gallagher (1980, 1988a) gives instructive overviews of the Irish party selectorate, the influences of both the electoral system and political culture on candidate selection, on the role of incumbents, and on the backgrounds of elected deputies, as well as detailed analyses of the members of the Irish Dail (1984, 1985, and 1993). Further studies on the Irish electoral system and its consequences for legislative recruitment include Marsh (1981) and Sinnott (1993).

Scandinavian Countries. For *Sweden* we have recent data on changes in the social and occupational background of MPs between 1906 and 1988 (Esaiasson and Holmberg 1996, 19–48). In this study, background data are combined with thorough analyses of the social representativeness of the Swedish Riksdag; of the links between social background and legislators' attitudes; and of the (weak, but significant) correlations between social affiliations and influence, with the latter operationalized as the possession of parliamentary positions. However, only scarce information about candidate selection and the selectorate proper is available (but compare Holmberg 1989 and 1994); thus, books on the Swedish Parliament, such as Isberg (1982), need to be consulted. Additional insights are offered by Brothén (1996) on seniority principles in the *Riksdag*, and Eduards (1991) on gender effects.

Parliamentary recruitment in *Norway* has been studied by Eliasson (1978; 1985), Heidar (1986; 1997), and Valen (1988). Here we learn quite a lot about party-specific procedures of candidate selection and selection criteria, about the degree of participation in this process, about ticket balancing, and about the social, educational, and political background of elected parliamentarians. Gender effects in selecting and electing candidates has recently been the topic of Matland (1993; 1994) and Nicholson (1993).

For *Finland*, Ruostetsaari (1993) offers a comprehensive analysis of the power elite. But MPs constitute only a small segment of this political elite, which is jointly analyzed with the Finnish administrative, business, mass media, and science elites. Parliamentary recruitment has been analyzed by Helander (1997).

In *Denmark*, Pedersen writes on the longitudinal aspects of legislative recruitment (1976; 1977) and on incumbency effects (1994). Further information and references are included in works by Damgaard (1980; 1997). Dahlerup (1988) has analyzed the role and recruitment of women.

Unfortunately, a number of articles and books likely to be useful on legislative recruitment in Scandinavia are written in Scandinavian languages mastered by only a small minority of European political scientists. There are, however, valuable comparative analyses of Nordic parliaments written in English by Arter (1984), Esaiasson and Heidar (1999), and Thomas (1985), and in German by Pappi and Schmitt (1994).

Benelux Countries. On average, we seem to know more about legislative recruitment in the Benelux countries than in Scandinavia. For *Belgium*, de Winter has presented an impressive book (1992) and valuable articles (1988; 1998). Using interviews with MPs as well as analyses of official documents and the literature, he describes intraparty rules and practices of candidate selection, the selectors' preferences, and the outcome of such recruitment and selection in terms of parliamentary composition and legislators' behavior.

Comparable data for the *Netherlands* can be found in Koole and Leijenaar (1988), where changes in recruitment patterns over the last decades are also reflected. A comprehensive study of the legislative recruitment and social background of Dutch MPs is Leijenaar and Niemöller (1997). Long-range changes in the social, regional, and political background of Dutch MPs between 1848 and 1967 are discussed in Daalder and van den Berg (1982). Irwin et al. (1979) present an analysis of social background and motivational factors in Dutch legislative careers. Gender effects have been analyzed by Leijenaar (1989) and Oldersma (1990a; 1990b). Secker (1995) covers the Dutch political-administrative elites as a whole, presenting data on social, educational, religious, and occupational background as well as age at retirement for ministers and MPs; his data even allow for comparisons of the 1946 and 1967 period with the years since then. Still, the most comprehensive information on Dutch parliamentarians can be found in Schendelen (1981a; 1981b).

German-Speaking Countries. All three (predominantly) German-speaking countries of Europe have federal systems with parliaments both on the national and on the *länder* or *cantonal* levels. Therefore, legislative recruitment and careers can be studied on two levels. For *Switzerland*, we have analyses of both *cantonal* Parliaments (Stadlin 1990) and the national Parliament (Kerr 1981a, 1981b; Riklin and Ochsner 1984). Most of them include at least basic information on legislative recruitment and careers. In addition, there are some studies of candidate selection and nomination (Gruner, Daetwyler, and Zosso 1975; Poledna and Kaufmann 1989). As in other countries, there is special concern for the recruitment, selection, and election chances of women (Fuchs 1994; Stämpfli and Longchamp 1990; Torracinta-Pache 1984).

We know even more about legislative recruitment in *Austria*. A valuable biographic dictionary of Austrian parliamentarians between 1918 and 1993 (Parlamentsdirektion 1993) allows for longitudinal analyses, and so does Dachs, Gerlich, and Müller (1995), a book on outstanding politicians of Austria's Second Republic. Stickler (1995) offers a comprehensive analysis of Austrian MPs between 1918 and 1975. An excellent article by Stirnemann (1988) covers the legal norms regulating legislative recruitment in Austria, the recruitment strategies and selection priorities of the Austrian political parties, the actual candidate selection within parties, the role of incumbents, career patterns and reasons for retiring, and the impact of political culture on the whole process. Whereas Stirnemann's focus is the national level, Wolfgruber (1997, 167–88) is concerned with recruitment at the *länder* level. Especially valuable is her analysis of the parties as the central selectorate and of women's chances of being selected and elected. Like Norris and Lovenduski, Wolfgruber uses interview and questionnaire data. Unfortunately, her study fails to include the standard social background data on Austrian state-level legislators. On the *länder* level, there are additional studies of candidate selection (Gratzer 1994), of the use of primaries (Sprenger and Nidler 1994), and of individual recruitment processes (Winderl 1991). Gender effects have also attracted special attention in Austria (Dyk 1986; Steininger 1992).

Legislative recruitment has been studied in *Germany* more than in any other European country, except possibly Great Britain. Regrettably, a comprehensive study like the one on Britain by Norris and Lovenduski (1995) is still missing for Germany. But there has been continuous work on this topic. At present, the best and most comprehensive overviews are Weßels (1997) and Roberts (1988). Weßels places his analysis in the framework of supply and demand approaches to legislative recruitment and carefully describes, on the national level, the effects of the electoral system, the structure of electoral competition, the most important trends in the changing social background of German candidates and MPs between 1949 and 1990, the relevant facts concerning turnover and seniority, and the pathways to the Bundestag. His quantitative and multivariate analysis of the social composition of the 3215 candidates for the 1994 federal elections is particularly valuable. Roberts (1988) assesses the German electoral system, then proceeds to a detailed account of candidate selection within the German parties, thereby paying special attention to the constituencies and party lists as central factors in this selection process. The consequences of the recruitment patterns discussed by Roberts include the close ties between deputies and parties, parliamentarians' linkages with interest groups, and the ability of the electorate to influence the recruitment process. Together, both articles offer a good picture of how legislative recruitment works in Germany. This picture may be supplemented by analyses of the selection and composition of the German political elite or of the political class as a whole, as given by Kaack (1980), Rebenstorf (1995), or Bürklin and Rebenstorf (1997).

Research on social background and parliamentary careers and on seniority and retirement of German national legislators is facilitated by the detailed data base maintained by the Bundestag and supplied by Schindler (1983, 112–215; 1988, 129–259; 1994, 233–351; 1995). It covers the German Bundestag between 1949 and 1991 and will be continued. (For a historical analysis of German MPs since 1848, see Best 1982, 1990.) Ismayr (1992, 50–70) compresses these (and further) data into a clear-cut picture of who the members of the Bundestag are and where they come from. On balance, one of the favorite subjects of research on legislative recruitment in Germany has been the composition of parliamentary parties, especially on the federal level, and the changes in the social, occupational, and educational backgrounds of parliamentarians (see Hess 1995; Kaack 1988a, 1988b; Müller 1988). But few studies have addressed the impact of social background on parliamentary behavior. Rebenstorf and Weßels (1989) contrast actual data on social background with electors' preferences concerning the composition of Parliament.

To Herzog (1975; 1979; 1990), we owe impressive research on the professionalization and career patterns of the German political and parliamentary elites. Further work on the professionalization of the latter has been done by Burmeister (1993) and Saalfeld (1997). Based on interview and questionnaire research conducted with parliamentarians on both national and state levels, Patzelt (1995, 265–321; 1996a; 1998) presents data on ambition and motivations leading into the legislatures, on political activities preceding the election to Parliament, on both the incentives and disincentives to a parliamentary career, and on recruitment problems as they are perceived by legislators themselves.

The basic procedures and guiding principles of German candidate selection are discussed in Kremer (1984). A general analysis of the recruitment market of the German political elite can be found in Kaltefleiter (1976), and of the intraparty ascent necessary for eligibility for nomination in Oberreuter (1994). Additionally, there is ample, but mostly outdated literature on the selection of candidates, especially in federal elections, and on the parties' roles as the central selectorate (as a recent study, see Porter 1995). We have some articles (such as Haungs 1970) on the rare intraparty primaries tested at the state level in the early seventies, and there is research on candidate behavior in campaigns (Horn and Kühr 1978; Staab 1986), and on how preference voting, possible in Bavaria, changes the (elsewhere fixed) party lists (Hübner 1979; compare James 1988). The advantages of incumbents are discussed in Boll (1994).

Due to Germany's federal structure, the regional analysis of candidates and MPs has also attracted much interest (see Hohmann 1987). A brief overview of the social background and the careers of MPs at the *länder* level is given by Holl (1989). The growing interest in political gender research is reflected by studies of the recruitment of women for political activity and parliamentary careers (e.g., Hoecker 1994, 1998; Kolinsky 1991; Penrose 1993; and Rusciano 1992). Biographical information on women legislators in German national parliaments from 1919 to 1983 is presented in Deutscher Bundestag (1983).

The recruitment of Eastern Germany's new parliamentarians after reunification was also an object of analysis. Data on the social composition, career patterns, and pathways to Parliament of this new political elite can be found in Lock (1998) and in papers by Derlien and Lock (1994), Glaeßner (1996), Patzelt (1996b; 1997), and Patzelt and Schirmer (1996). Parliamentary and post-legislative careers as chief executives at the *länder* level have been analyzed in Herzog (1977) and Plöhn (1984). For parliamentary socialization we can turn to Badura and Reese (1976), Patzelt (1998), and Sarcinelli (1989). On balance, though there is a large body of research on legislative recruitment in Germany, its pieces are not integrated enough to give a comprehensive picture, and German research still fails to offer a theoretical framework allowing for cross-national comparison.

Recruitment for the European Parliament. The European Parliament, which since 1979 has been elected on the basis of differing national electoral systems, could become an important object of comparative recruitment analysis. Playing an increasingly more important and yet rather opaque role in the process of European policy making, it is shaped much more than any of the national European parliaments by the personal political skills of its members and by the attractiveness—or lack thereof—of a "European career" for ambitious parliamentarians of the member states of the European Union. Therefore, we might expect numerous studies addressing the following issues: how divergent national recruitment systems may lead to relevant differences between the national groups of European MPs; how European legislative careers are embedded in diverse national patterns of political careers; or, the consequences of differing recruitment patterns and of informal national influence on the "parliamentary culture" at the European level.

But there is no significant body of such research as yet. The reason may be related to the general difficulties of comparative legislative research in Europe.

There is simply no truly *European* political science which would focus on European institutions. And to study the recruitment of all European legislators, using interview or questionnaire data, entails language problems that are serious obstacles to joint and comparative research. So we must rely on the few studies on national candidate selection for the European Parliament: for Britain by Westlake (1994), Holland (1986), and Gordon (1979); for France (but not exclusively focused on the European Parliament) by Kauppi (1996); and for Germany by Hrbek and Schweitzer (1989). Comparative studies of European legislative career paths like Scarrow (1997) are still rare. We have some specialized studies of the social and political background of the members of the European Parliament (see Thöne 1982; Kirchner 1983). The recruitment and representation of women on the European Parliament has also attracted a considerable amount of research (e.g., Kohn 1981; Vallance and Davies 1986). Finally, recruitment has been discussed in the context of European election studies by Boyce (1995), Irwin (1995), or Kolk, Schmitt, and Thomassen (1997). There is also some complementary research, such as that by Scholl (1986), who analyzes how the different electoral systems in Europe shape the constituency-oriented activities of the members of the European Parliament. On balance, the state of research on legislative recruitment on the European level is far from satisfying, and this is true for both the data collected and the efforts invested in theory construction.

An Expanding Subfield:
Gender Effects in Legislative Recruitment and Careers

Neither advances in theory and methodology nor the resurgence of democratic parliamentarism in Southern and Eastern Europe have provided European recruitment research with its single most important impulse. Rather, "feminist" social science and gender studies have played this role. As a consequence, an ever growing number of articles and books has been published on women and their still-limited chances for successful political careers since the seventies.

They include both general analyses of women's difficult entry into politics (see Hoecker 1986, 1987; Norris and Lovenduski 1993a; Skjeje 1991; Strecker and Lenz 1994) and a growing number of impressive comparative studies. Hoecker's review (1998) is a handbook on women's political participation in Europe; Norris (1985; 1997a) concentrates on women's parliamentary representation in Western Europe; Kohn (1980) compares women's opportunities of getting elected in six countries; and Rule (1987) covers no fewer than 23 democracies. In one way or another, these are contemporary follow-up studies to Comstock (1926), who analyzed women members of European parliaments more than sixty years ago.

Apart from studies that focus on special factors hindering or possibly improving women's selection and election chances, such as Heepe (1989) or Hills (1981), there are a number of explicitly comparative studies. Welch and Studlar (1990) compare Britain and the USA, Matland and Studlar (1996) Norway and Canada with regard to how electoral systems shape the election chances of women candidates. Hoecker (1996) compares procedures for promoting women candidates in British and German political parties, while Bendix (1994) compares Germany and Switzerland with regard to women's political participation in general. For the Scandinavian countries, we have the comparative studies of women's increasing political participation and growing recruitment success by Dahlerup (1988), Haavio-Mannilla et al. (1985), and Karvonen and Selle (1995). Fovenskov (1978a) analyzed why females in Denmark and Norway were so clearly underrepresented in Parliament.

On balance, comparative studies of the influence of gender on recruitment have produced more publications than comparative research on any other recruitment factors. The same picture emerges when we survey the share of gender studies in country-specific recruitment research. Unfortunately, this thematic emphasis is not caused by any breakthrough in legislative research itself, but only by the great popularity of gender studies in all fields of the social sciences. Certainly this has been a useful, and even necessary, corrective to the traditional ignorance displayed by (mostly male) political scientists about the problems of women's political participation and access to top positions. But we should strengthen our research efforts in the other fields of recruitment research to the same level.

What Do We Know, and What Should We Investigate in the Future?

What can we learn from the impressive body of European recruitment research? And where are the voids that we should fill in the future? To assess the *state of the art* (compare Gallagher and Marsh 1988, 1–19; Norris and Lovenduski 1995, 1–18), I will discuss the countries covered, the research questions asked, the methods applied, the theoretical frameworks used, and the general approaches taken by European recruitment research.

Cases Covered by European Recruitment Research

We have the most ample data base for Britain and Germany. Recruitment research in the Scandinavian and Benelux countries, deeply influenced by Anglo-American political science, has produced the second-largest body of data. French research in this field has been less prolific. Italy, Portugal, and Spain lag even further behind. And in spite of its fascinating possibilities for intra-institutional and cross-national comparisons, the European Parliament has attracted lamentably little interest.

Language problems impede European joint research to a great extent, while making collaboration indispensable. This language problem is also reflected in the fact that most research discussed in this article is in English or German, with far fewer references to French, Spanish, or Italian literature. Work in other languages obviously exists but is not part of the shared knowledge of scholars interested in comparative research—except among those few who are conversant with these other languages. The language obstacle can only be surmounted by bringing together English-speaking scholars from all European countries in conferences or workshops devoted to recruitment and retention research, and publishing their papers in volumes having a common theoretical framework. Gallagher and Marsh (1988), produced under the auspices of the European Consortium for Political Research, provides a good example of the way to go.

Research Questions and Collected Data

Some research on legislative recruitment is the incidental result of work on elections, parties, and the roles of parliamentarians. Such research generally does not employ the categories of recruitment theory, nor does it deal with the main questions in this field. For recruitment and retention research proper, we can group the most frequently asked questions and the available findings under the following headings: *eligibles, contenders, and members*; the *selectorate(s)*; the *electorate*; and the *opportunity structures* molding both the supply and the demand sides of legislative recruitment.

With regard to *eligibles, contenders, and members,* we know a great deal about the composition of Western European parliaments in terms of the social, political, regional, educational, occupational, and sometimes even religious background of their members; about the representation of women or minorities; and about age and seniority. We are well informed on political careers as a whole, a part of which may be in legislative service; about career patterns prior to becoming an MP; about professionalization in political careers; and about how, and how early, eligibles have to start if they want to become parliamentarians. We even know a lot about the role of incumbents and the factors that improve reelection chances.

There are, however, a considerable number of neglected questions as well. We do not know very much about the pool of eligible candidates and about what makes ordinary people run for elective offices. There has been little research in Europe on what constitutes a "political personality," on ambition, on the motivation for entering politics, and on the risks of political careers. We have also little research comparing successful with unsuccessful candidates.

Therefore, we have not yet learned enough about the effects of Western European recruitment systems on the quality of elected parliamentarians.

Data are scarce on the career patterns of parliamentarians, on the motivations for retirement, and on post-parliamentary careers. We should also know much more about candidates or incumbents as "political entrepreneurs." For what purposes, and under what circumstances, is it rational or rewarding to enter the political market? What are the resources required for successful campaigning? Who can get them, when and how? Finally, we need much more evidence on how the perception of all these facts affects the eligibles' decisions to run or not to run for candidacy or elected office.

As far as the *selectorate* is concerned, we know a great deal about how European parties work as the central selectorate. We have rich data on the formal and informal rules, procedures, priorities, and preferences according to which candidates are selected and promoted. We know about the relationship between the national and local party organizations and about the range of participants in the selection process. But there are other important gatekeepers on the way to parliament as well. Our knowledge of them is still very limited.

Most of all, we should know more about intraparty and other sponsorship of candidacies. Who is able and willing to offer such sponsorship, and why? What are the system-imposed limits on such sponsorship? How much "ticket-balancing" goes on? Other open questions include the following: Is party leadership a prerequisite or rather a consequence of becoming a member of parliament? To what extent are MPs needed by parties to secure media coverage, to obtain full-time party activists, and to establish efficient contacts with constituency and administrative elites? And what are the consequences of such considerations for actual recruitment mechanisms?

Although the mass media have played a less important role than have political parties in candidate selection, we should know more about their influence. Which kind of media coverage is necessary for becoming a successful candidate? What active role do media and journalists play in the process of the nomination of "normal" candidates? And in what way or degree do the media indirectly work as a selectorate by the effect that their criticism has on the supply-side of the recruitment process?

Surprisingly enough, there is also comparatively little systematic and theory-driven research on the *electorate* as an actor in legislative recruitment. The main reason seems to be that most polls concentrate on parties and their top candidates. So they usually do not offer data on "normal" candidates and on which characteristics affect the voter (see, as a rare exception, Borchers 1988 and Rebenstorf and Weßels 1989). But if we want to fully understand the legislative recruitment process, we certainly need research on what the voters expect, or at least tolerate, in candidates running for office.

As for the *opportunity structures*, there is ample work on the effects of electoral systems and the effects of these systems on party strategies and electoral campaigns. But we do not know enough about the relative attractiveness of political careers compared to alternative leadership careers, about the relative attractiveness of parliamentary salaries, and about post-parliamentary career opportunities. We also have little research on how individual careers, or at least hopes for a career, play out within the institutional settings and the various formal or informal role hierarchies of different parliamentary structures (compare Squire 1988a, 1988b). On balance, the interaction between motivation and opportunities needs more elucidation. Also the overall effects of regime structure on recruitment patterns deserve much more attention than they have been given. There are hardly studies on the distinctive opportunity structure offered by a federal system that permits politicians to shuttle back and forth between state and national legislatures, and between executive and legislative positions at both levels. Likewise, we have no studies comparing the attractiveness of legislative careers in presidential, semi-presidential, and parliamentary regimes.

A great deal of European research on legislative recruitment has been carried out in *historical* perspective since it was intended to allow for cross-historical comparisons. Countries that experienced major changes of their political systems, like France, Germany, Greece, Spain, and Italy, have particularly attracted historical research of political and parliamentary elites. The time-span covered goes back to the mid- or even early nineteenth century. Therefore we have a valuable body of historical knowledge about the changing social background of Western European legislators, and we know quite a bit about changing recruitment patterns. However, our historical knowledge of retention and (informal) careers in parliament is still very limited, and the questions that have failed to be addressed by research on contemporary parliamentary recruitment have also been neglected in historical research. This is true with respect to questions on eligibles, contenders, and members, on the selectorate and voters, and on the societal opportunity structure that has changed so much during the 200 years since the French Revolution and especially the half century since the end of World War II.

The study of patterns of historical change is, of course, not the only way to conduct theory-oriented *correlational analysis*. Most interrelations in the field of legislative recruitment have been studied on the basis of contemporary systems. Stemming from such research, we know a great deal about the correlations between recruitment mechanisms, the composition of parliamentary parties, and the behavior of MPs within their parliamentary parties. There are also considerable findings on how recruitment patterns affect the legislators' ties to their parties, to interest groups, and to the citizens in their voting districts. Additionally, we have analyses of the interrelations between the social background of MPs and some policy outcome of parliamentary activity. But although we have developed a good understanding of the principal factors that influence parliamentary recruitment, we have not yet systematically studied how these factors interact with each other and how these factors together relate to the capacity of parliamentarians and parliaments to provide political *leadership*. Much more interest has been paid to the effects of recruitment mechanisms or social background on parliamentary *responsiveness*.

Thus, while research on parliamentary recruitment in Europe has adduced extensive data on many aspects of the selection of MPs, many gaps remain. They are partly due to the fragmented and even isolated character of different traditions of European recruitment research, and partly due to a neglect of empirically grounded theory-building and the absence of a common theoretical framework. Finally, differences over research methods have proven to be an obstacle to systematic comparative research.

Research Methods and Their Limits

I will divide the discussion of research methods into three parts: methods for data collection, for data analysis, and for comparison. With regard to *data collection*, European research on legislative recruitment relies heavily on official or semiofficial data. They include lists of candidates, data on election outcomes, biographical data on MPs (often published by the parliaments themselves), and data made available by the research services of some legislatures. They also include legal documents that contain rules of nomination and election and newspaper accounts of contested intraparty candidacies and election campaigns. By comparison, interview and questionnaire data are rare. So European recruitment research is dominated by secondary analysis of already published data and shows a neglect of the gathering of data on individuals. This reflects the origins of European political science, which developed within the disciplines of history and law rather than within empirically-oriented sociology.

The lack of interview and questionnaire data helps to explain why we find factors like ambition, motivation, or perception to be so widely neglected in European recruitment research. Preferences for official and semiofficial data also brings European research to infer recruitment patterns from data on the social composition of parliaments rather than from interviews with key actors among the selectorate. Preferences in data collection also affect the choice of theoretical models. Rational-choice or psychological models, for instance, are rarely used in European studies of legislative recruitment and careers, and the main reason seems to be that tests of such models often require individual data, whereas European research tends to be satisfied with the analysis of easily accessible aggregate data.

The methods used for data collection also affect *data analysis*. In Europe, traditional interpretive analysis still prevails. Correspondingly, data have not generally been collected in machine-readable form, and thus statistical procedures cannot readily be used to analyze them. Moreover, statistical analysis often lacks sophistication. Where quantitative data are available and cannot be ignored—for instance on legislators' social background characteristics—their analysis normally ends with two-way tables and comparisons of means or percentages. Such limitations in the scope of methods are inevitably reflected in limits of research.

The predominant traditional approach of European recruitment research is mirrored in the *methods for comparison* as well. Since most research has dealt with individual countries, there has been only limited concern for comparison. When comparison has been undertaken, it has generally been case-oriented rather than variable-oriented. "Nation" has generally been used as the most important case-defining concept. While such an approach should not be abandoned but even be expanded in scope, the inclusion of a greater number of variables would make it possible to undertake the kinds of comparison suggested in the model by Norris and Lovenduski (1995) (see Figure 1).

Modern analytic tools would permit us to go much further without giving up the benefits of traditional European comparative methods. To begin with, more variable-oriented comparisons, based on multivariate statistical models, should be carried out. In such analyses, "nation" should be included as only one explanatory variable among others. Then appropriate models would allow us to detect factors that operate across the borders of national systems of recruitment or even on the European level. The project by Best and Cotta (1997) comes close to such an approach but is still exceptional on the European scene. Unfortunately, as long as we lack data on important variables for many countries, such an approach faces severe limitations. In particular, we still have too few well documented cases with the many variables that need to be included in a full model of recruitment.

In the face of this problem, the methodology of case-oriented macro-qualitative comparison seems to be an attractive supplementary strategy. It was developed by Ragin (1987) and has as its central idea the comparison of patterns of variable configurations across different cases. The comparison starts with writing down these individual variable configurations in an *is* and *is not* format. In a second step, the observed patterns are reduced, by use of Boolean algebra, to logically comprehensive minimal descriptions. In a third step, clusters of cases with common variable configurations can be identified; hypotheses on necessary or sufficient conditions for the occurrence of interesting effects can be falsified; and even theory-building can be inspired by the results of Ragin-type analyses. Unfortunately, this approach has not been widely used so far. Articles illustrating the road to be followed include Amenta and Poulsen (1994), Berg-Schlosser and Quenter (1996), and Ragin, Berg-Schlosser, and de Meur (1996). The necessary and easily available software is described in Drass (1992).

Theoretical Frameworks

Generally, European recruitment research has not been marked by a special concern for theory-building or theory-testing. (On theories of recruitment see, for instance, Beyme 1992; Black 1972; Borchert and Golsch 1995; Field, Higley, and Burton 1990; Fowler 1994; Norris 1997a, 1–14; Prinz 1993; Solvang 1982 and the literature reviewed there.) Until very recently, little effort has been invested in the construction of conceptual frameworks for common comparative research, a shortcoming apparently due to the neglect of comparative analysis itself. Rather, categories like social or political background, gender, age of parliamentarians, and seniority, have been treated as variables of self-evident importance. Sometimes, the easy accessibility of data rather than a concern for the theoretical relevance of the data seems to have been the guiding motive.

When recruitment research was placed into a broader theoretical context, this context was usually provided by representational theory in the sense of "descriptive" representation as discussed by Pitkin (1967, 61). Then the main questions were: How (and why) does the social composition of a representative assembly differ from that of the people represented, and what can be done to reduce this difference? Research on women legislators was notably inspired by this line of reasoning. Thus, "descriptive" representational theory led directly to social background analysis. The much more important "linkage perspective," which leads to political network analysis, was unfortunately employed only rarely, although its central question is of evident importance: How does the communicative efficiency of the network between parliament and society depend on the social composition of parliament and on the rooting of parliamentarians in society? Social background patterns tend to shape network patterns, and both enhance chances that legislators and parliaments are more responsive to certain segments of society than to others. But responsiveness is only one aspect of representation. Its twin aspect is leadership, which means influencing the political views of the voters. However, this leadership aspect of representation was neglected even more, and with it such questions as the political leadership capacity of MPs and the effect of recruitment patterns on this capacity.

According to the frequency of their use, we can rank the guiding theoretical concepts of European recruitment research as follows. In the top position we find concepts that describe the candidates' or parliamentarians' personal and social background. Analytically they have been used as indicators of recruitment patterns, and in the study of recruiting mechanisms both as dependent variables and as independent variables that affect outcomes like parliamentary responsiveness or legislative output. Sometimes, they have also been treated as "structural parameters" that indirectly shape other relevant interrelations. Second in rank is the concept of professionalization. It is meant to capture the essential changes between the "amateur parliamentarism" of the nineteenth century and the "professional parliamentarism" of today. This concept is usually linked to the concept of career, with much more attention given to pre-legislative careers than to legislative or even post-legislative careers. Concepts arising out of the supply and demand-analysis, ranking third, have reached a certain degree of popularity among researchers in the last few years. The same is true for the concept of (alternative) opportunity structures. Concepts like ambition or "political personality" are rarely used in academic empirical research, whereas they are popular in public political discussions. And the categories of rational-choice models, which are so widely employed in American recruitment research, are nearly absent. The different methodological and theoretical preferences in European and American recruitment research explain the differences over the use of such models. Concepts focusing on rational choice or "political personality" could, however, easily be integrated into the emerging European framework of supply and demand-analysis. In a next step of theory construction, this framework should be embedded in a linkage, leadership, and responsiveness approach of representational analysis.

Such an integration would open promising paths for further research and permit us to fill in the research gaps that I have identified. Together with some of the changes in methodology that I have suggested, and with collaborative work among multilingual scholars, it would be possible to overcome the "patchwork approach" that has marked so much of European recruitment research both geographically and conceptually.

Basic Approaches: Toward Normative Research

There are two basic, but complementary, approaches to the study of legislative recruitment and retention. First, we can treat it as a *dependent* variable and ask what factors contribute to the allocation of certain persons, or groups of eligibles, to relevant positions. This has been the main road of European recruitment research. Second, we can treat legislative recruitment and retention as an *independent* variable. Then our research questions will extend to how a given personal or social composition of parliament contributes to the integration and the stability, to the performance and the policy output of a legislature. Obviously, it is much more difficult to follow this second approach. There are serious problems in operationalizing and measuring the dependent variables; there are difficulties in analyzing data and making comparisons between the limited number of analyzable cases; and consequential theoretical questions need preceding answers: what compositional or structural features of a legislature are plausible determinants of both theoretically relevant and measurable dependent variables? Because of such difficulties it is no surprise that studies of legislative recruitment and retention as an independent variable have been rare.

But if legislative recruitment and retention can be neglected as a determinant of political performance and outcomes, then its importance as a dependent variable is also in question. If, however, legislative recruitment and retention really are major determinants of important systemic features like responsiveness or policy outcome, like capacity of parliamentary control and leadership, or like legitimacy as a whole, then its study as a dependent variable is crucial. If we can find a clear pattern of interrelations between the composition of parliaments and their output, then we could presumably consider how a modification of recruitment mechanisms might affect large consequences. Such findings would be of utmost practical importance.

Striving for such practically important results, we have to supplement an *empirical* approach with a *normative* approach. The central questions of such a normative approach would include the following: What are the personal features, practical skills, and linkages to society that our parliamentarians *ought* to possess? How can we determine the qualifications of a *good* member of parliament? What price in terms of acceptable inequality or practical privileges *should* we be willing to pay for them? And what types of legislative activity or outcome should we *want* to optimize by possible modifications of parliamentary recruitment? Such a normative and practical approach has not been very common in European recruitment and retention studies during the last decades. Therefore, we know, for instance, much more about professionalization among legislators than about the value of legislative professionalization and about the things parliamentarians should do in a more professional way. Reasoning on the latter questions has largely been left to general political discussions and to journalists; with only few exceptions such as Rebenstorf (1992) and Patzelt (1998). But on balance, European political scientists have been much better in the analysis of what is, or what has been, than in empirically grounded suggestions of what can and what should be done if we want to improve the mechanisms and results of political recruitment. However, political scientists should not limit their work to descriptions and explanations of legislative recruitment and retention; they should rather dare to go one step further: they should assess whether we really have the political personnel we need, and they should engage in political discussions of how our recruitment and retention systems might be reformed. After all, European political science started as practical philosophy, and there are no good reasons to cut off its roots.

NOTE

I am indebted to Steffen H. Elsner for his valuable bibliographic support and to Joachim Amm for his comments on an earlier draft of this paper.

REFERENCES

Acquaviva, Jean-Claude. 1997. *Les Députés. Élection-Mandat-Rôle-L'Assemblée Nationale.* Paris: Gualino Éditeur.
Amenta, Edwin, and Jane D. Poulsen. 1994. "Where to Begin: A Survey of Five Approaches to Selecting Independent Variables for Qualitative Comparative Analysis." *Sociological Methods and Research* 23:22–53.
Arter, David. 1984. *The Nordic Parliaments.* London: Hurst.
Badura, Bernhard, and Jürgen Reese. 1976. *Jungparlamentarier in Bonn. Ihre Sozialisation im Deutschen Bundestag.* Stuttgart/Bad Cannstatt: Frommann-Holzboog.
Bartolini, Stefano, and Roberto D'Alimonte. 1996. "Plurality Competition and Party Realignment in Italy: The 1994 Parliamentary Elections." *European Journal of Political Research* 29:105–42.
Bean, Clive, and Anthony Mughan. 1989. "Leadership Effects in Parliamentary Elections in Australia and Britain." *American Political Science Review* 83:1165–79.
Bendix, John. 1994. "Women and Politics in Germany and Switzerland." *European Journal of Political Research* 25:413–38.
Berg-Schlosser, Dirk, and Sven Quenter. 1996. "Macro-Quantitative vs. Macro-Qualitative Methods in Political Science. Advantages and Disadvantages of Comparative Procedures using the Welfare-State Theory as an Example." *Historical Social Research* 21:3–25.
Bermeo, Nancy. 1987. "Redemocratization and Transition Elections: A Comparison of Spain and Portugal." *Comparative Politics* 19:213–31.
Best, Heinrich. 1982. "Recruitment, Careers and Legislative Behaviour of German Parliamentarians, 1848–1953." *Historical Social Research* 23:20–54.
Best, Heinrich. 1990. *Die Männer von Bildung und Besitz. Struktur und Handeln parlamentarischer Führungsgruppen in Deutschland und Frankreich 1848 and 49.* Düsseldorf: Droste.
Best, Heinrich. 1997. "Politische Modernisierung und Elitenwandel 1848–1996. Die europäischen Gesellschaften im intertemporal-interkulturellen Vergleich." *Historical Social Research* 22:4–31.
Best, Heinrich, and Maurizio Cotta. 1997. "Elite Transformation and Modes of Representation since the Mid-Nineteenth Century: Some Theoretical Considerations." Paper presented at the Conference on Transformation of Political Representation in Europa, Jena. To appear in *The European Representative, Vol. 1, 150 Years of Parliamentary Representation in Comparative Perspective,* ed. Heinrich Best and Maurizio Cotta, 1999. Oxford: Oxford University Press.
Beyme, Klaus von. 1992. "Der Begriff der politischen Klasse—eine neue Dimension der Elitenforschung?" *Politische Vierteljahresschrift* 33:4–32.
Black, Gordon. 1972. "A Theory of Political Ambition: Career Choices and the Role of Structural Incentives." *American Political Science Review* 72:144–59.
Bochel, John, and David Denver. 1983. "Candidate Selection in the Labour Party: What the Selectors Seek." *British Journal of Political Science* 13:45–69.

Bogdanor, Vernon, ed. 1985. *Representatives of the People?* Aldershot: Gower.
Boll, Bernhard. 1994. "Parliamentary Incumbency in Germany: No Matter of Choice?" In *The Victorious Incumbent. A Threat to Democracy?*, ed. Albert Somit, Rudolf Wildenmann, Bernhard Boll, and Andrea Römmele. Aldershot: Dartmouth.
Boll, Bernhard, and Andrea Römmele. 1994. "Strukturelle Vorteile der Amtsinhaber? Wahlchancen von Parlamentariern im internationalen Vergleich." *Zeitschrift für Parlamentsfragen* 25:543–56.
Borchers, Andreas. 1998. "Im Hohen Haus regiert der Durschschnitt." *STERN*, September.
Borchert, Jens, and Lutz Golsch. 1995. "Die politische Klasse in westlichen Demokratien." *Politische Vierteljahresschrift* 36:609–29.
Boyce, Brigitte. 1995. "The June 1994 Election and the Politics of European Parliament." *Parliamentary Affairs* 48:141–56.
Brothén, Martin. 1996. "Anciennitetsprincipen i Sveriges riksdag." *Statsvetenskaplig Tidskrift* 99:37–52.
Budge, Ian, and Dennis Farlie. 1975. "Political Recruitment and Drop-out: Predictive Success of Background Characteristics over Five British Localities." *British Journal of Political Science* 5:33–68.
Bürklin, Wilhelm, and Hilke Rebenstorf. 1997. *Eliten in Deutschland. Rekrutierung und Integration.* Opladen: Leske + Budrich.
Burmeister, Kerstin. 1993. *Die Professionalisierung der Politik am Beispiel des Berufspolitikers im politischen System der Bundesrepublik Deutschland.* Berlin: Duncker und Humblot.
Campo, Salustiano del, José Félix Tezanos, and Walter Santin. 1982. "The Spanish Political Elite. Permanency and Change." In *Does Who Governs Matter? Elite Circulation in Contemporary Societies*, ed. Moshe M. Czudnowski. DeKalb: Northern Illinois University Press.
Cayrol, Roland, and Pascal Perrineau. 1982. "Governing Elites in a Changing Industrial Society: The Case of France." In *Does Who Governs Matter? Elite Circulation in Contemporary Societies*, ed. Moshe M. Czudnowski. DeKalb: Northern Illinois University Press.
Comstock, Alzada. 1926. "Women Members of European Parliaments." *American Political Science Review* 20:379–84.
Conley, Marshall W., and Patrick J. Smith. 1983. "Political Recruitment and Party Activists: British and Canadian Comparisons." *International Political Science Review* 4:48–56.
Cotarelo, R., ed. 1992. *Transición política y consolidación democrática en España.* Madrid: CIS.
Cotta, Maurizio, and Luca Verzichelli. 1994. Italy: The Breakdown of an Established Elite and the Rise of the New Politicians. Presented at the IPSA XVI World Congress, Berlin.
Criddle, Byron. 1988. "Candidates." In *The British General Election of 1987*, ed. Danuta Buttler and Dennis Kavanagh. London: Macmillan.
Cruz, M. Braga da, and M. Lobo Antunes. 1990. "Revolutionary Transition and Problems of Parliamentary Institutionalization: The Case of the Portuguese National Assembly." In *Parliament and Democratic Consolidation in Southern Europe: Greece,*

Italy, Portugal, Spain and Turkey, ed. Ulrike Liebert and Maurizo Cotta. London and New York: Pinter.
Czudnowski, Moshe M., ed. 1982. *Does Who Governs Matter? Elite Circulation in Contemporary Societies.* DeKalb: Northern Illinois University Press.
Daalder, Hans, and Joop Th. J. van den Berg. 1982. "Members of the Dutch Lower House: Pluralism and Democratization, 1848–1967." In *Does Who Governs Matter? Elite Circulation in Contemporary Societies*, ed. Moshe M. Czudnowski. DeKalb: Northern Illinois University Press.
Dachs, Herbert, Peter Gerlich, and Wolfgang D. Müller, eds. 1995. *Die Politiker. Karrieren und Wirken bedeutender Repräsentanten der Zweiten Republik.* Wien: Manzsche Verlags und Universitätsbuchhandlung.
Dahlerup, Drude. 1988. "From a Small to a Large Minority: Women in Scandinavian Politics." *Scandinavian Political Studies* 11:275–98.
Damgaard, Erik. 1980. "The Function of Parliament in the Danish Political System: Results of Recent Research." *Legislative Studies Quarterly* 5:101–21.
Damgaard, Erik. 1997. "The Political Roles of Danish MPs." In *Members of Parliament in Western Europe: Roles and Behavior*, ed. Wolfgang D. Müller and Thomas Saalfeld. London: Cass.
Denver, David. 1988. "Britain: Centralized Parties with Decentralized Selection." In *Candidate Selection in Comparative Perspective. The Secret Garden of Politics*, ed. Michael Gallagher and Michael Marsh. London: Sage.
Derlien, Hans-Ulrich, and Stefan Lock. 1994. "Eine neue politische Elite? Rekrutierung und Karrieren der Abgeordneten in den fünf neuen Landtagen." *Zeitschrift für Parlamentsfragen* 25:61–94.
Drass, Kris. 1992. *Qualitative Comparative Analysis 3.0.* Center for Urban Affairs and Policy Research, Evanston, IL: Northwestern University.
Dupeux, Louis, Raibner Hudemann, and Franz Knipping. 1996. *Eliten in Deutschland und Frankreich im 19. und 20. Jahrhundert. Strukturen und Beziehungen, Vol. 2.* Munich: Oldenbourg.
Dyk, Irene. 1986. "Frauen im österreichischen Parlament." In *Österreichs Parlamentarismus: Werden und System*, ed. Herbert Schambeck. Berlin: Duncker & Humblot.
Eduards, Maud L. 1991. "The Swedish Gender Model: Productivity, Pragmatism and Paternalism." *West European Politics* 14:166–81.
Eliassen, Kjell A. 1978. "Mass Mobilization and the Transformation of Parliamentary Elites in Norway." *Scandinavian Political Studies* 1:187–213.
Eliassen, Kjell A. 1985. "Rekruttering til Stortinget og regjeringen 1945–1985." In *Storting og regjering 1945–1985: Institusjoner-Rekruttering*, ed. Trond Nordby. Oslo: Kunnskapsforlaget.
Eliassen, Kjell A., and Mogens N. Pedersen. 1978. "Professionalization of Legislatures: Long-Term Changes in Political Recruitment in Denmark and Norway." *Comparative Studies in Society and History* 20:286–318.
Esaiasson, Peter, and Knut Heidar, eds. 1999. *Beyond Congress and Westminster. The Nordic Experience.* Columbus: Ohio State University Press.
Esaiasson, Peter, and Sören Holmberg. 1996. *Representation from Above: Members of Parliament and Representative Democracy in Sweden.* Aldershot: Dartmouth.

Farlie, Dennis, Ian Budge, and Galen A. Irwin. 1977. "Political Recruitment and Dropout: Extensions to the Netherlands and the United States." *British Journal of Political Science* 7:465–92.

Field, G. Lowell, John Higley, and Michael G. Burton. 1990. "A New Elite Framework for Political Sociology." *Revue Européenne des Sciences Sociales* 28:149–82.

Fowler, Linda L. 1994. "Theories of Recruitment in Comparative Perspective." Presented at IPSA XVI World Congress, Berlin.

Fuchs, Gesine. 1994. "Partizipation und Durchsetzungschancen von Frauen im Parlament. Das Beispiel des Kantonsparlaments von Basel-Landschaft." *Zeitschrift für Parlamentsfragen* 25:581–602.

Gallagher, Michael. 1980. "Candidate Selection in Ireland: The Impact of Localism and the Electoral System." *British Journal of Political Science* 10:489–503.

Gallagher, Michael. 1984. "Who Rule: The Dail Deputies of November 1982." *Economic and Social Review* 15:241–64.

Gallagher, Michael. 1985. "Social Backgrounds and Local Orientations of Members of the Irish Dail." *Legislative Studies Quarterly* 10:373–94.

Gallagher, Michael. 1988a. "Ireland: The Increasing Role of the Centre." In *Candidate Selection in Comparative Perspective. The Secret Garden of Politics*, ed. Michael Gallagher and Michael Marsh. London: Sage.

Gallagher, Michael. 1988b. "Conclusion." In *Candidate Selection in Comparative Perspective. The Secret Garden of Politics*, ed. Michael Gallagher and Michael Marsh. London: Sage.

Gallagher, Michael. 1993. "Parliament." In *Politics in the Republic of Ireland*, 2d ed., ed. John Coakley and id. Dublin and Limerick: Folens and PSAI Press.

Gallagher, Michael, and Michael Marsh, eds. 1988. *Candidate Selection in Comparative Perspective. The Secret Garden of Politics*. London: Sage.

Garrigue, Daniel, ed. 1992. *Le Député Aujourd'hui*. Paris: Assemblée Nationale.

Gaxie, Daniel. 1980. "Les Logiques du Recrutement Politique." *Revue Française de Science Politique* 30:5–45.

Giol, J. Capo, R. Garcia Cotarelo, López Garrido, and J. Subirats. 1990. "By Consociationalism to a Majoritarian Parliamentary System: The Rise and Decline of the Spanish Cortes." In *Parliament and Democratic Consolidation in Southern Europe: Greece, Italy, Portugal, Spain and Turkey*, ed. Ulrike Liebert and Maurizio Cotta. London and New York: Pinter.

Glaeßner, Gert-Joachim. 1996. "Regimewechsel und Elitentransfer. Parlamentarisch-politische und Verwaltungseliten in Ostdeutschland."*Deutschland Archiv* 29:849–62.

Gordon, Ian. 1979. *The Recruitment of British Candidates for the European Parliament*. Kingston. Mimeo.

Graham, James Q. 1982. "Legislative Careers in the French Chambers and U.S. House, 1871–1940." *Legislative Studies Quarterly* 7:37–56.

Gratzer, Christian. 1994. "Die Kandidatenauswahl der FPÖ, GABL, VGÖ und des Liberalen Forums anläßlich der Niederösterreichischen Landtagswahl 1993." *Österreichisches Jahrbuch für Politik* 1993:239–66.

Gretz, Winfried. 1993. *Politische Eliten im internationalen Vergleich. Eine Studie über die Parlamentsmitglieder in South Carolina und Baden-Württemberg*. Aachen: Shaker.

Gruner, Erich, Martin Daetwyler, and Oscar Zosso. 1975. *Aufstellung und Auswahl der Kandidaten bei den Nationalratswahlen in der Schweiz.* Bern: Forschungszentrum für schweizerische Politik, Universität Bern.

Guédé, Alain, and Serge-Alain Rozenblum. 1981. "Les Candidates aux Élections Législatives de 1978 et 1981: Permanence et Changements." *Revue Française de Science Politique* 31:982–98.

Gunther, Richard. 1992. "Spain. The Very Model of the Modern Elite Settlement." In *Elites and Democratic Consolidation in Latin America and Southern Europe*, ed. John Higley and Richard Gunther. Cambridge: Cambridge University Press.

Haavio-Mannila, E. et al. 1985. *Unfinished Democracy. Women in Nordic Politics.* Oxford: Pergamon Press.

Haungs, Peter. 1970. "Mitgliederbefragung zur Landtagskandidatenaufstellung. Das Experiment des CDU—Bezirksverbandes Rheinhessen—Pfalz." *Zeitschrift für Parlamentsfragen* 1:403–17.

Heepe, K. 1989. "Bessere Wahlchancen von Frauen durch Personenwahlsysteme?" *Zeitschrift für Parlamentsfragen* 20:102–13.

Heidar, Knut. 1986. "Party Organizational Elites in Norwegian Politics: Representativeness and Party Democracy." *Scandinavian Political Studies* 9:279–90.

Heidar, Knut. 1997. "Roles, Structures and Behaviour: Norwegian Parliamentarians in the Nineties." In *Members of Parliament in Western Europe: Roles and Behavior*, ed. Wolfgang C. Müller and Thomas Saalfeld. London: Cass.

Helander, Voitto. 1997a. "Finland." In *Passages to Power: Legislative Recruitment in Advanced Democracies*, ed. Pippa Norris. Cambridge: Cambridge University Press.

Herzog, Dietrich. 1975. *Politische Karrieren. Selektion und Professionalisierung politischer Führungsgruppen.* Opladen: Westdeutscher Verlag.

Herzog, Dietrich. 1977. "Partei- und Parlamentskarrieren im Spiegel der Zahlen für die Bundesrepublik Deutschland." *Zeitschrift für Parlamentsfragen* 7:25–42.

Herzog, Dietrich. 1979. "Karrieremuster von Abgeordneten in Deutschland—früher und heute. In *Politik als Beruf? Das Abgeordnetenbild im historischen Wandel. Protokoll eines Seminars der Deutschen Vereinigung fuer Parlamentsfragen,* ed. Bonn: Deutscher Bundestag, Presse- und Informationszentrum.

Herzog, Dietrich. 1990. "Der moderne Berufspolitiker. Karrierebedingungen und Funktion in westlichen Demokratien." In *Eliten in der Bundesrepublik Deutschland,* ed. Hans-Georg Wehling. Stuttgart: Kohlhammer.

Hess, Adalbert. 1995. "Sozialstruktur des 13. Deutschen Bundestages: Berufliche und fachliche Entwicklungslinien." *Zeitschrift für Parlamentsfragen* 26:567–87.

Higley, John, and Richard Gunther, eds. 1992. *Elites and Democratic Consolidation in Latin America and Southern Europe.* Cambridge: Cambridge University Press.

Higley, John, and Jan Pakulski. 1992. "Revolution and Elite Transformation in Eastern Europe." *Australian Journal of Political Science* 27:104–19.

Hills, John. 1981. "Candidates, the Impact of Gender." *Parliamentary Affairs* 34:221–32.

Hoecker, Beate. 1986. *Frauen in der Politik: Eine soziologische Studie.* Opladen: Leske + Budrich.

Hoecker, Beate. 1987. "Politik—noch immer kein Beruf für Frauen." *Aus Politik und Zeitgeschichte* B9–10:3–14.

Hoecker, Beate. 1994. "Parlamentarierinnen im Deutschen Bundestag 1949 bis 1990. Ein Postskriptum zur Abgeordnetensoziologie." *Zeitschrift für Parlamentsfragen* 25:556–81.

Hoecker, Beate. 1996. "Innerparteiliche Frauenförderung in Großbritannien und Deutschland." *Zeitschrift für Parlamentsfragen* 27:642–57.

Hoecker, Beate. 1998. *Handbuch politische Partizipation von Frauen in Europa*. Opladen: Leske + Budrich.

Hohmann, Johannes-Berthold. 1987. "Kandidaten und Abgeordnete von CDU und SPD in Berlin von 1946 bis 1963." *Historical Social Research* 41:51–71.

Holl, Stefan. 1989. *Landtagsabgeordnete in Baden-Würtemberg*. Sozialprofil, Rekrutierung, Selbstbild, Kehl a. R.: Engel.

Holland, Martin. 1986. *Candidates for Europe—The British Experience*. Aldershot: Gower.

Holmberg, Sören. 1989. "Political Representation in Sweden." *Scandinavian Political Studies* 12:1–36.

Holmberg, Sören. 1994. "Politische Repräsentation in Schweden." In *Parteien, Parlamente und Wahlen in Skandinavien*, ed. Franz Urban Pappi and Hermann Schmitt. Frankfurt a. M and New York: Campus.

Horn, Wolfgang, and Herbert Kühr. 1978. *Kandidaten im Wahlkampf: Kandidatenauslese, Wahlkampf und lokale Presse 1975 in Essen*. Meisenheim a. Glan: Hain.

Hrbek, Rudolf, and Carl-Christoph Schweitzer. 1989. "Die Deutschen Europa-Parlamentarier. Ergebnisse einer Befragung der deutschen Mitglieder des Europäischen Parlaments." *Aus Politik und Zeitgeschichte* B3:3–18.

Hübner, Emil. 1979. "Das Bayerische Landtagswahlrecht." In *Das Regierungssystem des Freistaates Bayern*, Vol. 2., ed. Reinhold L. Bocklet. München: Vogel.

Irwin, Galen A. 1995. "Second-order or third-rate: Issues in the Campaign for the Elections for the European Parliament 1994." *Electoral Studies* 14:183–98.

Irwin, Galen A., Ian Budge, and Dennis Farlie. 1979. "Social Backgrounds vs. Motivational Determinants of Legislative Careers in the Netherlands." *Legislative Studies Quarterly* 4:447–65.

Isberg, Magnus. 1982. *The First Decade of the Unicameral Riksdag: The Role of the Swedish Parliament in the 1970´s*. Stockholm: Stockholm University Research Reports.

Ismayr, Wolfgang. 1992. *Der Deutsche Bundestag. Funktionen, Willensbildung, Reformansätze*. Opladen: Leske + Budrich.

James, Peter. 1988. "The Bavarian Electoral System." *Electoral Studies* 7:33–39.

Kaack, Heino. 1980. "Zur Struktur der politischen Führungselite in Parteien, Parlament und Regierung." In *Handbuch des deutschen Parteiensystems*, Vol. I., ed. Reinhold Roth. Opladen: Leske + Budrich.

Kaack, Heino. 1988a. "Die soziale Zusammensetzung des Deutschen Bundestages." In *US-Kongreß und Deutscher Bundestag. Bestandsaufnahmen im Vergleich*, ed. Uwe Thaysen, Roger H. Davidson, and Robert G. Livingston. Opladen: Westdeutscher Verlag.

Kaack, Heino. 1988b. "Zur Abgeordnetensoziologie des Deutschen Bundestages: Zugehörigkeitsdauer und Altersschichtung." *Zeitschrift für Parlamentsfragen* 19:169–87.

Kaltefleiter, Werner. 1976. "The Recruitment Market of the German Political Elite." In *Elite Recruitment in Democratic Polities: Comparative Study Across Nations*, ed. Heinz Eulau and Moshe M. Czudnowski. London: Wiley and Sage.

Karvonen, Lauri, and P. Selle. 1995. *Women in Nordic Politics*. Aldershot: Dartmouth.

Kauppi, Niilo. 1996. "European Union Institutions and French Political Careers." *Scandinavian Political Studies* 19:1–24.

Kavanagh, Dennis. 1992. "Changes in the Political Class and its Culture." *Parliamentary Affairs* 45:18–32.

Kerr, Henry M. 1981a. *Parlement et société en Suisse. Une Analyse en Profondeur de la Démocratie Représentative Helvétique*. Saint-Saphorin (Suisse): Editions Georgi.

Kerr, Henry M. 1981b. *Unser Parlament*. Basel: Edition Heuwinkel.

Kim, Chong Lim, and Samuel C. Patterson. 1987. "Parliamentary Elites in Six Nations." *Comparative Politics* 20:379–99.

King, Anthony. 1981. "The Rise of the Career Politician in Britain—and its Consequences." *British Journal of Political Science* 11:249–85.

Kirchner, Emil J. 1983. "Background and Activities of Members of the European Parliament." *Res publica* 25:21–38.

Kohn, Walter S. G. 1980. *Women in National Legislatures: A Comparative Study of Six Countries*. New York: Praeger.

Kohn, Walter S. G. 1981. "Women in the European Parliament." *Parliamentary Affairs* 34:210–20.

Kolinsky, Eva. 1991. "Political Participation and Parliamentary Careers: Women´s Quotas in West Germany." *West European Politics* 14:56–72.

Kolk, Henk van der, Hermann Schmitt, Evi Scholz, and Jaques Thomassen. 1997. "The European Elections Study 1994." *European Journal of Political Research* 32:283–89.

Koole, Ruud, and Monique Leijenaar. 1988. "The Netherlands: The Predominance of Regionalism." In *Candidate Selection in Comparative Perspective. The Secret Garden of Politics*, ed. Michael Gallagher and Michael Marsh. London: Sage.

Kourvetaris, George A. 1989. "Political Elites and Party Organization in Greece: An Entrepreneurial Model." *Journal of Social, Political and Economic Studies* 14:189–214.

Kremer, Klemens. 1984. *Der Weg ins Parlament. Kandidatur zum Bundestag, 2. Aufl.* Heidelberg: Decker & Müller.

Legg, Keith. 1982. "Restoration Elites: Regime Change in Greece." In *Does Who Governs Matter? Elite Circulation in Contemporary Societies*, ed. Moshe M. Czudnowski. DeKalb: Northern Illinois University Press.

Leijenaar, Monique H. 1989. *De Geschade Heerlijkheid. Politiek Gedrag von Vrouwen en Mannen in Nederland. 1918–1988.* Den Haag: SDU.

Leijenaar, Monique H., and Kees Niemöller. 1997. "The Netherlands." In *Passages to Power: Legislative Recruitment in Advanced Democracies*, ed. Pippa Norris. Cambridge: Cambridge University Press.

Liebert, Ulrike, and Maurizio Cotta, eds. 1990. *Parliament and Democratic Consolidation in Southern Europe: Greece, Italy, Portugal, Spain, and Turkey.* London and New York: Pinter.
Lock, Stefan. 1998. *Ostdeutsche Landtagsabgeordnete 1990–1994.* Berlin: Verlag fuer Wissenschaft und Forschung.
Lovenduski, Joni, and Pippa Norris. 1989. "Selecting Women Candidates: Obstacles to the Feminisation of the House of Commons." *European Journal of Political Research* 17:533–62.
Masclet, Jean Claude. 1979. *Le Rôle du Député et ses Attaches Institutionelles sous la V République.* Paris: Libr. Gen. de Droit et de Jurisprudence.
Mastropaolo, Alfio. 1994. "Le elezioni politiche del marzo 1994. Vecchio e nouvo nel Parlamento italiano." *Storia Contemporanea* 196:461–70.
Matland, Richard E. 1993. "Institutional Variables Affecting Female Representation in National Legislatures: The Case of Norway." *Journal of Politics* 55:737–55.
Matland, Richard E. 1994. "Putting Scandinavian Equality to the Test: An Experimental Evaluation of Gender Stereotyping of Political Candidates in a Sample of Norwegian Voters." *British Journal of Political Science* 24:273–92.
Matland, Richard E., and Donley T. Studlar. 1996. "The Contagion of Women Candidates in Single-Member District and Proportional Representation Electoral Systems: Canada and Norway." *Journal of Politics* 58:707–33.
Morán, Maria-Luz. 1989. "Un intento de analisis de la 'clase parlamentaria' española: Elementos de renovación y de permanencia (1977–1986)." *Revista Española de Investigacionen Sociologicas* 45 and 1.
Müller, Emil-Peter. 1988. "Der Bundestag ist gebildeter geworden. Zur Entwicklung des Bildungsstandes der Bundestagsabgeordneten seit 1949." *Zeitschrift für Parlamentsfragen* 19:200–19.
Müller, Wolfgang C., and Thomas Saalfeld, eds. 1997. *Members of Parliament in Western Europe: Roles and Behavior.* London: Cass.
Narud, Hanne Marthe, and Henry Valen. 1999. "Does Background Matter? Social Representation and Political Attitudes." In *Beyond Congress and Westminster. The Nordic Experience,* ed. Peter Esaiasson and Knut Heidar. Columbus: Ohio State University Press.
Neisser, Heinrich, and Fritz Plasser, eds. 1992. *Vorwahlen und Kandidatennominierung im internationalen Vergleich.* Wien: Signum-Verlag.
Nicholson, Beryl. 1993. "From Interest Group to (Almost) Equal Citizenship: Women's Representation in the Norwegian Parliament." *Parliamentary Affairs* 46:254–63.
Nick, Rainer. 1992. "Vorwahlen in Österreich und in der Bundesrepublik Deutschland: Erfahrungen zur Kandidatennominierung aus mehr als zwei Jahrzehnten." In *Vorwahlen und Kandidatennominierung im internationalen Vergleich,* ed. Heinrich Neisser and Fritz Plasser. Wien: Signum-Verlag.
Norris, Pippa. 1985. "Women's Legislative Participation in Western Europe." *West European Politics* 8:90–101.
Norris, Pippa. 1993. "Conclusions: Comparing Legislative Recruitment." In *Gender and Party Politics,* ed. Pippa Norris and Joni Lovenduski. London: Sage.
Norris, Pippa. 1996. "Legislative Recruitment." In *Comparative Democratic Elections,* ed. Lawrence LeDuc, Richard G. Niemi, and Pippa Norris. Newbury Park: Sage.

Norris, Pippa, ed. 1997a. *Passages to Power: Legislative Recruitment in Advanced Democracies*. Cambridge: Cambridge University Press.
Norris, Pippa. 1997b. "Social Representation." *European Journal of Political Research* 32:185–210.
Norris, Pippa. 1997c. *Passages to Power: Legislative Recruitment in Advanced Democracies*. Cambridge: Cambridge University Press.
Norris, Pippa, and Joni Lovenduski. 1993a. "If Only More Candidates Came Forward: Supply-side Explanations of Candidates Selection in Britain." *British Journal of Political Science* 23:373–408.
Norris, Pippa, and Joni Lovenduski, eds. 1993b. *Gender and Party Politics*. London: Sage.
Norris, Pippa, and Joni Lovenduski. 1995. *Political Recruitment: Gender, Race and Class in the British Parliament*. Cambridge: Cambridge University Press.
Norton, Philip. 1980. "The Changing Face of the British House of Commons in the 1970s." *Legislative Studies Quarterly* 5:333–57.
Norton, Philip. 1994. "Parliament in the United Kingdom: The Incumbency Paradox." In *The Victorious Incumbent: A Threat to Democracy?*, ed. Albert Somit, Rudolf Wildenmann, Bernhard Boll, and Andrea Römmele. Aldershot: Dartmouth.
Oberreuter, Heinrich. 1994. "Die Ochsentour. Auswahl und Aufstieg von Parlamentariern." *Evangelische Kommentare* 27:11–13.
Oldersma, G. J. 1990a. "Vrouwen in Adviesraden." *Acta Politica* 4:467–85.
Oldersma, G. J. 1990b. "De Bouwstenen van Politieke Macht. Over Vrouwen in Nederlandse Adviesraden." In *Machten Onbehagen: Veranderingen in de Verhoudingen Tussen Vrouwen en Mannen*, ed. C. Bouw et al. Amsterdam: SUA.
Pappi, Franz Urban, and Hermann Schmitt, eds. 1994. *Parteien, Parlamente und Wahlen in Skandinavien*. Frankfurt a. M. and New York: Campus.
Parlamentsdirektion, ed. 1993. *Biographisches Handbuch der österreichischen Parlamentarier 1918–1993*. Wien: Österreichische Staatsdruckerei.
Pattie, Charles, Paul Whiteley, Ron Johnston, and Patrick Seyd. 1994. "Measuring Local Campaign Effects: Labour Party Constituency Campaigning at the 1987 General Election." *Political Studies* 42:469–79.
Patzelt, Werner J. 1993. "Zur Rekrutierungspraxis der Parlamente und zum internationalen Vergleich." In *Bitburger Gespräche*, ed. Gesellschaft für Rechtspolitik. München: Beck.
Patzelt, Werner J. 1995. *Abgeordnete und ihr Beruf. Interviews, Umfragen, Analysen*. Berlin: Akademie-Verlag.
Patzelt, Werner J. 1996a. "Deutschlands Abgeordnete. Profil eines Berufsstandes, der weit besser ist als sein Ruf." *Zeitschrift für Parlamentsfragen* 27:462–502.
Patzelt, Werner J. 1996b. "Repräsentanten und Repräsentation in den neuen Bundesländern." Dresden: Institute of Political Science. Research report.
Patzelt, Werner J. 1997. "Ostdeutsche Parlamentarier in ihrer ersten Wahlperiode: Wandel und Angleichung." *Historical Social Research* 22:160–80.
Patzelt, Werner J. 1998. "Parlamentarische Rekrutierung und Sozialisation. Normative Erwägungen, empirische Befunde und praktische Empfehlungen—aus deutscher Sicht." In *Wer soll uns vertreten? Professionsnormen für Politiker*, ed. Günther Burkert-Dottolo and Bernard Moser. Wien: Eigenverlag der Politischen Akademie.

Patzelt, Werner J., and Roland Schirmer. 1996. "Parlamentarismusgründung in den neuen Bundesländern." *Aus Politik und Zeitgeschichte* B26:3–11.
Peabody, Robert L. 1984. "Leadership in Legislatures: Evolution, Selection, Functions." *Legislative Studies Quarterly* 9:441–73.
Pedersen, Mogens N. 1976. *Political Development and Elite Transformation in Denmark.* Beverly Hills: Sage.
Pedersen, Mogens N. 1977. "The Personal Circulation of a Legislative: The Danish Folketing 1849–1968." In *The History of Parliamentary Behavior*, ed. William O. Aydelotte. Princeton: Princeton University Press.
Pedersen, Mogens. 1994. "Incumbency Success and Defeat in Times of Electoral Turbulances: Patterns of Legislative Recruitment in Denmark 1945–1990." In *The Victorious Incumbent. A Threat to Democracy?*, ed. Albert Somit. Aldershot: Dartmouth.
Penrose, Virginia. 1993. *Orientierungsmuster des Karriereverhaltens deutscher Politikerinnen: ein Ost-West-Vergleich.* Bielefeld: Kleine.
Pitkin, Hanna F. 1967. *The Concept of Representation.* Berkeley and Los Angeles: University of California Press.
Plöhn, Jürgen. 1984. "Ehemalige Bundestagsabgeordnete als Ministerpräsidenten der Länder—Ein etabliertes Karrieremuster." *Zeitschrift für Parlamentsfragen* 15:176–86.
Poledna, Tomas, and Christine Kaufmann. 1989. "Die parteiinterne Kandidatennomination—ein demokratisches Defizit? Eine Untersuchung am Beispiel der Nationalratswahlen im Kanton Zürich (1987)." *Schweizerisches Zentralblatt für Staats- und Gemeindeverwaltung* 90:281ff.
Porter, Stephen R. 1995. "Political Representation in Germany: The Effects of the Candidate Selection Committees." Ph.D. thesis. University of Rochester.
Prinz, Timothy S. 1993. "The Career Paths of Elected Politicians: A Review and a Prospectus." In *Ambition and Beyond: Career Paths of American Politicians*, ed. Shirley Williams and Edward L. Lascher. Berkeley: Institute of Governmental Studies Press.
Radice, Lisanne, Elizabeth Vallance, and Virginia Willis. 1990. *Member of Parliament: The Job of a Backbencher.* Basingstoke: Macmillan.
Ragin, Charles C. 1987. *The Comparative Method: Moving Beyond Qualitative and Quantitative Strategies.* Berkeley and Los Angeles: University of California Press.
Ragin, Charles C., Dirk Berg-Schlosser, and Gisèle de Meur. 1996. "Political Methodology: Qualitative Methods in Macropolitical Inquiry." *In A New Handbook of Political Science*, ed. Robert Goodin and Hans-Dieter Klingemann. Oxford: Oxford University Press.
Rasmussen, Jorgen. 1981. "Female Political Career Patterns and Leadership Disabilities in Britain: The Crucial Role of Gatekeepers in Regulating Entry to the Political Elite." *Polity* 13:600–20.
Rebenstorf, Hilke. 1992. "Steuerung des politischen Nachwuchses durch die Parteiführungen? Personalrekrutierung unter den Bedingungen gegenwärtiger Erfordernisse politischer Steuerung." *Aus Politik und Zeitgeschichte* B34–35:45–54.
Rebenstorf, Hilke. 1995. *Die politische Klasse: Zur Entwicklung und Reproduktion einer Funktionselite.* Frankfurt am Main: Campus.

Rebenstorf, Hilke, and Bernhard Weßels. 1989. "Wie wünschen sich die Wähler ihre Abgeordneten? Ergebnisse einer repräsentativen Bevölkerungsumfrage zum Problem der sozialen Repräsentativität des Deutschen Bundestages." *Zeitschrift für Parlamentsfragen* 20:408–24.

Recchi, Ettore. 1996. "Fishing the Same Schools: Parliamentary Recruitment and Consociationalism in the First and Second Italian Republics." *West European Politics* 19:340–59.

Reichel, Peter. 1974. *Bundestagsabgeordnete in europäischen Parlamenten: Zur Soziologie des europäischen Parlamentariers.* Opladen: Westdeutscher Verlag.

Riklin, Alois, and Alois Ochsner. 1984. "Parlament." In *Handbuch politisches System der Schweiz, Bd. 2: Strukturen und Prozesse,* ed. Ulrich Klöti. Bern and Stuttgart: Haupt.

Roberts, Geoffrey. 1988. "The Federal Republic of Germany: The Two-Lane Route to Berlin." In *Candidate Selection in Comparative Perspective. The Secret Garden of Politics,* ed. Michael Gallagher and Michael Marsh. London: Sage.

Rokkan, Stein. 1967. "Models and Methods in the Comparative Study of Nation-Building." Prepared for a Preparatory Meeting on Problems of Nation-Building, UNESCO, Brussels.

Rule, Wilma. 1987. "Electoral Systems, Contextual Factors and Women's Opportunity for Election to Parliament in Twenty-Three Democracies." *Western Political Quarterly* 40:477–98.

Ruostetsaari, Ilkka. 1993. "The Anatomy of the Finnish Power Elite." *Scandinavian Political Studies* 16:305–38.

Rusciano, Frank L. 1992. "Rethinking the Gender Gap: The Case of West German Elections. 1949–1987." *Comparative Politics* 24:335–57.

Rush, Michael. 1979. "The Members of Parliament." In *The House of Commons in the Twentieth Century,* ed. Shaft A. Walkland. Oxford: Oxford University Press.

Rush, Michael. 1986. "The Selectorate Revisted: Selecting Parliamentary Candidates in the 1980s." *Teaching Politics* 15:99–113.

Rush, Michael. 1988. "The Members of Parliament." In *The Commons Under Scruntiny,* ed. Michael Ryle and Peter G. Richards. London: Routledge.

Rush, Michael. 1994. "Career Patterns in British Politics: First Choose your Party ...." *Parliamentary Affairs* 47:566–82.

Saalfeld, Thomas. 1997. "Professionalisation of Parliamentary Roles in Germany: An Aggregate-Level Analysis." In *Members of Parliament in Western Europe: Roles and Behavior,* ed. Wolfgang Müller and Thomas Saalfeld. London: Cass.

Santamaria, J. 1994. "El Papel del Parlamento Durante la Consolidación de la Democracia y Después." *Revista de Estudios Politicos* 84:9–25.

Scarrow, Susan E. 1997. "Political Career Paths and the European Parliament." *Legislative Studies Quarterly* 22:253–63.

Schendelen, Marinus P. C. M. van. 1981a. *The Dutch Member of Parliament 1979–1980.* Rotterdam: Erasmus University Press.

Schendelen, Marinus P. C. M. van. 1981b. "Disaffected Representation in the Netherlands: A Nonaffected Reappraisal." *Political Behavior* 3:137–62.

Schindler, Peter. 1983. *Datenhandbuch zur Geschichte des Bundestages. 1949–1982.* Bonn: Abteilung Wissenschaftliche Dokumentation des Deutschen Bundestages.

Schindler, Peter. 1988. *Datenhandbuch zur Geschichte des Bundestages. 1980–1987.* Bonn: Wissenschaftliche Dienste des Deutschen Bundestages.

Schindler, Peter. 1994. *Datenhandbuch zur Geschichte des Bundestages. 1983–1991.* Bonn: Wissenschaftliche Dienste des Deutschen Bundestages.

Schindler, Peter. 1995. "Deutscher Bundestag 1976–1994: Parlaments- und Wahlstatistik." *Zeitschrift für Parlamentsfragen* 26:551–66.

Scholl, Edward L. 1986. "The Electoral System and Constituency-Oriented Activity in the European Parliament." *International Studies Quarterly* 30:315–32.

Searing, D.H. 1994. *Westminster's World. Understanding Political Roles.* Cambridge, MA: Harvard University Press.

Secker, Wilhelmina P. 1995. "Political-Administrative Elites in the Netherlands: Profiles and Perceptions." *Historical Social Research* 20:61–86.

Setzer, Hans. 1991. "Rekrutierung der politischen Führungseliten in Großbritannien. Kontinuität und Wandel in unserer Zeit." *Zeitschrift für Politik* 38:307–16.

Sidoti, Francesco. 1993. "The Italian Political Class." *Government and Opposition* 28:339–52.

Skjeie, Hege. 1991. "The Rhetoric of Difference: On Women's Inclusion into Political Elites." *Politics and Society* 19:233–63.

Solvang, Bernt Krohn. 1982. "Political Positions, Hierarchies and Political Markets: Towards a New Theory on Political Recruitment." *Scandinavian Political Studies* 5:149–67.

Somit, Albert , Rudolf Wildenmann, Bernhard Boll, and Andrea Römmele, eds. 1994. *The Victorious Incumbent. A Threat to Democracy?* Aldershot: Dartmouth.

Sprenger, Michael, and Peter Nidler. 1994. "Vorwahlen der Tiroler Volkspartei." *Österreichisches Jahrbuch für Politik* 1993:225–37.

Squire, Peverill. 1988a. "Career Opportunities and Membership Stability in Legislatures." *Legislative Studies Quarterly* 13:65–81.

Squire, Peverill. 1988b. "Career Opportunities and the Internal Organization of Legislatures." *Journal of Politics* 50:726–44.

Staab, Joachim Friedrich. 1986. "Direktkandidaten in den Bundestagswahlkämpfen 1969–1983. Erfahrungen im Umgang mit der lokalen und regionalen Tagespresse." *Publizistik* 31:296–314.

Stadlin, Paul. 1990. *Die Parlamente der schweizerischen Kantone.* Zug: Kalt-Zehnder.

Stämpfli, Rudolf, and Claude Longchamp. 1990. "Wie wird die Zukunft weiblich? Frauenförderung bei Wahlen und darüber hinaus." *Schweizerisches Jahrbuch für Politische Wissenschaft* 30:29–55.

Steininger, Barbara. 1992. "Frauen in der österreichischen Politik—eine empirische Analyse 1945 bis 1991." *Österreichisches Jahrbuch für Politik* 1991:643–66.

Stickler, Michael, ed. 1975. *Die Abgeordneten zum Österreichischen Nationalrat 1918–1975, und die Mitglieder des Österreichischen Bundesrates 1920–1975.* Wien: Verlag der Österreichischen Staatsdruckerei.

Stirnemann, Alfred. 1988. "Rekrutierung und Rekrutierungsstrategien." In *Das österreichische Parteiensystem*, ed. Anton Pelinka and Fritz Plasser. Wien and Köln and Graz: Böhlau.

Strecker, Gabriele, and Marlene Lenz. 1994. *Der Weg der Frau in die Politik.* Melle: Knoth.

Strøm, Kaare. 1997. "Rules, Reasons and Routines: Legislative Roles in Parliamentary Democracies." In *Members of Parliament in Western Europe: Roles and Behavior*, ed. Wolfgang D. Müller and Thomas Saalfeld. London: Cass.
Studlar, Donald T., Ian McAllister, and Alvaro Ascui. 1988. "Electing Women to the British Commons: Breakout from the Beleaguered Beachhead?" *Legislative Studies Quarterly* 13:515–28.
Studlar, Donald T., and Susan Welch. 1987. "Understanding the Iron Law of Andrarchy: Effects of Candidate Gender on Voting in Scotland." *Comparative Political Studies* 20:174–91.
Thiébault, Jean-Louis. 1988. "France: The Impact of Electoral System Change." In *Candidate Selection in Comparative Perspective. The Secret Garden of Politics*, ed. Michael Gallagher and Michael Marsh. London: Sage.
Thomas, Alastair H. 1985. "Members of Parliament and Access to Politics in Scandinavia." In *Representatives of the People? Parliamentarians and Constituents in Western Democracies*, ed. Vernon Bogdanor. Aldershot: Dartmouth.
Thöne, Eva M. 1982. "Das direkt gewählte Europäische Parlament. Ein Beitrag zur Abgeordnetensoziologie." *Zeitschrift für Parlamentsfragen* 12:149–80.
Torracinta-Pache, Claire. 1984. *Le Pouvoir est Pour Demain. Les Femmes Dans la Politique Suisse*. Lausanne: Editions de l´Aire.
Valen, Henry. 1988. "Norway: Decentralization and Group Representation." In *Candidate Selection in Comparative Perspective. The Secret Garden of Politics*, ed. Michael Gallagher and Michael Marsh. London: Sage.
Vallance, Elizabeth, and Elizabeth Davies. 1986. *Women of Europe. Women MEPs and Equality Policy*. Cambridge: Cambridge University Press.
Verzichelli, Luca. 1994. "Gli Eletti." *Rivista Italiana di Scienza Politica* 24:715–39.
Verzichelli, Luca. 1996. "La Classe Politica della Transizione." *Rivista Italiana di Scienza Politica* 26:727–68.
Wehling, Hans-Georg. 1990. *Eliten in der Bundesrepublik Deutschland*. Stuttgart: Kohlhammer.
Welch, Susan, and Donley T. Studlar. 1990. "Multi-Member Districts and the Representation of Women: Evidence from Britain and the United States." *Journal of Politics* 52:391–412.
Weßels, Bernhard. 1997. "Germany." In *Passages to Power: Legislative Recruitment in Advanced Democracies*, ed. Pippa Norris. Cambridge: Cambridge University Press.
Westlake, Martin. 1994. *Britain's Emerging Euro-elite? The British in the Directly Elected European Parliament*. Aldershot: Dartmouth.
Winderl, Thomas. 1991. "Fallstudie: Rekrutierungsmuster am Beispiel Dieter Lukesch." *Östereichisches Jahrbuch für Politik* 1990:793–802.
Winter, Lieven de. 1988. "Belgium—Democracy or Oligarchy?" In *Candidate Selection in Comparative Perspective. The Secret Garden of Politics*, ed. Michael Gallagher and Michael Marsh. London: Sage.
Winter, Lieven de. 1992. "The Belgian Legislator." Ph.D. thesis. European University Institute, Florence.
Winter, Lieven de. 1998. "The Belgian Parliament." In *World Encyclopedia of Parliaments and Legislatures, Vol. 1.*, ed. George T. Kurian and Lawrence D. Longley. Washington, DC: Congressional Quarterly.

Wolfgruber, Elisabeth. 1997. "Politische Repräsentation auf Länderebene: Die Landtage und ihre Abgeordneten." In *Länderpolitik. Politische Strukturen und Entscheidungsprozesse in den österreichischen Bundesländern*, ed. Herbert Dachs, Franz Fallend, and Elisabeth Wolfgruber. Wien: Signum-Verlag.

Wood, David, and Philip Norton. 1992. "Do Candidates Matter? Constituency-Specific Vote Changes for Incumbent MPs. 1983–1987." *Political Studies* 40:227–38.

Ysmal, Colette. 1994. "Incumbency in France. 1994: Electoral Instability as a Way to Legislative Turnover." In *The Victorious Incumbent. A Threat to Democracy?*, ed. Albert Somit, Rudolf Wildenmann, Bernhard Boll, and Andrea Römmele. Aldershot: Dartmouth.

Recruitment and Retention of Legislators in Brazil

Fabiano Santos

Introduction

This article discusses the issue of the recruitment and retention of legislators in Brazil since World War II. Its objectives are fourfold: a) to promote an assessment of existing studies on this subject; b) in light of this assessment, to discuss the possibilities for a comparison of the Brazilian experience with that of other countries; c) to identify the main theoretical challenges for developing such comparative research; and d) to locate existing obstacles to gathering empirical material on political careers in Brazil.

Before beginning the substantive analysis, an outline of Brazilian politics during this period is important and is divided into three phases.[1] The first, emerging from the fall of the so-called "Estado Novo" or "New State" (the name given to the dictatorial political system of Getúlio Vargas) spans the period from 1946 to 1964. It is often said that Brazil's first rehearsal of democracy occurred during this period, witnessing, as never before, the incorporation of the Brazilian population into institutionalized political competition. More specifically, beginning in 1946, there was an awesome growth in the electorate as a proportion of the population as a whole.

In addition, for the first time in the history of the Brazilian Republic, competition developed between political parties at the national level. During the so-called "República Velha" or "Old Republic" (the period preceding the Vargas dictatorship), parties were nothing more than state bodies. Thus, the nationally successful political coalitions resulted from the sum of local elites winning the domestic disputes.[2] With the creation of the national party system beginning in 1946, the Brazilian political society became something tangible, since interests and opinions transcending state borders gained representation. There were three main parties: the Partido Social Democrático (PSD) or "Social Democratic Party," the Partido Trabalhista Brasileiro (PTB) or "Brazilian Labor Party," and the

---

Reprinted with permission from *Legislative Studies Quarterly* 24, no. 2 (May 1999): 209–37.

União Democrática Nacional (UDN) or "National Democratic Union." The first two gravitated around the leadership of former dictator Getúlio Vargas, with the PSD based on state-level rural oligarchies and the PTB on trade union leadership stemming from the government-controlled corporatist scheme. The UDN represented political interests antagonistic to Vargas. Part of the local oligarchies, middle urban strata, and sectors of the industrial and financial bourgeoisie formed the mainstream of the opposition to the so-called *varguista* populism.

Finally, it is important to point out that electoral competition during the 1946–64 period was regulated by the Electoral Justice system. During the República Velha, deputies and senators-elect only took office after close scrutiny by the "Commission for Verification of Powers," a body composed of incumbent members of Congress whose purpose was supposedly to guarantee clean elections. In fact, the work of the "Commission" served the interests of state governors and the president, since the only legislators-elect it did not veto were those loyal to the factions in power.[3] By abolishing this fraudulent practice, the Electoral Justice system took a major step in making the ballot box reflect the will of the electorate.

In 1964, for various reasons,[4] a military coup d'état brought this short, rich democratic experiment to an end, launching a second phase in post-war Brazilian politics. The subsequent administrations canceled political rights, waged purges, tortured, and killed. Yet curiously, they maintained electoral and partisan competition and even the electoral calendar. They altered the electoral rules to decrease the opposition party's chances of expanding its congressional base. Nevertheless, the vote became an important tool in the peaceful transition to redemocratization. The old parties were eliminated by the military governments and their decrees. From 1966 to 1980, only two parties were allowed to compete, and even then only for legislative positions: the Aliança Renovadora Nacional (ARENA) or "National Renovative Alliance," supporting the military regime; and the Movimento Democrático Brasileiro (MDB) or "Brazilian Democratic Movement," in opposition to it.

This authoritarian period not only changed the political system itself, but produced an impressive transformation in the Brazilian economic system. Extremely high economic growth rates occurred year after year. With them, there was an equally important change in the country's social morphology. Urbanization, complexity, and social pluralism emerged as unanticipated effects of governments obsessed with economic modernization. And the transition to democracy acquired a body and pace.[5]

In 1980, party legislation was changed so as to allow other parties to be created. The 1982 elections included the Partido Democrático Social (PDS) or "Democratic Social Party," supporting the regime; the Partido do Movimento Democrático Brasileiro (PMDB) or "Party of the Brazilian Democratic Movement," consisting of members of the opposition who refused to split up the opposition bloc; the Partido Democrático Trabalhista (PDT) or "Democratic Labor Party," aiming to revive Vargas's old tradition of labor politics; the Partido Trabalhista Brasileiro (PTB) or "Brazilian Labor Party," with a conservative bent led by Getúlio Vargas's niece; and the Partido dos Trabalhadores (PT) or "Workers' Party," born of the independent trade union movement, associative movements, and leftist intellectual circles. In 1984, because of a break in the coalition supporting the regime, an interpartisan agreement elected the opposition candidate president.

Civilian government was thus reinstated in Brazil in 1985.[6] Along with it came the third phase in contemporary Brazilian politics. Party legislation was changed again, definitively eliminating restrictions on the creation of political parties. Since then, the Brazilian democracy has included participation by numerous parties, although only a few enjoy real electoral and congressional strength. In addition to the PMDB (center), PT and PDT (both left-wing), and PTB (right-wing), we now have other major parties like the Partido da Frente Liberal (PFL) or "Liberal Front Party" (center-right), the Partido da Social Democracia Brasileira (PSDB) or "Brazilian Social Democratic Party" (center-left), and the Partido Progressista Brasileiro (PPB) or "Brazilian Progressive Party" (right-wing).

This brief review of the country's recent political history illustrates the fluctuations in its political system and, by extension, in its system of representation. The legislative branch, parties, and leaders have not been immune to so many interruptions. Neither has political analysis. The discussion I propose in the following sections shows that the issues raised by researchers, the data gathered thus far, and the results obtained thereby have been profoundly marked by political events. This factor has taken political analysis away from the realm of the comparative research.

I will also argue that a comparative analysis on this subject cannot make theoretical headway without an understanding of the reasons by which different countries display different modes of interaction between the legislative branch and the broader political system. Comparative research including the Brazilian case is one thing, and comparative research per se is another. The latter can only be possible to the extent that we develop analytical tools to deal with the institutional variation observed in the various national and regional contexts. The most important implication of the argument, as we will see throughout this article, is that comparative-static analysis does not suffice to explain the variation in the institutional incentives orienting the rational behavior of political agents and the shaping of their careers.

In the second section, I discuss in greater depth the academic research concerning the Brazilian post-war experience. I note that the literature has been deeply marked by conjunctural political events, which explains the difficulties in promoting an assessment based on research approaches found in U.S. literature. Still, at the end of the section, I suggest that the more recent academic production has begun to incorporate issues and gather evidence that draw it closer to the international debate.

In the third section, I discuss some difficulties that comparative analysis must overcome in order for the conceptual discussion to make significant headway. I will argue that the concept of locked-in processes should be incorporated into the explanatory models, given that they deal with spatial and longitudinal variation in the relations between the pattern of recruitment and retention of legislators on the one hand and the insertion of the legislative branch into the broader political system on the other. In the fourth section, I discuss problems related to the gathering and analysis of empirical material for research on political careers in Brazil. My somewhat worrisome reading is that extensive research investment and effort must precede the gathering of evidence on this subject if one intends to make progress with comparative analysis. The last section is reserved for my concluding remarks.

Research on Recruitment and Retention of Legislators in Brazil

The literature on the recruitment and retention of legislators in Brazil is extremely limited. There are no lines of systematic research in which the academic debate, empirical analysis, and theoretical reflection are integrated so as to express agreement and disagreement on common issues. The picture becomes even more discouraging when one realizes that various issues pertaining to the current functioning of the legislative branch in Brazil appear to be closely linked to members' career profiles. Difficulty in establishing the seniority principle as a rule for internal ascent to positions of command, obstacles to acquisition of expertise by legislators, and the lack of reaction against the extreme control over the legislative agenda by the executive branch can be seen as originating (albeit partially) in the career incentives available to deputies and senators.[7]

In fact, the picture emerging from an analysis of the literature is that of a set of studies focusing on historically defined political problems. Brazil was experiencing an extremely delicate political moment when the first studies emerged on the political careers and social composition of the congressional elites. The authoritarian government that took power in 1964 waged purges and convicted the old political leadership. Its main goal was to replace the old political generation with a new one that would be less ideological and more focused on management problems. For this very reason, the underlying conceptual issue (on the occasions when it was laid out explicitly) was marked by the historical events experienced by researchers. The question can be formulated briefly as follows: to what extent is it possible to program the recruitment and retention of legislators without regard for the will of voters or even of the elected representatives themselves?

The Issue of Legislators' Political Socialization

Studies on political careers began to appear from the 1960s through the mid-80s, investigating the socioeconomic basis for the recruitment, political socialization, and perception of the role of representation by state deputies, federal deputies, and senators from the former State of Guanabara and subsequently from the city of Rio de Janeiro.[8] A group of researchers affiliated with the Institute of Public Law and Political Science at the Getúlio Vargas Foundation launched a series of publications on these themes.

Using a questionnaire, Pita and Arruda (1966) investigated the political socialization process for deputies elected to the Guanabara State Legislature in 1965. With a predominantly male membership (mostly highly educated physicians and lawyers), the state legislature confirmed the old maxim, according to which the legislature was inhabited by individuals who differed from the population as a whole. In other words, the study showed that just as in all legislative institutions around the world studied to date, there is a sociological bias in Rio's legislative branch. In addition, the authors were attempting to discover the local origins of the state deputies, as well as their sources of daily information and the political activities they exercised before entering the state legislature.

Moreira (1967), using the same research technique, expanded the field of observation to include deputies and senators among the interviewees. However, this study emphasized differences in relation to the same problem of political socialization among the members of the only two parties functioning at the time: ARENA and MDB.[9] The author explored questions like which (and how many) legislative positions the interviewees had held previously, as well as the representatives' political identity prior to the 1964 military coup d'état.

Parahyba, Maduro, and Vianna (1971) also interviewed a sample of candidates for various elective positions, in addition to deputies elected in the 1970 elections. Their main concern was how background variables affect the political perceptions of candidates and members of the legislature. Politicians' relationship to the social milieu, their opinions concerning the political system, and their role as representatives were also investigated in this survey. In this same volume, a research note by Maduro, Laranjeiras, and Vianna (1971) shows the questionnaire they used for deputies and senators.

Vianna, Maduro, and Parahyba (1971) interviewed another sample of 100 candidates for elective positions in order to discover their socioeconomic characteristics. Variables included gender, age, profession, place of birth, place of residence, and schooling. The main question was whether there was any difference in the recruiting pattern between the two parties running in 1970: ARENA and MDB. Was one party more elitist than the other? No significant difference was found. Parahyba (1973) changed the focus a bit and showed that the legislature recruited individuals seeking private benefits rather than those exercising a vocation for public service.

Maduro, Herescu, and Abreu (1980) performed a survey of 21 City Council members in order to identify the following: a) the socioeconomic profile of city legislators; b) their political socialization; and c) their perception of the role of a political representative. Regarding the first item, the authors observed a prevalence of upper-middle social strata; with regard to the second, they noted that City Council members' political initiation occurred through contact with political leaders; and finally, that the concept of the legislator's role was closely related to guidelines established by the leaders who had initiated them into public life.

Before formulating a critical view of this literature, it is important to mention several studies following this same approach, but which did not come from the same research group. Forjaz (1985), based on documentation published by the Chamber of Deputies itself (Barbosa 1981), performed a study on "the political/ideological behavior, social position, and political/institutional trajectory of the current leaders of the PMDB, PDS, PTB, and PT" (p. 49) in São Paulo. The argument was that patronage and co-optation politics had waned, increasing the importance of representative politics as a way of recruiting political elites in that state. The majority of the state deputies ranged in age from 55 to 64 years, were liberal professionals, and had risen to the State Legislative Assembly through either local legislative bodies or the government machinery. Private enterprise, the party machines, and other organizations from civil society did not serve as a channel to the National Congress. The main way by which Forjaz confirmed her point related to the actual introduction of multipartisan politics in São Paulo, a phenomenon that was not occurring in other parts of the country at the time.

Also over the course of the 1970s and 80s, David V. Fleischer made an important contribution through a series of publications based on joint research with professors and students at the Universidade de Brasília.[10] These studies can be divided into two groups: the first (including Fleischer 1973; 1977) deals specifically with the deputies elected by the State of Minas Gerais, while the second (Fleischer 1980; 1981a) focuses on legislative recruitment for the Chamber of Deputies as a whole. I will focus on these groups of studies one at a time.

The studies on representatives from the State of Minas Gerais investigated the social antecedents and career patterns of political leaders over the course of thirty years of legislative recruitment (1945–75). They addressed the following basic questions: What is the representatives' social, occupational, and educational background? What types of political careers do they pursue? How do the different political parties recruit their members? What changes resulted from the 1964 coup d'état and the subsequent adoption of the two-party system? What is the longevity and turnover of representatives by cohort and legislature? The conclusions were the following:

1. The most common professionals were members of the transportation industry and politically active attorneys. Overall educational level was relatively high. Different patterns were observed for entry into the legislature by different professions. Lawyers tended to enter politics earlier than physicians and businessmen, for example.
2. To a certain extent there was a "zig zag" upwards pattern. Once having entered the government machinery, candidates for the Chamber offered selective benefits to local leaders in exchange for the votes that the latter were expected to garner for the coming elections.
3. A different pattern of professional and regional recruitment of politicians occurred from one party to the next, both in the multipartisan period (1946–64) and during the military regime. During the 1946 Republic, the PSD and UDN recruited politicians in Minas Gerais from nearly all professions, while the PTB and PR recruited their candidates from a narrower range. During the bipartisan period, the ARENA played the same role as the PSD and UDN, while the MDB inherited the recruitment pattern of the PTB.
4. The main consequence of the 1964 military coup was to decrease the institutionalization of political recruitment in Minas Gerais. Representatives with less experience and legislative training were elected, as were those with less schooling.
5. From 1945 to 1964, the cohorts displayed a broader occupational distribution, more schooling, and greater longevity in Congress. Beginning in 1964—despite attempts by the military governments to replace the old political elite with another (trained at the municipal level and technically capable)—what actually happened was that the cohorts from 1967, 1971, and 1975 were very different from each other, with no common pattern in terms of longevity in Congress, origin, or schooling.

Fleischer's studies focusing on the Chamber of Deputies as a whole had specific objectives. Fleischer (1980) attempted the following: a) to show the turnover and retention pattern for Brazilian legislators in the 1978 elections; b) to perform a qualitative analysis of deputies' occupations, university training, and political experience; c) to identify affinities with the parties from the 1946 Republic; and, d) to simulate what the 1978 recruitment would have been like if the government had not altered the rules of the electoral game.[11]

The turnover rate was 56.6%, although it varied considerably from one region to another (higher in the Central West and lower in the Northeast, for example) and from one party to the next (higher in the MDB than in the ARENA). A controlled analysis of regional differences showed even more significant variations. The MDB had more lawyers, professors, and journalists than the ARENA, which in turn had more military officers, businessmen, ranchers, and public employees. Level of schooling was quite high, as was average age. There was an increasing mean rate of political experience. In 1979, level of identification with the old parties dropped as compared to the 1975 cohort. No relationship was found between the relative weight of the parties and the effects of the so-called "April Package."

In an article from 1981, Fleischer analyzed differences in the recruitment pattern for political parties in the 1946 Republic. Delving into the vast literature on Brazilian political parties from that period, the author at times confirmed but mostly invalidated the impression regarding the social underpinnings of the party system. Based on evidence concerning occupation, prior career, schooling, and degree of localism for the congressional representation of each party from that period, Fleischer showed that there were many more nuances than one might have imagined in the career profile and recruitment of Brazilian politicians during that period.

What can one make of this set of studies? First, it is important to comment on the empirical material used by the researchers from the Getúlio Vargas Foundation. As shown above, the analysis was entirely based on interviews with representatives and candidates from the State of Guanabara (later the city of Rio de Janeiro). Therefore, based on this analysis, nothing can be inferred about what happened in other parts of the country. Was there any regional variation? How? Why? These are questions that cannot be answered with the material used for this set of studies. Besides, all the studies were based on just one election. Thus, no conclusion can be drawn about longitudinal variation in politicians' response pattern. In fact, research results on the recruitment and retention of legislators taken from survey-type data are only valid for that point in time. Any extrapolation over time requires past and future surveys.

Forjaz's 1985 article, discussed above, was based not on a questionnaire but on a document published by the Chamber of Deputies, based in turn on the curricula presented by the deputies. This material is more flexible but still not totally satisfactory. I will comment on the problems involved in the use of this kind of source in a later section. For now, suffice it to note that the author limited her observations to members of the same legislature and from a single state. Again, therefore, one gets no idea of the magnitude and importance of longitudinal and spatial variations.

Fleischer's studies differ from previous ones because of the wealth of empirical material used. The articles dealing with the group of federal deputies from Minas Gerais (Fleischer 1973; 1977) overcame the problems observed in the studies on Rio de Janeiro and São Paulo. As shown above, Fleischer used a longer historical series, which allowed him to observe relevant variations over time in the recruitment and career profile. The empirical material was thus not gathered through surveys at single points in time, which allowed for an analysis of temporal series, and drew on numerous sources, providing the author with more reliable data than those used by Forjaz (1985). Obviously, the analysis of legislative recruitment in the State of Minas Gerais did not overcome the problem of spatial variation. Nevertheless, this problem was solved by the studies on the Chamber of Deputies as a whole (Fleischer 1980; 1981). It is thus valid to say that David Fleischer's studies on legislative careers solved the main empirical problems observed before then in the literature.

Yet the main problem in all these studies does not involve issues of an empirical nature. It relates to the conceptual dimension. At no stage, whether in the studies on recruitment in Guanabara and Rio de Janeiro, the article on São Paulo, or David Fleischer's work, are the authors' theoretical objectives explicitly laid out. What did they intend to explain? For what kind of phenomenon did the description of data serve to increase our understanding? Reading these articles leaves one in great doubt as to these questions. The overall impression from the literature, one is forced to admit, is that of a more or less sophisticated set of descriptive studies. Their importance is undebatable. Yet they are not sufficient to increase our knowledge of legislative institutions in general, or the recruitment and retention of Brazilian legislators in particular.

Albeit implicitly, one sees some conceptual development in the literature during the period analyzed. The goal of the next subsection is to show the substance of this development.

The Limits and Possibilities of Planned Recruitment

A book was published in 1975 on the role of the legislative branch in complex or developing societies, i.e., in countries whose economic and social problems require increasingly rapid and efficient responses by their respective governments (Mendes 1975). Yet is the contemporary legislature adapting to the new demands for production of public policies? This may have been the underlying question in the majority of the contributions to the book. The Brazilian legislature served as the theme for many of the chapters, not only because the organizer of the book was a Brazilian, but mainly because Brazil was experiencing an extremely delicate political moment at the time.

In 1974, the military regime installed in 1964 was celebrating its tenth anniversary. Albeit authoritarian, this regime did not interrupt Congress' activities, except for a brief period; neither did it interfere in the electoral calendar. The continued existence of an institution that was essentially democratic, yet had no decision-making or watchdog powers, was a veritable enigma. Regardless of the degree of precision in the answers produced at the time,[12] the important point is that what concerned the military governments was not just the retention (albeit formal) of the legislature as one of the branches of the Brazilian government, but also (in fact, mainly) to replace the old elites with a new generation of politicians, stripped of the old identity with and loyalty to the recent past and their respective parties.

It is thus understandable that the literature on legislative recruitment in Brazil was not directly concerned with the issues found in the U.S. literature. One could say that a major portion of the studies on political recruitment in Brazil during the 1960s, 70s, and 80s had the following conceptual question in mind: is it possible for any government to promote the replacement of congressional elites while disregarding the will of the electorate? To what extent were the military's interventions in the political world efficient in reshaping the profile of legislators?

It thus makes sense to highlight that the studies analyzed in the previous subsection are unanimous in their contention that the vast majority of deputies and senators under the new regime either were already part of the political world in the old democratic regime of 1946 or identified with some political party from that period. An identical observation was made by Astiz (1975) in the above-mentioned book: the occupational pattern of politicians in the post-1964 period did not change significantly as compared to 1946–64, and the same was true for the pattern of prior political activity. What did in fact change, and quite abruptly as observed by Astiz (1975), was the prestige ascribed to such positions as compared to 1946–64.

The doubt that remains is whether the intervention by the military in political institutions caused some relevant impact on the pattern of recruitment and retention of legislators in Brazil. This was the main concern of some studies published on the basis of research performed at the Instituto Universitário de Pesquisas do Rio de Janeiro during the 1970s, involving a survey of biographical data for legislators, government bureaucrats, and politicians in general. The research thus tapped a huge amount of primary and secondary sources, and several articles, documents, and reports were written based on this material. Unfortunately, few focused on the subject of interest herein. For the time being, I will refer only to the studies by Edson Nunes (1977; 1978; 1997).

In an article from 1977, Nunes explored the issue of replacement of the elites. Accepting the premise that the military planned to replace the Congressional elites, the author posed the following question: who would represent Brazilian society? The context of the experiment involved the elections for the Rio de Janeiro City Council in 1976, with the military regime in full force. Obviously, the problems occurred with the spatial and temporal extrapolation of his results. Nevertheless, the conceptual dimensions were made explicit in a way not found theretofore in the rest of the literature. The conclusion was thus considerably enriched, as follows: a) Rio de Janeiro City Council members did not belong to a new generation; b) their prior political experience came from family contacts and political old-timers; c) what was new was their disregard for party guidelines and their propensity for personal schemes for wooing voters; and d) voters stopped voting on the basis of issues and began to vote for candidates and parties that were virtually identical in their policy proposals.

Nunes 1978 (based on the same research used in his book from 1997) touches on a subject that interests us more. The question was the following: what change emerged from the military coup with regard to the recruitment of elites? Nunes starts with the observation that during the 1946–64 period the National Congress, especially the Chamber of Deputies, furnished the human resources to occupy the main positions of command in the public administration: the ministries and the state governorships. This meant that, in fact, the legislative career was a mandatory internship for whomsoever had progressive political ambitions, according to Schlesinger's conceptual scheme (1966). Voters, parties, and platforms dictated the rhythm of public administration because political representation constituted the main channel to access decision-making loci. With the military coup and the series of authoritarian governments, recruitment of elites in the executive branch changed considerably: on the one hand, the state governorships continued to be occupied by former members of the Chamber of Deputies, while the power of governors was substantially reduced; on the other hand, the ministries, with inflated prerogatives, were now occupied either by the military themselves or by technical bureaucrats with no electoral experience.

The arguments contained in the two studies by Nunes (1977; 1978) are actually identical. The military regime, by intervening in the pattern of recruitment and retention of Brazilian legislators, produced the opposite of the originally intended effect. The political representation process stopped recruiting prominent cadres from the public administration ensconced in the executive branch but continued recruitment of politicians linked to personalistic electoral schemes, where patronage and irresponsibility proliferated.

The New Phase in Research on Political Careers in Brazil: Institutionalization and Rational Choice by Legislators

With the demise of the military regime and redemocratization, the legislative branch regained important prerogatives that had been lost during the authoritarian period. The new Constitution in 1988 granted Congress a relevant role in the budget process and control over public expenditures, reduced the requirement for overriding presidential vetoes from two-thirds to an absolute majority, gave the legislative branch exclusive control over concessions for radio and television stations, and created the figure of terminative power for standing committees. According to this provision, given bills could be approved directly in the committees in which they were reviewed, with no need for agreement by the congressional plenary. This served as an incentive for decentralizing legislative work, besides encouraging deputies and senators to specialize in the pertinent themes under the jurisdiction of their committees.

Although it regained a major portion of its former capacity to legislate and intervene in the decision-making process, some recent analyses on relations between the executive and legislative branches in Brazil have shown that the National Congress has still not succeeded in overcoming a huge handicap vis-à-vis the president and his cabinet. Part of the explanation is to be found in the 1988 Constitution itself. Under Article 62, the president can issue decrees with the power of laws, the so-called *medidas provisórias* (provisory measures), to be reviewed by Congress within thirty days. If Congress fails to rule on such a decree, it is legally repealed. However, there is nothing to prevent reissuing the decree, meaning by avoiding the quorum to review the decree and reissuing it indefinitely, the administration acquires an important strategic recourse to make decisions without the legislature's explicit support. Besides, the new Constitution also allows the president a unilateral claim to urgent review of his bills. According to the urgent review process, Congress must vote on a bill within 45 days (beginning at the moment in which urgent status is granted). Such bills are thus transferred out of the committees within this deadline, regardless of whether their members have ruled on them or not.

Recent studies on the Brazilian legislative process show that since redemocratization, a major portion of the laws pertaining to administrative, financial, and economic policy issues have either been the object of provisory measures or received urgent status.[13] Meaning what? Basically, a downgrading in Congress's work in general, and specifically in the standing committees' activities. Deputies and senators will have no guaranteed return on their efforts to review given bills (for example, that their opinions will be considered when defining the content of issues to be submitted to the floor), and will hardly feel compelled to participate actively in the decision-making process of the standing committees. And if this is true, the legislature no longer has endogenous mechanisms to rely on for the specialization of its members.

Yet if it is true that the legislative branch's handicap vis-à-vis the executive branch lies in the Constitution itself, how can one explain the fact that deputies and senators fail to reform the Constitution to recover a balance of powers? Why do Brazilian legislators empower the executive branch to unilaterally define the country's economic and administrative agenda? It is highly probable that some kind of answer can be found by studying patterns in the careers and retention of representatives.

For example, the Brazilian legislature may well be facing difficulties in institutionalizing itself in the terms proposed by Polsby (1968). We know that the only way to clear up this doubt is by studying legislative careers. First, the borders between the legislative branch and the rest of the political and social world may still experience some ambiguity. Any conclusion hinges on investigating the profile of its members' previous and subsequent activities. Second, mechanisms for internal ascent may not be universal. The most efficient way to test this hypothesis is to determine to what extent the seniority principle prevails as a prerequisite for occupying leadership positions and chairing committees. Two recent studies on the Brazilian legislature have contributed to an understanding of these problems: André Marenco dos Santos (1997) and Argelina Figueiredo and Fernando Limongi (1996).

Santos (1997) investigated the recruitment pattern and careers of Brazilian federal deputies during two democratic cycles: 1946–62 and 1986–94. His initial premise was that one can measure the degree to which politics constitutes an autonomous sphere of social relations. The more that access to a seat in Congress requires specific training and techniques (the acquisition of which hinges on a background and career investment), the greater the autonomy of politics in relation to other social domains. Note that Santos's conceptual problem thus does not draw him directly towards Polsby's proposal. Nevertheless, both his research and conclusions help reflect on the problem of institutionalization of the legislature by studying the career patterns of deputies.

Santos used data taken from the *Repertório Biográfico* (Biographical Resumés), published by the Chamber of Deputies itself, based on curricula submitted by members of Congress when they join the House. I will comment later on the analytical problems involved in using such material. Still, I stress that working with this empirical material allowed the author to deal with the initially proposed conceptual question. An immediate observation is that there has been a sharp decline in the amount of prior experience for deputies beginning their first term. The type of previous occupation for first-term deputies and their age bracket changed considerably from one democratic cycle to the other. During the 1946–64 period, a large contingent of young people and public employees won seats in the House. Now, only 9% of the House is occupied by former public employees, and fewer than 20% are under thirty years of age. There are also major differences between these two periods with regard to prior party activity as a prerequisite for entering the House. While in the former period, militancy in some political party served as a funnel for running for a seat in Congress, in the latter period, half of the first-term deputies had only belonged to some party very briefly. Santos thus concluded the following:

> The political man, or at least the Brazilian version thereof, has been losing ground to outsiders who enter politics late (having already established a professional life) and win seats in Congress without having to climb all the steps in the career or spend a long internship inside the party organizations (1997, p. 99).

It becomes clear that Santos's core concern is not exactly the issue of institutionalization. The type of evidence employed does not allow one to state anything beyond the entry of first-term deputies into Congress. At any rate, based on the results, one can infer that the House is permeable to social agents with no links to the professional political world and whose commitment to the career and retention in the House is less than what would be expected had they invested more time in politics before joining Congress. But why would the recruitment pattern have changed from one democratic cycle to the other? Was there a break in the institutionalization of the Brazilian legislature? Could the military regime have been responsible for such an interruption? What was the relationship between the phenomenon observed by Santos and the pattern in the relationship between the executive and legislative branches? These are the questions raised by reading the article, but which remain unanswered.

The study by Figueiredo and Limongi (1996) tackles the institutionalization problem head-on. However, from a conceptual point of view, the authors take a position based frankly on the rational-choice theory.[14] Politicians' decisions on whether to remain in Congress hinge on an individual assessment in which the expected value of the term is the main determining factor. According to this approach, the capacity to retain politicians in the House is directly proportional to the political opportunities present therein. Thus, the more complex and numerous the career opportunities offered by Congress, the greater the expected benefit from remaining for more terms. Likewise, the more dependent internal ascent in the organizational structure is on seniority in the House, and the greater the expected value of such positions, the greater the capacity for retention in the legislature.

Using data from the *Diário Oficial* (the official Daily Federal Register), statistics from the TSE (Higher Electoral Court), and other sources referring exclusively to the Chamber of Deputies during the more recent period in Brazilian politics, Figueiredo and Limongi observed the following: a) capacity for retention in the Brazilian legislature is low. Numerous members of Congress have failed to run for reelection, others have resigned in the middle of their terms, and not all of those who run for reelection win;[15] b) the seniority principle as a rule for internal ascent is only valid for the positions of Speaker of the House and party whips and does not apply to committee chairs, thus proving that standing committees in the legislature fail to attract most deputies. In fact, the few pages of the article focusing on the problem of recruitment and retention of legislators serve basically as a theoretical and methodological orientation for what should be a study of political careers in the Brazilian democracy. In this sense, one could say that Figueiredo and Limongi have adequately combined their conceptual objectives with the empirical answers derived from their analysis.

Summary

The Brazilian literature on the recruitment and retention of legislators could be described as a set of studies focusing on historically defined political problems. As the Brazilian post-war political history was relatively volatile, it is not difficult to see why there are no lines of systematic research in which empirical analysis and theoretical reflection are integrated so as to express agreement and disagreement on common issues. As I showed, the underlying conceptual concerns were marked by the historical events experienced by researchers. The question now is how to deal with the issue of careers of politicians interacting in such a political environment? What are the main effects of political ups and downs upon the career profiles of deputies and senators? The next section suggests some possible answers to these questions.

Conceptual Obstacles to Comparative Research

First, there is still no detailed description of the structure for political opportunities in Brazil. Only by gaining a handle on such a structure and understanding the inherent risks and possibilities in running for the various political positions can one presume to know a representative's rational cost-benefit assessment. Where do legislators go after deciding not to run for reelection but to remain in political life? Why do certain legislators resign from their congressional careers? From the average political point of view, is the executive branch more attractive than the legislative? Why? What is the profile of the politician who stays in the legislature, in terms of prior experience and regional and occupational background?

Again, the answer to such questions obviously hinges on an accurate description of the structure for political opportunities in the Brazilian democracy. In this sense, and following Strøm's recommendation (1990; 1997), it is perfectly possible to describe such a structure based on Polsby's institutionalization indicators (1969) and to maintain its heuristic function as a set of incentives underlying legislators' strategic choices in their political careers. In other words, the first step towards obtaining answers to such questions may be to combine organizational approaches (emphasizing the institutionalization issue) and the rational-choice approach (stressing individual career objectives).

Even so, many doubts persist concerning the capacity of either the organizational or rational-choice approach to deal with the theoretical challenges arising from the relationship between the career profile of Brazilian legislators and the way by which the legislative branch participates in the broader political system. We have already seen that there may be a relationship between the typical career of a Brazilian politician and the pattern of executive-legislative branch interactions. The latter is marked by the executive's comparative advantage over the legislative in public policy-making. One of the causes of this phenomenon is the limited specialization of members of the National Congress. In other words, the Brazilian legislature lacks endogenous sources for creating expertise and thus depends on information generated by specialized agencies from the executive branch. The question is, why do deputies and senators not feel motivated to invest in specialization? Why are they not moved to serve on a standing committee for long periods of time?

The answer apparently lies precisely in the greater attraction exerted by jobs in the executive branch. That is, Brazilian politicians prefer to occupy positions in the executive, since they provide greater opportunities for intervening in the decision-making process; hence, they fail to invest in the legislative institution. If this is true, we are faced with an interesting phenomenon. On the one hand, the difficulties with institutionalization of the Brazilian legislature are related to what Fleischer has called the "zig zag" career profiles of its members. The limited ability to compete with the executive branch results from the limited investment by politicians in Congress itself. Still, the zig zag career profile in turn stems precisely from the limited institutionalization of the legislature. It is rational for politicians to aspire to positions in the executive, since chances are better there for intervening in the decision-making process.

Clearly, we are faced with a "locked-in" process.[16] The legislature cannot achieve institutionalization because the career incentives for deputies and senators point to the executive branch as the primary locus for intervening in relevant public decisions, and at the same time the career profile does not change to help retain politicians in the legislature because the latter is not sufficiently institutionalized (a process that would require exclusive career investments). So, when we observe the prevalence of certain legislative institutions we ". . . should then be cautious of the standard exercise that seeks the means by which the winner's innate 'superiority' came to be translated into adoption" (Arthur 1996, 27). Historically, once the legislature locks itself into an institutional path, any alternative solution for its organizational challenges turns incapable of "getting started."[17]

The presence of locked-in processes, in this case, implies that the reasons by which given legislative institutions fail to acquire autonomy vis-à-vis the more inclusive political world cannot be understood on the basis of a comparative-static analysis or identification of the degree of institutionalization. The first merely indicates the logic behind interaction at a certain point in time, given the institutional incentives conferring meaning and content to the rational choice, while the latter only provides a picture of how interaction occurs between the legislature and the rest of the political world. Neither is capable of revealing the dynamics behind certain fundamental historical choices, responsible precisely for the creation of the mechanisms on which rest both comparative-static analysis and an organizational and functionalist picture. Table 1 gives a more schematic idea of the argument.

Consider the following conceptual question: how do constitutional rules condition the profile of legislative careers? Suppose, and this is actually intuitive, that two aspects are particularly relevant: a) whether there is a limit to the number of terms members of Congress can serve (to facilitate the reasoning, suppose that there are only two possibilities, i.e., the legislator either is or is not allowed to run for reelection) and, b) whether there is some restriction to the legislator holding positions in the executive branch. Again, to make the argument more real, suppose that there are only two possibilities: legislators either are or are not allowed to hold positions in the executive branch without losing their legislative offices. Table 1 shows the four possibilities resulting from the combination of these two variables. More precisely, it contains four distinct institutional environments in which rational politicians may interact. One might naturally imagine that the recruitment and retention of legislators would be different for each of these possibilities.

If, in a given political system, legislators can be part of the executive branch and be indefinitely reelected, one might expect the zig zag career profile mentioned above. Neither the legislative, nor the executive branches could be the exclusive locus of political investment. This possibility is portrayed by quadrant 1 in the table. If, however, legislators can be reelected indefinitely and cannot be part of the executive branch without losing their legislative mandates, the legislature will probably be occupied by members with a strong desire to invest in their congressional careers. I call the resulting career pattern *long term*. If deputies are not allowed to run for consecutive reelection, but are not prevented from participating simultaneously in the executive branch, one would expect a certain lack of commitment to the legislative institution. I call the resulting pattern *short term*. Finally, if politicians are not allowed to run for consecutive reelection, and are prevented from participating in the executive, I call the resulting career profiles *alternating*. Consequently, the internal organization of the legislature and its relations to the outside world in the two cases, i.e., a diversity motivated by the different institutional incentives present in each possibility.

With the information at hand on the opportunity structure, it is possible to determine the expected value (for political agents) of competing for various

TABLE 1
Types of Legislative Careers

	May Take Jobs in the Executive	May Not
No term limits	zig zag	long term
Term limits	short term	alternating

Note: I thank Fernando Limongi for the suggestion (in an informal conversation) to construct this table using these two variables.

available positions. The greater the anticipated value, the greater the probability that the agent will compete for the position. The retention rate of any given legislature will increase in proportion to the expected value of retaining the congressional seat and inversely to the expected value of occupying other positions. Thus,

$$E(a_1) = P(O_1).U(O_1) - C(a_1) \qquad (1)$$
$$E(a_2) = P(O_2).U(O_2) - C(a_2) \qquad (2)$$

where, $E(a_i)$ is the expected value of acquiring position i;
$P(O_i)$ is the probability of acquiring position i;
$U(O_i)$ is the utility resulting from the previous event; and,
$C(a_i)$ is the cost of acquiring position i.

$E(a_1)$ represents the expected value of remaining in the legislature and $E(a_2)$ represents the expected utility of winning any given position other than a congressional seat. Thus, the retention rate increases in proportion to the difference between $E(a_1)$ and $E(a_2)$ for the average legislator. Observing now the institutional possibilities shown in Table 1, one could imagine intuitively that the cost of obtaining any given position outside the legislature would be relatively high in quadrant 2, since this would automatically mean a loss of one's seat in Congress. This increases the value of $C(a_2)$, thus reducing the value of $E(a_2)$. In quadrant 1, on the other hand, the value of $C(a_2)$ is reduced. Seeking other political positions would not involve losing one's congressional mandate, i.e., where legislators are not forbidden from occupying positions in the executive branch during their terms in Congress. Thus, the average legislator would expect to obtain a relatively high utility for $E(a_2)$.

Again, the point deserving attention is that the equilibrium for an average legislator in the institutional context portrayed by possibility 2 is clearly different from that emerging from institutional context number 1. What is the meaning of the equilibrium in each case? The typical political career pattern should vary as follows: politicians who interact in quadrant 1 should adopt a zig zag career path. Retention and ascent in political life should be gained without major risks or costs by means of occupying different positions in different spheres of government. Thus, there will be no institutional investment focusing exclusively on the legislature. Institutional context number 2 consists of politicians lacking attractive alternatives outside the legislature itself. Few such legislators risk seeking ascent by way of positions in the executive branch. Such undertakings entail high risk and are thus only taken on by politicians with high visibility or real chances of winning. At any rate, one would expect in this situation that the institutional development of the legislature would be a priority for a major portion of the legislators. One could thus conclude that—*ceteris pari-*

bus—the institutionalization of the legislature would be greater in quadrant 2 (filled by legislators with protracted careers) than in quadrant 1 (filled by "zig zag" politicians).

The remaining doubt concerns the direction of the causal chain. In other words, what determines what? Which is the dependent variable and which the independent? Suppose that some institutional engineer made a diagnosis of the problems involved in the institutionalization of the legislature in quadrant 1 and prescribed some changes in the constitutional rules, such as prohibiting access to positions in the executive branch during one's term in Congress. What would the reaction by legislators be, since after all, they are in charge of changing the rules of the game? One easily realizes that the changes would not meet the politicians' career interests. In other words, such changes will not be introduced endogenously, since it would not be rational to change rules which, from the legislators' point of view, favor their career ambitions.

Suppose again that the same institutional engineer attempted to promote a change in the rules of the game in quadrant 2. Suppose that public opinion is reacting to the lack of congressional turnover and to what is perceived as institutional sclerosis. Our engineer should propose that more flexible rules be adopted, allowing for the emergence of zig zag-type careers. Suppose, furthermore, that such changes are actually adopted. What would be the expected reaction of the politicians? Obviously, legislators whose visibility is restricted to the districts that elected them, i.e., the majority, should stay put, for two reasons: first, because in this highly institutionalized legislature, the chances would be good for intervening in the decision-making process; second, because the chances would still be limited for gaining any political position except for one's seat in Congress. Such changes would no doubt be harmless in terms of their original objective.

Locked-in processes are precisely the kinds of phenomena whose basic elements feed on themselves. They do not change as solutions that are "superior," from the point of view of an outside observer, are found. Therefore, they display a high degree of resistance to endogenous changes. Institutional incentives and the recruitment pattern in the above example combine in such a way that the changes are either not introduced in the first place or do not produce the desired effect when they are. Equilibrium analysis and identification of the degree of institutionalization are only capable of diagnosing any given situation as a locked-in process, but are incapable of indicating the ultimate cause of the resulting type of interaction. The latter can only be identified through historical investigation. I will explain why.

By way of illustration, consider the analysis performed by Gary Cox (1987) on the development of partisan government in England. Based on Polsby's indicators (1968), the British Parliament may be the least institutionalized legislature in the Western world. The relevance of Cox's study is precisely to have shown how changes in legislative rules in the British Parliament in the mid-nineteenth century ended up transferring all decision-making authority to the executive branch. Besides, as an effect of the same cause, legislators' political careers became entirely focused on occupying positions in the cabinet.

Cox also shows how changes in the British legislative process were motivated by an excess amount of work, and problems demanding answers by the public sector. The solution was to relieve the agenda by transferring decision-making power to the ministers. But why was this solution adopted? Why not divide up the work internally by way of specialized standing committees, as occurred at almost the same time in the United States Congress? Pure and simple comparative-static analysis is incapable of answering such questions, simply because the answer lies in contingent, unpredictable aspects of the historical process.

I think one can now begin to answer the questions formulated at the end of the last section by a rather simple suggestion:

More historical research (and not just more comparative-static analysis and measures of institutionalization) is needed for the investigation concerning the cause of the emergence of a certain career pattern (as opposed to another) to move beyond a mere description of lock-in processes.

Critical Assessment of Research Sources

The principal research source for the recruitment and retention of legislators is a series of publications entitled *Deputados Brasileiros: Repertório Biográfico* (Biographical Data on Brazilian Deputies (Brazil)). The volumes are published at the beginning of each legislature, usually a few months before the first session. The purpose is to publish biographical data on all the deputies taking office. The information is gathered through interviews. In addition to personal data, it includes the deputies' main prior activities. The first edition was published in 1967, when a new legislature was being inaugurated. During the 1970s, under the coordination of David Fleischer, a special edition published the biographical data on deputies from the legislatures spanning the period from 1946 through 1967 (Fleischer 1981b).

The publication improved steadily over time: while the initial volumes included little information (and of dubious accuracy at that), the most recent issue, pertaining to the current legislature, has much more (and more precise) information. There are still two major limitations: a) it was only during the 1991–95 legislature that the data began to be updated periodically instead of being gathered only at the beginning of the first legislative session; and, b) the information is reported by the deputies themselves. What are the consequences for research? I will take the answer by parts.

1. To restrict biographical information to those taking office at the beginning of the legislature (and at the precise moment in which it is inaugurated), makes it impossible to observe crucial evidence. For example, based on the *Repertório* it is impossible to answer the following questions: what is the career path of a given representative inside the House? Was he/she transferred to some position in the executive branch, whether elective or otherwise? Did he/she resign? It is only possible to retrieve information on deputies' career paths if and when they are reelected. However, we know that it is essential for research on recruitment and retention to examine the destination of all legislators. Resignation and migration are as important as retention.
2. To work with information provided by the members of Congress themselves can introduce a bias in the analysis in various ways, of which I offer just two examples:

    a) when asking about their occupation, among other things, one wants to know if their insertion in economic life allows one to classify them as high, middle, or low class. For a long time in Brazil, landowners constituted the country's economic elite. Besides, albeit in an impressionist way, it was known that the vast majority of the state and national deputies were members of the agrarian elite themselves or had relatives inside it. Yet the most common professionals among deputies, as stated in the *Repertório*, are lawyers and physicians, because legislators state the profession from their university diplomas. Such self-reported information obviously produces a considerable bias, since a major portion of the elite Brazilians aspiring to political careers study law. Consequently, such information fails to detect any variation in national political representation in the relative weight of various elites. In short, we do not know precisely when the landowners lost their predominance in the Chamber of Deputies.

    b) the relevance of investigating average level of schooling is closely linked to the problem of the origin of the deputies' status. To determine the magnitude of the discrepancy between the general population and its elected deputies is essential for an analysis of regional and longitudinal variations in the electoral context, as defined by Prewitt and Eulau (1971). Might the turnout and eviction rates be higher in electoral contexts with less educational discrepancy? The problem is that one cannot trust in a representative's self-reported information on schooling. Since there is no educational prerequisite to be elected (except that one must be literate), it is perfectly plausible that deputies overstate their own cognitive capacity due to issues of peer relationship.

Why is it important to have a diagnosis of these research sources?[18] The basic purpose is to map out the problems involved in comparative research on the legislature, specifically on the recruitment and retention of legislators. To make such research possible, one must accept the challenge of overcoming the poor quality of information contained in the main sources.

Consider the following conceptual question: how do constitutional rules influence the career profile of legislators? Let us recall from Table 1, in which two variables were presented as particularly relevant: a) permission for (or prohibition of) consecutive terms, i.e., whether legislators may or may not run consecutively and indefinitely; and, b) whether legislators may occupy or compete for positions in the executive branch without automatically losing their seats in Congress. For example, an implicit hypothesis in constructing this table is that in certain institutional contexts characterized by quadrant 2, political careers are oriented primarily towards the legislative branch, or at least to a greater degree than those developed in institutional contexts characterized by quadrant 3. Furthermore, this is due naturally to the expected value of obtaining different political positions in one case as compared to the other.

Although the argument is convincing, its empirical validation requires comparative research, and that requires a minimum standardization of relevant information. To examine to what extent the politicians belonging to the different systems are grouped in the respective quadrants demands detailed knowledge of the trajectory of each representative and senator, including prior experience and positions occupied before, during, and after their terms. As we noted at the beginning of this section, hard work and perseverance are needed to overcome existing obstacles to such research in Brazil.

Conclusion

The following is a summary of the article's main conclusions, in light of prospects for performing comparative research:

1. the Brazilian bibliography on recruitment and retention of legislators has the following limitations:

    a) Part of it is historically dated. Its theoretical concern pertains to the attempts by military governments to replace congressional elites in planned fashion. The obligatory conclusion is that this was not possible. Various degrees of methodological sophistication and awareness of the conceptual problem characterized the literature on this subject through the 1980s.

    b) The recent literature, albeit theoretically and methodologically stronger, is still extremely limited. The current academic debate still does not allow for the shaping of a context favorable to comparative research.

    c) Comparative analytical perspectives will only be successful to the extent that they incorporate concepts and analytical methods capable of dealing with locked-in processes. The role played by contingent historical events appears to be crucial for an understanding of the diversity of experiences in the political sphere, particularly in the relations between legislative careers and performance by the legislative branch.

2. Research work must overcome major obstacles in order to achieve the desired degree of standardization of evidence and information, with a view towards comparing different international experiences, for the following reasons:

   a) The existing data are based on biographical testimony provided by the legislators themselves, which can entail a series of distortions in the relevant information.

   b) The existing data on a major portion of the cohorts of post-World War II legislators refers exclusively to first-term deputies and senators. Much work remains to be done in order to provide a full picture of the career paths of Brazilian legislators.

Finally, despite all the difficulties, one may still be rather optimistic with regard to research on legislative recruitment and retention in Brazil. This theme appears to be the key to several enigmas surrounding the functioning of democratic institutions in Brazil. The time is thus ripe for research efforts aimed at leveraging and providing greater consistency to this fascinating subject.

NOTES

Prepared for presentation at the Shambaugh Comparative Legislative Research Conference, Iowa City, Iowa, April 17–18, 1998. I would like to thank Gerhard Loewenberg, Peverill Squire, and Renato Boschi for their helpful comments on this paper. I would also like to thank the research assistants Acir dos Santos Almeida and Andrea Schreder.

1. The studies on post-war political parties, elections, representation, and political behavior in Brazil deserve a chapter of their own, due to their enormous diversity. I would cite just two bibliographical reviews for those interested in gathering material on the subject: Lamounier and Kinzo 1978 and Lima Junior, Schmitt, and Nicolau 1992.

2. For an analysis of this period, see Lessa 1988.

3. See Lessa 1988.

4. Regarding the causes of the collapse of democracy in Brazil, see Almeida 1998, Figueiredo 1993, Furtado 1969, and Santos 1986.

5. There is abundant literature dealing with the changes in the Brazilian socioeconomic system starting in the post-war period. For an example, see Santos 1985.

6. The bibliographical review by Lima Junior, Schmitt, and Nicolau (1992) also includes references to the transition to democracy in Brazil.

7. On this point, see Figueiredo and Limongi 1995 and 1996, and Santos 1997a and 1997b.

8. What is now the city of Rio de Janeiro was the capital, first of the Empire from 1822 to 1889, and later of the Republic from 1889 to 1960. Since 1960, the country's capital has been Brasília, in the State of Goiás. In 1960 the city of Rio de Janeiro became a city-state called Guanabara. Then, in 1975, the city of Rio de Janeiro merged with the surrounding State of Rio de Janeiro, an old, traditional province dating back to the Empire and which had become a unit in the Federal Republic. The State of Guanabara was thereby eliminated as such, and the city of Rio de Janeiro became the capital of the (merged) state by the same name.

9. A bibliographical review of political parties from this and other periods can be found in Lamounier and Kinzo 1978 and Lima Junior, Schmitt, and Nicolau 1992.

10. Fleischer published more political career studies than are analyzed in this article. However, I believe that the main points from his arguments are well represented by the studies mentioned herein.

11. In April 1977, the Geisel administration issued a decree establishing a series of changes in electoral legislation, with a view towards increasing the chances of the pro-military regime party. These measures came to be known as the *pacote de abril* or "April package."

12. The most famous paper in this vein is that of Packeham (1966), arguing that Congress was kept functioning to serve as an escape valve for political pressure. The legislature thereby helped legitimate the regime. For a similar analysis, see Mezey 1985. For a critique of the functionalist perspective, see Huber 1996, especially in the introduction. That author's main objection rests on what he calls the "anthropomorphization" of the legislature by the functionalist authors. According to Huber, the legislature cannot be considered an actor with ends or goals (such as institutionalizing itself) that are independent of its members' individual preferences.

13. See works by Diniz (1995), Figueiredo and Limongi (1995 and 1996), and Monteiro (1995).

14. For a proposal aimed at an integration of the organizational-functionalist and rational-choice approaches, see Strøm 1990 and 1997. Strøm's argument is that the legislature's degree of institutionalization as measured by the organizational-functionalist approach serves as a parameter for legislators' strategic choices, such as the concept of representation to be adopted and the cost-benefit analysis as to whether to participate in a pro-administration coalition. However, Strøm emphasizes that such choices are never made in disagreement with the representatives' individual objectives.

15. For a proposal of a rigorous measure of congressional turnover taking the eviction rate into account, see Santos 1997.

16. For locked-in processes in the economy, see Arthur 1996, especially chapter 2.

17. See Arthur (1996, 19).

18. To a certain extent, the limitations of the Repertório can be overcome by consulting the Dicionário Histórico-Biográfico Brasileiro (Brazilian Historical and Biographical Dictionary), published by Beloch and Abreu (1984). However, many deputies received nothing more than brief notes on their careers. Information on alternates and resignations can be gathered from Deputados Brasileiros: 1826–1976 (Brazil), also published by the Chamber of Deputies. Finally, data concerning the internal organization of the House, i.e., Speaker, committees, and party whips, must be researched in the Diário do Congresso (Congressional Daily (Brazil)), published by the Higher Electoral Court, with data on politicians' voting records.

References

Almeida, Alberto Carlos. 1998. *Presidencialismo, Parlamentarismo e Colapso da Democracia.* Niterói: EDUFF.
Arthur, W. Brian. 1996. *Increasing Returns and Path Dependency in the Economy.* Ann Arbor: The University of Michigan Press.
Astiz, Carlos A. 1975. "O Papel Atual do Congresso Brasileiro". In *O Legislativo e a Tecnocracia*, Candido Mendes (org.). Rio de Janeiro: Imago.
Barbosa, Humberto G. 1981. *Deputados Brasileiros (46ª Legislatura, 1979–1983).* Brasília: Centro de Documentação e Informação da Câmara dos Deputados.
Beloch, Israel e Alzira Alves de Abreu (eds.). 1984. *Dicionário Histórico-Biográfico Brasileiro, 4 vols.* Rio de Janeiro: Forense Universitária.
Brazil. *Dados Estatísticos do TSE.* Brasília: Superior Tribunal Eleitoral.
Brazil. *Deputados Brasileiros: 1826–1976.* Brasília: Centro de Documentação e Informação da Câmara dos Deputados.
Brazil. *Deputados Brasileiros - Repertório Biográfico,* 5 vols. Brasília: Centro de Documentação e Informação da Câmara dos Deputados.
Brazil. *Diário do Congresso Nacional.* Rio de Janeiro e Brasília: Imprensa Nacional.
Carey, John M. 1996. *Term Limits and Legislative Representation.* Cambridge: Cambridge University Press.
Cox, Gary. 1987. *The Efficient Secret: The Cabinet and the Development of Political Parties in Victorian England.* Cambridge: Cambridge University Press.
Diniz, Eli. 1995. "Governabilidade, Democracia e Reforma do Estado: Os Desafios da Construção de uma Nova Ordem no Brasil dos Anos 90." *Dados* 38:385–415.
Figueiredo, Argelina. 1993. *Democracia ou Reformas? Alternativas à Crise Política: 1961–1964.* São Paulo: Paz e Terra.
Figueiredo, Argelina e Fernando Limongi. 1995. "Mudança Constitucional, Desempenho do Legislativo e Consolidação Institucional." *Revista Brasileira de Ciências Sociais* 29:175–200.
Figueiredo, Argelina e Fernando Limongi. 1996. "Congresso Nacional: Organização, Processo Legislativo e Produção Legal." *Cadernos de Pesquisa CEBRAP* 5.
Fleischer, David. 1973. "O Trampolim Político: Mudanças nos Padrões de Recrutamento Político em Minas Gerais." *Revista de Administração Pública* 7:99–116.
Fleischer, David. 1977. "A Bancada Federal Mineira: Trinta Anos de Recrutamento Político, 1945/1975." *Revista Brasileira de Estudos Políticos* 45:7–58.
Fleischer, David. 1980. "Renovação Política—Brasil 1978: Eleições Parlamentares Sob A Égide do 'Pacote de Abril'." Trabalhos em Ciências Sociais. Série Sociologia. UNB. (mimeo).
Fleischer, David. 1981a. "O Pluripartidarismo no Brasil: Dimensões Sócio-Econômicas e Regionais Do Recrutamento Legislativo, 1946–1967." *Revista de Ciência Política* 24:49–75.
Fleischer, David. 1981b. *Deputados Brasileiros—Repertório Biográfico dos Senhores Deputados abrangendo o período de 1946–1967.* Brasília: Centro de Documentação e Informação da Câmara dos Deputados.
Forjaz, Maria Cecília Spina. 1985. "Os Deputados de São Paulo: Trajetória social e política." *Revista de Administração de Empresas* 25:49–56.

Furtado, Celso. 1969. "Political Obstacles to Economic Growth." In *Obstacles to Change in Latin America*, ed. Cláudio Velliz. London: Oxford University Press.

Lamounier, Bolivar, and Maria D'Alva Gil Kinzo. 1978. "Partidos Políticos, Representação e Processo Eleitoral no Brasil, 1945–1978." *Boletim Informativo Bibliográfico* 5:11–32.

Leopoldi, Maria Antonieta Parahyba. 1973. "Carreira Política e Mobilidade Social: O Legislativo Como Meio de Ascenção Social." *Revista de Ciência Política* 7:83–95.

Lessa, Renato de A. 1988. *A Invenção Republicana: Campos Sales, as bases e decadência da Primeira República Brasileira*. São Paulo: Vértice.

Lima Jr., Olavo Brasil de, Rogério A. Schmitt, and Jairo M. Nicolau. 1992. "A Produção Recente sobre Partidos, Eleições e Comportamento Político: Balanço Bibliográfico." *Boletim Informativo Bibliográfico* 34:3–66.

Maduro, Lídice Aparecida Pontes, Sônia Maria Guimarães Laranjeiras, and Maria Lúcia Teixeira Werneck Vianna. 1971. "Nota De Pesquisa—Estudo Da Representação Política No Estado Da Guanabara: Eleitos Em 15–11–70." *Revista de Ciência Política* 5:89–103.

Maduro, Lídice Aparecida Pontes, Mariana Herescu, and Regina Lucia Farias de Abreu. 1980. "Os Representantes do Município do Rio de Janeiro." *Revista de Ciência Política* 23:193–239.

Matthews, Donald R. 1985. "Legislative Recruitment and Legislative Careers." In *Handbook of Legislative Research*, ed. Gerhard Loewenberg, Samuel C. Patterson, and Malcolm E. Jewell. Cambridge, MA: Harvard University Press.

Mendes, Candido, org. 1975. *O Legislativo e a Tecnocracia*. Rio de Janeiro: Imago.

Mezey, Michael L. 1985. "Functions of Legislatures in the Third World." In *Handbook of Legislative Research*, ed. Gerhard Loewenberg, Samuel C. Patterson, and Malcolm E. Jewell. Cambridge, MA: Harvard University Press.

Monteiro, Jorge Vianna. 1995. "O Poder de Propor: Ou, a Economia das Medidas Provisórias." *Revista de Administração Pública* 29:59–72.

Moreira, Maria Terezinha V. 1967. "A Renovação dos Quadros Políticos na Guanabara." *Revista de Ciência Política* 1:47–74.

Nunes, Edson de Olveira. 1977. "Quem Representa o Carioca?" *Dados* 16:97–107.

Nunes, Edson de Olveira. 1978. "Legislativo, Política e Recrutamento de Elites no Brasil." *Dados* 17:53–78.

Nunes, Edson de Olveira. 1997. *A Gramática Política do Brasil*. Rio de Janeiro: Jorge Zahar Editor.

Packenham, Robert. 1970. "Legislatures and Political Development." In *Legislatures in Developmental Perspectives*, ed. Alan Kornberg and Lloyd D. Musolf. Durham, NC: Duke University Press.

Parahyba, Maria Antonieta de A. G., Lídice Aparecida Pontes Maduro, and Maria Lúcia Teixeira Werneck Vianna. 1971. "Candidato *versus* Sistema Político–Notas De Uma Pesquisa Sôbre O Acesso Aos Cargos Legislativos na Guanabara." *Revista de Ciência Política* 5:29–42.

Pitta, Nilda Agueda Martinez, and José Maria Arruda. 1966. "Composição Sociológica da Assembléia Legislativa do Estado da Guanabara." *Revista de Ciência Política* 9:120–44.

Polsby, Nelson. 1968. "The Institutionalization of the U.S. House of Representatives." *American Political Science Review* 62:144–68.

Santos, André Marenco dos. 1997. "Nas Fronteiras do Campo Político: Raposas e *outsiders* no Congresso Nacional." *Revista Brasileira de Ciências Sociais* 33:87–101.
Santos, Fabiano. 1997a. Democracy and Legislative Dynamics in Brazil. Presented at the annual conference of the Institute of Latin American Studies, University of London.
Santos, Fabiano. 1997b. "Patronagem e Poder de Agenda na Política Brasileira." *Dados* 40:465–92.
Santos, Wanderley Guilherme dos. 1985. "A Pós-Revolução Brasileira." In *Brasil: Sociedade Democrática*, ed. Hélio Jaguaribe et al. Rio de Janeiro: José Olympio.
Santos, Wanderley Guilherme dos. 1987. *Sessenta e Quatro: Anatomia da Crise*. São Paulo: Vértice.
Santos, Wanderley Guilherme dos. 1997. "Da Poliarquia à Oligarquia: Eleições e Demanda por Renovação Parlamentar." *Sociedade e Estado* 7:11–56.
Schlesinger, Joseph A. 1966. *Ambition and Politics: Political Careers in the United States*. Chicago: Rand McNally.
Strøm, Kaare. 1990. *Minority Government and Majority Rule*. Cambridge: Cambridge University Press.
Strøm, Kaare. 1997. "Rules, Reasons and Routines: Legislatives Roles in Parliamentary Democracies." *Journal of Legislative Studies* 3:155–73.
Vianna, Maria Lúcia Teixeira W., Lídice Pontes Maduro, and Maria Antonieta de A. G. Parahyba. 1971. "Notas de Pesquisa–Estudo De Representação Política No Estado Da Guanabara: Candidatos E Eleitos No Pleito De 15/11/1970." *Revista de Ciência Política* 5:97–121.

Part 3
Legislative Representation

Electoral Systems and the Representation of Minority Interests in Legislatures

David T. Canon

The rules and institutions used to translate preferences into electoral outcomes have a profound impact on the nature of representation provided in a political system. The alternative electoral institutions the Founders created to elect House members, senators, and the president in the United States are testimony to their instinctive belief in this proposition. Other electoral arrangements, such as proportional representation, single nontransferable votes, majority runoffs, cumulative voting, and ethnic quotas have provided fertile ground for comparative analysis. The topic has taken on great political significance as constitutional engineers in emerging democracies around the world act on Giovanni Sartori's observation that electoral systems are "the most specific manipulative instrument of politics" (1968, 273). This paper will touch on these electoral systems in the comparative context, but will focus on the most recent effort to alter electoral arrangements and representation in the U.S. Congress: the creation of minority-majority districts in 1992 and their impact on the Congressional Black Caucus (CBC). I will focus on black representation, rather than representation of minority interests more broadly.

General Overview

There are many electoral institutions that have an impact on representation in the United States that I will not discuss in great detail. Instead, I will briefly outline the main topics and some of the relevant research. The topics I cover here—redistricting, the majority runoff provision, at-large and single-member districts, and staggered terms—have general representational consequences and important implications for minority representation. This relatively ambitious list only begins to scratch the surface of possible topics. Grofman and Lijphart (1986, 2–3) list 18 electoral institutions that have representational consequences.

Reprinted with permission from *Legislative Studies Quarterly* 24, no. 3 (August 1999): 1–32.

Some of these that will not be discussed here include the following: ballot format (office-block vs. party list), cross-endorsements and cross-filings, district magnitude, size of the legislature, ease of voter access to the electoral process, nonpartisan primaries, campaign timing rules, number and type of offices subject to electoral choice, sequencing and regularity of elections, and mechanisms for voter initiative, referendum, and recall. Recent research on campaign finance and historical research in the "new institutionalist" tradition (Crook and Hibbing 1997; Katz and Sala 1996; Swift 1996) are also important for this topic, but will not receive attention here.

Redistricting

Racial redistricting (which I will examine in the next section) has drawn more attention than any other electoral institution in the 1990s, but drawing district lines has many other representational consequences as well. The manipulation of redistricting for partisan gain predates racial gerrymandering by more than a century. The term "gerrymander" comes from the original manipulation of district lines in Massachusetts in 1811, when Governor Elbridge Gerry signed a bill that created a district in the shape of a salamander to promote his party's interests. For at least 80 years, scholars have been interested in determining what explains the shape of district lines and the partisan composition of districts. (The earliest citation I found was to a 1918 *APSR* article entitled "Geography and the Gerrymander" by C.O. Sauer.)

One subset of this research has focused on the complexity introduced by competing values and principles of redistricting. Butler and Cain (1992, ch. 4) present several considerations involving the form of districts: equal population, respect for natural frontiers (including local boundaries, communities of interest, and lines of communication), compactness, and contiguity. They also discuss considerations involving outcomes: party fairness, ethnic and racial fairness, and party competition. Niemi et al. (1990, 1155) focus on compactness, which became very important in litigation over racial redistricting. They provide multiple measures of compactness based on perimeter, dispersion, and either geography or population. While they advocate the use of multiple measures, the measures tend to converge on the same conclusion concerning the relative compactness of a given district. While work on this topic is extremely useful for understanding the competing goals of redistricting and providing tools for assessing these goals, it does not explain why one goal is pursued over another.

Another part of the literature attempts to explain specific patterns of redistricting and their consequences by focusing on institutional and political factors. Most of this work operates at the aggregate level, looking at the impact of institutional characteristics (such as partisan control of the state legislature and governorship) on the distribution of congressional or state legislative seats.

Glazer, Grofman, and Robbins (1987) reject two political explanations for the motivations behind congressional districting: partisan advantage and incumbency protection. With a few possible exceptions, they find that the 1970s round of redistricting served to protect the status quo; that is, "neither party gained at the expense of the other, and incumbents did not benefit at the expense of challengers, with the qualification that incumbents were not forced to run against each other" (680). Peverill Squire (1995) concurs with this finding of limited partisan effects in the 1970s. Niemi and Winsky (1992) find a partisan advantage in the election of 1972, but this effect diminished over time and disappears entirely by the end of the decade. Richard Born (1985), in one of the few studies to examine as many as four reapportionment cycles (1952–82), concludes that unified partisan control of the redistricting process produced modest effects that diminished in the post-"one person-one vote" era.

The 1980s round of redistricting produced greater partisan effects. Squire (1995, 229) shows that parties that controlled the process generally won more seats than they had before redistricting and also that they won a greater proportion of seats than percentage of the vote. Alan Abramowitz (1983) examines the 1982 redistricting and finds that the Democratic party realized the greatest seat dividend (as measured by the swing ratio) in the 17 states in which they had complete control of the redistricting process. Campagna and Grofman (1990, 1254–55) point out that Abramowitz is describing responsiveness rather than bias and that he fails to control for states in which redistricting was controlled by the courts or Justice Department. They also find that states that had unified party control of the legislative process had the largest partisan bias, for Republicans as well as Democrats, and that redistricting enhances the responsiveness of the system. This latter point runs counter to the typical view that redistricting helps incumbents, but this finding was later supported by Gelman and King (1994). Basehart and Comer (1995, 241) find similar results for state legislatures in the 1980s. States that had partisan control of the process showed the greatest partisan bias; those with bipartisan control showed limited partisan effects; and those that were nonpartisan (parties were excluded from the process) also had limited partisan effects, but these states created districts that were the least "incumbent friendly." Analysis of the 1990s round of congressional redistricting reveals more limited effects. Niemi and Abramowitz (1994, 811) conclude that "partisan control of state government did little or nothing to enhance partisan gains from redistricting."

In sum, these aggregate-level results range from those who find a significant relationship between partisan control of the redistricting process and partisan bias, to those who find limited effects that dissipate over time or no effects at all. Gelman and King (1994, 543) provide a nice resolution to these conflicting results: they argue that both sides are right. A partisan process produces partisan bias compared to what would have happened if the other party controlled the process, but any kind of redistricting "actually reduces the degree of bias as compared to no redistricting." (See King 1989a for a first cut at some of these issues.)

Runoff Elections

Anecdotal evidence points to obvious representational implications of majority runoff elections: if a black candidate is running in a district that has a substantial African American population, he or she could win a plurality of votes in the first-round primary with a unified black vote over two or more white candidates who split the white vote in a polarized election. The white voters then unite, giving the second-place white candidate a majority of the votes in the runoff. This happened in North Carolina in 1982 when Mickey Michaux, a black state representative, won the first primary with 44% of the vote over two white candidates in the 40% black district, but then lost to Tim Valentine in the runoff by a 56–44 margin (Patterson 1983, 238–41). Systematic analysis of this topic is relatively rare because there are no comprehensive records kept of the race of candidates who lose elections. In one of the best studies of the racial consequences of runoff elections, Bullock and Smith (1990) examine 401 county races between 1970 and 1984. They find that the black front-runner in the first primary who faces a white candidate in the runoff wins the nomination only 50% of the time compared to white candidates who lead a black in the first round, who win 83.8% of the time (the baseline success for front-runners winning the nomination when both candidates were white was 71.3%) (Bullock and Smith 1990, 1212). However, since 1977 this effect has diminished greatly (white front-runners won 80.8% of their runoffs against a black candidate between 1978 and 1984, compared to black front-runners who won 71.4% of their runoffs against white candidates). They also find that black front-runners are more likely to win the nomination in relatively wealthy districts and when they have a larger margin of victory in the initial primary (Bullock and Smith 1990, 1215). (See Bullock and Johnson 1992 for a more comprehensive treatment of this topic.)

At-Large Versus Single-Member Districts

At-large electoral districts also undermine minority representation. If five representatives are to be elected in a racially polarized multimember district that is 40% black, the majority of whites could conceivably fill all five seats. If the seats are allocated by single-member districts and residential patterns are relatively segregated, blacks could elect two of the five members. Dozens of studies of local elections confirm that blacks are far more likely to be elected in single-member districts than in at-large districts (see Davidson and Grofman 1994, 6–11, for a review of this literature). A few scholars have argued that this tendency has weakened as whites have become more willing to vote for blacks (Thernstrom 1987, 240–44). But Susan Welch (1990, 1069) finds that while blacks have made gains on city councils elected in at-large elections since the 1970s (using 1988 data), they still are underrepresented when compared to single-member district elections. Welch also examines representation of Hispanics on city councils but does not find any clear impact of the electoral system; at-large systems appear to offer slightly better representation, but mixed systems are more representative at lower levels of Hispanic population. Rabinovitz and Hamilton (1980) argue that mixed district/at large plans maximize levels of black representation, but Moncrief and Thompson (1992) show that blacks are more likely to be elected from single-member districts and women are more likely to be elected from multimember districts. Both effects are more pronounced in urban areas.

Staggered Terms

Another electoral institution that was alleged to dilute minority voting power is the staggered terms of political office (Senate 1982, 47). The Justice Department and the courts have both referred to staggered terms as one of the factors that may be used under a "totality of circumstances" test to determine whether there is a Section 2 vote dilution claim, or as grounds to deny preclearance to covered jurisdictions under Section 5 of the Voting Rights Act. Twenty-seven state senates use staggered terms, as do many city councils. However, the most systematic study of this issue, which examined all 50 state senates (1973–83) and 250 city councils (in 1985), showed that staggered terms actually had small positive impact on the probability of electing a black. This study also confirmed the negative impact of at-large representation on the probability of electing blacks, though the impact was relatively small (Bullock and MacManus 1987).

Should Minorities Receive Special Consideration?

Given the distinctive nature of black interests,[1] at least over a range of relevant issues, how should these interests be represented in Congress? Can white politicians adequately represent African American interests? Should African Americans have congressional districts explicitly drawn to maximize their political power, even if it requires tortuous district lines? Once the districts are created, should black representatives focus their attention on black constituents, or attempt to represent the entire district? What impact do they have on the nature of representation, accountability, legitimacy, and equality?

One basis for answering these questions is found in the debate in the minority politics and women's studies literature concerning the "politics of difference" versus the "politics of commonality" (Connoly 1991; Eisenstein 1988;

Gilligan 1982; Gitlin 1993; MacKinnon 1987; Young 1993) and the broader literature on community, identity, and democracy (Beitz 1989; Gates 1992; Gutmann and Thompson 1996; Kymlicka 1995; Phillips 1995; Streich 1997; Taylor 1992). I cannot do justice to the complexity and scope of the normative literature on these topics,[2] but I will briefly outline its contours.

The literature on identity, community, and democracy helps sort out the general principles that should govern the relationships among groups and between politicians and constituents. Stated in general terms, the questions on racial politics posed above are: Should government treat everyone as individuals or recognize group differences? If group differences are recognized, what are the proper mechanisms for ensuring fair representation? Should group differences be confined to the private sphere and only tolerated in the public sphere within a broader Madisonian system of majority rule (Rawls 1971), or should identity politics be embraced, recognizing that permanent majorities may be tyrannical (Guinier 1994)?

These questions reveal the central fault lines in current democratic theory. There are a myriad of combinations across competing principles: does the ideal democracy place more emphasis on individualism or identity, community or liberty, rights or responsibility (for citizens), accountability or autonomy (for politicians), authenticity or assimilation, equality of opportunity or outcomes? There are no obvious groupings across all these dimensions that can be captured in a single belief system or theory, nor could consistent choices across pairs be made by those who seek racial justice and equality.

Can Minorities Receive Special Consideration?

The goal of enhancing racial representation through redistricting was challenged in the landmark decision *Shaw* v. *Reno* (1993), which held that bizarrely shaped black majority districts violated the rights of white voters if they were created solely on the basis of race and ignored traditional districting practices. Justice O'Connor, in the most widely quoted passage of the decision, argued that the challenged reapportionment plan

> . . . bears an uncomfortable resemblance to political apartheid. It reinforces the perception that members of the same racial group—regardless of their age, education, economic status, or the community in which they live—think alike, share the same political interests, and will prefer the same candidates at the polls. We have rejected such perceptions elsewhere as impermissible racial stereotypes (*Shaw* v. *Reno* 1993, 2827).

This decision created a new basis for challenging the constitutionality of a voting district. Prior to *Shaw*, there were only two bases upon which to challenge a district: "one person one vote" and vote dilution. This new analysis emphasized "traditional districting practices" for the first time, citing the importance of compactness, contiguity, and respect for political subdivisions (respect for "communities defined by actual shared interests" was added in *Miller*). Or in O'Connor's words "we believe that reapportionment is one area in which appearances do matter" (1993, 2827).

Subsequent decisions expanded the scope of judicial scrutiny. *Miller* v. *Johnson* (1995) established that congressional districts were unconstitutional if race was the "predominant factor" in their creation, while moving away from the importance of the appearance of the district. Bizarrely shaped districts were no longer a threshold requirement for an equal protection claim. *Miller* also held that compliance with Section 5 preclearance was not an adequate reason for creating a black-majority district, even when the Justice Department insisted that additional black-majority districts be added. *Bush* v. *Vera* (1996) established that protecting incumbents was not a strong enough reason to dislodge race as the predominant factor when both motivations were present. *Abrams* v. *Johnson* (1997) upheld the dismantling of two of Georgia's black-majority districts that followed the *Miller* decision, even though the state legislature had shown a clear preference for keeping one of those two districts during the redistricting process. This decision signals that the courts are becoming increasingly activist in this area of litigation, rather than allowing the elected institutions to settle the issue.

Critics of *Shaw* and its progeny are plentiful. Richard Engstrom suggests that the reasoning in *Shaw* has no basis in the Constitution or federal statute and created a confusing "conceptual thicket" to compound the difficulties posed by the "political thicket" of redistricting that for decades the Court was loathe to enter (Engstrom 1995, 323–24; also see Kousser 1995, 1; see Grofman 1995, and Peterson 1995 for more positive assessments of *Shaw*). Other critics see judicial activism as the greatest failing of the *Shaw* decision. Christopher Eisgruber argues, ". . . this judgement (*Shaw* v. *Reno*) is empirically contingent in a way that makes it appropriate for legislative, rather than judicial, resolution. That is why I think *Shaw* is a monster: not because I agree with the policy it declared unconstitutional (I don't), but because the *Shaw* Court wrongly interfered with legislative discretion to treat America's most severe and most intractable problem, the problem of racial inequality" (Eisgruber 1996, 525). Ironically, liberals on the bench are the ones talking about self-restraint and states' rights.

Partisan Implications of Racial Redistricting

The partisan implications of creating minority-majority districts became immediately obvious as the 1990s redistricting commenced. The literature reveals two important ways in which partisan calculations are mixed with racial motivations, one from the Democrats' perspective and the other from the Republicans' vantage point; both are rooted in the tremendous loyalty that black voters show for Democratic candidates. Neither has been recognized as a central legal principle in the post-*Shaw* court cases, but both were critical in the pre-*Shaw* redistricting process.

The first involved the Democratic party's effort to balance the need to create new black-majority districts and the desire to protect white Democratic incumbents. Creating black-majority districts may hurt white Democratic incumbents because surrounding districts lose substantial numbers of black voters who tend to vote Democratic (see Brace, Grofman, and Handley 1987 for a balanced argument based on the pre-1990s redistricting data). Consequently, Democratic-controlled state legislatures often attempted to mitigate the damage through very creative cartography. North Carolina produced one of the most successful efforts in 1992 as they added two new black districts while protecting all the white Democratic incumbents (one of the new black members replaced a retiring white incumbent). Thus, the massive defeat of wounded white Democratic incumbents did not materialize in 1992 as only a few were defeated due to racial redistricting (Bob Benenson [1992] puts the number at three, Kevin Hill [1995] says four; and David Lublin [1997, 112] says "five or six"). In 1992, the main effect of the racial redistricting on the surrounding districts was not to hurt white Democratic incumbents, but to make Republican incumbents' districts become more secure. This had very little impact on the representation of black interests because most Republicans are not sympathetic to black interests (Overby and Cosgrove 1996; Swain 1993, 13–19).

Some have argued that the impact of black-majority districts on white Democrats was far greater in 1994, but it is difficult to sort out the confounding influence of the general Republican landslide (Engstrom 1995). The range of estimates of Democratic losses caused by racial redistricting in 1994 vary from one seat (NAACP 1994), to seven seats (Lublin 1997, 114), or 17 seats over the 1992–94 cycle (Swain 1995, 78–83; see Lublin 1997, 111–14 for a summary of this conflicting research). In any event, it seems clear that white incumbents have not been as harmed as Democratic partisans feared, nor as much as Republican partisans hoped. I should also note that the anticipated Democratic payoff from dismantling some of the black districts did not materialize in 1996. In Georgia where the shift of black voters to white-majority districts was most dramatic, all Republican incumbents were able to win. Nor did black incumbents suffer; all were comfortably reelected.

Are Minority Interests Represented in Legislatures?

The representational consequences of racial redistricting are more subtle than simple wins and losses. The potential cost of black-majority districts for black representation is not only that Republicans will win more seats, but that the Democrats who survive will have fewer black voters and therefore not be as sensitive to their needs. Two basic approaches in the representation literature have been used to examine these effects: descriptive and substantive representation.

Descriptive Representation. A first set of concerns is rooted in the politician's side of the relationship. Does the member of Congress "look like" the constituent? Is the member black or white, male or female, Catholic or Protestant? There are three positions on the value of descriptive representation. The first argues that there is a distinct value in having role models and notes the benefits that come from the simple act of being represented by someone who shares something as fundamental as skin color. For example, Davidson and Grofman quote Tom McCain, a black politician from South Carolina: "There's an inherent value in office holding that goes far beyond picking up the garbage. A race of people who are excluded from public office will always be second class citizens" (Bianco 1997; Davidson and Grofman 1994, 16; Mansbridge 1996; Thernstrom 1987, 239).

The other two groups argue that descriptive representation by itself is not useful unless it is linked to substantive representation; the left-of-center perspective argues that having "black faces in high places" may come at too high a price. Robert C. Smith says, "Like the transformation of black music, it will be a hollow victory if in order to achieve equitable descriptive-symbolic representation blacks are required to sacrifice their substantive policy agendas. The new black politician would then be a shell of himself, more like a Prince or Michael Jackson than a B.B. King or Bobby Bland" (Smith 1990, 161). (Jones 1985 and Pinderhughes 1987, xix make similar arguments.) The right-of-center perspective recognizes the value of descriptive representation in some limited contexts, but points out that whites can adequately represent black interests and that descriptive representation comes at a price (as noted above).

Anne Phillips (1995) argues that empirical research has focused almost exclusively on representation of "ideas" (substantive) rather than "presence" (descriptive). While substantive representation receives a disproportionate share of attention, there are many studies that focus on descriptive representation. These works either describe how the presence of blacks in Congress has grown in the past century (Clay 1993, Appendices A and B; Lublin 1997, ch. 2; Swain 1993, 20–34), or provide explanations for how blacks get elected (Cameron, Epstein, O'Halloran 1996, 803–05; Grofman and Handley 1989; Grofman, Griffin, and Glazer 1992; Handley and Grofman 1994; Lublin 1997, ch. 3). All of this work concludes that there are significant differences in racial representation between the South and non-South (a greater percentage of black voters is needed to elect a black member in the South than in the non-South), and between Democrats and Republicans (above 40% black population it is extremely unlikely that a Republican would be elected). Grofman and Handley (1989; Handley and Grofman 1994) make the strongest statement that black majority districts are nearly a necessary condition to elect blacks to office.

Descriptive representation is also important because the political world has recently shown a much greater sensitivity to having leaders who "look like America." The Clarence Thomas hearings created the perception that the "old white guys" on the Senate Judiciary Committee "just didn't get it" (Sapiro and Soss, forthcoming). President Clinton's well-publicized efforts to appoint a diverse cabinet brought more attention to the importance of descriptive representation. Congress watchers, such as *Congressional Quarterly* and the *National Journal* also mention the racial, gender, and even occupational composition of every new Congress and every Congress textbook dutifully mentions the similar sets of demographic figures.

Substantive Representation. While descriptive representation supplies an important dimension to a complete theory of representation, it only goes so far. As A. Phillips Griffiths pointed out, we do not expect lunatics to be represented by crazy people. "While we might wish to complain that there are not enough representative members of the working class among Parliamentary representatives," he says, "we would not want to complain that the large class of stupid or maleficent people have too few representatives in Parliament; quite the contrary" (quoted in Phillips 1995, 39).

Substantive representation moves beyond appearances to specify *how* the member serves the interest of the constituents. Two models go back at least until the time of Edmund Burke: 1) the trustee who represents the interests of constituents from a distance, weighing a variety of national, collective, local, and moral concerns, and 2) the delegate who has a simple mandate to carry out the direct desires of the voters. Hannah Pitkin advanced the discussion by noting that both of these perspectives are right and that true representation must combine both approaches (Pitkin 1967, 209–10). The most demanding theory of representation, known as "policy responsiveness," requires that voters express basic policy preferences, representatives respond to those desires, and then voters monitor and assess the politician's behavior (Miller and Stokes 1963). Other scholars paint a more subtle picture, pointing to congressional interpretations of constituency preferences (Kingdon 1989), the heterogeneity of a district (Fiorina 1974), segments of the constituency (Fenno 1978), differences across issue areas (Clausen 1973), and "potential preferences of inattentive publics" (Arnold 1990, 68–71).

Applying these basic components of representation to race adds a layer of complexity (Carmines and Stimson 1989). At the constituency level, the racial composition of the district intersects with Fenno's concentric circles (1978). Within the district, reelection, and primary constituencies (and to some extent the personal constituency, depending on the politician), race overlays a complex set of relationships that vary from district to district. Black constituents have distinct needs and interests that differ from the white constituency (Swain 1993, 7–10). Blacks are disproportionately affected by problems such as crime, drugs, poverty, discrimination, and poor health. Politicians representing districts with a substantial African American population differ in their responsiveness to the needs and interests of these constituents. Some members of Congress focus on one race within their reelection constituency, others give attention to both races within one party, while some may focus on a single race at the district level. These patterns of representation obviously vary across issues. Most issues that are addressed in Congress do not have any direct racial content, others are centrally concerned with race, and another substantial portion may or may not concern race depending on the member's framing of the issue (Canon 1999, ch. 4).

Measuring Racial Representation. Early work on racial representation focused on urban politics, which is where African Americans first achieved significanct political power. Blacks in Congress had almost no power, so they were largely ignored by scholars (of 350 citations in McClain and Garcia's (1993) extensive review of the minority politics literature, only seven concerned African Americans in Congress). This lack of attention may also be attributed to the perception that the CBC was weak and ineffective through its first 20 years (see Swain 1993, 37–39 for a review of various studies that make this argument). One of the most favorable studies concluded on the pessimistic note, "(U)nless the Caucus is able to increase its size sufficiently to have a significant impact on roll-call divisions and manages to free itself from submersion within the larger Northern Democratic sea, it appears unlikely that the Black Caucus will be able to add substantive success to its already impressive organizational and operational successes" (Levy and Stoudinger 1978, 332). Elsewhere, the same authors wondered if the CBC was destined to become "little more than a generalized publicity organ" (Levy and Stoudinger 1976, 44). Loomis (1981, 210) notes that the CBC started to play a more substantive role in the late 1970s, but that "the CBC remains most successful as a symbolic focus for many national black concerns." Loomis argues that this symbolic focus poses a problem for the CBC because their constituents expect substantive results that are difficult to deliver. Rep. William Clay's book, *Just Permanent Interests* (1993), is a good insider account of the history and evolution of the CBC. Clay recognizes some of the difficulties pointed out by the academic accounts, but emphasizes the role of the CBC as the voice for black Americans.

Subsequent work has demonstrated that the CBC has played a more prominent role in Congress since 1993, when its numbers increased by 50%. Canon (1995) shows that the CBC played a pivotal role on 9 of the 16 "key votes" identified by *Congressional Quarterly* in the first session of the 103d Congress; increased their presence on most committees, especially constituency committees on which they were underrepresented before 1993; held three full committee chairs and 16 subcommittee chairs; and played a larger role in the whip system (see Singh 1998, ch. 7, for similar evidence). Singh (1998, 202) points out that the Republican takeover of Congress forced the CBC back into their more confrontational role; he also sees the increased diversity within the CBC as a source of weakness rather than strength. He argues that despite the CBC's increased institutional clout, it has not had much policy success in terms of improving the lives of black constituents. However, Singh does not provide an operational definition of "success," nor does he consider that the CBC can be influential on issues that do not narrowly concern race. Cobb and Jenkins (1996) show that the CBC is a powerful voice for black interests within the House, introducing a disproportionate share of the legislation that offered symbolic benefits and direct and indirect economic and social benefits for blacks.

Other scholars shifted focus from the internal political clout of the CBC to the responsiveness of members of Congress to their black constituents. Carol Swain employs participant observation, detailed case studies of 13 districts, and quantitative analysis of roll-call voting in her analysis of racial representation in Congress. Her central conclusion is that black representatives and white Democrats both do a good job of representing black interests. In fact, when controlling for party, region, percentage urban, and percentage black, the race of the member is not a significant predictor of LCCR scores, COPE scores, or alternative roll-call ratings. These results lead Swain to conclude that, "Redrawing boundaries to create additional districts with large black majorities . . . appears not to be the most effective way to increase the representation of black interests" (1993, ix). Swain argues that creating black-majority districts is a self-limiting strategy (due to the relatively few numbers of such districts that could be drawn), and that blacks are better off entering biracial coalitions with whites to elect more blacks and counting on whites to represent their interests.

Swain's argument has been controversial. Grofman, Handley, and Niemi (1992, 135) agree with Swain that creating black-majority districts to enhance racial representation has a self-limiting logic, but they disagree that biracial coalitions to elect whites are the answer; they say, "Here, although we recognize the white liberal legislators may vote similarly to their black counterparts on roll-call votes, this does not mean that they have the same commitment to a leadership role on civil rights or on economic issues of concern to the black community. Also, the view that black votes should be used to (re)elect white liberals is a variant of a very old style of paternalism. The rejection of black claims to self-representation in favor of the interests of white incumbents has been a factor retarding black representation." Swain's finding that the race of the member had no impact on roll-call scores was contradicted by Cobb and Jenkins (1996), Whitby (1997), and Canon (1999). Also, Swain's conclusion that whites adequately represent blacks is not supported by my analysis of a broader range of legislative behavior than she considers. The difference in our results may be explained by the selection of cases. Her analysis of Peter Rodino, Lindy Boggs, Robin Tallon, and Tim Valentine serves as the strongest basis for her conclusions, whereas I analyze all white members in the 103d Congress who represent districts that are at least 25% black (total population). Boggs and Rodino were well-known for representing their black constituents, while Tallon and Valentine were clearly not "old South" Democrats. Thus, Swain did not have a representative sample of the Democrats and Republicans who represent districts with substantial black populations. However, Swain's book is an extremely rich and useful source of information on racial representation and set the stage for much of the research that was done on the topic over the next five years.

Another body of work focuses on the internal dynamics of the CBC—its level of cohesion (Levy and Stoudinger 1978; Pinney and Serra 1995; Walton 1995) and the sources of cues (Levy and Stoudinger 1976; Menifield 1996; Pinney and Serra 1995). This work reveals that the CBC is a cohesive group (as measured by the standard deviation of their ADA scores) that becomes even more cohesive in response to presidential agendas that are adverse to its interests (Pinney and Serra 1995, 20). They are extremely liberal as a group, but the younger generation of members is introducing more diversity (Walton 1995, 15–16). Menifield (1996, 24–41) examines a series of key votes on foreign, economic, and social policy to determine the relative influence of the CBC, the Hispanic Caucus, and the Women's Caucus. The CBC was the strongest source of cues (they had a statistically significant impact on 12 of the 20 key votes he examined compared to 9 of 20 for the Hispanic Caucus and 2 of 20 for the Women's Caucus). Menifield also interviewed members of Congress to ask them to rate their most important sources of information and the "top three items that affect votes" (1996, 11), but this part of the study was not incorporated into the preliminary version of his analysis reviewed here. While this body of work makes a useful contribution to the literature, more explicit linkages need to be made to policy and broader questions of representation. Ideology and cohesion are not important for their own sake, but for how they affect the ability of various groups within Congress to meet their goals and serve their constituents.

Most of the literature cited above on responsiveness, cohesion, and ideology share one common problem: an exclusive use of roll-call votes to measure congressional behavior. The standard approach regresses district-level characteristics on various interest group ratings such as ADA (Americans for Democratic Action), COPE (Committee on Political Education), or LCCR (Leadership Conference on Civil Rights), or Poole and Rosenthal's NOMINATE scores (1996). This practice can be explained largely by the "law of available data." Roll-call data, especially interest group ratings, are readily available and easily analyzed but are not accurate measures of a member's overall behavior in Congress because of the "censored sample problem" (Di Lorenzo 1997, 1742–43; Hall 1996; Hall and Wayman 1990, 801; and King 1989b, 208–13 make similar arguments in different contexts). Furthermore, general ideological ratings are not an especially good measure of black interests because most of the issues they include in their measure of support are not of central importance to the African American community. Even LCCR scores, which are supposed to be the most closely related to race, do not reflect a racial agenda. One can say very little about the extent of black representation based on roll-call votes, or the interest group support scores that are based on roll-call votes.

Some recent work attempts to overcome this problem by employing a broader range of measures of congressional behavior. Vincent Di Lorenzo (1997) and Cobb and Jenkins (1996) both examine sponsorship of legislation of interest to black constituents, arguing that this alternative measure of legislative behavior is a good indicator of the intensity of commitment to black interests. Di Lorenzo sees the activity of members of the CBC in the area of "truth in lending" legislation as an indication of their "legislative heart." While I did not find much value added from his use of chaos theory, this piece represents an important step away from the over-reliance on roll-call voting. Similarly, Cobb and Jenkins (1996) find that black members of the House disproportionately sponsor legislation on issues that were of direct and indirect significance to black voters on economic and social issues in the 103d Congress. My research on racial representation in Congress examines sponsorship and cosponsorship of legislation, speeches on the floor of the House, amendments offered, committee assignments, leadership positions, constituency newsletters, the location of district office, the racial composition of the staff, and newspaper coverage of members (in addition to roll-call voting) in all districts that were at least 25% black in the 103d Congress. I conclude that black members of Congress do a better job of representing a balance of racial interests than do white members, and that there are important differences in the representational styles of members of the CBC. Some are explicitly biracial in their politics, while others continue to practice a "politics of difference" (Canon 1999, chs. 4 and 5).

Johnson and Secret (1996) pursue a different approach, returning to the sociological conception of "legislative roles" (Davidson 1969; Wahlke et al. 1962). They interviewed 18 members of Congress in 1992 (12 African American and 8 Hispanic) and asked them about their representational focus. They report an extremely diverse set of responses (1996, 255, 263), but overall, members expressed both a strong district focus and a sense of responsibility to represent minority constituencies nationwide. This finding is consistent with Clay's (1993) argument about the role of the CBC and other interview-based research on the CBC (Swain 1993). It would have been useful to have included some white members of Congress as a basis for comparison; nonetheless, this study helps provide a better understanding of how minority members of the House resolve conflicting representational pressures.

The collective impact of this recent research that looks at a broader range of legislative behavior is to demonstrate that the race of the member matters. These findings contradict the research by Swain (1993), Cameron, Epstein, and O'Halloran (1996), Thernstrom and Thernstrom (1997, ch. 16), and others who are more inclined to the "color-blind" approach to racial representation.

Racial Redistricting and Turnout

Turnout. Redistricting can have an impact on turnout by generating interest in the electoral process among groups of voters who previously felt alienated from the system. Brace et al. (1995) analyzed homogeneous precincts in Florida (defined as at least 90% black or Hispanic) to see whether turnout changed after the creation of a minority-majority district. They found that turnout increased in the new congressional districts by 8%, compared to 4.5% in districts that did not change between 1988 and 1992. The same analysis for state House seats was less clear because of a more limited number of precincts. They also used cross-sectional data in the 1992 Florida legislative elections and found that turnout was higher in new black-majority congressional and state house seats but not in state senate seats. Ronald Weber's analysis (1995) of turnout in the 1994 elections, however, showed that some of these gains may have been short-lived, as black turnout in the new black districts did not remain as high as turnout in the older districts.

Alternative Electoral Institutions

Interest in alternative electoral systems has exploded both in the U.S. and around the world. In the U.S., dissatisfaction with racial redistricting has spurred an examination of alternative mechanisms to represent minority interests. The proliferation democracy in the last decade has raised awareness that creating stable political systems that address the needs of various groups may be facilitated by picking the right type of electoral institutions (Zimmerman 1994). One study on South Africa noted, "Electoral-system design is increasingly being recognized as a key lever than can be used to promote political accommodation and stability in ethnically divided societies" (Reynolds 1995, 86).

Cumulative Voting

Some critics of racial redistricting argue that alternative electoral institutions, such as proportional representation or cumulative voting, may provide a more efficient voice for minority interests in a majority rule political system than do majority-minority districts (or single-member, geographic representation more generally). Richard Morrill says, "With single-member districts, it is manifestly impossible to satisfy any but one dimension of these interests—that of the majority" (1996, 4). Lani Guinier's advocacy of these positions, in addition to her even more controversial views on minority veto powers, supermajorities, and cumulative voting on legislation of interest to the minority community in Congress (1991a, 1991b, 1994) led to the demise of her nomination as Assistant Attorney General for Civil Rights in the spring of 1993. These views constitute a subtle but important shift from voting rules that favored black candidates to rules that would favor black interests. Guinier's position is based on the belief that the "right to fair representation" under the Voting Rights Act should be measured by "the extent protected minority groups are provided meaningful voice in government" (1994, 93). While Guinier's proposals for procedural changes in the legislative process are extreme (and in my view, unworkable), her cumulative voting plan (which she calls "semi-proportional representation") is more plausible. Conventional proportional representation systems will be discussed below.

Cumulative voting works in the following fashion: members of the legislature would be elected from multimember districts in which voters would have one vote per legislative seat. Voters could allocate their votes between the candidate in any proportion, including "plumping" their votes by casting them all for one candidate. Thus, minorities who comprised at least $1/n^{th}$ of the district (where n is the number of legislative seats) should be able to elect at least one of their preferred candidates. This electoral arrangement has received some attention in the popular press and among empirical scholars and formal theorists.

Formal theorists have long been interested in the process of aggregating individual preferences into collective outcomes. When more than two options are presented, there is no voting system that produces consistently fair and just results (see Riker 1982, ch. 4, for a summary of the various voting methods). While cumulative voting cannot satisfy all the conditions of a fair voting system, formal work suggests that it can serve as a mechanism for increasing minority representation. Most formal work has focused on the optimal voter strategies to elect candidates of their choice under various voting systems. Merrill (1981) finds that under cumulative voting in multimember districts, cumulating votes for a preferred candidate is an undominated strategy. Cox (1984) found that in two-member districts under straight voting, it is optimal to "plump" votes for a single candidate. He also finds that in multimember districts, cumulative voting promotes a dispersion of ideological positions among the candidates (Cox 1990, 927). Gerber, Morton, and Rietz (1998) find that under straight voting, the majority candidates in a three-candidate two-seat election (with two majority and one minority candidate) constitute one equilibrium. However, they also find that there are equilibria that predict either a close three-way race, or even the minority candidate winning. Under cumulative voting in the same context, minority candidates win when minority voters have no preference between the majority candidates, and cumulate their votes for their first choice. However, if the minority voters split their votes, the majority candidates can win (141–42). Burt Monroe (1995) proposes a "fully proportional representation" system in which voters could express preferences over a full slate of candidates rather than being allowed to only express their first preferences, as in all existing electoral systems. While this system has no empirical referent in the political world, it raises intriguing possibilities for providing richer and deeper representation of political views.

The empirical literature is relatively thin on the topic of cumulative voting in the United States because there are only a few offices for which the practice is used. The most commonly cited examples in the literature are Chilton County, Alabama; Peoria, Illinois (which only held one election under cumulative voting); Alamogordo, New Mexico (which ended its experiment in 1994); and the Illinois General Assembly from 1870–1982 (Adams 1996; Issacharoff and Pildes 1996; Sawyer and MacRae 1962; Van Biema 1994). Engstrom (1994, 687) points to "over 50 local governing units (that) have adopted either limited or cumulative voting systems in response to dilution allegation." Adams (1996) provides strong empirical evidence that the cumulative voting system in Illinois produced more ideologically extreme members of the state assembly than those who were elected by the single-member district system that was employed in 1982. Chilton County, Alabama, which is 12% black, used cumulative voting to elect its first black commissioner since Reconstruction, Bobby Agee. In the second election under cumulative voting, Issacharoff and Pildes (1996) report that white candidates were courting black voters, and Agee was able to attract a few more white votes. In addition to providing descriptive representation, cumulative voting may help break down racial barriers.

However, there are several potential problems with cumulative voting: 1) it is relatively complex and produces voter confusion, at least in the short term; 2) it will shift power to groups of voters with higher turnout rates (elderly, wealthy, highly educated, whites); 3) it would benefit minorities of the right; 4) multimember districts in which the cumulative voting would occur would be so large as to virtually do away with the concept of geographic representation that is so central to American politics (Morrill 1996, 4–5); and 5) it could produce a less stable, more fractured political system (Forest 1996, 10). One other unintended effect often not mentioned by proponents of the system: Republicans are likely to benefit from cumulative voting even more than they did from the creation of black-majority districts. If Republicans "plump" their votes, they should be able to elect candidates roughly in proportion to their population, just like minorities would. For example, in Chilton County, an area where Republicans rarely won local office, three of the seven commission seats went to Re-

166   Legislatures

publicans. Furthermore, minorities would need to construct powerful slating organizations to limit the supply of candidates, or risk splitting their limited voting power. In Centre, Alabama, another community that tried cumulative voting, a black city councilman was elected when the plan was implemented in 1988. But in 1992, he had black competition and the city council reverted to all-white (Van Biema 1994, 43). The practice is clearly not a panacea for minority representation.

Proportional Representation vs. Plurality Elections

Much of the comparative literature on this topic is more concerned with the impact of electoral institutions on parties, competition, and the division of power than on ethnic and racial politics. This highly technical literature attempts to define proportionality (usually in terms of the deviation of the party's shares of seats from its share of votes) and how to measure deviations from proportionality.[3] However, the literature that examines racial and ethnic representation and electoral systems is substantial and growing. The consensus of this literature is that proportional representation (PR) and parliamentary governments are better for minority representation than are plurality elections and presidential governments. PR systems are fairer than plurality systems, they are more inclusive, they promote power-sharing and consociational democracy, and thus, they provide a greater voice for ethnic and racial minorities. Shugart and Carey (1992, 28–43) point out three characteristics of presidential governments that are especially bad for racially or ethnically diverse societies: "temporal rigidity, majoritarianism, and dual democratic legitimacy." The worst of these is the winner-take-all quality of majoritarianism in a presidential system; minorities that fear permanent majority tyranny will have little incentive to buy into a zero-sum game.

However, this view is not universally held. Supporters of plurality elections (Barkan 1995; Horowitz 1991; Lardeyret 1991) identify a range of problems with PR that are similar to the drawbacks of cumulative voting that I noted above. These critics point out that large, broad-based, and ethnically diverse political parties in a plurality system are more likely to promote stable, democratic politics than the politically extreme, racially homogeneous, regional parties that may be produced in a PR system. The Sri Lankan case provides evidence for both sides of the debate. For many years it provided a relatively rare example of a less-developed country with a parliamentary democracy and fair and regular elections. This stability may be attributed to its plurality, single-member elections that were instituted in 1947. However, by the 1970s, extreme minority parties that were shut out of the system, such as the militant Tamil party, eventually "undermined the democratic aspects of the system" and led to ethnic conflict (Shastri 1991, 344).

Proportional representation also benefits women. Wilma Rule (1994) provides compelling evidence that single-member districts are much less likely to elect as many women as PR systems. She says, "Electoral arrangements are not neutral; they are the means used to exclude or include groups. The arrangements are amenable to change faster than social biases and other barriers to women's election opportunity and fair representation" (689). She shows that of the 27 "long established democracies," the nine with the highest proportion of women in the lower houses of parliament are all PR systems. Of the next 17, eight are single-member and nine are PR. The mean percentage of women parliament members for the PR nations was 18.4% compared to 10.1% in the single-member nations. Even more telling are the figures on the upper and lower houses of parliament in Australia, Japan, and Germany: these nations use PR in the upper house where an average of 25.3% of members are women, while the lower houses use single-member districts (or "small districts" in the case of Japan) and have an average of 7% women. A similar bit of evidence from the United States shows that in the 15 states that have multimember districts for their state legislatures, 21.8% of the legislators are women, compared to 12.4% in the 35 states with single-member districts. While the causal mechanisms that produce these relationships are still not entirely clear (see Matland and Studlar 1996, for one attempt to explain this pattern based on "contagion theory"), electoral systems are not neutral when it comes to electing women (see Rule and Zimmerman 1994, for a more complete analysis of these and other data on the representation of women and minorities in different types of electoral systems).

Mixed Systems

Some of the emerging democracies in Eastern Europe have adopted mixed systems that attempt to combine the advantages of PR and plurality systems, such as the Additional-Member system (in Hungary and Bulgaria) and Single Transferable Vote (STV—in Estonia). John Ishiyama finds that the Additional Member system in Hungary has promoted a stable coalition government with substantial representation for minority parties. However the STV system was abandoned in Estonia because "STV does not provide an incentive for parties to adopt national rather than regional programs, although it does provide for minority representation. It is especially dangerous in a situation where a substantial Russian minority is regionally concentrated in the northeastern part of Estonia" (Ishiyama 1996, 505–06). Other nations attempt to achieve proportional representation for racial and ethnic groups through non-PR methods, such as ethnic geographic districts, optional ethnic districts, and ethnically proportional slates. Lijphart reviews these alternative arrangements in Belgium, Cyprus, Lebanon, New Zealand, West Germany, and Zimbabwe, and discusses the pros and cons of each, relatively to simple PR. He concludes that in most cases, PR is preferable (1986, 122–23).

The skeptical Americanist may argue that this comparative work is interesting but irrelevant for the American case because practical politics dictate that PR or alternative electoral systems will never be implemented in the U.S. However, 22 municipalities used some type of proportional system between 1915 and 1964 (Weaver 1986, 141) and many jurisdictions continue to employ multimember districts that could easily be converted to cumulative voting. Even if practical politics precludes certain options, the theoretical and normative literature in American politics needs to incorporate the experiences of other nations when analyzing the range of possibilities.

Future Directions for Research

Historical and State-Level Research

There has been tremendous variation in electoral institutions over the course of our nation's history. Some members of the U.S. House were elected from multimember districts until 1842, a uniform date for federal elections was not set until 1845, some states elected House members in odd numbered years until 1880, the secret ballot was not widely used until the 1890s, district size varied dramatically until the 1960s (Jacobson 1997, 7–12). State legislatures provide even more variation with multimember and single-member districts, and the instance of cumulative voting in Illinois, mentioned above. Scholars have only begun to uncover the representational consequences of these changes in electoral institutions and the cross-sectional variation at the state level.

Recent Reforms: Campaign Finance and Term Limits

Campaign finance reform and term limits were two of the most significant changes in electoral institutions to emerge in the 1990s. Neither has been implemented at the national level, as term limits for Congress were struck down by the Supreme Court and campaign finance reform languishes in Congress. However, states continue to serve as laboratories of experimentation in both areas. Given the recent implementation of laws in both areas, there is relatively little empirical work on these topics. However, state-level variation in the versions of campaign finance and term limits allows some additional leverage on representational questions; research on these topics should help inform the debates at the national level. What impact does public financing have on candidate recruitment and competition in state legislative elections (Mayer and Wood 1995), or on broader representational questions? Does public financing help control the influence of special interests, or do they simply find other outlets for their money? What are the implications of limited or lengthened terms for representation (Keech 1986)? Are term-limited members more responsive to the public? Is there a transfer of power to special interests and the "permanent" bureaucracy, as some critics maintain?

Policy Consequences

Davidson and Grofman (1994, 14) identify a "fourth generation" of work on voting research that examines the political process's "output so far as minority citizens at the grassroots are concerned." That is, what difference does it make *for minority citizens* that minority politicians are in office? What policies are implemented that otherwise would not have been, and what impact do they have? Policy evaluation is always a tricky business, but especially when involving counterfactual scenarios. Perhaps because of this complexity, this is an area where very little work has been done (for one good example of this type of research see Button 1988). However, the ultimate significance of electoral institutions for representation lies in this generation of research.

Elite-Centered Research

We also know very little about the impact of electoral institutions on political elites and their second-stage effects at the individual level. Armand Derfner (1973, 555–56) outlines eight "candidate diminution" tactics used by southern states to discourage black candidates from running. Even more benign practices, such as redistricting that was intended to promote black representation, can create uncertainty and influence the nature of the candidate pool that emerges (Canon, Schousen, and Sellers 1994). Candidate slating groups, initially used in the South to dilute black voting power, may become essential to *maintain* black voting power in a system of cumulative voting. Even in black-majority districts with sizable white populations, black candidate slating organizations may be necessary to prevent a split black vote from allowing a white candidate to win. In the era of candidate-centered elections, such slating groups tend not to have much power, but perhaps they can be more effective in racially homogeneous communities. There are few accounts of these groups beyond the anecdotal level (Canon, Schousen, and Sellers 1994). What impact do the various electoral institutions mentioned here and elsewhere in this essay have on the type of candidate who runs for office, and ultimately, how does this influence the nature of representation? Are slating groups consistent with participatory democracy?

Conclusion

This essay should leave little doubt that electoral institutions have significant implications for representation. Politicians will attempt to manipulate institutions for partisan gain and political scientists will continue to examine the contours of this relationship. The productiveness and quality of the latter enterprise will substantially improve if scholars venture across subdisciplinary boundaries. Subfields that ignore each other's work are mutually impoverished. Empirical, normative, legal, and formal scholars all have something to contribute to our understanding of the impact of electoral systems on representation. The obstacles to cross-fertilization are high: jargon may be frustrating, and quantitative work and formal theory may be intimidating to the uninitiated. Truly integrating comparative work into American politics is, perhaps, even more daunting because anything more serious than casual dabbling and borrowing involves extensive retooling and retraining. However, the potential payoff is high. Adequately representing divergent group interests is a problem that bedevils most countries. While the racial divide in the United States is not as severe as racial or ethnic divisions in South Africa, the former Yugoslavia, India, or many other nations, American political scientists (and citizens) who are interested in helping bridge the racial divide can learn from the comparative experience.

NOTES

1. See Swain 1993, ch. 1; Canon 1999, ch. 1; and Thernstrom and Thernstrom 1997, ch. 1 for a review of the literature on the various ways to define black interests, and the data on the objective and subjective indicators of black interests.
2. Greg Streich's dissertation (1997; cited above) spends more than 300 pages analyzing and critiquing this literature. Even his thorough presentation is not exhaustive.
3. See Riedwyl and Steiner (1995) for a brief overview of the different electoral systems (such as the d'Hondy, Saint-Lague, Hare, and Droop methods). Gallagher (1991) reviews three of these measures and applies them to 83 elections in 23 countries from 1979 to 1989. He finds that the measures correlate highly, but there are differences. Cox (1996) and Cox and Niou (1994) examine the impact of the single non-transferable vote on the electoral success of small and large parties. Part I of Grofman and Lijphart (1986) examines the impact of election type on political competition.

REFERENCES

Abramowitz, Alan I. 1983. "Partisan Redistricting and the 1982 Congressional Elections." *Journal of Politics* 45:767–70.
Adams, Greg D. 1996. "Legislative Effects of Single-Member vs. Multi-Member Districts." *American Journal of Political Science* 40:129–44.

Arnold, R. Douglas. 1990. *The Logic of Congressional Action*. New Haven: Yale University Press.
Barkan, Joel D. 1995. "Debate: PR and Southern Africa Elections in Agrarian Societies." *Journal of Democracy* 6:106–16.
Basehart, Harry, and John Comer. 1995. "Redistricting and Incumbent Reelection Success in Five State Legislatures." *American Politics Quarterly* 23:241–53.
Beitz, C.R. 1989. *Political Equality: An Essay in Democratic Theory*. Princeton, NJ: Princeton University Press.
Benenson, Bob. 1992. "GOP's Dreams of a Comeback Via the New Map Dissolve." *Congressional Quarterly Weekly Report* 50 (November 7):3580–81.
Bianco, William T. 1997. "Evaluating Descriptive Representation: When Will Constituents Do Better with 'Someone Like Them?'" Working paper, Department of Political Science, Penn State University.
Born, Richard. 1985. "Partisan Intentions and Election Day Realities in the Congressional Redistricting Process." *American Journal of Political Science* 79:305–19.
Brace, Kimball, Bernard Grofman, and Lisa Handley. 1987. "Does Redistricting Aimed to Help Blacks Necessarily Help Republicans?" *Journal of Politics* 49:169–85.
Brace, Kimball, Lisa Handley, Richard Niemi, and Harold Stanley. 1995. "Minority Turnout and the Creation of Majority-Minority Districts." *American Politics Quarterly* 23:190–203.
Bullock, Charles S. III, and A. Brock Smith. 1990. "Black Success in Local Runoff Elections." *Journal of Politics* 52:1205–20.
Bullock, Charles S. III, and Loch K. Johnson. 1992. *Runoff Elections in the United States*. Chapel Hill: University of North Carolina Press.
Bullock, Charles S. III, and Susan A. MacManus. 1987. "Staggered Terms and Black Representation." *Journal of Politics* 49:543–52.
Butler, David, and Bruce Cain. 1992. *Congressional Redistricting: Comparative and Theoretical Perspectives*. New York: Macmillan.
Button, James W. 1988. *Blacks and Social Change: The Impact of the Civil Rights Movement in Southern Communities*. Princeton: Princeton University Press.
Cameron, Charles, David Epstein, and Sharon O'Halloran. 1996. "Do Majority–Minority Districts Maximize Substantive Black Representation in Congress?" *American Political Science Review* 90:794–812.
Campagna, Janet, and Bernard Grofman. 1990. "Party Control and Partisan Bias in 1980s Congressional Redistricting." *Journal of Politics* 52:1242–57.
Canon, David T. 1995. "Redistricting and the Congressional Black Caucus." *American Politics Quarterly* 23:159–89.
Canon, David T. 1999. *Race, Redistricting, and Representation: The Unintended Consequences of Black Majority Districts*. Chicago: University of Chicago Press.
Canon, David T., Matthew M. Schousen, and Patrick J. Sellers. 1994. "A Formula for Uncertainty: Creating a Black-Majority District in North Carolina." In *Who Runs for Congress: Ambition, Context, and Candidate Emergence*, ed. Thomas A. Kazee. Washington, DC: CQ Press.
Carmines, Edward G., and James A. Stimson. 1989. *Issue Evolution: Race and the Transformation of American Politics*. Princeton, NJ: Princeton University Press.

Clausen, Aage R. 1973. *How Congressmen Decide: A Policy Focus*. New York: St. Martin's Press.

Clay, William. 1993. *Just Permanent Interests: Black Americans in Congress, 1870–1992*. New York: Amistad Press.

Cobb, Michael D., and Jeffrey A. Jenkins. 1996. "Who Represents Black Interests in Congress?: Sponsoring and Voting for Legislation Beneficial to Black Constituents." Presented at the annual meeting of the Midwest Political Science Association, Chicago.

Connoly, William. 1991. *Identity/Difference: Democratic Negotiations of Political Paradox*. Ithaca, NY: Cornell University Press.

Cox, Gary W. 1984. "Strategic Electoral Choice in Multi–Member Districts: Approval Voting in Practice?" *American Journal of Political Science* 28:722–38.

Cox, Gary W. 1990. "Centripetal and Centrifugal Incentives in Electoral Systems." *American Journal of Political Science* 34:903–35.

Cox, Gary W. 1996. "Is the Single Nontransferable Vote Superproportional? Evidence from Japan and Taiwan." *American Journal of Political Science* 40:740–55.

Cox, Gary W., and Emerson Niou. 1994. "Seat Bonuses under the Single Nontransferable Vote System: Evidence from Japan and Taiwan." *Comparative Politics* 27:221–36.

Crook, Sara Brandes, and John R. Hibbing. 1997. "A Not-So-Distant Mirror: The 17th Amendment and Congressional Change." *American Political Science Review* 91:845–53.

Davidson, Chandler, and Bernard Grofman, eds. 1994. *Quiet Revolution in the South: The Impact of the Voting Rights Act, 1965–1990*. Princeton, NJ: Princeton University Press.

Davidson, Roger. 1969. *The Role of the Congressman*. New York: Pegasus.

Derfner, Armand. 1972. "Racial Discrimination and the Right to Vote." *Vanderbilt Law Review* 26:523–84.

Di Lorenzo, Vincent. 1997. "Legislative Heart and Phase Transitions: An Exploratory Study of Congress and Minority Interests." *William and Mary Law Review* 38:1729–1815.

Eisenstein, Zillah. 1988. *The Female Body and the Law*. Berkeley: University of California Press.

Eisgruber, Christopher L. 1996. "Ethnic Segregation by Religion and Race: Reflections on *Kiryas Joel* and *Shaw v. Reno.*" *Cumberland Law Review* 26:515–26.

Engstrom, Richard L. 1994. "The Voting Rights Act: Disenfranchisement Dilution and Alternative Election Systems." *PS: Political Science & Politics* 27:685–88.

Engstrom, Richard L. 1995. "Voting Rights Districts: Debunking the Myths." *Campaigns and Elections* April:24–46.

Fenno, Richard F. 1978. *Home Style: House Members in Their Districts*. Boston: Little, Brown.

Fiorina, Morris P. 1974. *Representatives, Roll Calls, and Constituencies*. Lexington, MA: Lexington Books.

Forest, Benjamin. 1996. "Where Should Democratic Compromise Take Place?" *Social Science Quarterly* 77:6–13.

Gallagher, Michael. 1991. "Proportionality, Disproportionality, and Electoral Systems." *Electoral Studies* 10:33–51.

Gates, Henry Louis, Jr. 1992. *Loose Canons: Notes on the Culture Wars*. New York: Oxford University Press.
Gelman, Andrew, and Gary King. 1994. "Enhancing Democracy Through Legislative Redistricting." *American Political Science Review* 88:541–59.
Gerber, Elisabeth R., Rebecca B. Morton, and Thomas A. Rietz. 1998. "Minority Representation in Multimember Districts." *American Political Science Review* 92:127–44.
Gilligan, Carol. 1982. *In a Different Voice: Psychological Theory and Women's Development*. Cambridge: Harvard University Press.
Gitlin, Todd. 1993. "Universality to Difference: Notes on the Fragmentation of the Idea of the Left." *Contention: Debates in Society, Culture, and Science* 2:15–40.
Glazer, Amihai, Bernard Grofman, Marc Robbins. 1987. "Partisan and Incumbency Effects of 1970s Congressional Redistricting." *American Journal of Political Science* 31:680–707.
Grofman, Bernard. 1995. "*Shaw* v. *Reno* and the Future of Voting Rights." *PS: Political Science and Politics* 28:27–36.
Grofman, Bernard, and Lisa Handley. 1989. "Minority Population Proportion and the Black and Hispanic Congressional Success in the 1970s and 1980s." *American Politics Quarterly* 17:436–45.
Grofman, Bernard, Robert Griffin, and Amihai Glazer. 1992. "The Effect of Black Population on Electing Democrats and Liberals to the House of Representatives." *Legislative Studies Quarterly* 17:365–79.
Grofman, Bernard, and Arend Lijphart, eds. 1986. *Electoral Laws and Their Political Consequences*. New York: Agathon Press.
Grofman, Bernard, Lisa Handley, and Richard Niemi. 1992. *Minority Representation and the Quest for Voting Equality*. New York: Cambridge University Press.
Guinier, Lani. 1991a. "The Triumph of Tokenism—The Voting–Rights Act and the Theory of Black Electoral Success." *Michigan Law Review* 89:1077–1154.
Guinier, Lani. 1991b. "No 2 Seats—The Elusive Quest for Political Equality." *Virginia Law Review* 77:1413–1514.
Guinier, Lani. 1994. *The Tyranny of the Majority: Fundamental Fairness in Representative Democracy*. New York: Free Press.
Gutmann, Amy, and Dennis Thompson. 1996. *Democracy and Disagreement: Why Moral Conflict Cannot be Avoided in Politics and What To Do About It*. Cambridge, MA: Harvard University Press (Belknap).
Hall, Richard L. 1996. *Participation in Congress*. New Haven, CT: Yale University Press.
Hall, Richard L., and Frank W. Wayman. 1990. "Buying Time: Moneyed Interests and the Mobilization of Bias in Congressional Committees." *American Political Science Review* 84:797–820.
Handley, Lisa, and Bernard Grofman. 1994. "The Impact of the Voting Rights Act on Minority Representation: Black Officeholding in Southern State Legislatures and Congressional Delegations." In *Quiet Revolution in the South: The Impact of the Voting Rights Act: 1965–1990*, ed. Chandler Davidson and Bernard Grofman. Princeton, NJ: Princeton University Press.

Hill, Kevin. 1995. "Does the Creation of Majority Black Districts Aid Republicans? An Analysis of the 1992 Congressional Elections in Eight Southern States." *Journal of Politics* 57:384–401.

Horowitz, Donald. 1991. *A Democratic South Africa? Constitutional Engineering in a Divided Society*. Berkeley: University of California Press.

Ishiyama, John T. 1996. "Electoral Systems Experimentation in the New Eastern Europe: The Single Transferable Vote and the Additional Member System in Estonia and Hungary." *East European Quarterly* 29:487–507.

Issacharoff, Samuel, and Richard H. Pildes. 1996. "All for One: Can Cumulative Voting Ease Racial Tensions?" *The New Republic* November 18, 10.

Jacobson, Gary C. 1997. *The Politics of Congressional Elections*, 4th ed. New York: Longman.

Johnson, James B., and Philip E. Secret. 1996. "Focus and Style Representational Roles of Congressional Black and Hispanic Caucus Members." *Journal of Black Studies* 26:245–73.

Jones, Mack H. 1985. "The Voting Rights Act as an Intervention Strategy for Social Change: Symbolism or Substance?" In *The Voting Rights Act: Consequences and Implications*, ed. Lorn S. Foster. Westport, CT: Praeger.

Katz, Jonathan N., and Brian R. Sala. 1996. "Careerism, Committee Assignments, and the Electoral Connection." *American Political Science Review* 90:21–33.

Keech, William R. 1986. "Thinking about the Length and Renewability of Electoral Terms." In *Electoral Laws and Their Political Consequences*, ed. Bernard Grofman and Arend Lijphart. New York: Agathon Press.

King, Gary. 1989a. "Representation through Legislative Redistricting: A Stochastic Model." *American Journal of Political Science* 33:787–824.

King, Gary. 1989b. *Unifying Political Methodology: The Likelihood Theory of Statistical Inference*. Cambridge: Cambridge University Press.

Kousser, J. Morgan. 1995. "*Shaw* v. *Reno* and the Real World of Redistricting and Representation." California Institute of Technology Working Paper #915.

Kymlicka, Will. 1995. *Multicultural Citizenship: A Liberal Theory of Minority Rights*. New York: Oxford University Press.

Lardeyret, Guy. 1991. "The Problem with PR." *Journal of Democracy* 2:30–35.

Levy, Arthur B., and Susan Stoudinger. 1976. "Sources of Voting Cues for the Congressional Black Caucus." *Journal of Black Studies* 7:29–45.

Levy, Arthur B., and Susan Stoudinger. 1978. "The Black Caucus in the 92nd Congress: Gauging Its Success." *Phylon* 38:322–32.

Lijphart, Arend. 1986. "Proportionality by Non–PR Methods: Ethnic Representation in Belgium, Cyprus, Lebanon, New Zealand, West Germany, and Zimbabwe." In *Electoral Laws and Their Political Consequences*, ed. Bernard Grofman and Arend Lijphart. New York: Agathon Press.

Loomis, Burdett A. 1981. "Congressional Caucuses and the Politics of Representation." In *Congress Reconsidered*, ed. Lawrence C. Dodd and Bruce I. Oppenheimer. Washington, DC: CQ Press.

Lublin, David Ian. 1997. *The Paradox of Representation: Racial Gerrymander and Minority Interests in Congress*. Princeton, NJ: Princeton University Press.

Lublin, David Ian, and Katherine Tate. 1992. "Black Officeseeking and Voter Turnout in Mayoral Elections." Presented at the annual meeting of the American Political Science Association, Chicago.

MacKinnon, Catherine A. 1987. *Feminism Unmodified: Discourses on Life and Law.* Cambridge: Harvard University Press.

Mansbridge, Jane. 1996. "In Defense of Descriptive Representation." Presented at the annual meeting of the American Political Science Association, San Francisco.

Matland, Richard E., and Donley T. Studlar. 1996. "The Contagion of Women Candidates in Single–Member District and Proportional Representation Electoral Systems: Canada and Norway." *Journal of Politics* 58:707–33.

Mayer, Kenneth R., and John M. Wood. 1995. "The Impact of Public Financing on Electoral Competitiveness: Evidence from Wisconsin, 1964–1990." *Legislative Studies Quarterly* 20:69–88.

McClain, Paula D., and John A. Garcia. 1993. "Expanding Disciplinary Boundaries: Black, Latino, and Racial Minority Groups in Political Science." In *Political Science: The State of the Discipline II*, ed. Ada W. Finifter. Washington, DC: American Political Science Association.

Menifield, Charles E. 1996. "Caucuses as Sources of Cues: A Look at the Black, Women's, and Hispanic Caucuses." Presented at the annual meeting of the Midwest Political Science Association, Chicago.

Merrill, Samuel III. 1981. "Strategic Decisions Under One-Stage Multi-Candidate Voting Systems. *Public Choice* 36:115–34.

Miller, Warren E., and Donald E. Stokes. 1963. "Constituency Influence in Congress." *American Political Science Review* 57:45–56.

Moncrief, Gary F., and Joel A. Thompson. 1992. "Electoral Structure and State Legislative Representation: A Research Note." *Journal of Politics* 54:246–56.

Monroe, Burt L. 1995. "Fully Proportional Representation." *American Political Science Review* 89:925–40.

Morrill, Richard L. 1996. "Territory, Community, and Collective Representation." *Social Science Quarterly* 77:3–5.

NAACP. 1994. "Report of the NAACP Legal Defense and Educational Fund: The Effect of Section 2 of the Voting Rights Act on the 1994 Congressional Elections." Mimeo, November 30.

Niemi, Richard G., and Alan I. Abramowitz. 1994. "Partisan Redistricting and the 1992 Congressional Elections." *Journal of Politics* 56:811–17.

Niemi, Richard G., and Laura R. Winsky. 1992. "The Persistence of Partisan Redistricting Effects in Congressional Elections in the 1970s and 1980s." *Journal of Politics* 54:565–72.

Niemi, Richard G., Bernard Grofman, Carl Carlucci, and Thomas Hofeller. 1990. "Measuring Compactness and the Role of Compactness Standard in a Test for Partisan and Racial Gerrymandering." *Journal of Politics* 52:1155–81.

Overby, L. Marvin and Kenneth M. Cosgrove. 1996. "Unintended Consequences? Racial Redistricting and the Representation of Minority Interests." *Journal of Politics* 58:540–50.

Patterson, Beeman C. 1983. "The Three R's Revisited: Redistricting, Race, and Representation in North Carolina." *Phylon* 44:232–43.

Peterson, Paul E. 1995. "A Politically Correct Solution to Racial Classification." In *Classifying by Race*, ed. Paul E. Peterson. Princeton, NJ: Princeton University Press.

Phillips, Anne. 1995. *The Politics of Presence*. New York: Clarendon Press/Oxford University Press.

Pinderhughes, Diane M. 1987. *Race and Ethnicity in Chicago Politics*. Urbana: University of Illinois Press.

Pinney, Neil, and George Serra. 1995. "The Congressional Black Caucus: Group Agreement and Voting Influences." Presented at the annual meeting of the American Political Science Association, Chicago.

Pitkin, Hanna F. 1967. *The Concept of Representation*. Berkeley: University of California Press.

Poole, Keith, and Howard Rosenthal. 1996. *Congress: A Political–Economic History of Roll-Call Voting*. New York: Oxford University Press.

Rabinovitz, Francine F., and Edward K. Hamilton. 1980. "Alternative Electoral Structures and Responsiveness to Minorities." *National Civic Review* 69:371–401.

Rawls, John. 1971. *A Theory of Justice*. Cambridge, MA: Belknap/Harvard University Press.

Reynolds, Andrew. 1995. "Constitutional Engineering in Southern Africa." *Journal of Democracy* 6:86–99.

Riedwyl, Hans, and Jürg Steiner. 1995. "What is Proportionality Anyhow?" *Comparative Politics* 28:357–69.

Riker, William H. 1982. *Liberalism Against Populism: A Confrontation Between the Theory of Democracy and the Theory of Social Choice*. San Francisco: W.H. Freeman.

Rule, Wilma. 1994. "Women's Underrepresentation and Electoral Systems." *PS: Political Science & Politics* 27:689–92.

Rule, Wilma, and Joseph F. Zimmerman, eds. 1994. *Electoral Systems in Comparative Perspective: Their Impact on Women and Minorities*. Westport, CT: Greenwood Press.

Sawyer, Jack, and Duncan MacRae, Jr. 1962. "Game Theory and Cumulative Voting in Illinois:1902–1954." *American Political Science Review* 56:936–46.

Sapiro, Virginia, and Joe Soss. Forthcoming. "Spectacular Politics, Dramatic Interpretations: Multiple Meanings in the Thomas/Hill Hearings." *Political Communication*.

Sartori, Giovanni. 1968. "Political Development and Political Engineering." In *Public Policy*, ed. John D. Montgomery and Albert O. Hirschman. New York: Cambridge University Press.

Sauer, C.O. 1918. "Geography and the Gerrymander." *American Political Science Review* 12:403–26.

Senate. 1982. Voting Rights Act Extension, Report of the Subcommittee on the Constitution of the Committee on the Judiciary. Senate report 97–417, 97 Congress, 2d session. Washington, DC: Government Printing Office.

Shastri, Amita. 1991. "Electoral Competition and Minority Alienation in a Plurality System: Sri Lanka 1947–77." *Electoral Studies* 10:326–47.

Shugart, Matthew, and John Carey. 1992. *Presidents and Assemblies: Constitutional Design and Electoral Dynamics*. New York: Cambridge University Press.

Singh, Robert. 1998. *The Congressional Black Caucus: Racial Politics in the U.S. Congress.* Thousand Oaks, CA: Sage Publications.

Smith, Robert C. 1990. "Recent Elections and Black Politics: The Maturation or Death of Black Politics?" *PS: Political Science and Politics* 23:160–62.

Squire, Peverill. 1995. "The Partisan Consequences of Congressional Redistricting." *American Politics Quarterly* 23:229–40.

Streich, Gregory W. 1997. *After the Celebration: Theories of Community and Practice of Interracial Dialogue.* Unpublished Ph.D. dissertation. University of Wisconsin, Madison.

Swain, Carol M. 1993. *Black Faces, Black Interests: The Representation of African Americans in Congress.* Cambridge, MA: Harvard University Press.

Swain, Carol M. 1995. "The Future of Black Representation." *American Prospect* Fall:78–83.

Swift, Elaine K. 1996. *The Making of an American Senate: Reconstitutive Change in Congress, 1787–1841.* Ann Arbor: University of Michigan Press.

Taylor, Charles. 1992. *Multiculturalism and the 'Politics of Recognition.'* Princeton, NJ: Princeton University Press.

Thernstrom, Abigail. 1987. *Whose Votes Count? Affirmative Action and Minority Voting Rights.* Cambridge, MA: Harvard University Press.

Thernstrom, Stephan, and Abigail Thernstrom. 1997. *America in Black and White: One Nation, Indivisible: Race in Modern America.* New York: Simon and Schuster.

Van Biema, David. 1994. "One Person, Seven Votes." *Time* 143:17 (April 25):42–43.

Vanderleeuw, James M., and Glenn U. Utter. 1993. "Voter Roll-Off and the Electoral Context: A Test of Two Theses." *Social Science Quarterly* 74:664–73.

Wahlke, John, Heinz Eulau, William Buchanan, and Leroy C. Ferguson. 1962. *The Legislative System.* New York: John Wiley.

Walton, F. Carl. 1995. "The Congressional Black Caucus and Its Liberal Ideology: A Search for Explanation." Presented at the annual meeting of the American Political Science Association, Chicago.

Weaver, Leon. 1986. "The Rise, Decline, and Resurrection of Proportional Representation in Local Governments in the United States." In *Electoral Laws and Their Political Consequences*, ed. Bernard Grofman and Arend Lijphart. New York: Agathon Press.

Weber, Ronald E. 1995. "The Unanticipated Consequences of Race-Based Districting: The Impact on Electoral Competition and Voter Participation." Presented at the annual meeting of the Midwest Political Science Association, Chicago.

Welch, Susan. 1990. "The Impact of At-Large Elections on the Representation of Blacks and Hispanics." *Journal of Politics* 52:1050–76.

Whitby, Kenny J. 1997. *The Color of Representation: Congressional Behavior and Black Interests.* Ann Arbor: University of Michigan Press.

Young, Iris M. 1993. "Justice and Communicative Democracy." In *Radical Philosophy: Tradition, Counter-Tradition, Politics*, ed. Roger S. Gotlieb. Philadelphia: Temple University Press.

Zimmerman, Joseph F. 1994. "Alternative Voting Systems for Representative Democracy." *PS: Political Science & Politics* 27:674–76.

The Study of Japan's Medium-Sized District System

Sadafumi Kawato

This essay deals with the study of Japan's electoral institution called *Chû Senkyoku Sei* (the medium-sized district system, MDS) and the political reform to replace MDS with a new electoral system. MDS was first adopted for the House of Representatives election in 1925 and was used in all subsequent elections but 1946. It was finally replaced in 1994 with a dual system of single-member districts (SMD) and proportional representation districts (PR). MDS had important consequences for the representation of parties and interests in the Diet. Among other things, during most of the postwar period under MDS the Liberal Democratic Party (LDP) had been the dominant party. At the same time, the party was characterized by its factionalized structure. MDS has been extensively studied in Japan. Foreign researchers also find Japan's electoral institution to be key to understanding the Japanese political process; they bring new perspectives to the study.

Since MDS is defined as a system with medium-sized district magnitude, it implies the existence of other systems with large and small district magnitude. In the classification scheme used in Japan, MDS refers to the system with a district magnitude of three to five, while the "small" district system (SDS) has the district magnitude of one, and the "large" district system (LDS) has a district magnitude of six or more. This classificatory scheme goes back to the enactment of the first electoral law for the House of Representatives in 1889. Since then, Japan has adopted two SDSs, two MDSs, and two LDSs (see table 1). MDS was adopted in 1925 after SDS and LDS were tried and proved unfit to Japan's political conditions. When Japan found MDS no better some seventy years later, it adopted the dual SMD-PR system.

Under MDS, winners were determined by the order of finish in each district. For example, in a district where four members were elected, the top four finishers were given seats. Voters cast a single vote for a candidate regardless of the number of seats allotted to the district. "Votes are not transferable to other candidates of the same party in the event that a voter's first choice has already made it past the post, as is the case in the single transferable-vote systems in

Ireland and Finland" (Ramseyer and Rosenbluth 1993, 21). Thus, it is called a single nontransferable vote (SNTV).

Interestingly, foreign researchers prefer to call the postwar pre-1994 system SNTV, and they are sometimes careful in not using the term MDS. For example, Ramseyer and Rosenbluth (1993) only depict it as having two- to six-member districts; thus translators of the Japanese edition had to insert the term *Chû Senkyoku Sei*. Specialists sometimes note that MDS is a unique Japanese term, which is understood to be equivalent to SNTV in the Western literature (Miyake 1989). As table 1 shows, MDS is not identical with SNTV, for SNTV was adopted along with all three types of electoral systems.

TABLE 1
Japanese Electoral Systems

Law	Name of Electoral System	District Magnitude (DM)	Mean (DM)	Electoral Formula	Number of Ballots
1889	Small district system	1 to 2	1.17	Plurality	1 to 2
1900	Large district system	3 to 12 (prefectures); 1 to 11 (cities and islands)	6.58; 1.33	SNTV	1
1919	Small district system	1 to 3	1.24	SNTV	1
1925	Medium district system	3 to 5	3.82	SNTV	1
1945	Large district system	4 to 14	8.79	Limited Vote	2 to 3
1947	Medium district system	Typically 3 to 5 (1, 2, 6)	3.98	SNTV	1
1994	SMD-PR dual system	1 (SMD); 7 to 33 (PR)	1; 18.18	Plurality; d'Hondt	2 (each for SMD and PR)

In the subsequent sections, I show how different research efforts contributed to unveiling the working of MDS. The first section considers the origins of MDS and SNTV. The second section reviews the literature on the working of MDS. The third section deals with the political reform process and the effects of the new electoral system as topics of the growing literature. Throughout this essay, I hope to show that studying MDS and studying SNTV are two different approaches to (presumably) the same electoral system (for convenience, I call them MDS research and SNTV research, respectively). The former is concerned with differences among MDS, SDS, and LDS as well as other accompanying institutional features of MDS. SNTV itself rarely receives attention because it is a rather general feature of Japanese electoral systems. Parties were nurtured in SNTV with different district magnitudes. Thus, MDS research tends to treat party as the dependent variable and focuses on how MDS has affected candidates and parties. Researchers do not believe in party's ability to effectively control and coordinate candidates and incumbent politicians. A party is thought to be nothing but a coalition of factions or, in the extreme case, simply an aggregate of like-minded incumbent members.

SNTV research, on the other hand, gives most attention to the postwar, pre-1994 electoral system. It contrasts SNTV with other popular electoral systems such as majoritarian and PR systems. Building upon the rational choice approach, researchers regard SNTV as a rule of the game, which imposes constraints on self-interested political actors. Incentives and strategies of actors are analyzed, and outcomes are explained as an equilibrium. Some employ rigorous formal models, others present reinterpretations of Japanese political process with the rational choice flavor. Researchers are interested in how parties, factions, and candidates managed to overcome the difficulties posed by SNTV. Other features of the Japanese electoral system are rarely given attention. SNTV research tends to evaluate parties' ability highly, claiming that parties are successful in coping with the problems.

The Origins of MDS-SNTV

If one is interested in MDS, its origins can be found in the legislative processes of the electoral laws of 1925 and 1947. But if one is concerned with SNTV, it can be traced back to the 1900 electoral law. Fortunately, the Minutes of the Diet and relevant committees are readily available from their establishment in 1890, as are memoirs of politicians, official documents, and reports prepared by bureaucrats. I find Shûgiin [House of Representative] and Sangiin [House of Councillors] (1961, 1990) and Jichishô Senkyobu (1990) useful.

In prewar Japan, the House of Representatives (Lower House) was the sole popularly elected part, which struggled for government control against the nonelected part, or the oligarchic bureaucrats (Miyazaki 1984). Parties made their way to the party-based cabinet era of the 1920s by extending suffrage and consolidating their support base in the electorate (Kawato 1992). Parties and the oligarchs were well aware that the choice of an electoral institution would greatly affect their fortunes. An electoral system was enacted through a legislative process in which a law must be approved by the Privy Council and passed by the Lower House and the House of Peers. The oligarchs dominated the Privy Council and the House of Peers. Thus, the choice of electoral institutions involved the social choice problem among groups of people with conflicting goals. One hypothesis on the choice of institutions posits that participants seek alternatives that favor their desired policies, or further their own electoral ends (Bawn 1993; Kohno 1997a). It is interesting to explore whether this hypothesis is substantiated in the institutional choice in Japan.

The Adoption of LDS-SNTV

Ramseyer and Rosenbluth (1995) succinctly explain why the Meiji oligarchs adopted LDS-SNTV in 1900. The initial SDS of 1889 was advantageous to large parties that continuously resisted the oligarchs' fiscal policies. Citing Soma (1986), they argue that Prime Minister Yamagata devised an electoral system to keep parties as weak and fractious as possible. The idea was to force any party seeking to win or maintain a legislative majority to field multiple candidates in most districts. They claim Yamagata was able enough to piece together a barely sufficient alliance through promises and cash within the anti-Oligarch Diet. This is a brilliant argument on how the Meiji oligarchs were able to thwart the development of parties, although whether Yamagata really intended so is controversial. Ito (1996) reviews their book and sharply criticizes it. Pointing to the well-known fact that it was not Yamagata but Ito who initially proposed LDS-SNTV, he notes that their argument was mere conjecture. Ito (1996) argues that the truth is that Yamagata successfully cooperated with the Kensei Party leader Hoshi to pass the revised bill (see also Ito 1991).

SNTV researchers assume that the institution designers and parties were fully aware of the difficulties SNTV would pose for large parties. Thus, it becomes a puzzle why parties agreed to install such an antiparty electoral system. When the multifaceted nature of the problem is considered, it may not be so difficult to understand. The literature is rich with analysis of the legislative process and the intentions and preferences of Ito, Yamagata, and major party leaders (Oka 1958; Sakagami 1990; Ito 1991; Mitani 1995; Soma 1986; Tomita 1979; Matsuo 1989; Banno 1971). The 1900 law had four major features: (1) the installation of city independent districts; (2) relaxing the suffrage requirements to be more favorable to city merchants and industrialists; (3) the creation of large prefectural districts; and (4) the adoption of SNTV. Ramseyer and Rosenbluth treat (3) and (4) as a single feature. But they are separable and separate. The existing parties representing rural landowners were initially against (1) and (2), but the Kensei Party leader Hoshi persuaded the party to seek to extend support from the urban districts as well (Banno 1971). As to (3), one might think large parties did not desire LDS because the existing SDS was more favorable to them.

In fact, SDS was not popular among party candidates. Small district size encouraged corrupt campaign practices that cost the family fortune of candidates. There were within-party quarrels over candidacy in many districts composed of multiple counties, similar to those seen in the mid-nineteenth-century U.S. congressional districts (Banno and Ito 1965; Kernell 1977). Thus, parties had proposed revisions to install LDS with bloc vote during the 1890s (Shûgiin and Sangiin 1961). As to (4), secretary of the House of Representatives Hayashida proposed LDS with SNTV in 1893 as a system to promote minority representation, and he drafted the LDS-SNTV bill in 1898 as secretary general upon Prime Minister Ito's direction (Sakagami 1990; Mitani 1995). Then why did Ito choose LDS-SNTV in light of the fact that he had planned to form a party and in 1900 became the president of the Seiyûkai, the largest party in the Diet? Mitani (1995) argues that by enlarging the district size and making the election of national notables easier than that of local notables Ito wanted to strengthen the foundations of parties. In contrast with Ito, Yamagata was a stubborn antiparty oligarch. He feared that the extension of suffrage entailed in Ito's bill was so close to universal suffrage that it would soon lead to party-based cabinets (Ito 1991). Therefore, by manipulating the House of Peers, he successfully set the suffrage requirements as high as possible. Thus the choice of LDS-SNTV was much more complex than Ramseyer and Rosenbluth argued. But it clearly reflected the preferences of the relevant actors.

In response to the 1900 electoral law, parties devised a strategy of dividing a large prefectural district into small "private districts" and letting each branch nominate a candidate (Kawato 1992). This strategy is well known as *jiban-wari* (dividing the support base). Candidates cultivated their *jiban,* and the role of parties in the campaign became minimal. Competition under LDS was no different from that under SDS. SNTV did not necessarily intensify competition among candidates of the same party. Rather, because they shared the same local interests, they belonged to the same faction in the party. Thus, prewar factions were based on the regional connections (Sato and Matsuzaki 1986). The overall relationship between votes and seats was close to that of the PR system (Kawato 1997).

The Adoption of MDS-SNTV in 1925 and 1947

The electoral law of 1925 introduced MDS along with universal manhood suffrage as well as the ban on door-to-door canvassing and other campaign restrictions. In the MDS research tradition, each of the three features is analyzed in full detail. Matsuo (1989) is mainly concerned with universal suffrage, and Soma (1986) focuses on the restrictive nature of the law. The literature shows that the adoption of MDS was a compromise decision of the three coalition parties. They agreed to replace the existing SDS with MDS because it would give each candidate of the coalition parties a reasonable chance to win seats in a district (see also Fukui 1988; Furuya 1994; Masumi 1979).

Parties dreaded the first election under the new electoral system not because it was MDS but because it increased the number of eligible voters from 3 million to 12 million. The electoral law promoted candidate-centered campaigns, and MDS was in principle favorable to small parties. Nevertheless, the two-party system was consolidated because the control of the cabinet was at stake in elections (Awaya 1988). Candidates of the small parties fared badly compared to those of the two major parties.

The first postwar election in 1946 was held under extraordinary circumstances eight months after Japan's defeat in World War II. The new electoral law with LDS and universal suffrage was hastily passed by the Diet in the fall of 1945. The commonly accepted view is that there was no intervention from the General Headquarters of the Allied Occupation Forces (GHQ) (Masumi 1983; Soma 1986; Fukunaga 1986).[1] Home Ministry bureaucrats conceived LDS as a more appropriate system than MDS in order to undermine the support basis of the existing parties and to promote election of popularly supported national notables and newcomers suitable for the new situations. The use of large prefectural districts was a means to accommodate the massive movement of the population caused by the war damages. A question that can be raised here is why PR was not installed instead of LDS with the limited vote. The Home Ministry rejected it on the grounds that the ministry was not prepared for it, parties were still underdeveloped, and the electorate's level of political sophistication was low (Fukunaga 1986; Jichi Daigakkôu 1961). Kohno (1997a) analyzes how parties' preferences for electoral systems affected the final outcome. He stresses that the reaction of the parties to the LDS bill was consistent with their electoral strengths and incentives, but fails to note that the initiative was not in their hands.

In the 1946 general election under LDS, more than 2,700 candidates with more than 250 party labels jumped in the race. Newcomers and women fared well in the election. About 80 percent of the winners were newly elected. Of the 79 women candidates, 39 won seats. No party commanded a majority. LDS promoted a multiparty system. These results invited criticism against LDS that voters did not cast their second and third votes seriously (Jichi Daigakkôu 1961). The Yoshida cabinet and conservative parties agreed to reinstall MDS-SNTV. They did not let the Home Ministry bureaucrats take initiative. This time, a GHQ official objected to the proposal of Home Minister Uehara. Then Yoshida brought this to GHQ commander Douglas MacArthur and obtained his permission. MDS was proposed as a revision to the government bill by the Liberal Party and passed (Furuya 1994; Soma 1986; Fukunaga 1986). Kohno (1997a) is correct in pointing out that the choice of electoral system involved high stakes for parties, and they chose the one that would further their own interests. After all, MDS was an acceptable choice for all parties, though it may not be the best one.

The Working of MDS-SNTV

The pre-1994 MDS can be described as a simple extension of the Anglo-American single-member district system, except that the district magnitude was not fixed at one but ranged from two to six. Voters cast a single ballot and the top M vote-getters win seats, where M is district magnitude. Since 511 members of the House of Representatives were elected from 129 constituencies, any party seeking to win a majority of 256 seats and thus take power was forced to run two or more candidates in every district. The result—candidates of the same party running against each other—was a unique consequence of MDS.

Under MDS, partisan competition and competition among candidates took place at the same time. Broadly, two major questions have been asked. First, how did individual candidates compete under MDS? Second, what was the role of parties in elections? SNTV research offers new perspectives to analyze the pre-1994 system.

Competition among Candidates

MDS researchers stress that elections were extremely competitive in Japan. Under MDS, each candidate's victory or defeat was crucially influenced by the pattern of competition within a district (Abe, Shindo, and Kawato 1994). The percentage of votes a candidate could expect to get depended largely on the district magnitude and the number of candidates in a district (Kawato 1987; Nishihira 1972). A sufficient vote percentage for winning a seat in an M-member district is $(100 / [M + 1])$ percent, while Ishikawa (1978) shows that the actual mean vote percentage of the Mth finishers (i.e., winners with the fewest votes) was several percent below that. He also shows that 40 to 50 percent of the districts were marginal in the sense that the difference in votes between the lowest-ranking winner and the highest-ranking loser was less than 1 percent of the total electorate. Incumbents who had finished at the top in a district sometimes lost in the next election, and candidates who had placed highest among the losers often won in their subsequent election effort (Curtis 1992).[2] The proportion of incumbents reelected was 80 percent or so. In a relative sense, reelection was not something one could easily get under MDS (Kawato 1992; Reed 1994).

Although the number of candidates in a district varied greatly, researchers have long known that there were serious candidates and fringe candidates (Stockwin 1982). If we concentrate on serious candidates, 92 percent of them were in contests where $M + 1$ to $M + 3$ serious candidates competed for M seats (Kawato 1987). Reed (1991) goes one step further by extending Duverger's (1954) law to MDS and proposing an $M + 1$ rule, which states that Japanese MDS tended to produce competition among $M + 1$ candidates. Cox (1994) formally proves this as an equilibrium of a contest in which voters undertake strategic voting to make the most of their votes.

The fact that there were multiple candidates from the same party in most districts had important implications. First, MDS researchers observed that campaigns were centered upon individual candidates rather than the party. Candidates could not rely on the party to win organizationally or policy-wise. Thus, they had to secure their seats by cultivating personal votes. *Kôenkai,* or personal support organizations maintained by candidates and elected politicians, developed from around the general election of 1958 and have become a permanent part of campaign tactics (Abe, Shindo, and Kawato 1994). In so doing, politicians established a direct link with tens of thousands of individual voters (Masumi 1969; Curtis 1971; Ishikawa and Hirose 1989). Kôenkai also attended to and helped with the demands of the locality for budgetary assistance for new facilities, road repairs, and other construction (Hirose 1989a). Maintaining such a huge human organization naturally cost a huge amount of money (Hirose 1989b; Iwai 1990; Sone and Kanazashi 1989). Thus, MDS promoted money politics.

Second, researchers see the campaign regulations introduced together with MDS in 1925 as having important consequences (Sakagami 1990). The electoral law stipulated that a person who wants to run for election should report his candidacy and that election campaign activities are only permitted for a candidate and his election office staff. Parties were allowed to engage in campaigns only by issuing letters of recommendation and making election speeches. Postwar liberalization of campaigns did not last long. Several 1952 electoral law revisions introduced restrictions on political activities of parties during the campaign period. Those political activities of parties that were hardly distinguishable from campaign activities were banned. A limited range of those activities was permitted to the "confirmed parties" with twenty-five candidates or more in the general election. Thus, the electoral law minimized the role of parties in the campaign (Kyôgoku 1969). These restrictions have worked to reinforce candidate-centered campaigns. Various campaign restrictions on candidates were instrumental in standardizing and equalizing the campaign activities and thus making them almost identical among candidates. Kôenkai has been construed as a free political activity conducted before the official campaign period. Thus it has flourished.

Third, researchers claim that electoral competition under MDS encouraged the development of factions within the LDP (Watanabe 1958; Kitaoka 1985). The rivalries among LDP candidates within the same districts strengthened the ties of each to different power-holders within the party. Intense campaign conflict enhanced the need to mobilize electoral support through fund-raising, local pork-barreling, and high-profile activity on the national level. By joining a faction, one can obtain financial help, promises of pork, and appointment to cherished posts in the cabinet, party, and parliament. Thus, Sato and Matsuzaki (1986) describe the LDP as having a loose organizational structure whose basic constituent elements are factions and kôenkai.

Consequences for Parties

Researchers ask how MDS affected the structure of the LDP. As Curtis (1988) aptly describes, the widely embraced model of modern party organization in Japan is the mass membership party with clearly defined programs and policy goals. What actually formed was a decentralized, politician-based organization with incessant factional strife. Some see this as reflecting the backwardness of Japan's political culture. Watanuki (1997) explains that Japan has skipped the stage of mass and class parties. Sato and Matsuzaki (1986) praise the LDP as a modernized party with decentralized and loose organizational characteristics that has adjusted itself to the needs of constituent factions by adopting seniority rule and an interfactional balancing rule (see also Kawato 1996; Epstein, Brady, Kawato, and O'Halloran 1997; Kohno 1997a). The foremost purpose of forming a faction was to secure the members' vote for the LDP presidential election. MDS contributed to factionalism by motivating rival members from the same districts to join different factions (Kitaoka 1985; Cox and Rosenbluth 1993). The LDP's internal political process has been described as factional politics; it is a game of coalition building for the LDP presidency with cabinet posts allocated among factions as its payoff (Leiserson 1968; Kawato 1996; Ishikawa and Hirose 1989).

The number of factions was eight at the first presidential election in 1956, and it gradually decreased and stabilized at five. It used to be said that the optimal size for a faction was between thirty and fifty members, for a faction with fewer than thirty members was too small to be effective in securing cherished posts, but one larger than fifty exceeded the fund-raising capability of a faction leader (Abe, Shindo, and Kawato 1994). But the 1975 revision of Political Fund Regulation Law changed the role of factions in fund-raising. After that, instead of gathering and distributing money to members, faction leaders let them raise money by endorsing them to contributors (Sato and Matsuzaki 1986; Iwai 1990). Thus, the upper limit to the size of a faction disappeared.

Some researchers question how MDS affected the factional structure and the party system—specifically, how MDS affected the number of factions in the LDP and the number of parties. Both questions are not framed well because they essentially assume some indirect relationship. Ishikawa (1981) was the first to suggest that the optimal number of parties in MDS is the largest $M + 1$, or six, because five-member districts would allow for six-party competition. He also suggested that the optimal number of LDP factions is the largest $M - 1$, or four, because at least one seat would go to the opposition parties. Kohno (1997a) tried to extend Reed's $M + 1$ rule to the evolution of Japanese party system, saying that the maximum number of parties that can exist was six. He claims that the maximum number of LDP factions that could have existed was five because the LDP should not field more than M candidates. Anyway, both predictions/explanations are not and cannot be distant from the reality under the pre-1994 MDS: five parties and five factions within the LDP.

Parties did not loom large in the minds of Japanese electorate. Voters have been asked in surveys whether they vote on the basis of party or on the basis of an individual candidate. Until 1967, citizens voting on the basis of candidate outnumbered those voting on the basis of political party. This pattern was reversed in the 1969 election, but since then, party orientations have not intensified, and in recent elections they have been only slightly stronger, with an exception in 1993 when candidate orientations were stronger (Miyake 1989, 1999).

Proportionality of Electoral Results

MDS creates a unique relationship between the share of the votes a party receives and the number of parliamentary seats it wins. In general, the discrepancy between votes and seats is small in PR systems and large in the majoritarian systems; Japan's MDS falls between the two. Various indexes of proportionality measure the difference between vote shares and seat shares. An index of proportionality in Japan is similar to those of the less proportional PR systems but also to those of the more proportional non-PR systems. In this respect, it indeed behaves like a semiproportional system (Lijphart, Pinter, and Sone 1986). However, Nishihira (1981) claims that this characterization is wrong, because the seat shares are not proportional to the vote shares at all. He points to the fact that the LDP always enjoyed a sizable seat bonus (the percentage of seats won minus the percentage of votes won), while the JSP fared less well in this term, and other parties could not secure seat shares comparable to the vote shares. Thus, MDS constantly brought about results advantageous to the largest LDP. When the seat bonus for any party is zero, Gallagher's (1991) index of disproportionality will be zero too. If one calls this pure-proportionality, then seat bonus is a measure to indicate the divergence from the pure-proportionality. If we call electoral systems that give large parties seat bonuses *sub-pure-*

proportional, and systems that give small parties seat bonuses *super-pure-proportional*, MDS is definitely the former.

In an analysis of Japan's pre-1994 SNTV, Lijphart et al. (1986) found that it poses difficult problems for large parties (see also Lee 1992; Cox 1997; Cox and Niou 1994; Cox and Rosenbluth 1994, 1996). The larger parties have to solve two serious problems. That is, in order to maximize the number of seats for a given share of votes in a district, a party must field an optimal number of candidates and equalize the votes among its candidates. If it fails to do so, it would get fewer seats and benefit other parties. Using the electoral data in the 1980 election, Lijphart et al. (1986) showed that the LDP committed three kinds of strategic errors (overnomination, undernomination, and vote equalization error), which cost the party seats. They question the seeming paradox that SNTV presents handicaps for the LDP while the party still earns some seat bonus. They conclude that the seat bonus (and thus the overrepresentation of the largest party under SNTV) is mainly due to the low district magnitude.

Cox (1991) and Lee (1992) have formally shown that the maximum number of seats a party can win under SNTV in a district is the number of seats it could have won if the d'Hondt formula of PR were used instead of SNTV. Thus with the district magnitude held constant, large parties fare worse under SNTV than they would under d'Hondt. Taagepera and Shugart (1989) and Christensen and Johnson (1995) claim that SNTV is more proportional (superproportional) than d'Hondt. To avoid confusion, let me call it super-d'Hondt proportional. Thus Lijphart (1994) categorized the postwar, pre-1994 SNTV into the middle PR category, more proportional than d'Hondt but less proportional than LR-Hare. He argues it is sufficiently similar to PR that it can be included in the comparative analyses of all PR systems.

That SNTV is theoretically super-d'Hondt does not mean it is actually so. Thus Cox and Niou (1994) undertook an empirical analysis to find how often LDP committed strategic errors and found the LDP's error rate declined over time. However, they formulated the problem by stating that they "investigate the apparent discrepancy between theoretical expectation—that SNTV hurt large parties—and empirical fact—that the large parties regularly do well." They seem to equate d'Hondt proportionality with pure-proportionality and thus speculate that super-d'Hondt proportionality and sub-pure-proportionality are not compatible. They seem to conclude that the super-d'Hondt proportionality does not materialize because the structural difficulties posed by SNTV for large parties are more than counterbalanced by structural difficulties of a slightly different kind faced by small parties. They pointed to the inefficient fractionalization of opposition parties and the inherent advantage of the LDP as a governing party.

Because d'Hondt is known as the least pure-proportional among PR formulas (Lijphart 1994), that SNTV is super-d'Hondt does not mean it is any closer to pure-proportionality. Indeed, Taagepera and Shugart (1989) reported simulated effects of district magnitude on deviation from pure-proportionality (Loosemore-Hanby index) under the d'Hondt formula. The average deviation from pure-proportionality for district magnitude of three to five is 17.6 percent, while the actual deviation from pure-proportionality for the 1983 election in Japan (SNTV) is 6.9 percent. Evidently, SNTV is super-d'Hondt because it produced smaller deviation. But most of the deviation from pure-proportionality is caused by the seat bonus for the LDP. Thus, it is also sub-pure-proportional. SNTV is sub-pure-proportional and super-d'Hondt at the same time.

Christensen and Johnson (1995) also questioned where the LDP seat bonus comes from. By isolating and measuring the seat bonus components, they showed the LDP received most of its seat bonus from district magnitude and to a lesser degree from malapportionment. Moreover, in contrast with Cox and Niou's expectation, they showed the LDP made more errors than the opposition. Thus SNTV is super-d'Hondt theoretically as well as empirically.

All of the above arguments are confined to the postwar MDS. Thus, Kawato (1997) analyzes the prewar MDS from 1928 to 1937 where the Seiyûkai and the Minseitô competed as the two major parties. He shows that the error rates for both parties were not high compared with the postwar LDP, and that the electoral results were close to those under the d'Hondt formula. Thus, unlike the LDP, the two parties were not hurt by SNTV under the prewar MDS. The prewar MDS was not super-d'Hondt. He explains that each of the two parties benefited from other's errors, which lessened the disadvantage under SNTV; the existence of huge national swings between the two parties made the subtle nomination strategies unimportant and unnecessary. Kawato (1999a) undertakes a comprehensive analysis of MDS for the period 1928 through 1993, comparing the largest party's actual seat shares with estimated seat shares under the d'Hondt formula and under pure-proportionality. It shows MDS has always been super-d'Hondt proportional and sub-pure-proportional.

SNTV and Parties

The controversy over sub- or super-d'Hondt proportionality is closely related to how one understands one-party rule by the LDP. As Cox (1996) succinctly states, if SNTV is subproportional (favorable to large parties), then the use of this system in Japan may help explain the long tenure in power of the LDP. On this point, Miyake's (1989) view is representative of MDS researchers. He clearly states that MDS is neither a necessary nor a sufficient condition for one-party rule, because Japan experienced a two-party system, multiparty system, and predominant party system under MDS. But even though SNTV is super-d'Hondt, the LDP might have done best in unfavorable circumstances. Cox (1996) shows that the conservatives were more efficient than the opposition when they faced the task of winning the same number of seats but they were less efficient overall because they faced a harder mix as the largest party.

Ramseyer and Rosenbluth (1993) also address the problem that the LDP confronted under SNTV. They are more interested in how the LDP succeeded in coping with the problem than whether it ever succeeded or not. They claim the solution to the problem was that the LDP allowed its candidates access to government resources with which to compete for votes. According to them, to even out its votes the LDP used its control over government to build its candidates' personal support networks. That is, LDP politicians differentiated themselves from one another by specializing in particular types of constituency services and in so doing building and maintaining kôenkai to satisfy their own supporters. They also tended to choose different division memberships in the Policy Affairs Research Council so as to prevent needless competition from the same districts (see also McCubbins and Rosenbluth 1995; Inoguchi and Iwai 1987).

This is a coherent explanation of how the LDP rationally reached an equilibrium under SNTV. Several points are of interest here because of the sharp contrast with MDS research. First, it is one thing to claim d'Hondt and SNTV are equivalent, but another to posit that the LDP formulated their problems and tried to solve them. For most MDS researchers, the problems the large party faced under SNTV are more conceptual than real. A late colleague of mine pointed out in personal conversation that the proposition that d'Hondt and SNTV are equivalent is valid only when the party knows the election results in advance and has full control over nomination of candidates. Thus, this proposition is understood to simply mean that the LDP naturally falls short of d'Hondt results.

Second, for all practical purposes, it is impossible to predict the percentage of votes a party will earn. Without reliable estimates of votes, the LDP had no way of knowing ex ante whether they would commit errors of any kind. That is why 15 percent of incumbent LDP members lost reelection bids, and 64 percent of nonincumbent LDP candidates got elected during 1958 through 1990. It is often the case that the intraparty competition affected the overall electoral results in the district. At times battles between rival LDP candidates led to a division of the LDP electorate in the district such that neither got enough votes to win. At other times, such rivalries led to intense battles to get out the party faithful, and the resulting tide of LDP voters going to polls swamped the opposition.

Third, MDS researchers believe no secretaries-general or members of the electoral strategy committee of the LDP saw the problem as formulated this way. To be sure, they knew that overnominating candidates would hurt the LDP's chances for maximizing the seats. But they had no idea how they could equalize the votes among the LDP candidates. There is no evidence that the LDP tried to do that. Whether kôenkai contributed to vote equalization among LDP candidates has not been empirically tested, and the vote equalization errors did not decrease at all during the whole period of the LDP one-party rule (Kawato 1999a).

Fourth, the question boils down to how researchers understand the LDP's ability to control and coordinate candidates. Ramseyer and Rosenbluth essentially argue that it was the party that arranged the whole thing. But the same empirical facts (e.g., kôenkai, pork barrel politics, money politics) have already been explained in terms of candidates' needs for reelection. Thus their approach certainly enriches Japanese political research but stops short of yielding new empirical predictions.

Political Reform

Senkyo Seido Shingikai (the Eighth Election System Council) was convened in 1989 to consider fundamental reform of both the electoral system and the system of financing parties and elections. The council pointed to the defects of MDS as follows:

> Under the current medium-sized district system, any party seeking a majority and control of government must field multiple candidates in the same districts. For those candidates election becomes a personal strife rather than a partisan, issue-based competition. In such a candidate-centered election, the social climate in Japan promotes campaign and political activities that depend heavily on the personal relationship between candidates and voters, causing an increase in the campaign fund.
>
> Moreover, under this medium-sized district system, since the partisan balance has not changed and turnover of the party in power did not occur for many years, all the suspense goes out of politics and corruption sets in. (Senkyo Seido Shingikai 1990)

The council claimed that these problems could not be remedied through operations of the existing institution and proposed to replace MDS with a dual SMD-PR system to bring about issue-oriented, party-centered election. The council also proposed public financing of parties and severe restrictions on corporate contributions to individual politicians. Political reform was accomplished four years later by the non-LDP Hosokawa cabinet after two LDP cabinets failed. Various alternatives for electoral systems were proposed during the process. But the one finally adopted was strikingly close to the council's proposal.

The literature on the political reform process is growing (Narita 1996, 1997; Tanaka 1997; Uchida et al. 1994; Otake 1995; Kawato 2000). The election was held under the new system in 1996 and 2000. Researchers started to analyze how the electorate voted and what the emerging party system would be (Reed

1999; Kohno 1997b; Sato 1997; Kitaoka 1997; Suzuki et al. 1998; Suzuki 1999, 2000). I would like to discuss a few points that might be interesting to explore further. First, political reform is an institution design problem. Thus, one can ask questions similar to those raised about past electoral system changes. The proposal of a dual SMD-PR system was a departure from the traditional Japanese systems, and it involved a potential for party system change. As an SMD portion would favor large parties, no parties other than the LDP had incentives to adopt it. The LDP was naturally reluctant as the largest party under MDS. Thus, why and how the non-LDP coalition government pursued and accomplished political reform can be a major question. An analysis should examine electoral and other incentives of parties and individual politicians and the institutional contexts (see Kawato 2000). That the parties other than the LDP groped for survival once the reform was complete should also be taken into account.

A second major question is how the political reform package would affect elections and parties. The working of SMD-PR is obviously interesting. Given two separate votes, voters might cast them strategically. Duverger's law would work in SMD to bring about two-party competition, while PR favors multiparty competition. How the new system would affect features associated with MDS such as factionalism, pork barrel politics, kôenkai, and personalized election campaign style is also interesting. By analyzing how they would change under the new system and comparing the behavior of politicians under SMD-PR with that under MDS, we are in a better position to assess the effects of electoral systems on various characteristics of Japanese politics. Research on these topics would help further our understanding of the Japanese political-electoral process.

Third, political reform introduced several new institutions beside SMD-PR. Thus, one should be careful in assessing the political consequences of the electoral law. Revised political fund regulation law stipulated that politicians receiving contributions of ¥50,000 or more are required to report names of contributors. This has made transparent the flow of political money, and a comprehensive analysis of politics and money has been conducted (Sasaki et al. 1999; Kawato 1999b). A less noticed but important reform is the introduction of party-centered campaigns. Parties are now permitted to conduct election campaigns for their candidates. Moreover, publicly financed broadcasts of candidates' political views have been replaced with those of political platforms and introduction of candidates by parties. Thus, running as an independent has become the least attractive option. Public financing of parties also affects the behavior of parties. Some ¥30.9 billion is annually allocated to parties having five or more Diet members, or earning 2 percent or more of the vote in the most recent national elections, in proportion to their number of Diet members and the vote shares previously won. This was one major reason for the breakup of the New

Frontier Party in December 1997. While electoral necessity may push politicians to form a large opposition party, the provision gives a party of several Diet members a handsome subsidy. Thus members who have secured personal votes can make and break parties. On the other hand, the provision makes it difficult for small parties to submit a joint list for PR because the subsidy is given to a party, not to a group of parties. This might mean a large opposition party tends to be formed as an election comes closer, but also tends to break up after that unless it takes power or shows good prospects for power.

Conclusion

This essay has chosen three topics in the research on Japanese electoral systems and briefly reviewed them. The importance of electoral institutions in understanding the Japanese political process is widely acknowledged. I showed how two approaches to the same institution are different in their understanding of the nature of parties and individual politicians. MDS research is better equipped with detailed knowledge of various aspects of electoral systems. A lesson one can learn from MDS research may be that how politicians understand the electoral system definitely affects the working of the system. SNTV research introduced new perspectives into the electoral research in Japan. It presented theoretically important insights into Japan's electoral systems and guided recent innovative research. Perhaps the greatest contribution is that it has made the study of Japan accessible to a broader audience in the political science community. Both approaches have contributed to enriching Japanese electoral research.

NOTES

I would like to thank Peverill Squire, Gary W. Cox, Steven W. Reed, Ofer Feldman, Junko Kato, Motoshi Suzuki, Masaru Kohno, and Aiji Tanaka for helpful comments.

1. Ishikawa (1984) suspects there might have been at least some guidance from GHQ because SNTV was more natural to the Japanese mind while the limited vote was actually adopted. He later corrects his error by describing that the 1945 electoral reform was most unusual in that there was no intervention from GHQ (Ishikawa 1995).

2. Of the top finishers in the 1990 election, 117 ran for reelection in 1993, and 27 were defeated. In the same election, 77 runners-up in the 1990 election sought seats, and 47 won (Asahi Shimbun 1993).

REFERENCES

Abe, Hitoshi, Muneyuki Shindo, and Sadafumi Kawato. 1994. *The Government and Politics of Japan*. Tokyo: University of Tokyo Press.

Asahi Shimbun. 1993. *Asahi Senkyo Taikan: Dai 40 Kai Shûgiin Sôsenkyo; Dai 16 Kai Sangiin Tsûjo Senkyo* (Asahi Overview of Elections: The Fortieth House of Representatives Election and the Sixteenth House of Councillors Election). Tokyo: Asahi Shimbunsha.

Awaya, Kentaro. 1988. *Shôwa no Seitô* (Political Parties in the Showa Era). Tokyo: Shôgakkan.

Banno, Junji. 1971. *Meiji Kenpô Taisei no Kakuritsu* (Establishment of the Meiji Constitutional System). Tokyo: University of Tokyo Press.

Banno, Junji, and Ito Takashi. 1965. "Sugita Teiichi Tsubota Jinbee Kankei Monjo ni miru Meiji 20 Nendai no Senkyo to Chihô Seiji" (Elections and Local Politics during the Meiji 20s Analyzed through Sugita Teiichi and Tsubota Jinbee Documents). *Shakai Kagaku Kenkyû* 17 (1).

Bawn, Kathleen. 1993. "The Logic of Institutional Preferences: German Electoral Law as a Social Choice Outcome." *American Journal of Political Science* 37:965–89.

Christensen, Raymond V., and Paul E. Johnson. 1995. "Toward a Context-Rich Analysis of Electoral Systems: The Japanese Example." *American Journal of Political Science* 39:575–98.

Cox, Gary W. 1991. "SNTV and d'Hondt Are 'Equivalent.'" *Electoral Studies* 10:118–32.

Cox, Gary W. 1994. "Strategic Voting Equilibria under the Single Nontransferable Vote." *American Political Science Review* 88:608–21.

Cox, Gary W. 1996. "Is the Single Nontransferable Vote Superproportional? Evidence from Japan and Taiwan." *American Journal of Political Science* 40:740–55.

Cox, Gary W. 1997. *Making Votes Count*. New York: Cambridge University Press.

Cox, Gary, and Emerson M. S. Niou. 1994. "Seat Bonuses under the Single Nontransferable Vote System: Evidence from Japan and Taiwan." *Comparative Politics* 26:221–36.

Cox, Gary W., and Frances Rosenbluth. 1993. "The Electoral Fortunes of Legislative Factions in Japan." *American Political Science Review* 87:577–89.

Cox, Gary W., and Frances Rosenbluth. 1994. "Reducing Nomination Errors: Factional Competition and Party Strategy in Japan." *Electoral Studies* 13:4–16.

Cox, Gary W., and Frances Rosenbluth. 1996. "Factional Competition for the Party Endorsement: The Case of Japan's Liberal Democratic Party." *British Journal of Political Science* 26:259–69.

Curtis, Gerald L. 1971. *Election Campaigning Japanese Style*. New York: Columbia University Press.

Curtis, Gerald L. 1988. *The Japanese Way of Politics*. New York: Columbia University Press.

Curtis, Gerald L. 1992. "Japan." In *Electioneering*, ed. David Butler and Austin Ranney. Oxford: Clarendon.

Duverger, Maurice. 1954. *Political Parties*. London: Methuen.

Epstein, David, David Brady, Sadafumi Kawato, and Sharyn O'Halloran. 1997. "A Comparative Approach to Legislative Organization: Careerism and Seniority in the United States and Japan." *American Journal of Political Science* 41:965–88.

Fukui, Haruhiro. 1988. "Electoral Laws and the Japanese System." In *Japan and the World*, ed. Gail Lee Bernstein and Haruhiro Fukui. London: Macmillan.

Fukunaga, Fumio. 1986. "Sengo ni okeru Chû Senkyoku Sei no Keisei Katei" (Formative Process of Medium-Sized District System in the Postwar Period). *Kôbe Hôgaku Zasshi* 36 (3): 403–58.

Furuya, Takayoshi. 1994. "Chû Senkyoku Sei ni kansuru Oboegaki (1)" (A Memorandum on Medium-sized District System, Part 1). *Jichi Kenkyû* 70 (5): 3–20.

Gallagher, Michael. 1991. "Proportionality, Disproportionality and Electoral Systems." *Electoral Studies* 10 (1): 33–51.

Hirose, Michisada. 1989a. *Hojokin to Seikentô* (Government Subsidy and Governing Party). Tokyo: Asahi Shimbunsha.

Hirose, Michisada. 1989b. *Seiji to Kane* (Politics and Money). Tokyo: Iwanami Shoten.

Inoguchi, Takashi, and Tomoaki Iwai. 1987. *"Zoku Giin" no Kenkyû* (A Study of "Policy Tribes"). Tokyo: Nihon Keizai Shimbunsha.

Ishikawa, Masumi. 1978. *Sengo Seiji Kôzo Shi* (History of Postwar Political Structure). Tokyo: Nihon Hyôron Sha.

Ishikawa, Masumi. 1981. *Nihon Seiji no Ima* (Contemporary Japanese Politics). Tokyo: Gendai no Riron Sha.

Ishikawa, Masumi. 1984. *Deeta Sengo Seiji Shi* (A Data History of Postwar Politics). Tokyo: Iwanami Shoten.

Ishikawa, Masumi. 1995. *Sengo Seiji Shi* (History of Postwar Politics). Tokyo: Iwanami Shoten.

Ishikawa, Masumi, and Michisada Hirose. 1989. *Jimintô: Chôki Shihai no Kôzô* (LDP: The Structure of Long-Term Rule). Tokyo: Iwanami Shoten.

Ito, Yukio. 1991. "Rikken Seiyûkai Sôritsuki no Gikai" (The Diet around the Time the Seiyûkai Was Established). In *Nihon Gikai Shiroku* (Historical Record of the Japanese Diet), vol. 1, ed. Kenzo Uchida, Samon Kinbara, and Tetsuo Furuya. Tokyo: Daiichi Hôki.

Ito, Yukio. 1996. "Gôriteki Sentaku Moderu to Kindai Nihon Kenkyû" (Rational Choice Model and Modern Japanese Study). *Revaiasan* (Leviathan) 19:146–56.

Iwai, Tomoaki. 1990. *Seiji Shikin no Kenkyû* (Research on Political Campaign Financing). Tokyo: Nihon Keizai Shimbunsha.

Jichi Daigakkôu. 1961. *Sengo Jichishi IV* (Postwar History of Local Government). Tokyo: Bunsei Shoin.

Jichishô Senkyobu. 1990. *Senkyohô Hyakunenshi* (A Hundred Year's History of Electoral Laws). Tokyo: Daiichi Hôki.

Kawato, Sadafumi. 1987. "Chû Senkyoku Sei ni okeru Tokuhyôritsu no Bunpu" (The Distribution of the Vote in Medium-sized District System). *Hokudai Hôgaku Ronshû* (Hokkaido Law Review) 38 (2): 341–404.

Kawato, Sadafumi. 1992. *Nihon no Seitô Seiji 1890–1937* (Party Politics in Japan, 1890–1937: Parties in Parliament and in Elections). Tokyo: University of Tokyo Press.

Kawato, Sadafumi. 1996. "Shinioriti Rûru to Habatsu: Jimintô ni okeru Jinji Haibun no Henka" (The Development of Seniority and Interfactional Balancing Rules in the LDP). *Revaiasan* (Leviathan) (special issue, winter): 111–45.

Kawato, Sadafumi. 1997. "Senkyo Seido to Seitô Sei" (Electoral Systems and Party Systems). *Revaiasan* (Leviathan) 20:59–83.

Kawato, Sadafumi. 1999a. "Chû Senkyoku Sei ni okeru Seitô kan Kyôsô: Sûpâ donto Puropôshonariti to Dai Seitô" (Partisan Competition in the Medium-sized District

System: Super-d'Hondt Proportionality and Large Parties). *Senkyo* (Election) September 1999.
Kawato, Sadafumi. 1999b. "Seiji Shikin to Senkyo Kyôsô" (Political Money and Electoral Competition). *Revaiasan* (Leviathan) 25:52–77.
Kawato, Sadafumi. 2000. "Strategic Contexts of the Vote on Political Reform Bills." *Japanese Journal of Political Science* 1 (1): 23–51.
Kernell, Samuel. 1977. "Toward Understanding Nineteenth Century Congressional Careers: Ambition, Competition, and Rotation." *American Journal of Political Science* 21:669–93.
Kitaoka, Shin-ichi. 1985. "Jiyû Minshutô: Hôkatsu Seitô no Gôrika" (The LDP: The Rationalization of a Catch-All Party). In *Gendai Nihon no Seiji Kôzô* (The Political Structure of Contemporary Japan), ed. Jiro Kamishima. Tokyo: Hôritsu Bunkasha.
Kitaoka, Shin-ichi. 1997. "Yotô to Yatô no Seiji Rikigaku" (Political Dynamics of Governing Parties and Opposition Parties). *Shokun* (January) 112 (1): 28–37.
Kohno, Masaru. 1997a. *Japan's Postwar Party Politics*. Princeton: Princeton University Press.
Kohno, Masaru. 1997b. "Turnout and Strategic Ticket-Splitting under Japan's New Electoral Rules." *Asian Survey* 37 (5): 429–40.
Kyôgoku, Jun-ichi. 1969. *Gendai Minshusei to Seijigaku* (Modern Democracy and Political Science). Tokyo: Iwanami Shoten.
Lee, Kap Yun. 1992. "Seats and Votes in Japanese Lower House Elections (1958–90)." *Revaiasan* (Leviathan) 10:109–31.
Leiserson, Michael. 1968. "Factions and Coalitions in One-Party Japan: An Interpretation Based on the Theory of Games." *American Political Science Review* 62:770–87.
Lijphart, Arend. 1994. *Electoral Systems and Party Systems*. Oxford: Oxford University Press.
Lijphart, Arend, R. L. Pinter, and Y. Sone. 1986. "The Limited Vote and the Single Nontransferable Vote: Lessons from the Japanese and Spanish Examples." In *Electoral Laws and Their Political Consequences,* ed. B. Grofman and A. Lijphart. New York: Agathon.
Masumi, Junnosuke. 1969. *Gendai Nihon no Seiji Taisei* (Contemporary Japanese Political System). Tokyo: Iwanami Shoten.
Masumi, Junnosuke. 1979. *Nihon Seitôshiron,* vol. 5 (A Treatise on the History of Japan's Political Parties). Tokyo: University of Tokyo Press.
Masumi, Junnosuke. 1983. *Sengo Seiji,* vol. 1 (Postwar Politics). Tokyo: University of Tokyo Press.
Matsuo, Takayoshi. 1989. *Futsû Senkyo Seido Seiritsushi no Kenkyû* (Research on the History of the Establishment of the Universal Suffrage Electoral System). Tokyo: Iwanami Shoten.
McCubbins, Mathew D., and Frances M. Rosenbluth. 1995. "Party Provision for Personal Politics: Dividing the Vote in Japan." In *Structure and Policy in Japan and the United States,* ed. Peter F. Cowhey and Mathew D. McCubbins. Cambridge: Cambridge University Press.
Mitani, Taichiro. 1995. *Zôho Nihon Seitô Seiji no Keisei* (Formation of Japan's Party Politics, enlarged edition). Tokyo: University of Tokyo Press.

Miyake, Ichiro. 1989. *Tôhyô Kôdô* (Voting Behavior). Tokyo: University of Tokyo Press.
Miyake, Ichiro. 1999. "Seitô Tôhyô to Kôhosha Tôhyô no Baransu" (The Balance between Party Voting and Candidate Voting). *Revaiasan* (Leviathan) 25:7–31.
Miyazaki, Ryûji. 1984. "Senzen Nihon no Seiji Hatten to Rengô Seiji" (Political Development and Coalition Politics in Prewar Japan). In *Rengô Seiji I* (Coalition Politics I), ed. Hajime Shinohara. Tokyo: Iwanami Shoten.
Narita, Norihiko. 1996. "Seiji Kaikaku Hôan no Seiritsu Katei" (Legislative Process of Political Reform Bills). *Hokudai Hogaku Ronshû* (Hokkaido Law Review) 46 (6): 1895–1976.
Narita, Norihiko. 1997. "'Seiji Kaikaku no Katei' Ron no Kokoromi" (An Essay on the Process of Political Reform). *Revaiasan* (Leviathan) 20:7–57.
Nishihira, Shigeki. 1972. *Nihon no Senkyo* (Japanese Elections). Tokyo: Shiseidô.
Nishihira, Shigeki. 1981. *Hirei Daihyô Sei* (Proportional Representation Systems). Tokyo: Chûô Kôronsha.
Oka, Yoshitake. 1958. *Yamagata Aritomo*. Tokyo: Iwanami Shoten.
Otake, Hideo. 1995. "Jimintô Wakate Kaikakuha to Ozawa Grûpu" (LDP Young Reformists and Ozawa Group). *Revaiasan* (Leviathan) 17:7–29.
Ramseyer, J. Mark, and Frances McCall Rosenbluth. 1993. *Japan's Political Marketplace*. Cambridge: Harvard University Press.
Ramseyer, J. Mark, and Frances M. Rosenbluth. 1995. *The Politics of Oligarchy: Institutional Choice in Imperial Japan*. New York: Cambridge University Press.
Reed, Steven R. 1991. "Structure and Behaviour: Extending Duverger's Law to the Japanese Case." *British Journal of Political Science* 20:335–56.
Reed, Steven R. 1994. "The Incumbency Advantage in Japan." In *The Victorious Incumbent: A Threat to Democracy?* ed. Albert Somit et al. Aldershot: Dartmouth.
Reed, Steven R. 1999. "Strategic Voting in the 1996 Japanese General Election." *Comparative Political Studies* 32 (2): 257–70.
Sakagami, Nobuo. 1990. *Gendai Senkyo Seido Ron* (An Essay on Contemporary Electoral Systems). Tokyo: Seiji Kôhô Sentâ.
Sasaki, Takeshi, Shin-ichi Yoshida, Masaki Taniguchi, and Shuji Yamamoto, eds. 1999. *Daigishi to Kane* (Dietmembers and Money). Tokyo: Asahi Shimbunsha.
Sato, Seizaburo. 1997. "Senkyo Seido Kaikakuronsha ha Haiboku Shita" (Electoral System Reformists Were Defeated). *Chûô Kôron* (January).
Sato, Seizaburo, and Tetsuhisa Matsuzaki. 1986. *Jimintô Seiken* (The LDP Administration). Tokyo: Chûô Kôronsha.
Senkyo Seido Shingikai. 1990. *Tôshin* (Reports).
Shûgiin and Sangiin, eds. 1961. *Gikai Seido Nanajûnenshi* (A Seventy Years' History of the Parliament). Tokyo: Ôkurashô Insatsukyoku.
Shûgiin and Sangiin, eds. 1990. *Gikai Seido Hyakunenshi* (A Hundred Years' History of the Parliament). Tokyo: Ôkurashô Insatsukyoku.
Soma, Masao. 1986. *Nihon Senkyo Seido Shi* (History of Japan's Electoral Systems). Fukuoka: Kyûshû University Press.
Sone, Yasunori, and Masao Kanazashi. 1989. *Nihon no Seiji* (Japanese Politics). Tokyo: Nihon Keizai Shimbunsha.
Stockwin, J. A. A. 1982. *Japan: Divided Politics in a Growth Economy*. London: Weidenfeld and Nicolson.

Suzuki, Motoshi. 1999. "Shûgiin Shin Senkyo Seido ni okeru Senryakuteki Tôhyô to Seitô Shisutemu" (Strategic Voting and the Party System under Japan's New Electoral Law). *Revaiasan* (Leviathan) 25:32–51.

Suzuki, Motoshi. 2000. "Heiritu Sei ni okeru Tôhyô Kôdô Kenkyû no Tôgôteki Bunseki Apurôchi" (An Integrative Approach to Analyzing Voter Behavior under Japan's Mixed Electoral System). *Senkyo Kenkyû* (Japanese Journal of Electoral Studies) 15:30–41.

Suzuki, Motoshi, Yutaka Shinada, and Masahiko Tatebayashi. 1998. "Sophisticated Voting and the Formation of a Coalition Government under Japan's New Electoral Law." Paper presented at the Annual Meeting of the American Political Science Association, Boston.

Taagepera, Rein, and Matthew Shugart. 1989. *Seats and Votes*. New Haven: Yale University Press.

Tanaka, Munetaka. 1997. *Seiji Kaikaku Roku Nen no Dotei* (The Six Years' Path to Political Reform). Tokyo: Gyosei.

Tomita, Nobuo. 1979. *Meiji Kokka no Kunô to Hen-yô* (Anguish and Transformation of the Meiji State). Tokyo: Hokuju Shuppan.

Uchida, Kenzo, Tooru Hayano, and Yasunori Sone. 1994. *Dai Seihen* (Great Political Change). Tokyo: Toyo Keizeii Shimposha.

Watanabe, Tsuneo. 1958. *Habatsu*. Tokyo: Kôbundô.

Watanuki, Joji. 1997. "Japan–From Emerging to Stable Party System?" Research Paper Series A-67, Institute of International Relations, Sophia University.

Part 4
Party Structures in Legislatures

Divided Parties, Divided Government

Michael Laver

Relations between Legislature and Executive

Every modern democratic regime relies fundamentally upon institutional linkages between a legislature, charged with representing the will of the people in the process of making the laws of the land, and an executive, charged with implementing these laws. A key distinction between types of democratic regimes concerns the sources from which these two branches of the governmental system derive their legitimacy and thence their right to be respected and obeyed by the public at large, even when particular decisions they make are unpopular.

One model can be found in European-style "parliamentary government." In this model both legislature and executive share the same source of legitimacy—the periodic free election of public representatives to a legislature which in turn makes and breaks the executive. The executive in a parliamentary government system has no independent source of legitimacy, being indirectly responsible to the electorate via a representative legislature. An alternative model can be found in U.S.-style "presidential government." In this model both legislature and executive, each with significant overlapping powers, have independent sources of legitimacy—periodic free elections both to the legislature and to the position of chief executive.

While there are many procedural and institutional details that separate presidential from parliamentary government systems, the key distinction we are concerned with here is the existence of shared versus independent sources of legitimacy for the legislature and the executive. What we think of as "divided government" is observed when governance structures with independent sources of legitimacy have the potential to come into conflict. If there are significant overlapping powers between the two structures, then divided government creates the possibility of deadlock in the governmental system.

Reprinted with permission from *Legislative Studies Quarterly* 24, no. 1 (February 1999): 5–29.

There are several reasons why independent sources of legitimacy may come into conflict. Elections to different bodies may be held at the same time on different bases—perhaps using different constituency structures or different electoral formulas. They may be held on the same basis on different dates, reflecting two different snapshots of public opinion. The may even be held at the same time on the same basis if voters "split their ticket" and use different criteria for making their choices in, for example, legislative and executive elections.

A final, and for this paper, crucial source of conflicting legitimacies can arise, even in a parliamentary system, as a result of the politics of coalition. When no one party wins a majority in the legislature, coalitions of parties are needed to secure legislative majorities. It can then happen that one particular legislative coalition puts the executive in place during the government formation process, a different legislative coalition might sustain the executive in a vote of confidence that decides its future, while yet another legislative coalition enacts measures that thwart or obstruct the day-to-day business of the executive.

Such conflicts between legislature and executive are most likely to arise in European political systems when there are "minority" cabinets. Minority cabinets occur when the parties participating in the cabinet do not themselves control a majority of the legislature, despite having won the explicit or implicit support of a legislative majority in order to be installed in office.[1] It can then happen that members of a legislative majority leave the incumbent executive in place, not breaking the government in a confidence/no confidence motion despite having the legislative numbers at their disposal to do so, while continuing to vote against the government's legislative proposals. Laver and Shepsle (1991) explored the comparison between U.S.-style divided government and European-style minority government, and Strøm (1990) provides an extensive treatment of minority government in Europe.

Another source of division between executive and legislature in parliamentary government systems can arise if we relax the party-as-unitary-actor assumption and lift the lid on intraparty politics. The making and breaking of governments may then pull different sections of the same party in different directions. Conflicts between legislature and executive may then become an intrinsic feature of internal party politics, as executive and legislative elements of the same party pursue different strategies in particular circumstances relevant to the future of a given government. In the extreme, parties may risk splitting over the making and breaking of governments while majority governments, even one-party majority governments, may find themselves defeated on particular legislative proposals as a result of the breakdown of party discipline.

The focus of the argument that follows is upon this latter type of interaction between intraparty politics and the operation of parliamentary government. This interaction may result in conflict between legislature and executive that is the European equivalent of the U.S. phenomenon of divided government. Such conflict may become more common if there is a decline in the cohesion of political parties, with a consequent decline in the ability or willingness of cabinet ministers to deliver the legislative support of their party in a disciplined and predictable manner. The result of this decline would be a narrowing of the gap between "divided" government U.S.-style and European "unified" government. Divisions within parties could manifest themselves as divisions between legislature and executive.

The next section reviews the interaction between intraparty politics and the making and breaking of European governments in general terms. The third section describes and begins to analyse a formal model of this interaction and explores some of its implications. The fourth section describes and analyses one recent confrontation between executive and legislature in the Netherlands, a confrontation brought about because executive and legislative branches of the same party behaved in different ways. The final section presents some more general thoughts about the link between intraparty politics and the potential for conflict between legislatures and executives in Europe.

Party Discipline and Legislative-Executive Relations in Europe

Most accounts of parliamentary government in modern Europe are explicitly or implicitly grounded in the assumption that political parties behave as unitary actors. This does not mean, of course, that those who write about parliamentary government are blind to the intricacies of intraparty politics. Rather it means that the unitary-actor assumption not only makes the modelling of many key political processes far more tractable, but it also seems to be an empirically reasonable working assumption, given the high levels of legislative party discipline we do tend to find in most parliamentary democracies. In reviewing the empirical plausibility of this assumption, for example, Laver and Schofield (1990) found that, whatever their internal decision-making processes, it was almost invariably the case that parties enter and leave governments as coherent units. It is almost never the case that only a section of a party joins a government while another section stays outside. Almost never does a section of a party leave a government while another section stays in office. This is an extremely strong empirical regularity—parties do seem to act as unified blocs when making and breaking governments.

Some of the sources of coherence in the behaviour of political parties are analysed in Gary Cox's classic book, *The Efficient Secret*. This looks at the nineteenth-century evolution of modern party politics in Britain and emphasises the relationships between three closely interlocking processes (Cox 1987). The first is the emergence of a mass franchise in elections to a legislature increasingly concerned with public rather than private legislation—this underpinned the developing electoral value of a party label. The second is the consolidation of a unified system of government in which the executive is derived from the legislature—this established the primary career path to executive power as one of rising through the ranks of legislators. The third is the emergence of increasingly disciplined parliamentary parties, in which discipline is enforced by sanctions imposed by party hierarchs who both control access to the valuable party label and act as gatekeepers in the political career structure.

While the political histories of different parliamentary government systems obviously differ, these processes are far more general in their implications. Stable parliamentary government depends crucially on the ability of the executive to forecast and rely upon stable voting alignments in the legislature. Given the size of most modern parliaments, this vital structuring of legislative behaviour is provided by the disciplined affiliation of legislators to political parties.

Going one step further, by far the most straightforward way for an executive in a parliamentary government system to gain and maintain power is for the cabinet to comprise senior members of one or more political parties that between them command the loyalties of a majority of legislators. We think of this as a "majority government." Majority governments thus derive their character axiomatically from the ability of party leaders in the executive to command the loyalty of legislative party members, in other words, upon party discipline. Without such party discipline, the stability of the executive may be undermined.

Thus, even a single-party government with a huge parliamentary majority can maintain its grip on power only by having a disciplined legislative party. If such a party splits in a significant way, and if the rebels are prepared to vote against the government, then even the most formidable of majorities may count for nothing. In this very real sense, every government is a coalition government. If it is not a coalition of different parties, then it is at least a coalition of factions within the single governing party—factions that may be explicit or implicit, with members whose preferences may well diverge in relation to particular issues, but who make the strategic decision to stay together within the same party.

A good example of this can be found in the interaction between the Europhile and Europhobe wings of the British Conservative Party. Even at the height of the Conservatives' legislative majority, the issue of Europe always had the potential to split the Conservatives and destroy the government. Managing this potential confrontation was one of the most important jobs of any Conservative leader who wanted to remain Prime Minister.

Party discipline is also crucial to minority government, in which the parties in the executive do not themselves control a legislative majority, yet can nonetheless rely upon legislative support from parties outside the executive.

The stability of such "outside" support obviously has a crucial bearing upon the stability of minority governments, a stability that is enhanced, other things being equal, if outside support is structured in disciplined blocs.

Most theoretical accounts of parliamentary government, furthermore, take political parties to be not only unitary actors but also as fixed elements of the political scene. Parties are treated as exogenous inputs to whatever process is being modelled, whether this is the making and breaking of governments, the fighting of elections, or anything else. Events that run counter to this view, for example party splits or (much less common) fusions between two parties, are typically treated as exogenous shocks to the system, not as endogenous outputs of party competition.

All of this results in many political scientists taking a remarkably anthropomorphic view of political parties. These are modelled in accounts of political competition as having "ideal points" and "indifference curves," for example, as if each party had a single brain. At best, the party is seen in these terms as a sort of insect hive, comprising physically distinct individuals but working intellectually to a single coherent design.

Side-by-side with such simple models, there are obviously many "thickly descriptive" case studies of particular political parties that describe very complex internal processes. These accounts tend to be detailed stories of individual cases, however. Apart from being sources of inspiration for more generally applicable ideas, such thick descriptions do not yet form the basis of any more comprehensive account of party competition and parliamentary government.

Lifting the lid off intraparty politics when we model interparty competition in a parliamentary government system is much more easily said than done, however. Nobody denies that it is an important project, but knowing how to go forward in a systematic and rigorous manner is another matter entirely. One of the more ambitious moves in this direction was made by Luebbert (1986) in an account of political parties that gave a central role to party leaders whose main motivation was to remain party leaders, who needed to win the intraparty political game in order to achieve this, and for whom interparty politics, even participation in government, was a secondary concern.

Luebbert's argument was informal. Laver and Shepsle (1996) attempted to build intraparty politics into a model of interparty competition over the making and breaking of governments, showing by example within their model of government formation that intraparty diversity of preferences, and variations in intraparty decision-making regimes, can have an impact upon the partisan composition of equilibrium governments. They fell far short, however, of proposing a rigorous model that fully integrated intraparty politics into interparty competition, implicitly demonstrating by example how very difficult this is going to be.

I do not set out to propose such an overall model in this paper. Rather, I hope to put a piece of the puzzle into place. I do this by looking at one particular way in which relaxing the party-as-unitary-actor assumption has a bearing upon interparty competition in general, and the phenomenon of legislative-executive conflict in particular. This has to do with what happens if government parties cannot, or will not, discipline the actions of their members in the legislature. In other words, the discussions that follow treat intraparty discipline as an endogenous outcome of, rather than as an exogenous input to, interparty competition in parliamentary government systems. As we shall see, this will force us to reconsider what we understand by the concepts of majority and minority government, and in this way will hopefully throw new light on the phenomenon of legislative-executive conflict in Europe.

The Interparty Implications of Intraparty Discipline

There are many different theatres of interparty competition; we tend to use different conceptions of a political party in each of them. Thus, if we are dealing with party competition in some local district during an election campaign, then we will be interested in party candidates, party activists, and voters, with senior party politicians perhaps making an occasional appearance as part of a wider political game. We will quintessentially be interested in autonomous political actors who operate *within* political parties. Any notion of the party as a unitary actor will be utterly unsustainable. If, on the other hand, we look at the making and breaking of national governments in the period between elections, then we may well choose to concentrate upon interactions between quite a small number of elite politicians. We may even feel that we can tell a good enough story if we treat only party leaders as being autonomous political actors, and thus focus exclusively upon interactions between these people. In doing this we are not treating each party as a *unitary* actor in the sense that every aspect of a party's actions are determined by a single autonomous decision maker, but we are certainly treating each party as a *unified* actor in the sense that party members behave *as if* their actions were determined by a single autonomous decision maker.

The traditional recourse of focusing on party leaders is clearly a product of the desire for analytical tractability. It is also, however, a political reality that when party leaders negotiate with each other over the making and breaking of governments, a key presumption is that, if they commit their party to a certain course of action, then they will be able to deliver. If party leaders cannot deliver on commitments that their parties will behave in certain ways, then the entire system of parliamentary government has the potential to become chaotic and unpredictable.

Lifting the lid on intraparty politics thus forces us to treat the making and breaking of governments as being determined by two interlocking political games, rather than as a simple interaction between party leaders. At one level, party leaders do interact with each other, as modelled by classical coalition theorists. At another level, each decision a party leader makes has to be carried through within the party's internal political system—and of course party leaders will anticipate the need to do this when making commitments to other party leaders.

One important consequence of modelling the making and breaking of governments in terms of two interlocking political games is that a party leader's failure to deliver on commitments may be seen either as a straightforward reneging on the part of the leader, or as a political failure by the leader to carry the commitment within party. This failure to carry the party may further be the result of weakness, stupidity, lack of effort, or bad luck on the part of the leader. It may also have been anticipated quite accurately by a party leader who cynically made a commitment to others in the clear expectation that this could not be carried within his or her own party. This raises, as we shall see, the clear possibility of shirking by party leaders, who may not put in the effort needed to ensure fulfillment of commitments that have become inconvenient. These different potential reasons why a party leader might fail to honour commitments may well have a bearing upon how other political actors react to such failure. We quickly find ourselves in muddy strategic waters.

We can attempt to make progress in this area by giving some shape to two political games that interact with each other. First, consider an interparty game that is in effect the one dealt with by classical coalition theorists. To keep things simple, concentrate for the moment on interactions between two parties over the making and breaking of governments. If these parties are negotiating to go into a coalition government together, then they negotiate a coalition agreement. This agreement may be more, or less, explicit.

The ideal-type coalition agreement defines a mutually agreed strategy for each coalition partner in every foreseeable political circumstance, together with a procedure for dealing with unanticipated political shocks. Real-world coalition agreements will, of course, remain silent on many potential future political circumstances. There will probably be excellent strategic reasons for doing this. Two parties may, for example, be quite unable to agree upon what to do in some particular eventuality—but they may also be prepared to take a chance that this situation will not in fact happen. They may furthermore be unable to agree, before a government is formed, on what to do about something that they are almost certain will happen in the future, but may feel that the potential for future agreement between them will be greater once they have lived together in office for a while, and have thus learnt whether or not to trust each other.

Failing to specify in advance a strategy for each coalition partner in some particular circumstance involves an implicit agreement to activate the default interparty negotiating procedure if this circumstance arises. In this sense, we can think of any coalition agreement between two parties as being complete, even if it does not explicitly specify a course of action for all players in every conceivable political circumstance.

In general terms, therefore, an interparty coalition agreement specifies, for any given situation, either a course of action for each party or recourse to further interparty negotiations of some form. When the specified course of action involves more than just the party leader, and since all concerned do know that parties are not unitary actors, a coalition agreement at least implies the actions a party leader should take to ensure the compliance of his or her party to fulfill the agreement. However, much to the regret of many of them, no doubt, most party leaders are not all-powerful dictators within their own parties. This embeds an intraparty political game within the interparty game of making and breaking governments.

For the purposes of developing a simple model, we can divide the actions available to a party leader when dealing with his or her own party into two categories: *apply party discipline* and *allow independent decision making by internal party actors*. In the context of voting behaviour in parliament, we can think of these choices as being *apply party whip* and *allow free vote* on the issue in question. Allowing a free vote imposes no further intraparty obligations on the leader involved in relation to the issue at stake. Mutual acceptance that a party leader may allow a free vote effectively takes the issue out of interparty politics. Applying the party whip, however, implies an obligation on the party leader to ensure that the whip is obeyed. This involves a cost, in terms of both intraparty and interparty credibility, if the whip is not, in fact, obeyed.

The universal doctrine of *collective cabinet responsibility* in western European parliamentary systems means that, once some matter has been decided by coalition partners in cabinet, however controversial and divisive this decision was, then all cabinet members are collectively responsible for implementing the decision. This applies even to members who in cabinet discussions vigorously opposed the eventual option chosen. The only constitutional recourse for a cabinet member who cannot go along with a cabinet decision is to resign and oppose this decision from the opposition benches.

In the context of parliamentary government and cabinet coalitions, the doctrine of collective cabinet responsibility translates into an obligation on the party leaders involved in cabinet decisions that they should do whatever it takes to deliver the compliance of their respective parties, unless otherwise specified. If a party leader loses a battle in cabinet and then does not raise a finger to deliver the support of his or her legislative party, then this would quite clearly be refusing to accept collective responsibility for implementing cabinet decisions. Such a situation would lead to the possibility that any cabinet decision, once taken, could be overturned in the legislature by an alliance of the losing party or parties in cabinet and members of the cabinet's legislative opposition.

Divided Parties, Divided Government 209

This implies that issues subject to a free vote and therefore not requiring legislative discipline on the part of government parties must be explicitly set out in a coalition agreement. Indeed, we might even take this to be one of the defining characteristics underpinning the system of party politics that makes parliamentary government viable. Therefore, in what follows, I concentrate upon those situations in which, explicitly or implicitly, the doctrine of collective cabinet responsibility imposes an obligation on party leaders in cabinet to deliver the legislative support of their parties for cabinet decisions, leaving for later work the interesting strategic matter of when party leaders going into government together might agree to a free vote on some issue.

We are now in a position to explore the sequence of decisions that begins when a party leader—the leader of Party P—must take action to ensure the compliance of his or her party with some element of a decision made jointly with a coalition partner—Party Q. The most interesting case, of course, is when, other things being equal, both the leader and rank-and-file elements of Party P would prefer not to comply with the decision at issue. In other words, we are most interested in the case in which a party leader is being asked to deliver on some concession made during cabinet decision making. This means that, if the party leader could get away with failing to deliver, then he or she would do so, and some positive payoff would result. (Call this the "defection" payoff, p, for the leader of Party P, and call it p' for some legislator in Party P.)

Since the issue concerned does not involve a free vote, the doctrine of collective cabinet responsibility obliges the party leader to whip the party in order to ensure compliance. Assume that, if Leader P does not apply the whip, then the vote will be lost. If the vote is lost, then *both the leader and the legislators* in Party P receive the defection payoff from not delivering on a promise to coalition partners, while the party leader suffers a loss of credibility in potentially valuable future negotiations. (Call this reputational hit c_3.) The promise made by Leader P is valuable to Leader Q, who faces a cost if the promise is not honoured. (Call this cost -q.)

Leader Q must now decide how to react to this reneging by Leader P. Assume that the options for Leader Q are either accepting the reneging or withdrawing from the government and bringing it down. If Leader Q accepts reneging from a coalition partner, then he or she must also suffer a loss of credibility in future negotiations, being seen as someone who does not punish people who fail to honour their deals. (Call this reputational hit k_3.)

If Leader Q does leave and bring down the government, then this is a bad outcome for all concerned. (The payoff for this has been fixed arbitrarily at -1 for each player, in contrast to the payoff of zero that arises from the outcome envisaged in the coalition agreement, whereby the whip is applied and obeyed, the vote is carried and the government stays in office.) This sequence of events is described in the bottom branch of the game tree in Figure 1, which also

FIGURE 1
The Whipping Game

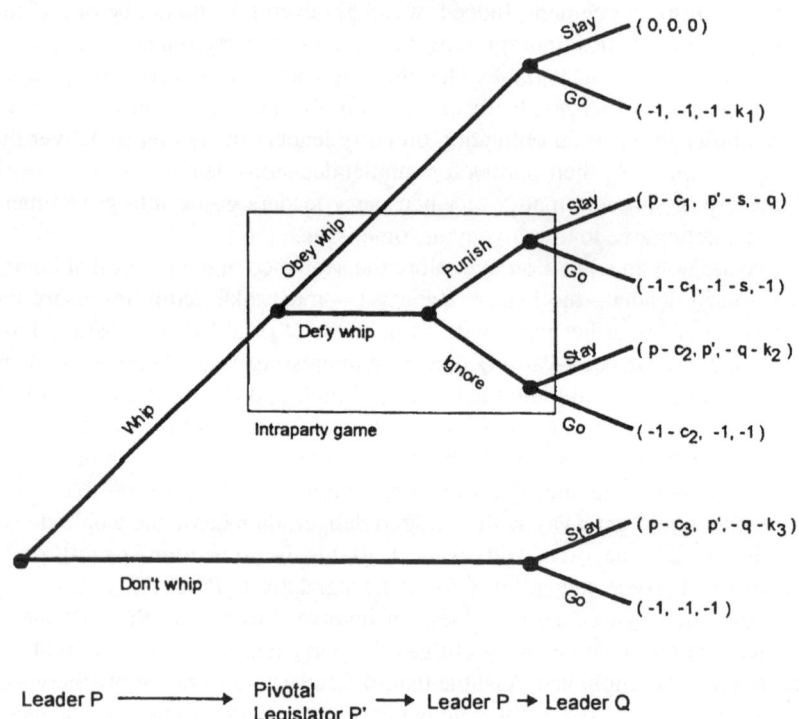

Key:
- p = payoff to Leader P from reneging on deal with Leader Q
- q = cost to Leader Q of Leader P reneging

- p' = defection payoff to pivotal Legislator P
- s = sanction applied by Leader P to pivotal Legislator P if latter defects
- c_1 = cost to Leader P of applying sanction to pivotal Legislator P
- k_1 = credibility hit to Leader Q from leaving cabinet even after Leader P applies whip

- c_2 = credibility hit to Leader P from refusing to sanction those who defy whip
- k_2 = credibility hit to Leader Q from accepting Leader P's refusal to sanction those who defy whip

- c_3 = credibility hit to Leader P from refusing to apply whip at all
- k_3 = credibility hit to Leader Q from accepting Leader P's refusal to apply whip

shows the payoffs for the three key actors: the leader of Party P, a pivotal Party P legislator, and the leader of Party Q.

If the leader of Party P does not whip the party, then the leader of Party Q must decide either to stay in the government or to go. If the leader of Party Q stays, then the leader of Party P gets the payoff, p, from reneging on the agreement, but suffers a credibility hit, c_3, arising from a naked refusal to apply the whip when it was clearly understood that this should be done. The legislator from Party P gets the defection payoff, p'. The leader of Party Q suffers the loss from being reneged on, -q, and the credibility hit, k_3 from not punishing this, particularly when the reneging has happened in such a naked way. If, on the other hand, the leader of Party Q brings down the government, then the matter at issue remains unresolved and all involved pay the price of the fallen government.

The alternative course of action for Leader P is to apply the whip. This involves instructing party legislators to vote in a particular way and imposing a sanction on each that fails to do so. Call this sanction s. For the sake of simplicity, we concentrate here upon a pivotal party legislator or faction of legislators, whose vote makes the difference between success and failure for the vote in question. Having been whipped to vote in a particular way, the legislator(s) concerned must decide whether to obey the whip or not. If they obey the whip, the vote is won. If they defy it, the vote is lost. This takes us to the intraparty game that can be found inside the box in Figure 1.

If the whip is obeyed, then the vote is carried and the promise is delivered upon by Party P, provided that Leader Q does not behave in a very peculiar way, bringing down the government despite the fact that his or her coalition partner had delivered on its promises to the letter (and thus taking a big reputational hit, k_1, in the process).

If the whip is defied and the vote is lost, then *both party leader and party legislator* reap gains (of p and p' respectively) from not having to deliver on the promise to the coalition partner. Legislators face the threatened sanction, s, from the party leader, while the party leader must decide whether actually to impose the sanction. Applying the sanction has a cost, c_1, for Leader P—we may take c_1 to impound both the cost of imposing the sanction and the reputational hit for the party leader in imposing a whip that is defied. If Leader P decides to ignore, and not to punish, those who defy the party whip, then this course of action has its own costs c_2. We can take c_2 to impound both the intraparty reputational hit of threatening a sanction and then not imposing it, and the interparty reputational hit of being under an obligation to impose sanctions on internal party dissidents and then not doing so.

If the whip is defied and the vote is lost, then Leader Q must decide how to respond, though the precise response may depend upon whether or not Leader P punishes the internal party dissidents whose actions defeated the vote. Once more, assume Leader Q can either accept the indiscipline within Party P that led to the failure to deliver on coalition obligations, and stay in the government, or can bring the government down. Assume that, if Leader Q accepts the dissidence in Party P, then this involves no reputational hit if those dissidents are punished as per the implicit deal. Assume however that the leader of Party Q will take a reputational hit (of k_2) for staying in government if Leader P does not punish the dissidents who prevented Party P from meeting its coalition obligations.

Before moving on to explore the implications of the game set out in Figure 1, we need to make a couple of simple assumptions involving the relative size of the various reputational hits we have been talking about. First, considering the potential reputational damage faced by Leader P, we assume that the biggest reputational hit for Leader P is not even to pretend to apply the whip when facing an obligation to do so. Next comes applying the whip but failing to punish dissidents. The smallest reputational hit arises from applying the whip, facing some dissidence, but punishing this. (In other words, $c_3 > c_2 > c_1$.) Considering the potential reputational hits faced by Leader Q, all we need to assume is that he or she takes a bigger reputational hit from accepting Leader P's refusal to apply the whip when obliged to do so than from accepting Leader P's applying the whip and then failing to punish dissidents. (In other words, assume that $k_3 > k_2$.)

The Whipping Game

The confrontations between legislature and executive explored below all turn upon defiance of the party whip by party legislators. This defiance arises because the costs of defying the whip, in terms of sanctions applied by the party leadership, are less than the defection payoffs arising from doing so. This in effect allows parties to renege on commitments to coalition partners and possibly to get away with this. For any given promise made to a coalition partner, the key strategic variable is the scale of the sanction applied by the party leader to those who defy the whip.

This creates a situation in which party leaders may have an incentive to "shirk" by applying sanctions too small to bring about the level of compliance with the whip that is required if they are to honour their commitments to other party leaders. Thus, they may appear to be honouring their commitments, applying the whip and punishing defectors, but may be doing this in the knowledge that their whipping activities will be ineffective. The net result of this ineffective whipping will be positive for both leaders and their parties.

We can divide the whipping game into four broad cases, depending on the relative size of the reputational hits suffered by Leader Q and the cost to Leader Q of Party P failing to honour its coalition promises and explore these by backward induction.

Case 1: q > 1

In this case Leader Q would rather bring down the government than pay the price of Leader P reneging—Leader P's promise is very valuable indeed to Leader Q. If q > 1, then

$q + k_2 > 1$ (and thus $-q - k_2 < -1$)
$q + k_3 > 1$ (and thus $-q - k_3 < -1$)

This implies that, in the final stage of the game, Leader Q will always bring down the government unless Leader P applies the whip and Party P legislators obey it. This in turn implies that Leader P will always punish defiance of the whip in the previous stage of the game, since $-1 - c_1 > -1 - c_2$. This further implies that the pivotal legislator will obey the whip in the stage before this, since $0 > -1 - s$. This in turn implies that Leader P will apply the whip in the first stage, since $0 > -1$. Thus, if Leader Q values Leader P's promise very highly, as assumed in this case, then the equilibrium path through the game will be WHIP–OBEY–STAY, as anticipated in the coalition agreement.

Case 2: (i) q < 1 and (ii) q + k₂ > 1

Condition (i) implies that, forgetting about reputational effects, Leader Q would prefer to see the government remain in place and accept not getting the promised concession from Leader P. Leader P's promise is less valuable to Q than in Case 1. However, taking reputational hits into account, Leader Q would rather bring down the government than accept both Party P's failure to deliver and the reputational hit arising from accepting Leader P's failure to punish dissidents. This implies, in the final stage, that Leader Q stays in government as long as Leader P punishes party dissidents. As before, this implies that Leader P will punish dissidents this time, since $p - c_1 > -1 - c_2$.

There are now two subcases, depending upon whether or not $p' - s < 0$, in other words, upon whether or not the sanction for defecting is greater than the defection payoff for Legislator P'.

Case 2.1: $p' - s < 0$. In this case, the net payoff to Legislator P' from defying the whip is negative, since the sanction is greater than the defection payoff. Legislator P' thus obeys the whip. This implies that Leader P imposes the whip in the first stage and the equilibrium path through the game is once more WHIP–OBEY–STAY.

Case 2.2: $p' - s < 0$. In this case, the sanction is less than the defection payoff and Legislator P' defies the whip. Leader P's choice in the first stage of the game depends upon whether or not $p - c_1 > -1$. It seems extremely unlikely that $p - c_1 < -1$, since this implies a massive c_1 reputational hit, which arises for the relatively minor transgression of applying the whip, not being obeyed, and punishing defectors—a hit greater than the combined value of the government not falling AND the defection payoff. So we assume $p - c_1 > -1$. In this event Leader P will apply the whip in the first stage of the game, and the resulting equilibrium path is WHIP–DEFY–PUNISH–STAY.

This is the first case in which Leader P does not deliver on his or her promise to Leader Q. We note that Leader Q stays in the coalition because Leader P punishes dissidents. We also note that the sanction applied to dissidents is not sufficient to deter their defiance of the whip. Strikingly, provided the c_1 reputational hit is not too large for Leader P (i.e., $p > c_1$), both the leader and the pivotal legislators of Party P are better off in this situation than they are in delivering upon their promises to Leader Q. In effect, Leader P applies the whip and slaps dissidents gently on the wrist for defying it and all in Party P are better off as a result.

In the context of the main theme of this paper, this is the first clear case of conflict between legislature and executive. What we find is a section of the government's ostensible legislative majority defecting to defeat it, as a result of what is a quite rational and strategic, and possibly even stage-managed, breakdown in party discipline.

Case 3: (i) $q < 1$ and (ii) $q + k_2 < 1$ and (iii) $q + k_3 > 1$

In this case, Leader Q prefers to accept the failure to deliver on the promise and is also prepared to take a k_2 reputational hit rather than bring down the government, provided that Leader P whips Party P. Leader Q is not prepared to take the k_3 reputational hit arising from accepting Leader P's blatant refusal to whip at all, however. In other words, Leader P's promise is less valuable to Leader Q, all things being equal, than in cases 1 and 2. In the final stage of the game, Leader Q stays in government provided Leader P applies the whip, regardless of whether or not dissidents are punished, and leaves only if Leader P refuses to apply the whip. This implies that Leader P punishes dissidents in the penultimate stage, since $p - c_1 > p - c_2$. There are then two subcases, exactly as in Cases 2.1 and 2.2, with an identical analysis.[2] Thus

Case 3.1: $p' - s < 0$. This implies that Leader P imposes the whip in the first stage, and the equilibrium path through the game is WHIP–OBEY–STAY.

Case 3.2: $p' - s < 0$. This implies Leader P will apply the whip in the first stage of the game, and the resulting equilibrium path is WHIP–DEFY–PUNISH–STAY.

We thus have another case of conflict between legislature and executive in which party leaders in the government, despite applying the whip to parties controlling a legislative majority, are defeated in the legislature on a key coalition proposal.

Case 4: (i) $q < 1$ and (ii) $q + k_2 < 1$ and (iii) $q + k_3 < 1$

In this case, Leader Q never brings down the government in the final stage, regardless of what Leader P does, staying in government even if Leader P refuses to apply the whip. In effect, of the various possibilities we have analysed, Leader P's promise is least valuable to Leader Q in this case, holding constant the cost of the various reputational hits. Leader P punishes defiance of the whip in the penultimate stage $(p - c_1 > p - c_2)$. There are then two subcases, depending upon whether or not $p' - s < 0$.

Case 4.1: $p' - s < 0$. Once more, because the sanction for defying the whip is greater than the payoff, pivotal legislators will obey the whip at the second stage. However, Leader Q's almost total unwillingness to break the government in this case presents Leader P with other strategic options. We have just seen that, if the whip is applied, then it will be obeyed and the agreed coalition deal will be delivered. However, it may be that Leader P can do better simply not applying the whip, breaking the deal, and gaining a defection payoff, offset against the price of a reputational hit. This will be the case if $p - c_3 > 0$. In this event the equilibrium path through the game will be a naked reneging by Leader P: DON'T WHIP–STAY.

This case results in a legislative defeat for a majority government, but is less a case of conflict between legislature and executive, however, than of straightforward reneging by one party leader on obligations due to the other. Indeed, in this scenario, Leader P short-circuits compliance with the deal by refusing to apply the whip in the first place.

If the cost of the reputational hit for such blatant perfidiousness is greater than the defection payoff, however $(p - c_3 < 0)$, then Leader P will apply the whip, and the equilibrium path will be the WHIP–OBEY–STAY implied in the coalition deal.

Case 4.2: $p' - s < 0$. In this case, as before, the anticipated sanction is insufficient to prevent the pivotal legislator from defying the whip. This changes Leader P's calculations on applying the whip in the first place. Knowing it will be defied, Leader P does apply the whip, even in the knowledge that Leader Q would stay in office if it were not applied. There is no need for the blatant defection of refusing to apply the whip since Leader P knows that, because the whip will be defied if applied, the promise will not be honoured anyway. The reputational hit for applying the whip unsuccessfully and punishing defectors is less than naked refusal to apply it in the first place (i.e., $p - c_1 > p - c_3$). In this event, the equilibrium path through the game is WHIP–DEFY–PUNISH–STAY.

As we have seen, this generates a form of conflict between legislature and executive in which party leaders in government are defeated in the legislature, despite leading parties commanding a legislative majority, as a result of a breakdown in party discipline.

Sanctions for Defying the Party Whip

The interactions explored above place the sanctions with which potential party dissidents are threatened under intense scrutiny. Parties can renege on their coalition commitments by applying sanctions that are too small to have the required effect. The types of punishments that can be meted out by party leaders make these very hard to monitor at the level of detail required, however. The meagre penalties that can be applied derive from the party political game itself, and typically involve banishing dissidents from some or all of the benefits of party membership. This might involve expulsion from the party, temporary suspension, demotion on a PR list, and so on.

The difficulty is that those who are banished can be unbanished quite easily, those who are demoted can be promoted again, and the possibility of thus reversing sanctions is one way in which party leaders can pull their punches in a manner that can be difficult to track. A legislator may be demoted on a party list for example, only to be re-instated once the government involved has fallen anyway, an election is due to be held, and any reaction to the reinstatement by a cheated coalition partner is no longer effective. A banished dissident whose action had defeated a government proposal may be let back into his or her party somewhat earlier than anticipated. Even if the coalition concerned is still in power, the strategic question that arises is whether readmitting a dissident in this way is sufficient grounds for the thwarted coalition partner now to bring down the government. Yet who is to say, looking at matters such as this from outside the party, that a nudge and a wink were not exchanged between punisher and punished at the time when mutually beneficial party indiscipline was being mooted? Given the very nature of the sanctions involved in enforcing party discipline, therefore, shirking by party leaders is going to be difficult indeed to monitor.

Party Indiscipline and Conflict between Legislature and Executive

The simple legislative game discussed above shows a number of cases in which conflict between legislature and executive can arise in a European-style "unified" government system, even when the incumbent government has an ostensible legislative majority. In every one of the cases discussed, whether or not a leader delivers a unified party to honour a particular coalition commitment is an intensely strategic matter rather than something that can be taken as given. One case arises when a party leader simply refuses to whip his or her party when under an obligation to do so—openly reneging on the obligations imposed by collective cabinet responsibility. A more subtle set of cases arises when legislators in government parties behave in an undisciplined manner.

This indiscipline arises as a result of the interaction of two things. The first is the value attached by a party to having a coalition partner honour a commitment. If a party feels strongly about the commitment concerned, or manages to convey the impression to others that it cares strongly, then there will be no incentive for reneging. Fear of provoking a coalition partner into bringing down the government will be sufficient to ensure internal party discipline.

The possibility of government defeats arises once a party values the survival of the government more than the issue at stake and is prepared to accept the application of the whip and the punishment of those who defy it as a sign of the good faith of coalition partners. This opens up the possibility—as in Cases 2.2, 3.2, and 4.2 above—that the party leader says one thing, committing the party to a course of action and applying the whip in this direction, while sections of his or her party do something else. The net result is that a government that appears to command a generalised legislative majority may in practice face majority opposition in the legislature on the issue in question.

This type of conflict between legislature and executive arises out of divisions (at least of role if not of opinion) within a government party—the unitary status of which is traditionally held to be one of the keys to European-style parliamentary government. We can find such intraparty divisions in practice, furthermore, not just in simplified theoretical models, as the following example shows.

Conflict between Legislature and Executive in the Netherlands

In order to get a feel for the way in which intraparty politics can generate this type of conflict between legislature and executive, this section provides a brief sketch of an intriguing event in recent Dutch politics.[3] This concerns a long-running policy problem offering two possible solutions. A cabinet with a secure legislative majority decided on one option, though this was opposed by one of the government parties. Legislators from the dissenting government party combined with those from the opposition to vote against the government and defeat its proposals in the legislature. As a result of the behaviour of legislators from one of the government parties, the legislature defeated this government proposal and substituted the alternative. The government accepted this outcome.

The government that took office after the 1994 general election in the Netherlands was a "purple" coalition of the Labour Party, Democrats '66 (D66), and the Liberal Party. Table 1 shows the distribution of seats in the 150-seat legislature between key parties after the election and estimates of party policy positions on three key policy dimensions, derived from an expert survey conducted at the time. These dimensions are as follows: all-important economic policy; immigration policy, the most important and divisive non-economic dimension; and the environmental policy at issue in this case (Laver 1995).

The purple coalition took 111 days to form and, as can be seen from Table 1, combined two parties whose policy positions on key dimensions were quite similar, Labour and D66, with a third party, the Liberals, who had radically different positions on each key dimension. Labour and the Liberals took five cabinet portfolios each, while D66 took four. The Prime Minister was Wim Kok of Labour.

The Christian Democrats, who had been in power continuously since 1917, were excluded from office despite their central position in the Dutch policy space, a position that would have made them members of the equilibrium governments predicted by almost any extant theoretical model of government formation (Laver 1995). This deviation from equilibrium can be put down in part to personal animosities between leaders of Labour and the Christian Democrats, who had been in office together in the previous coalition, as well as a growing feeling among all of the other Dutch parties that the Christian Demo-

TABLE 1
Seats Won by, and Policy Positions of Larger Dutch Parties after the 1994 General Election

Party	Seats	Taxation vs. Spending	Immigration	Environment
Labour	37	8.48	7.07	9.07
Christian Democrats	34	12.70	10.46	12.81
Liberals	31	17.31	15.00	15.96
D66	24	10.56	7.04	7.44

Sources: Policy positions: Laver (1995); Seats: Lucardie and Voerman (1995).
Note: All party positions are the mean judgments of the experts surveyed on the dimensions in question, on a 1–20 scale.
Dimension definitions:
Taxation vs. spending: Promote raising taxes to increase public services (1) *versus* Promote cutting public services to cut taxes (20)
Immigration: Accept immigration and promote policies helping immigrants (1) *versus* Oppose immigration and oppose any policies helping immigrants (20)
Environment: Promote environmental protection, even if this slows economic growth (1) *versus* Promote economic growth, even if this damages environment (20)

crats had been in government far too long, so that the benefits of getting them out came to be seen as exceeding any policy costs.

The issue at stake was the location of a major new motorway, the A73, planned to run through the southern province of Limburg. Cabinets and parliaments had been discussing this issue for 30 years—the two main alternative routes were championed by those in favour of industrial development, on the one hand, and those in favour of protecting the environment, on the other. Conveniently for our current purposes, one of these routes (D1) was on the east bank of the river Maas, while the other was on the west bank (D2). Industrial interests and regional politicians favoured the eastern alternative, since this would be shorter and lead through major population centres. Environmental movements wanted the road on the western bank of the Maas, since fewer acres of protected land would then have to be sacrificed.

The main political parties were also divided on the issue. The Christian Democrats, with a stronghold in Limburg because of its large Catholic population, backed the provincial politicians and the eastern route, D1. The Liberals, defenders of industry, were also strongly in favour of the eastern route. For Labour and D66, the environmental arguments were dominant and they supported the western route, D2. Table 1 confirms that, if this issue is seen as one defined along the environmental policy dimension, then the Christian Democrats and Liberals are aligned on the "pro-growth" side of the spectrum, with Labour and D66 aligned on the "pro-environment" side.

The issue led to several heated debates within the cabinet. Three cabinet portfolios were involved—Transport and Public Works (held by the Liberals), Housing, Planning and Environmental Management (held by Labour) and Agriculture, Nature Management and Fisheries (Liberals). After several postponements, the decision of the cabinet represented a numerical victory for Labour and D66 ministers. The cabinet decision thus favoured the environmentally friendly western route, D2.

Once a cabinet decision has been taken, under the rules of the parliamentary government system, all ministers are expected to defend it. It was thus the task of the Liberals' Annemarie Jorritsma-Lebbink, the minister of Transport and Public Works, to present the cabinet decision in parliament and justify the choice of the western route that her party had in fact opposed. Her parliamentary speeches on this matter were lacking in conviction, by all accounts—she even admitted in these to being unhappy with the cabinet decision she was now responsible for implementing, since this had not been her first choice. The other main political parties stuck to their stated positions—the Christian Democrats favouring the eastern route, Labour and D66 favouring the western route. The smaller left-wing parties supported the cabinet, as did one conservative orthodox-Christian party. The minister did not succeed in convincing the other smaller, conservative parties.

At the end of the debate, Liberal and Christian Democrat legislators put down a motion proposing the eastern alternative. After a lot of head counting and several unsuccessful attempts to locate a nonpaired absent Labour member of parliament, the motion proposing the eastern alternative was carried by 71 to 70. Immediately after this, the cabinet announced that it would abide by the wishes of parliament and build the road on the eastern bank of the Maas. The cabinet and the legislature had come into conflict and, in this case, the legislature had won. The cabinet gave in to the parliamentary majority and neither the responsible minister, nor the whole cabinet, resigned and left office. No sanction was applied by the Liberal leadership against Liberal legislators who had voted against the decision of a cabinet of which the Liberals were members.

In terms of the model set out in Figure 1, this case fits either in the category "DON'T WHIP–STAY" or "WHIP–DEFY–IGNORE–STAY," depending upon how we interpret the evidently half-hearted attempts of the Liberal minister to convince deputies from her own party to support the cabinet decision. Either way, the outcome is explicable only if the issue at stake was of very little importance to the government parties who were reneged upon by the Liberals (q was very small), and if these parties did not set great store by their credibility in forcing cabinet colleagues to abide by collective cabinet decisions (k_3 was very small too). Knowing that Labour and D66 politicians would rather shoulder all of these costs than bring down the government, Liberal legislators could then act with impunity. Despite losing the argument in cabinet, the Liberals were in this way able to end-run their cabinet colleagues and get what they wanted in the legislature.

The Dutch situation is somewhat complicated by questions as to who is the "real" party leader in Holland. Is this the leader of the parliamentary party, or the leader of the Liberal ministers in cabinet? It might well be argued by experts on Dutch politics that the "real" Liberal Party was the parliamentary party, that the "real" party position was that the road should be built on the eastern bank of the Maas, that Liberal ministers simply failed to carry the day as no more than agents of the party in cabinet, and that the cabinet should have expected to have been defeated in the legislature. But such an argument would not gainsay the point that collective responsibility—one of the fundamental sources of stability for cabinet government in parliamentary democracy—was not operating in this case.

Conclusions

A single case can do no more, of course, than put a little flesh on the bare bones of a general argument. Set in the context of the model developed above, however, this Dutch case does paint one possible picture of how conflict between legislature and executive can arise in a European parliamentary democracy.

If the pattern described in the previous section were to become an established norm, then cabinet government as Europeans now know it would evolve into something quite different from what is seen as the classical system of unified government. The result would be a shift towards something more closely akin to the type of legislative-executive relations to be found in the U.S. Any cabinet decision would be liable to be overturned by a legislative coalition between the parliamentary opposition and losing factions in the cabinet. In short, the current European system of cabinet government depends upon tight party discipline and is liable to change quite radically if party discipline begins to break down.

This concentrates our attention upon the factors that facilitate indiscipline in parliamentary parties and thereby open up the possibility of conflict between legislative and executive sections of the same party. One important factor arises when, as we have just seen in the Dutch case described above, there are different leaders of the party as a whole and the parliamentary party. In such cases, senior party politicians may go into government, but the leader of the parliamentary party may stay outside, with the potential to promote the interests of backbench party politicians when these conflict with those of the government. This is of course less a form of indiscipline than a way of running the party that keeps legislative and executive elements quite distinct. What is important in the present context, however, is that the internal affairs of a party in government are subject to conflict between executive and legislature.

One obvious and well-known source of indiscipline has to do with the electoral system. Some systems, for example first-past-the-post, attach great value to membership of one of the very few large parties that are not massively underrepresented by the method of turning votes into seats. In this environment, it may be much easier for leaders to punish dissidents by banishing them from the party. In highly proportional list-PR systems, in contrast, dissidents may well have much more realistic opportunities to form a credible new party, and for this reason be harder to discipline. To set against this, electoral systems in which people cast votes for individual candidates, such as first-past-the-post, single transferable vote, and preferential list-PR systems, allow individual legislators to build their own power bases and thereby insulate themselves from the potential sanctions of party leaders. Non-preferential list-PR systems, in contrast, make it easier for party leaders to promote or demote party legislators on the list, according to how well-behaved they have been. In short, there are complex interactions between the electoral system and the intraparty whipping game, but electoral systems do have a considerable bearing upon how easy it is for party leaders to deliver upon their promises to others.

The internal governance structures of political parties also have a major impact upon the extent to which party leaders can impose their will upon the rank and file. Important matters in this regard include the way in which the party leader is chosen, the way in which party candidates for legislative office are selected, the role of the party conference and/or executive in setting party policy and mandating decisions on government formation, and so on. Some parties may well have an internal governance structure that makes them inherently more difficult to discipline. This will obviously have a bearing upon how they are viewed by others as potential partners in the making and breaking of governments.

There are plenty of complex interactions to explore here but the important thing to bear in mind is the extent to which a party leader can ensure the compliance of internal elements of the party when it comes to delivering upon promises made to others. Parties are clearly not unitary actors, and function as unified actors only to the extent that their leaders are able to maintain disciplined behaviour among the rank and file. The less able leaders are to maintain such discipline, the greater the potential in Europe for the same type of conflict between legislature and executive that can arise under the U.S. system of divided government.

The main way out of this would be a reassertion by cabinet parties of a practical strategic interpretation of the doctrine of collective cabinet responsibility to mean that all parties in a cabinet agree to abide by, and do their best to implement, cabinet decisions, even when they disagree with them. This would be backed up by the matching obligation that, when this compliance does not happen, cabinet parties who are reneged upon should withdraw from cabinet and bring down the government, however much they might wish in the short term not to have to do this. The reputational costs of failure to enforce the implicit bargain at the heart of the parliamentary government system would otherwise only lead to further reneging, further potential for conflict between legislature and executive, and a drift towards the type of legislative gridlock that can be facilitated by divided government, U.S.-style.

NOTES

An earlier version of this paper was presented at the Comparative Legislative Research Conference held at The University of Iowa, 17–18 April 1998. I am very grateful to Gerhard Loewenberg and David Mayhew for their constructive comments on an earlier version.

1. Implicit support may arise, for example, from the strategic abstention of certain actors in circumstances where voting against a proposed government would result in its defeat. It may also arise when there is no formal investiture requirement, but when the incoming government can only in practice take office if it can expect to win any early vote of no confidence it might have to face.

2. The cases have the same outcome because the change in conditions between Case 2 and Case 3 in effect change only the relative attractiveness of options for Leader Q that are off the equilibrium path.

3. I am indebted to Monique Leijenaar for providing the details of this case.

REFERENCES

Cox, Gary. 1987. *The Efficient Secret.* Cambridge: Cambridge University Press.
Laver, Michael. 1995. "Party Policy and Cabinet Portfolios in the Netherlands, 1994." *Acta Politica* XXX:3–29.
Laver, Michael, and Kenneth A. Shepsle. 1991. "Divided Government: America is Not Exceptional." *Governance* 4:250–69.
Laver, Michael, and Kenneth A. Shepsle. 1996. *Making and Breaking Governments.* Cambridge: Cambridge University Press.
Lucardie, Paul, and Gerrit Voerman. 1995. "The Netherlands." *European Journal of Political Research. Data Issue* 28:427–36.
Luebbert, Gregory. 1986. *Comparative Democracy: Policy Making and Governing Coalitions in Europe and Israel.* New York: Colombia University Press.
Strøm, Kaare. 1990. *Minority Government and Majority Rule.* Cambridge: Cambridge University Press.

Positive Theories of Congressional Parties

Steven S. Smith

We often think that the era of positive theories of congressional politics began with Mayhew's *Congress: The Electoral Connection*. In fact, studies of congressional parties had a positive emphasis from the start of the behavioral era. This is not true of studies of most other features of congressional politics (committees, voting behavior, norms, deviance), but studies of congressional parties have long emphasized the strategic and contingent relationship between legislators, their parties, and party leaders. Recall three articles published in the *American Political Science Review* in the 1960s. Huitt (1961) considered informal and weak Senate party leadership to be a function of strong constituency orientation among senators facing periodic election in diverse states.[1] When Froman and Ripley (1965) wrote of the "conditions of party leadership," they emphasized how reelection-oriented members become less influenced by party leaders as they move from legislative settings that have few electoral consequences to those that have greater potential electoral consequences. Jones (1968, 481) asked two questions in the first major treatment of the minority party: "What are the principal policy-making strategies of the minority party? What political conditions determine the range of strategies available to it in any one Congress?" While each of these essays is usually relegated to the category of "traditional" studies of Congress, each considers parties and their leaders' behavior to be the product of goal-driven strategies.

In recent years, positive theories of congressional parties have been elaborated to encompass a variety of institutional features. The seasoning of the field is reflected in its contrasting theoretical accounts of the existence of parties and their effects, and the return to empirical evidence in a set of insightful studies of modern congressional decision making. My purpose is to provide a critical review of this recent literature, much of which is still unpublished, and contribute, in a modest way, to the ongoing development of theory in this field.

Reprinted with permission from *Legislative Studies Quarterly* 25, no. 2 (May 2000): 193–215.

Key Arguments

The central questions are: Do congressional parties matter? and, If so, why? These issues have been approached in a variety of ways. Most recent studies treat congressional parties as exogenous features of their (implicit or explicit) models, then observe or posit that parties and their leaders enjoy certain parliamentary privileges. It is then argued that these parliamentary advantages, particularly for the majority party, influence legislators' committee and floor behavior and legislative outcomes. But this is not where recent studies of congressional parties and leadership began. Instead, Cooper and Brady (1981) argued that parties, and leadership powers, are endogenous to electoral outcomes and the membership's policy preferences and so have little independent effect on behavior and outcomes, contrary to recent claims. I begin with their study.

The Cooper-Brady Argument

Until the late 1990s, most scholars in the field seemed persuaded by the Cooper-Brady argument (1981), an argument introduced in the authors' previous works (Brady 1973; Cooper 1975). Cooper and Brady proposed that the ebb and flow in the centralization of power in House majority party leadership is a function of intraparty cohesiveness and interparty polarization, which, they argued, paralleled party polarization in the electorate.[2] The theory is that legislators' policy preferences are determined by the outcome of elections, the distribution of preferences determines whether the parties differ greatly and whether the parties are internally cohesive, and that internally cohesive, polarized parties generate centralization. The integrative capacity of party leadership flows primarily from "party strength," defined as cohesiveness in policy preferences. Writing before the resurgence of partisanship in the 1980s, Cooper and Brady (1981, 424) observed that "the degree of power dispersion now present is explicable in terms of present weaknesses in party unity or coherence." The degree of party unity, that is, the distribution of preferences among legislators, shaped the decision-making process; the legislative process did not determine the degree of party unity. Thus, the suggestion of a relationship between party leaders' activity and legislative outcomes is spurious. Both leaders' activity and legislative outcomes are determined primarily by the distribution of preferences within the membership.

The core features of the Cooper-Brady thesis have been adopted in the work of Sinclair (1983, 1995), Deering and Smith (1997), Rohde (1991), and Aldrich and Rohde (1997) on the modern Congress. All of these scholars note the importance of changing policy alignments for the centrality of party leaders in policy-making in the House. Aldrich and Rohde (1997, 3), reflecting the views of the others, argued that intraparty cohesiveness and interparty polarization lead members of the majority party to "grant their partisan institutions—their party conference/caucus, leaders, and other such institutional mechanisms—more powers and resources, and more latitude to use these powers and resources, to achieve collectively desired outcomes." While most of these scholars make explicit their view that factors other than election outcomes (including leadership strategies) contribute to party cohesiveness, they appear to accept the view that election outcomes are the primary determinant of the policy alignments, which in turn determine the role of partisan institutions and policy outcomes.

These more detailed studies of congressional party leadership in the 1980s and 1990s challenge an important argument of Cooper and Brady. They claim that party leadership activity matters. Rohde (1991, 192) makes the claim in the concluding sentence of his book: "Parties are consequential in shaping members' preferences, the character of the issues on the agenda, the nature of legislative alternatives, and ultimate political outcomes, and they will remain important as long as the underlying forces that created this partisan resurgence persist." While terms like "consequential" and "important" leave plenty of analytical "wiggle room," the clear thrust of these studies has been that the parties and their leaders matter. Rohde, like Cooper and Brady, considers only the House.

Sinclair (1995) was the first to assess directly the consequences of House party leadership involvement for policy-making. Others, including Cooper and Brady, had more to say about leadership resources and activity than about leadership influence on members' behavior or legislative outcomes. And even then, most studies relied on qualitative secondary accounts to characterize party leadership activity. Sinclair, too, relies on secondary accounts of individual legislative battles but systematically codes for evidence of leadership and presidential involvement in specific legislative battles. For five selected Democratic Congresses of the 1969–90 period, she reports (1995, 300) that "even after the character of the floor coalition is taken into account, leadership involvement in interaction with presidential position significantly influenced the success of committees on the House floor."[3] Aldrich and Rohde (1997), with less systematic evidence, reached similar conclusions.[4]

The Pivotal-Politics Thesis

Krehbiel (1998) challenges the view that parties matter and, in doing so, implicitly endorses the Cooper-Brady argument that suggestions of party-outcomes or party-floor behavior relationships are spurious. Like the Cooper-Brady thesis, Krehbiel's case is predicated on a spatial view of lawmaking. He holds that the pivotal voter (the median voter in a single chamber under simple majority rule) in a unidimensional alignment determines a chamber's choices. Parties play no formal role in the theory. Instead, the pivotal voter's location, which varies with the decision rule, determines the outcome. Krehbiel does not argue that parties are inconsequential. Rather, he argues (1998) that "competing party organizations bidding for pivotal votes may roughly counterbalance one another, so final outcomes are not different from what a simpler but completely specified nonpartisan theory predicts." Krehbiel, who finds some small but measurable "party effects" of various kinds in different aspects of congressional activity, nevertheless argues that those effects are marginal at best and may be the by-product of poor measures of legislators' preferences in the equations estimating preference and party effects. Properly measuring and controlling for preferences, Krehbiel contends, leaves little room for party in a parsimonious explanation of individual behavior or majority policy choices. Krehbiel, no doubt, would not find the Sinclair and Aldrich-Rohde analyses persuasive because they do not directly account for the underlying policy preferences.

A spatial perspective might provide the basis for a theory of congressional parties (and obviously has for other theorists)—like-minded legislators create party organizations in order to enhance their effectiveness as a policy coalition. Krehbiel's pivotal politics is simply silent on the creation and development of congressional parties. The argument is largely empirical and contemporary: because controlling for preferences leaves little for parties to explain, modern parties are not essential to explaining policy choices and so need not complicate the theory.

The Conditional Party Government Thesis

Attempts to rescue party have been offered by Aldrich and Rohde (1997) under a label proposed by Rohde (1991), "conditional party government."[5] In the Aldrich-Rohde account, House party organizations and leadership are important for policy-making when the party polarization condition suggested by Cooper and Brady is met. When the parties are polarized, the majority party organizes to control the agenda, to offer inducements to median-range legislators, and to otherwise pull policy choices toward the median preference of the majority party. The inducements are possible through voluntary contributions from members to their parties. Moreover, the majority party enjoys significant institutional advantages because majority rule confers on it the ability to shape the rules in its members' interest, constrained only by the few procedures specified in the Constitution. Aldrich and Rohde seek to illustrate these party effects by identifying policies that appear to have been shaped by actions of party leaders under conditions that should generate party government.

The Electoral Connection Thesis

While spatial theorists usually associate legislators' policy preferences with constituency preferences, they posit that policy preferences rather than the goal of reelection motivate the strategies of politicians once they are in office. Electoral considerations influence legislative politics exclusively through the legislators' policy preferences, which in turn shape legislators' policy and institutional strategies. The perspective is similar to the "policy domain" theory of Clausen (1973), who argued that, within broad domains of policy, legislators develop stable policy positions that represent a composite of policy influences, including constituency pressures, personal ideology, the constellation of interest group influences, and so on. Spatial theorists, however, make no theoretical claim about policy domains, although some fall back on first-dimension D-NOMINATE scores or other unidimensional rankings to operationalize preferences.

A second class of theories keeps the electoral goal of legislators central to their calculations about party and other institutional arrangements. This perspective has multiple origins (for example, Arnold 1990, Mayhew 1974) and is best articulated in Kiewiet and McCubbins (1991) and Cox and McCubbins (1993). Cox and McCubbins (1993, 109) defend their use of the electoral goal as a foundation for a party theory by arguing that "although we do not assume that legislators are 'single-minded' in their pursuit of reelection (Mayhew 1974), we do believe that is an important component of their motivation and that, to begin with, it is reasonable to consider this goal in isolation." In fact, the goal is *the* foundation for collective party action in their theory.

Cox and McCubbins observe that a party's record has electoral consequences for individual legislators. Maintaining or enhancing party reputation is a collective good with attendant coordination problems that are managed with the creation of party organization and leadership. Implicitly, the thesis is that party organization and leadership vary with the particularities of the task of maintaining and enhancing the party reputation. Cox and McCubbins note that the electoral relevance of committees' jurisdictions varies, and so party effort to control committees varies across committees (on this point, see also Maltzman 1997).

The party theory of Cox and McCubbins is important because it posits that legislators carrying the same brand name, a party label, have a common interest even if there is substantial variance in their policy preferences. Party leaders and organizations enhance the efficiency of building a favorable party record, so legislators are motivated to grant leaders special powers and resources. Once in place, leaders' powers and resources can be employed to buy the support from wayward colleagues, enforce deals, and in other ways protect their parties' records.

The importance of the electoral connection is also central to Sinclair's arguments about party leadership in the House. She argues, following Fenno (1973), that legislators have a mix of goals (reelection, good public policy, and influence), which makes it unlikely that they will be fully satisfied with any delegation of power to party organs and leaders (Sinclair 1995, 17). And party leaders' contributions to policy often can be understood only in terms of multiple goals. For example, House majority party leadership may direct the design of special rules restricting floor amendments so that legislators are not forced to choose between a vote in their electoral interest and a vote for their policy preference. Such strategic dilemmas are especially common on omnibus budget and tax bills, where the need for "political cover" is frequently observed (Sinclair 1995, 1999; Smith 1989). Sinclair (1999) demonstrates that a substantial number of majority party members vote for a special rule restricting amendments but vote against the bill on final passage even when it was not changed on the floor, indicating that revealed procedural and policy preferences are not identical. The disparity increases with the restrictiveness of the rule.

Recent Evidence

Several recent papers provide evidence of party effects, controlling for preferences. In each case, the partisan theory is more fully elaborated and party effects are found. The studies emphasize varying mechanisms for party influence or effect. Several recent studies emphasize agenda control by the majority party—in particular, the House majority party—in order to make explicit the view that the majority party can affect outcomes without party leaders directly influencing individual legislators. Others still emphasize direct party influence on individual legislators, usually implying that leaders apply pressure on individuals.

Sinclair (1999) reports two patterns of behavior on procedural matters in the House that are consistent with a party effect on outcomes. First, she demonstrates that "measures on which the committee was partisan were much more likely to be considered under restrictive rules than were those on which the committee was not partisan." Second, she finds that majority party members often vote for a special rule for a bill but against final passage of that bill, even when the bill is not modified on the floor. That is, a special rule that provides for the consideration of a bill is often supported by legislators who oppose the bill. Thus, in two ways, party effects appear to be substantial at the agenda-setting stage of House action.

Cox and McCubbins (1999) posit a model of agenda control by the majority party. Operationally, the majority party keeps legislation opposed by the party majority off the floor, even if the legislation is favored by a chamber (cross-party) majority. This should yield a pattern of outcomes on final passage motions in which the majority party wins, the floor median's relationship to the majority party median is unrelated to outcomes (because only bills acceptable to both the majority party median and floor median make it to the floor), and the behavior of the minority party on the bills considered on the floor is a function of the minority's distance from the floor median. For the 45th–99th Congresses, Cox and McCubbins model the House majority party's "roll rate," the percentage of votes on which the party lost when a majority of the party voted in favor of passage. Roll rates are unrelated to the majority party's distance from the chamber median but strongly related to the minority party's distance from the chamber median (policy locations measured in NOMINATE scores), as the agenda control model predicts.

Lawrence, Maltzman, and Smith (1999) find a consistent pattern of voting, using the individual member as the unit of analysis, that reflects an asymmetric party effect similar to the one predicted and measured by Cox and McCubbins. On House final passage votes in each of nine recent Congresses, majority party members consistently exhibit little variation and high rates of personal success, whatever their policy preferences, while minority party members' success rates are nearly perfectly related to policy preferences. The pattern holds for both Democratic and Republican majorities and demonstrates the inappropriateness of a naive test using a measure of preferences and a dummy variable for party.

Lawrence, Maltzman, and Smith also distinguish two models of asymmetric party effects. One assumes that parties are electoral cartels but that the majority party has the strongest electoral incentive to behave cohesively. This model predicts unity among majority party members. The second assumes that the majority party's median controls the floor agenda but all members, including majority party members, vote as the policy preferences dictate. This model predicts that majority party members vary in their frequency of winning as a function of their policy distance from the majority party median. The second model consistently performs better than the first.

Notably, Lawrence, Maltzman, and Smith find few party effects in the Senate, where a purely preference-based model of voting appears to fit best. This finding, combined with the more direct evidence of agenda-setting influence in the House, suggests that the institutional setting influences the exhibition of party effects. This is a potentially significant observation—if true, then current institutional arrangements cannot be viewed as simply the product of current preferences.

Heckman and Snyder (1997) propose, and Snyder and Groseclose (1999) apply, a technique for estimating both preferences and party effects from roll-call data. On the assumption that party effects are important only for close votes, the technique begins by estimating ideal points (preferences) from a dimensional analysis of the votes with a lopsided majority—greater than a 65–35 split. Then party effects are estimated by ordinary least squares with the legislators' votes (yea versus nay) from the set of roll-call votes, with closer divisions as the dependent variable and the preference measure and a dummy variable for party as the independent variables. Examining House roll-call behavior for the period since World War II, Snyder and Groseclose find substantial party effects on a sizable proportion of votes and across a wide variety of types of votes (substantive and procedural).[6] McCarty, Poole, and Rosenthal (1999) are quick to point out, however, that the estimation of preferences from the lopsided votes generates potentially serious errors in estimating the preferences of legislators in the middle of the policy spectrum (those who are responsible for making votes close). Because party captures much of the variation in preferences for that middle group, the Heckman-Snyder technique is likely to overstate the significance of party.

McCarty, Poole, and Rosenthal uncover another piece of evidence of party effects. They isolate the 19 senators and representatives who switched parties in the past several decades and examine changes in "revealed" preferences using the DW-NOMINATE procedure for estimation (McCarty, Poole, and Rosenthal 1999). They find that the party switchers exhibit far greater than average changes in behavior. The authors note that the mechanism generating this effect cannot be inferred from the observed behavior, but they seem to prefer to ascribe electoral interests to many of the switchers—they moved to the party more popular in their districts. Still, they conclude that party is "a part of a legislator's overall environment that forms her induced preferences" (30).

Ansolabehere, Snyder, and Stewart (1999) replicate the analysis of McCarty, Poole, and Rosenthal with Americans for Democratic Action (ADA) scores to reconfirm the changes in behavior. But the electoral misfortunes of the switchers lead them to question whether switching was truly motivated by electoral interests. Instead, they find qualitative evidence that legislators' discomfort with being ideological misfits (say, conservatives in the Democratic caucus) accounts for switching. The source of the behavioral change, however, is not explicitly addressed in this report. We are left with the impression that party switching relieves members of unwanted pressure from their old parties and allows them to behave in a manner more consistent with their own preferences.

Wilson (1999) extends the analysis of party and NOMINATE-based scores back to 1879. For every House roll-call vote between 1879 and 1997, Wilson compares the observed median (defined by legislators' D-NOMINATE scores) with medians generated in simulations of each roll-call vote in which no partisanship is allowed. The simulations generate predicted medians based on preference-only behavior. In this way, Wilson accounts for that fact that the D-NOMINATE scores are based on behavior that may be influenced by preferences, party, and other factors. He finds a general shift of the observed median toward the majority party and away from the median predicted by a variety of purely preference-based models. Sharp shifts in the observed medians, relative to the simulated medians, occur whenever there is a change in majority party control.

Finally, Ansolabehere, Snyder, and Stewart (1999) use a survey-based measure of preferences to avoid the problem of dependence between the measure of preferences and the voting-based dependent variables used in most of these analyses. The surveys were conducted during the 1996 and 1998 election cycles by Project Vote Smart, which asks all candidates for Congress to answer a battery of questions about many policy issues in a written questionnaire for the purpose of voter education. The validity of the measure is asserted on the basis of face validity and a .76 correlation with district presidential vote. For their preference measure, which they call "electorally revealed preferences," Ansolabehere, Snyder, and Stewart extract the first principal component from the elected members' responses. Estimates of a model of voting scores (W-NOMINATE or factor scores) with the preference measure, a dummy variable for party, and district presidential vote as independent variables show consistently large preference and party effects (and no presidential vote effects) in the 103d–105th Congresses (1993–98). In an analysis of preference and party effects on individual votes, Ansolabehere, Snyder, and Stewart show that party effects are stronger on close votes than on lopsided votes, very strong on procedural votes, and moderately strong on passage votes. Further, party effects are more modest on amendment votes and stronger on social welfare and budgetary votes than on other votes.

Preliminary Assessment

Do parties matter? The recent debate addresses this issue from one, narrow perspective—are party effects detectable once we account for legislators' preferences? Other sources of influence—constituency preferences, interest group demands, campaign contributors' expectations, and so on—are not incorporated explicitly into most of the recent theories and statistical models. There are good reasons to be concerned about preference and party effects, to be sure, but there also is reason to argue that more fully specified models are essential to calculating unbiased estimates of those effects.

In defense of the recent literature, it might be argued that preferences are the compound product of constituency, group, and contributor influence—something like the "electorally revealed preference" described by Ansolabehere, Snyder, and Stewart or the constituency-generated preferences emphasized by Cooper and Brady. Furthermore, party might be considered an immediate influence that is sometimes incompatible with preferences so conceived. In this way, preferences reflect sources of influence external to Congress, party reflects sources of influence internal to Congress, and contrasting preference and party effects is appropriate. Unfortunately, the internal/external distinction is entirely arbitrary. Party is an external as well as an internal source of influence. Similarly, the internal counterparts to constituency and group influence—member caucuses, factional groups, and so on—cannot be ignored.

Still, it is worth considering the current debate on its own terms because of the insights that it has produced about the nature of party effects in Congress. I begin with the pivotal-politics thesis.

The Pivotal-Politics Thesis

Krehbiel was correct when he once noted the scarcity of direct evidence for the proposition that parties matter. The proposition underpins most studies of congressional parties, even those studies that (partially) accept the Cooper-Brady thesis. Krehbiel also approaches the question properly by advancing a theory (in his case, a spatial theory based on policy preferences), generating a counterhypothesis to the "parties matter" proposition, and seeking to test for party effects, controlling for preferences.

The evidence that policy alignments shape outcomes is indisputable, but the empirical case against parties is unconvincing and appears to be fading as new evidence is marshaled. Several limitations of the pivotal-politics thesis warrant attention.

1. The pivotal-politics thesis leaves us without an explanation of parties, whose activities, internal rules and practices, and leadership consume so much time and effort on the part of legislators (Rohde 1995, 125–29). If legislators only care about their policy gains and losses, and if parties are irrelevant to policy outcomes, why parties? That there is so much superfluous activity should concern theorists seeking to account for the major features of Congress with consequentialist arguments.

A possible response to this criticism is that parties tend to neutralize each other. As one party devises a useful strategy for appealing to median range legislators, the other party counters with its own useful strategy. In this way, the parties are active, but neither party gains a net advantage. Party can be safely set aside in theory and application.

This "mutually assured futility" perspective turns on two assumptions. The first, fully consistent with the underlying theory, is that the parties engage in instantaneous mutual adjustment. The assumption of perfect information allows for this. In practice, surprise strategies and lagged responses may be important. The second assumption is that the only viable party strategy is to offer another policy proposal (on the policy dimension at issue). Under Krehbiel's theory, in which the median voter controls the nature of the rule under which a bill and amendments are debated, we could assume that the minority party has an opportunity to offer a proposal to improve the outcome for the median voter. In practice, a majority party created for other nonpolicy (say, electoral) purposes may have resources valued by the median voter that cannot be matched by the minority party.

2. The operationalization of preferences involves a decomposition of the theoretical construct and a selective focus on one component. Spatial theories treat preferences as ideal points at the moment of decision. Theoretically, preferences can be influenced by any consideration up to the point of decision. In this way, the theory readily incorporates party or committee influences, electoral influences, and so on, at least in principle. These influences are merely causally antecedent to preferences and, as such, outside the scope of the theory itself. The preferences are a composite of these influences and, in theory, can be changed. Strictly speaking, then, controlling for preferences leaves nothing for other influences (constituency, party, committee) to explain. To explain behavior with preferences in this way is trivial and uninteresting.

In empirical applications, preferences often are operationalized with interest-group ratings, NOMINATE scores, or some other measure that aggregates over another period of time. In this way, preferences are treated something like long-term policy dispositions. In other studies, preferences are assumed to be similar to constituency preferences, so that district presidential vote, demographic characteristics, or even poll results can be used as a surrogate for members' preferences. In all such treatments of preferences, the measured policy dispositions may be viewed as long-term or stable components of a decomposed preference, which also is shaped by short-term influences (constituency, party, committee). Policy dispositions, we might think, are the product of legislators' long-term personal policy commitments and constituency expectations and can be changed by short-term influences.

Reducing preferences to policy dispositions has consequences. Plainly, a policy disposition theory, not the original spatial theory, is tested. In fact, it is difficult to see how we can test the original spatial theory against any other theory. After all, the original theory excludes any political influence separate from preferences because it is considered a causally antecedent influence on preferences. But on the upside is that the policy dispositions are what Cooper and Brady, Aldrich and Rohde, Sinclair, and others have in mind. A policy disposition, in contrast with a preference, provides a basis for thinking that legislators' strategies will not be erratic and thus generate rapidly changing policy and institutional choices.

3. The argument that preferences are not entirely exogenous to party is credible. They probably are, as Rohde (1995) claims, partly shaped by party activity within Congress. Krehbiel is surely correct in insisting that we find evidence that leaders have persuaded a legislator to do something he or she is unlikely to have done otherwise. But there is a catch. The usual linear models will not suffice. As we have discovered in studies of party identification, issue evaluations, and presidential voting, accounting for nonrecursive relationships can substantially change our inferences about the importance of a variable.

Unfortunately, serious technical obstacles stand in the way of estimating the indirect effects of party, the most important of which is isolating exogenous variables for party and preferences. Thus, while Krehbiel's tests of preferences and party effects are unconvincing, we are unlikely to improve on them.

4. While claims about wide variation in party influence are common, no one has claimed that leaders' influence over individual legislators is widespread. To the contrary, party leaders can greatly influence a policy outcome by having only marginal influence on the behavior of a few legislators. Whip polls, task force head counts, consultations with lobbyists, and so on are all a part of identifying a few members whose support might be gained by well-focused leadership effort. Because these few members are pivotal, statistical estimates of variance explained by a dummy variable for Democrats and Republicans will not identify the critical effect of party on outcomes. Very little variance in individual behavior may be explained by a party dummy variable when the difference between winning and losing turned on effective leadership strategy. Statistically small effects of party on individual behavior, controlling for preferences, is what I would expect, based on my reading of insider accounts (for example, Sinclair 1983, 1995). That is what Krehbiel finds (1998, ch. 8). We need to measure specific acts of leadership or party effort and substitute corresponding variables for the dummy party variable employed by Krehbiel (and others).

5. Isolating the effects of preferences and party on outcomes is difficult in an institutional setting in which party pervades the decision-making process. Preferences, Krehbiel correctly observes, are difficult to measure independently of observed behavior. Party is, too. To control for party with a dummy variable in an equation that includes preferences does not account for the way party may have constrained the alternatives over which variance in preferences is measured. Because party is the basis for making committee assignments, delegating responsibility within committees, scheduling and organizing floor activity, appointing conferees, and structuring other features of congressional decision making, the indirect effects of party are difficult to assess for a narrow range of behavior at any one stage in the process, say, roll-call voting.

6. The pivotal-politics thesis fails to explain important institutional features. Why would the median voter in the House or Senate adopt a supermajority decision rule (suspension of the rules, cloture, tax measures)? One possibility is that the majority seeks to make its current decisions more binding on subsequent majorities, as we frequently see in rules governing the adoption of constitutional amendments. But this obvious response does not explain rules that are binding in the current Congress. Another possibility is that one majority, say a party majority, seeks to raise the threshold for other majorities that might form in the current Congress. But, such a possibility undermines the basic thesis.

7. The pivotal-politics thesis rests on the assumption that there is a pivot—which is certain only when the policy space is unidimensional. While there is evidence that the liberal-conservative continuum is the most common dimension underlying congressional policy alignments (McCarty, Poole, and Rosenthal 1999; Smith 1989), it is highly probable that the dimensionality of the policy space is more complex on important legislative measures—appropriations bills, major re-authorization bills, reconciliation bills, and so on. If so, it is not clear which median dictates the outcome. Party strategies may influence the dimension that is privileged or the way the positions of the competing medians are compromised.

Conditional Party Government

The conditional party government argument of Aldrich and Rohde is evolving through their papers, but it appears to be going a step further than the Cooper-Brady thesis. Cooper and Brady emphasize that the appearance of party strength varies with polarization of preferences by party, but it is the cohesiveness of the majority and sharp interparty differences, not the action of the party or its leaders, that determine outcomes. Aldrich and Rohde, in various papers, argue that there are significant party effects beyond preferences that kick in when the party government condition is met. Have they confirmed this proposition? The answer seems to be no. This is a work in progress, but two points can be made about the arguments to date.

1. In a 1997 exposition of the argument, legislators volunteer utiles (formal power, resources) to the party for it to organize and influence outcomes. However, in the spatial account offered by Aldrich and Rohde, it is unclear why legislators should contribute utiles to party organizations when they only care about the spatial location of the policy outcome. Moreover, the argument for *majority* party advantage is itself contingent on the institutional context—the majority party must have the power, under the rules, to impose changes when it is motivated by interparty competition and is sufficiently cohesive to do so. This is more institutional apparatus than Aldrich and Rohde's exposition of the core theory allows. As an empirical matter, the majority party may not have been able to impose desired rules changes in the House before the late 19th century and probably still does not in the modern Senate.

In this presentation of the argument, Aldrich and Rohde reach beyond spatial theory to elaborate the foundations of congressional parties. In fact, they observe that their "story can be enriched" by the Cox-McCubbins perspective. They even appear to employ the perspective when they make observations that rely on electoral considerations, rather than purely policy considerations, such as this one:

It is also important to note that such packages [as the reconciliation bill] provide political cover for members, masking their support for policies that would be unpopular with their constituents by combining them with other things, and making it easier for them to go along with the leadership (Aldrich and Rohde 1997, 16).

Aldrich and Rohde then cite ways in which the majority party leadership uses control over the floor agenda to avoid embarrassing its party colleagues with floor defeats or votes on proposals crafted by the minority party. These observations are entirely consistent with Sinclair's (1995) convincing argument that the use of special rules can only be explained in terms of *both* policy and electoral objectives.

Still, Aldrich and Rohde (1997, 7–8) attempt to retain a strictly spatial perspective when outlining the way in which the Cox-McCubbins enrichment can be incorporated in their theory. They translate the party-record thesis by operationalizing the party record as the mean ideal point of the party's legislators and by equating a legislator's electoral needs with her ideal point. Necessarily, a strategy that suits the member's policy interests suits her electoral interests in the same degree. And, necessarily, the only source of variation from election to election is the fit of the party record to a district's preferences. By itself, this operational treatment of the party record adds nothing to the ability of the conditional party government thesis to explain policy choices (or processes) beyond the sketchy model suggested by Cooper and Brady, nor does it supply the missing motivation for members to create parties and contribute utiles to them.

Aldrich and Rohde (1997, 8) suggest an additional elaboration: "Further, we could imagine dividing the individual candidate characteristics into those that are related to policy dimensions and those advantages that are independent of policy (the typical litany of incumbent advantages serve as illustrations)." These nonpolicy advantages also are the basis for selective incentives, allocated by leaders, to entice members to vote in the direction of the party median. Unfortunately, this elaboration renders members' behavior even less predictable—policy and nonpolicy advantages must be balanced in some way. Furthermore, we still do not know why a member would empower her party to undermine her leverage as a median member of the chamber. And Aldrich and Rohde do not explain how their initial equation of policy and electoral interests can be maintained when advantages that are independent of policy are introduced. In the end, the attempt to incorporate the Cox-McCubbins perspective with the conditional party government thesis does little to sustain the core spatial argument.

These elaborations have an important implication for a theory of party development that is ignored in the recent debates. If we concede that legislators value the *popularity* of party activity (so they care about more than just the policy choice) and other *nonpolicy* benefits that might be bestowed by party, we must admit that the gains from coordination generated by parties are not entirely policy gains. In fact, policy gains from coordination may not have been the primary basis for the development of important features of congressional parties. Gains in party reputation or the allocation of the perquisites of office (patronage, for example) may be essential to explaining the organization of parties and their subsequent policy significance.

2. The theoretical challenge for Aldrich and Rohde is to demonstrate that party effects can be generated from a spatial model in which legislators are motivated by policy preferences alone (i.e., by minimizing the distance between their ideal points and the outcome). In a 1998 paper elaborating on the 1997 paper, Aldrich and Rohde present a game with two dimensions, three players (two majority party, one minority party) with different ideal points, and a status quo located within the triangle formed by the players' positions. A majority party player makes a proposal b at the center of her party, the minority party player offers an amendment, and votes are cast on the amendment and proposal (as amended, if amended). Aldrich and Rohde argue that if the condition for party government is met—the parties are polarized so that the ideal points form an isosceles (elongated) triangle—the majority party can produce an outcome at its own center.

There are two points to be made about the Aldrich-Rohde game. First, as Krehbiel and Meirowitz (1999) observe, the Aldrich-Rohde inference from the simple spatial model is wrong. While the majority party proposer can improve her position by offering a bill away from the status quo, the minority party player can offer an amendment that is noncentral to the majority party that will be approved. The outcome makes one of the majority party players better off but not both (in Figure 1, a^* beats both the bill b^* and the status quo q).

Second, the "party-ness" of the model comes in the form of an *exogenous* procedural privilege granted to a particular majority party player to make the first proposal and the right of the minority party player to offer an amendment, with no other proposals allowed. Setting aside the question of how such (fixed) rights get established by players who care only about policy outcomes, variation over time is explained entirely by variation in ideal points (as Cooper and Brady argued). There is no sharp phase transition in the location of the outcome as the condition of party government is more fully met—only a gradual shift in policy outcomes to the majority end as the majority becomes more cohesive (see Krehbiel and Meirowitz 1999, Figure 7). The preferences of the players, combined with exogenously imposed rules and party membership, generate the outcome. No independent influence of "party strength" exists.

In sum, the conditional party government argument, in emphasizing the consequences of variation in the distribution of policy preferences, captures an

FIGURE 1
Three-Player Legislature with Bill **b** and Amendment **a**

Figure 1a. Players Equidistant Apart with Majority Party (Republican) Proposal Power

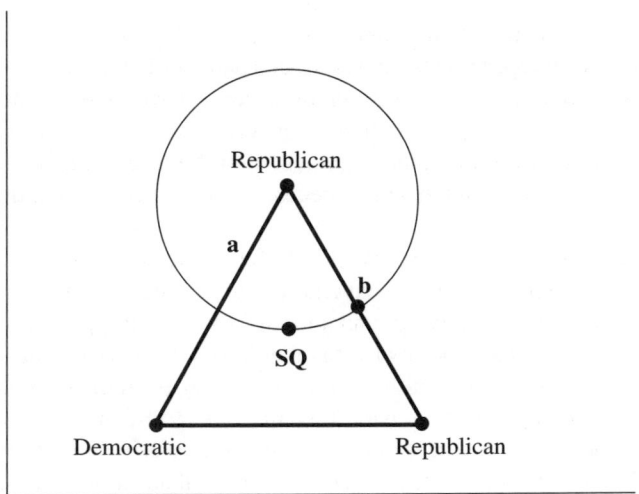

Figure 1b. Polarized Parties with Majority Party (Republican) Proposal Power

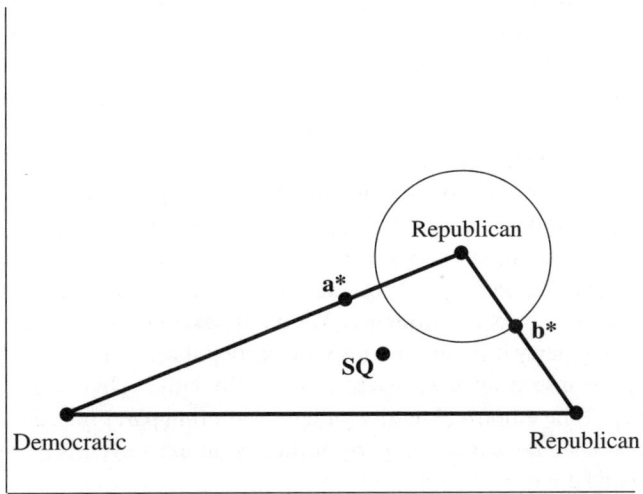

important source of variation in the assertiveness of party leaders and party success, as Cooper and Brady argued, but it does not yet account for the existence of parties or for party effects on outcomes beyond preferences. Electoral forces shape preferences, Aldrich and Rohde emphasize, but their theory begins with preferences and does not explicitly account for the role that common electoral interests might play in generating and maintaining congressional parties.

If we treat seriously the claimed empirical relationship between interparty polarization, intraparty cohesiveness, and party influence, the lack of an adequate spatial theory poses a problem, at least if we expect spatial theory to establish sufficient conditions for party government. In fact, while spatial theory offers reason to believe that the alignment of preferences will contribute to party influence, it does not yet establish necessary or sufficient conditions for party influence.

The argument has two parts. First, the greater the potential policy gains are, the greater the incentive to expend resources. Thus, the greater the distance is between the parties, the greater the incentive for the parties to deploy resources to buy votes. In this way, the condition of polarized parties motivates the use of party resources, although it does not by itself create additional party resources or make the use of party resources more effective.

Second, party resources must exist for some reason other than the achievement of policy goals. As we have seen, the spatial account provides no policy-related incentive for a legislator to volunteer resources to a party that will use them to pry her away from her ideal point. A party with multiple collective goals may find that it can deploy resources that might be used for another purpose. For example, a party leader might use a committee assignment that could be used to enhance one member's electoral prospects instead to induce another member to support the party position. When such resources exist and the policy stakes are high, the party is encouraged to use its resources to influence the outcome.

All things being equal, greater party polarization produces a greater commitment of resources and, presumably, greater leadership influence on the outcome. But conditions vary (all things may not be equal), so party polarization will not be found to be a necessary or a sufficient condition for party influence. Instead, polarization is an important contributory factor that helps to account for the variance in party influence. We would expect, as several scholars have claimed, that party influence varies with party polarization even if the former is not a necessary or sufficient condition for the latter. This argument does not relieve us of the empirical burden of demonstrating party influence, but it does provide a basis for expecting party influence to exist even if there is no sufficient spatial condition for it.

Recent Empirical Evidence

The recent empirical studies of party effects are important for two reasons. First, after a long delay, the studies take up Cooper and Brady's challenge to demonstrate that party activity is not merely spuriously related to legislative behavior and outcomes. The studies have shown that *voting behavior* is structured by party, when controlling for preferences, at least at some important stages in the process. Moreover, a couple of studies have demonstrated more directly that *outcomes* on final passage votes show evidence of party influence.

Second, the empirical studies have made some limited progress in specifying the mechanisms of party influence. The use of a dummy variable is justified in many studies on the grounds that there are compound forms of party influence. But if legislative behavior or outcomes reflect asymmetric patterns of partisan advantage and influence, the dummy variable may underestimate party effects. The studies by Cox and McCubbins (1999) and Lawrence, Maltzman, and Smith (1999) already provide evidence of this problem.

Conclusion

Recent work on party effects in Congress represents real progress. Theories of congressional parties have become more precise. Theories now explicitly account for the endogeneity of legislative parties to legislators' political goals. This logic has long been recognized but, until recently, had been developed and applied unsystematically, even casually. Theories that specify the mechanisms of party influence have proven particularly insightful, if not always successful. Empirical work has addressed the issue of controlling for preferences in assessing party effects, and it has become more historical and more sensitive to legislative context as scholars have sought better evidence on party effects.

Still, important conceptual and empirical issues remain. Theoretical claims about the relationship between preferences and party influences remain ambiguous. The validity of measures of preferences and party effects remains suspect. An exclusively spatial foundation for congressional parties is yet to be defined; a richer multiple-goals perspective remains to be developed. And studies of the origins of party organization and leadership in the House and Senate, which would strengthen the empirical basis for claims about the functions of parties as solutions to problems of cooperation and collective action among legislators, remain to be done.

NOTES

I thank Sarah Binder, Eric Lawrence, D. Roderick Kiewiet, and Forrest Maltzman for their comments on an early draft of this essay.

1. Huitt also emphasized the formal power of committees and their chairs. He deals with this issue only briefly but clearly treats committee power as exogenous to party power rather than treating both as products of senators' choices.

2. Earlier studies frequently noted the incohesiveness of congressional parties and its consequences for the nature of congressional parties and leadership. Brady and Cooper made this notion more rigorous by identifying the importance of both interparty distance and intraparty cohesiveness. Brady later developed this argument for several periods of realignment and for the Senate (Brady 1988; Brady, Brody, and Epstein 1989).

3. The character of the floor coalition is measured as 1 for a partisan division, −1 for a North/South split (presumably among Democrats), and 0 for other divisions.

4. The Cooper-Brady school of studies now includes the historical studies of Binder (1997) and Dion (1997) on the evolution of rules related to minority rights in the House. These studies go beyond an explanation of party centralization to explain formal rules changes by the House. This is an important move. Rather than resting with some account of party centralization, these studies seek to explain changes in chamber rules. Binder, for example, demonstrates that the strength of the parties (their size and cohesiveness) influences the creation and suppression of minority rights. For this class of rules, these studies persuasively argue that party matters. They do not assess the policy consequences of rules changes or party.

5. David Rohde (1995) elsewhere argues for retaining a multiple-goal perspective on legislators' motivations.

6. Snyder and Groseclose find significant party effects for about half of all votes in the period since the 40th Congress.

REFERENCES

Aldrich, John, and David Rohde. 1997. "Balance of Power: Republican Party Leadership and the Committee System in the 104th House." Presented at the annual meeting of the Midwest Political Science Association, Chicago.

Aldrich, John, and David Rohde. 1998. "Measuring Conditional Party Government." Presented at the annual meeting of the Midwest Political Science Association, Chicago.

Ansolabehere, Stephen, James M. Snyder, and Charles Stewart III. 1999. "The Effects of Party and Preferences on Congressional Roll-Call Voting." Unpublished manuscript. Massachusetts Institute of Technology.

Arnold, R. Douglas. 1990. *The Logic of Congressional Action*. New Haven: Yale University Press.

Binder, Sarah. 1997. *Minority Rights, Majority Rule*. Cambridge: Cambridge University Press.

Brady, David. 1973. *Congressional Voting in a Partisan Era*. Lawrence: University of Kansas Press.

Brady, David. 1988. *Critical Elections and Congressional Policy Making*. Stanford: Stanford University Press.

Brady, David, Richard Brody, and David Epstein. 1989. "Heterogeneous Parties and Political Organization: The U.S. Senate, 1880–1920." *Legislative Studies Quarterly* 14:205–23.

Clausen, Aage. 1973. *How Congressmen Decide.* New York: St. Martin's Press.
Cooper, Joseph. 1975. "Strengthening the Congress: An Organizational Perspective." *Harvard Journal of Legislation* 12:307–68.
Cooper, Joseph, and David Brady. 1981. "Institutional Context and Leadership Style: The House from Cannon to Rayburn." *American Political Science Review* 75:411–25.
Cox, Gary, and Mathew McCubbins. 1993. *Legislative Leviathan.* Berkeley: University of California Press.
Cox, Gary, and Mathew McCubbins. 1999. "Agenda Power in the U.S. House of Representatives." Presented to the Conference on the History of Congress, Stanford University.
Deering, Christopher J., and Steven S. Smith. 1997. *Committees in Congress.* Washington, DC: CQ Press.
Dion, Douglas. 1997. *Turning the Legislative Thumbscrew.* Ann Arbor: University of Michigan Press.
Fenno, Richard F., Jr. 1973. *Congressmen in Committees.* Boston: Little, Brown.
Froman, Louis, and Randall Ripley. 1965. "Conditions for Party Leadership." *American Political Science Review* 59:52–63.
Heckman, James J., and James M. Snyder. 1997. "Linear Probability Models of the Demand for Attributes with an Empirical Application to Estimating the Preferences of Legislators." *RAND Journal of Economics* 28:S142–S189.
Huitt, Ralph. 1961. "Democratic Party Leadership in the Senate." *American Political Science Review* 55:333–44.
Jones, Charles. 1961. "Representation in Congress: The Case of the House Agriculture Committee." *American Political Science Review* 55:358–57.
Jones, Charles. 1968. "The Minority Party and Policy-Making in the House of Representatives." *American Political Science Review* 62:481–93.
Kiewiet, D. Roderick, and Mathew McCubbins. 1991. *The Logic of Delegation.* Chicago: University of Chicago Press.
Kingdon, John. 1973. *Congressmen's Voting Decisions.* New York: Harper and Row.
Krehbiel, Keith. 1998. *Pivotal Politics.* Chicago: University of Chicago Press. References to manuscript.
Krehbiel, Keith, and Adam Meirowitz. 1999. "Parliamentary Rights and Party Power." Mimeo. Stanford University.
Lawrence, Eric, Forrest Maltzman, and Steven S. Smith. 1999. "Who Wins? Party Effects in Legislative Voting." Presented at the annual meeting of the Midwest Political Science Association, Chicago.
Maltzman, Forrest. 1997. *Competing Principals: Committees, Parties, and the Organization of Congress.* Ann Arbor: University of Michigan Press.
Mayhew, David. 1974. *Congress: The Electoral Connection.* New Haven: Yale University Press.
McCarty, Nolan, Keith T. Poole, and Howard Rosenthal. 1999. "The Hunt for Party Discipline in Congress." Presented at the annual meeting of the Midwest Political Science Association, Chicago.
Rohde, David. 1991. *Parties and Leaders in the Postreform House.* Chicago: University of Chicago Press.

Rohde, David. 1995. "Parties and Committees in the House: Member Motivations, Issues, and Institutional Arrangements." In *Positive Theories of Congressional Institutions*, ed. Kenneth Shepsle and Barry Weingast. Ann Arbor: University of Michigan Press.

Sinclair, Barbara. 1983. *Majority Leadership in the U.S. House*. Baltimore: Johns Hopkins University Press.

Sinclair, Barbara. 1995. *Legislators, Leaders, and Lawmaking: The U.S. House of Representatives in the Postreform Era*. Baltimore: Johns Hopkins University Press.

Sinclair, Barbara. 1999. "Do Parties Matter?" Presented to the Conference on the History of Congress, Stanford University.

Smith, Steven S. 1989. *Call to Order: Floor Politics in the House and Senate*. Washington, DC: Brookings.

Snyder, James M., and Timothy Groseclose. 1999. "Party Influence in Congressional Roll-Call Voting." Unpublished manuscript. Massachusetts Institute of Technology.

Wilson, Rick. 1999. "Here's the Party: Group Effects and Partisan Advantage." Presented at the annual meeting of the Midwest Political Science Association, Chicago.

Part 5

Rules and Procedures in Legislatures

On the Effects of Legislative Rules

Gary W. Cox

Introduction

In this essay, I consider how a legislature's rules of procedure can affect both the process and the outcome of legislation. By legislative rules of procedure I mean both the standing orders the legislature may establish for itself and those statutory or constitutional provisions that materially affect the legislature's processing of bills (e.g., urgency provisions in Latin America). The discussion is divided into two main parts.

First, I consider whether or not rules of procedure should have any effects at all, given that they can often be changed by simple majorities of legislators. One way that this concern can be expressed is in terms of policy instability. In multidimensional spatial models of legislative decision making under pure majority rule, the *generic* result is instability—that is, there almost never exists a policy that cannot be defeated in a pairwise majority vote by some other policy (McKelvey and Schofield 1986; Saari 1997). Riker (1980) has argued that rules are valued primarily for their anticipated effect on policy outcomes, so that generically there will be no stability in the choice of rules, just as there is none in the choice of policies. By this argument, one cannot point to the rules as playing any systematic role in determining legislative outcomes. Here, I do not consider Riker's "inherited instability" argument based on the multidimensional spatial model but instead focus on a related argument based on the unidimensional spatial model.

The second part of the essay classifies the effects that rules have. Rules can change the set of bills that plenary sessions of the legislature consider; they can change the menu of amendments to any given bill considered in the plenary; they can affect how members vote; and—putting the first three effects together—they can affect which bills pass. I review evidence that rules do in fact have the suspected effects.

Reprinted with permission from *Legislative Studies Quarterly* 25, no. 2 (May 2000): 169–92.

Can Legislative Rules Have Any Effects, If They Can Be Changed by the Assembly?

In studying how rules of procedure affect legislative outcomes, we must make an important initial distinction between exogenous rules and endogenous rules. Exogenous rules are those that cannot legally be changed by the legislature itself; changes require the assent of some other actors separate from or external to the legislature. Endogenous rules, in contrast, are those that can legally be changed by the legislature itself.[1]

Most studies of the effects of legislative rules take them to be exogenous. For example, in the 1970s and 1980s, much of the literature stressing the importance of committees in the U.S. Congress assumed, either implicitly or explicitly, that the committees' jurisdictions were stable and that the seniority norm was essentially inviolable. Studying the effects of rules by assuming that they are exogenous is a useful endeavor, but it can be analogous to studying presidential vetoes in the U.S. under the assumption that vetoes cannot be overridden. When rules can be overturned by the very actors whose behavior is supposedly constrained by the rules, doubts are legitimately raised about how effective those rules can be.[2]

Suppose, for example, that the current rules of procedure in some legislature promote a particular policy choice, X, but that a majority exists in the legislature that would prefer a different policy, Y. In this case, the majority preferring Y could replace the current rules with ones consistent with passing Y, and then pass Y. Knowing this, any agents empowered under the current rules might acquiesce in Y's passage rather than obstructing it or amending it, as they would be able to do were the rules exogenous. Thus, one might argue that stable rules of procedure must either be inherently neutral as far as policy choice is concerned or they must be consistent with the equilibrium policy choice under majority rule. For example, in the case of a unidimensional policy space, the equilibrium policy choice under majority rule is the median voter's ideal point (Black 1958). It should not be possible to maintain rules that potentially interfere with the selection of the median voter's ideal policy unless that potential is never actualized.

Although scholars used to take the effectiveness of rules of procedure for granted, arguments such as the one just given have suggested that rules might have no independent causal force, at least when they can be changed by a simple majority of those subject to the rules (Krehbiel 1991, 1993). Reacting against this sort of argument, scholars have suggested a variety of ways in which the causal impact of rules, which continues to be widely accepted as an empirical matter, can be theoretically explained. I consider three such arguments next.

The Rules Are in the Constitution (or Otherwise Entrenched)

A first possibility is that the legislature's internal rules of procedure are stable because they are stipulated in the constitution and the constitution cannot be amended by a simple majority of the assembly. If some legislative rules are entrenched in the constitution, and they lead to a policy choice, X, will that be stable? If a coalition (of legislators and nonlegislators) existed that was large enough to amend the constitution, preferred Y to X, and could find a set of rules that yielded Y, then X would not be stable and neither would the rules leading to it.[3] But, if one continues to assume a unidimensional policy space, then constitutionally entrenched rules will enable the stabilization of nonmedian policy outcomes. For example, if the constitution requires a three-fourths majority of the assembly to amend, then the range of stable policies expands from the median to the interquartile range; if the constitution requires another body to concur by majority, then anything between the medians of the two bodies would be stable, and so forth.

Empirical examples of entrenched rules of procedure include both constitutional stipulations such as the *vote bloqué* in France (cf. Huber 1996) or the urgency procedure in Brazil and Chile and nonconstitutional stipulations such as the U.S. Senate's filibuster and cloture provisions (Binder 1997; Binder and Smith 1997). More generally, Döring (1995b, 36) reports that, of 16 countries covered in a multiauthor study of Western European legislatures, 6 required supermajorities to change the legislative rules of procedure, while Cox and Morgenstern (2000) report that in 7 Latin American countries the president has entrenched agenda-setting powers of one sort or another.

The Rules Suit the Majority Party and It Can Protect Them

If party leaders can expel members from legislative caucuses, deny them renomination, or deny them future office opportunities, then the majority party (or coalition) may be able externally to enforce a given set of rules. Cox and McCubbins (1994) tell such a story for the U.S. House of Representatives. Whatever one thinks of their story in the U.S. case, something like it seems plausible in countries such as Costa Rica, the United Kingdom, Venezuela, and Taiwan.

The Legislators Are Too Busy to Change the Rules

Legislation is more like research and development than it is like choice among already known alternatives. Members of most major legislatures are thus constantly strapped for time.

But overriding any legislative decision made pursuant to the rules takes time and effort, and overturning the rules themselves takes even more time and effort. The costs entailed in overturning rule-based decisions and rules are thus *largely exogenous*: they are the costs in terms of time and effort needed to construct a strategy for overturning the decision and to assemble the required coalition in support of change. If one believes these claims—that it is costly to overturn rule-based decisions and more costly to overturn rules, and that the costs entailed are largely exogenous opportunity costs—then one must also believe that rules have consequences.

Consider, for example, the ability to "veto" bills that U.S. committees are routinely alleged to possess. As bills can be discharged, one might argue that committee vetoes can be overridden whenever a floor majority wishes. But suppose a member files a discharge petition on a particular bill. She now tries to get other members to sign her petition but finds that hardly anyone knows what the bill is about. They are too busy with their own issues. When asked to sign, the other members face a choice. They can take the petitioner's word that it is in their interests to sign. They can take the committee's word that it is in their interests not to sign. Or, they can allocate scarce resources to investigate the matter for themselves. Unless the petitioner can find enough members who either already know about the issue at stake and agree with her or are willing to take her cue over the committee's, the petition may stall because the other potential signatories are too busy to investigate the matter.

Suppose that the petitioner thinks she might get enough signatures from members who already know their preferences or are willing to take her cue. She now faces another hurdle. There is not enough time on the floor to pass every bill on the calendars, much less every bill in committee. Does a majority of the House prefer that the to-be-discharged bill take an increment of time on the floor, at the cost of not being able to proceed with some other bill (or bills) in the queue? Which other bill(s) will be sacrificed? Unless these issues can be negotiated as well, the petition will still fail, even if in a world of complete information (all members costlessly know their operative political preferences) and zero transaction costs (no time budget constraint on the floor) it would pass.

For important enough bills, the two costs suggested above will be lower: more members will already know about the bill and have clear preferences, and more will be willing to bump something else off the floor in order to proceed with it. But for less important bills, the costs can be prohibitive. Thus, even when vetoes can be overridden by a simple majority, and even when the bill vetoed would improve policy for some majority on the floor, the veto can stand. If one wishes to reject this conclusion, one must believe that every bill that would improve the status quo policy for some majority is identified and passed in each Congress.

The general point is this: Even "suspensory vetoes" are important and consequential in an assembly in which time is short. As I shall argue below, positive agenda power—the ability to initiate the next step in a bill's progress toward passage, at a given time—is even more important and harder to overturn.[4]

If Rules Have Effects . . .

Suppose that one believes that rule-based decisions are costly to overturn and that the rules themselves are even more costly to overturn. This is enough to motivate a belief that rules will have causal effects but not enough to say much about what those effects might be. In the next sections, I consider some of the effects that rules have.

Rules can have proximal, intermediate, and final effects. The proximal effects of rules are to distribute resources (e.g., staff) and agenda power (e.g., a suspensory veto subject to discharge).[5] The distribution of resources and agenda power stipulated by the rules in turn affects the menu of policy choices with which members are faced and how members vote on any given policy choice (intermediate effects). Finally, the ability to set the menu of policy choices and to affect voting behavior may lead to an impact on the policy actually chosen.

The proximal effects of rules are the easiest to describe, although even here there is a wide range of specific techniques (see, e.g., Döring 1995c). In the next two sections, I will consider the intermediate effects—how rules affect the menu of choices and voting behavior.

How Rules Affect the Menu of Choices

Agenda powers can be classified in two broad categories:[6]

1. The power to put bills on or keep them off the floor agenda (thereby determining whether or not the floor has the chance to alter policy along a given dimension);
2. The power to protect bills from amendment on the floor.

Each of these species of agenda power is differently allocated in different assemblies. In each case, the question is whether the rules that allocate agenda power produce *agendas* that are consequentially different from those that would have been constructed by floor majorities (whether or not these agendas then lead to different policy outcomes is considered later).

Setting the Floor Agenda

In considering how the plenary agenda is set, I shall build on the work of Shepsle (1979) and Cox and McCubbins (1999). Shepsle's model begins with two main elements: a set of w issues, or policy dimensions, that the legislature must decide, and a set of n legislators, each with strictly quasi-concave preferences defined over the policy space. The issues are partitioned into a number of jurisdictions. The members are divided into a number of committees (with membership on more than one committee possible), each with its own jurisdiction. Committees are given the exclusive right to propose bills in their jurisdictions, but a committee's jurisdiction may itself be the union of smaller subjurisdictions (possibly, though not necessarily, attached to subcommittees). A committee with a complex jurisdiction may propose a separate bill for each of its subjurisdictions, but it cannot propose one omnibus bill dealing with all at once.

The sequence of events in Shepsle's model is (1) the committees propose bills—i.e., put them on the plenary agenda,[7] (2) the plenary amends each of the bills put on its agenda by the committees, as its members see fit, and (3) each bill, as amended, is put to a final up or down vote. Although this particular sequence is not followed in all legislatures, something like it is followed in many.

Cox and McCubbins alter Shepsle's model in three main ways. First, they consider fully strategic actors instead of "sincere" legislators. In this respect, they follow Denzau and Mackay (1983) and Krehbiel (1985). Second, they divide Shepsle's committee stage into separate agenda-setting, amendment, and final passage substages. Just as the floor legislative process can be divided into these stages, so the committee legislative process can, too. Third, they consider two polar distributions of agenda power—the floor agenda model and the partisan agenda model.

In the first model, the floor agenda is determined as if by majority vote in the plenary session. One way to interpret this model is literally. In some cases (e.g., Denmark in the 1980s—see Damgaard and Svensson 1989; the U.S. in the 1790s), much of the plenary agenda is decided by the plenary itself. Shepsle's model can formally accommodate such cases by assuming that there is just one committee—a committee of the whole. Another way to interpret the floor agenda model is to say that there are in fact a number of distinct committees but that the floor can extract bills from any committee it chooses (via a discharge petition in the United States, for example); thus, the committees cannot bottle up bills that a floor majority wishes to consider.

In the second model, the floor agenda is determined as if by majority vote in the majority party caucus.[8] Again one might interpret this literally—as a model of those few periods in the U.S. House's experience when the majority party caucus seemed to rule the roost—or indirectly—as a model of committees which must anticipate the reaction of control committees or majority party leaders (Cox and McCubbins 1993).

A key consideration in the model is the location of the status quo point on each dimension. Normalizing, one can take F_j, the location of the median legislator on the floor on the jth dimension, to be $F_j = F = 0$. That is, we locate the zero point on each dimension at the floor median on that dimension. This is done without loss of generality since the scale is arbitrary. The location of the status quo point, SQ_j, varies with j. Positive values of SQ_j indicate right-of-center status quo points, while negative values indicate left-of-center status quo points.

Now consider how the plenary agenda is set. Suppose first that there is a separate floor vote on whether or not to consider each of the w dimensions of policy. Suppose also that every member votes his or her own constituents' interests (or his or her personal beliefs) rather than following the party line. If the motion to consider dimension j is passed, the ultimate consequence will be that policy on dimension j is moved from SQ_j to F.[9] If the motion fails, then policy will remain at SQ_j. Thus, a member will vote to consider dimension j if and only if she prefers F to SQ_j. An agenda formed by a sequence of floor votes on what to consider next would thus produce an agenda that consisted of all dimensions with status quo points not equal to F.

Nota bene that constructing agendas by pure majority vote in the plenary does not offer any inherent advantage to the majority party or coalition. Suppose that a majority party exists and is left-leaning, so that most of its members are to the left of F, while most of the minority party's members are to the right of F. The bills that the median legislator decides to proceed with concern the dimensions with status quo points not equal to F. These status quo points can be put in four basic categories. First, "far left" status quo points are so far left that even a majority of the left-leaning majority party prefers F to the status quo (as does a majority of the minority party). Second, "near left" status quo points are such that a majority of the majority prefers the status quo to F (with a majority of the minority preferring the reverse). Third, "near right" status quo points are such that a majority of the majority prefers F to the status quo, but a majority of the minority party prefers the status quo to F. Finally, "far right" status quo points are such that majorities of both parties prefer F to the status quo.[10]

From these four possible locations for the status quo emerge three possible voting patterns. If the status quo is either far left or far right, then majorities of both parties will support placing a bill on the agenda. If the status quo is near left, then a majority of the majority party will oppose placing the bill on the agenda, but lose. If the status quo is near right, then a majority of the minority party will oppose placing the bill on the agenda, but lose. *Thus, in the floor agenda model, whether the majority party does better or worse than the minority in terms of setting the agenda for plenary action depends entirely on the location of the status quo points on the various dimensions.* If the distribution of status quo points is symmetric about F, then the majority party should lose as often as the minority party loses. If the distribution of status quo points is skewed to the right, then the majority party (assumed left-leaning) should lose less often than the minority. Finally, if the distribution of status quo points is skewed to the left, then the majority should lose more often than the minority.

An alternative model of how the plenary agenda is set, the partisan agenda model, assumes that the majority party has a veto over the placement of any issue on the floor agenda. More specifically, if a majority of the majority party opposes placing a particular bill on the agenda, it can prevent its appearance. I shall be less concerned with how such an agenda selection mechanism might arise[11] than with what the consequences would be, were it to exist. The most obvious consequence would be that no status quo preferred by a majority of the majority party to the floor median—no near-left status quo in the example above—could gain a place on the floor agenda. Thus, under this model, one should never observe the majority party unsuccessfully opposing the placement of a bill on the plenary agenda.

Comparing Point Estimates. Cox and McCubbins pose two questions to assess the success of the majority party in controlling the floor agenda. First, how frequently is the majority party *rolled* on agenda-setting votes? A roll is counted when a majority of the majority party opposes the placement of a bill on the floor agenda, but loses. If the majority can veto agenda items, then its agenda-setting roll rate should be zero. Second, how frequently does a majority of the majority coalition oppose the final passage of a bill, but lose? If the only issues that were placed on the agenda by a left-of-center party were those on which the status quo was right-of-median, then the worst that could happen to these bills would be that they were amended to the floor median, in which case the median legislator and all to her left would still prefer passing the bill to rejecting it. Thus, the majority's final passage roll rate should also be near zero.

To address the first question, Cox and McCubbins examined all 5,789 bills that originated in the House in eight selected congresses and were reported out of committee. They found that in only four of these cases (or 0.07%) did a majority of the majority party's committee members dissent from the committee report. Indeed, majority dissent of any magnitude was quite rare. Thus, in the House at least, the majority's record of avoiding issues that produce serious splits on initial report was nearly perfect.

What about the majority coalition's final passage roll rate? In the 45th to 99th Congresses, Cox and McCubbins find that the modal roll rate for the majority party on final passage votes is *zero*, with an average of *3%*.

The majority's low roll rates—0.07% at the agenda-setting and 3% at the final passage stage—contrast with rather higher figures for the minority: about 5% at the agenda-setting and 25% at the final passage stage. Thus, in the U.S. case, the preliminary evidence tends to reject the floor model in favor of the partisan (or "cartel") model.

A similar study of the Japanese Diet (Cox, Masuyama, and McCubbins 2000) finds a similar pattern. Governing parties in Japan are virtually never rolled. Opposition parties' roll rates generally range from 7% to 50%. Although similar studies have not been performed for other legislatures, for many of them the expected result of a comparable study seems clear. In the U.K. House of Commons, the French National Assembly, or the German Bundestag, for example, the government seems clearly to control the agenda. Issues do not come out of committee unless the government wants them to come out, nor do governments sustain defeats on the floor. There are, however, assemblies where the agenda-setting and final passage roll rates for the government are much higher, such as Denmark (De Winter 1995, 145).

Comparative Statics. The conflicting point estimates of the floor and partisan models are important in indicating the central differences between them. However, the equilibrium point estimates of the two models could be perturbed by any of a number of small changes in the model, such as introducing a small amount of uncertainty about the location of status quo points or a small opportunity cost to action. Such amendments are less likely to affect the two models' comparative statics predictions than their point estimate predictions, and so the former are more important from the point of view of empirical testing.

To explain the two models' comparative statics, we will let M_j denote the majority party's median and m_j the minority party's median. Under the floor agenda model, Cox and McCubbins (1999) show that the probability of the majority party losing an agenda-setting or final passage vote increases with the distance between M_j and $F_j = F = 0$ for all j, while the probability that the opposition loses an agenda-setting or final passage vote increases with the distance between m_j and F for all j. Under the cartel agenda model, the second of these comparative statics expectations holds—the opposition should lose more often since its median member is more distant from the floor median—but the first does not—the majority party should never lose and any fluctuations in its roll rate should be unrelated to the distance between the majority party and floor medians.

Cox and McCubbins (1999) find support in the U.S. case for the cartel model and reject the floor agenda model. In particular, while the majority party's roll rate is unrelated to the distance between the party's median (as measured by Poole-Rosenthal W-NOMINATE scores)[12] and the floor median (measured in the same way), the minority's roll rate is significantly related to the distance between the minority and floor medians.

In the United States, it is often said that it is not surprising to find the majority party winning votes—after all, they are the majority. But this observation is specious in the context of a unidimensional spatial model in which members are assumed to vote their own interests solely. Suppose the Democrats are in the majority. If the status quo on a particular dimension is to the left of the floor median, then the vote will go against the majority party (the Democrats). The median voter and all to her right will favor pulling the leftward status quo to the floor median, while many of those to her left will oppose such a move. Precisely how many oppose the move depends on how far left the status quo is, but for status quo points that are preferred by the median Democrat to the floor median, a majority of the Democrats will vote against passing the bill. In that sense, the party will lose. If, on the other hand, the status quo is to the right of the floor median, then the vote will go against the minority party. So, in a world in which all issues are unidimensional, most of the battle is to decide which issues to consider at all. Once a given issue is chosen, and assuming that nongermane amendments can be beaten off, the amendment structure and the twisting of arms at vote time are marginal considerations.

The prediction that government roll rates will not vary with the distance between the government's and the assembly's medians, while opposition roll rates will vary with the distance between the opposition's and assembly's medians, is also borne out in the case of Japan (Cox, Masuyama, and McCubbins 2000). While there are thus far no other similar studies, it seems clear that for some, such as the U.K. House of Commons, the results will be comparable to those in the United States and Japan.

Regulating Debate and Amendment on the Floor

But what happens if exogenous events (e.g., Saddam Hussein's invasion of Kuwait) force an issue onto the agenda? What happens if the Senate is held by the other party, which does its best to force issues onto the agenda? What happens, in other words, if the majority coalition in a particular chamber cannot perfectly control its plenary agenda and ensure that only unidimensional bills of a coalition-friendly sort appear on the agenda?

In these cases, controlling the flow of amendments on the floor may be especially important. The reaction of the majority to an unavoidable but unpleasant issue may be to package it with several other issues to create an omnibus that is at least palatable to the majority. But then the majority will need to ensure that the package is not picked apart on the floor, which will entail restricting the range and nature of amendments offered.

Do majority parties or coalitions actually have the ability to restrict amendments on the floor in ways that the median voter (on some particular dimension) might not agree with? It seems clear enough that the French government has such an ability via the package vote (Huber 1996), that the U.K. government has such an ability via the guillotine (Dion 1997), and that several Latin American presidents have a similar ability (Cox and Morgenstern 2000). Even in the U.S. House, where there are not constitutionally entrenched agenda-setting powers, there is a wide array of case-study evidence that the majority party uses restrictive procedures on the floor to protect majority party legislation. More systematically, Sinclair (2000) shows that bills reported from committee on partisan votes have been more likely to receive restrictive rules in the House.[13]

How Rules Affect Voting Behavior

Rules affecting the distribution of resources and agenda power can affect the voting behavior of members in two broad ways: (1) by allowing agenda setters to manipulate who can monitor votes, and (2) by providing the wherewithal to make side payments. Let us consider each of these points in turn.

One way to view legislators' voting behavior is as the net result of various different considerations that can be divided into three main categories: constituents' preferences, personal preferences, and party preferences. If a legislator's constituents' interests, his or her personal beliefs, and his or her party's desires coincide, voting decisions are easy (Kingdon 1989). If these considerations conflict, however, then manipulating the observability of members' actions becomes particularly important (Arnold 1990). Governing or majority coalitions with agenda control can frame issues in ways that protect their members from the scrutiny of their constituents or expose them to the scrutiny of their party leaders.

An example of protection from constituents, or "providing cover," is an omnibus bill that includes a controversial provision or two, along with many popular or necessary provisions. Members can vote for the whole and justify their votes as ways to secure the (locally) popular bits, while decrying or disowning the (locally) unpopular bits. Restrictive procedures can be used to ensure that the members are never faced with an amendment that proposes to remove just the unpopular parts. Another example of protection from constituents is a vote of confidence. In the unlikely event that she is challenged, a member can apologetically explain that the vote was really about the continuation in office of the government, so that she was not at liberty to vote simply on the merits of the issue (on which, of course, she is 100% in accord with her aggrieved constituents).

An example of exposure to party leaders' scrutiny is Willy Brandt's "stay in your seat" confidence vote. Worried that some of his backbenchers might support the no-confidence motion confronting his government if allowed to vote anonymously, Brandt ordered his troops to stay in their seats and took advantage of the German requirement that an absolute majority of legislators must support the no-confidence motion in order to bring the government down.

Agenda power and other resources (e.g., staff) distributed by rules can also provide the wherewithal to make side payments to members. For example, if party leaders control assignment to committees or portfolios, desired assignments can be held out as inducements to good behavior. In the United States, Cox and McCubbins (1993) provide and review evidence showing how parties use party assignments to shore up loyalty on the margin. A similar story seems to play out in Europe, both in terms of the initial trading of ministerial portfolios for party support of a government and in terms of party leaders handing out plum assignments in the committee or party hierarchy to more loyal followers (Damgaard 1995). Even in Brazil, Santos (1999) reports that party loyalty enhances a member's chance of being appointed to the more important committees for some parties.

Two further points about side payments ought to be made. First, side payments are often used to clinch deals or clear legislative hurdles. Particularistic benefits may be ends in themselves for the ordinary member, but for party leaders they are also means to the accomplishment of broader goals. Second, positive and negative side payments intended to influence members' voting behavior are a *part* of any healthy legislative leviathan, but they are of quite variable importance. In electoral systems that foster personal votes, it is not even in the party's best interest to "force" their members to vote in particular ways, since this substantially reduces their probabilities of reelection, thus damaging the party's prospect of attaining or retaining majority status. In the United States, the typical procedure is for majority party leaders to "buy" no more votes than they must in order to secure a legislative victory.

The bottom-line question, of course, is whether or not attempts by parties to manipulate who can monitor members' votes and to distribute side payments do in fact influence members' voting behavior. In parliamentary systems, the ability of parties to control their members' voting behavior by making issues matters of confidence is widely accepted (although questions have been raised about the credibility of government threats to resign). In contrast, legislative parties in presidential systems do not have the big gun of confidence to enforce discipline at the voting stage. Strong correlations still typically exist between voting behavior and partisan affiliation in such systems, but it is hard to say whether these correlations arise simply because members join parties with which they tend to agree or whether there is also some party influence above and beyond what would be expected on the basis of members' preferences.

So, how can one detect the influence of party on roll-call voting? Some headway has recently been made in solving this methodological problem. If House members vote with their parties only when the party position is congenial to their constituents and/or to their personal ideologies, then (1) their voting behavior should not change when they switch parties (unless their constituency or ideology changed when they switched); (2) there should be no systematic relationship between members' reelection success and how frequently they vote with their party on key party votes (by assumption, no one is casting "tough"—i.e., electorally costly—votes for their party; thus, if one member is more loyal to the party than another on key votes, this can only be because his or her constituency is more in tune with the party's position, and such members will be no more likely to suffer larger-than-average vote drops or actual defeat than less loyal members); and (3) members should be no more likely to support their party than would be expected on the basis of the positions they advocate in elections. Yet, (1) several analyses of party-switchers over the postwar era have found significant changes in voting behavior toward greater agreement with the newly joined party (see, e.g., Ansolabehere, Snyder, and Stewart 1999; McCarty, Poole, and Rosenthal 1999); (2) several studies find systematic correlations between party loyalty and electoral risk (Brady et al. 1996; Jacobson 1996); and (3) Ansolabehere, Snyder, and Stewart (1999) find that members of the U.S. House are more likely to support their party than would be expected from their responses to electoral questionnaires. It is hard to explain these results on the assumption that parties do not influence their members' voting behavior.

How Rules Affect Final Policy Choices

In this section, I consider how rules might affect final policy choices. I first consider how the rules enable the majority party or coalition to get what it wants, then how they can simplify legislative negotiations.

Helping the Majority "Get Its Way"

Rules can empower the majority party or coalition, when there is one, at three broad stages of the legislative process: at the agenda-setting stage, at the amendment stage, and at the voting stage. I shall consider each of these stages, in reverse order. In each case, the question addressed is how power at a particular stage can lead to final policy outcomes favored by the majority.

The Whip Model. Perhaps the most frequently mentioned way in which a majority party or coalition can get its way is by exerting discipline over its members when they vote. While this technique may be important in parliamentary systems with strong parties, in some of the presidential systems of Latin America and the United States, this technique is important only on the margins. Rather than insisting on a solid block of party votes to ensure passage of their legislation, parties in some presidential systems allow their members to dissent more often but still seek to corral a few pivotal votes when needed. The evidence that parties can actually pressure their members into voting has already been reviewed. Are the votes in fact pivotal, so that they make the difference between winning and losing?

The evidence here is largely anecdotal, but there are a lot of anecdotes, at least for the United States. The standard operating procedure for Speakers in the U.S. House on close votes is to have a certain number of "vest pocket" or "just-in-case" votes lined up in advance. If the bill appears ready to fail, the

Speaker then calls in as many of these votes as are needed to ensure victory, in some cases even stopping the clock to provide time to find the needed votes.[14]

The Restrictive Rule Model. One step earlier in the legislative process than votes on final passage are votes on amendments to bills. And before the actual amendments come, decisions must be made about which amendments will be in order. In cases where the government has the power to prevent all amendments and hence present members with take-it-or-leave-it choices, it can clearly affect the final outcome.

Theoretically, the impact of this sort of power on the legislative outcome is captured in the widely known setter model (Rosenthal 1990). In the United States, the partisan effect of restrictive rules on outcomes is contested (Krehbiel 1991, 1997a, 1997b). But there is certainly evidence that the majority party uses restrictive rules on partisan issues and that the minority complains about it. More compellingly, members' voting behavior on (rule/bill) pairs is what one would expect on the hypothesis that *members* believe that the rule will have an effect on the outcome.

To explain this last point, due to Sinclair (2000), we must remember that under House procedure a "special rule" is sometimes adopted to regulate plenary debate and amendment activity on a particular bill. Members vote first on the issue of whether to accept the rule, then on the substance of the bill. Suppose the majority party fashions the proposed rules in order to prevent amendments that the minority would like to move and that all members know this. Suppose further that the electoral consequences of votes on rules are murky: members can always talk about fairness or efficient transaction of business or minority stalling and majority bullying to shield themselves from any claim that a vote for a rule, R, that facilitates passage of a bill, B, is really a vote for B, or that a vote against R is really a vote against B. Suppose finally that all members believe that R will *in fact* facilitate passage of B and that both parties are pressuring their members to support the party position.

Given these three assumptions, one expects the following patterns in voting behavior on (rule/bill) pairs. Some majority party members will have constituencies that support the substance of the bill. They will vote both for the rule and for the bill. Other majority party members will have constituencies that oppose the substance of the bill. These members are likely to vote against the bill because to do otherwise incurs electoral risk. Put another way, it will be relatively expensive for the party to buy these members' votes on the bill. In contrast, it may be considerably cheaper to buy their votes on the rule, depending on how securely shielded from electoral retribution they feel. The party need offer no side payment at all to members who personally favor the bill. Members who are personally indifferent or mildly opposed can be bought by compensating them just for their personal distaste; they need not be compensated for electoral risk (or, at least, the electoral risk is reduced and hence the needed compensation).

All told then, one expects majority party members whose constituents oppose the bill either to vote against both the rule and the bill or to vote for the rule but against the bill (with only a few voting for both). A similar argument leads one to expect minority party members to fall mostly into two camps: those voting against both rule and bill, and those voting against the rule but for the bill. Sinclair (2000) shows that these opposed expectations about majority and minority voting on (rule/bill) pairs do obtain, suggesting support for the underlying assumption that members believe rules to have causal force. At present, this is probably the best statistical evidence we have that rules affect outcomes.

The Partisan Agenda Model. Before a bill gets to the stage at which permissible amendments on the floor are decided, it has to get out of committee. The power to decide which bills make it to the floor is arguably the least appreciated but most fundamental power in terms of influencing final outcomes.

Recall that under the partisan or cartel agenda model, the majority coalition monopolizes the plenary agenda, in the sense that it is able to prevent the appearance on the floor agenda of any bill with which a majority of the majority would prefer not to deal. With this sort of agenda selection power, the issues that actually make it to the plenary will all have status quo points that are either to the minority's side of the floor median or so far to the majority party's side that a majority of the party would prefer pulling them back to the median. Thus, even if every separate decision taken by the House is unidimensional and ends up at the floor median, the policy location in the multidimensional space in which the whole sequence of decisions takes place will be substantially biased from what it would have been under a neutral agenda structure. If the majority is left-leaning, movements will be made leftward on a good number of dimensions with relatively fewer rightward movements (and those only to correct "far left" status quo points). Few rightward movements from the "near left" are passed because no resources are devoted to finding such moves, and if they do crop up, considerable resources are deployed against them. The net result is that policy will be more leftist than would have been the case under a neutral agenda.

Simplifying Legislative Negotiations

Besides privileging the majority coalition over other legislative majorities, rules of procedure can also make commitments to pass complex packages of legislation more credible, hence less costly to negotiate.

Concentrated Agenda Power Leads to Fewer but More Complex Conflictual Acts. Döring (1995a) and Henning (1995) consider a model in which the government is a monopoly supplier of legislation. The government can choose either to produce fairly simple and nonconflictual bills, whose passage will not require the use of agenda power, or to produce more complex and conflictual bills, whose passage will be facilitated by agenda power. They argue that increasing the concentration and amount of agenda power in the hands of the government lowers the "price" of the more complex and conflictual bills, while leaving the price of simple nonconflictual bills unchanged. Accordingly, a government will increase its "purchase" of complex conflictual bills when its agenda power increases, assuming that all else is equal and that complex conflictual bills are normal goods (in the economist's sense). Since (1) complex and conflictual bills always require more time to process than simple and nonconflictual bills, even when the government has strong agenda powers, and (2) the government faces a fixed, hard time constraint, any increase in the percent of complex bills that the government undertakes will necessarily mean a lower volume of legislation overall. Thus, all told, one expects fewer but more complex conflictual bills and acts (given the high success rate of governments) when agenda power is higher.

Döring (1995a) provides some cross-national evidence for part of this story in a study of Western European legislatures. Ranking 18 European assemblies in terms of the agenda powers given to the government, then correlating this ranking with the volume of legislation enacted in each country, Döring finds a negative and significant relationship. This finding addresses the issue of the overall volume of legislation but not the issue of how conflictual the acts are, which Döring leaves for a later time.

Some evidence that agenda powers are in fact brought to bear mostly on complex and conflictual bills can be gleaned from single-country studies. Many studies of the use of restrictive rules in the U.S. House find that they are more often used on omnibus or multiply-referred—which is to say, more complex—bills (Sinclair 1995, 2000). Similarly, some studies find these rules used more often in cases of partisan conflict (Sinclair 2000). Huber's (1996) study of the use of restrictive rules in France finds similar tendencies.

Concentrated Agenda Power Leads to Quicker Negotiations over Government Formation. De Winter (1995, 143) argues that "in countries where institutional arrangements give the executive extensive legislative agenda setting powers, government formation will consume less time, as most matters can be settled 'on the road'. On the other hand, in countries where the legislature has a relatively strong hold on its own agenda, coalition parties will prefer to settle all or most potential disputes before a cabinet is formed and, thus, formalize agreements in a written contract. . . ." De Winter finds support for this idea in the fact that Döring's index of government agenda control correlates negatively and significantly with the length of coalition negotiations in Western Europe.

There are different possible interpretations of this argument. First, perhaps parties without agenda power view themselves as not having any ability to *imple-*

ment agreements on the road. Thus, they negotiate more in advance. But why are their initial negotiations able to be implemented? Second, perhaps it is possible for parties to agree on a distribution of portfolios, rather than a detailed policy platform, in systems with strong agenda power. Third, perhaps some of the contingencies that must be negotiated in systems without concentrated agenda power can be prevented from ever arising by appropriate use of agenda power.

Conclusion

Legislative rules have effects because they distribute real resources whose effects cannot be undone without incurring real costs in time and effort, because they confer benefits that parties find worth preserving through extralegislative means, and because they are sometimes entrenched legally. In a world in which time is short, the power to delay or expedite can be crucial, even if decisions to decelerate or accelerate a particular bill can be appealed to the plenary. In a world in which the effects of rules on final outcomes are obscure to voters, members fear electoral retribution from their constituents less than they would on straightforward votes on substance. Moreover, the obscurity of procedural rules' effects makes it easier for parties to maintain control of procedural votes than to maintain control of substantive votes.

The actual effects rules have are sorted here into three categories: effects on the menu of choices (which bills are considered on the floor? which amendments are allowed?), effects on voting behavior, and effects on the final legislative outcome (which bills pass?). Evidence of such effects is visible in most of the legislatures that have actually been studied, although the quality of the evidence varies widely, since it is difficult to make the necessary counterfactual comparisons (e.g., what would the agenda have been had the rules been different?) cleanly.

Typically, the effect of rules is most visible in conjunction with a majority party or coalition's efforts to push through its legislative agenda against opposition. If one ordered the world's legislative parties from those with the greatest incentives to push through their legislative agendas to those with the fewest incentives, the ordering would put parliamentary parties at the top (the government falls if its program fails); proactive congressional parties, such as those in the United States, next (where the legislative parties are sometimes viewed as having electoral incentives to prosecute agendas [Cox and McCubbins 1993]); and reactive congressional parties, as in Latin America, last (where the party label means less and, relatedly, there are fewer incentives to prosecute a party agenda).

It is interesting to examine the structure of agenda power across these three levels of incentive. Control of the agenda is firmest in the parliamentary regimes, especially the more Westminsterian ones. It is lodged, moreover, in the hands of legislative party leaders (who typically assume executive office). Control of the agenda is next firmest in the United States. It is again lodged in the hands of legislative party leaders (who, due to the separation of powers, do not assume executive office). Control of the agenda is weakest in Latin America. It is lodged partly in the hands of the president, an executive official who often attempts to be "above parties," and partly in the hands of the *mesa directiva*, typically composed of legislative party leaders.

It is interesting to note also that the meaningfulness of party labels, in terms of the policies that each party is likely to pursue, is ordered roughly the same way as are the incentives to legislate: European parliamentary democracies first, U.S. presidential systems second, Latin American presidential systems last. There appears, in other words, to be a positive correlation between (1) legislative parties' incentives to legislate (and the frequency with which they actually do legislate), (2) the extent to which agenda power is centralized in the hands of legislative party leaders of the majority coalition, and (3) the electoral meaningfulness of the party label in policy terms.

NOTES

I thank the participants at the Shambaugh Conference, University of Iowa, for their comments on an earlier draft of this paper, and Chris Den Hartog for assistance in preparing the manuscript.

1. The best examples of exogenous rules are those stipulated in constitutions, at least when the constitution cannot be amended by the legislature alone but also requires, say, presidential approval, approval by state assemblies, or approval in a national referendum. Clear examples of endogenous rules would be the standing orders of the U.S. House of Representatives, which can be changed or maintained at the sole discretion of the House (the courts have repeatedly declined to review these rules, citing Article I, Section 5 of the Constitution which stipulates that "Each House may determine the Rules of its Proceedings. . . .").

2. An analogous concern has frequently been raised about electoral rules. See Cox 1997, chapter 2.

3. This would be the typical result if the policy space were of high enough dimensionality, since then even super- or concurrent majority requirements would not suffice to stabilize policy (see Cox and McKelvey 1984; McKelvey and Schofield 1986; Saari 1997). But note that these results from cooperative game theory assume that it is costless to change the rules—no time elapses, no one needs to examine the consequences of changing to a particular new set of rules as such consequences are utterly transparent to all, and so forth. Note also that noncooperative approaches can give quite different results—consider Diermeier and Feddersen 1998.

4. If rule-based decisions—such as a committee deciding not to proceed with a bill—are costly to overturn, what about ripping up the rules themselves? Instead of discharg-

ing the committee of a particular bill, would it be cheaper to abolish the committee, pack it, or strip it of jurisdiction? One supposes that the answer is "no" in this particular example and more generally.

5. Another important proximal effect that rules can have, which I do not consider here, is to delineate informational requirements—e.g., the requirement that committees file written reports to accompany bills, with documentation of those supporting and dissenting from the report.

6. Another important power that might be classified as an agenda power is that of setting the reversionary policy outcome.

7. In some legislatures, such as the U.S. House, bills proposed by committees are not guaranteed a hearing on the floor; they are simply eligible for such a hearing but must still pass other hurdles.

8. The model assumes the existence of a majority coalition. Here I consider the case of a majority party.

9. This follows if one assumes that nongermane amendments (i.e., amendments that bring in other policy dimensions) are not allowed and that an amendment to substitute the policy F for whatever policy the bill proposes is in order.

10. The boundaries between these four regions can be defined as follows. Let M_j be the median ideal point of the majority party and m_j be the median ideal point of the minority party and assume that $M_j < F < m_j$. Let $R(M_j)$ be the point to the majority median's left that gives utility equal to F (given symmetric utility functions, this will be the point $2M_j - F$). Similarly, let $R(m_j)$ be the point to the minority median's right that gives utility equal to F (given symmetric utility functions, this will be the point $2m_j - F$). Then every point to the left of $R(M_j)$ is "far left," every point between $R(M_j)$ and F is "near left," every point between F and $R(m_j)$ is "near right," and every point to the right of $R(m_j)$ is "far right."

11. In the U.S. case, likely institutional bases for a majority party veto over the placement of items on the plenary agenda include: the scheduling power of sub-committee and committee chairs, the requirement that every "spending bill" pass through both an authorizing committee and the appropriations committee (on which the majority party is disproportionately represented), the requirement that most important bills pass through the Rules Committee (on which, again, the majority party is disproportionately represented), and the Speaker's and Majority Leader's control over floor scheduling.

12. See Poole and Rosenthal 1997.

13. As Sinclair 2000 points out, this pattern is precisely opposite to what a majoritarian (or "neutral rules") model would expect (cf. Krehbiel 1991).

14. The only argument that this does *not* represent evidence that the majority party is "buying" pivotal votes is Krehbiel's suggestion that both parties buy about the same number of votes on any given bill, thus canceling out each other's efforts. There is no evidence for this "canceling conjecture," however, and there is considerable reason to doubt it. For example, the majority party has more resources with which to reward and punish than the minority, which should lead to better success in the vote-buying market. Also, if party efforts do routinely cancel out, one would expect minority party leaders to be just as prominent in last-minute vote buying as majority party leaders, which is certainly not the picture painted in the qualitative literature. Also, why are there not as many anecdotes about minority party leaders pulling out last-minute victories as there are about majority party leaders? Either the agenda has been stacked or the majority has a bigger bag of side payments.

REFERENCES

Ansolabehere, Stephen, James M. Snyder, and Charles Stewart III. 1999. "The Effects of Party and Preferences on Congressional Roll-Call Voting." Unpublished typescript. Massachusetts Institute of Technology.
Arnold, R. Douglas. 1990. *The Logic of Congressional Action*. New Haven, CT: Yale University Press.
Binder, Sarah. 1997. *Majority Rule, Minority Rights*. Cambridge: Cambridge University Press.
Binder, Sarah, and Steven Smith. 1997. *Politics or Principle? Filibustering in the United States*. Washington, DC: Brookings Institution Press.
Black, Duncan. 1958. *The Theory of Committees and Elections*. Cambridge: Cambridge University Press.
Brady, David W., John F. Cogan, Brian J. Gaines, and Douglas Rivers. 1996. "The Perils of Presidential Support: How the Republicans Took the House in the 1994 Midterm Election." *Political Behavior* 18:345–67.
Cox, Gary W. 1997. *Making Votes Count*. Cambridge: Cambridge University Press.
Cox, Gary W., and Mathew D. McCubbins. 1993. *Legislative Leviathan*. Berkeley: University of California Press.
Cox, Gary W., and Mathew D. McCubbins. 1994. "Bonding, Structure, and the Stability of Political Parties: Party Government in the House." *Legislative Studies Quarterly* 19:215–31.
Cox, Gary W., and Mathew D. McCubbins. 2000. "Agenda Power in the U.S. House of Representatives, 1877 to 1986." In *Essays on the History of Congress*, ed. David W. Brady and Mathew D. McCubbins. Palo Alto, CA: Stanford University Press (forthcoming).
Cox, Gary W., and Richard D. McKelvey. 1984. "A Ham Sandwich Theorem for General Measures." *Social Choice and Welfare* 1:75–83.
Cox, Gary W., and Scott Morgenstern. 2000. "Reactive Assemblies and Proactive Presidents: A Typology of Latin American Presidents and Legislatures." In *Comparative Politics* (forthcoming).
Cox, Gary W., Mikitaka Masuyama, and Mathew D. McCubbins. 2000. "Agenda Power in the Japanese House of Representatives." Unpublished typescript. University of California, San Diego.
Damgaard, Erik. 1995. "How Parties Control Committee Members." In *Parliaments and Majority Rule in Western Europe*, ed. Herbert Döring. Berlin: Campus Verlag.
Damgaard, Erik, and Palle Svensson. 1989. "Who Governs? Parties and Policies in Denmark." *European Journal of Political Research* 17:731–45.
Denzau, Arthur T., and Robert J. Mackay. 1983. "Gatekeeping and Monopoly Power of Committees: An Analysis of Sincere and Sophisticated Behavior." *American Journal of Political Science* 27:740–61.
De Winter, Lieven. 1995. "The Role of Parliament in Government Formation and Resignation." In *Parliaments and Majority Rule in Western Europe*, ed. Herbert Döring. Berlin: Campus Verlag.
Diermeier, Daniel, and Timothy Feddersen. 1998. "Cohesion in Legislatures and the Vote of Confidence Procedure." *American Political Science Review* 92:611–22.

Dion, Douglas. 1997. *Turning the Legislative Thumbscrew*. Ann Arbor: University of Michigan Press.
Döring, Herbert. 1995a. "Fewer Though Presumably More Conflictual Bills: Parliamentary Government Acting as a Monopolist." In *Parliaments and Majority Rule in Western Europe*, ed. Herbert Döring. Berlin: Campus Verlag.
Döring, Herbert. 1995b. "Institutions and Policies: Why We Need Cross-National Analysis." In *Parliaments and Majority Rule in Western Europe*, ed. Herbert Döring. Berlin: Campus Verlag.
Döring, Herbert. 1995c. "Time as a Scarce Resource: Government Control of the Agenda." In *Parliaments and Majority Rule in Western Europe*, ed. Herbert Döring. Berlin: Campus Verlag.
Henning, Christian. 1995. "A Formal Model of Law Production by Government as a Natural Monopoly." In *Parliaments and Majority Rule in Western Europe*, ed. Herbert Döring. Berlin: Campus Verlag.
Huber, John. 1996. *Rationalizing Parliament: Legislative Institutions and Party Politics in France*. Cambridge: Cambridge University Press.
Jacobson, Gary C. 1996. "The 1994 House Elections in Perspective." *Political Science Quarterly* 111:203–23.
Kingdon, John W. 1989. *Congressmen's Voting Decisions*, 3d ed. Ann Arbor: University of Michigan Press.
Krehbiel, Keith. 1985. "Obstruction and Representativeness in Legislatures." *American Journal of Political Science* 29:643–59.
Krehbiel, Keith. 1991. *Information and Legislative Organization*. Ann Arbor: University of Michigan Press.
Krehbiel, Keith. 1993. "Where's the Party?" *British Journal of Political Science* 23:235–66.
Krehbiel, Keith. 1997a. "Rejoinder to 'Sense and Sensibility.'" *American Journal of Political Science* 41:958–64.
Krehbiel, Keith. 1997b. "Restrictive Rules Reconsidered." *American Journal of Political Science* 41:919–44.
McCarty, Nolan, Keith Poole, and Howard Rosenthal. 1999. "The Hunt for Party Discipline in Congress." Unpublished manuscript. Carnegie Mellon University.
McKelvey, Richard D., and Norman Schofield. 1986. "Structural Instability of the Core." *Journal of Mathematical Economics* 15:179–98.
Poole, Keith T., and Howard Rosenthal. 1997. *Congress: A Political-Economic History of Roll Call Voting*. New York: Oxford University Press.
Riker, William H. 1980. "Implications from the Disequilibrium of Majority Rule for the Study of Institutions." *American Political Science Review* 74:432–46.
Rosenthal, Howard. 1990. "The Setter Model." In *Advances in the Spatial Theory of Elections*, ed. James Enelow and Melvin Hinich. Cambridge: Cambridge University Press.
Saari, Donald. 1997. "The Generic Existence of a Core for q-rules." *Economic Theory* 9:219–60.
Santos, Fabiano. 1999. "Party Leaders and Committee Assignments in Brazil." Presented at the annual meeting of the American Political Science Association, Atlanta, Georgia.

Shepsle, Kenneth. 1979. "Institutional Arrangements and Equilibrium in Multidimensional Voting Models." *American Journal of Political Science* 23:27–59.

Sinclair, Barbara. 1995. *Legislators, Leaders and Lawmaking*. Baltimore: Johns Hopkins University Press.

Sinclair, Barbara. 2000. "Do Parties Matter?" In *Essays on the History of Congress*, ed. David W. Brady and Mathew D. McCubbins. Palo Alto, CA: Stanford University Press (forthcoming).

Parliamentary Floor Voting Procedures and Agenda Setting in Europe

Bjørn Erik Rasch

Introduction

Which voting agendas do European parliaments use when they need to choose between several mutually exclusive alternatives? Do the details of floor voting procedures matter for legislative outcomes? Over the last decades, it has been shown that aggregation of preferences by means of voting is burdened with a variety of difficulties. Three topics relevant to legislative research are discussed extensively in the social choice literature. The first is the assumed prevalence of cycles in majority voting. Plott (1967) demonstrated that the existence of an unambiguous majority alternative in spatial voting games required voters' preferences to be distributed highly symmetrically in policy space, and it is unlikely that we find this symmetry condition satisfied in practice. Nevertheless, few clear-cut instances of majority cycles have been reported in the literature on legislative voting, and claims have been made to the effect that the empirical relevance of the "generic" instability of majority rule still remains unclear (Green and Shapiro 1994; but see Van Deemen 1998).

The second basic insight is the importance of institutional arrangements (McKelvey 1976; Shepsle 1979). Majority rule can be institutionalized in different ways to handle multiple alternatives. Theoretical arguments as well as experimental results support the view that decision-making procedures and the details of legislative agendas to a large extent determine outcomes, particularly in the case of majority cycling.

The third important theme taken from the social choice literature is related to the use of strategy and skill in voting processes (Farquharson 1969). All voting institutions are vulnerable to manipulation; regardless of the institutional framework, there will be occasions on which some voters can achieve a better outcome from their point of view by voting contrary to their true preferences

---

Reprinted with permission from *Legislative Studies Quarterly* 25, no. 1 (February 2000): 3–23.

(Gibbard 1973; Satterthwaite 1975). That is, when decision processes are manipulable, voters may have incentives to vote against alternatives they actually prefer or in favor of something they dislike, in order to make the final outcome of the process as good as possible. To analyze this kind of sophisticated action, voting institutions normally are modeled as non-cooperative games (McKelvey and Niemi 1978). Note however that strategic voting potentially will produce outcomes reflecting voters' preferences more closely than would be the case under sincere, non-sophisticated voting. In addition, other forms of strategic maneuvers may be available to decision makers, as for instance vote trading or logrolling, manipulation of voting sequences, and insincere additions or removals of motions to consider and vote on (Riker 1986).

The aim of this paper is primarily to give an account of floor voting procedures in European parliaments, and to indicate some consequences of the various approaches to voting for legislative outcomes. Along the way, I review relevant parts of the literature related to the three key social choice problems mentioned above. Throughout, I concentrate on methods for voting on bills and amendments in lower or single houses of national parliaments only. Parliaments might use different methods for voting on ordinary (law) bills and other types of proposals (e.g., resolutions, constitutional amendments, the state budget, or financial legislation); lower and upper houses also might approach voting problems differently. Furthermore, the procedures described in this paper are never used for elections within assemblies (e.g., to elect the Speaker).

The paper is organized as follows. First, floor-voting procedures in a number of European parliaments are outlined. Data is provided by legislative experts throughout Europe. In the second section, various order-of-voting rules that parliaments employ are presented and discussed. Agendas largely seem to be based on principles that make it likely that "true" majority alternatives—whenever they exist—will be adopted by sincere voting. The third and last section contains concluding remarks.

Parliamentary Floor Voting Procedures

Voting procedures are mechanisms by which individual votes on possible outcomes are translated into collective choices. To be able to work on any number of feasible alternatives, voting procedures consist of two components: a balloting method and decision rules, which may be more or less complex. The first specifies how and in what form votes are cast, whereas the latter specifies how votes are summed up or aggregated in order to produce an outcome. Decision rules include both a dominance relation that defines the requirements for winning—for instance, the majority principle—and a voting sequence, in the event that more than one ballot is necessary.

If an assembly needs to make a choice between three or more mutually exclusive alternatives, a large number of procedures—each with different properties—could be used (see e.g., Miller 1995; Nurmi 1987; Riker 1982). In the parliamentary setting, however, it turns out that only two main approaches are followed. National parliaments tend to apply either a variant of the *amendment procedure*, or some sort of *successive procedure*. The amendment procedure—or *elimination procedure* as it is also called—has received comprehensive scholarly attention, mainly because it is used in the Anglo-American world, while the successive procedure has been studied more sporadically (but see Bjurulf and Niemi 1981; Grofman 1981; Miller 1995).[1]

To define the procedures, let us suppose parliamentarians are to select one alternative from a fixed and finite set of feasible outcomes. The alternatives are mutually exclusive options, meaning that motions and alternatives, in practice, need not be the same (Ordeshook and Schwartz 1987, 183). Alternatives first have to be arranged in some sequence, i.e., a predetermined voting order. The successive procedure now works by voting on the alternatives one-by-one, up or down, in the order specified. Thus, the initial ballot clarifies whether a majority supports the first alternative or not. If this single alternative receives a majority of votes, it is adopted and no more votes need to be taken; all other alternatives—not compatible with the accepted one—are automatically eliminated. If, however, a majority decides against the first alternative, this alternative is removed and will not gain further consideration. The assembly then moves on to the second alternative specified by the voting order selected. The third stage of the voting process is reached only if the second alternative is voted down. Voting proceeds until one alternative obtains a majority. At least one of the two alternatives remaining at the last possible step (the k-1'th ballot with k alternatives) has to be the outcome, if no single alternative at an earlier stage of the voting process has been able to attract a majority. The structure of the successive procedure is shown in Figure 1, assuming four mutually exclusive options a, b, c, and d and the voting order abcd.[2]

If none of the alternatives before the parliament has a clear-cut majority of first preference votes, the outcome at least partly has to be based on ex ante or ex post subsidiary voting (in addition to first preference votes). In the latter (ex post) case, a member of parliament votes in favor of a lower ranked alternative only after higher ranked options are eliminated. Thus, the legislator votes directly in accordance with his or her preferences; whenever two alternative sets are compared, the one containing the alternative highest on the legislator's preference scale is chosen. This behavior is termed *sincere* or nonstrategic voting, as voting is based solely on the voter's own preferences. *Strategic* voting, however, requires information on others' preferences and likely behavior and takes the form of ex ante subsidiary voting. Thus, an actor votes in favor of some single alternative although it is not the highest ranked one of the remaining

FIGURE 1
Structure of Successive Procedure and Amendment Procedure with Four Alternatives

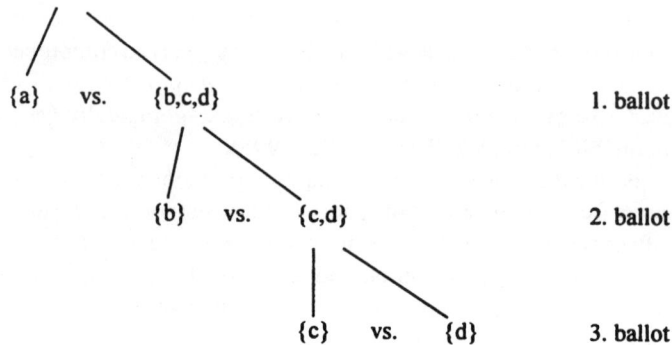

Successive Procedure

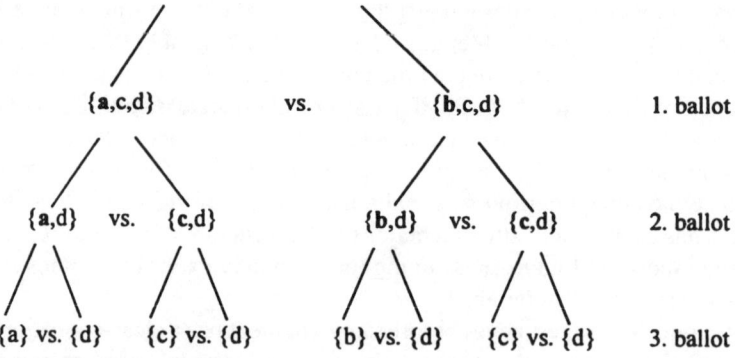

Amendment Procedure (or Elimination Procedure)

Note: Figure 1 represents the structure of the successive procedure and the amendment procedure with four alternatives (possible outcomes) *a, b, c,* and *d*. The voting order assumed is abcd. Both methods are binary, multistage approaches, and proceed by comparing various (sub)sets of alternatives. (Under the amendment procedure, alternatives under consideration for elimination before the final stage of the voting process are boldfaced.)

options. The purpose is to secure the best possible outcome. Note that under the successive procedure, as long as a voting order is specified, no voter can gain by voting in favor of a worst alternative or against a best alternative. In this sense, then, it is not possible to gain by voting *contrary* to one's preferences.[3] Sophisticated legislators will try to make the best possible use of their votes, meaning that their sophisticated strategies or plans may or may not imply strategic voting.

The standard amendment procedure proceeds by comparing pairs of alternatives and removing one of the two at every voting stage.[4] After arranging the alternatives in some order, the initial poll is taken between the first two alternatives. The winner of this contest is paired against the third alternative of the predetermined voting order. The majority winner at this second stage then goes on to meet the fourth alternative on the list, and so on. With k alternatives on the agenda, exactly k-1 ballots are carried out. During the voting process, alternatives are always eliminated one-by-one, and in this sense, we are dealing with a strictly sequential elimination process. Contrary to what might be observed in connection with the successive procedure, a winner is never selected before the final ballot; victories at earlier stages are only preliminary.

Sincere voting in the case of the amendment procedure also means voting strictly in accordance with one's own preferences. Strategic voting, however, implies voting contrary to true preferences at earlier stages of the voting process, i.e., in favor of the lowest ranked of two alternatives, to make the final outcome as good as possible given the preferences and likely actions of others. Thus, the legislator may gain by voting against his or her best alternative, or in favor of the worst alternative. Sophisticated strategies, however, under the amendment as well as the successive methods, do not necessarily involve strategic voting.

Table 1 indicates the main approaches to legislative voting on multiple alternatives in parliaments of Western Europe and East-Central Europe, as well as the European Parliament. Also, the U.S. and Canadian legislatures are added. The successive procedure is predominant, while the only other main scheme to be found in this area is the amendment procedure. With the exception of Scandinavian countries, the table is not based on a close inspection of voting practices. Rather, the information on European legislatures contained in the table is provided by legislative specialists in the various countries.[5] Whenever possible, other sources of information (other informants or literature) have been brought in as a check.[6]

One possible basis for misclassification does exist. Because parliaments often vote laws in smaller parts (e.g., article by article), it is possible to misinterpret this practice and say that a successive procedure is used, although, in fact, the parliament in question leans toward an amendment procedure. To misinterpret the successive approach as one of amendment voting should be much less likely. Also, because the new democratic institutions of East-Central Europe are in a phase of consolidation, voting practice should be expected to be more mixed and ambiguous than it is in established democracies. The latter consideration seems to be of particular relevance to the case of the highly fractionalized Polish Sejm. To conclude, we have traced the two main approaches to parliamentary voting in Europe, however, it is not yet possible to tell just how stringently the two procedures are applied in day-to-day proceedings.[7]

If we concentrate on Europe (the countries included in Table 1), parties controlling a majority of seats in parliament are hardly found, except, of course,

TABLE 1
Legislative Floor Voting Procedures in European National Parliaments

Successive Procedure (Alternatives voted "one-by-one")	Amendment (Elimination) Procedure (Alternatives voted "two-by-two")
Austria	Finland
Belgium	Sweden
Denmark	Switzerland
France	United Kingdom
Germany	
Greece	
Iceland	
Ireland	
Italy	
Luxembourg	
Netherlands	
Norway	
Portugal	
Spain	
Czech Republic	
Hungary	
Poland	
Slovakia	
Slovenia	
	(Canada)
(European Parliament)	(USA)

Sources: See Rasch (1995) and Döring (1995, 13–23) on Western Europe; questionnaire answered by legislative specialists in East-Central Europe (Gabriella Ilonszki, Irena Jackiewicz, Jana Reschova, Danica Sivakova, and Drago Zajc). On USA, see e.g., Strom (1990), Sullivan (1984), and Ordeshook and Schwartz (1987). Flanagan (1997) gives information on parliamentary voting in Canada.

for the United Kingdom. Typically, multipartyism without majority parties dominates the picture. More often than not, however, majority governments are formed also when no party holds a majority of seats in parliament, and governing multiparty coalitions tend to act as fairly unitary blocks. In the latter case, assuming a disciplined majority coalition, the details of voting procedures outlined above would hardly be more important for the outcome than situations involving a disciplined majority party. In parliamentary systems, which are generally known for high levels of party discipline, voting procedures are most likely to play a role in practice—if at all—under minority governments. Floor voting could affect the outcome if the governmental party or parties have failed to build majority support for their initiative through bargaining and deliberation during the preparatory stages of the lawmaking process.[8] Predictions concerning what would happen on the floor if attempts to form majority support for a proposal fail, may, of course, influence negotiations at pre-voting stages.

Does it matter which voting scheme is used? Which one of the procedures is best suited for parliamentary decision making? It is not possible to give simple answers to such questions. Let me point to some relevant characteristics to consider. First, related to implementation and decision-making costs, amendment voting easily gets more complex and impermeable for the decision makers than successive voting as the number of amendments to decide on increases. Higher speed in voting is possible within the simpler successive framework. It likely will be easier for voters to ascertain the implications of particular voting orders, which is a factor that might reduce the potential power of an agenda setter.

Second, the outcome of amendment voting may be less dependent on the actual voting order selected than under successive voting. At least this is true if a Condorcet winner exists (among the limited alternative set considered), and if the legislators do not vote strategically.[9] Under these conditions, the standard amendment procedure always picks the Condorcet winner. The Condorcet winner may, however, lose under successive voting if this alternative is voted on too early, meaning that it will be deprived from receiving enough subsidiary votes to win. The higher degree of voting-order dependency in successive voting also may result in increased power to those responsible for forming the voting order, or, alternatively, to those most knowledgeable in these matters. The voting order, of course, is irrelevant to the result if one alternative commands a majority of first-place preferences. This is true for both procedures. Politically, however, the order of voting may be important under the successive procedure, even if an alternative supported by a majority exists. Unless this alternative is voted on last, the voting process will terminate before each and every alternative has had a try.

None of the procedures makes it possible for very weak alternatives, such as a Condorcet loser, to be adopted. However, neither the standard amendment framework nor the successive scheme are able to guarantee that Pareto-dominated alternatives will be defeated, assuming sincere voting (see e.g., Grofman 1981; Straffin 1980).[10]

Third, which one of the voting procedures is the approach most susceptible to strategy and skill by the legislators? Voting outcomes may be manipulated in many ways. The set of alternatives available at the floor can be influenced by strategic additions or deletions of proposals. Several papers have, for example, pointed to the possibility of introducing amendments either to save a losing bill or to kill a winning bill, assuming the use of the amendment procedure (Enelow and Koehler 1980). Agenda manipulation (with a fixed set of alternatives) may be related to the choice of voting method, the choice of order in which alternatives are considered, or the labeling of the alternatives (which may affect the ordering). Further, strategic voting is a way to manipulate, but also, under some circumstances, a way to counteract strategic maneuvers related to agenda setting.

The successive procedure, on the one hand, seems to be more sensitive to order-of-voting effects than the amendment procedure, in principle opening up vast opportunities to affect the outcome by manipulating the voting order (particularly if voting is sincere). On the other hand, amendment voting over multiple alternatives might easily become much more complex than successive voting, allowing some voters to take others by surprise during the process of sequential elimination of single alternatives. Findings in empirical studies trying to discover whether legislators do vote strategically are, however, mixed. Furthermore, most of the work analyzes case studies in voting bodies where the amendment procedure is used (Bjurulf and Niemi 1978; Calvert and Fenno 1994; Krehbiel and Rivers 1990). It is hard to tell how relevant theoretical possibilities to manipulate outcomes are to members of European parliaments, and how frequently such possibilities in fact are exploited in practice.[11]

Principles of Agenda Formation

It is well known among analysts as well as politicians that the outcome of parliamentary voting may depend on the order in which feasible alternatives are voted upon on the floor. Arguments have been forwarded to the effect that for the standard amendment scheme, "given sincere voting, the later any motion enters the voting order, the greater its chances of adoption" (Black 1958, 40). A similar assertion has been made with respect to successive voting. However, if legislators are expected to vote strategically, it might be advantageous to have one's first choice voted upon earlier rather than later (Farquharson 1969, 62).[12] In this section, some important principles guiding the choice of voting order for a fixed set of alternatives will be discussed. Again, information is provided by legislative specialists in the various countries. They have consulted standing orders and in some cases asked parliamentary staff for clarification, but they do not build on systematic analyses of actual voting practices.[13]

McKelvey's (1976) demonstration of conditions for unlimited agenda control in spatial voting games may serve as a point of departure. It is unlikely that there will be a Condorcet winner in multi-dimensional space, and when such an alternative is lacking, the majority cycle encompasses the entire policy space. Thus, *any* two alternatives in the space are linked in a cycle, making it possible to start majority voting from any one of them, just to terminate with the other one as the outcome. The situation is completely open and might be exploited by monopolistic agenda setting. Under some conditions, an agenda setter is able to design a sequence of pairwise ballots that yields the agenda setter's own ideal point (first preference) as the majority decision, no matter how extreme this ideal point might be relative to others' first place preferences. Clearly, with this background, social choices of majority-rule institutions appear to be highly dependent on the agenda mechanism that is used, and unlimited control of the agenda might mean total control of legislative outcome.

Several authors have warned that the practical importance of McKelvey's agenda theorem should not be overstated. It is based on an extremely sparse institutional framework, as well as rather unrealistic behavioral assumptions. Introducing conditions that are more adequate clearly entails limits on possibilities for agenda control. For one thing, institutional structures common to legislative assemblies, most notably a system of standing committees where each committee is responsible for preparing decisions within quite narrow jurisdictions, should make actual majority-rule cycles in floor voting less likely (Shepsle 1979). But even if cycles remain, opportunities for agenda control are largely undermined. There are four reasons why this is so.

First, it is a lot easier to move agenda processes (of the McKelvey type) in a centrist rather than in a non-centrist direction of the multi-dimensional policy space (Feld, Grofman, and Miller 1989). Thus, non-centrist agenda setters normally will need to employ very long and ingenious sequences of pairwise ballots to reach favorable alternatives, typically not conforming to agendas observed in parliamentary voting. Second, the agenda theorem assumes that the agenda setter acts strategically in designing the voting sequence, while everyone after that votes sincerely. In fact, the ordinary members of the legislature play no role beside revealing preferences on pairs of alternatives (i.e., voting "yea" or "no" to those single alternatives the agenda setter finds it advantageous to bring forward at each step of the process). However, if one opens up for sophisticated voting, the set of reachable alternatives in policy space may shrink (depending on the voting procedure). As long as the standard amendment scheme is used, the agenda setter will not be able to yield outcomes outside the "uncovered set" (Shepsle and Weingast 1984).[14] Strategic voting requires that the entire agenda is fixed and announced to the legislators before any voting takes place, but still the agenda setter alone is assumed to pick the alternatives for consideration and to determine the order of voting. Third, then, agenda-setting processes might not be as centralized—or monopolistic—as in the McKelvey case. In completely open, decentralized agenda formation, assuming sophisticated behavior, majority rule will not wander anywhere in policy space.[15] Possible outcomes under amendment voting again belong to the uncovered set (Miller 1980; Shepsle and Weingast 1984). Fourth, the voting order in the case of the agenda theorem is "forward" moving. A single alternative is introduced and placed against the status quo, then a second alternative is paired with the winner of the first vote (the new status quo), and so forth. Thus, the status quo can be said to be voted upon first. The forward moving process also implies that the voters "discover" the agenda while voting. Therefore, they have no alternative but to behave sincerely at each voting stage. A "backward" moving agenda, on the other hand, takes the order in which alternatives are moved as the point of departure and establishes a voting sequence in exactly the reverse order from this. An implication is that status quo is voted upon last. It should be noted that backward moving agendas, with sophisticated voters, tend to constrain outcomes more than forward moving agendas (Shepsle and Weingast 1984; Wilson 1986). Thus, the potential power of an agenda setter may be reduced.

How are agendas formed in real-world legislatures? The rules of agenda building in the U.S. Congress have been extensively analyzed, and it is often claimed that very similar rules are found in other legislatures. I will now give an account of agenda principles in European parliaments, and also indicate some likely effects of the way agendas normally are designed. Three observations should be emphasized.

First, determination of the voting order in European parliaments is far from monopolistic. On the one hand, in most parliaments the threshold to formulate motions is quite low. Individual legislators normally only meet mild restrictions if they want to make proposals, be it an issue already on the parliamentary agenda or completely new initiatives (see Mattson 1995). On the other hand, the initial order of voting (for a fixed set of alternatives) is, with few exceptions, suggested by the Speaker or president of the assembly. Before announcing the voting order on the floor, the presiding officer typically will have been in contact with relevant party or committee leaders and legislative staff if doubts on which order to choose arise or if other difficulties are anticipated. We should also bear in mind that the level of information on the standpoints of various party groups may be quite high at this final stage of the legislative process, i.e., after the preparatory work in governmental offices and parliamentary committees is done (including lobbying and hearings), after negotiations and deliberation in committee rooms and corridors are brought to a close, and after the general, plenary debate is ended. The role of presiding officers, furthermore, often can be regarded as less party-oriented and conflictual than that of ordinary members of parliament.[16] Procedures for electing Speakers are also typically complex, multi-round majority runoff arrangements, leaving only candidates with rather broad appeal any chance of winning.[17]

What if the voting order suggested by the Speaker nevertheless does not conform to the wishes of the majority of the legislators? Then, as indicated in Table 2, the majority in most parliaments is free to revise the voting order. In other words, the Speaker proposes the legislative agenda under an open rule, which gives legislators an opportunity to suggest revisions of the voting order. But, as we shall see, this opportunity is constrained by some general principles. In forming the agenda the Speaker most probably will try to anticipate whether the voting order will eventually be revised on the floor, and avoid agendas unacceptable to a majority of legislators.[18] It is tempting to conclude that as far as presiding officers are concerned, they have neither the incentives nor the means to exert strict control of the legislative agenda. Other potential agenda-setting candidates, as parliamentary governments or legislative committees, should be similarly limited by the open rules described above.

As a second observation, it is not always the case in European parliaments that the status quo (if this option is present at all) is voted upon last. In this sense then, European legislatures deviate from the practice followed by the U.S. Congress. About half the countries in Table 2 do not necessarily leave status quo to the final stage of the floor-voting process.[19] On the occasions when status quo is *not* voted upon last and the amendment procedure is used, outcomes outside the win set of the status quo become possible.[20] With respect to the successive procedure, outcomes outside the win set of the status quo are possible even if status quo is voted upon last. The provision to vote upon status quo last under the successive voting scheme thus puts status quo in a privileged position (sincere voting) but does not by itself constrain outcomes as clearly as in the case of amendment voting.

Most legislative decision-making processes in parliamentary countries originate in governmental offices.[21] Often the governmental bill, probably as the bill is formulated after being reviewed by a legislative committee, has a privileged position in voting. The original bill functions, so to speak, as an anchor in floor voting and is typically voted upon late. It is not unusual to see a final vote between the governmental bill and the status quo.

This is the third observation: In most of the European countries it is customary to look at the *content* of motions, not only their formal properties or labeling (such as "original motion," "amendment to original motion," "amendment to the amendment," etc.). More specifically, if multiple alternatives exist, one tries to vote on the most far-reaching or extreme alternatives first and to approach more moderate ones gradually. The (original) governmental bill or the committee bill may serve as a point of reference—or anchor—for the comparisons. In practice, definitions and interpretations of "most extreme" will rest on the discretion of the speaker and the floor majority. To vote on the most deviant proposals first is an approach most readily found in countries using the successive procedure, that is, in countries using the procedure which is most sensitive to voting order effects. Finland illustrates that the norm to vote upon extreme alternatives first is also applied in the case of the amendment procedure.

TABLE 2
Order-of-Voting Rules in European Parliaments
(1 = yes; 0 = no)

Country	Always Vote on Status Quo Last	Always Vote on Most Extreme Alternative First
Austria	0	1
Belgium	0	0
Czech Republic	1	(0)
Denmark	0	1
Finland[Am]	1	1
France[1]	1	1
Germany	1	1
Greece	1	1
Hungary	0	1
Iceland	0	1
Ireland[1]	1	1
Italy[1]	1	1
Luxembourg	0	0
Netherlands	1	1
Norway	0	1
Poland	1	1
Portugal	0	0
Slovakia	1	(0)
Slovenia	0	1
Spain	0	1
Sweden[Am]	0	0
Switzerland[Am]	1	0
UK [Am,1]	0	0
European Parliament	1	1

Sources: See Rasch (1995) and Döring (1995, 13-23) on Western Europe; questionnaire answered by legislative specialists in East-Central Europe (Gabriella Ilonszki, Irena Jackiewicz, Jana Reschova, Danica Sivakova, and Drago Zajc).
[Am]Countries using the amendment procedure for legislative voting in lower or single house.
[1]Floor majority may not have opportunity to revise initial proposal of voting order.

Earlier, a distinction was made between forward and backward moving agendas. In the latter case, labeling becomes essential. Status quo is voted on last. The original bill is introduced at the penultimate division, after an amendment to the bill has been considered. Before that, votes may have been taken on an amendment to the amendment, a substitute, and an amended substitute. The latter two of the six alternatives described are thus voted on first. Although labeling might be important in some European legislatures, the norm to vote on the most extreme proposal first indicates a third kind of legislative agenda formation (beside forward- and backward-moving agendas). We can use the term *median agenda* for a voting order introducing the most extreme of the remaining alternatives at each stage of the voting process. Legislators focus on the content of proposals rather than labeling or other formal properties in formulating the voting order, and this often amounts to the same as considering the preferences of various parties more directly.[22] Note that if a Condorcet winner exists, median agendas often can be expected to introduce this alternative late (probably even last).

Finally in this section, I will point to some implications of the principles guiding agenda formation in European parliaments. If the preferences of members of parliament are single-peaked or nearly so, the practice of starting with extreme positions according to the underlying policy dimension results in the Condorcet winner as the outcome. This is true for both the amendment and the successive procedure. Voting, in other words, takes the form of eliminating the most extreme points of view first, gradually moving towards the center of the distribution of preferences.[23] It does not matter for the final outcome whether voting begins at one extreme of the underlying dimension or, alternatively, from both ends of the scale successively. (Also, if no Condorcet winner exists in spatial voting games, median agendas are likely to constrain the set of possible outcomes.)

Furthermore, if preferences are single-peaked or nearly so, and median agendas are used, no legislator can be better off by voting strategically rather than sincerely (Hylland 1976; Rasch 1987). This holds for the amendment procedure as well as the successive procedure. Thus, most European legislatures seem to have developed voting schemes that are strategy-proof for single-peaked preferences. If unidimensionality in parliamentary decision making is not exceptional (partly because of the kind of structural and procedural features pointed out by Shepsle 1979 and others), this is all the more important.

Conclusion

When parliaments have to choose between several mutually exclusive alternatives, only two voting methods seem to be applied. Use of the successive procedure is more widespread in European parliaments than the familiar, Anglo-

American standard amendment scheme. Both procedures may be sensitive to the order of voting; in some cases, the legislative outcome rests entirely on the order in which proposals are considered, rather than the preferences of the members of the voting body. It has been central to this paper, therefore, to give an account of the principles guiding voting order formation in the European context. We have seen that the possibilities for any agenda setter to control the voting order are limited. With respect to the ordering of alternatives, status quo alternatives are not always voted on last (as in the U.S. Congress). In many legislatures, more extreme alternatives are voted on before less extreme ones. Agendas based on the latter approach, termed median agendas in the paper, have two interesting properties (in the case of unidimensionality). First, Condorcet alternatives will be adopted. Second, there is nothing to gain by strategic voting. There is no difference in this respect between the successive procedure and the standard amendment procedure.

As the analysis mainly rests on institutional data, it strongly needs to be elaborated with adequate data on actual voting practices. We will then be able to describe actual procedures and principles of agenda formation more closely and will get a reasonably firm understanding of how frequently multi-alternative situations emerge on the floor of national parliaments.

NOTES

This research has been supported by the Research Council of Norway. A first version of the paper was presented at the Shambaugh Comparative Research Conference, University of Iowa, Iowa City, April 16–19, 1998. I thank Rod Kiewiet, Herbert Döring, Gary Cox, Gerhard Loewenberg, Hannu Nurmi, and Drago Zajc for helpful comments.

1. For example, Nurmi's 1983 very useful review of normative properties of various voting procedures lacks the successive procedure.
2. With respect to the successive procedure, Riker (1982, 73) writes that "if at the end no winner has been selected, the procedure is abandoned or repeated." The successive procedure, as normally defined, is however decisive. One of the two single alternatives compared at the last stage of the voting process will be the outcome if this stage is reached at all.
3. The reason is that as soon an alternative gets a majority of votes, it also becomes the decision of the legislature in question. If a voter feels that this outcome is the worst possible, he or she will of course oppose it. Likewise, if one believes that the alternative being voted on is the best possible, one will always hurt its chances of adoption by voting against it.
4. As Figure 1 shows, the procedure in reality compares subsets of alternatives. The comparisons, however, are done in such a way that the subsets have all but one element in common.
5. The legislative specialists answered a questionnaire. All questions were institutional rather than behavioral. In answering, the specialists used the standing orders and other

documents of the various parliaments, and some specialists also contacted parliamentary staff to obtain more precise or reliable information. Most of the respondents could not be considered specialists in social choice theory but were highly experienced legislative scholars (cf. Döring 1995).

6. For example, Pappi 1992 (on the German Bundestag) and Ramstedt 1961 (on the Nordic countries, France, Germany, Switzerland, UK, and various international organizations). Wolters (1980 and 1984) says that Dutch voting is based on the standard amendment procedure, while we claim that the successive structure in fact is the one used for voting on law bills. However, voting practices are not necessarily unique, and different procedures might be used for different types of legislative decisions.

7. Ordeshook and Schwartz (1987) observed a mix of different procedures or agendas in the U.S. Congress. (For example, the October 8, 1998 House roll calls to authorize an impeachment inquiry of President Clinton seem to be based on a successive approach.) The same could be true at least for other countries mainly following the amendment framework. Voting in the Norwegian Parliament has been studied extensively, and in this case, the successive procedure—together with a number of more specific order-of-voting rules—is entirely predominant.

8. Some data from Norwegian roll-call voting might be illustrative. Minority governments occur quite frequently (about 63% of the governments 1884–1997) and more often than the average for Western Europe (for comparison, Strøm 1990 reports that 35% of the governments in 15 parliamentary democracies in Western Europe during 1945–87 were minority governments). Only 5 of 25 elections after 1905 (i.e., after dissolution of the union with Sweden) have resulted in a majority of parliamentary seats for any single party. In the beginning of the 1980s, on average about 15% of all floor-voting situations contained three or more mutually exclusive alternatives (N each parliamentary year ranges from 1271 to 1612; time period 1980-86). However, at most 6% of all situations had three or more mutually exclusive alternatives, none of which commanded a majority of first place preferences. Under the non-socialist majority government 1983–84, this percentage of potentially problematic voting situations was only 0.2 ($N = 1416$). In other words, actual voting-order difficulties were almost nonexistent. For details, see Rasch 1988. In systems with weak party discipline, voting-order problems easily become more significant than the data above indicate.

9. An alternative is a *Condorcet winner* if it beats every other (feasible) alternative in pairwise majority contests. A *Condorcet loser* is an alternative that is beaten by every other available alternative.

10. If two alternatives a and b exist and everybody prefers a to b, this means that there are situations where b will be the outcome. It is easier to imagine realistic situations of this type under successive voting than with respect to the amendment procedure. Here is an illustration: Assume that three parties I, II, and III of about equal size deal with four alternatives $a, b, c,$ and d. The preferences are I: a>b>c>d, II: c>a>b>d, and III: d>a>b>c, with a as Condorcet winner. Every actor prefers a to b, so b is Pareto dominated. Nevertheless, voting order acdb leads to b as the result of voting (provided voting is sincere). Now, if a is a proposal to postpone the decision in the case at hand, and b is the status quo, the suggested voting order also should be entirely realistic in a setting of successive voting. When the standard amendment procedure is used, Pareto-dominated alternatives will not be the sincere voting outcome as long as a Condorcet winner exists.

11. Several instances of strategic voting in the Swedish Riksdag have been reported in the literature (Bjurulf 1973; Bjurulf and Niemi 1978; Hadenius 1981; Lewin 1988). Similarly, with respect to the Finnish Riksdag, Nurmi (1997, 43) writes that "legislative majorities almost routinely resort to the preference misrepresentation in order to maneuver the weakest possible contestant to confront their favorite candidate in the final pairwise vote." Both Sweden and Finland use the amendment procedure. In Norway, using the successive procedure, it has been hard to come up with any clear-cut cases of strategic voting in Parliament (see Rasch 1990, where an instance of strategic voting is analyzed). This simple observation could indicate a general pattern with respect to the frequency of strategic voting under the amendment procedure and the successive procedure respectively.

12. See Jung (1990) and Miller (1995, 93–96) for precise statements with respect to the most favorable voting order positions, cf. also Niemi and Gretlein (1985) and Niemi and Rasch (1987).

13. For Scandinavian parliaments, details on voting practices can be found in Ramstedt (1961), Bjurulf and Niemi (1978), and Rasch (1987).

14. The covering relation is defined in this way. An alternative a is said to *cover* alternative b if, and only if, a beats b and every other alternative beaten by b. The *uncovered set* is then those alternatives not covered by any other alternatives (in the feasible set) (cf. Miller 1980). The uncovered set is a subset of Pareto optimal outcomes.

15. If voters act sincerely, however, the final outcome under open agenda formation entirely will depend on details of the voting procedure (i.e., the stopping rule).

16. This is also reflected in the way ties on ordinary motions are handled. Only in four of the Western European legislatures does the Speaker have a casting vote (Ireland, Norway, Switzerland, and United Kingdom). In Sweden, ties on ordinary motions are resolved by drawing lots, and in all other countries, a tied vote implies that the status quo prevails.

17. Procedures used for electing Speakers in parliaments in Western Europe are described in Rasch (1995). Jenny and Müller (1995) discuss to what extent presidents of parliaments in Western Europe can be regarded as neutral chairmen of the respective assemblies or not.

18. In the Norwegian Parliament, from 2 to 6 times each parliamentary year a vote has been taken on which voting order to follow. In no case have the parliamentarians had more than two voting order proposals from which to choose. The successive procedure is known to be highly sensitive to voting order effects. These data do however indicate that conflicts related to the order of voting are exceptional, partly because, of course, difficult multi-alternative situations (where no alternative has a majority of first place preferences) are relatively rare.

19. Herbert Döring and his collaborators have collected information on legislation covering working time and working conditions in 18 countries of Western Europe for the period 1981–91. Out of a total of 541 bills, a final vote on the totality of the bill was taken in almost 73% of the cases. Finland, Ireland, Portugal, Spain, Sweden, and United Kingdom, for some reason, were the countries most reluctant to vote on final passage of the bills included in the data set. Not surprisingly, a vote on final passage of the bill was much more common in cases when voting on the bill was conducted clause by clause (about half of the cases).

20. The win set of the status quo consists of alternatives that (various) majorities of the assembly in question prefer to the status quo.

21. Governments thus obviously have agenda power associated with when and how to make proposals, and this kind of influence is not dealt with here (see e.g., Döring 1995b).

22. As an illustration of this type of agenda, see the following formulation in the Standing Orders of the Slovenian Parliament: "If several amendments are proposed to an article of a proposed law, deputies shall vote first on the amendment which departs most from the content of the article in the proposed law, and then, following this criterion, on other amendments" (Article 192).

23. Heckscher (1892) discusses the practice of voting on extreme motions first. The way he defends this principle of agenda formation is close to anticipating Black's (1958) median theorem.

REFERENCES

Austen-Smith, David. 1987. "Sophisticated Sincerity: Voting over Endogenous Agendas." *American Political Science Review* 81:1323–29.

Bjurulf, Bo. 1973. "A Simulation Analysis of Selected Voting Procedures." *Statsvetenskaplig Tidskrift* 76:1–61.

Bjurulf, Bo, and Richard G. Niemi. 1978. "Strategic Voting in Scandinavian Parliaments." *Scandinavian Political Studies* 1:5–22.

Bjurulf, Bo, and Richard G. Niemi. 1981. "Order-of-Voting Effects." In *Power, Voting, and Voting Power,* ed. Manfred J. Holler. Würzburg: Physica-Verlag.

Black, Duncan. 1958. *The Theory of Committees and Elections.* Cambridge: Cambridge University Press.

Calvert, Randall L., and Richard F. Fenno. 1994. "Strategy and Sophisticated Voting in the Senate." *Journal of Politics* 56:349–76.

Denzau, Arthur, William Riker, and Kenneth Shepsle. 1985. "Farquharson and Fenno: Sophisticated Voting and Home Style." *American Political Science Review* 79:1117–34.

Döring, Herbert. 1995. "Introduction." In *Parliaments and Majority Rule in Western Europe*, ed. Herbert Döring. Frankfurt/New York: Campus Verlag/St. Martin's Press.

Döring, Herbert. 1995b. "Time as a Scarce Resource: Government Control of the Agenda." In *Parliaments and Majority Rule in Western Europe*, ed. Herbert Döring. Frankfurt/New York: Campus Verlag/St. Martin's Press.

Enelow, James M., and David H. Koehler. 1980. "The Amendment in Legislative Strategy: Sophisticated Voting in the U.S. Congress." *Journal of Politics* 42:396–413.

Farquharson, Robin. 1969. *Theory of Voting.* New Haven: Yale University Press.

Feld, Scott L., Bernard Grofman, and Nicholas R. Miller. 1989. "Limits on Agenda Control in Spatial Voting Games." *Mathematical and Computer Modelling* 12:405–16.

Flanagan, Thomas. 1997. "The Staying Power of the Legislative Status Quo: Collective Choice in Canada's Parliament after *Morgentaler.*" *Canadian Journal of Political Science* 30:31–53.

Gibbard, Allan. 1973. "Manipulation of Voting Schemes." *Econometrica* 41:587–601.
Green, Donald P., and Ian Shapiro. 1994. *Pathologies of Rational Choice Theory. A Critique of Applications in Political Science.* New Haven: Yale University Press.
Grofman, Bernard. 1981. "The Theory of Committees and Elections: The Legacy of Duncan Black." In *Towards a Science of Politics: Essays in Honor of Duncan Black*, ed. Gordon Tullock. Blacksburg, VA: Virginia Polytechnic Institute and State University.
Hadenius, Axel. 1981. *Spelet om skatten. Rationalistisk analys av politiskt beslutsfattande.* Stockholm: Almqvist & Wiksell.
Heckscher, Alb. 1892. *Bidrag til Grundlæggelse af en Afstemningslære.* Copenhagen: Universitetsbokhandler G.E.C. Gad.
Hylland, Aanund. 1976. "Strategy-proof voting procedures for single-peaked preferences." Unpublished paper. Department of Political Science, University of Oslo.
Jenny, Marcelo, and Wolfgang C. Müller. 1995. "Presidents of Parliament: Neutral Chairmen or Assets of the Majority?" In *Parliaments and Majority Rule in Western Europe*, ed. Herbert Döring. Frankfurt/New York: Campus Verlag/St. Martin's Press.
Jung, Joon Pyo. 1990. "Black and Farquharson on Order-of-Voting Effects: An Extension." *Social Choice and Welfare* 7:319–29.
Krehbiel, Keith. 1988. "Spatial Models of Legislative Choice." *Legislative Studies Quarterly* 13:259–319.
Krehbiel, Keith, and Douglas Rivers. 1990. "Sophisticated Voting in Congress: A Reconsideration." *Journal of Politics* 52:548–78.
Lewin, Leif. 1988. *Ideology and Strategy: A Century of Swedish Politics.* Cambridge: Cambridge University Press.
Mattson, Ingvar. 1995. "Private Members' Initiatives and Amendments." In *Parliaments and Majority Rule in Western Europe*, ed. Herbert Döring. Frankfurt/New York: Campus Verlag/St. Martin's Press.
McKelvey, Richard D. 1976. "Intransitivities in Multidimensional Voting Models and Some Implications for Agenda Control." *Journal of Economic Theory* 12:472–82.
McKelvey, Richard D. 1979. "General Conditions for Global Intransitivities in Formal Voting Models." *Econometrica* 47:1085–1112.
McKelvey, Richard D., and Richard G. Niemi. 1978. "A Multistage Game Representation of Sophisticated Voting for Binary Procedures." *Journal of Economic Theory* 18:1–22.
Miller, Nicholas R. 1980. "A New Solution Set for Tournaments and Majority Voting." *American Journal of Political Science* 24:68–96.
Miller, Nicholas R. 1995. *Committees, Agendas, and Voting.* Chur: Harwood Academic Publishers.
Niemi, Richard G., and R. Gretlein. 1985. "A Precise Restatement and Extension of Black's Theorem on Voting Orders." *Public Choice* 47:371–76.
Niemi, Richard G., and Bjørn Erik Rasch. 1987. "An Extension of Black's Theorem on Voting Orders to the Successive Procedure." *Public Choice* 54:187–90.
Nurmi, Hannu. 1983. "Voting Procedures: A Summary Analysis." *British Journal of Political Science* 13:181–208.
Nurmi, Hannu. 1987. *Comparing Voting Systems.* Dordrecht: D. Reidel Publishing Company.
Nurmi, Hannu. 1997. "Referendum Design: An Exercise in Applied Social Choice Theory." *Scandinavian Political Studies* 20:33–52.

Ordeshook, Peter C., and Thomas Schwartz. 1987. "Agendas and the Control of Political Outcomes." *American Political Science Review* 81:179–99.

Pappi, Franz Urban. 1992. "Die Abstimmungsreihenfolge der Anträge zum Parlaments- und Regierungssitz am 20. Juni 1991 im Deutschen Bundestag." *Zeitschrift für Parlamentsfragen* 23:403–12.

Plott, Charles R. 1967. "A Notion of Equilibrium and Its Possibility under Majority Rule." *American Economic Review* 57:787–806.

Ramstedt, Tolle. 1961. *Parlamentarisk beslutsteknik.* SOU 1961:21 Författningsutredningen.

Rasch, Bjørn Erik. 1987. "Manipulation and strategic voting in the Norwegian parliament." *Public Choice* 52:57–73.

Rasch, Bjørn Erik. 1988. "Political Legitimacy and Collective Rationality of Parliamentary Voting Procedures." In *Rationality and Legitimacy. Essays on Political Theory*, ed. Dag Anckar, Hannu Nurmi, and Matti Wiberg. Helsinki: The Finnish Political Science Association.

Rasch, Bjørn Erik. 1990. "Lokket av Pandoras krukke: En voteringsteoretisk analyse av Stortingets Hurum-vedtak." In *Oppstyr og styring rundt flyplass - Hurum, Fornebu, Gardermoen?,* ed. Knut Midgaard. Oslo: Dreyer.

Rasch, Bjørn Erik. 1995. "Parliamentary Voting Procedures." In *Parliaments and Majority Rule in Western Europe*, ed. Herbert Döring. Frankfurt/New York: Campus Verlag/St. Martin's Press.

Riker, William H. 1982. *Liberalism Against Populism. A Confrontation Between the Theory of Democracy and the Theory of Social Choice.* San Francisco: Freeman.

Riker, William H. 1986. *The Art of Political Manipulation.* New Haven, CT: Yale University Press.

Satterthwaite, Mark. 1975. "Strategy-Proofness and Arrow's Conditions." *Journal of Economic Theory* 10:187–217.

Schofield, Norman. 1978. "Instability of Simple Dynamic Games." *Review of Economic Studies* 45:575–94.

Shepsle, Kenneth A. 1979. "Institutional Arrangements and Equilibrium in Multidimensional Voting Models." *American Journal of Political Science* 23:27–59.

Shepsle, Kenneth A., and Barry R. Weingast. 1984. "Uncovered Sets and Sophisticated Voting Outcomes with Implications for Agenda Institutions." *American Journal of Political Science* 28:49–74.

Straffin, Phillip D., Jr. 1980. *Topics in the Theory of Voting.* Boston: Birkhäuser.

Strom, Gerald S. 1990. *The Logic of Lawmaking. A Spatial Theory Approach.* Baltimore: The Johns Hopkins University Press.

Sullivan, Terry. 1984. *Procedural Structure.* New York: Praeger.

Van Deemen, Adrian. 1998. "The Condorcet Paradox: A Review of Research Results." Paper for the ECPR Joint Sessions of Workshops, Warwick, March 23–28, 1998.

Wilson, Rick K. 1986. "Forward and Backward Agenda Procedures: Committee Experiments on Structurally Induced Equilibrium." *Journal of Politics* 48:390–409.

Wolters, Menno. 1980. "Strategic Voting: An Empirical Analysis with Dutch Roll Call Data." In *Models of Political Economy*, ed. Paul Whiteley. London: Sage.

Wolters, Menno. 1984. *Interspace Politics.* Leiden: University of Leiden.

Part 6

The Evolution of Legislatures

Transitional Governance in the United States: Lessons from the First Federal Congress

Rick K. Wilson

Introduction

Over the past decade, legislative scholars have witnessed a remarkable transformation among many legislative institutions, particularly those in Central and Eastern Europe. While the scope of this transformation seems radical, it is by no means historically unique. The transition in the United States from the Continental Congress to the Federal Congress in the 1780s was no less interesting for understanding institutional change. Moreover, there are shared characteristics of institutional change that span two hundred years and quite different cultures. The perspective taken here is that institutional change can be understood by appealing to a common set of theoretical puzzles. These include problems of coordination, collective action, and collective choice. At the same time the study of institutions has produced systematic ways of disentangling institutional change. In this paper I pinpoint several components of institutions that enable scholars to calibrate institutional change.

I begin by noting that institutional change is typically endogenous, caused by the very actors populating the institution. Such actors are purposive and motivated to find advantage where they can (for a general discussion, see Knight 1992). This means that the design of institutions may take many forms. Trying to characterize an "ideal type" for a legislative mechanism is a pointless exercise. So too is the search for optimal institutional design. Institutional change reflects the compromises and advantages achieved by the actors.

This does not imply that we lack a metric for understanding institutional change and adaptation. As Carey, Formanek, and Karpowicz (1999) argue in this volume, scholars must be attentive to issues of both legislative effectiveness and legislative autonomy. For now I sidestep the issue of how legislatures

---

Reprinted with permission from *Legislative Studies Quarterly* 24, no. 4 (November 1999): 543–68.

are separated from a powerful executive or the ties of strong party discipline. Instead I focus on legislative effectiveness, which I take to mean the capacity of institutions to grapple with three common problems. Unless they are solved, the legislature will fail; and failure can be catastrophic for the polity. While these problems are familiar social dilemmas, the discussion here is limited to problems facing actors within the legislative institution.

The first problem is one of coordination. Here actors have common preferences but face multiple equilibria. They do not care which equilibrium is selected, so long as one is chosen. Coordinating actors to select one, however, is problematic. The second problem is one of collective action. Again, actors have common preferences, but now have incentives to let someone else solve the problem while "free riding" on their efforts. Volumes have been written on this problem, but it is no less important for a legislature. The third problem is one of collective choice. Here actors have quite different preferences and are in conflict. At worst the failure to solve this problem is inconsistency and incoherence in outcomes, which in turn is likely to engender gridlock within the institution. All three problems pose serious challenges for legislative institutions. Observing how transitional institutions grapple with these problems provides a common template for understanding institutional change.

If there are many institutional solutions to these problems, then where does one start when trying to analyze institutional change and variation? I adopt components of the Institutional Analysis and Design (IAD) framework proposed by Ostrom et al. (1994). Drawing on a rich tradition taken from public choice, principle-agent models, the New Institutional Economics and game theory, the IAD framework pinpoints crucial institutional features that deserve scrutiny. In particular, this approach requires a clear description of actors, admissible actions, levels of information, and a mapping of actions into outcomes. Institutional features, including representational rules, decision rules, and even quorum rules, combine to mediate individual strategic behavior. A sketch of this approach is offered in a subsequent section.

In this paper I compare two institutions over time—the Continental Congress and the First Federal Congress—and ask how each confronted the problems of coordination, collective action, and collective choice. The first institution was an objective failure (it withered away), while the second laid the groundwork for success.

I argue that similar comparative studies might be exceedingly useful. While different actors may adopt different institutional choices in the design of legislatures, the success of those legislatures resides with how well these three social dilemmas are handled. It is likely that the richest treasure trove of data will lie with those legislatures that have most recently experienced democratic transitions.

Social Dilemmas

At the outset, I noted that any legislature must deal with three generic social dilemmas. In this section, these are detailed and discussed with respect to the Continental Congress. There is widespread agreement among historians and political scientists that the Continental Congress was a failed institution. In part this was because the body could not come to grips with the economic chaos following the end of the Revolutionary War. Another part, however, was the failure of actors within the Continental Congress to deal with problems of coordination, collective action, and collective choice. Each failure undermined the capacity of members to find solutions for the beleaguered new nation.

Coordination Problems

The problem of coordination is perhaps the simplest of the three social dilemmas to overcome. Because actors share preferences, the problem they face is to coordinate the selection of one equilibrium from among many. Any will suffice. In a legislature this corresponds to a setting in which many different versions of a bill are floated, each of which is acceptable to the members, but over which there is little agreement about which version should be brought to the fore. In the contemporary U.S. Congress, such coordination problems are rare because an enormous institutional apparatus exists, ranging from party caucus mechanisms to standing committees. A variety of mechanisms often serves to focus the choice by members on a single piece of legislation.

An especially important coordinating mechanism involves political leadership. Leaders do a number of things for followers. They bear the costs for providing pure public goods (Kiewiet and McCubbins 1991); they structure the agenda, thereby limiting decision costs for followers (Wilson 1996); they often provide leadership in its traditional sense of getting followers to pay attention to novel ideas and solutions (Burns 1978); and finally, they serve as a focal point around which followers can rally (Calvert 1992). It is this last point that is especially important for this discussion. In another context Wilson and Rhodes (1997) show just how effective leaders can be for solving coordination problems. They find that followers quickly and easily rally around a leader signaling a specific equilibrium.

Leadership was practically nonexistent in the Continental Congress. This effectively eliminated a potentially important coordinating device for the membership. The circumstances that confronted the delegates to the First Continental Congress did not call for a powerful presiding officer. Rather, what was deemed necessary was to create a forum open to the diverse ideas and opinions of the participants. Each delegate was keenly aware that he bore the responsibility of representing his colony during a crisis in which a false step or statement might lead to charges of treason or perhaps even to the onset of war. Moreover, the crisis had induced each state to send its most experienced political leaders. The 56 men who journeyed to Philadelphia for the First Continental Congress claimed nearly 500 years of legislative experience (the average was eight and one-half years). Fully 12 of them from 9 different colonies had presided over their colonial legislature. Not surprisingly then, delegates were reluctant to assign great power and discretion to any one of their number.

This is of particular interest because a wide range of precedents concerning the powers and prerogatives of the men who presided over the lower houses of the colonial legislatures were well known to the members of the First Continental Congress. All of the southern legislatures except North Carolina's allowed their Speakers to appoint committees and to prepare an agenda for the floor; among the legislatures of the middle Atlantic region, there was a mix of strong Speakers, as in Maryland and Pennsylvania, and of weak Speakers, as in New Jersey and Delaware; while in New England only Massachusetts allowed its Speaker to appoint committees and wield great influence on the floor.

Moreover, Peyton Randolph, the man elected President of Congress in both 1774 and 1775, was the sitting Speaker of the Virginia House of Burgesses. The Speaker in Virginia had, since 1682, been empowered to appoint all standing and ad hoc committees and to name their chairmen (Greene 1959, 486; Griffith 1963, 3; Harlow 1917, 107; Luce 1922, 106). Similarly, the Pennsylvania Assembly, meeting immediately upstairs from the Congress, with its *Records* and precedent books lining the walls and easily available to the president and members of Congress, had in its rules of 1703 awarded its Speaker both committee appointment and agenda-setting powers.

Despite these well known precedents, the powers granted by the First Continental Congress to its president did not extend beyond presiding over the discussions that occurred among his colleagues on the floor. Within six weeks of the opening of the Congress, the Connecticut delegates reported to their governor that, "our president, though a gentleman of great worth, and one who fills and supports the dignity of his station to universal acceptance, yet cannot urge forward matters to an issue with that dispatch, which he might in a different assembly." In this assembly, the delegates explained, "every one must be heard, even on those points or subjects, which are in themselves not of the last importance" (Burnett *Letters* 1, 70).

Congress never strengthened the role of its president, and no alternative leadership positions were ever created. A set of precedents, norms, and expectations was developed in the first Congress and carried intact into the second. This set was maintained through the history of the institution and gave the president no assignment powers, no power to appoint members to standing or ad hoc committees, and no power to control the flow of business out of committees and back to the floor. Instead, assignment powers and committee appointment powers were held by and exercised on the floor of Congress. In addition, resolutions, bills, and reports coming out of committee and back to the floor were, first by norm and then by formal rule, taken up in the order in which they were delivered to the secretary. Any questions arising over the priority among items lying on the table were settled by a majority vote of the states. Once the floor decided what it would consider, the president monitored the conduct of the debate and little more (Johnson 1964, 316–17; Sanders 1930, 39). While the office of president had minor consequence, it was sufficiently innocuous that through most of its history, the office passed in yearly rotation among the states.

In short, the office of the president did little to coordinate the membership. While deference was usually paid to the occupant, rulings by the president did not go unchallenged. Nor did any other office take on the qualities of a leadership position. Robert Morris, Superintendent of Finance in the early 1780's, tried, without success, to engineer consequential legislation to provide revenue and repay debts. However, his efforts, and those on his behalf, failed. Leadership, whenever it was exercised, was quickly opposed. Delegates were deliberate in preventing the design of institutional positions of leadership and were quick to undermine those who sought to lead. After all, the principle of state dominance was clear.

Collective Action Problems

Collective action problems are also endemic to any political institution. Such problems arise when actors have congruent preferences. However, taking action is individually costly and everyone would prefer that someone else pay the cost. For example, while the collectivity understands that a tariff bill for raising revenue would be a valuable thing, no one wants to make the effort to frame the initial draft of a very complex piece of legislation. As a consequence the legislation goes undrafted. Almost any legislative activity benefits from the attention of a smaller subset of members who spend the time and resources to research, examine, and inform the deliberative body. However, few volunteer to bear those costs, while everyone benefits from someone else's efforts.

Many collective action problems are associated with workload concerns. Typically these workload problems are handled by shifting the burden to a subset of the members—usually in the form of a committee. Appointing a committee pushes the costs for information gathering onto a subset of legislators. This produces one solution to the problem of collective action. Of course, committees are not the only mechanism for handling collective actions problems, but they are an important tool in most legislative assemblies.

The work of the modern Congress is done in its standing committees. The substantive jurisdiction of each committee is fixed in the rules of the institution.

Moreover, members seek standing committees of particular substantive jurisdiction on the basis of their own and their constituent's interests, and members hold their committee seats as a property right once they are appointed. Whether this results in an effective vehicle for "gains-in-trade" (Shepsle and Weingast 1987), or a vehicle for an "informational rationale" (Krehbiel 1991) is of no matter here. The direct or indirect cause of establishing a committee system is to foster expertise in which those experts bear the costs for legislating. The question posed here is: did the Continental Congress divide its workload among a series of standing committees of stable and exclusive jurisdiction in order to foster substantive expertise, minimize collective costs, and enhance the quality of information flowing to the floor? It did not.

Despite several reform attempts, the Continental Congress always depended heavily upon large numbers of ad hoc committees. Each was instructed and guided by the results of open debate in the Committee of the Whole. The first phase in the history of Congress's committee system relied upon an extensive network of ad hoc committees. This was the original foundation of the committee system in the Continental Congress, and it was never supplanted as the dominant mode of handling the workload. It was, however, supplemented at various stages of the Continental Congress's history by standing committees, boards, and executive departments.

Each of these standing committees, boards, and departments proved to be less successful than hoped, largely because myriad ad hoc committees were created to oversee and investigate them within their putative fields of jurisdiction. In addition, ad hoc committees invariably were charged to reconsider and often recast the reports and recommendations that the standing committees, boards, and departments sent to the Congress. As a result, ad hoc committees always remained the standard mechanism employed by the Congress to prepare issues for final deliberation on the floor.

Nothing more clearly demonstrates the general character of the committee system in the Continental Congress than the method for calling new committees into existence and selecting members to them. Committees were appointed when a majority of the states voted in favor of a motion to appoint a committee. Any delegate could make such a motion on any issue before the Congress. When a motion to appoint a committee passed, nominations of delegates to fill positions on the committee were offered from the floor (*Journals* 2:79, 3:266; Burnett *Letters* 2:74, 2:83–84). Once every member who wished to make a nomination had done so, each member cast a secret ballot for one of the nominees. The Secretary of Congress tabulated the ballots and the president announced the names of the members elected. The individuals receiving the most votes were elected to the committee, with the top vote-getter serving as committee chair. "Grand Committees," composed of one member from each state, were occasionally selected to consider critical issues. In these instances, each delegation was allowed to nominate their own member and then the slate was approved by a ballot of all members. These procedures guaranteed that the members on the floor controlled the committees of the Congress, and that any significant divisions on the floor would be reproduced in each committee.

The Continental Congress was relentless in its determination to insure that concentrations of power and influence either on or off the floor were difficult, if not impossible, to generate and sustain. First, there were an incredible number of committees created in the Congress. Jillson and Wilson (1994) note that 3,249 separate committees were *elected* between 1774 and 1788. Second, the vast majority of the committees employed each year were small ad hoc committees. More than three-quarters (76.8%) of the committees created by the Congress had only three members. Another 17.7% had five members. Clearly, Congress habitually (fully 94.5% of the time) elected small, odd numbered, ad hoc committees to handle the issues that came before the body. For a body that rarely had more than 35 members present, this proliferation of ad hoc committees generated an enormous and varied workload for most delegates. At the extreme, delegates like Abraham Clark (NJ), Hugh Williams (NC), and James Duane (NY) served on more than 300 committees. Ad hoc committees dominated the congressional landscape and did little to minimize collective costs or build substantive expertise.

In an effort to curb and focus the workload, early in 1776 delegates began to experiment with standing committees and later with boards, commissions, and even Executive Departments. Figure 1 highlights the all-too-temporary effects of the various reforms of the committee system. Each data point on the plot represents a three-month moving average of the number of ad hoc committees appointed between May 1775 and December 1788. The effect of this "smoothing" is to dampen some of the variation in the data from month to month, providing a clearer picture of the general trend during this 14-year period. Also on the figure are points at which reforms of the committee system were implemented (for a more extensive discussion, see Jillson and Wilson 1994). Clearly, while each reform to the committee system had a temporary effect, none held, and Congress invariably returned to a full dependence on myriad, small, ad hoc committees.

Members were always reluctant to have decisions of any kind, let alone critical decisions in the areas of defense, foreign policy, and finance made off the floor of Congress. Therefore, they elected increasing numbers of ad hoc committees to monitor their putative agents in the standing committees, boards, and departments.

While committees could have been important vehicles for solving important collective action problems with respect to workload, they did not offer such a solution. Expertise was seldom fostered, with members winning election to committees based on factors other than specialized knowledge. Even standing committees were subject to substantial scrutiny (although absenteeism ensured that no such committee could accumulate much in the way of either expertise or power). Nor was it the case that workload was reduced. With so many commit-

FIGURE 1
Smoothed Monthly Committee Appointments, 1775–88

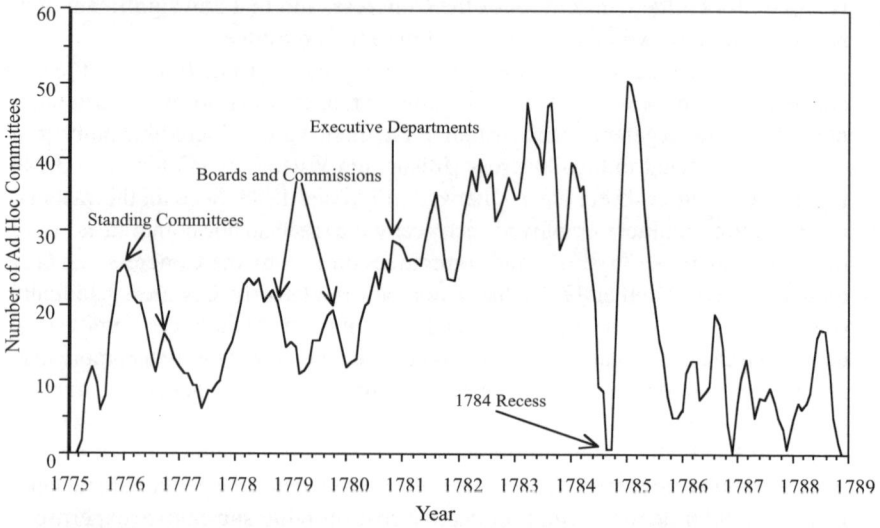

tee appointments—on practically any matter—delegates were constantly busy. Moreover, when matters returned to the floor, committee efforts were quickly forgotten.

The Collective Choice Problem

The collective choice problem is a familiar problem for political scientists. It is characterized by actors holding different interests and finding that there may exist no consistent, predictable outcomes under the voting rules. An extensive literature on social choice extending from Arrow (1963) forward points out that outcomes are manipulable and that no particular voting mechanism guarantees consistency or coherence in choice (see the discussion by Riker 1980). This can be especially problematic in legislative institutions in which those bodies are expected to bring closure over issues. If they cannot, and the same issues are continually revisited, then the institution is quickly undermined.

A great deal of effort has been expended investigating institutional configurations that bring about equilibrium. This search for structure induced equilibrium (SIE) has turned the focus toward mechanisms that bring closure and yield consistency in choice. Such mechanisms are often located in the rules governing floor behavior and voting.

The Continental Congress, by contrast with many contemporary legislatures, was the quintessential egalitarian institution. It did most of its work in the

Committee of the Whole where every member could be present and play an equal role. Its procedures guaranteed open discussion on the floor, ensured that no faction gained monopoly agenda setting powers, and provided delegates with ample opportunity for discussion, amendment, obstruction, and delay. In short, prior to March 1781 the Continental Congress was remarkably similar to the abstract collective choice settings studied by McKelvey (1976, 1979), Schofield (1978), and Riker (1980).

Instead of adopting rules that awarded subsets of delegates special agenda powers (the leadership or an equivalent of the modern Rules Committee), adopting rules that narrowly proscribed when motions and amendments were in order (closed or modified rules), or adopting rules that allowed the formulation of complex legislative packages (omnibus bills), the Continental Congress relied on very minimal rules (Oleszek 1989, 74–76, 124–27). This combination of an open agenda, limited agenda-setting powers in the chair and committees, and issue by issue consideration of legislative matters meant that no faction in Congress was able to introduce and carry through a coherent program around which permanent, or even stable, coalitions might form.

No resolution, bill, or committee report making it to the floor was able to lay claim to a closed rule. Initially, any motion, germane or otherwise, was in order with respect to any bill, report, or resolution before the Congress. This led George Wythe (VA) to observe on October 21, 1775, that "The rule, that the question should be put upon the last motion that is made and seconded, is productive of great confusion in our debates; six or seven motions at once" (*Journals* 3:500).

South Carolina's Christopher Gadsden, in this same debate, succinctly echoed this concern, saying "I wish we could keep to a point" (*Journals* 3:501). Eight months later, in a diary entry dated May 6, 1776, John Adams (MA) was still complaining about: "the art and skill with which the General's letters, Indian affairs, revenue matters, naval arrangements, and twenty other things, many of them very trivial, were mixed, in those committees of the whole, with the great subjects of government, independence, and commerce. Little things were, designedly, thrown in the way of great ones, and the time consumed upon trifles which ought to have been consecrated to higher interests" (Adams *Works*, 3:43). To correct these concerns, a standing rule was adopted on July 17, 1776, that prevented a second motion from being offered before one already on the floor was resolved (*Journals* 5:573–74). However, amendments to the main question continued to be frequently offered.

Despite Congress's attempt to regularize its procedures, members continued to complain of unpredictability, volatility, and inefficiency in both legislation and administration. On September 5, 1777, less than two months before he was elected President of Congress, Henry Laurens wrote to fellow South Carolinian John Gervais that he had "been witness to a Report made by a Committee of the Whole, which had been entered upon the Journal, superseded by a new Resolution even without reference to the Report. A Resolution carried almost *Nem Con*—entered, and half an hour after reconsidered and expunged. When I add that such irregularity is the work of almost every day, you will not wonder that I wish to be any where but in Congress" (Smith *Letters* 2:482, see also 2:488).

Not surprisingly, Laurens's experience as president increased his frustration with the legislative procedures employed in Congress. In a letter of April 17, 1778, to James Duane (NY), a bewildered Laurens complained that: "Long and warm debates for many a day had led us to the threshold of the Report from the Committee of the Whole. We had Entered fairly the Door, by reading the whole for information, the first Clause for debate, and received an amendment which was read by the Chair and the question half put, when we were turned out by a New Motion—debates arose upon the point of order" (Burnett *Letters* 3:170, see also 6:21).

Debates upon points of order were frequent in the Congress precisely because so little order existed. In August 1779, Thomas Burke (NC) wrote a long and thoughtful letter to the North Carolina Assembly concerning the political dynamics at work in a legislative setting where pure majority rule reigned. Interestingly, Burke recognized that instability characterized more than the outcomes of debate and decision, it characterized the rules by which debate and decision was to occur. Burke explained that "circumstances make rules of order . . . very arbitrary and uncertain, hence frequent disputes arise thereon . . . and the decisions at length depend upon the Integrity of the Majority. Thus Rules of order cease to be, what they ought, common checks upon excesses" (Burnett *Letters* 4:367–68). Rules could not constrain willful majorities.

Clearly, "instability" was what members of the Continental Congress confronted every day. The observations by Adams, Laurens, and Burke presented above suggest that pure majority rule engendered instability on the floor and that this instability infected, or was "inherited" by, the rules that were supposed to govern debate and decision in the Congress. When delegates did not like the potential effect of rules on outcomes they simply set the offending rule aside by majority vote. Because majorities changed frequently, rules of legislative procedure were uncertain.

Prior to March 1781, the Continental Congress was the prototype pure majority rule legislative institution. Adoption of the Articles of Confederation on March 1, 1781 altered, in two decisive respects, the rules under which the Congress operated. These new rules converted the fundamental dynamics of the institution from pervasive fluidity to an equally pervasive rigidity.

Following the adoption of the Articles of Confederation in 1781, the problems facing delegates to the Continental Congress were compounded by several changes in floor procedures. From the outset the Continental Congress operated under the "unit rule" in which each state was accorded a single vote that was a function of a simple majority of each state's delegation. The Articles changed the number of positive votes needed to decide issues in Congress. Before the Articles were approved, a simple majority of the states present and voting could decide matters. After the Articles were ratified, seven positive votes were required to conclude regular business, and nine positive votes were required to decide important business. The latter included the ratification of treaties and all matters of great financial concern.

These constitutional provisions governing congressional procedures dramatically affected the performance of the institution. Almost overnight Congress traded pervasive instability for a perverse stability in which the status quo on all issues was powerfully privileged. As Figure 2 shows so starkly, the effect of requiring seven- and nine-state majorities in Congress was immediate. The figure tracks the percentage of motions that passed in Congress by congressional year. Also reconstructed, beginning in 1781, the percentage of all motions that would have passed if the old rules were retained.[1] The solid line, indicating the percentage of successful motions by congressional year, drops sharply in 1781 following ratification of the Articles and implementation of the new majority requirements. The broken line shows the percentage of motions that would have passed had no rule change taken place. Prior to March 1, 1781,

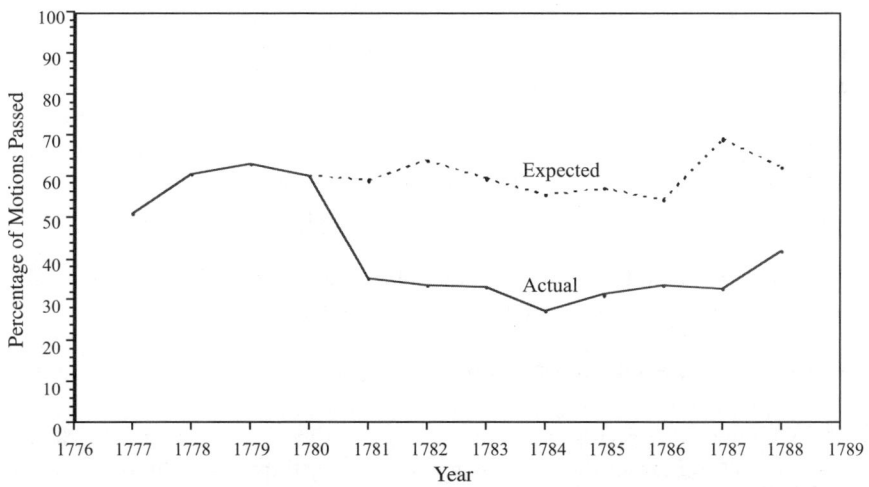

FIGURE 2
Actual and Expected Passage of Legislation
in the Continental Congress, 1777–88

Source: Compiled from data in Inter-University Consortium for Political and Social Research, Roll Calls of the Continental Congress.

60% of the motions offered in Congress passed; after March 1, only 30% of the motions offered in Congress passed. Delegates turned almost immediately from complaining about instability to complaining just as vociferously about deadlock.

In early March 1784, no less a figure than Thomas Jefferson explained to a correspondent what the rules embedded in the Articles meant for the conduct of business in the Congress. Jefferson wrote that "a ninth state appeared today, but eight of the nine being represented by two delegates each, all important questions will require not only an unanimity of states, but of members, for which we have no reason to hope. I very much apprehend we shall be unable to get through even those [questions] which seem indispensable" (Burnett *Letters* 7:458, see also 8:15). Fixed supermajority requirements, in the face of low attendance, pushed what would have been a stiff supermajority requirement (9 of 13 states or 69%), toward a requirement of virtual unanimity both of states and individuals, for which, as Jefferson noted, there was "no reason to hope."

Attendance remained so low that David Ramsay, chairman of Congress during the first half of 1786 (John Hancock failed to come forward and assume his post as president), wrote to "Certain states," saying, "three months of the federal year are now completed and in that whole period no more than seven states have at any one time been represented. No question except that of adjourning day to day can be carried without perfect Unanimity. The extreme difficulty of framing Resolutions against which no exception can be taken by any one State, can scarcely be conceived. . . . Sorry I am to add that the most essential interests of the United States suffer. . . . The disposition of our western Territory, An American Coinage, Commercial arrangements with European powers, particularly Great Britain, and a variety of other matters are of immense and pressing importance, but for want of an additional number of States nothing can be done" (Burnett *Letters* 8:291).

What Jefferson, Ramsay, and others understood from painful experience, was that the move from pure majority to supermajority rules dramatically restricted the opportunity to resolve issues that came before the Congress. Rather than conferring positive powers for decision making to a majority, supermajority rules typically award negative decision powers to a minority. As Jillson and Wilson (1994) detail, minority factions were abundant in the Continental Congress, and few hesitated to use the power to obstruct.

Institutional Analysis and Design

The Continental Congress failed to solve these three critical social dilemmas. As noted at the outset there are many possible institutional solutions to these dilemmas. Post hoc explanations (like those offered above) easily explain failures. But where does one turn to disentangle an institution in a systematic fashion? What elements of institutions deserve careful scrutiny in order to understand the incentives for and constraints on actors?

Elinor Ostrom and her colleagues have spent a great deal of time struggling with understanding the elements that make up institutions. Ostrom et al. (1994) point to an "institutional analysis and design" framework that provides a basis for disentangling institutions. In short, this framework is an organizing tool to identify the broad working parts of an "action arena" and the relationships among those parts. This action arena is the conceptual unit of analysis. Given my interests in institutional solutions to social dilemmas facing legislatures, focusing on the Continental Congress as a decision making body makes sense. If my concerns extended to the problems of repaying debts incurred during the Revolutionary War, then the action arena would be expanded to incorporate state assemblies and their decisions.

Although carefully specifying the unit of analysis may not seem to be an innovation, Ostrom et al. go on to argue that there is a minimal set of elements that characterize the action situation within which individuals interact. They note a "minimal action situation is characterized using seven clusters of variables: (1) participants, (2) positions, (3) actions, (4) potential outcomes, (5) a function that maps actions into realized outcomes, (6) information, and (7) the costs and benefits assigned to actions and outcomes" (1994, 29). For anyone familiar with game theory, these are central components of constructing a game. Carefully developing these minimal elements and the ways in which they encourage or constrain the strategic behavior of actors is important for explaining institutions—including legislatures.

To illustrate the value of this framework and to show its application to understanding transitional legislatures, I focus on two components that were of special importance for the shift between the Continental and Federal Congresses: (1) participants and (2) actions. What is meant by these two with respect to the IAD framework, and what do they tell us about the transitional period?

The concept of "participants" has to do with who is involved in the institutional setting. At its most fundamental level this cuts to the question of representation. In the case of a legislature, it is the questions of who is the representative and who is being represented. Under the Continental Congress, the states were the unit of representation and State Assemblies were the represented. By the First Federal Congress, representation had been split, with states represented in the upper chamber and citizens being represented in the lower chamber. This simple change in the institutional basis of representation changed the incentives for representatives. No longer were they bound to the instructions of their State Assemblies. Instead representatives now were bound to geographically centered constituents. As I argue later, this freed representatives to engage in logrolling and deal making in ways that were impossible in the Continental Congress.

The concept of "actions" is equivalent to defining the allowable moves in a game. It characterizes the rules and procedures defining what actors may or may not do and the sequence in which they may act. While the First Federal Congress adopted most of the rules and procedures of the Continental Congress, there were several important differences. Foremost was the shift from voting by state "unit-rule" to voting by individual members. Under "unit-rule" the state delegation was polled and the majority position of that state then became its vote. Even though senators in the Federal Congress represented state interests, they too were able to cast individual ballots. This shift was critical for the strategic coalition building.

Struggle Over Representation

The struggle over representation is key for any legislative body. In the contemporary period this is driven home in debates over using a "first-past-the-post" versus a proportional representation system. Clearly, who is admitted to a deliberative body and who they represent constitute fundamental first principles.

In the Continental Congress, members quickly decided these issues. From the outset, the members thought of themselves as delegates, acting as a delegation and representing their respective colony. As the Continental Congress matured, appointments were routinized and made by state assemblies, with delegations reporting back to their assembly. Many delegations awaited instructions from their state and were often reticent to take a lead on issues (see the general discussion by Jillson and Wilson 1994).

The locus of representation was abruptly changed with the First Federal Congress. While state representation was maintained in the upper chamber, each state's delegation was equal in size—two senators for each state. In the Continental Congress, state delegations varied in size, depending on how many delegates the state assembly wanted to appoint and how many could be coaxed to attend. While some delegations rarely had a minimum of two members, others might have as many as seven. In the First Federal Congress, each state was required to appoint two delegates, inequities in the size of delegations were no longer of concern and senators were freed to vote as individuals. This latter opened the possibility for building coalitions of like-minded senators, rather than building upon state coalitions.

That members were freed to vote their interests was even more true in the House. The new constitution mandated that representatives be elected to represent populations within the states, rather than the states themselves. In the Continental Congress there had been some discussion over representation by population. However, because there was no reliable census of the states, delegates were skeptical of apportioning power based on estimates of state size (and unwilling to cede state claims to representation).

While the different states defined their own methods for popular election (in several of the states, members ran in at-large districts), the movement in the Federal Congress was for geographical representation in the states. This created very different incentives for representatives, who now had identifiable constituencies whose interests might be opposed to those of other members in the same state, and whose interests might be shared with members from other states. This introduced the possibility for factions arising across the states and the breakdown of state delegations. Equally important, it meant that coalitions could easily be broken apart as new issues were introduced on the floor. This offered the possibility for greater fluidity and flexibility in the House. Most importantly, it provided the basis for political entrepreneurs to press new agendas.

Severing the tie of representatives with their state legislature created new incentives for members. While few members of the House regarded congressional service as the *sine qua non* of political service, most members were highly motivated to represent the interests of their constituents. Their attachments to views represented in their own state legislatures were more a matter of class, kinship, and friendship ties, than direct ties. Even senators, with little stake in remaining in office, could differ quite substantially from their fellow delegation member. Depending on the state, legislative turnover could be enormous (with yearly elections being quite common). As a consequence, state delegations could be quite fractious and, within the space of two years, appoint very different types of senators.

Rules, Structure, and Procedure

By and large, the First Federal Congress adopted the rules and procedures of the Continental Congress. While other scholars note that the minimal set of rules and procedures adopted in the First Federal Congress had their roots in English Parliamentary procedure and the various Colonial Assemblies, Jillson and Wilson (1994) argue that these precedents were melded into the Continental Congress and then resurfaced in the Federal Congress.

Consider Galloway's (1958) assessment of the floor rules and procedures adopted in the First Congress. He notes

> Decorum and debate, motions and balloting, were governed by the second standing rule. No member could speak more than twice to the same question without leave of the House. No member could vote on any questions in the result of which he was immediately and particularly interested; or in any other case where he was not present when the question was put. Every member present in the House when a question was put was required to vote for or against it, unless excused. The previous question was to be admitted upon demand of five members and its form was defined. And any fifteen members could compel the attendance of absentees (Galloway 1958, 457).

These rules were similar to those adopted in the Continental Congress. The exceptions pertained to the previous question (whereby any member could call for it) and compelling attendance (which was problematic for the Continental Congress because requiring members to attend was in the purview of the states).

A fundamental difference, however, was tied to the manner of voting. In the Continental Congress, all voting took place via the "unit rule," in which each member of a state delegation was polled for his ballot. These ballots were then calculated, with the majority position serving as the state vote. With an even number of delegates, ties occasionally would arise and that state's vote was left uncounted.

In the Continental Congress two problems arose that were compounded by the unit rule. The first had to do with a strict quorum rule and the second had to do with the way in which coalitions were formed. Under the former, in order for legislation to pass, a majority of the states (not states present) had to vote in favor of the bill. This meant that a vote by seven states was needed. For much of the mid- and late-1780's it was rare for ten states to be present. In effect this required an extraordinary majority of the states—something that was often difficult to obtain. Second, the strategy of finding a common ground among members and building a coalition was exceedingly difficult in the Continental Congress because individual votes were rarely important; only a state's vote mattered. For example, if a state was represented by three delegates, two would have to be won over in order to gain the state's vote. This enormously complicated the task for political entrepreneurs.

The shift in voting rules, in the First Federal Congress, from "unit rule" to "everyone rule" provided political entrepreneurs opportunities to build bundles of legislation around majority coalitions of individual members. By bringing individuals into new coalitions the cleavages that separated northern and southern states were overcome and old issues that had stymied the Continental Congress could now be resolved. What is amazing is that the set of actors (and their preferences) did not change—but rather the rules of procedure changed and opened the possibility for different outcomes. The next section describes exactly such an instance.

Cooking a Deal in 1790

Aldrich, Jillson, and Wilson (1998) compare a handful of issues left unresolved in the Continental Congress and then revisited and quickly decided in the First Federal Congress. In March 1783, representatives to the Continental Congress considered two significant issues, neither for the first nor the last time. The first concerned the location of the capital for the fledgling nation. Selecting a permanent site was preferable, but failing that, settling on a temporary location was critical. Between March 6 and 8 alone, 15 roll-call votes were cast, with votes on March 6 rejecting seven states. (In the order voted down they were Rhode Island, New York, New Jersey, Pennsylvania, Delaware, Maryland, and Virginia; that is to say all of the centrally located and therefore feasible states.) Another 18 roll-call votes were cast over the following two weeks, considering (sometimes several times) a variety of potential sites, including the banks of the Potomac. Also considered were dual capitals, rotating the honor every six months. Eventually, however, nothing was decided.

The second issue was the fiscal plan submitted by Superintendent of Finance Robert Morris. Led on the floor by James Wilson (PA) and Alexander Hamilton (NY), Morris's plan had been introduced in 1781 and had been debated off and on since that time. On March 20, the same day that dual capitals on the Delaware and the Potomac Rivers was defeated, fiscal moderates led by James Madison (VA) defected from the Morris coalition and defeated key provisions of the plan by a vote of 4 states aye, 7 nay, 1 divided, and 1 abstention. While a more moderate measure proposed by Madison eventually passed the Continental Congress, it included a provision that required adoption by each state government before it would go into effect; a provision all knew doomed the measure.

The First Federal Congress took up these two matters again in 1790. For a considerable portion of that First Congress, now Treasury Secretary Hamilton and Rep. Madison and 11 others who were in Congress in 1783 and 1790, revisited their struggle over these issues, sometimes in identical form.

After inconclusive action in the upper chamber, then Senator Robert Morris (PA) proposed the temporary location of the new capital in Philadelphia, a move many believed would become the permanent location. His coalition lost 11 to 13, however, when Gunn (GA), Paterson (NJ), and both North Carolina senators defected from their previous support. With the Senate now delaying action, Rep. FitzSimons (PA) introduced Morris's motion in the House and, on May 31, the motion passed 38–22. On June 8, the Senate again voted 11–13, defeating the House resolution. Finally, on June 11, the House voted 31–28 to replace Philadelphia with Baltimore. The bill thus amended passed the House easily, in large part because all understood that the Senate's repeated rejection of Baltimore meant that the House's "decision" left the matter stalemated and perhaps unresolvable.

Earlier, on January 9, 1790, Alexander Hamilton responded to the Congress' request and submitted the first of his Reports on the Public Credit. In contrast to the Continental Congress, the new Congress relatively easily agreed to provisions for the funding of the federal debt, largely because Madison's proposal to discriminate between original and succeeding holders of its debt instruments was defeated on February 22. The question revolved around the federal assumption of state debt. On March 8, the House endorsed the assumption of debt on an unrecorded vote of 31 to 26 in the Committee of the Whole. This statement of principle was reversed on April 12, however, when Madison, after many of his amendments had been turned aside, finally succeeded in defeating this key aspect of Hamilton's Plan by an un-recorded (but scholarly reconstructed) vote of 29–31, also in the Committee of the Whole. Thus, as summer approached, both siting of the capital and assumption of state debt (and thus adoption of the fiscal Plan) were blocked.

This deadlock must have aroused concern that the new Congress and its enabling Constitution might fail, just as certainly and over the same issues, as the Continental Congress and the Articles of Confederation did. But both issues were resolved just two months later, after Jefferson, Madison, and Hamilton had struck a deal over dinner at Jefferson's lodgings. Madison's defeat of assumption was reversed, and Hamilton's Plan was enacted in a form nearly identical to that which he had proposed—and in a form quite similar to that which Morris had proposed 9 years earlier. In August 1790, the new government also agreed to siting the capital temporarily in Philadelphia, awaiting construction of a permanent residence on the banks of the Potomac. Not only were these policies thus adopted, but unlike so many resolutions in the old order, they were settled once and for all.

While the discussion, maneuvering, and voting touched on all the nerves that were laid bare in the Continental Congress, by 1790 the issues could be laid to rest. Several factors were responsible for that change. The most proximate causes were the entrepreneurial leadership of Madison and the end of the unit rule. The ultimate causes were fundamental changes in representation and basic rules and procedures.

In the First Federal Congress, Madison, Jefferson, and Hamilton could link issues, exert leadership, and get representatives to commit to specific votes. Largely through Madison's efforts, a handful of representatives were convinced to change their votes on the siting issue and then on the issue of assumption. As Aldrich, Jillson, and Wilson (1998) show, the deal reached by Madison required considerable entrepreneurial skill. Moreover they show that under the unit rule the task of winning either vote would have been impossible. The handful of votes that were changed would not have affected the votes by state delegations. Only under the new representational rules was it possible to end a stalemate that had been ongoing for almost a decade.

Transition Governments

So what has been learned? What lessons can be drawn from the tasks and problems faced in the First Federal Congress as it made a transition from a failed institution to one that, by all appearances, was a success? At the same time, what lessons can be distilled for current transitional governments?

Carey et al. (1999) make the important distinction between legislative effectiveness and legislative autonomy. The latter deals with the capacity of the legislative body to make binding decisions independent of other actors. The early U.S. legislative experience was different. The Continental Congress was "the only game in town" in the sense that there were no other competitors for national policy-making. Despite the addition of a second chamber and two more branches of government under the new constitutional system, Congress remained the center for national policy-making and, as a consequence, was largely autonomous. In this sense it had already overcome a major hurdle that most contemporary transitional governments must clear.

On the other hand, legislative effectiveness relates more closely to the problems of coordination, collective action, and collective choice faced by autonomous legislative institutions. Once a legislature defines itself, it does not escape those dilemmas. The institutional design of a legislature is crucial. The story for the early period of the U.S. involves a transition from a failed institution to one that has been long lived. My claim is that longevity was enabled by ensuring institutional effectiveness.

The literature on transitional governments bounces back and forth between issues of autonomy and institutional design. Given my interests, I concentrate on the ways in which rules and procedures change when moving from one regime to another. Welsh (1994) distills a number of common elements to the transitional processes in Central and Eastern Europe. Table 1, taken from her Table 1, notes the major commonalities related to legislative institutions. It is instructive to compare these elements to the American transition.

The first two items from Table 1 are nearly identical to those discussed above—representational reforms and procedural reforms. As noted earlier, the redesign of modes of representation may affect the incentives of representatives in important ways. Likewise, simple restructuring of rules and procedure can be critical. Both were central issues for members overseeing the transition from the Continental Congress to the Federal Congress. The discussion in the main body of this paper provides some insight as to why. As well, these arenas appear important for contemporary transition governments, although how and under what circumstances remains part of a rich research agenda.

Table 1 also points to the importance of developing a new elite and/or prosecuting and purging that elite. Much of the current literature on transitions assumes that the old elite must be removed. It is not clear that this is a necessary or sufficient condition for transitional processes. If the institutions are well designed (and those institutions bind member's behavior) then who participates is of less concern. It is often voiced that if the old elite is allowed into new institutions, then they will work to undermine those institutions and revert to old patterns of behavior. Barbara Geddes (1995) is a bit more circumspect concerning what is called the "Leninist legacy."

TABLE 1
Major Transitional Processes in Central and Eastern Europe and a Comparison with the U.S. Transition

Current Transitional Governments	U.S. Transition
1. Reform of electoral system	1. Reform of electoral system
2. Reform of structure of government	2. Reform of rules and procedures
3. Selection of new political elite	3. Retention of political elite
4. Prosecution/purge of old elite	4. Reliance on old elite
5. Constitution writing	5. Constitution writing
6. Development of new institutions for interest articulation	6. Gradual development of a party system
7. Restitution of past injustices	7. Debt repayment
8. Reform of media sector	8. No concern with media

Source: Adopted from Welsh 1994, 382.

In her view, the institutions that have been adopted, while not perfect, serve to have a moderating effect on the old elite and force them to play by the same rules as everyone else. To be successful, the old elite needs to abandon its old ways or it "withers away" (see also Ishiyama 1995 who makes a similar point).

Technically purging the old elite was not a concern in the First Federal Congress. However, this was only because the Revolutionary War ensured that British loyalists had fled and effectively were disenfranchised. The old elite under the Articles of Confederation became the new elite under the Federal Congress—the revolutionaries were not displaced. This ensured that the transition was smoother in the U.S. system. Members of the new Congress well understood the problems that had been faced in the Continental Congress—largely because many of those members had served in that earlier body. Those members were quite familiar with which procedures worked and which obstructed. At least in the First Federal Congress the accumulated skill and experience of members was important for resolving issues that long had been stalled.

Table 1 also makes clear that constitution writing is essential. There is no doubt that the process of writing and building a constitution is essential for a transitional government. However, it is not the process of writing the constitution that is important. Instead, what is critical is the discussion over fundamental principles and the involvement of the governed in the process of ratification. This was absolutely critical for the American experience (see Riker 1996).

A sixth feature noted by Welsh (1994) is the development of new institutions for interest articulation. By this she means the development of new parties and interest groups. As Remington and Smith (1995) noted in their study of Russia, confusion over the institutional rules and unsettled policy preferences by voters makes it difficult for parties to develop and congeal. The same was true in the First Federal Congress, although there the members were fearful that parties and factions might arise. Yet even the First Congress witnessed the formation of clear coalition patterns—things that looked like nascent parties (see Hoadley 1986). It is not clear that well-defined parties are a necessary condition for a successful transition. Partisanship in the Federal Congress waxed and waned over the early period. Ordinarily it was the array of issues that defined the coalition composition and members were not compelled to toe a particular, consistent, party line. This added to flexibility in resolving issues that previously had been in stalemate.

Welsh also notes the concerns with restitution. These certainly involve important issues—issues I think are related to the redefinition of property rights. This issue was of little concern for the First Federal Congress, except as it related to repayment of debts incurred by the various states for fighting the Revolutionary War. As noted above, this was a contentious issue because some states had tried to repay their debt, while others did not. Getting the states to agree that the Federal government should assume all debts was a major step forward. However, it involved little in the way of a major redefinition of property rights.

Finally, Table 1 notes the importance of transforming the media. Obviously this was of concern for contemporary governments in which the media had previously been controlled by a single state entity. It is not clear, once again, whether this is a necessary condition for a successful transition. Once a centralized media is broken apart, it appears that the usual outcome is a very fragmented media. If the concern is that a fragmented media will produce biased information, does this adversely affect the legislature? This is an interesting question. However, the experience of the First Federal Congress would suggest that a fragmented media has no effect. The media in the early period of American politics was very partisan and often quite vicious. However, it had little impact on what was accomplished within the Congress.

In conclusion, my claim is that legislative effectiveness is largely going to be measured by how well legislatures grapple with fundamental social dilemmas. Any transitional government will confront such problems and they need to be addressed. There is no single template for solving these problems. However, it appears that the lessons to be drawn from the U.S. experience and what has been observed in contemporary transitional governments is to focus on representational issues and explicit rules and procedures internal to the legislature. The IAD framework provides a way of thinking through institutional design in a systematic manner. Such an approach can be useful in focusing our research questions.

NOTES

This paper was originally prepared for presentation at the Comparative Legislative Research Conference, April 17-18, 1998, held at The University of Iowa. The National Science Foundation bears no responsibility for the content of this paper. The author is grateful for the comments of John Aldrich, Cal Jillson, Rod Kiewiet, Jerry Loewenberg, and Pev Squire. Like the NSF, they are absolved of any errors that remain.

1. Of course I can only speculate whether such motions would have passed. Members might have played quite different strategies under the old rules. Nonetheless, the differences are striking and support the claim about the impact of this rule change.

REFERENCES

Adams, Charles Francis. 1851–56. *The Works of John Adams*, 9 vols. Boston: Little, Brown.
Aldrich, John, Calvin C. Jillson, and Rick K. Wilson. 1998. "Why Congress? What the Failure of the Continental and the Survival of the Federal Congress Tell Us about the New Institutionalism." Presented at the Stanford Conference on Political History, Stanford, CA.
Arrow, Kenneth. 1963. *Social Choice and Individual Values*. New Haven, CT: Yale University Press.
Burnett, Edmund C., ed. *Letters of the Members of the Continental Congress,* 8 vols. Washington, DC: Carnegie Institution, 1921–36.
Burns, James MacGregor. 1978. *Leadership*. New York: Harper and Row.
Calvert, Randall L. 1992. "Leadership and Its Basis in Problems of Social Coordination." *International Political Science Review* 13:7–24.
Carey, John M., Frantisek Formanek, and Ewa Karpowicz. 1999. "Legislative Autonomy in New Regimes: The Czech and Polish Cases." *Legislative Studies Quarterly* 24:569–603.
Galloway, George. 1958. "Precedents Established in the First Congress." *Western Political Quarterly* 11:454–68.
Geddes, Barbara. 1995. "A Comparative Perspective on the Leninist Legacy in Eastern Europe." *Comparative Political Studies* 28:239–74.
Greene, Jack P. 1959. "Foundations of Political Power in the Virginia House of Burgesses, 1720–1776." *William and Mary Quarterly*, 3d series. 16:485–506.
Griffith, Lucille. 1963. *Virginia House of Burgesses, 1750–1774*. Alabama: Colonial Press.
Harlow, Ralph V. 1917. *The History of Legislative Methods in the Period Before 1825*. New Haven, CT: Yale University Press.
Hoadley, John F. 1986. *Origins of American Political Parties, 1789–1803*. Lexington: University of Kentucky Press.
Ishiyama, John T. 1995. "Communist Parties in Transition: Structure, Leaders, and Processes of Democratization in Eastern Europe." *Comparative Politics* 27:147–66.

Jillson, Calvin, and Rick K. Wilson. 1994. *Congressional Dynamics: Structure, Coordination, and Choice in the First American Congress, 1774–1789.* Stanford, CA: Stanford University Press.

Johnson, Herbert A. 1964. "Toward a Reappraisal of the 'Federal' Government: 1783–1789." *The American Journal of Legal History* 8:314–25.

Journals of the Continental Congress, 1774–1789. Edited by Worthington C. Ford and others. Washington, DC: US Government Printing Office, 1904–37.

Kiewiet, D. Roderick, and Mathew D. McCubbins. 1991. *The Logic of Delegation: Congressional Parties and the Appropriations Process.* Chicago: University of Chicago Press.

Knight, Jack. 1992. *Institutions and Social Conflict.* Cambridge: Cambridge University Press.

Krehbiel, Keith. 1991. *Information and Legislative Organization.* Ann Arbor: University of Michigan Press.

Luce, Robert. 1922. *Legislative Procedure: Parliamentary Practices and the Course of Business in the Framing of Statutes.* New York: Houghton-Mifflin.

McKelvey, Richard D. 1976. "Intransitivities in Multidimensional Voting Models and Some Implications for Agenda Control." *Journal of Economic Theory* 12:472–82.

McKelvey, Richard D. 1979. "General Conditions for Global Intransitivities in Formal Voting Models." *Econometrica* 47:1085–1112.

Oleszek, Walter. 1989. *Congressional Procedures and the Policy Process,* 3d ed. Washington, DC: CQ Press.

Ostrom, Elinor, Roy Gardner, and James Walker. 1994. *Rules, Games and Common-Pool Resources.* Ann Arbor: University of Michigan Press.

Remington, Thomas F., and Steven S. Smith. 1995. "The Development of Parliamentary Parties in Russia." *Legislative Studies Quarterly* 20:457–89.

Riker, William H. 1980. "Implications from the Disequilibrium of Majority Rule for the Study of Institutions." *American Political Science Review* 74:432–55.

Riker, William H. 1996. *The Strategy of Rhetoric: Campaigning for the American Constitution.* New Haven, CT: Yale University Press.

Sanders, Jennings B. 1930 (reprinted 1971). *The Presidency of the Continental Congress 1774–1789: A Study in American Institutional History.* Gloucester, MA: Peter Smith.

Schofield, Norman. 1978. "Instability of Simple Dynamic Games." *Review of Economic Studies* 45:575–94.

Shepsle, Kenneth A., and Barry R. Weingast. 1987. "The Institutional Foundations of Committee Power." *American Political Science Review* 81:85–104.

Smith, Paul H. 1976. *Letters of Delegates to Congress, 1774–1789,* 20 vols. Washington, DC: Library of Congress.

Welsh, Helga A. 1994. "Political Transition Processes in Central and Eastern Europe." *Comparative Politics* 26:379–94.

Wilson, Rick K. 1996. *Expensive Choices.* Unpublished manuscript, Rice University.

Wilson, Rick K., and Carl M. Rhodes. 1997. "Leadership and Credibility in N-Person Coordination Games." *Journal of Conflict Resolution* 41:767–91.

Politicians, Bureaucrats, and Interest Groups in Japan: Transformation from One-Party Predominance or Not?

Junko Kato

The strength of the Japanese bureaucracy is common knowledge in comparative politics although scholars attach various reasons for it, such as the necessity for state intervention in late industrialization (Gershenkron 1962) and the instability of the power base of the elites during the process of democratization (Silberman 1993). During the postwar period, however, another critical factor that explains the political dynamics in Japan is the long-term predominance of the Liberal Democratic Party (LDP) from 1955 to 1993. The presence of the same incumbent party and a stable bureaucratic organization provides a good case for examining the relationship between incumbent politicians and bureaucrats when both have competitive policy expertise. The liaison with interest groups adds another twist to the competition between these policymakers. Whereas the incumbent politicians are more sensitive to the demands of interest groups and their effects on election and are thus more motivated to articulate those interests, bureaucrats are more attentive to the general activities of interest groups and thus easily collect a variety of information. The interest groups judge which is the more effective for pressing their policy demands—incumbent politicians or bureaucrats. In a situation of one-party dominance, the legislative liaison with bureaucrats and interest groups becomes more important in policy-making.

Thus, the LDP's thirty-eight-year governance made the incumbent party the center of policy-making. Although the LDP held a clear majority in both Houses of the Diet during most of the period from 1955 to 1993, the Diet was not the place for interaction between incumbent politicians, bureaucrats, and interest groups. Those negotiations and bargainings took place within the party. They preceded the Diet process where the incumbent LDP made compromises with opposition parties in policy-making. The uninterrupted presence of the same strong party is peculiar to Japan during this period, but this stability in party politics provides some general implications for the relationship between politicians, bureaucrats, and interest groups. The first section will introduce these implications after illustrating the characteristics of their relationship during the period of one-party predominance.

In 1993, the LDP's one-party dominance was thwarted by its own sudden breakup. The party could not regain in the ensuing general election the number of seats that it had lost by the preelection defection. The LDP sought to ally with other parties but failed, and a non-LDP coalition government was formed by former opposition parties and splinter parties. After about a year, the LDP returned to office in 1994. It allied with the Social Democratic Party of Japan (SDPJ), which had been a major but perennial opponent during the LDP dominance, and the Harbinger, which is a smaller splinter party from the LDP. The LDP regained a majority in the House of Representatives of the Diet in 1997 when members from other parties, most of whom had been its own members, joined it. However, after it failed to restore a majority in the House of Councillors in the 1998 election the LDP formed an alliance with the LP[1] and then with the Clean Government (*Komei*) Party in 1999. Other parties have continued to merge and break up, and, even inside the LDP, competing strategies to ally with other parties remain a potential threat to unity. In the general election in 2000, the LDP failed to maintain a majority for itself in the House of Representatives, and its coalition with other parties has become normal in party politics.

The second section will deal with how the relationship between elected politicians, bureaucrats, and interest groups has changed. More specifically it will show that the interruption of the long-term LDP rule in 1993 and the emerging coalition bargaining between parties have added other elements to their relationship. It will also examine the validity of the general implications introduced in the first section against observations and evidence provided during this period.

1. Policy Expertise and Interest Representation under One-Party Dominance

Japan was an "uncommon" democracy from 1955 to 1993 in the sense that the LDP controlled votes and seats (i.e., obtained a plurality of votes and a majority in the Diet) and dominated the policy agenda and cabinet portfolio. During this period its electoral support declined once in the 1970s, and it lost its majority in the House of Councillors in 1989, but the party's governance was regarded as the most clear-cut case of one-party dominance in a comparative perspective (Pempel 1990). The dominant view in the existing literature describes the characteristics of the policy-making process, more specifically, the legislative process under the LDP's rule, as follows.[2] First, until the early 1970s, the deliberation process in the Diet was considered rather unsubstantial, and the Diet rarely modified the government bills that the bureaucrats wrote. Second, the incumbent LDP passed bills with a majority of support except when the bills were clearly counter to their constituencies' interests. From 1955 to the early 1970s, the government budget continued to expand as the Japanese economy recovered from the war damage, facilitated industrialization, and recorded a high rate of growth. In such an economy, budget allocation was not a zero-sum game, and it was possible to arrive at policy solutions in which opposing interests were made compatible through the allocation of abundant public money. Third, during this period, the most dominant models of policy-making were the bureaucratic dominance model (Johnson 1982) and the "triad" elite model in which policies were made as the result of coordination among the LDP, bureaucracy, and major business associations (Kaplan 1972; Yanaga 1968).

The political dynamics of the 1970s replaced the stability of LDP rule. First, there was a decline in popular support for the LDP that became apparent first in opinion polls, then in electoral votings, and was the result of more party independents and floating votes. This occurred almost at the same time as the end of high economic growth symbolized by the rapid upsurge in the price of oil (oil crises) and the termination of the link between the dollar and gold. Second, the LDP's delayed response to new policy demands for environmental protection and welfare provision shifted popular support to opposition parties that had responded more quickly. In terms of the legislative relationships between bureaucrats and interest groups, two changes were observed. First, there were more substantial modifications to government bills in the Diet as a result of a closer numerical strength between the LDP and opposition parties; the LDP made more compromises with the opposition camp, and, subsequently, the opposition parties contributed to modifications in the government bills (Krauss 1984; Mochizuki 1982). Second, new interest groups emerged that were related to the new issues of environmental and welfare policies and citizen and consumer groups.

In 1980, popular support for the LDP was explicitly restored by the elections of both Houses of the Diet (the so-called conservative resurgence). The LDP finally caught up with policy demands and came to be intimately associated in the public mind with relatively good economic performance (compared with other industrial democracies) after the global economic changes in the mid-1970s. The LDP rule was not only stable again but also strengthened in the 1980s. Based on this situation, a view emerged in the literature of the LDP's increased policy-making power, which had been cultivated by the party's long experience of governance and its abilities to adjust to a new policy environment, especially, budget deficits since the mid-1970s. More specifically, according to this view, scarcity in financial sources for budget allocations constrained policy choices, and the incumbent politicians had to intervene on details of policy-making. Policy-making had been delegated entirely to bureaucrats in the 1960s when increasing tax revenues had exceeded public expenditures. But special tax treatment and regulation of business activities had become critical means for incumbent politicians to serve the interests of their constituents during times of budget deficits since the late 1970s (Kishiro 1985, 52).

The LDP's regained strength in the 1980s brought two phenomena to the forefront of scholarly interest. The first is, as described already, the competition between incumbent politicians and bureaucrats. The deliberation process inside the LDP before the Diet convened was an important place for bureaucrats to persuade incumbent politicians to support proposed bills and for politicians to modify substantially or even block bureaucratic proposals. The Diet once again became a place of secondary importance in policy-making. The relationship between politicians and bureaucrats was previously regarded as collusive or overtly advantageous for bureaucrats. In the 1980s, however, the question was whether the bureaucrats were still influential, even though the LDP had increased its policy-making expertise.

A second interesting phenomenon is the ever-increasing importance of the relationship between the LDP and interest groups. During the period of one-party dominance in particular, the interest groups usually chose which incumbent party or bureaucratic organizations they would press for their interests. The attitude of interest groups is another important measure of the relative influence between incumbent politicians and bureaucrats. The LDP's strong connection with interest groups gave it an advantage over bureaucrats: the close connection enabled the incumbent politicians to get policy information, articulate vested interests, and make feasible policies. For example, in the mid-1980s the LDP was reported to have very close relationships with 1,225 groups, though this number had been as low as about 600 in the mid-1970s (Sato and Matsuzaki 1986, 109). If the groups are classified according to their socioeconomic activities, the shares of individual categories have constantly changed along with the transformation of the Japanese industrial structure (Sato and Matsuzaki 1986, 110–11). This shows that the LDP not only represented as many interest groups as possible but also tried to strengthen the relationship with the groups in new and/or important policy fields.

Observing that transformation in the 1980s, scholars attempt to explain Japanese politics using various pluralist models in which important common elements are the LDP's supremacy over bureaucrats and the representation of pluralistic interests throughout the LDP organization (Inoguchi 1983; Sato and Matsuzaki 1986; Muramatsu and Krauss 1984). Other researchers point to the intimate link between policymakers and interest groups (Pempel 1982; Samuels 1987; Okimoto 1989) and agree with the pluralist models at least about the increasing influence of the LDP, although they express many other important differences in the explanation of the policy-making process.

The stability of LDP rule in the 1980s causes scholars to agree about the increasing LDP influence in details of policy-making but disagree about the relative shift in influence between incumbent politicians and bureaucrats. For example, one view, expressed mostly by pluralists and rational choice scholars (Ramseyer and Rosenbluth 1993), argues the supremacy over the bureaucracy of the LDP that has accumulated policy knowledge. The opposing view, held mostly by statists in the tradition of a bureaucratic dominance view, argues the maintenance of bureaucratic dominance despite the increasing policy expertise of incumbent politicians. These competing views present a contradictory evaluation of the relative power of incumbent politicians and bureaucrats but concur on the existence of a trade-off between the influence of incumbent politicians and bureaucrats. A common implicit assumption here is that policy expertise acquired by incumbent politicians poses a threat to bureaucrats who once dominated policy information and knowledge.

In a previous study (Kato 1994) I examined the relationship of incumbent politicians, bureaucrats, and interest groups using the Japanese tax reform case from 1979 to 1989 and focusing on the introduction of the unpopular new tax, the value-added tax. Tax policy is a good subject to explore these relationships. First, tax policy is highly specialized and technical and thus requires a high level of policy expertise. The necessity of policy expertise influences the relative power of incumbent politicians and bureaucrats. Second, tax policy is destined to influence a wide range of interest groups and constituencies and is thus highly political. The introduction of a value-added tax and the accompanying income tax cut in Japan in the 1980s are no exceptions, and many interest groups as well as the unorganized public had vested interests in the existing tax system. In this regard, the tax reform is a good case to illuminate the relationship between politicians, bureaucrats, and interest groups.

In terms of the first point, this case shows that increasing the policy expertise of incumbent politicians augments their influence in policy-making but not necessarily at the expense of bureaucratic influence. If incumbent politicians have been in power for a long time and if they have concentrated on specific policies, they are often as familiar with details of policies as bureaucrats who have been trained as generalists and frequently change positions. This situation, however, is not necessarily disadvantageous for bureaucrats. What the existing literature fails to emphasize is that the competence of incumbent politicians hinges on how long they can continue to exploit the bureaucratic organization to obtain and accumulate policy information. In Japan, incumbent politicians cannot obtain enough staff support for policy-making outside the bureaucratic organization, for example, inside the legislature or in a party. The sharing of policy information between experienced politicians and bureaucrats is likely to contribute to a similar attitude and mind-set about policy-making. These politicians serve as powerful cooperators with bureaucrats in policy-making. This increases the possibility that they will agree on a specific policy proposal. In the tax reform case, the final introduction of the unpopular new tax in 1989, which the bureaucrats had originally proposed in the late 1970s, would have been impossible without experienced politicians who understood that it would be a technically superior measure for raising revenue. Therefore, the most effective exercise of bureaucratic influence is dependent upon the cooperation of incumbent politicians. In this regard, the postwar bureaucracy is distinct from the prewar one though several organizational legacies and inertias remain.[3]

Another important finding concerns the policymakers' relationship with interest groups. Incumbent politicians who are concerned with reelection are sensitive to the demands of interest groups. However, the experienced incumbents who cooperate with bureaucrats tend to have stable support bases for reelection and to underestimate the opposition of interest groups. As policy specialists, they are likely to support an unpopular policy if it is a feasible choice from the perspective of policy experts. One expects a disagreement inside the party between these experienced members and other line members with short tenures and weak electoral support bases, but party discipline enables the experienced politicians who lead the party to make formal party decisions against the line members. The ironic implication here is that experienced politicians are less sensitive to opposition from interest groups and thus may fail to compromise enough to cultivate their opposition. Referring to the tax reform case, despite strong opposition inside the party the LDP decided to introduce the value-added tax with initiative from experienced members who cooperated with the bureaucrats. In the general election, the LDP lost a majority in one House of the Diet for the first time since 1955. One of the major reasons for this loss was the unpopularity of the new tax.

The discussion above illuminates a relationship between incumbent politicians, bureaucrats, and interest groups that is diametrically opposed to that of the existing view. They are summarized as competing hypotheses:

HYPOTHESIS 1:
The policy expertise of incumbent politicians helps them increase their influence over policy-making at the expense of bureaucrats; increasing the policy expertise of incumbent politicians is counter to bureaucratic influence.

The party that has been in office for a long time is good at articulating and representing the interests of a wide range of groups in society. As a result, interest groups come to regard that party as a reliable channel for influencing policy-making that is alternative to and competes with that of the bureaucracy.

HYPOTHESIS 2 (based on the discussion here):
Incumbent politicians without staff support outside bureaucratic organization are important cooperators for bureaucrats; the increased policy expertise of politicians goes hand in hand with bureaucratic influence.

The party in office for a long time establishes a strong link with interest groups. But, at the same time, it also tends to be less sensitive to the demands and opposition of interest groups. This risk is high, especially when the party politicians develop policy expertise by collecting information from bureaucrats.

The interruption of LDP rule in 1993 and subsequent developments in party politics will provide us for the first time with cases against which to examine these hypotheses.

2. The Impact of Partisan Dynamics since 1993

In June 1993 the LDP broke up, and two splinter parties were formed. In the subsequent general elections, the LDP failed to get a majority of the House of Representatives although it retained almost the same number of seats as before the elections. The changes in 1993 are expected to have a substantial impact on the policy-making process, on the relationship between politicians, bureaucrats, and interest groups, and on the role of the Diet. With respect to the relationship between the three political actors, distinct changes are expected based on the two sets of hypotheses presented in the previous section. According to hypothesis 1, the influence of bureaucrats is expected to increase at the expense of the parties, especially the LDP, which has lost its one-party dominance; and interest groups are expected to become more reliant upon the bureaucracy as party politics become unstable. The LDP's connection with interest groups will be weakened. According to hypothesis 2, although the influence of the LDP is expected to decline, the bureaucrats will also have a hard time influencing the policy-making process without stable cooperation from the incumbent party. Under the decreasing stability of party politics, although the interest groups are expected to be more in touch with the bureaucracy than before, the parties are generally becoming more sensitive to the demands of interest groups.

Although the view based on hypothesis 1 involves a clear trade-off in influence between the incumbent party and the bureaucracy, both in policy-making in general and in the relationship with interest groups in particular, the implication based on hypothesis 2 denies such a trade-off and thus provides a mixed evaluation of the influence of the party. Although the lack of stability of party politics often precludes such demands from being reflected in policies, the parties themselves are more attentive to the pressure of interest groups. Although both views agree on the declining influence of the LDP, the overall picture of policy-making is different because of the diametrically opposed expectations of bureaucratic influence. Therefore, this section first focuses on the bureaucracy and then on the changing party politics including the dynamics inside the Diet. The relationship between policymakers and interest groups after the change in 1993 will be speculated upon, thereby extending the preceding discussion.

Bureaucratic Influence in Decline: Political Neutrality, Disclosure of Corruption, and Administrative Reform

Immediately after the interruption of LDP rule in 1993, most observers of Japanese politics did not expect that the bureaucrats would be as cooperative with the new incumbent coalition parties as they were with the LDP. The non-LDP coalition parties in 1993 included two splinter parties from the LDP and, at the same time, all the former opposition parties except the Japan Communist Party (JCP). If bureaucrats have a propensity to stay away from parties that have not been in office and/or are distant from their conservative ideology, it is reasonable to expect that the Japanese bureaucrats would stay away from the newly formed coalition parties and give them a hard time.

This point is related to a common problem in comparative politics: that is, whether bureaucrats are politically neutral in the sense that they are willing to provide staff assistance to parties that have come to power after they were long out of office and/or are ideologically distinct from themselves. For example, the bureaucrats in France were expected to be unsupportive when the French Socialists came to office in the 1980s after the long-term conservative hegemony of the Gaullists.

The French bureaucrats have supported the Socialists and proved to be politically neutral in this regard, and so have the Japanese bureaucrats. More specifically, the Japanese bureaucrats tried to forge a new cooperative relationship with incumbent politicians when the LDP was out of office. The bureaucrats sought cooperation in policy-making from the non-LDP incumbent politicians who were familiar with the policies instead of choosing to keep them ignorant of the policies. A notable example of this cooperation is the proposal in February 1994 of the People's Welfare Tax by Prime Minister Morihiro Hosokawa of the first non-LDP coalition cabinet, which aimed to increase the rate of the consumption tax from 3 to 7 percent. This proposal was withdrawn immediately due to opposition from the public as well as from inside the coalition government. Although the tax increase was desired by the Ministry of Finance (MOF), which was looking for a new financial source to cope with budget deficits, many coalition members apparently had not known about the proposal in advance. More precisely, the MOF bureaucrats, aided by the Japan Renewal Party (JRP) leaders, persuaded Prime Minister Hosokawa to propose it.[4] For one year during the non-LDP government, the former incumbent LDP was alienated from the policy information that bureaucrats provided mainly to the non-LDP coalition parties. In other words, the intimate and close relationship between the LDP and bureaucrats had been cut off, and this certainly influenced their relationship after the LDP returned to office in 1994.

In this respect what is to be noted is the disclosure of scandals and corruption involving several ministries from 1993 to 1996. The Ministry of Health and Welfare came under public criticism because of its alleged slow and inappropriate response to the prevention of HIV infection and the implications of top bureaucrats in briberies and corruption involving subsidies for the construction of nursing homes for the elderly. A collusive relationship between the Ministry of Construction and major construction companies that involved the allocation of public works was revealed. The most prolonged and damaging disclosure is the one about the MOF. As a massive deregulation of the financial market was being pushed, a fraudulent relationship between the MOF and financial industries was revealed. Some top bureaucrats took responsibility and resigned. Other bureaucrats, including the most privileged ones who aspire to top positions on the fast track, have been arrested for taking bribes. These disclosures of scandals involving powerful bureaucrats severely hurt their reputation in society as well as their credibility in advancing policy proposals. This situation was not directly caused by the change of the governing parties in 1993, but, the LDP, even after it returned to power, has kept its distance from the bureaucratic organization and has not been very eager to defend it from public criticism.

The proposal for administrative reform is another even more explicit example of the distant relationship between the LDP and the bureaucracy. The Japanese government attempted to reform its administrative organization in the 1960s and again in the 1980s, but the organization of ministries at the center of the government was intact. However, a proposal made in 1997 involved the massive reorganization of administrative organizations, more precisely, the merging and transforming of a prime minister's office and twenty-one ministries and agencies into a newly established Cabinet Office and twelve ministries and agencies starting from January 2001. For example, eleven ministries and agencies were to merge into four ministries, the Environmental Agency was to be a ministry, and other ministries and agencies were to revise their functions. Of course, the magnitude of the changes in numbers and names of bureaucratic organizations should not be equated with the impact of organizational reform. The immediate consequence of the reform is mixed. Many ministries have tried to merge without losing their previous function. Many of the highest positions in the existing ministries remain in newly integrated or merged ministries and thus are not reduced in the same way as the number of organizations. The total number of bureaus is reduced but not in half. The powerful Ministry of International Trade and Industries (MITI) has been preserved, though its name has been changed. The MOF, which has changed its name in Japanese, preserves its policy-making power in both public finance, while the newly established Financial Supervision Agency has become responsible for private finance. The controversial proposal to privatize the postal service has not been decided. However, such a major reform proposal has not been made since the mid-1940s, so the importance and substance of this reform proposal cannot be denied.[5]

The most critical change in terms of the relationship between incumbent politicians and bureaucrats is strengthening the power of the cabinet. The Cabinet Office will be created to coordinate policy-making that is otherwise divided along the boundary of ministries and to set up major policy directions including the budget size and public financial management. Two to six political appointees besides a minister are assigned to each ministry and agency. The consequence of the reform will be great although it will not be realized immediately. It will take at least twenty to thirty years. Since the Japanese bureaucratic organization has stable members who tend to work for the same ministry and agency for life, the policy attitude and orientation inherited in each organization will be preserved until most of the members recruited under the name of old ministries and agencies have retired.

Consequently, the bureaucracy has failed to establish an intimate relationship with any party other than the LDP. It has also failed to restore a close relationship with the LDP, even though that party is back in office. This is also consistent with the implication of hypothesis 2. At the same time, however, one needs to be cautious about expecting the level of bureaucratic influence to come close to its former level as the LDP regains its seats. The LDP won several seats but less than a majority in the general election in October 1996. It then regained a majority in 1997 by accepting defectors from other parties most of whom had been former LDP members. Faced with the prospect of governing without the allegiance of other parties, the LDP became less enthusiastic about administrative reform. Many drawbacks and concessions described above were attributed to waning enthusiasm on the side of the LDP in addition to resistance from the bureaucracy. This is a reasonable response if a stable incumbent party needs bureaucratic cooperation to exercise influence in policy-making. This consequence implies that the relationship between the incumbent parties (most likely including the LDP) and the bureaucracy will be cooperative rather than zero-sum (as implied in the hypothesis 2).

Declining Party Discipline and the Changing Role of the Diet

As already briefly reviewed, the Japanese Diet has been regarded in the existing literature as weak, but the reason given for its weakness has differed from one period to another. In the 1960s the Diet was regarded as a rubber stamp that served to pass, by the majority power of the LDP, the bills written by bureaucrats. Through the 1970s, when the LDP had a close margin with the opposition camp in the number of seats in the Diet, there were more substantial revisions and modifications as a result of compromises between the incumbent LDP and opposition parties. In the 1980s, however, the Diet was again regarded as weak though not because of bureaucratic dominance. The LDP began to intervene in the details of policy-making—not in the Diet, but rather inside the party before the submission of the bills to the Diet. In other words, ironically, the situation in the 1980s implies that the presence of a strong incumbent party and its stable majority did not strengthen but rather weakened the role of the Diet.

This situation may be explained as a result of the rational responses of the incumbent party and the bureaucracy. For the incumbent party, even if it is a majority power, the Diet process is more uncertain than the deliberation process inside the party. In addition, the best strategy for passing the bills that the party favors is to arrive at a policy consensus within the party and leave as much time as possible for bargaining with opposition parties in the Diet. The pre-Diet deliberation process inside the incumbent party provides a better prospect for bureaucrats to pass the bills in the Diet: they can expect full support from the incumbent party for the bills in the Diet if the bills have incorporated the party's demands. The pre-Diet deliberation inside the party is counter to the interests of the opposition parties, but they have no power to prevent it.

Keeping this in mind, volatile party politics and the absence of a stable majority in the Diet since 1993 are not necessarily factors that weaken the Diet. Actually, the Diet process has increased in importance since 1993. The bargaining between the governing coalition parties outside the Diet does not work as effectively as the pre-Diet deliberation inside the LDP, and the lack of discipline within all the parties has made it difficult to predict the results of Diet deliberations. A consensus often fails to be reached before parliamentary votes, the members vote against the party's decision, or the parties fail to impose a voting decision on their members. The result is increasing uncertainty in the Diet process.[6]

In this regard, the Diet has come to serve a more substantial role. It has become the place where the final decision is substantially made on bills, and the outcome of these decisions is much harder to predict than before. The Diet is still not a powerful legislative body where bills are actually written, but it is also no longer a rubber stamp to ratify the decisions that have already been made elsewhere. Future changes in party politics will determine whether this situation will be consolidated or not.

Responses from Interest Groups

The relationship between politicians and interest groups was expected to change after the interruption of LDP rule in 1993. First, apart from the specific context of Japanese politics, the ousting from office of a long-term incumbent party should have some impact on the link between interest groups and policymakers that has been nurtured under its governance. Second, in the context of Japanese politics in the 1990s, reforms of the election system and political finance that have been implemented are expected to change the way interest groups try to reflect their interests or demands in policy-making. The LDP breakup in 1993 was triggered by a disagreement over the reforms of the election system and political finance. The non-LDP coalition party government agreed to implement the reforms and managed to form a consensus to introduce a mixed system of single-member district system and proportional representation (to replace the medium-sized election district system with a single nontransferable vote) and publicly fund party activities. It is too early to obtain evidence to examine the influence of these specific reforms on interest representation. Thus, this section will speculate about the impact of the interruption of the LDP rule using the recent survey data about interest group activities.

A comprehensive survey of interest groups and empirical data about their relationship with policymakers are in short supply in any industrial democracy, but in the Japanese case, there are comparable survey data available both at the height of the LDP dominance (for 1980) and immediately after the 1993 change (for 1994) (Ito, Muramatsu, and Tsujinaka 1986; Muramatsu 1998; Tsujinaka and Ishio 1998; Akizuki 1998). Both surveys posed the same or comparable questions to the same (major) interest groups and attempted to figure out their day-to-day activities and interactions with policymakers. The more recent survey has published neither the entire raw data nor a complete analysis of it, but the published results and analysis, though limited, illuminate crucial transformations in the attitude of interest groups toward politicians and bureaucrats. First, the survey found a clear shift from party to bureaucracy when interest groups chose to which policymakers they effectively made their policy demands. For example, in 1980, 46.4 percent of the groups chose party and 47.6 percent chose bureaucracy, whereas in 1994, only 31.2 percent chose party and 60.7 percent chose bureaucracy. In 1980, 50.4 percent of the groups supported the LDP to a lesser or greater extent, and in 1994 this dropped to 28.3 percent (Muramatsu 1998, 13). Combining these results, in 1980 most groups believed the LDP represented and protected their interests effectively. In 1994, both support for and expectation from the LDP sharply declined. This result appears obvious, considering that the LDP lost its privileged status as a one-party incumbent. However, the survey results include two other interesting findings.

First, both the number of interest groups that said they trusted the party and the number that trusted the bureaucracy have declined. The proportion of interest groups that answered that they trusted party dropped from 77.0 to 45.0 percent, and the ones that answered that they trusted the bureaucracy dropped from 77.6 to 59.5 percent (Akizuki 1998, 70). This result means that interest groups have increased their exposure to the bureaucracy, but this shift from party to bureaucracy does not necessarily mean an increase in their absolute reliance on bureaucracy (Muramatsu 1998, 18–19; Akizuki 1998, 70). Rather, the results imply that, because the party is not to be relied upon, the bureaucracy appears to be a better choice for interest groups. In this respect, the survey results are more consistent with the image based on hypothesis 2, which has some reservation about the strengthening relationship between bureaucrats and interest groups.

Another interesting implication of the reports on the survey data is that the shift from party to bureaucracy may have been going on from the mid-1980s well before the change in 1993. The reports use other literature (Kume 1990) as evidence of this or come to this conclusion by extending the interpretations of the survey data (Akizuki 1998, 71). The evidence is not strong enough to make an argument for this shift, but the idea is interesting in the sense that the change in party politics in 1993 appears to be limited to the relationship between policymakers and interest groups—at least, more limited to it than the relationship between policymakers, that is, between bureaucrats and incumbent politicians.

Conclusion

Although it is difficult to draw an overall picture of the relationship between incumbent politicians, bureaucrats, and interest groups in a period of transformation of Japanese party politics, a couple of important findings have resulted from the sudden change in party politics in 1993. First, the subsequent change in the relationship between incumbent politicians and bureaucrats after the end of one-party dominance provides evidence that the presence of a long-term incumbent party whose members have policy expertise promotes instead of thwarts the bureaucratic attempt to influence policy-making. Bureaucratic influence goes hand in hand with the influence of incumbent politicians. Only when the incumbent party can rely on competent staff support for policy-making outside the bureaucracy (i.e., in the legislature and party organization) is this unlikely to be the case.

Another finding is that the bureaucracy appears to be more effective (though in relative terms) in responding to the demands of interest groups independent of the change in party politics in 1993. This remains speculation but is a curious possibility if one accepts the emerging view that parties in industrial democracies tend to transform into a cartel party that penetrates deeply into the government to allocate resources to social interests (Mair 1997). The concept of a cartel party assumes some merging of the functions of bureaucracy and parties inside the government, and this assumption has a strong affinity with the argument that bureaucratic and political influence strengthen each other. This is yet another possibility for generalizing this argument, but whether it will be confirmed hinges on broad changes in party politics in Japan, including that of party organization.

NOTES

1. In 2000, the LP ended its coalition with the LDP. The LP broke up over this decision and a part of the LP members formed the Conservative Party and continued to ally with the LDP.
2. For more detailed reviews of the existing literature and views, including complete references and citations, please see Kato 1994, 45–56.
3. In the study of the Japanese bureaucracy, there are competing views to regard the prewar and postwar bureaucracies as continuous and as discontinuous. Please see Muramatsu 1981, 13–17.
4. The JRP included many experienced politicians. The disharmony inside the coalition government caused by this tax proposal led to the disintegration of the coalition and ended with the resignation of the prime minister himself and defections of the SDPJ and Harbinger. In other words, the incumbent politicians with policy expertise were ready to cooperate with the bureaucrats, even if doing so meant risking the disintegration of their own governing coalition.
5. For more details about administrative reform see Mabuchi 1999, Masujima 1999, and Shinoda 1999.
6. For example, in the first ordinary Diet session after the 1996 general election, party discipline over parliamentary votes was lifted in a way that had rarely occurred before, and the result was an increase in noncompliance of members with formal party voting decisions. Among six major pieces of legislation passed in this session, only three budget and financial bills (the 1996 Supplementary Budget Bill, the 1997 Budget Bill, and the Revision of the Bank of Japan Bill) were passed on the basis of voting along strict party lines with the compliance of every party member. However, even for these bills, the legislative support coalition was different from one bill to another. Also in the deliberation of the bill to determine a new security relationship with the United States in the ordinary Diet session from 1998 to 1999, the LDP in alliance with the Liberal Party sought two strategies to compromise with one or two opposition parties and, at the last moment, decided to compromise only with the Clean Government Party while refusing to accept the demands of the Democratic Party.

REFERENCES

Akizuki, Kengo. 1998. "Bunsuireiniaru Nihonno Atsuryoku Dantai." *Leviathan* (special issue): 57–72.
Cowhey, P., and M. McCubbins. 1995. *Structure and Policy in Japan and the United States*. Cambridge: Cambridge University Press.
Gershenkron, A. 1962. *Economic Backwardness in Historical Perspective*. Cambridge: Harvard University Press.
Inoguchi, T. 1983. *Gendai Nihon Seiji Keizai no Kozo*. Tokyo: Toyokeizai Shiposha.
Ito, M., M. Muramatsu, and Y. Tsujinaka. 1986. *Sengo Nihon no Atsuryoku Dantai*. Tokyo: Toyokeizai Sinposha.
Johnson, C. 1982. *MITI and the Japanese Miracle: The Growth of Industrial Policy, 1925–1975*. Stanford: Stanford University Press.

Kaplan, E. J. 1972. *Japan: The Government-Business Relationship.* Washington, DC: U.S. Department of Commerce.

Kato, J. 1994. *The Problem of Bureaucratic Rationality: Tax Politics in Japan.* Princeton: Princeton University Press.

Kishiro, Y. 1985. *Jiminto Zeiseichosakai.* Tokyo: Toyokeizaishimposha.

Krauss, E. 1984. "Conflict in the Diet." In E. Krauss, T. P. Rohlen, and P. G. Steinhoff, eds., *Conflict in Japan.* Honolulu: University of Hawaii Press.

Kume, I. 1990. "Gyoseikikanno Jiritsusei to Noryoku." *Kobe Hogaku Nenpo* 6:225–77.

Mabuchi, M. 1999. "Henkanaki Kaikaku, Kaikakunaki Henka." *Leviathan* 25 (spring): 7–24.

Mair, P. 1997. *Party System Change.* Oxford: Oxford University Press.

Masujima, T. 1999. "Chuoshochoto Kaikakukihonho Gyokaku no Tokushoku to Monedaiten." *Leviathan* 25 (spring): 25–49.

Mochizuki, M. M. 1982. "Managing and Influencing the Japanese Legislative Process: The Role of Parties and the National Diet." Ph.D. diss. Harvard University.

Muramatsu, M. 1981. *Sengo Nihon no Kanryosei.* Tokyo: University of Tokyo Press.

Muramatsu, M. 1998. "Atsuryokudantaino Seijikodo." *Leviathan* (special issue): 7–21.

Muramatsu, M., and E. Krauss. 1984. "Bureaucrats and Politicians in Policymaking: The Case of Japan." *American Political Science Review* 78 (1): 124–46.

Okimoto, D. 1989. *Between MITI and the Market: Japanese Industrial Policy for High Technology.* Stanford: Stanford University Press.

Pempel, T. J. 1982. *Policy and Politics in Japan: Creative Conservatism.* Philadelphia: Temple University Press.

Pempel, T. J., ed. 1990. *Uncommon Democracies: The One-Party Dominant Regime.* Ithaca: Cornell University Press.

Ramseyer, J., and F. Rosenbluth. 1993. *Japan's Political Marketplace.* Cambridge: Harvard University Press.

Samuels, R. 1987. *The Business of the Japanese State.* Ithaca: Cornell University Press.

Sato, S., and T. Matsuzaki. 1986. *Jiminto Seiken.* Tokyo: Chuokoronsha.

Shinoda, T. 1999. "Hashimoto Gyokaku no Naikakukino Kyokasaku." *Leviathan* 25 (spring): 51–77.

Silberman, B. 1993. *Cages of Reason.* Chicago: University of Chicago Press.

Tsujinaka, Y., and Y. Ishio. 1998. "Riekidantai Nettowakukozoto Seikenhendo." *Leviathan* (special issue): 22–43.

Yanaga, C. 1968. *Big Business in Japanese Politics.* New Haven: Yale University Press.

Change Is Short but Continuity Is Long: Policy Influence of the National Assembly in Newly Democratized Korea

Chan Wook Park

Introduction

The main purpose of this essay is to discuss how the Korean National Assembly has changed in its performance of policy activity during the country's democratic transition. Over the past decade or so, Korea has periodically held competitive elections. Its citizens have been given opportunities for participation and enjoyed enhanced civil and political rights. Democratization has provided the National Assembly with a propitiously wider political environment for institutional evolution. In the authoritarian past, executive dominance was a salient characteristic in the legislature's policy activity, including lawmaking, budget review, and legislative oversight. To what extent has the National Assembly shaken off these old practices since democratic transition? The essay is going to address this question by seeking to find differences in the legislature's policy influence between the authoritarian Fifth and democratic Sixth Republics.

Before examining the National Assembly's policy activity, this essay first investigates temporal change and continuity in various aspects of that activity, including the context of the legislative institution (e.g., the historical dimension, constitutional framework, and the country's political culture). This study also looks at the party factor that has an impact internally or externally on the workings of the legislature. In addition, the study briefly turns to legislative organizational features delineating possibilities and limitations for the legislature to exert policy influence: typically, legislative members, committees, and staff resources. By highlighting these conditions, one can find clues explaining why the National Assembly has or has not varied over time in its policy activity.

Conditions of the National Assembly's Policy Activity

The Democratization of the Korean Polity: Historical Context

Contemporary South Korean political history has been marked by frequent regime changes. From the inception of the First Republic in 1948 through the current Sixth Republic, Korea has undergone a series of political upheavals. Despite its founding ideology of liberal democracy, the First Republic soon degenerated into authoritarianism where President Syngman Rhee wielded his arbitrary power. The Rhee government's flagrant rigging of the 1960 presidential election triggered the student uprising that led to the downfall of the First Republic. During the Second Republic, Koreans briefly experienced democratic politics and a parliamentary system of government. But the Second Republic was toppled by the military under General Park Chung Hee's command in May 1961. After ruling the country for two and a half years as the junta leader, Park was elected president of the Third Republic. In October 1972, President Park fortified his dictatorial rule by proclaiming martial law and instituting the Fourth Republic. In October 1979, Park was assassinated, which invited another round of military intervention led by General Chun Doo Hwan. Chun rose to the presidency of the Fifth Republic. Faced with massive pro-democracy citizen demonstrations in June 1987, Chun conceded to popular demands, including direct popular election of the president. With a new democratic constitution, the Sixth Republic started off in February 1988.

As shown in table 1, the whirlwind of regime changes made the national legislature discontinue its institutional life or unexpectedly abridge its term on several occasions. The term of the Fourth Assembly was cut short because of the April 1960 uprising and its ensuing constitutional revision. The Fifth Assembly was dissolved as a result of a military coup d'état in 1961. The Eighth Assembly underwent a dissolution with the opening of the Fourth Republic under the name of *Yushin* (revitalizing) reform. Again, the Tenth Assembly was closed by military intervention following President Park's death. Finally, the Twelfth Assembly came to an early end amid the recent democratic transition.

Notwithstanding its past political turbulence, Korea in the recent decade has moved ahead toward democracy. Formally, its recent transition to democracy began on June 29, 1987, when Roh Tae Woo, then the ruling party's presidential candidate handpicked by President Chun, announced a concession to enormous popular pressure for the restoration of democracy. Shortly afterward, political leaders and their parties negotiated the new constitutional framework. In December 1987, Roh was elected president by direct popular vote for the first time in sixteen years. Roh emerged victorious largely due to the fact that two prominent civilian leaders, Kim Young Sam and Kim Dae Jung, split the opposition vote. Kim Young Sam, who joined President Roh's ruling party in early 1990, won the 1992 presidential election. Kim Young Sam was the first civilian president since the military intervention in 1961. In December 1997, Kim Dae Jung was elected in his fourth presidential bid. This marked the first peaceful change of presidential power to the opposition.

Despite these achievements, however, Korea still has a long way to go for the maturing of democratic order. The consensus on the rules of the political game among the political elite remains shallow and fragile. Some politicians want to change the present presidential system of government into a parliamen-

TABLE 1
A Chronology of the Korean National Assembly

Republic	Regime Type	System of Government	Assembly	Term
First	Authoritarian	Presidential	Constituent	May 1948–May 1950
			Second	May 1950–May 1954
			Third	May 1954–May 1958
			Fourth	May 1958–May 1960 (curtailed due to the student uprising)
Second	Democratic	Parliamentary	Fifth	July 1960–May 1961 (dissolved by the military coup)
Third	Authoritarian	Presidential	Sixth	December 1963–June 1967
			Seventh	July 1967–June 1971
			Eighth	July 1971–October 1972 (dissolved due to martial law)
Fourth	Authoritarian	Presidential	Ninth	March 1973–March 1979
			Tenth	March 1979–October 1980 (dissolved by the military coup)
Fifth	Authoritarian	Presidential	Eleventh	April 1981–April 1985
			Twelfth	April 1985–May 1988 (curtailed due to pro-democracy protest)
Sixth	Democratic	Presidential	Thirteenth	May 1988–May 1992
			Fourteenth	June 1992–May 1996
			Fifteenth	May 1996–May 2000
			Sixteenth	May 2000–present

tary one. There exists ongoing controversy over the revision of the current electoral system for the National Assembly. Complaints about the prosecution's lack of political impartiality are often heard, and political donations from business still disproportionately favor the ruling coalition against the opposition. Despite their commitment to democratic ideals, citizens are not very supportive of democracy in action and even have nostalgia for the authoritarian past due to the country's troubled economy. All in all, the Korean polity is currently a fledgling democracy that needs to be consolidated (see Shin and Diamond 1999, 1–42).

Political Culture and Legislative Support

Due to the lack of a democratic political tradition, Koreans have yet to develop the political culture favorable to legislative politics that involves pragmatic bargaining and compromise over substantive issues among equal competitors. Some significant elements of the old Confucian tradition still persist. Norms for resolving conflict among those on an equal footing have not taken root. There is also a strong tendency toward formalism, which refers to the emphasis on the form or style of an action. Politicians show inadequate concern about the substantive issues having direct bearing on citizens' daily lives. Being more often than not focused on some abstract principles or formal propriety, legislative conflict is not likely to be easily resolved through negotiated compromise (see C. L. Kim and Pai 1981, 5–22; C. L. Kim 1988a; Park 1993a).

When legislative support is conceived in a highly abstract sense, the Korean people can be seen as supportive all the time. Even in the authoritarian era of the Fourth Republic, a majority of them recognized the necessity of the National Assembly as such in expectation of its positive role for democratization. On the other hand, one can define legislative support in a more concrete sense as the approval of the legislature existing at a specific point of time. This conception of legislative support is hardly distinguishable from the evaluation concerning the particular legislature's performance of its proper functions. In this concrete version, only a minority of Koreans gave their support to the National Assembly in the authoritarian era (C. L. Kim and Pai 1981, 38, 251–94; C. L. Kim, Barkan, Turan, and Jewell 1984, 159–203).

Existing survey results about public perceptions of the National Assembly and its members in the democratic era suggest the following. During the early phase of democratization, Korean citizens developed high expectations about what the National Assembly could do in the new political environment. Amid a sense of euphoria from democratic transition, Koreans revealed a more positive and supportive attitude toward the National Assembly than they did in the authoritarian past. However, as they have recognized a serious gap between their expectations and the legislature's actual job performance, they have increasingly withdrawn their support for the National Assembly. Particularly, in the second half of the Thirteenth Assembly, there occurred a sharp decline in legislative support (K. Kim and Park 1991, 84–85). A survey administered in 1996 indicated that only three out of seven citizens were satisfied with the way the national legislature worked (Shin and Van Der Slik 1997, 39–64).

Constitutional Change

Each constitution of the Fifth and Sixth Republics provided a presidential system of government. However, there could be found a striking contrast between these two constitutions. Stronger presidential power was given under the Fifth Republic constitution than the Sixth Republic one. The military leadership imposed the Fifth Republic constitution, whereas the Sixth Republic constitution was negotiated among political parties. Based on its substantive content as well as on its adoption procedure, the Fifth Republic constitution was not democratic. Under this constitution, the president was clearly predominant over the National Assembly. The president had the right to dissolve the National Assembly whenever the leader considered it necessary for national security reasons. In case of serious turmoil, the president could exercise emergency measures covering the whole range of national affairs. The total annual number of days during which the National Assembly was in session was limited to one hundred and fifty. On the other hand, the Sixth Republic constitution has allowed the National Assembly a stronger position than before. The president cannot dissolve the National Assembly. There is no limit to the total annual number of its session days. The National Assembly has restored its power to inspect all aspects of executive operations during every annual regular session.[1]

Still, one cannot say that the present constitution makes the president and National Assembly equal in power. Unlike the U.S. prototype of presidency, the Korean presidency has tipped the power balance toward the president. There can be found several constitutional constraints on the national legislature in extending its regular or extraordinary session, deliberating the national budget, and so on. During periods of serious turmoil, the president can exercise emergency powers bypassing the National Assembly, although these powers have a more limited definition in the constitutional text than they did previously.

Political Parties and Interparty Dynamics

A typical Korean political party is personality-dominated and rallies around a particular boss to maintain its vigor. As people know a *chaebol* conglomerate by the owner's name, a political party is identified with its leader: the nation's president for the ruling party, and a charismatic or popular leader for an opposition party. Although factions may exist within a party, power and influence in the party tend to gravitate toward one person. A party without a strong focal leader will become fragile and is likely to fall apart. It is no exaggeration to say that the fate of a party, including a split or the formation of a new party, hinges on decisions made by its leader.

Political parties do not diverge much in ideology or policy direction. The political parties represented in the National Assembly are all centrist or conservative, the ideological horizon of Korean politics having been substantially reduced since the partition of the Korean peninsula. A progressive party is hardly viable in politics built around existing parties and established politicians. Politicians with progressive tints gain access to the national legislature through the conduit of existing parties.

In the authoritarian era, the issue of industrialization versus democratization divided the ruling and opposing parties. In the democratic era, this issue has lost much of its vigor, but no other major ideological or policy issue has crystallized in its stead. Of course, on some policy issues, existing parties may claim different positions even within a limited range of the ideological spectrum. But no party has fully and consistently translated its advocated ideological stance into a concrete policy program. A party's crucial electoral base is its leader's native region. The word *regionalism* succinctly describes Korean party politics.

Personality dominance, bossism, and lack of ideological distinction all contribute to the instability of the party system. Prominent political leaders make and unmake political parties all the time. Members of the National Assembly change party affiliation according to their relationships with the leaders or political convenience. The ever-shifting parties, none of which lasts long enough for a voter to develop an attachment, confuse ordinary citizens. Indeed, many people have become disillusioned with existing parties.

In the Thirteenth Assembly election, after the democratic transition, the president's party failed to gain a majority for the first time in Korea's legislative politics, with the National Assembly split among four parties (Park 1988c; H. N. Kim 1989). This kind of divided government generated an opportunity for developing the politics of coalition building among multiple parties. The National Assembly became much more assertive, independent, and vigorous than in the authoritarian past. For example, in the first half of the Thirteenth Assembly, three opposition parties together could even reject some important presidential proposals in the legislature. However, in early 1990, the ruling Democratic Justice Party, having found it both time-consuming and difficult to build working majorities, merged with two opposition parties to form the Democratic Liberal Party. The mammoth ruling party could command over a two-thirds majority. In the second half of the Thirteenth Assembly, the ruling party railroaded executive proposals in the legislature.

In the elections for the Fourteenth and Fifteenth Assemblies, the president's party (the Democratic Liberal Party and its successor the New Korea Party, respectively) was not able to obtain a majority of legislative seats, either (Lee 1994; Park 1993b; Leuthold 1997). But after these elections, the ruling party drew in some opposition and independent legislative members, manufacturing a majority status eventually. Kim Dae Jung rose to the presidency in the second year of the Fifteenth Assembly. At that time, President Kim's National Congress for New Politics, a former opposition party, could not command a legislative majority, even when combined with its junior coalition partner, the United Liberal Democrats. Again, there emerged a possibility of the power balance between the executive and legislative branch. But this possibility has vanished as the two parties in the ruling coalition have gradually recruited some legislative members from the other side of the aisle and finally attained a combined majority status. The Grand National Party, formerly the ruling New Korea Party, remained a minority, though the largest party, in the second half of the Fifteenth Assembly.

The Sixteenth Assembly election held on April 13, 2000, produced a semblance of a two-party system in which no single party won a majority of the legislative seats. The opposition Grand National Party finished first, but four seats short of a simple majority. President Kim Dae Jung's party, which changed its name from the National Congress for New Politics to the New Millennium Democratic Party less than three months before the election, gained the second largest share of the seats. The United Liberal Democrats, the previous junior partner in the ruling coalition, finished a far distant third, winning less than twenty seats. By the National Assembly law, this party has not been allowed to form its own legislative party group. Even when the president's party would team up again with the United Liberal Democrats, this ruling coalition could not make a legislative majority. In the beginning of the Sixteenth Assembly, whenever a major issue comes up for decision, the ruling coalition and the main opposition party will struggle against each other to woo support from a tiny number of legislative members unaffiliated with either side.

In both the authoritarian and democratic eras, the norm of strong party discipline is firmly embedded in the legislative process. Legislative members risk party expulsion if they dare to defy party lines on major issues (C. L. Kim 1988a; C. L. Kim and Kim 1995). Strong party discipline, especially that of the ruling party, reins in legislative members and restricts the policy influence of the National Assembly. There exist strong electoral incentives for a member to obey the directives from his leaders. The exclusive power to nominate a candidate rests with party leadership, which makes a member's partisan loyalty an important condition for renomination. Also, the party's financial and organizational support is crucial for his electoral campaigns and for constituency representational activities (Park 1988a, 1988b). Moreover, a legislative member loyal to the party leadership can be rewarded for legislative work. For instance, the party whip may assign the member to a preferred standing committee.

Intense partisan conflicts in the National Assembly devastate cross-party accommodation and cooperation in the legislature. Throughout its history, there have existed numerous examples of fierce skirmishes waged on the floor resulting in legislative deadlock or one party's unilateral domination (Park 1993a; Kang 1988). In the Twelfth Assembly of the Fifth Republic, most of its energy was consumed in arguing over whether to rewrite the constitution. Likewise, the second half of the Thirteenth Assembly was characterized by the routinization of standoff and stalemate over major issues of partisan interests. The Fourteenth Assembly did not proceed smoothly, either. In the regular session of 1994, the legislature did not properly deliberate the budget proposal due to political tension prompted by the issue of whether or not to prosecute those involved in the military takeover in 1979.

The Fifteenth Assembly was also notorious for its recurrent paralysis because of severe interparty strife. In March 1998, when President Kim Dae Jung asked the National Assembly to approve his nomination of Kim Jong Pil as the prime minister, the opposition majority Grand National Party attempted to disapprove it. The vote-taking on this matter was abruptly interrupted and afterward remained pending for several months since the parties disagreed over the balloting procedure. In the middle of 1998, the ruling coalition intentionally made the national legislature virtually dormant for three months without the speaker, vice speakers, and committee chairs being chosen after the completion of their two-year terms. In the meantime, the ruling coalition transformed its former minority status into the majority one by recruiting opposition legislative members. In protest, the opposition boycotted the legislative session and took to the streets. A series of deadlocks occurred over controversial issues, such as the prosecution's attempt to arrest an opposition legislative member on charges of illegally raising funds in the last presidential campaign, the government's alleged spying on legislative members, and the ruling coalition's unilateral passage of some major legislative measures. One impasse after another hindered the Fifteenth Assembly from effectively exercising its policy influence.

Legislative Members, Committees, and Staff Resources

Legislatures with significant policy influence are characterized by a low rate of membership turnover, measured by the percentage of freshmen members (Mezey 1979, 249–51). Membership stability is likely to indicate the presence of career politicians with policy expertise. The military leadership of the Fifth Republic barred most existing politicians from running for the Eleventh Assembly, which raised the percentage of first-term legislative members to 79 percent of the total membership. In the wake of lifting the political ban, the comparable figure dropped to 39 percent in the Twelfth Assembly. With the democratic opening of the Sixth Republic, the percentage in the Thirteenth Assembly increased again to 55 percent. It went down to 41 percent for the Fourteenth Assembly, showed a slight increase for the Fifteenth Assembly (46 percent), but then decreased a bit to 41 percent for the Sixteenth Assembly. This suggests that legislative members were and are, on the whole, not much experienced in their legislative work.

The committee system has yet to take firm root in the deliberative process of the National Assembly. Formally, an elaborate system of specialized committees exists, but this system does not function as effectively as originally intended. Committee deliberations over important matters are highly amenable to partisan skirmishes. Important characteristics of committees in a legislature with robust policy influence are missing, such as a sense of corporate identity, a high level of expertise, and the practice of in-depth review (Park 1998b).

Staff resources for legislative work have increased steadily, but they are not adequate enough to help legislative members exercise their policy leverage. For instance, the total number of committee staffers was 73 for the Eleventh Assembly, 84 for the Twelfth Assembly, 134 for the Thirteenth Assembly, and 136 for the Fourteenth Assembly. Currently, the size of personal staff available to each legislative member is 6, of which 3 can provide the member with policy assistance. There are also a dozen policy specialists for each legislative party group. In addition, there exist support agencies, such as the Office of Legislative Research and Analysis and the Office of Legislation and Budget.

The Policy Activity of the National Assembly

Lawmaking

Not only the members of the National Assembly but also the executive branch can introduce legislative bills. The latter type of legislative proposal is called a government bill. Table 2 shows that the average number of bills introduced per year was 122 in the Eleventh Assembly and 126 in the Twelfth Assembly. But it almost doubled in the Thirteenth and Fourteenth Assemblies (235 and 225 bills, respectively) and roughly quadrupled in the Fifteenth Assembly (488 bills). This surely indicates a sharp increase in legislative needs and workload. It may result from a growing necessity for specialized laws and proliferating popular demands for government action in a newly emerging democratic regime. It would have motivated legislative members to propose many more bills than before. The recent remarkable surge in the number of introduced bills is mainly due to the policy action taken by the Kim Dae Jung government for economic structural adjustment and reform. However, an increase in the sheer load of legislation by itself should not lead one to conclude that the National Assembly has strengthened its legislative activism and influence vis-à-vis the executive branch.

The portion of member bills among the total introduced bills is sometimes used as a surrogate measure that indicates the legislative initiative taken by legislative members relative to the executive branch. A relevant question to be raised in this analysis is whether members' legislative initiative has become more visible in the democratic era than in the authoritarian era. The portion of member bills was 41.3 percent in the Eleventh Assembly and 55.7 percent in the Twelfth Assembly. The comparable figures for the Thirteenth, Fourteenth, and Fifteenth Assemblies were 60.7, 35.5, and 58.6 percent, respectively. This reveals that the regime's democratization has no consistent effect on the pattern of members' legislative initiative.

The executive branch takes the initiative to draft legislative proposals to a greater extent than suggested by these figures. In every session, the ruling party's legislative members introduce some bills prepared by the executive branch. "Reform measures," such as public officials' ethics law, election law, and the like, were enacted in the Fourteenth Assembly. This assembly even made a special law to prosecute those involved in the military coup d'état and brutal crackdown of the Kwangju Uprising, including two former presidents. Actually, most of these bills were initiated and prepared by presidential aides, then delivered to the ruling party's legislative members for their formal introduction.

The extent to which a legislature exercises a legislative influence over the executive branch is affected by its capacity to determine the legislative agenda on its own. As far as government bills are concerned, the National Assembly is

TABLE 2
Number of Bills Introduced

Bill Introduction	Fifth Republic Assembly		Sixth Republic Assembly		
	Eleventh	Twelfth	Thirteenth	Fourteenth	Fifteenth
Member	202 (41.3)	211 (55.7)	570 (60.7)	321 (35.6)	1,144 (58.6)
Government	287 (58.7)	168 (44.3)	368 (39.3)	581 (64.4)	807 (41.4)
Total	489 (100.0)	379 (100.0)	938 (100.0)	902 (100.0)	1951 (100.0)
Number of bills introduced per year	122	126	235	226	488

Source: The Secretariat of the Korean National Assembly, *Compiled Materials on the National Assembly* 1995, 386; *Report on the Proceedings of the 14th National Assembly* 1997, 171; and http://www.assembly.go.kr (all sources in Korean).
Note: Numbers in parentheses are percentages.

fundamentally unable to control the agenda for reviewing them. It is a long-established pattern that the introduction of government bills is heavily concentrated in the annual regular session. For instance, in 1993, about 82 percent of the total government bills were introduced immediately before the opening of or during the regular session (Committee on Institutional Improvements, Korean National Assembly 1994, 269). This suggests that the legislature is considerably constrained by the government in controlling its own legislative agenda.

The success rate of introduced bills can give a significant clue to the extent of a legislature's policy influence. In table 3, one can find that the passage rate of government bills in the democratic era is on the whole lower than that in the authoritarian era. It was lowest in the Fifteenth Assembly. Still, even in this legislature, approximately 79 percent of government bills were adopted. In contrast, the highest passage rate of member bills was only about 41 percent in the Eleventh Assembly. These data point to the continuation of executive dominance in the democratic era.

The extent of the legislature's modification of government bills suggests its policy influence through lawmaking. In the National Assembly, the notion of bill amendment refers mostly to changes in a bill's title, improvements in wording and legal formalities, and other minor adjustments. The backbone of an executive proposal remains intact regardless of such amendments. Moreover, the National Assembly does not allot an adequate amount of time to add significant amendments to a bill. Committee and floor procedures for legislation proceed too hastily. The average time elapsed between a bill's introduction

TABLE 3
Number of Bills Passed

Bill Introduction	Fifth Republic Assembly		Sixth Republic Assembly		
	Eleventh	Twelfth	Thirteenth	Fourteenth	Fifteenth
Member	83	66	171	119	461
	(41.1)	(31.3)	(30.0)	(37.2)	(40.3)
Government	257	156	321	537	659
	(89.5)	(92.9)	(87.2)	(92.4)	(81.7)
Total	340	222	492	656	1,120
	(71.4)	(58.6)	(52.5)	(72.8)	(57.4)

Source: The Secretariat of the Korean National Assembly, *Compiled Materials on the National Assembly* 1995, 387; *Report on the Proceedings of the 14th National Assembly* 1997, 171; and http://www.assembly.go.kr (all sources in Korean).
Note: The percentages in parentheses are computed based on the number of bills proposed in each category.

and its final passage was seventy-four days in the Eleventh Assembly; eighty in the Twelfth Assembly; forty-five in the Thirteenth Assembly; sixty-one in the Fourteenth Assembly; and forty-nine in the Fifteenth Assembly (see the Committee on Institutional Improvements, Korean National Assembly 1994, 94; K. Kim 2000, 40). This vindicates the belief that a heavier load of legislative work in the democratic era is handled more cursorily than in the authoritarian era. The actual time given to the deliberation of a bill at committee and plenary meetings is likely to be a tiny portion of the elapsed time: probably some hours or even several minutes. The National Assembly is habituated to terminating deliberation in a hurry and deciding upon a number of bills in clusters at the end of the session.

The National Assembly's inability to reject the passage of bills against executive preference is most apparent when the president's party or coalition rams through a bill quickly with a snap vote, dubbed *nalch'igi t'onggwa* (snatching the passage of a proposal). When an important bill supported by the president is strongly opposed by the minority, the president's majority party or coalition often ignores the legal framework for passing bills. The speaker or other presiding officer loyal to the president curtails questions and debates even when objections are raised. Then the majority party finally railroads the bill through floor votes. This kind of practice has continued in the democratic era except for the first half of the Thirteenth Assembly. An example in the first half of the Fifteenth Assembly was the passage of two controversial bills concerning labor rights and the National Security Planning Agency (later, the National Intelligence Service). Both were favored by President Kim Young Sam but objected to by the opposition parties. In the early morning hours of December 26, 1996, only the legislative members of the ruling New Korea Party sneaked into the National Assembly building and rushed through the bills to obey the presidential directive.

More recently, on January 6, 1999, President Kim Dae Jung's ruling coalition unilaterally rammed 66 legislative measures through as the opposition Grand National Party unsuccessfully attempted to block vote taking. The measures included a motion for giving consent to the Korea-Japan fisheries accord, the teachers' union bill, and economic reform bills. On the next day, the ruling majority coalition broke through the opposition's blockade to pass its plan for the upcoming investigative hearing on the former government's economic mismanagement, as well as four other bills. Again, on May 4, 1999, amid a bruising scuffle between the legislative members of opposing parties on the floor, the vice speaker affiliated with the ruling coalition completed a few-minutes-long procedure to pass the government reorganization bill plus four other pieces of controversial legislation.

Under the checks-and-balances constitutional system, the presidential use of his veto power or threat of using it shows the dynamics of conflict and cooperation between the president and the legislative branch. In the authoritarian Fifth Republic, the president never found it necessary to exercise his veto power.

In the current Sixth Republic, the presidential veto was used only during the first half of the Thirteenth Assembly (when it was exercised seven times). At that time, the combined opposition majority passed some important legislative bills through the legislature against the president's will. What is meant by the lack of presidential veto during the Fifth Republic and most of the Sixth Republic? Certainly, it does not stand for close cooperation between the president and the legislature as equal partners. But it rather implies the legislature's docile subordination to the executive.

Has any change been observed in the policy interaction between legislative members and interest groups? In the authoritarian era, the major target that interest groups desired to influence and get access to was the executive branch. The National Assembly had little significance as a point of access or as a target for lobbying. In the regime where the norm of executive dominance was strong in the policy process, interest groups strove to approach and influence the executive branch, including the president, and other high-level officials (see Yoon 1975). On the legislative members' side as well, it was suggested that they seldom came into contact with interest group representatives for legislative work (C. L. Kim and Pai 1981, 155).

Evidence indicates that legislative lobbying has gained some significance in the democratic era. Immediately after the democratic transition, former government officials who had been discharged by force in 1980 by the military were organized. The group made a petition to the National Assembly to receive compensation from the government. In response, the Thirteenth Assembly in its first half, swayed by the opposition majority, enacted such law. The president initially vetoed the passed bill. But the legislature passed a modified version, and the president finally signed it (J. Kim 1989). With the democratic transition, despite the persistent tendency of executive dominance in the policy process, there has been some expanded room for legislative lobbying (Y. R. Kim 1992).

Budget Review

The National Assembly should approve the government budget proposal prior to its execution. In the course of its examination, the National Assembly hears the budget statement from the executive branch in the plenary session, then sets committee review procedures in operation. Each standing committee examines the portion of the budget that concerns the committee's jurisdictional counterpart in the executive branch. At the next stage, the special committee on budget and accounts embarks on an overall examination. After the special committee on budget and accounts adopts a modified budget proposal, it is reported back to the plenary session for final approval.

The extent of final modifications made by the National Assembly in the original budget proposal is strictly bounded. In the Fifth and Sixth Republics alike, changes have come within just 1 percent of the original proposal, with a single exception, the budget for fiscal year 1990. Before the Fifth Republic, the last time that the legislature altered the budget proposal by more than 1 percent was the calendar year of 1974, that is, for fiscal 1975. The legislature is such a passive reviewing body that its budgetary power cannot be a decisive source of leverage in its dealings with executive agencies.

There is no major discernible change in the pattern of the National Assembly's budget review between the authoritarian and democratic eras. The legislature's budget review continues to be limited in many important ways. First, the time schedule remains much the same and is hardly conducive to a thoroughgoing review. A standing committee's preliminary review lasts five or six days. The overall review of the budget and accounts committee is conducted within at most two weeks or so. Second, there is a significant constitutional constraint on the deliberation in the National Assembly. If the legislature wants to increase the amount of any item of expenditure or create any new item in the budget, it must obtain the consent of the executive branch in advance. Third, the National Assembly law itself is restrictive in this regard, too. A motion for amending the budget proposal in the plenary session requires support by at least fifty members. Furthermore, the budget for the National Intelligence Service[2] is only subject to preliminary review by the intelligence committee in a closed session. It bypasses a comprehensive review by the budget and accounts committee. Last but not least, until the beginning of the Sixteenth Assembly, the budget and accounts committee worked as a temporary special committee that changed membership every year and did not deal with fiscal matters on a continuous basis.

Legislative members themselves are well aware that the National Assembly exercises little control over the budget in its review process. Those members, both in the ruling and opposition parties, lobby the executive branch for making budget funds available to their district projects during the hot summer days when the Finance and Economy Ministry prepares for the budget proposal to be submitted to the legislature (*Chosun Ilbo,* November 2, 1996). Indeed, it is well known that legislative members frequently seek favor from bureaucrats outside of the deliberative process. Legislative members intercede with the bureaucracy by paying personal visits or making phone calls in order to provide particularized services to individual constituents. Also, by doing so, they try to influence the specific allocation of scarce governmental resources for the benefit of their districts (C. L. Kim and Pai 1981, 186–217; Kim, Barkan, Turan, and Jewell 1984, 128; Park 1988a, 1988b).

Legislative Oversight and Control of the Bureaucracy

The National Assembly is constitutionally provided with various means of legislative oversight and control. Major ones include annual inspection, specially arranged investigations, and interpellation for questioning ministers orally or in writing.

Annual inspection. At the outset of the regular session, the National Assembly establishes a period of twenty days or less for conducting inspections of government operation. Each standing committee oversees government ministries or agencies under its jurisdiction. Inspection is conducted in committee rooms or on the spot, that is, at agencies or other places visited by legislative members. The National Assembly had once lost this inspection power during the authoritarian Fourth and Fifth Republics, but has regained it thanks to democratic transition.

Based on its substance, legislative inspection can be divided into two types: One is "policy-oriented" inspection (*chŏngch'aek kamsa*), whereas the other is "politics-dominated" inspection (*chŏngch'i kamsa*). The former focuses on the analysis and evaluation of policies, aiming at identifying and solving policy problems. In this type of inspection, legislative members draw on obtained documents and their expertise, and they apply objective standards, such as efficiency and instrumental rationality. On the other hand, the latter is concerned with the question of who is right or wrong concerning political issues, leading to the exposure of irregularities and accountability problems. In such inspections, legislative members are highly sensitive to public opinion. They apply "the logic of politics" and seek partisan interests. At the early phase of the democratic era, in the late 1980s and early 1990s, annual inspections were to a large extent politics-dominated. But later inspections have become increasingly policy-oriented (H. Kim 1996, 27–30).

When it comes to the effectiveness of annual inspections in the National Assembly, multifaceted shortcomings and drawbacks are found. Typical problems arising from legislative members' incapacity to organize and operate inspection have been identified (H. Kim 1996; Park and Lim 1996, 85). Among them the committees for inspection every year choose too many agencies. Some agencies are subject to inspection by multiple committees in the same year. Others are only superficially inspected. Still others undergo no inspection even after they have been selected for the inspection purpose.

Legislative members demand agencies to submit irrelevant documents in unreasonably large quantities. For information indispensable to inspection, they rely on administrative agencies more than on their personal staff or other legislative support personnel. Administrative agencies and bureaucrats are reluctant to disclose their information to the public. Information asymmetry is serious between legislative members and bureaucrats.

Too many witnesses are summoned. Legislative members do not call witnesses selectively to take evidence, but blindly choose blocks of bureaucrats, including agency heads. Most witnesses are questioned perfunctorily. There are several cases in which some witnesses' testimonies are canceled after they have been chosen.

During the inspection, legislative members behave inappropriately. They question in an authoritarian manner. Their questions are wide of the mark, and reveal the lack of expertise. They raise questions without basic research and on rumors' grounds. They seek their own visibility excessively, and also put too much emphasis on their own partisan or district interests. They are obsessed with exposing irregularities. They fail to check up bureaucrats' follow-up actions to correct problems revealed in past inspections.

On the other hand, there are also problems with bureaucrats' behavior patterns. The bureaucrats under inspection are said to be lukewarm, passive, uncooperative, and sluggish in responding to legislative members' requests for information, documentation, and answers to queries. Administrative agencies do not expeditiously respond to legislative members' demands for rectifying past malfeasance and inaction pointed out during the inspection and taking further appropriate measures (H. Kim 1996, 42–43).

A host of problems with legislative inspection, as listed earlier, suggest that legislative members are deficient in their competence and information for performing substantive oversight of the bureaucracy. The standard view established in the authoritarian era but still prevailing in this democratic era refutes legislative dominance but indicates bureaucratic dominance. Administrative agencies are not responsive to the national legislature. Bureaucrats seem to be responsive only to the president, given the president's strong and highly centralized decision-making power.

Special investigations. The National Assembly is also empowered to investigate specific matters. The legislature may have a standing or special committee conduct such an investigation. One-third or more (later, in the Sixteenth Assembly, a quarter or more) of the total membership may request this investigation, but the plan for carrying it out must be approved in advance by a simple majority in the plenary session. The investigative hearing may be held as a way of obtaining evidence and testimony. The National Assembly's right to special investigation was not annihilated in the authoritarian Fifth Republic, but it was never exercised at that time. In the Eleventh Assembly, the opposition submitted motions for legislative investigation eleven times, but all these attempts aborted mainly because of the then-ruling Democratic Justice Party's objections. The Thirteenth Assembly of the democratic Sixth Republic, in its first half, was the most active in performing legislative investigation activities. The legislature launched a series of probes into the brutal crackdown of the Kwangju Uprising, the egregious abuses of power, and the wrongdoing under the rule of President Chun. This former president could not escape from testifying at a hearing before a panel organized jointly by two special investigative committees. In the Fourteenth Assembly, three investigations were launched about corruption practices and another regarding the collapse of a huge department store building. But no single investigative hearing was held as part of the probe, and in two of the four cases the investigation could not be completed due to interparty disputes.

The onset of an investigation by the National Assembly depends on the changing political climate. During most of the Fourteenth Assembly, when President Kim Young Sam enjoyed high popularity and had a good grip on the ruling party, the incumbent government was not subject to any serious investigation. When the political situation and public opinion do not press for a legislative investigation, there is only a slim chance that the National Assembly will carry one out.

In early 1997, a major financial scandal surrounding the Hanbo business group broke out. Together with the controversial passage of two bills in late 1996, the scandal made presidential popularity plummet. Political parties agreed to organize a temporary special committee to investigate the scandal in the first half of the Fifteenth Assembly. The committee held a chain of investigative hearings. This investigation not only reached senior politicians, an incumbent cabinet minister, and a presidential aide, but it escalated to probing influence-peddling and bribery charges against the president's second son. This kind of investigative activity, never attempted in the authoritarian era and rarely even in the normal years of this democratic era, may suggest that the legislature can dare to defy the president only when the political tide is strongly against the leader.

Despite the possibilities of investigative hearings serving as a forum for executive accountability, the hearings organized by the National Assembly in the democratic era have not borne fruit enough to dispel public suspicion about the matter under investigation. Two investigations pursued in the second half of the Fifteenth Assembly illustrate this point well. In the so-called furgate or boutique scandal, a business tycoon was imprisoned on charges of smuggling huge sums of U.S. dollars abroad and embezzling company funds. In attempting to save him from criminal prosecution, the wife of the minister for national unification affairs allegedly asked the businessman's wife to pay for furs bought by the justice minister's wife. The prosecution's hasty investigation could not clear public suspicion about this matter, and so the legislation and judiciary committee of the National Assembly conducted a series of hearings. Key female witnesses involved in this scandal gave contradicting testimony covered live on television. The investigation hardly progressed in getting to the truth as expected.[3] Another scandal involved the former head of the public security department, the supreme prosecutors' office. He was indicted on charges of instigating a labor strike at the Korea Minting and Securities Printing Corporation in order to take credit for cracking down on the illegal strike and facilitating the corporation's restructuring efforts. To probe into this case, the National Assembly organized a special hearing panel. Again, it failed to dissipate public misgivings.

Legislative members had difficulty taking evidence and getting access to documents. The members showed limited skill in handling witnesses who evaded testimony unfavorable to them or who perjured themselves for fear of prosecution. There was a temporary surge in sensationalism at the time of the legislative investigation, but later there was not much concrete change in executive decision making and implementation. Criticism of the National Assembly's unsuccessful investigations finally led the legislature to pass the independent counsel law demanded by the opposition in the second half of the Fifteenth Assembly.

Interpellation. The plenary session may request the presence of the prime minister, ministers, or other government representatives for interpellation, a procedure through which a legislative body calls the government to account. The legislative member who wishes to question a minister or government representative must submit to the speaker in advance a summary of questions and the length of time needed. The speaker transmits the summary to the government at least forty-eight hours prior to the interpellation. The speaker is also responsible for deciding, in consultation with floor leaders, the length of an interpellation period, the number of interpellators in each party group, and their order. From the Eleventh Assembly through the first half of the Fourteenth Assembly, an interpellator was normally given no more than thirty minutes. But since the second half of the Fourteenth Assembly the time limit for an interpellating speech has been set to fifteen minutes. In addition, the legislative member may submit written questions through the speaker to the government.

In the democratic Sixth Republic, both ordinary people and legislative members enjoy a much greater freedom of speech about politically sensitive matters than in the previous authoritarian regime. On paper, the constitution of the Fifth Republic guaranteed legislative members protection of parliamentary privileges and immunities, such as the exemption of legal accountability for their opinions officially expressed in the legislature. However, in reality there were unwritten taboos, called *sŏngyŏk,* about what was not to be spoken out loud in the legislature. These referred to critical remarks about the existing constitutional order, about the behavior of the president and his extended family, and about the president's major policies (C. L. Kim 1988a). In the Twelfth Assembly, an opposition legislative member was arrested because of his speech criticizing President Chun's authoritarian regime during the interpellation hours. To dodge the controversy concerning the member's privileges and immunities, the prosecution technically indicted him on a charge of distributing materials containing antistate remarks to reporters prior to his speech made in the legislature. By contrast, in the Sixth Republic, legislative members are not prohibited from dealing with any kind of topic in the legislature. This leads one to expect the interpellation time to serve as a forum for executive accountability.

Despite members' enlarged freedom of speech, it is hard to say that floor interpellation now really serves its intended purposes. Legislative members rarely raise concise and genuine questions. Some hopeless legislative members, forgetting their proper role of lawmaking, ask a cabinet minister if he or she has any intention to make such and such laws. There is much doubt about whether legislative members' questions will ensure executive accountability for policy actions or contribute to the information base upon which they exert policy influence. Cabinet ministers often do not seem to provide sincere answers to the questions raised. Interpellation remains tedious and unmoving, no more than a blunt warning against executive mismanagement.

Conclusion

Concerning the National Assembly's policy influence, two conflicting images exist. One image is an old one that was built in the long years of authoritarianism and has a lasting impact. This portrays the legislature as a weak and marginal policy actor that takes little policy initiative. Its policy deliberation is of a perfunctory, superficial, and limited nature. Modifications of a major executive proposal are not often made, and such proposals are seldom rejected. In brief, the legislature is unable to exercise policy influence independent of the executive. The other image is that of a significant and relatively strong policy actor. This image is a future-oriented one that has emerged in the newly democratized context, but it still remains fragile and shaky. The legislature is able to react to the executive's policy initiative. In the process of deliberation, it represents diverse opinions and interests, altering important executive proposals in a meaningful way and sometimes even rejecting them. It may play a secondary policy-making role relative to the executive, but shows institutional and functional autonomy to a considerable extent.

In the early phase of the democratic era, a shift from the old image to a new one seemed certain. In the first two years of the Thirteenth Assembly, the president's party was in the position of legislative minority and often overwhelmed by the legislative initiative taken by opposition legislative members. At that time, the legislative arena began to gain increasing importance as an access point for interest groups. Owing to the National Assembly's newly provided constitutional powers, significant effects of activism on legislative oversight could be seen. These new practices of legislative politics have created an alternative image of legislative influence. This new image, however, has never become prevalent. From the second half of the Thirteenth Assembly on, the legislature has increasingly become relegated to being a modest policy actor. The image of the national legislature overshadowed by the executive has turned out to be perennial and predominant. Change is short, but continuity is long for Korean legislative politics.

Why does the National Assembly not so readily evolve toward a much stronger policy actor than it used to be in the authoritarian past? This puzzle prods one to look at continuity and change in the conditions impinging on the legislature's policy influence. The current constitution has set the National Assembly free from the shackles of the previous authoritarian regime and provided it with appropriate means of checking the president and executive agencies. When it comes to the realities of party politics, however, tenacious old practices die hard. Political parties are not accustomed to making compromises. Party discipline, especially in a party on the ruling side, never ceases to be strict. Even in the democratic era, the president and his close aides direct the ruling majority's floor strategies for major bills or other important matters on the legislative agenda. Ongoing partisan conflicts inhibit the National Assembly from collectively exercising a policy influence. The legislative organizational characteristics also show deficiencies in the maintenance of institutional autonomy in relations with the executive branch. The National Assembly lacks the old-guard type of skilled and experienced members in dealing with the president and other high-level officials. The committee system has not taken firm root in the legislative process. Specialized staff service remains scantily available to the legislature and its members. Except for constitutional change, all other key conditions remain unfavorable for the strengthening of legislative influence even in the democratic era.

This essay does not toll a bell at the death of the newly emerging image about the policy activity of the National Assembly. The image of the national legislature as a robust policy actor still lingers, but it remains feeble and largely irrelevant to the grim actualities of Korean legislative politics. This compels the unceasing search for legislative reform.

NOTES

1. The Korean National Assembly meets either in the regular or extraordinary (special) session. The regular session opens annually on September 10 or the next day if the day is a holiday. The duration of this session may not exceed one hundred days. An extraordinary session may be convened at the request of the president or at least one-fourth of the total membership. Its duration is limited up to thirty days. Among the works contributing to our understanding of the Korean National Legislature are C. L. Kim (1988b), Lowenberg and Patterson (1979), Mezey (1979; 1993), Paik (1985), Park (1997; 1998a, b, c; 1999; 2000), Shin (1996), and Yoon (1975; 1986).

2. The agency has changed its name twice. It was originally the Central Intelligence Agency, later the National Security Planning Agency, and finally was given the current name.

3. Later, this scandal led to the justice minister's dismissal and arrest.

REFERENCES

Committee on Institutional Improvements, Korean National Assembly. 1994. *Compiled Materials* (in Korean).
Kang, Jang-seok. 1988. "Conflict Management in Divisive Legislatures." Ph.D. dissertation, University of Hawaii.
Kim, Chong Lim. 1988a. "The Unwritten Rules of the Game in the National Assembly of the Fifth Republic." *Asian Perspective* 12 (2): 5–34.
Kim, Chong Lim. 1988b. "The Keystone of Korean Democracy: Conflict and Cooperation in Legislative-Executive Relations." In *Proceedings of the Seminar on Political Conflicts in Korea,* 33–54. Seoul: Graduate School of Policy Studies, Korea University.
Kim, Chong Lim, Joel D. Barkan, Ilter Turan, and Malcolm E. Jewell. 1984. *The Legislative Connection: The Politics of Representation in Kenya, Korea, and Turkey.* Durham, NC: Duke University Press.
Kim, Chong Lim, and Yong-Gwan Kim. 1995. "The Evolution of Obedience Norms in the National Assembly: A Study of the Repeated Carrot-and-the-Stick Game." *Asian Perspective* 19 (2): 243–70.
Kim, Chong Lim, and Seong-Tong Pai. 1981. *Legislative Process in Korea.* Seoul: Seoul National University Press.
Kim, Hong Nack. 1989. "The 1988 Parliamentary Elections in South Korea." *Asian Survey* 29 (5): 481–95.
Kim, Hyun-koo. 1996. "Kukchongkamsa Siltaebunsokkwa Gaesonbanghyang" (Realities of Inspection on Government Affairs and Directions of Its Improvement) (in Korean). Paper presented at a seminar hosted by the Legislative Research and Training Institute.
Kim, Ji-soo. 1989. "Han'gukipbopkwachong'eso Ŭihoe, Hangchongbu, Iikjiptankanŭi Tongtaejok Sanghojakyong'ekwanhan Yon'gu" (A Study of the Dynamic Interactions among the Legislature, Executive Branch, and Interest Groups) (in Korean). M.A. thesis, Korea University.
Kim, Keon-oh. 2000. "Jesipodae Kukhoeŭi Ŭianchori Hyonhwangbunsok" (An Analysis on the Deliberation of Legislative Matters in the Fifteenth Assembly) (in Korean). *Kukhoebo* (National Assembly Review) 403:38–45.
Kim, Kwang-Woong, and Chan Wook Park. 1991. "Political Attitudes toward the National Legislature and Its Members in the Six Republic of Korea." *Korea Journal* 31 (2): 78–92.
Kim, Young Rae. 1992. "Korean Labor Movement and Political Participation." *Korea Observer* 23 (1): 1–18.
Lee, Kap-yun. 1994. "Democratization, Party Failure and the Emergence of the Unification National Party." *Korea and World Affairs* 18 (4): 749–71.
Leuthold, David A. 1997. "Further Steps toward Democracy: The 1996 National Assembly Elections." *Korea Observer* 28 (1): 1–24.
Loewenberg, Gerhard, and Samuel C. Patterson. 1979. *Comparing Legislatures.* Boston: Little, Brown.
Mezey, Michael L. 1979. *Comparative Legislatures.* Durham, NC: Duke University Press.

Mezey, Michael L. 1993. "Legislatures: Individual Purpose and Institutional Performance." In Ada W. Finifter, ed., *Political Science: The State of the Discipline II*, 335–64. Washington, DC: American Political Science Association.

Paik, Young-Chul. 1985. "Legislative Institutionalization and Political Instability in the Modernization Process." Ph.D. dissertation, University of Hawaii.

Park, Chan Wook. 1988a. "Constituency Representation in South Korea: Sources and Consequences." *Legislative Studies Quarterly* 13 (2): 225–49.

Park, Chan Wook. 1988b. "Legislators and Their Constituents in South Korea: The Patterns of District Representation." *Asian Survey* 28 (10): 1049–65.

Park, Chan Wook. 1988c. "The 1988 National Assembly Election in South Korea: The Ruling Party's Loss of Legislative Majority." *Journal of Northeast Asian Studies* 7 (3): 59–76.

Park, Chan Wook. 1993a. "Partisan Conflict and *Immobilisme* in the Korean National Assembly: Conditions, Processes and Outcomes." *Asian Perspective* 17 (2): 5–37.

Park, Chan Wook. 1993b. "The Fourteenth National Assembly Election in Korea: A Test for the Ruling Democratic Liberal Party." *Korea Journal* 33 (1): 5–16.

Park, Chan Wook. 1997. "The National Assembly in the Consolidation Process of Korean Democracy." *Asian Journal of Political Science* 5 (2): 96–113.

Park, Chan Wook. 1998a. "Korea, South." In George Thomas Kurian, ed., *World Encyclopedia of Parliaments and Legislatures,* vol. I, 393–401. Washington, DC: Congressional Quarterly.

Park, Chan Wook. 1998b. "The Organization and Workings of Committees in the Korean National Assembly." *Journal of Legislative Studies* 4 (1): 206–24.

Park, Chan Wook. 1998c. "The National Assembly of the Republic of Korea." *Journal of Legislative Studies* 4 (4): 66–82.

Park, Chan Wook. 1999. "Legislative-Executive Relations and Legislative Reform: Toward the Institutionalization of the Korean National Assembly." In Doh C. Shin and Larry Diamond, eds., *Institutional Reform and Democratic Consolidation in Korea*, 73–95. Stanford: Hoover Institution.

Park, Chan Wook. 2000. *Korea's 16th National Assembly Elections.* New York: Asia Society.

Park, Jong-Heup, and Jong-Hoon Lim. 1996. "Che Sipsadae Kukhoe Kukchongkamsa: Bunsokkwa P'yongka" (A Retrospective on the General Inspection of Government Affairs by the 14th National Assembly) (in Korean). *Ŭicho ng'Yo n'gu* (Korean Journal of Legislative Studies) 2 (1): 56–86.

Secretariat of the Korean National Assembly. 1995. *Compiled Materials on the National Assembly* (in Korean).

Shin, Doh Chull, and Larry Diamond. 1999. "Introduction." In Shin and Diamond, eds., *Institutional Reform and Democratic Consolidation in Korea,* 1–42. Stanford: Hoover Institution.

Shin, Doh Chull, and Jack R. Van Der Slik. 1997. "The Democratization of Legislative Politics in Korea." *Korea Journal* 37 (4): 39–64.

Shin, Myungsoon. 1996. "Change and Continuity of Parliamentary Politics in Democratizing Korea." Paper presented at the Conference on Democratic Institutions in East Asia, Duke University.

Yoon, Hyoung Sup. 1975. "Taehankyoyukyonhaphoeŭi Kuchowa Iikp'yoch'ulekwanhan Yon'gu" (A Study on the Organizational Structure and Interest Articulation of the Korean Teachers' Association) (in Korean). *Sahoekwahaknonjip* (Social Science Review) 7:1–37.

Yoon, Young O. 1986. "Policy-making Activities of the South Korean National Assembly." *Journal of Northeast Asian Studies* 10 (1): 29–48.

Legislative Autonomy in New Regimes: The Czech and Polish Cases

John M. Carey, Frantisek Formanek, and Ewa Karpowicz

Introduction

The wave of democratization worldwide from the late 1970s through the early 1990s has focused the attention of those who study political institutions on the evolution of legislatures in new democracies. The interest is motivated both by the windfall of empirical cases triggered by regime transitions, and by a normative commitment to the idea that strong legislatures are essential to the performance of democratic institutions. Arguments that place high value on the representation of societal diversity (Lijphart 1984; 1994), those that emphasize deliberation as a means of honing policy alternatives and producing consensus (Miller 1993), and those focusing on regime stability (Shugart and Carey 1992) all imply the importance of legislatures as fora for making key policy decisions.

Among students of legislatures in newly democratic regimes, much of this discussion revolves around the concepts of effectiveness and autonomy. Wilson (1999) has examined historical evidence from the United States to trace the origins of what is widely regarded as the prototypical strong legislature, in which strength is measured as effectiveness in reaching policy decisions. In recent transitions, where potent executives—either presidential, parliamentary, or hybrid—exist alongside new legislatures, it is necessary to distinguish the idea of legislative autonomy from that of effectiveness. A good deal of recent work on legislatures in Latin America (Figuereido and Limongi 1998; Jones 1997; Nacif 1997) and post-Communist Europe (Olson 1998) is devoted to evaluating nascent legislative autonomy in current new democracies. This paper follows a similar path in an effort to evaluate the evolution of legislative autonomy in Poland and in the Czech Republic during the 1990s. Before beginning discussion of the empirical cases, however, we must clarify the idea of legislative autonomy and the sort of evidence relevant to assessing it. In particular, we note

---

Reprinted with permission from *Legislative Studies Quarterly* 24, no. 4 (November 1999): 569–603.

that what counts as autonomy tends to vary with the constitutional format of the regime under consideration.

The paper proceeds as follows. First, we discuss the related ideas of legislative effectiveness and autonomy, underscoring the centrality of the second concept in studies of recent democratic transitions. Next, we introduce the two cases under examination here, Poland and the Czech Republic, beginning with a brief discussion of the status of their legislatures both before and during the era of Communist rule. We then review the changes in the institutional and partisan characteristics prompted by the transitions to democracy in the early 1990s. We focus on the dominant, lower legislative chamber in each country, describing the evolution over the past decade of the party and committee systems, the structure of legislative leadership, and its relationship to the executive. Finally, we examine the role of the legislature in drafting and overseeing the execution of policy, paying particular attention to budget bills as bellwethers of legislative autonomy and the cohesiveness of parties and coalitions. We conclude that both the Polish Sejm and the Czech Parliament have developed much of the internal institutional framework to support legislative autonomy, and that in the Czech case in particular, recent experiences with minority government are contributing to this trend.

Effectiveness, Autonomy, and the Executive

In his article on the evolution of legislative effectiveness in the United States from the Continental Congress to the First Federal Congress, Wilson (1999) emphasizes collective action, coordination, and social choice as fundamental challenges that legislatures must overcome to perform as effective policy-making institutions. The early U.S. congresses faced problems of developing expertise about complex policies and establishing orderly control over the agenda, as well as voting procedures, so that legislators' diverse preferences could be translated expeditiously into coherent and stable policy decisions. Their solutions, as identified by Wilson, included the development of a committee system with stable membership and distinct jurisdictions so that members were willing to develop specialized policy expertise; the establishment of legislative leadership offices with control over the legislative agenda; and the adoption of majoritarian voting rules. These developments, which distinguished the First Federal from the Continental Congress, established Congress as an effective policy maker.

The themes of informational capacity and decisiveness are central to analyses of legislative capacity in current transitional regimes as well, but the point of reference against which legislative effectiveness is evaluated distinguishes these cases starkly from the early United States. Especially under the Articles of Confederation, the absence of a strong executive meant that the default, in lieu of congressional action, was a policy vacuum. In this context, it makes sense to evaluate, first, can the legislature inform itself? And, second, can it decide? Among transitional regimes in the late twentieth century, in contrast, one can generally stipulate the existence of an executive with substantial constitutional policy-making authority. Studies of current transitional legislatures, therefore, tend to distinguish legislative autonomy from effectiveness. If effectiveness is the legislature's ability to make informed decisions, autonomy is its capacity to gather information, cultivate policy expertise, and make decisions—*independently from other institutions*. In considering the institutional point of reference against which autonomy is evaluated, the constitutional structure of a regime becomes relevant.

Students of presidential and parliamentary systems alike regard the executive as the point of reference against which legislative autonomy is measured. Autonomous legislatures are those that can and do make decisions and take actions independently from the executive. Access to information and expertise on policy from sources independent of the executive, generally through a stable and specialized system of legislative committees, is widely regarded as a necessary condition for legislative autonomy, regardless of regime type (Carey 1998; Norton 1994; Schüttemeyer 1994; Ström 1990). On matters of control over the legislative agenda and party discipline, however, evaluations of what characteristics imply legislative autonomy tend to vary with the constitutional structure of the regime studied.

Students of pure presidential systems define strong legislatures as those that can perform effective oversight, and introduce and pass legislation independently from presidential leadership, and even against presidential opposition where relevant (Morgenstern 1999). These activities require effective coordination and voting discipline in legislatures, the principal sources of which are legislative leadership offices and parties (Mainwaring and Scully 1995). Various studies, for example, attribute policy gridlock in Brazil to low levels of party discipline and the absence of effective leadership control over the legislative agenda (Ames 1994; Geddes and Ribeiro Neto 1992; Mainwaring and Perez Liñan 1997). In pure presidential systems, legislative and party leadership offices are constitutionally distinct from the executive office. As a result, strong leadership control over the legislative agenda and tight party discipline—which in turn foster legislative decisiveness—are yardsticks of legislative effectiveness. The relationship among party discipline, centralized agenda control, and legislative autonomy in parliamentary systems is less straight-forward. First, as theories of parliamentary government increasingly acknowledge, legislators who belong to the governing coalition may have preferences that differ from those of the cabinets officials they support (Huber 1996; Laver 1999; Laver and Shepsle 1996, ch.12). In this context, if legislative party leaders are independent from cabinet pressure, strong party discipline may facilitate legislative decisiveness, as under presidentialism; but if the legislative parties are subordinate to leaders who also occupy cabinet posts, airtight discipline may imply executive dominance (Bagehot 1966; Cox 1987).

Hybrid regimes add one more layer of complexity. These regimes, where an independently elected president coexists with a cabinet subject to parliamentary confidence, offer two viable points of reference against which one might assess legislative autonomy—president or cabinet. Which point of reference dominates evaluations of legislative autonomy typically depends on whether the president effectively controls the composition of the cabinet. An example is Russia, where the configuration of constitutional authorities over the cabinet means it has acted more as an agent of Yeltsin than the Duma during the 1990s: prominent legislative studies have therefore focused on the development of Duma factions as effective and cohesive collective actors (Hapsel, Remington, and Smith 1998; Remington and Smith 1995). In Poland, on the other hand, where post-transition precedent, the Little Constitution, and the 1997 Constitution all provide a stronger link between Sejm support and cabinet survival, insiders tend to evaluate legislative autonomy as *independence from partisan control* of individual legislators and committees.

To sum up, there is consensus that legislative autonomy involves accumulating information and policy expertise, conducting oversight of policy implementation, and effectively demanding policy changes from the executive. Active and specialized standing committees are widely regarded as necessary for autonomy. The role of disciplined parties, on the other hand, tends to be assessed differently in different institutional environments. Under presidentialism, with separate elections for the branches, and where cabinet ministers are generally not drawn from among the ranks of the legislature, there is frequently little or no overlap between partisan leadership across branches——particularly under the common scenario of divided government (Shugart 1995). The capacity for decisiveness, therefore, is the indicator of legislative strength, and party discipline contributes to decisiveness. Under parliamentarism, where overlap between the leadership in the branches is often considerable, to the extent that executive and leadership coincide, strong parties may imply executive dominance. In hybrid regimes, the executive reference point for legislative autonomy may be either the president or the cabinet.

Before the Revolution, Parties, and the "Leading Role"

In both Poland and Czechoslovakia, the formal position of Parliament has been formidable, even prior to the transitions to democracy in the 1990s. During the period of Communist rule in both countries, constitutions enshrined Parliaments as the highest political authorities. In practice, however, the relevance of parliaments as arenas for deliberation and substantive policy negotiations was practically nullified by the absence of competitive elections and the strict control exercised by Communist and allied parties over their deputies.

The Sejm in the Polish People's Republic

The Sejm has always been central to Polish democratic aspirations. As one of Europe's oldest parliaments, it was symbolically important both when Poland was partitioned and during the Communist era, when the country's sovereignty was restricted, but the Sejm was allowed to conduct activity on a limited scale. The constitutional provisions concerning the position and powers of Parliament were never challenged under Communist rule. However, any prospect for the Sejm to represent the diversity of national opinion was thwarted by the leading role of the Communist Party (PZPR).

The Constitution of 1952 established the principle of *unity of authority* and the supremacy of the Sejm within the state (Articles 20–29). The Sejm was "the representative organ of the State's uniform authority," "its highest organ," "the highest body expressing the will of the Nation, appointed to realize its sovereign rights" (Articles 20 [1] and [2]). Parliament was "to exercise supreme control over the social, economic and political life" (Article 20 [3]), apparently establishing its political rank as higher than that of any other institution of authority. The Constitution was vague, however, about the specific powers of the Sejm. Advocates of Parliament initially postulated that there was a need to "thicken" the regulatory structure of the constitution by introducing amendments that specified Parliament's functions and scope of authority, but no consequential specification of authorities was ever elaborated. During the 1970s, the PZPR bureaucracy increased its control over the state bureaucracy in the name of greater administrative efficiency, bypassing both the nominal control of the Sejm and even the party's collective bodies. The process culminated with constitutional amendments in 1976 that significantly reduced even the Sejm's authority over the administration, and limited what little control its committees had exercised.

The extended period of workers' mass protests beginning in August 1980 triggered reforms designed to give the Sejm a greater role. Constitutional amendments in 1980 and 1982 aimed to provide deputies with greater authority to oversee executive decisions, and throughout the decade a growing number of voices advocated expanding and specifying the Sejm's authority in areas as diverse as the following: economic and financial planning, ratifying international agreements, passing amnesty laws, and appointing the Prosecutor General. By late 1988 and early 1989, the opposition stepped up pressure for change in the structure of authority and, finally, in the Round Table negotiations secured an agreement on amendments to the constitution, providing for a new bicameral Parliament and the establishment of a presidency with broad powers.

Despite its broad range of formal authorities, an assessment of the Sejm during the People's Republic must be short and unequivocal—it had virtually no say in any matter. Elections presented voters with no genuine alternatives to candidates from the PZPR and its sanctioned allies. Parliament in session was a mere voting device; it danced to the tune played by the Communist Party. Disputes about the scope of authority between the Sejm and the government were feigned. This situation was similar to that of other Communist bloc countries, with the exception that, after 1956, the Sejm had a group of "dissidents" representing Catholic communities who received mandates (from the party rather than the nation) and formed their own parliamentary caucus. This provided an outlet for public opinion and allowed the authorities to promote the idea that the Sejm was pluralistic and that deputies were free to offer critical opinions. However, this can in no way affect the assessment of the Sejm as a whole.

The Czech Parliamentary Experience, 1918–89

On October 28, 1918, Czech independence from the Austrian Empire was declared at a spontaneous demonstration in Prague. On the same day, and without knowledge of the national movement in their homeland, a meeting of the Czechoslovak foreign resistance and politicians in Geneva, Switzerland, established the foundations of the new state as a republic with a parliamentary system of government. Although the winning powers recognized the new state toward the end of the First World War, the exact demarcation of Czechoslovak frontiers required an extended period of negotiation with neighboring states, because the Czech and Slovak lands had been parts of different state formations for hundreds of years. One side effect was that the republic could not define constituencies precisely or hold national elections immediately.

By 1920, the new Czechoslovak Constitution established a congruent bicameral Parliament, with members of the Chamber and the Senate selected from the same electoral districts and by the same proportional electoral system. The duration of the period of interwar democracy was marked by extraordinary centralization of control over Parliament by central party organizations. The parties determined the positions of candidates on electoral lists, thereby reducing deputies' constitutionally guaranteed independence. Prospective candidates were regularly required to proffer undated resignation letters for their political parties, which could be used against them at any time. Moreover, all important proposals were subject to negotiation by leaders of the five major political parties (Social Democrats, National Socialists, Agrarians, People's Party, and National Democrats) before they came to the Parliament. Finally, a Permanent Committee, composed of 16 deputies and 8 senators by proportional partisan representation, could issue provisions with the force of law in many policy jurisdictions when the Assembly was not in session. Because it had only 24 members, this so-called "small Parliament" was much more easily controlled by party leaders than was the full legislature and was a favored forum for policy making.

The Communist period after World War II was distinct from the interwar period in the suppression of free and competitive elections but was consistent in the tendency toward strict partisan control over parliamentary deputies. In the first post-war elections, the Czechoslovak Communist Party (KSC) became the decisive political force, based on support from the Soviet Union and its popularity as a victorious power. Both the Peoples' Democratic Constitution of 1948 and the Socialist Constitution of 1960, passed by the Communist parliaments, acknowledge Parliament as the supreme law-making authority. But the basis of constitutional rule was undermined by the ominous provision guaranteeing the "leading role of the KSC" (Czechoslovak Constitution, Art. 4).

The members of the National Assembly (1948–68) and the bicameral Federal Assembly (1969–89), elected in controlled elections, were effectively appointed by the General Committee of the KSC. The Parliament had an unvarying proportion of Communists, members of the other two collaborating parties (the Socialist Party and the Peoples' Party), nonpartisans, representatives of different nationalities and various professions. Parliament met a few times each year in a general session and generally voted 100 percent for bills created by the Communist government. The members of Parliament spent the rest of their time "with their constituencies in the voting districts" and they were supposed to work at their original professions, retaining close links with the people. After a short period of liberalization in 1968, the Soviet crackdown prompted purges disqualifying all who had protested the invasion, not only from political activity, but from higher education and teaching positions, professional advancement, and travel. These draconian steps, in turn, generated a gradual loss of most citizens' interest in politics and made room for the exclusive appointment of Communists to all levels of the government.

To sum up, the "leading role" of Communist parties in both Poland and Czechoslovakia subsumed the constitutional supremacy of both Parliaments. Through its committee system and the allocation of a limited number of seats to nominal opposition parties, the Sejm provided an occasional forum for criticism of government policies but only to the extent tolerated by the party. In Czechoslovakia, the trend toward dominance of central party leaders over deputies dated back to the interwar era of parliamentary democracy, then reached its zenith during the Communist period. In both cases, Parliaments were decisive but not autonomous. That is, these legislatures were ineffective not because of coordination failure or the inability to reach collective decisions; rather, they were ineffective because they were not repositories of policy expertise or arenas of deliberation independent from the Communist Party bureaucracies, which also controlled the respective executives and state bureaucracies.

Transitions, Movements, Elections, and New Party Systems

In both Poland and Czechoslovakia, legislative marginalization was a product of the centralized control over legislators by party leaders coupled with controlled elections. Perhaps not surprisingly, then, the movements that led opposition to the Communist regimes, and eventually deposed them, rejected the principle of tight party discipline—indeed, they initially questioned the centrality of parties as mechanisms of legislative organization altogether. The transition periods in both Poland and Czechoslovakia were dominated by nonparty movements and marked by fluid legislative coalitions. In both countries, however, this period was short-lived. Both the political ambitions of leading politicians and the demands of legislative decision making encouraged the formation of parliamentary blocs, which in turn developed reputations with electoral value. In Poland, an initial experiment with a highly proportional electoral system encouraged enormous party fragmentation in the early 1990s, which then prompted the adoption of a legal threshold for representation in parliamentary elections. By the late 1990s, both elites and voters appear to have adjusted to the reform, generating a legislative party system with around three effective parties (Laakso and Taagepera 1979). In the Czech Republic, the early establishment of a restrictive legal threshold encouraged rapid consolidation of the new legislative party system.

The "Contractual Sejm," Fragmentation, and Party System Shakedown in Poland

As a result of the Round Table negotiations in the spring of 1989, the Polish Communist government agreed to hold contested elections for 35% of the Sejm and all of the newly created Senate. In the Sejm, the contested seats were filled by majority vote both for individual candidates and for one nationwide list; in the Senate, candidates were elected by majority vote in two- or three-member districts. All opponents of the PZPR and its allies coalesced under the banner of the Citizen's Parliamentary Club, the electoral manifestation of Solidarity, and won all 161 available Sejm seats (of 460, total) as well as 99 of 100 seats in the Senate. The stunning scope of the Solidarity victory triggered further dramatic changes in the legislative party system. The deputies representing the government side (the *ancien régime*) did their best to change their image as representatives of the former system and opportunists who had entered Parliament under the political contract rather than as a result of a free election. The pressure to implement change was so strong that the PZPR's vassal parties—and even many Communist deputies—beat a hasty retreat, voting for many bills proposed by the opposition. The Solidarity side, holding that it was elected with a clear mandate, ceased to act as an opposition despite being a parliamentary minority. Its deputies closed ranks and jointly formed a parliamentary club. In part, the goal was to be better placed to fight (or to cooperate if need be) with the Communists, but the goal was also to be perceived by society as a carrier of values, a representative of an ethos, of an attitude which was moral rather than political in nature.

The most important events in the life of this Sejm included the appointment of the non-Communist prime minister, the revision of the Constitution, and the passage of several economic laws. The government, which was referred to as "ours" (because it was non-Communist), and the Sejm, which was called "contractual," were guided by identical objectives. Initially, during Sejm debates, deputies came up with arguments in favor or against, but when it came to voting they usually said "aye." In a little more than two years, the contractual Sejm adopted 160 resolutions, passed 250 laws, and significantly amended the constitution including, in September 1990, greatly strengthening the presidency and providing that the office be filled by direct election.

Despite its accomplishments and its initial momentum, however, the second year of the contractual Sejm was characterized by growing political conflicts. The election of Lech Walesa to the presidency in November 1990, his confrontational leadership style, and ensuing divisions within the Solidarity group, all contributed to increasing divisiveness. The erosion of consensus that marked the transition period, however is also reflected in the increasingly fragmented structure of the parliamentary clubs and caucuses. There were seven parliamentary clubs in July 1989, eleven by the end of 1990, and fifteen by October 1991. The initial period of pan-partisan unanimity gradually gave way to fragmentation and a reconfigured party system, complicating the process of collective choice. By the middle of 1991, there was agreement that the best way to resolve this problem was to hold a new, totally free election.

Under a law adopted during the contractual Sejm, a group of fifteen persons could be registered as a party, and the Sejm was selected from large-magnitude districts, including a 69-seat national district, with no minimum threshold for representation. In the context of intense party fragmentation after the 1991 election (see Table 1), it took 9 months to form even a minimally stable government coalition. The short existence of this Parliament was characterized by conflicts between the Sejm and the President, and among parliamentary parties, and by frequent changes of the government.

In raw numbers, legislative productivity fell off some from the contractual Sejm, but there were substantial accomplishments nonetheless, most notably agreement on an interim, "Small Constitution," which clarified the relative authorities of the president, premier, and Parliament over the composition and survival of the executive branch. The most important innovation here was establishing the principle of the division of authority, replacing the principle of

TABLE 1
Polish Electoral Results and Representation in the Sejm, 1989–97

	1989	1991		1993		1997	
Party	% Seats[a]	% Vote	% Seats	% Vote	% Seats	% Vote	% Seats
OKP	35.0						
PZPR	37.6						
ZSL	16.5						
SD	5.9						
PAX	2.2						
UChS	1.7						
PSCU	1.1						
PCD		2.4	1.1				
PWU		0.2	0.9				
CD		1.1	0.9				
SAM		0.4	0.4				
PPPP		3.3	3.5				
URP		2.3	0.7	3.2	—		
Party "X"		0.5	0.7	2.7	—		
WAK		8.7	10.7	6.4	—		
POC		8.7	9.6	4.4	—		
KLD		7.5	8.0	4.0	—		
PL		5.5	6.1	2.4	—		
Samoobrona				2.8	—		
KdR				2.7	—		
BBWR				5.4	3.5		
UD		12.3	13.5	10.6	16.1		
KPN		7.5	10.0	5.8	4.8		
SLD		11.8	13.0	20.4	37.2	27.1	35.7
PSL		8.7	10.4	15.4	28.7	7.3	5.9
AWS		5.1	5.9	4.9	—	33.8	43.7
UP		2.1	0.9	7.3	8.9	4.4	—
GM		1.2	1.5	0.4	0.7	0.1	0.4
UW						13.4	13.0
ROP						5.6	1.3
KPEiP						2.7	—
KPEiRRP						1.5	—
UPR						2.3	—
Others		10.7	2.2	1.4	0.2	1.9	—
	$Neff_s$	$Neff_{vb}$	$Neff_s$	$Neff_v$	$Neff_s$	$Neff_v$	$Neff_s$
	3.4	14.0	10.8	9.8	3.9	4.6	3.0

(notes to Table 1 on next page)

*a*Under the Round Table agreement, two-thirds of Sejm seats were reserved for representatives of the PZPR and its allied parties. The seat distribution reflects both the reserved seats and the contested ones, which were swept by the OKP. Data on the vote distribution across party lists in the two-round elections for contested seats are unavailable.
*b*Votes and seats for "Others" are omitted in calculating Number of effective parties (Neff). Were the lump vote and seat totals included in the calculation, they would skew the measure upward substantially. Omitting them invariably skews the final figures downward, but only by a minuscule amount, as the votes/seats are widely dispersed across marginal lists.

Parties:
PZPR, Polish Unit Workers' Party; OKP, Citizen's Parliamentary Club; SLD, Democratic Left Alliance; PSL, Polish Peasant Party; UW, Union of Freedom; AWS, Solidarity Electoral Alliance; UL, Union of Labor; KPN, Confederation for an Independent Poland; BBWR, Nonparty Bloc to Support Reform; GM, German Minority; WAK, Catholic Electoral Action; POC, Center Alliance; KLD, Congress of Liberal Democrats; UD, Democratic Union; PL, People's Alliance/Agrarian Alliance; PPPP, Friends of Beer; ZSL, United Peasants' Party; SD, Democratic Party; ROP, Movement for the Reconstruction of Poland; PAX, Association of Lay Catholics; UChS, Social Christian Union; PSCU, Polish Social Catholic Union; KPEiP, National Pensioners' Party; KPEiRRP, National Agreement of Old Age and Disability Pensioners; UPR, Rightist Union of the Republic; PCD, Party of Christian Democrats; PWU, Polish Western Union; CD, Christian Democracy; URP, Union of Realpolitik; Samoobrona, Self-Defense; KdR, Coalition for the Republic; SAM, Silesian Autonomy Movement.

Sources:
Facts on File News Services. World News Digest With Index. K-III Reference Corp.
Hellman, Joel. 1999. *NCSEER Post-Communist Elections Project Home Page.* (http://www.fas.harvard.edu/~jtucker/pcelections.html).
Keesing's Record of World Events. Longman.
National Endowment for Democracy. 1998. "Elections Watch: Poland." *Journal of Democracy* 9(1) (January).
http://www.agora.stm.it/elections/election/country
Vinton, Louis. 1993. "Poland Goes Left." RFE/RL Research Report. October 8.
Webb,W.B. 1992. "The Polish General Election of 1991." *Electoral Studies* 11:166–70.

unity of authority, which had been expressed and guaranteed by the formal supremacy of the Sejm over state organs. Technically, the Sejm's loss of "supremacy" implied a limitation of its legislative powers, some of which were allocated to the Senate, the president, the cabinet, and the Supreme Court. De facto, however, Sejm supremacy had always been a myth, under Communism because of PZPR dominance and subsequently because of conflicts with Walesa over the relative powers of the president and Parliament over the cabinet. The Small Constitution formally established both the primacy of the Sejm in naming the government, and the responsibility of the government to the Sejm—principles that would eventually be codified in the permanent Constitution of 1997.[1] In doing so, the Small Constitution established that the relevant yardstick by which to evaluate Sejm autonomy, as in parliamentary systems, is the independence of Sejm deputies and parties (clubs) from sub-ordination to cabinet directives.

Notwithstanding the accomplishment of the Little Constitution, party system fragmentation undermined the ability of the first freely elected Sejm to maintain a stable government. In response, the electoral law was amended, establishing 5% national vote-share threshold for parties, and an 8% threshold for coalitions, to win representation. New elections were held in October 1993. The successor parties to Solidarity for the most part failed to coalesce to form lists capable of clearing the threshold. As a result, the number of lists winning representation fell, nearly 30% of the vote was captured by lists that won no representation, and the two main Communist successor parties—the Social Democrats (SLD) and Peasant Party (PSL)—captured a secure majority of Sejm seats based on little more than a third of the vote.[2]

A critical development, then, during the second Sejm, was the shakedown of the legislative party system into a smaller number of electoral parties, which corresponded increasingly with the membership in parliamentary clubs. The decreased number of partisan actors facilitated much greater stability in the government coalition, which was controlled by the Social Democrats and the Peasant Party for the entire 1993–97 term. By 1997, moreover, the trend toward partisan consolidation was even more pronounced. The post-Solidarity groups that had been penalized by the 5% threshold in 1993 coalesced to form a reconstituted Solidarity Electoral Alliance (AWS), which won a plurality of the votes and seats, and the Union of Freedom (UW), formed from the merger of the Congress of Liberal Democrats (KLD) and the Democratic Union (UD), establishing itself as a pivotal coalition partner for any viable government.

Table 1 illustrates the trajectory of legislative party system fragmentation and subsequent reconsolidation during the 1990s. In addition to changes in the number of parties for which we have vote and seat data, the table shows the dramatic decline since 1991 in the share of votes and seats in the "Others" category, which is comprised of multiple marginal parties. Changes in the effective number of vote- and seat-winning parties also indicate the extent to which both voters and party leaders responded, albeit not perfectly and not immediately, to the adoption of the 5%/8% threshold in 1993.

To summarize, after the initial success of Solidarity as an anti-system and anti-party movement during the transition period of the contractual Sejm, the first democratically elected Sejm illustrated the problems of instability of collective choice and gridlock associated with intense party system fragmentation. These problems were largely resolved under the second Sejm, but at the cost of excluding from representation parties that had secured a substantial portion of the popular vote. By the third Sejm, the post-Solidarity groups appeared to have recognized the need for a more unified partisan structure, both for electoral and governing purposes.

The Civic Forum and the Post-Divorce Czech Party System

Czech parliamentary evolution during the 1990s bears general resemblance on some counts to that in Poland: the initial commitment to rolling back the domination of Parliament by the Communist Party bureaucracy, leadership by broad anti-Communist movements, the dissolution of these movements into multiple factions, followed by the eventual consolidation of partisan blocs for both elections and organizing legislative behavior. The Czech case, of course, is distinguished by a number of important factors: the breakup of Czechoslovakia during the first two years after the end of Communist rule; the absence of a popularly elected presidency that challenged Parliament for control over the government; and also the more rapid establishment of a restrictive electoral system that deterred legislative party system fragmentation.

Among the most important goals of the Czech Civic Forum (OF) and the Slovak Public Against Violence (VPN) movements during the "velvet revolution" in late 1989 were free elections to the Parliament and the repeal of constitutional Article 4 on the "leading role of the Czechoslovak Communist Party." The Communist Party-dominated legislature initially presented an obstacle in this regard. However, confronting massive protests, the government in December acceded to the inclusion of a majority of non-Communists in the cabinet and President Gustav Husak resigned. This, under the then-current constitution, required the election of a new president by the Federal Assembly. The question then became whether the Parliament would vote for a nonpartisan candidate. Hundreds of thousands of people on the streets every day produced a similar phenomenon among the old cadres as the 1989 election results had in Poland. On the last day of 1989, the Communist deputies raised their hands as one man for Vaclav Havel.

After the presidential elections, the Czechoslovak Communist regime totally broke up. In January 1990, a nonpartisan majority was co-opted into the Federal Assembly, and in February into the Czech National Council, the Slovak National Council, and all regional, district, and municipal governments, providing interim, transitional governing structures. These institutions amended the constitution and passed a new electoral law, providing for elections in June 1990 for a Federal Assembly with a shortened, two-year transitional term. Apart from these accomplishments, overall legislative output was low, and work in committees practically nonexistent, due to legislative and procedural inexperience.

Although more than 100 political parties registered before the June elections, the immediate establishment of a 5% vote threshold for representation, combined with massive support for the opponents of the *ancien regime*, discouraged party system fragmentation and generated legislative supermajorities (3/5 required for constitutional amendments) for the Civic Forum/Public Against Violence coalition. Almost immediately, however, conflicting tendencies within these umbrella-groups asserted themselves. Consensus on legislation grew increasingly difficult to negotiate, and two factions in the Parliament, the Liberal Club and Interparliamentary Conservative Right Club, were established as the nuclei of two major political parties, the Civic Movement and Civic Democratic Party. By March 1991, partly in anticipation of the upcoming 1992 electoral campaign, the Civic Forum formally split into political parties.

In the wake of the June 1992 election, legislative action and constitutional reforms were further complicated by the bicameral structure of the Czechoslovak Federal Assembly, which consisted of two houses with 150 seats each—the House of the People, apportioned according to population (101 Czech mandates and 49 Slovak mandates), and a House of Nations (75 Czech mandates and 75 Slovak mandates). The nationalistic core of Slovak parliamentarians, headed by Valdimir Meciar and his Movement for Democratic Slovakia, held all action in the House of Nations hostage to their demands for independence, accelerating the division of the Czech and Slovak Federal Republic on December 31, 1992.

After the velvet divorce, the new Czech Constitution provided for a bicameral Parliament, with a 200-seat Chamber of Deputies and an 81-seat Senate. The existing Czech National Council, which had served as a subnational legislature in the old Czechoslovakia, and had been renewed in 1992, assumed the role of the Chamber. It is elected by closed-list proportional representation in large districts but also with a 5% threshold. Elections to fill the Senate were delayed due to disputes over what powers the body should exercise, and whether a Senate is necessary at all in the unitary Czech state. Finally, in 1996, the Senate was filled by majority elections (with run-offs, where necessary) in single-member districts, but the Senate's formal powers over legislation are minimal and the government is now responsible exclusively to the Chamber.

The 1992 Chamber (National Council) elections produced a center-right majority coalition of parties descended mostly from the Civic Forum (OF). Vaclav Klaus's Civic Democratic Party (ODS) was the largest, with about a third of the seats, and joined in forming a government by the Civic Democratic Alliance (ODA), the Christian Democratic Union (KDU), and the Christian Democratic Party (KDS), which eventually merged with the ODS. The government coalition effectively controlled the daily work of the Chamber as its narrow majority of seats increased as it picked up some defectors from other parties. But it could not adopt constitutional changes, which required 3/5 supermajorities, without support from at least part of the opposition, which was composed mainly of the Left Bloc (LB), the Communist Party (KSCM), the Social Democrats (CSSD), and the Republicans (RPR).

TABLE 2
Czech Electoral Results and Representation in the Parliament, 1990–98

Party	1990[a] % Vote	1990[a] % Seats	1992[a] % Vote	1992[a] % Seats	1996 % Vote	1996 % Seats	1998 % Vote	1998 % Seats
Civic Forum	53.2	67.3						
KDU/SMS	8.7	8.9						
AFC	3.8	—						
Green Party	3.1	—						
MSD	7.9	8.9	5.9	7.0				
LSU			6.5	8.0				
PCETF			3.2	—				
CM			4.6	—				
Left Bloc			14.1	17.5	1.4	—		
KSCM	13.5	14.9			10.33	11.0	11.0	12.0
CSSD	3.9	—	6.5	8.0	26.4	30.5	32.3	37.0
ODS/KDS			29.7	38	29.6	34	27.7	31.5
KDU/CSL			6.3	7.5	8.1	9.0	9.0	10.0
SPR/RSC			6.0	7.0	8.0	9.0	3.9	—
DZJ			3.8	—	3.1	—	3.1	—
ODA			5.9	7.0	6.4	6.5		
DEU					2.8	—	1.4	—
SD/LSNS					2.1	—		
Independents					0.5	—		
US							8.6	9.5
Others	5.9	—	7.5	—	1.3	—	3.0	—
	$Neff_v$ 3.13	$Neff_s$ 2.04	$Neff_v$ 7.01	$Neff_s$ 4.8	$Neff_v$ 5.33	$Neff_s$ 4.15	$Neff_v$ 4.73	$Neff_c$ 3.71

[a]Results are from the Czech National Council, which became the Parliament of the Czech Republic after the separation of Czechoslovakia into the Czech Republic and Slovakia in 1992.

Parties:
ODS/KDS, Civic Democratic Party/Christian Democratic Party; ODA, Civic Democratic Alliance; CM, Civic Movement; US, Freedom Union; KDU/SMS, Christian Democratic Union/Christian Democratic Movement; KDU/CSL, Christian Democratic Union/People's Party; SPR/RSC, Rally for the Republic/ Republican Party; CSSD, Czech Social Democratic Party; KSCM, Communist Party Bohemia/Moravia; MSD, Movement for Self-Governing Society for Moravia/Silesia; LSU, Liberal Social Union; AFC, Alliance of Farmers in Countryside; DZJ, Pensioners for a Secure Life; PCETF, Party of Czechoslovak Entrepreneurs Tradesmen and Farmers; DEU, Democratic Union; SD/LSNS, Free Democrats/Liberal National Socialist Party.

Sources:
Hellman, Joel. 1999. *NCSEER Post-Communist Elections Project Home Page* (http://www.fas.harvard.edu/~tucker/pcelections.html).
http://www.agora.stm.it/elections/election/country
Klima, Michal. 1998. "Consolidation and Stabilization of the Party System in the Czech Republic." *Political Studies* 46:492–510.
Olson, David M. 1998. "Party Formation and Party System Consolidation in the New Democracies of Central Europe." *Political Studies* 46: 432–64.

The balance of forces shifted some as a result of the 1996 elections, with the parties of the governing coalition falling just short of a Chamber majority, while the Social Democrats and Communists made substantial gains. But the heterogeneous opposition groups were unable to form a government, instead tolerating the perpetuation of a Klaus-led minority cabinet. The next two years were marked by tedious negotiation on each bill, followed by ultimata from the Social Democrats prompting repeated government crises, by deputies moving among the parties, and finally by the collapse of the government and early elections. The June 1998 elections similarly failed to produce a majority coalition. After prolonged negotiations, the Civic Democratic Party agreed to support a minority government led by Milos Zeman and the Social Democrats in exchange for parliamentary leadership positions.[3]

Institutional Structure of the Sejm and Czech Parliament

In turning our attention to the institutional structures of the Polish Sejm and Czech Parliament in the late 1990s, we focus on four areas: legislative careers; formal leadership organs within the chambers; the committee systems; and the legislative parties (also known as parliamentary clubs). In the first instance, we are interested in what motivates legislators' behavior, and specifically, whether service in Parliament is a viable and desirable political career (Polsby 1968). To the extent that it is, we can expect high reelection rates and, potentially, the accumulation of policy expertise and the willingness of legislators to challenge executives. On the other hand, if legislative turnover is high—for example, because service is poorly compensated or widely regarded as a mere stepping-stone to other office—then expertise should be low and independence compromised. Second, leadership structures within legislatures are of interest to the extent they are endowed with the authority to set legislative agendas and to coordinate negotiations among various actors to facilitate collective decision making. Third, committee systems are widely regarded by students of legislatures as potential sources of specialized policy expertise. We are interested here in the degree of stability in the structure of the committee system and its membership, their staff resources, and the overall level and nature of committee activities. Finally, we evaluate whether the parliamentary clubs are cohesive legislative actors and how independent they are from the executive. In each case, we mean to assess the development of institutional resources that we regard as reflecting the legislature's capacity for effective and autonomous action. The accumulation of legislative experience through reelection and specialized expertise within committees indicates the capacity of legislatures to develop and defend policy preferences independently from executives, while the establishment of internal leadership structures with control over the legislative agenda

TABLE 3
Previous Parliamentary Experience of Deputies to Polish Sejm III (elected 1997)

Total Number of Previous Terms Served in Sejm (including Communist Era)					
0	1	2	3	4	5
225 (49%)	131 (29%)	64 (14%)	36 (8%)	3 (1%)	1 (0%)

Experience of Deputies in the Sejm III in Previous Legislatures					
Contractual Sejm, 1989–91	Sejm I, 1991–93	Sejm II, 1993–97	Senate I, 1989–91	Senate II, 1991–93	Senate III, 1993–97
48 (10%)	132 (29%)	178 (39%)	7 (2%)	3 (1%)	7 (2%)

Source: Authors' research.

indicates the ability of these branches to act collectively (Wilson 1999). The import of party cohesiveness for autonomy, in turn, hinges on whether legislative parties are effectively subordinate to executive branch officials.

The Sejm

The Sejm elected in 1997 embodies considerable legislative experience and patterns of reelection, coupled with what appears to be stabilization of the party system in the mid–1990s, suggesting that levels of experience among deputies should continue to rise.

On close daily observation of the Sejm, it is evident that with each successive term since the transition, deputies are increasingly inclined to invest time and effort on Sejm-specific activities—that is, those that contribute to institutional capacity. The number of the deputies focusing their professional life exclusively on parliamentary work is increasing, to the point where almost all are effectively full-time legislators, and do not engage in any other professional activity during their period in office. The small number of deputies who do sustain parallel careers are mostly from the peasant parties, who still administer their agriculture units, although in many cases only theoretically. The decision by most deputies (and senators) to forego professional activity outside politics often implies substantial financial and career sacrifices—e.g., for lawyers or doctors, who may not earn as much as deputies as they could in practice. This is not to say that legislative work is selfless, nor that opportunities to use legislative office for personal gain are absent or irrelevant to deputies. The fact is, however, that the prospect of a Sejm career has become more reliable over time and that the job itself has become increasingly demanding since the 1980s, not to mention the previous decades.

The formal leadership structures of the Sejm include the Marshall, the Presidium, and the Council of Seniors. The Marshall is elected by majority vote of all members for the full four-year term of the legislature, subject to confidence of the majority. As chair of the Presidium (Sejm Standing Orders, Art. 12), the Marshall exerts substantial influence over the work of the Sejm. In addition to the Marshall, the Presidium includes four vice-Marshalls. This executive committee operates by majority rule—although its deliberations are generally closed—and determines the schedule of sessions, the consideration of bills, their referral to committees, and the admissibility of amendments on the floor. The Presidium also proposes the membership slates of all Sejm committees to the floor for ratification, and in doing so serves as gatekeeper of valued committee positions. In conducting these tasks, the Presidium consults with the Council of Seniors, composed of the leaders of all parliamentary clubs (Standing Orders, Art. 13). In short, the Presidium serves as a forum for coordinating the activities of a 460-member legislature, and it is endowed with substantial authority over the agenda.

Most of the substantive work of the Sejm is conducted in standing committees. Parliamentary clubs are allotted committee seats in proportion to their representation in the Sejm, with the specific committee rosters composed by the Presidium and approved by majority vote. There are no formal rules regulating the allocation of committee chairmanships, and this can become a subject of intense bargaining among parliamentary clubs. There is a hierarchy of committees in terms of importance, and the norm is that the chairs of the most powerful committees, such as Budget, Defense, Justice, and Foreign Affairs, are controlled by members of the government coalition, whereas chairs of lesser committees may be left to opposition deputies.

The specialization of Sejm committees has gradually increased during the 1990s as the number of committees has grown from 23 during the first Sejm, to 25 in the second, to 27 currently. Most committee jurisdictions mirror the activity of executive ministries.[4] Narrowing committee jurisdictions encourages the development of increasingly specialized policy expertise by members, and it facilitates oversight by allowing committees to focus resources intensely on particular executive policy domains. There is some concern that fragmentation of committee jurisdictions complicates the process of drafting legislation on complex policy issues, which may span multiple committee jurisdictions. To the extent that this is so, the influence of the Presidium and of parliamentary club leaders (through the Council of Seniors) in coordinating legislative activities across various committees may rise with the number of committees.

Although the specialization of Sejm committees has grown somewhat over the past ten years, their resources remain sparse. Most committees are allotted only three to four staff members, who provide purely clerical support. Deputies' budgets for expenses and staff are likewise minimal (around U.S.$2,000 per year each). The Chancellery of the Sejm provides some counsel on such matters as legal language for drafting legislative proposals, but overall, the informational resources available to legislators are limited, and the sophistication of legislative proposals initiated inside the Sejm—as opposed to in the executive ministries, for example—is often low. One result is that deputies and committees frequently rely on outside sources, such as academics, journalists, unions, and interest groups, for information about the policy implications of legislative and executive decisions.

The partisan units of legislative organization in the Sejm are clubs and caucuses—the former must have at least 15 members and are guaranteed representation on the Council of Seniors, and the latter must have three members. The Sejm's club structure reflects the electoral party structure; thus legislative party fragmentation decreased considerably in 1993 with the imposition of the 5% threshold and the exclusion of many post-Solidarity parties from the Sejm. In 1997, the electoral surge of the AWS—the newly reconstituted Solidarity alliance—brought a particularly diverse club to prominence in the Sejm, including in its ranks liberals, trade unionists, Catholic groups, and nationalists. Thus, within Solidarity in particular, there are frequent disagreements over club policy. All clubs decide internally whether specific bills are matters of discipline or not. Sanctions range from nothing to expulsion from the club. The latter is not unprecedented,[5] but it is rare, despite the fact that dissidence by deputies is common (Olson 1998, 462).

Czech Republic

As in Poland, parliamentary service in the Czech Republic has become highly professionalized. Table 4 shows that levels of legislative experience in the Parliament elected in 1998 are strikingly similar to that in the Sejm, with more than half of the incumbents winning reelection and around 20% having served more than one previous term. As in Poland, moreover, most deputies regard service in Parliament as the top rung of the political career ladder, rather than as a way station to another position. As a result, legislators invest considerable effort in

TABLE 4
Previous Parliamentary Experience of Deputies
Elected to Czech Parliament in 1998

	Deputies Serving Continuously Since Election of:		
	1990	1992	1996
Deputies	13 (6.5%)	25 (12.5%)	70 (35%)

Source: Authors' research.

both securing their own reelection and seeking advancement within the Parliament: for example, to party leadership positions, to the Organizing Committee, to committee chair. Although the infrastructure of Parliament was grossly insufficient in the first years after the transition, the physical space has been upgraded considerably, and deputies are now provided with office space and sufficient support to maintain a staff member or two, both in Prague and in their district. Appointments in the executive branch to ministerial or vice-ministerial office are also coveted, but advancement within Parliament is generally regarded as a step toward such positions, so is highly valued. Other aspirations clearly matter as well. It would be misleading to suggest that deputies do not seek to represent particular policy interests through legislative service, but the most effective way of doing so is to secure reelection and advance through the ranks of leadership. Beginning in the mid–1990s, the issue of compatibility between legislative service and private business or professional activity grew increasingly prominent, with a number of cases in which serious questions arose regarding conflicts between deputies' public and private financial interests. With regard to legislative professionalization, however, the bottom line is that politicians value parliamentary service, and such service represents an increasingly viable path to a political career.

The formal leadership structure of the Chamber of Deputies includes a Chairperson, Deputy Chairs (the number of which to be determined by the Chamber; Rules of Procedure, Art. 26), and since 1995, an Organizing Committee. The Chairperson is elected by majority vote of the Chamber, in a run-off election if necessary, for the four-year term of the Parliament, subject to confidence of the majority. The Organizing Committee effectively combines the functions of the Sejm Presidium and Council of Seniors. That is, it determines the Chamber schedule, the admissibility of bills and amendments, the order on which items are voted, the reference of bills to committees, and proposes the rosters for committee membership to the full Chamber for approval. The Organizing Committee is chaired by the Chamber Chair and is composed of the Deputy Chairs as well as the leaders of the parliamentary clubs. The structure of this executive committee is distinct from that of the Sejm, however, because club representation is proportional to shares of Chamber seats, whereas in Poland, each club is entitled one delegate to the Council of Seniors. Thus, the Czech Organizing Committee provides a slightly more majoritarian instrument of agenda control within the Chamber than the Presidium/Council of Seniors structure does in the Sejm.

The most striking development in the evolution of the Czech parliamentary leadership structure in the 1990s is the agreement under which its control passed to the government's main opposition after the 1998 elections. The elections initially produced a stalemate in the Chamber over the formation of a new government. The previous government of Vaclav Klaus, an ODS-ODA-KDU (that is, Civic Democratic Party—Civic Democratic Alliance—Christian Democratic Union) minority coalition, had been under attack, largely due to charges of corruption. The ODA did not win representation in 1998, and the newly formed Freedom Union (US), which won 19 seats, had initially formed via a split from the ODS club during the 1996–98 term. In short, prospects for continued coalition among parties on the right were strained. Similarly, the Social Democrats, now the plurality party with 74 seats, had publicly committed not to coalesce with the Communists in an effort to establish their centrist credentials. After prolonged negotiations in which an explicit Social Democrat-Civic Democratic Party coalition was ruled out, the Civic Democrats finally agreed to support the establishment of a Social Democratic minority cabinet. The main concession extracted in exchange was that the Chamber Chair would go to Klaus, relying on the implicit support of Social Democratic deputies. This configuration represents a significant step toward the independence of Chamber leadership structures from subordination to the executive, albeit one imposed by the imperatives of minority government and subject to its precarious survival. The configuration of partisan forces, and the specific agreement reached by the Civic Democratic Party and Social Democrats, leading to the establishment of opposition control in the Chamber may well contribute to a precedent of legislative autonomy from executive control in the Czech Republic.

In contrast to these developments in leadership, the committee system of the Czech Parliament has not yet acquired the trappings of stability and specialization that are generally associated with legislative autonomy. Committee slots are distributed proportionally across clubs at the beginning of each Parliament. In addition to the Organizing Committee, the current Chamber includes only eleven standing committees: Budget, Economy, Foreign Affairs, Constitutional-Legal, Defense-Security, Health and Social Welfare, Mandate-Immunity, Agriculture, Petition and Human Rights, Public Administration-Regional Development-Environment, and Science-Education-Culture-Youth-Physical Fitness. The jurisdictions of Czech parliamentary committees are sufficiently broad to preclude as much specialization on policy by their members as in the Sejm.

More importantly, neither committee membership nor the configuration of committees themselves have remained stable across the various Parliaments convened in the 1990s. Deputies serving in successive Parliaments are frequently assigned to different committees, thus undermining the accumulation of personal expertise on policies within committee jurisdiction. The effect was amplified by two waves of committee restructuring and reconfiguration of jurisdictions. The first, following the 1992 election, consisted in part of simply renaming committees still carrying their Communist-era monikers (e.g., "Budget and Control" became "Budget"; "National Economy" became "Economy"), but some committees (e.g., "Church," "Trade and Tourism," "Environment and Urbanism") were dissolved and their jurisdictions absorbed by others. The second wave of committee reforms followed the establishment of a new set of rules of parliamentary procedure in 1995 and entailed clarification of committee jurisdictions as well as the replacement of the old Chamber Presidium as the chamber's governing board with the Organizing Committee. One of the main questions associated with the period of minority government and opposition control of the Chamber in the late 1990s is whether parliamentary committees will be increasingly relied upon—and will be provided the resources to serve—as important arenas for policy deliberation, oversight of the government, and the development of policy expertise.

The fundamental unit of organization in the Czech Parliament is the parliamentary club. Clubs must have 10 members to be awarded representation in Chamber committees, including the Organizing Committee.[6] At the outset of each Parliament throughout the 1990s, the configuration of clubs has reflected that of electoral lists and alliances, but there has been substantial fluidity in the affiliation of deputies with clubs during each Parliament. As the electoral party system consolidates around a smaller number of parties, policy reputations strengthen, and voters increasingly coordinate around viable parties, it is reasonable to expect that inter-electoral club switching among deputies will decline.[7] This pattern is suggested, at the bottom of Table 5, by the decline over the two most recent Parliaments in the rough measure of club membership instability, although the aggregate nature of the measure and the shorter life span of the latter Parliament suggest caution in interpreting numbers.

TABLE 5
Membership in Czech Parliamentary Clubs, 1992–98

Club	After 1992 Election	Before 1996 Election	After 1996 Election	Before 1998 Election	After 1998 Election
ODS	66	72	68	39	63
US	0	0	0	30	19
ODA	14	16	13	12	0
KDU/CSL	15	24	18	18	20
KDS	10	0	0	0	0
SPR/RSC	14	5	18	18	0
Left Bloc	35	23	0	0	0
CSSD	16	22	61	58	74
KSCM	0	10	22	22	24
MSD	14	0	0	0	0
LSU	16	0	0	0	0
Independents	0	7	0	3	0
Others	0	21	0	0	0
Aggregate switches (/2)		61		38	

Source: Klima (1998) Table 5, as well as data provided by the authors.

The fluidity of their membership notwithstanding, Czech parliamentary clubs are cohesive in their voting. On average, over the first eight years after the transition, the mean proportion of club members voting together on legislation on the Chamber floor was over 90%.[8] Clubs determine internally whether particular votes are to be matters of discipline, and club leaders have proven willing to act aggressively to deter independent voting by deputies. Among the innovations in Chamber Rules of Procedure adopted in 1995 was the requirement to record votes upon the first readings of legislation, before bills are referred to committees. Thus the position of each club, and each of its deputies, is recorded before the committees study the legislation, in an effort to deter deputies from straying from club lines in the course of committee deliberations (Klima 1998, 502). Czech party leaders also use control over electoral lists to deter deputies from breaking party ranks. A key distinction here between the Czech Chamber and the Sejm is that the elections to the former are from effectively closed party lists, whereas those to the latter are from lists that are open.[9] As a result, Czech party leaders can fine-tune legislators' reelection prospects by controlling list rankings, even short of denying incumbents renomination altogether. Maverick legislators are demoted on party lists, effectively crippling their reelection chances (Klima 1998, 500). In the most extreme cases, clubs have proven willing to expel deputies immediately for violations of discipline— most notably after the December 1996 vote on the first reading of the 1997 budget, in which two Social Democratic deputies broke ranks, providing Klaus's minority government the slim Chamber majority necessary to pass the budget over Social Democratic opposition. Both deputies were expelled immediately.

To sum up this section, as the electoral party systems in each country shake down and stabilize somewhat, both the Sejm and Czech Chamber appear to be heading toward increasing rates of membership stability and cumulative experience. The leadership structures in each case have been stable during the 1990s and, apart from the brief period of the first Sejm, have proven effective in controlling agendas, preventing instability in collective decisions and during prolonged periods of legislative deadlock. The committee system in the Sejm is more stable, more highly specialized, and more independent in its deliberations than that in the Czech Chamber, which has been marked by assertive and disciplined parliamentary clubs. The notable control by club leaders—in conjunction with executive and national party leaders—over rank-and-file deputies up through 1997 (Klima 1998) suggested the possibility that decision making in the Czech Chamber would become subordinate to partisan or coalitional decisions taken outside the legislature. However, the agreement on minority government and opposition control of Chamber leadership positions struck in 1998 suggests that strong club discipline, if maintained, could actually fortify the ability of the Czech legislature to rival executive control over policy making.

Legislatures and Policy Making

Although both the Polish and Czech Parliaments are bicameral, the lower chambers in each country are clearly dominant. In both systems, newly appointed governments are subject to investiture votes in their respective lower chambers. Cabinet ministers are responsible both individually and collectively to the Sejm (Constitution, Art. 159), and collectively only to the Czech Chamber (Constitution, Art. 68), whereas in neither country does the Senate have any formal control over the formation or survival of cabinets. Similarly, the lower chambers have superior lawmaking authorities. In both countries, any Senate amendments or objections to legislation produced by the lower chamber can be overridden by majority votes in the lower chamber (Czech Constitution, Art. 47; Polish Constitution, Art. 121).[10] The Czech Senate, moreover, does not even consider budget legislation (Art. 42).

Despite its constitutionally privileged position in the law-making process, Parliament is not the origin of most legislation in either country; rather, due to the superiority of informational resources in the executive, most legislation is drafted in the ministries and sent to Parliament for review. This does not distinguish Poland and the Czech Republic from most other regimes—parliamentary, presidential, or hybrid—nor is it necessarily indicative of the relative influence of the branches over policy outcomes (Carey and Shugart 1998; Cox and McCubbins 1993). We do not pretend to offer a comprehensive analysis of legislative-executive power; rather, in this section, we discuss some specific examples of legislative involvement in policy making and oversight in which the structural characteristics of each legislature are manifest.

Sejm Committee Desiderata

Beyond their role in drafting, amending, and deliberating over legislation, Sejm committees exert influence over policy through the use of *desiderata*, which are formal declarations by Sejm committees to members of the executive regarding the execution of law. *Desiderata* are primarily mechanisms of legislative oversight. To the extent that they are honored by ministries, they allow committees to draw on the expertise of sources outside the legislature in assessing policy,[11] to fine-tune policy as it is implemented, and to do so in a manner not dependent on the explicit approval of floor majorities or parliamentary clubs. The stimuli for *desiderata*, and their substantive content, range from broad policy concerns of the entire Sejm, which are pursued by the committee of jurisdiction, to particularistic petitions on behalf of narrow constituent groups. Executive officials whose actions are subject to *desiderata* are obliged to provide formal responses to the committees, although deputies are frequently dissatisfied with the level of detail provided, or with the responsiveness of executive officials to specific recommendations included in *desiderata*. A few examples from the second Sejm will serve as illustrations.

In the category of broad policy issue oversight, the Committee for Social Policy and the Health Committee issued an initial joint *desideratum* requesting information about the implementation of anti-abortion legislation. Both committees found deficient the quality of information provided by the executive regarding how portions of the law concerning education, contraception, and prenatal assistance were to be administered. Mid-level ministry officials sent by the government to an initial hearing were rebuffed by the committees as being of insufficient rank to speak on the government's behalf to the Sejm. After subsequent hearings with senior government representatives, the committees issued *desiderata* criticizing the scarcity of shelters for single mothers provided by the government, the availability of benefits for mothers with small children, and the influence of Catholic Church teachings on the content of public school textbooks' discussion of abortion.

At a slightly more particularistic level, committees occasionally use *desiderata* to avoid the constitutional restriction on amendments to budget legislation originating outside the cabinet (Art. 221). As examples, in 1997, the Committee on Social Policy issued *desiderata* criticizing as insufficient the government's specific budget items appropriating subsidies for veterans' phone service, and those subsidizing the purchases of sanitary materials for families of persons with chronic diseases. In another instance, the board of directors of the State Archives petitioned the Committee on Education, Science, and Technical Progress about insufficient financing and space constraints. After site visits from committee members in both 1996 and 1997, the committee issued *desiderata* requesting increased funding, which were in turn honored by the government. In 1997, the same committee issued a *desideratum* criticizing the quality of the teacher evaluation program in public schools and attributing the problem to insufficient funding to pay salaries to the superintendents who conducted the evaluations.

In short, *desiderata* are the manifestation of the Sejm committee system's improvisational ability to gather information about policy and to apply direct pressure on the executive branch to alter policy implementation in ways that directly matter to constituents, interest groups, and other government institutions. Notably, there is no evidence that these instruments are subject to pressure from the Sejm leadership or from parliamentary clubs. Rather, the *desideratum* process suggests that Sejm committees are becoming points of access to lawmakers for interest groups with specialized policy interests, and that committees provide such lawmakers with bases of policy entrepreneurship from which to challenge the executive.

Coalitional Improvisation on Budgets

The 1999 budget negotiations strikingly illustrate the prominence of the legislature in Czech policy making. The 1998 agreement by the Civic Democratic Party (ODS) to support a Social Democratic minority government did not entail a commitment to support specific executive policy initiatives. Thus, each bill must be negotiated separately, and legislative coalitions do not necessarily coincide with the partners to the original government accord. This separation of legislative from government coalitions represents the disruption of the "fusion of powers" and executive dominance that can characterize cabinet government under parliamentary systems (Bagehot 1966; Cox 1987). The rejection of the government's budget proposal—arguably the most important piece of legislation considered in any given year—and the subsequent construction of a budget coalition distinct from that on which the government was originally founded indicates the centrality of the Czech Chamber as a critical arena of policy making under minority government.

In September 1998, Zeman's Social Democratic government submitted a budget to the Chamber that included the first projected deficit since the transition (RFE/RL 1998a). An ODS spokesman immediately disavowed the bill as fiscally irresponsible, predicting that it had "no real chance of making it through the Parliament" without being substantially amended. Similar criticisms were lodged by the Christian Democratic Union and the Freedom Union (RFE/RL 2(178) 1998). Over the ensuing months, budget negotiations were accompanied by open debates, both among and within parties, on the feasibility of alternative coalitions in various contexts—electoral, executive, and legislative. The discussion was stimulated by elections in November to renew one-third of the Senate. The majority format provided a week between rounds of balloting in which parties whose candidates had been eliminated weighed the question of which candidates to endorse in run-off elections. In apparent contradiction to his party's refusal to consider a governing coalition with the Communists, a Social Democratic leader in the Senate openly called on Social Democratic voters to support Communist candidates in the final electoral round, in districts where Social Democrats had been eliminated (RFE/RL 2(224) 1998). Shortly thereafter, based on electoral gains in the Senate elections by both the Christian Democrats (KDU) and Communists (KSCM), Christian Democratic deputy Cyril Svoboda, who was considered a candidate for chairman of the party, openly reflected on the possibility of an eventual KDU-KSCM governing coalition, and alliance running directly counter to the current Christian Democratic platform (RFE/RL 2(227) 1998).

By the end of the month, attention had turned from electoral and governing alliances back to legislation, but the final Chamber coalition on the budget—Social Democrat, Christian Democrat, and Communist—reflected the various projected partisan coalitions of previous weeks. It is also noteworthy that, despite its objections to Zeman's original proposal calling for a deficit of almost U.S.$900 million, the Christian Democrats eventually signed off on a bill projecting a deficit over U.S.$1 billion. This suggests that a traditional legislative logroll was necessary to assemble sufficient votes in the Chamber. Legislative prominence in budget making may come with a substantial price tag (RFE/RL 2(229) 1998).

The events surrounding the 1999 budget underscore the importance of the Czech Chamber as an arena for policy bargaining. During the initial period of majority government under Klaus, consultation among national party leaders, executive officials, and parliamentary club leaders—all within the governing coalition—produced decisions that were fairly routinely ratified in the Chamber (Klima 1998, 503). In contrast, the current period of minority government is stimulating coalitional flexibility and improvisation, which, in turn, increases the prominence of the legislature.

Concurrent with the budget negotiations in the Czech Republic, severe strains were becoming evident within the majority Solidarity-Freedom Union coalition government in Poland—also over budget issues. In early November 1998, Solidarity deputies, together with deputies from the Peasant Party, Nasze Kolo,[12] and some independents coalesced to support, on the first reading, legislation establishing a series of tax exemptions for families with children. The bill was vehemently opposed by Finance Minister and Freedom Union Chairman Leszek Balcerowicz, who stated that Solidarity voted "against their own government, their own prime minister, and their own budget" (RFE/RL 2(216) 1998), thus implying that the bill reflected not only a rift between the parties, but also between government and Sejm leaders within Solidarity. Solidarity deputies eventually withdrew support for tax exemptions before final passage. An ardent budget hawk, Balcerowicz has been equally and openly critical of Solidarity for its responsiveness to the demands by trade unions for protection from market forces and for agricultural subsidies (RFE/RL 2(228) and 2(233) 1998). These tensions between Solidarity and the Freedom Union reflected the fragility of the Polish governing coalition formed in 1997. It showed that bill-specific Sejm coalitions behind specific pieces of legislation sometimes challenge government policies.

Conclusion

We began this essay by noting the widespread consensus that effective legislatures are critical to the democratic regime performance and that the idea of legislative autonomy from the executive is central to the current literature on comparative legislatures. We examined the sources of legislative information and decisiveness in the post-Communist regimes of Poland and the Czech Republic, following on some of the same themes as Wilson's (1999) study of the early U.S. congresses, but also emphasizing the importance for legislative autonomy of the parliamentary and hybrid structure of these two regimes.

In both countries, initial moments of movement-led anti-partism were followed eventually by party system shakedown and consolidation—after a period of intense party fragmentation and government instability in Poland, and a corresponding period of national dissolution leading to the establishment of the Czech Republic. By the mid–1990s, a limited number of prominent partisan actors was identifiable in each country, both in elections and in legislative organization and bargaining. In neither system are the levels of staff and support resources sufficient that legislators can rely primarily on their own infrastructure for the development of policy initiatives. Yet if the party systems continue to stabilize and average levels of legislative tenure rise, as appears likely, the informational capacities of these Parliaments should increase as well. On this dimension, Poland appears to have progressed further than the Czech Republic, particularly with respect to the stability, specialization, and activism of its committee system. The most noteworthy development in the Czech case, on the other hand, is the development of the legislature as an alternative arena for coalition building on important policies, stimulated by the minority governments of the late 1990s. The award of the Chamber's top leadership post to an opposition leader in 1998 suggested this trend; negotiations surrounding the 1999 budget confirmed that the Chamber is not a rubber stamp for executive proposals, that the ultimate shape of coalitions on particular bills—and, it follows, their content—is indeterminate until resolved by the Chamber.

NOTES

Special thanks to Beth Wilner for her expert research assistance.

1. The Small Constitution implied that the president retained responsibility for defense, security, and foreign policy, although the language here was sufficiently vague that disputes ensued over whether this means the president must approve of those holding cabinet posts in these areas.
2. Six parliamentary clubs and one caucus formed after the election; by the end of its four-year term, this configuration would change to five clubs and six caucuses. Clubs must have a minimum of 15 members and are guaranteed representation in the Sejm Presidium; caucuses must have 3 members and do not have representation in the Presidium.
3. "Elections Watch," *Journal of Democracy* 9:177.
4. In the Sejm III (elected in 1997), those that mirror ministry jurisdictions: Foreign Affairs; National Defense; Justice and Human Rights; Health; Education, Science and Youth; Public Finance; Economics; Transport and Communications; Physical Planning,

Construction and Housing; Agriculture and Rural Development; Local Self-Government and Regional Policy; Environment Protection, Natural Resources and Forestry; Administration and Internal Affairs; State Treasury, Enfranchisement and Privatization; European Integration; Physical Education and Tourism; Culture and Media; Liaison with Poles Abroad; Small and Medium Enterprise; Special Services; Competition and Consumer Protection; State Control (created in December 1998). Those that do not are the committees on: Deputies Ethics; Rules and Deputies' Affairs; Family Affairs; Social Policy; Constitutional Accountability; and National Minorities.

5. For example, in July 1998, an AWS deputy was expelled for refusing to vote with the club on a critical bill to reform the administrative structure of regional governments.

6. It is noteworthy, however, that the distribution of committee seats across clubs is not adjusted throughout the term should various clubs lose or gain members, or new clubs form (Rules of Procedure, Art. 77).

7. In 1995, the Rules of Procedure of the Chamber were changed, increasing from five to ten the number of deputies required to form a club, in an explicit effort to deter the "political terrorism" of club switching and fragmentation.

8. This rough indicator, of course, does not distinguish among parties, nor does it weight votes according to whether they were divisive across parties or matters of consensus. Future work will examine patterns of floor voting in the Czech Republic and Poland in more detail, comparing levels of voting unity, not only among different parties and coalitions within each Parliament, but also cross-nationally, along the lines suggested in Carey (1999).

9. Czech voters can cast preference votes for specific candidates, but in order to reorder the ranking established by the party, thresholds of 10% of all the party's voters nationwide, then of 10% of its voters in a district, must reorder lists in a compatible manner. The effect has been to render the preference vote moot (Klima 1998, 505). In Poland, conversely, the allocation of seats among each list's candidates is determined entirely by preference votes. The difference between these systems implies that Polish deputies face a stronger imperative than their Czech counterparts to cultivate personal reputations among voters, distinct from the collective reputations of their parties (Carey and Shugart 1995).

10. In Poland, of course, the president is a distinct, and constitutionally powerful, legislative actor, whose veto can only be overridden by a 3/5 majority in the Sejm.

11. These are "fire alarms" (c.f. McCubbins and Schwartz 1984), who are better informed about the connection between legislative content and effects than legislators themselves are likely to be, perhaps because of firsthand experience with how the law is already being administered.

12. Christian Party (ZChN), whose members were initially elected as a part of the AWS list, then decided not to remain members of the parliamentary club.

REFERENCES

Ames, Barry. 1994. "Electoral Strategy under Open-List Proportional Representation." *American Journal of Political Science* 39:406–33.
Bagehot, Walter. 1966. *The English Constitution.* Ithaca, NY: Cornell University Press.

Carey, John M. 1998. "Parties, Coalitions and the Chilean Congress in the 1990s." Unpublished paper.
Carey, John M. 1999. "Measuring Party and Coalition Unity in Multiparty Legislatures." Washington University Department of Political Science Working Paper.
Carey, John M., and Matthew S. Shugart. 1995. "Incentives to Cultivate a Personal Vote: A Rank Ordering of Electoral Systems." *Electoral Studies* 14:417–39.
Carey, John, and Matthew S. Shugart, eds. 1998. *Executive Decree Authority*. New York: Cambridge University Press.
Cox, Gary W. 1987. *The Efficient Secret*. New York: Cambridge University Press.
Cox, Gary W., and Mathew D. McCubbins. 1993. *Legislative Leviathan: Party Government in the House*. Berkeley: University of California Press.
Figuereido, Argenlina Cheibub, and Fernando Limongi. 1997. "Presidential Power, Legislative Organization, and Party Behavior in the Legislature." Centro Brasileiro de Análise e Planejamento working paper.
Geddes, Barbara, and Artur Ribeiro Neto. 1992. "Institutional Sources of Corruption in Brazil." *Third World Quarterly* 13:641–61.
Haspel, Moshe, Thomas F. Remington, and Steven S. Smith. 1998. "Electoral Institutions and Party Cohesion in the Russian Duma." *Journal of Politics* 60:417–39.
Huber, John. 1996. "The Vote of Confidence in Parliamentary Democracies." *American Political Science Review* 90:269–82.
Jones, Mark. 1997. "Federalism and Discipline in the Argentine Congress." Presented at the Conference on Latin American Legislatures. Centro de Investigaciones y Docencia Económica, Mexico City.
Klima, Michal. 1998. "Consolidation and Stabilization of the Party System in the Czech Republic." *Political Studies* 46:492–510.
Laasko, Markku, and Rein Taagepera. 1979. "Effective Number of Parties: A Measure with Application to West Europe." *Comparative Political Studies* 12:3–27.
Laver, Michael, and Kenneth Shepsle. 1996. *Making and Breaking Governments: Cabinets and Legislatures in Parliamentary Democracies*. New York: Cambridge University Press.
Laver, Michael. 1999. "Divided Parties, Divided Government." *Legislative Studies Quarterly* 24:5–29.
Lijphart, Arend. 1984. *Democracies: Patterns of Majoritarian and Consensus Government in Twenty-One Countries*. New Haven, CT: Yale University Press.
Lijphart, Arend. 1994. *Electoral Systems and Party Systems*. New York: Oxford University Press.
Mainwaring, Scott, and Aníbal Pérez Liñán. 1997. "Party Discipline in the Brazilian Constitutional Congress." *Legislative Studies Quarterly* 22:453–83.
Mainwaring, Scott, and Timothy R. Scully. 1995. "Party Systems in Latin America." In *Building Democratic Institutions*, ed. Scott Mainwaring and Timothy R. Scully. Stanford, CA: Stanford University Press.
McCubbins, Mathew, and Thomas Schwartz. 1984. "Congressional Oversight Overlooked: Police Patrols Versus Fire Alarms." *American Journal of Political Science* 28:165–79.
Miller, David. 1993. "Deliberative Democracy and Social Choice." In *Prospects for Democracy*, ed. David Held. Stanford: Stanford University Press.

Morgenstern, Scott. 1999. "U.S. Models and Latin American Legislatures." In *Legislatures in Latin America*, ed. Scott Morgenstern and Benito Nacif. Unpublished.

Nacif, Benito. 1997. "The System of Governance in the Mexican Chamber of Deputies: Changing Partisan Balance and Persistent Patterns of Behavior." Presented at the Conference on Latin American Legislatures. Centro de Investicagiones y Docencia Económica, Mexico City.

Norton, Philip. 1994. "Representation of Interests: The Case of the British House of Commons." In *Parliaments in the Modern World: Changing Institutions*, ed. Samuel C. Patterson and Gary W. Copeland. Ann Arbor: University of Michigan Press.

Olson, David M. 1998. "Party Formation and Party System Consolidation in the New Democracies of Central Europe." *Political Studies* 46:432–64.

Polsby, Nelson. 1968. "The Institutionalization of the U.S. House of Representatives." *American Political Science Review* 62:144–68.

Remington, Thomas F., and Steven S. Smith. 1995. "The Development of Parliamentary Parties in Russia." *Legislative Studies Quarterly* 20:457–89.

RFE/RL. 1998a. Radio Free Europe/Radio Liberty. *Newsline* Vol. 2, No. 177, Part II, September 14.

RFE/RL. 1998b. *Newsline* Vol. 2, No. 178, Part II, September 15.

RFE/RL. 1998c. *Newsline* Vol. 2, No. 216, Part II, November 9.

RFE/RL. 1998d. *Newsline* Vol. 2, No. 224, Part II, November 19.

RFE/RL. 1998e. *Newsline* Vol. 2, No. 227, Part II, November 24.

RFE/RL. 1998f. *Newsline* Vol. 2, No. 228, Part II, November 25.

RFE/RL. 1998g. *Newsline* Vol. 2, No. 229, Part II, November 30.

RFE/RL. 1998h. *Newsline* Vol. 2, No. 233, Part II, December 4.

Schüttemeyer, Suzanne S. 1994. "Hierarchy and Efficiency in the Bundestag: The German Answer for Institutionalizing Parliament." In *Parliaments in the Modern World: Changing Institutions*, ed. Samuel C. Patterson and Gary W. Copeland. Ann Arbor: University of Michigan Press.

Shugart, Matthew S. 1995. "The Electoral Cycle and Institutional Sources of Divided Government in Presidential Systems." *American Political Science Review* 89:327–43.

Shugart, Matthew Soberg, and John M. Carey. 1992. *Presidents and Assemblies: Constitutional Design and Electoral Dynamics*. New York: Cambridge University Press.

Strøm, Kaare. 1990. *Minority Government and Majority Rule*. New York: Cambridge University Press.

Wilson, Rick K. 1999. "Transitional Governance in the United States: Lessons from the First Federal Congress." *Legislative Studies Quarterly* 24: 543–68.

OTHER SOURCES

Barta, Jan. 1993. *Legal Context of the Independence of the Czech Republic*. Prague: Pravnik.

Czech Bulletin on Human Rights. 1996. March 1. Prague: IDEU.

Formanek, Frantisek. 1990. *Candidate of Civic Forum*. Prague: KCOF.

Formanek, Frantisek. 1992. *Political Parties in 1992 Federal Elections*. Prague: IDEU.
Jiraskova, Vera. 1997. *Constitutional Reforms*. Prague: Legal Horizon.
Klimek, Antonin. 1997. *The Beginning of Parliamentary Activity in Czechoslovakia*. Prague: PZ.
Klokocka, Vaclav. 1996. *Constitutional Systems of European States*. Prague: Linde, Inc.
Mikule, Vladimir, and Vladimir Sladecek. 1994. *Constitutional Justice and Human Rights*. Prague: Codex.
Parliamentary Bulletin (Parlamentni zpravodaj). 1993–98. Prague: IDEU.
Pavlicek, Vaclav, and Jiri Hrebejk. 1998. *The Constitution and the Constitutional Order of the Czech Republic*. Prague: Linde, Inc.
Samalik, Frantisek. 1991. *Legal State contra Stalinism*. Prague: Svoboda.

Part 7
Conclusions

Assessing Comparative Legislative Research

Kenneth A. Shepsle

At the conclusion of a volume like the present one, it is appropriate to sit back and take stock of the field. The authors of these fine essays, however, are hardly a representative sample of legislative scholars, so generalizations about the field based on their work should be offered with caution. Yet, since they are among the leaders in comparative legislative studies, their collective wisdom may be taken as a reliable indicator of the significant directions taken in this field in recent years, and as a harbinger of things to come.

In underscoring and elaborating upon some of this wisdom, I will not take up each essay seriatim in this brief essay, but instead will address some of the (mainly methodological) issues raised in many of them (and in the discussions surrounding them at the 1998 Shambaugh conference at the University of Iowa where they were first presented). In doing so I echo some of the sentiments expressed in another afterword (Fiorina 1995), one commissioned by Barry Weingast and me for an earlier collection of essays (Shepsle and Weingast 1995b). I think it is significant that the issues that animated that volume—a volume focusing on formal theories of *congressional* institutions—are also front and center in the present volume on comparative legislative studies. The two subfields of congressional studies and comparative legislative studies, once so separate and insulated from one another, are converging. What once was an obstacle to generalization and cross-fertilization—the apparent uniqueness of the U.S. Congress among the world's legislative bodies—is now no longer seen as so disabling. In fact, it is appropriate to begin my concluding remarks with the issue of American exceptionalism. In my view, for too many years the work of congressional scholars was *improperly* portrayed as irrelevant to the comparative study of legislatures by appeal to this reason.

1. American Exceptionalism

A few years ago, just after I had moved my own research activity from writing mainly about the U.S. Congress to studying parliamentary institutions, I teased an eminent congressional scholar, David Rohde, about the parochialism of American politics. "American politics," I said contemptuously of my recently deserted field, "is nothing more than the largest area-studies program in political science." He responded in defense (but not at all defensively): "The field of American politics is not an area-studies program; it is a *methodology*." He went on persuasively to describe how, despite the exceptionalism of its history and institutional practices, American politics has served the wider political science community by forging scientific tools and providing a laboratory in which they are tested, perfected, and prepared for export.

Over the past three-quarters of a century, innovations have ranged from empirical tools, including quantitative measurement, scaling and other data techniques, statistical inference, simulation, experimental approaches, survey research, and elite interviewing, to theoretical developments like systems theory, exchange theory, and rational choice theory. Moreover, among students of American politics more generally, the legislative scholar, I believe, was nearly always one of the very first to take up new empirical procedures, to be self-consciously theoretical in his or her work, and to be the most open to these new innovations and least tied to a methodological or theoretical status quo. Some may find this too self-congratulatory and rosy a picture (though Fiorina's essay cited above shares my view), but it is not much of a distortion to claim that students of American politics have been the principal (though not exclusive) initiators and diffusers of modern scientific tools and approaches to the broader political science profession, and congressional and state legislative scholars have been in the vanguard of this movement.[1]

Needless to say, America's exceptionalism often means that details of operationalization and implementation require adjustment before tools can be exported (to other fields and to other places). These tools and approaches are not off-the-shelf, garden-variety widgets, but more like electrical plugs—implements serving the same purposes in principle everywhere, but in practice differing in important details from place to place (some two-pronged, others three-pronged; some with a round prong, others a flat one). The necessary adaptations almost always require imagination, are often difficult and far from straightforward, and have only fairly recently been done successfully.

Consider some illustrations. Theories of policy-making based on the premise of delegation to decentralized agents received their initial inspiration from the example of jurisdictional authority delegated from the full chamber to committees in the (atypical) committee system of the U.S. Congress (see, e.g., Kiewiet and McCubbins 1991). Once it was realized that the principle of delegation was applicable to many legislative settings, then despite the fact that it was forged in the exceptional American setting, it could nevertheless be widely disseminated, applied, say, to parliamentary cabinets and ministries (Laver and Shepsle 1996).

Likewise, the proposal and veto powers of committees in the American legislative context are but special instances of a more general agenda power common to collegial bodies everywhere. The technology used to study the exercise of sequenced power in the American legislative setting, tools that include the analysis of winsets, the methodology of backward induction and subgame perfection, and other game-theoretic techniques, could be applied to great advantage in parliamentary settings (as is evident in Baron 1998, Diermeier 1995, Huber 1996, Tsebelis 1995, and the fine essays by Laver and Rasch in this collection).

Once it is recalled, to take a final example, that America was the "first new nation" (Lipset 1967) with an Articles-of-Confederation legislature that failed to solve problems of coordination, collective action, and collective choice, requiring it to be reengineered under the Constitution of 1787 (Wilson, this volume), one can begin to theorize—comparably and comparatively—about newly designed legislative institutions in the emerging democracies of the contemporary world (as is done in Carey, Formanek, and Karpowicz, this volume).

In short, the conclusion that American exceptionalism is grounds for rejecting rational choice theory, or experimental methods, or quantitative modeling, or variants of the "new institutionalism" as a basis for understanding legislative practices and behavior elsewhere is refuted by much recent work on legislatures outside the United States, and notably by the essays in this volume. It should not dissuade the student of another legislature, or of comparative legislatures, or of legislative-like bodies in the private sector or the international arena, from adapting theories and methods that happened to have had their origins in the study of an exceptional legislature.

2. Models

It is striking, as one reads through the essays in this collection, how pervasive is the commitment to modeling and, relatively speaking, how diminished are the traditions of thick description and descriptive empiricism. Legislative studies, both congressional and comparative, today reflect an allegiance to a progressively more demanding set of scientific criteria than in the past. Let me be clear that I do not mean that *all* legislative scholarship is formal political theory of the Teutonic axiom-theorem-proof variety (though some of it is). I do mean, and the essays in this volume amply demonstrate, that it is no longer atypical nowadays for a piece of legislative research to begin explicitly with premises—colors nailed to the mast—and then to trace their implications—sometimes formally, other times more casually—with an eye to bringing contemporary data or historical cases to bear on them. The Cox, Laver, and Rasch essays in this volume are excellent illustrations of the ways in which relatively simple theoretical premises contain a mother lode of empirically testable implications. They also exemplify the methodological attitude that *hypotheses should be theory-driven,* not merely interesting speculations. (As provocative as the latter may be, it is theory-driven hypotheses that cumulate.) Even less formal approaches borrow heavily from the language of models, employing principal-agent, electoral-connection, or spatial metaphors, for example (see Kato's contribution in this volume on party-bureaucracy relations in Japan as an illustration).

It is also apparent that rationality is the principal modeling flavor of choice at present. Kiewiet et al. have already noted in their introductory essay that the rationality assumption is a garment that is gracefully and unself-consciously worn by legislative scholars. (In an earlier era, however, the same might have been said about sociological assumptions—where legislators were characterized more in terms of attitudes and roles than rationality-based categories like preferences and beliefs.) It is utterly uncontroversial today to assume that legislators are naturally purposeful, and only somewhat more controversial to claim they are calculators of benefits and costs, indeed maximizers of utility on every margin (though Smith qualifies and clarifies this in his essay, noting that the goals are multiple and not always Mayhewian, a point to which I return below). In a second sense the rationality hypothesis is favored in this literature because legislative institutions are easily thought of as mechanisms whose operating characteristics are understandable—either intuitively by politicians or after they have acquired some experience in the institution. Consequently, these procedures, practices, and arrangements can be seized upon by actors for instrumental purposes. Finally, rationality fits with a modern attitude toward institutional change: while not always working out as purposeful agents intend, institutional practices are *designed* and *selected,* at least in part, by decisive coalitions of institutional actors with particular ends in mind. (For a macrohistorical, almost mystical view of institutional change standing in stark contrast to rationality-based thinking—where coral reefs serve as a metaphor for institutional practices and changes in them—see Sait 1938.)

Missing, or at least considerably less frequently in evidence, are thickly descriptive intellectual *tours d'horizon.* Park's essay (this volume) on the history of the Korean assembly comes closest. Wilson's piece on the lessons of the early Federal Congresses in the United States and Carey et al.'s on the emergence of revitalized legislatures in the Czech Republic and Poland read more like analytical narratives in the spirit of Bates et al. (1998). These reflect the theory-driven requirements increasingly common in comparative legislative scholarship. (One may accept this as progress, while still hoping that it does not discourage entirely those historical-institutional essays, e.g., Cooper 1970, that provide rich contextual materials.) Also of diminishing frequency are those quantitative descriptive pieces and empirical hypothesis-testing exercises that lack theoretical scaffolding with which to organize inquiry. It is my sense that each of these trends is more sharply evident in the congressional and American state legislative context than in comparative legislative studies, but convergence is nevertheless apparent.

The principal reason for the success of modeling in the legislative field, it should be noted, is that it *works* much of the time. It enhances clear thinking (Fiorina 1974 has always set the standard in my mind). It identifies inconsistencies and anomalies (Krehbiel 1999 is a controversial yet impressive example). It encourages cumulativeness (Laver and Schofield 1990 and Cox and McCubbins 1993 display this in the literature on parliamentary coalitions and positive theories of Congress, respectively). It directs the acquisition of new data sets and the reanalysis of existing ones (Poole and Rosenthal 1997). From time to time, models even enlighten, generating altogether original insights and explanations (good examples, of which there are many, include Cox 1999, Krehbiel 1998, and Laver, this volume). Modeling, in short, has come into prominence in legislative scholarship because it often enables or delivers results not easily available to ordinary-language approaches.

3. Modeling Issues

With modeling a growing presence in legislative studies, scholars struggle with a number of modeling issues, several of which have preoccupied authors in the present volume.

Endogeneity. Smith, in his informative and insightful essay on positive theories of legislative organization, wonders how far "upstream" one needs to back things up in a model. In modeling a legislative decision, for example, is it enough to specify legislator preferences, that is, take them as exogenous, or must we rationalize them by modeling the process by which legislators are (s)elected. That is, must we *endogenize* preferences? If the latter, is modeling the (s)election process enough or must we back things up even further to explain the essence of (s)elector preferences—deriving them, for example, from a theory of wealth maximization, the psychology of partisan attachments, or a sociocultural basis? It is always a judgment call when it comes to determining how to bound one's inquiry. If one takes too many things for granted, then the exercise in which he or she engages becomes trivial; if, on the other hand, too few things are taken for granted, the task confronting the scholar becomes impossibly general. In the first case too many interesting things are taken as fixed and outside the boundaries of inquiry; in the second, too many are taken as "in play" and inside the boundaries.

In our model of government formation in parliamentary democracies (Laver and Shepsle 1996), for example, Laver and I chose to take the spatial policy position and parliamentary weight of each party as exogenous—as having been determined elsewhere (party conferences and electoral arena, respectively). We were interested in identifying how a distribution of party weights and positions, *once determined,* map into a government (a distribution of cabinet portfolios). Given our focus on this institutional arena, we were less concerned with how each party arrived at its manifesto position, how voters decided, and hence how the weights and spatial positions of parliamentary actors were determined. Our model was confined to the government formation process; we did not, in Smith's words, back up the analysis all the way to the electoral process.

Others have sought to model the "big game"—the entire sequence of party positioning, election, and then government formation. They have been more ambitious in the sense that they sought to endogenize more of the sequence. Austen-Smith and Banks (1988, 1990), for example, provide a sequential, game-theoretic analysis of this problem, but restrict their analysis to a one-dimensional policy space. Baron (1998) moved the analysis to a multidimensional space, but restricted it to but three parties. This suggests that it is indeed possible to endogenize factors previously treated as exogenous. Sometimes this can be done at no cost to generality; at other times it may be necessary to introduce qualifications or restrictions (e.g., three parties, unidimensionality). The real lesson here is that it is important to get started, produce some results, and only then interrogate one's model further to see whether features taken as fixed and exogenous can be brought into the model's domain.

Observational equivalence. The editors, in their introductory essay, express concern about the unpleasant fact that competing theories often share some (many?) common implications. Consequently, these implications cannot be used to discriminate among the theories that share them in common. While this is certainly true, I don't see it as a basis for concern. If Theory A implies X, and Theory B implies X, then, in accounting for regularity X, it really doesn't matter whether we attribute it to A or B. Put differently, it only matters to those who compulsively believe we need to come to a definitive conclusion about attribution. I am not a member of this tribe. A gunfight among theories is best staged in empirical territories where their implications and predictions differ.

Where theories differ, there is in principle the basis for a decisive test. But decisive in what sense? I suspect that we never really *reject* theories so much as we learn where they do and do not provide much explanatory leverage. Fiorina (1995), for example, observed that, in the controversy between proponents of distributive and informational rationales of legislative organization and practice, each appealed to data drawn from different historical eras. Distributive theories seemed to work in the "textbook Congress" era (Shepsle 1989), whereas informational rationales did its heavy lifting in the postreform era. It is likely in my view that as we evolve and extend our theories to a broader cross-section of legislatures, then what had been treated as competing explanations will be transformed into a synthesis of formerly opposing elements. In this respect I find it likely that our future theories of congressional organization, and, a fortiori, of the vast variety of parliamentary institutions, will contain elements drawn from the imperatives of distributive politics, the requirements for information, the inevitability of partisan forces, and the desirability of delegation. Success here will constitute finding ways for pork barrel politics, informational rationales, legislative leviathans, and principal-agent relationships to reside within the same framework (see Shepsle and Weingast 1995a and Gilligan and Krehbiel 1995 for opposing views on this).

Institutions as equilibria. As a last modeling issue, let me comment briefly on the equilibrium orientation of many of the models developed or described in the essays of this volume (see especially Hibbing, Laver, Smith, Cox, Rasch, and Wilson). In a sense there is a growing recognition that many elements of legislative life are best conceived of as hanging together, rather than as part of a causal chain. Perturbations to one or more of these elements ripple through the entire arrangement. That is, the elements are portrayed as constituting an equilibrium relationship, and perturbation is treated via comparative statics analysis. If one were to measure the impact of a change in some relevant parameter on some other variable, it would be necessary to measure not only the direct effect of the one on the other (as a causal framework would require) but the indirect effects of the changed parameter on third variables which in turn had effects on the variable in question. Symbolically, if x, y, and z stand in an equilibrium relationship, and some shock affects x, then this change in x will not only change y directly, it will also change z, which in turn will affect y (and possibly even x). An increase in incumbent resources for electoral purposes, for example, may well increase an incumbent's probability of reelection. This may directly increase the probability that a particular incumbent will survive long enough to become the chair of his or her committee. But the perturbation will also increase the probability of reelection for *other* incumbent committee members (in particular, those with higher seniority than the incumbent in question), thereby diminishing his or her prospects of becoming chair. In the new equilibrium after the shock, the prospects for the incumbent in question may hardly be improved at all. An appropriate equilibrium analysis will want to take account of both direct and indirect effects.

An equilibrium may be robust or not. Hibbing (this volume), for example, gives Polsby's (1968) more sociological conception of institutionalization an equilibrium flavor by suggesting that, in terms of individual careers, an institutional equilibrium is robust when the comings and goings of particular legislators don't have much impact on institutional life, that is, when membership turnover is inconsequential. Thus, in contrast to Polsby, Hibbing claims that the measure of robustness is not *declining* membership turnover but its *inconsequentialness* for the life of the institution.

An equilibrium may be instantaneous or emergent. For example, there is an argument, elaborated by Cox (1997) and dating back to Duverger (1954), that derives a very close connection between the electoral and legislative party systems of a political order. But it should not be anticipated, by students of the newly emerging democracies of Eastern Europe, for instance, that this connection will become immediately apparent. It may take some time for the dust to settle—for intraparty discipline to emerge and interparty deals to be cooked among "strategic elites." To illustrate, I once constructed a time-series of the number of political parties in the West German Bundestag from 1949 until the unification with East Germany. There were somewhere on the order of fifteen parties in the early years, and it took three elections before the number stabilized at about four. It took time for fusions, takeovers, and mergers among parties to be accomplished; but once done, the number of parties remained quite stable.

An equilibrium may persist or self-destruct (or first one and then the other). This may, at first, seem like a peculiar way to talk about an equilibrium. And this is because our formal theories have not grappled successfully with phenomena involving the disruption of one equilibrium and the selection of another. To illustrate what I have in mind, consider that twice in American political history relatively stable arrangements have disintegrated. Jillson and Wilson (1994) describe one—the period of the Articles—which produced equilibrium in the form of gridlock (no one said an equilibrium has to be good!), then self-destruction, and finally the emergence of a new constitutional order. The second, described by Riker (1982, chap. 9), was the persistence of the Jeffersonian-Jacksonian coalition for much of the first four decades of the nineteenth century, a period that ended in drift and eventually civil war. As these examples show, there may be (long) periods of partisan or institutional invariance, interrupted by an event or a shock that undermines the equilibrium. Equilibria are not forever. A set of elements that hang together may be vulnerable to a destabilizing event that undermines the connection.

What I am really saying here is that I think it constitutes a mark of scientific progress in the legislative field that an empirical regularity is now identified as an equilibrium pattern about which it is asked: "What else must be true of a world in which this empirical regularity holds?" Equilibrium analysis, in this way, becomes a discovery tool as well as a form of explanation.

4. Concluding Thoughts

Comparative legislative studies will in the coming years proceed pretty much in the ways they always have. Scholars will continue to follow their curiosity; the world of phenomena will continue to present us with events, regularities, and anomalies in need of account; intellectual entrepreneurs and arbitrageurs will continue to float novel applications and interpretations. Rather than speculate about how these things will play out—an activity fraught with risk (not to speak of presumption)—let me conclude by drawing three concepts from recent research that distinguish themselves in my mind as requiring further attention and elaboration for future progress in the field.

Multiple goals. Smith (this volume) and others (Fenno 1973; Sinclair 1995; Maltzman and Smith 1995; Parker 1996; Maltzman 1997) have commented on the strain sometimes evident in congressional theories that rely upon legislators motivated exclusively by the electoral connection. Mayhew (1974), following Downs (1957), moved theorizing ahead light-years by assuming just this. Nevertheless, most scholars are prepared to concede that legislative maximizing behavior entails trade-offs on many margins and among competing objectives—not every legislator in all circumstances is prepared to sell his or her mother down the river for a handful of votes.

The crudest statements of the Mayhewian premise are even more tenuous as we move beyond the American scene. An electoral system is a selection mechanism, not only in the obvious sense that it determines the winners, but also in the sense that it *selects for* certain kinds of characteristics and therefore *encourages* certain types of candidacies. Indeed, some (Parker 1996) would argue that there is a perverse quality to the American selection system—it selects for rent-seeking types. In any event, as one moves away from first-past-the-post (FPP), single-member-district (SMD), weak-party (WP) electoral arrangements, the system that seems most likely to select ruggedly individualistic, Mayhewian types, a much greater dispersion of types emerges. Certainly we find politicians in non—FPP/SMD/WP legislatures with electoral ambitions, but we find some different types as well—those with partisan ambitions, ministerial ambitions, extragovernmental (corrupt) ambitions, even ideological ambitions. In some ("amateur") legislatures we find legislators with little ambition at all (except to return home). Thus, as we bring the nature of the selection mechanism (read: electoral system) and type of legislature into the discussion, it becomes increasingly less tenable for a single-minded electoral ambition to be taken as typical. Legislators are still mostly ambitious, but the electoral and legislative systems play a decisive role in channeling that ambition and encouraging multiple types.

One way forward on the matter of multiple goals is to endogenize legislator types as determined by the electoral arrangements in place, rather than taking them exogenously as Mayhewian. This is a genuinely comparative project that requires thinking of the distribution of types in a legislature—and hence the multiplicity of goals pursued in Smith's sense—as being bound up in the variation in electoral rules. Mayhew (1974) must be wedded to Cox (1997).

Strategic elites. I have little in particular to say about Cox's (1999) utilization of the strategic-elites concept in his recent essay on electoral mobilization, except to encourage its broad adoption. His application is particularly intriguing because he takes on the so-called "paradox that ate rational choice" (Fiorina 1990). More generally, though, Cox's focus on strategic elites complements Smith's on multiple goals. It invites hard thinking about the politician's institutional world and the various kinds of things he or she instrumentally pursues there. Moreover, as Cox makes evident, this focus—the political supply side, so to speak—lends itself more naturally to the machinery of rational choice theory than does the more amorphous and fluid world of mass political behavior.

Parties. In congressional studies, parties are definitely back in fashion. Most of the 1990s has witnessed a simmering debate on the role of party in the American Congress. Rohde (1991) and Cox and McCubbins (1993) make powerful cases for the ebbs and flows of party influence over the course of congressional history. Krehbiel (1993, 1999), on the other hand, challenges these interpretations. Whether correct or not, these challenges have provided a number of researchers with grounds to look hard at the evidence and to think hard about their theories. Can one find residues of party separate and apart from those of interest and preference?

Europeans, I suspect, find all this amusing. It would be hard for them to imagine a parliamentary world without parties. This attitude, however, is slightly smug, for Krehbiel's challenges require answers of them as well. Laver (this volume) has charted an interesting and promising direction—namely, to dispatch with the assumption of parties as *unitary actors*. By "deconstructing parties" and "lifting the lid" on the internal life of a party, Laver proposes a means by which to reinterpret the very foundations of parliamentary government, namely, the relationship between executive and legislature. In doing so he provides a vantage point from which to take up issues of relevance to the Krehbiel critique. In particular, he puts the magnifying glass on the stresses and strains on backbenchers going along with the deals cut by their leaders, as well as on the nature of partisan loyalty, defection, and punishment. If party is to have content and meaning apart from preference and interest, it ought to be found in these organizational and institutional properties.

In sum, there has for some time been an active conversation in place among congressional scholars—a conversation between formal theorists and empiricists, game theorists and multidimensional scalers, historians and elite interviewers, scientists and soakers and pokers. This conversation has now engaged the broader community of comparative legislative scholars. The comparative enterprise will benefit; so will the conversation.

NOTE

The author was a participant of the Shambaugh Conference on Comparative Legislative Research, University of Iowa, April 1998, where the essays in this volume were originally presented. I was asked by the conference organizers, who are also the editors of this volume, to sit in the back of the room, to keep a running tally of interesting issues, and ultimately to organize them into a concluding essay. The remarks presented here are the result of this exercise, as well as of a reading of revised versions of each article and some reflection a year and a half after the conference. The editors provided superb advice on an earlier draft which is reflected in this final version.

1. The flow of ideas has certainly not been in one direction only, especially if one takes a longer view. Although Americanists in recent years can claim much credit for exporting ideas about legislatures, we have been considerable importers as well—some would say *net* importers. The eighteenth- and nineteenth-century classics by Borda, Condorcet, and Bagehot (the latter acknowledged by Woodrow Wilson among others), along with twentieth-century contributions ranging from James Bryce to Harold Laski to Duncan Black to Maurice Duverger, are obvious examples.

REFERENCES

Austen-Smith, David, and Jeffrey Banks. 1988. "Elections, Coalitions, and Legislative Outcomes." *American Political Science Review* 82:405–22.
Austen-Smith, David, and Jeffrey Banks. 1990. "Stable Governments and the Allocation of Policy Portfolios." *American Political Science Review* 84:891–906.
Baron, David. 1998. "Comparative Dynamics of Parliamentary Governments." *American Political Science Review* 92:593–610.
Bates, Robert, Avner Greif, Margaret Levi, Jean-Laurent Rosenthal, and Barry Weingast. 1998. *Analytical Narratives.* Princeton, NJ: Princeton University Press.
Cooper, Joseph. 1970. *The Origins of the Standing Committees and the Development of the Modern House.* Houston: Rice University Studies.
Cox, Gary. 1997. *Making Votes Count.* New York: Cambridge University Press.
Cox, Gary. 1999. "Electoral Rules and the Calculus of Mobilization." *Legislative Studies Quarterly* 24:387–419.
Cox, Gary, and Mathew McCubbins. 1993. *Legislative Leviathan: Party Government in the House.* Berkeley: University of California Press.
Diermeier, Daniel. 1995. "Commitment, Deference, and Legislative Institutions." *American Political Science Review* 89:344–55.
Downs, Anthony. 1957. *An Economic Theory of Democracy.* New York: Harper and Row.
Duverger, Maurice. 1954. *Political Parties.* London: Methuen.
Fenno, Richard. 1973. *Congressmen in Committees.* Boston: Little, Brown.
Fiorina, Morris. 1974. *Representatives, Roll Calls, and Constituencies.* Boston: D.C. Heath.
Fiorina, Morris. 1990. "Information and Rationality in Elections." In *Information and Democratic Process,* ed. John A. Ferejohn and James H. Kuklinski. Urbana: University of Illinois Press.
Fiorina, Morris. 1995. "Afterword (But Undoubtedly Not the Last Word)." In *Positive Theories of Congressional Institutions,* ed. Kenneth Shepsle and Barry Weingast. Ann Arbor: University of Michigan Press.
Gilligan, Thomas W., and Keith Krehbiel. 1995. "The Gains from Exchange Hypothesis of Legislative Organization." In *Positive Theories of Congressional Institutions,* ed. Kenneth Shepsle and Barry Weingast. Ann Arbor: University of Michigan Press.

Huber, John. 1996. *Rationalizing Parliament.* New York: Cambridge University Press.
Jillson, Calvin, and Rick K. Wilson, 1994. *Congressional Dynamics: Structure, Coordination, and Choice in the First American Congress, 1774–1789.* Stanford: Stanford University Press.
Kiewiet, D. Roderick, and Mathew McCubbins. 1991. *The Logic of Delegation: Congressional Parties and the Appropriations Process.* Chicago: University of Chicago Press.
Krehbiel, Keith. 1993. "Where's the Party?" *British Journal of Political Science* 23:235–66.
Krehbiel, Keith. 1998. *Pivotal Politics.* Ann Arbor: University of Michigan Press.
Krehbiel, Keith. 1999. "Paradoxes of Parties in Congress." *Legislative Studies Quarterly* 24:31–64.
Laver, Michael, and Norman Schofield. 1990. *Multiparty Government.* New York: Oxford University Press.
Laver, Michael, and Kenneth A. Shepsle. 1996. *Making and Breaking Governments: Cabinets and Legislatures in Parliamentary Democracies.* New York: Cambridge University Press.
Lipset, Seymour Martin. 1967. *The First New Nation.* Garden City: Doubleday-Anchor.
Maltzman, Forrest. 1997. *Competing Principals.* Ann Arbor: University of Michigan Press.
Maltzman, Forrest, and Steven S. Smith. 1995. "Principals, Goals, Dimensionality, and Congressional Committees." In *Positive Theories of Congressional Institutions,* ed. Kenneth Shepsle and Barry Weingast. Ann Arbor: University of Michigan Press.
Mayhew, David. 1974. *Congress: The Electoral Connection.* New Haven: Yale University Press.
Parker, Glenn R. 1996. *Congress and the Rent-Seeking Society.* Ann Arbor: University of Michigan Press.
Polsby, Nelson. 1968. "The Institutionalization of the U.S. House of Representatives." *American Political Science Review* 62:144–68.
Poole, Keith, and Howard Rosenthal. 1997. *Congress: A Political-Economic History of Roll Call Voting.* New York: Oxford University Press.
Riker, William H. 1982. *Liberalism Against Populism.* San Francisco: Freeman.
Rohde, David. 1991. *Parties and Leaders in the Postreform House.* Chicago: University of Chicago Press.
Sait, Edward McChesney. 1938. *Political Institutions: A Preface.* New York: Appleton-Century-Crofts.
Shepsle, Kenneth. 1989. "The Changing Textbook Congress." In *Can the Government Govern?* ed. John Chubb and Paul Peterson. Washington, DC: Brookings Institution.
Shepsle, Kenneth, and Barry Weingast. 1995a. "Positive Theories of Congressional Institutions." In *Positive Theories of Congressional Institutions,* ed. Kenneth Shepsle and Barry Weingast. Ann Arbor: University of Michigan Press.
Shepsle, Kenneth, and Barry Weingast, eds. 1995b. *Positive Theories of Congressional Institutions.* Ann Arbor: University of Michigan Press.
Sinclair, Barbara. 1995. *Legislators, Leaders, and Lawmaking.* Baltimore: Johns Hopkins University Press.
Tsebelis, George. 1995. "Decisionmaking in Political Systems: Presidentialism, Parliamentarism, Multicameralism, and Multipartism." *British Journal of Political Science* 25:289–325.

Contributors

David T. Canon is Professor of Political Science, University of Wisconsin, Madison.

John M. Carey is Associate Professor of Political Science, Washington University, St. Louis.

Gary W. Cox is Professor of Political Science, University of California, San Diego.

Frantisek Formanek is the Executive Director of the Institute for Democracy and European Unity (IDEU), Prague.

John R. Hibbing is Professor of Political Science, University of Nebraska—Lincoln.

Ewa Karpowicz is a Senior Specialist in the Research Bureau, Chancellery of the Sejm, Warsaw.

Junko Kato is Associate Professor, Graduate School of Arts and Sciences, University of Tokyo.

Sadafumi Kawato is Professor of Political Science, School of Law, Tohoku University, Japan.

D. Roderick Kiewiet is Professor of Political Science, California Institute of Technology.

Michael Laver is Professor of Political Science and Director of the Policy Institute, Trinity College, Dublin, Ireland.

Gerhard Loewenberg is Professor of Political Science, the University of Iowa.

Gary F. Moncrief is Professor of Political Science, Boise State University.

Chan Wook Park is Professor of Political Science, Seoul National University.

Werner J. Patzelt is Professor of Comparative Government, Institut für Politikwissenschaft, Dresden University of Technology.

Bjørn Erik Rasch is Professor of Political Science, University of Oslo.

Fabiano Santos is Associate Professor of Political Science at the Rio de Janeiro Graduate Research Institute.

Kenneth A. Shepsle is Professor of Government, Harvard University.

Steven S. Smith is Professor of Political Science and Director of the Weidenbaum Center on the Economy, Government, and Public Policy at Washington University, St. Louis.

Peverill Squire is Professor of Political Science, the University of Iowa.

Rick K. Wilson is Professor of Political Science, Rice University.

Index

Abrams v. Johnson (1997), 155
Abreu, Regina Lucia Farias de, 124
actions, 304
activities, members everyday, 5
Adams, John, 299
additional-member system, 167
ad hoc committees, 296–98
administrative reform, 322–23
administrative state, 11
advertising, 5
agenda
　control of, 13, 122, 229, 263–64, 338–39
　formation, 276–81
　plenary, 252
agenda-setting process, 230, 235, 251–56, 277–81
　centralization of, 278
　importance of, 7, 8
　parliamentary, 269–87
Aldrich, John, 225–26, 236–41
Aliança Renovadora Nacional (ARENA), 120, 123–24, 126
allow free vote, 208
alternative roll-call ratings, 160
amateurs, congressional, 53
ambition
　and behavior, link between, 51
　constraints on, 57
　as motivation for candidacy, 51
　progressive, 54
　in state legislative studies, 57
　theory, 51
　types of, 51, 59–61
amendment activity, 4
amendment procedure, 271–76

amendments, regulating, 256–57
American exceptionalism, 387–89
Americans for Democratic Action (ADA), 161
annual inspection, 343–44
Ansolabehere, Stephen, 13, 231–32
anti-abortion legislation, 375
applicability of congressional research, 3
apply party whip, 208
apprenticeship norm, 33
arrangements, organizational, 36
Arruda, José Maria, 123
Articles of Confederation, 353
　effects of, 300–302
assumptions, Congressional, 8
Astiz, Carlos A., 128
at-large districts, 152–53
attendance in Congress, 302
Austria, 92
autonomy, 353–55, 367–68
　defined, 354
　legislative, 352–83

Balcerowicz, Leszek, 378
balloting method, 270
behavior
　congressional, 161
　inappropriate, 344
behavioral era, 224
Belgium, 91
Berkman, Michael, 60
Best, Heinrich, 80, 86–87, 101
bills introduced, number of, 337
Biographical Data on Brazilian Deputies, 138

401

Boggs, Lindy, 161
bossism, 334
Brady, David, 225, 232, 240
Britain. *See* United Kingdom
budget
  allocation, 316
  deficits, 316
  process, control of, 129
  reviews, 341–42
budgets, 377–78
Bundestag, 255, 394
bureaucratic dominance model, 316
bureaucratic influence, 320–23
bureaucratic unsticking services, 6
bureaucrats, 314–28
Burke, Thomas, 300
Bush v. Vera (1996), 155
business associations, 316

cabinet, Japanese, 323
campaign
  contributors, 232
  finance reform, 168–69, 191
  war chests, 68
candidacy, research needs, 55
candidate
  competition, 184–86
  emergence, 53–54, 66
  pool, 67
  recruitment, 66
candidate selection
  in German parties, 93
  process, 85
  Western European, 85
Candidate Selection in Comparative Perspective, 84–86
Canon, David T., 52–53
capital, permanent, location of, 306–8
career
  decision, congressional, 5
  linkages between Congress and state legislatures, 47
  paths, 83, 204
  sacrifices, 368
careerism, 15, 48, 54, 336, 367, 370–71

defined, 59
legislative, 56–61
in state legislatures, 47, 58
careers, legislative, 25–45, 31–38, 40, 61–62, 367
  desirability of, 28
  end of, 26
  future research on, 29–38
  internal, 26
  research on, 25–29
Carey, John M., 65–66, 389, 390
cartel agenda model, 255, 261
censored sample problem, 162
chambers, interaction between, 7
chaos theory, 162
check-kiting scandal, 63
Chû Senkyoku Sei, 178–98
Chun Doo Hwan, 330, 344
Citizen's Parliamentary Club, 359
city independent districts, 181
Clark, Abraham, 297
Clay, William, 159
closeness of elections, 184
coalition
  agreement, 207
  building a, 306
  government, 204
  politics of, 202
coalitions, 377–78
cohesiveness, 225, 240
collected data, 97–100
collective action problems, 292, 295–98, 353, 389
collective cabinet responsibility, 208–12, 220, 222
collective choice problem, 292, 298–302, 389
Commission for Verification of Powers, 120
committee
  membership, 4
  structures, 37
  system, 337, 353, 367, 372, 374, 388
committee assignments, 235
  retention of, 16–17

committee deference, 14
committee *desiderata,* 375–76
Committee of the Whole, 299
Committee on Political Education (COPE), 161
committees
  deference to, 10
  role of, 7
Communist Party (PZPR), 356
Communist rule, 355–58
compactness, 150, 155
comparative research, 3–22, 387–98
  conceptual obstacles to, 133–38
  difficulties of, 80–82, 121
  lack of, 3
  prospects for, 140
  recent, 82–87
compensation, member, 37
concentrated agenda power, 261–63
conditional party government, 227, 236–41
conflict between legislature and executive, 217–20
Congressional Black Caucus (CBC), 149, 159–63
congressional historical studies, 15–17
congressional institutions, 387
congressional parties, 224–44
Congress: The Electoral Connection, 224
connection, electoral, 8
constituency preferences, 232, 257
constitutional constraints, 342
constitutional design, 35
constitutional engineering, 4
constitution writing, 310
contiguity, 155
Continental Congress, 291, 293–311
continual assignments, 57
contribution limits, 192
Cooper, Joseph, 31, 225, 232, 240
Cooper-Brady thesis, 225–26, 236
coordination problems, 292, 293–95, 353, 389
COPE scores, 160
correlational analysis, 99

corruption, Japanese, 322
Costa Rica and term limits, 65
Cotta, Maurizio, 80, 86–87, 101
Council of Seniors, 369
country studies, 88–95
Cox, Gary, 13, 137–38, 203, 228, 229–30, 236–37, 241, 249, 251–52, 254–56, 257, 263, 389, 393
credit claiming, 5
cues, sources of, 161
cumulative voting, 163–66
  See also proportional representation
cycles in majority voting, 269
Czech
  Organizing Committee, 371, 373
  party system, 364–67
Czechoslovak Communist Party (KSC), 358
Czechoslovakia
  breakup of, 364
  transition period, 359
Czech Parliament
  1918–89, 357–58
  institutional structure, 367–74
Czech Republic, 352–83, 370–74

data
  analysis, 100–101
  collection, 100
  cube, 86
  macrolevel, 6
deadlock, 201
debate, regulating, 256–57
decision rules, 270
decisiveness, 353
defeat, electoral, 62
defection payoffs, 209, 212
deliberation, pre-Diet, 324
Dellums, Ron, 33
democratic political tradition, lack of, 332
democratization, 314
Denmark, 91
descriptive representation, 157–58
design, constitutional, 35

De Winter, Lieven, 262
Diet, 178, 180, 192, 254, 314–20
　role of, 323–24
differentiation, societal, 37
direct popular election, 330
disadvantaged groups, 87
discipline
　club, 374
　expulsion from party, 374
　intraparty, 206–12
　party, 203–6
　See also party discipline
disincentives for serving, 57
distributional hypothesis, 8
district magnitude, 178–98, 184–86
door-to-door canvassing, 182
Döring, Herbert, 262
Dreier, David, 33
dual democratic legitimacy, 166
Duane, James, 297, 300
Duma, 355

economic performance, 316
education in candidates, 85
effectiveness, 353–55
Efficient Secret, The (1987), 203
egalitarian assembly, 16
Eisgruber, Christopher, 155
election law reforms, 16
elections, 202
election system, reforms of, 325
electoral accountability, 11
electoral connection, 5, 227–29, 395
electoral institutions, alternative, 163–68
Electoral Justice system, 120
electoral laws, changes in, 16
electoral success. *See* reelection
electoral systems, 99, 149–77, 221
　impact of, 85
　restrictive, 364
electorate, 98
elements of an action situation, 303
eligibles, contenders and members, 97
elimination procedure. *See* amendment procedure

elite
　purging of, 309
　recruitment, 48
elite-centered research, 169
elites
　and loss of position, 87
　power base of, 314
empirical approach, 104
empirical material, 126–27, 131
endogeneity, 391–92
endogenous rules, 248–51
English as dominant political science language, 81
environmental protection, 316
equal competitors, 332
equilibrium
　approach, 7, 136, 393–94
　governments, 218
　policy choice, 248
Estado Nova, 119
European Consortium for Political Research, 81
European Parliament, 94–95
European recruitment research, 96–97
European Representative, The (1999), 86
evidence and inference, 13–15
exceptionalism, American, 65, 387–89
exchange theory, 388
executive accountability, 347
executive branch
　attraction of, 134
　initiatives, 338
Executive Departments, 297
executive, strong, absence of, 353
exogenous rules, 248
expectations of members, 13
expected utility maximization, 5
experience of members, 310
exportation of political ideas, 388
expulsion from party, 374

factions, 186
failure to carry the party, 207
federal assumption of state debt, 307–8
federal systems, German, 91–94

female candidates, bias against, 55
female legislators, 28–29
Fenno, Richard F., 61–62
Fifth Republic, 329–48
Figueiredo, Argelina, 131–32
final policy choices, 259–63
financial sacrifices, 368
Finland, 91
Fiorina, Morris, 5–6, 56, 387
First Federal Congress, 291–313, 304–11
  rules and procedures, 305–6
first-past-the-post, 221
First Republic, 330
fiscal plan, 307–8
Fleischer, David V., 124–27, 134, 138
floor agenda model, 252, 255
floor voting procedures, parliamentary, 269–87
Forjaz, Maria Cecília Spina, 124, 126
formalism, 332
Formanek, Frantisek, 389
Fourth Republic, 330
Fowler, Linda, 51
fragmentation, 360, 363
France, 89
Franco regime, changes after, 88–89
functionalism, structural, 6
fusion of powers, 377
future research, 96–104

Gadsden, Christopher, 299
gains from exchange hypothesis, 8
gains-in-trade, 296
Gallagher, Michael, 84–86, 90
game theory, 6, 303
gatekeepers, political role of, 49
Geddes, Barbara, 309
gender effects, legislative, 95–96
General Headquarters of the Allied Occupation Forces (GHQ), 183
generalization of research, 3
geographic representation, 165
Germany, 92–94
Gerry, Elbridge, 150
gerrymandering, 150

Gervais, John, 299
"get along by going along," 33
Gingrich, Newt, 33
goals, multiple, 228–29, 395
government, divided, 201–23
governments, equilibrium, 218
Grand Committees, 296–97
Great Britain. *See* United Kingdom
Greece, 89
gridlock, legislative, 222
Groseclose, Tim, 12, 230
Guinier, Lani, 164

Hall, Richard, 63
Hamilton, Alexander, 307–8
Hancock, John, 302
Havel, Vaclav, 364
Heckman, James J., 230
Herescu, Mariana, 124
Hibbing, John R., 62, 393
Hispanic Caucus, 161
historical studies
  of Congress, 15–17
  European, 99
Hosokawa, Morihiro, Prime Minister, 321
House of Commons, 255, 256
House of Peers, 181
Husak, Gustav, 364
hypotheses, 8, 319–20, 390

ideological distinction, lack of, 334
incentives, for serving, 57
income tax cut, 318
incumbency protection, 151
incumbent politicians and bureaucrats, competition between, 317
incumbents, position on, 85
independent decision making, 208
indiscipline, 216–17, 221
industrialization, late, 314
inference and evidence, 13–15
informational capacity, 353
informational rationale, 296
informational resources, 375

initiatives, 39
Institutional Analysis and Design (IAD), 292, 302–6
institutional arrangements, 269
institutional change, 31–38, 291
institutional design, 309
institutionalization, 31, 37–38, 129–32
  and career length, 32
  desirability of, 39–41
  legislature's stage of, 27
  potential for, 40
institutionalized parties, 34–35
institutions
  as equilibria, 393–94
  shaping of, 29–31
institutional structure
  Czech Parliament, 367–74
  Sejm, 367–74
interest groups, 54, 232, 314–28
  as gatekeepers, 49
  importance of, 317
  target, 341
interest representation, 315–20
  gap in, 87
interfactional balancing rule, 186
internal dynamics of the CBC, 161
interparty polarization, 240
interpellation, 346–47
interplay, three-way, 7
interpretive analysis, 100–101
interview data, lack of, 100
intraparty cohesiveness, 240
intraparty discipline, 206–12
intraparty politics, 202, 205
Ireland, 90
issues, modeling, 391–92
Italy, 88
Ito, Hirobumi, Prime Minister, 181–82

Japan, 178–98, 254, 256, 314–28
  bureaucracy, strength of, 314
  corruption, 322
  political parties, 315
  power of cabinet, 323
  scandals, 322

Jefferson, Thomas, 16, 308
Jeffersonian-Jacksonian coalition, 394
jiban-wari, 182
Jorritsma-Lebbink, Annemarie, 219
judicial activism, 155
Just Permanent Interests (1993), 159

Karpowicz, Ewa, 389
Kato, Junko, 390
Katz, Jonathan, 16
Kernell, Samuel, 16–17
Kiewiet, D. Roderick, 390
Kim Dae Jung, 330–31, 335, 336, 340
Kim Jong Pil, 336
Kim Young Sam, 330–31, 340
Klaus, Vaclav, 365, 371–72, 374, 378
kôenkai, 185–86, 190
Kok, Wim, 218
Korea
  National Assembly, 329–51
  political history, 330–32
  political parties, 333–36
Krehbiel, Keith, 8, 12, 30, 37, 226–27, 233–35
Kwangju Uprising, 344

language barriers, 81, 97
large district system, 178, 181–82
Largent, Steve, 33
Laurens, Henry, 299–300
Laver, Michael, 389, 391, 393, 396
law of available data, 161
lawmaking activity, 62, 337–41
Lawrence, Eric, 230, 241
LCCR scores, 160
leadership, 100, 102, 293
  ladders, 60
  organs, 367
Leadership Conference on Civil Rights (LCCR), 161–62
leaving the institution, 62–64
legislative agenda, control of, 122
legislative amendments, 338–39
legislative autonomy, 309, 352–83

legislative body, understanding of a certain, 26–27
legislative campaign committees, 54
legislative capacity, 58
legislative careers, 25–45, 31–38, 40
  desirability of, 28
  end of, 26
  future research on, 29–38
  internal, 26
  research on, 25–29
legislative controls, 342–47
legislative effectiveness, 292, 309
legislative gridlock, 222
legislative institutions, 15
legislative lassitude, 10–11
legislative leadership offices, 353, 354
legislative organization, 7–8
  design of, 4
  positive theories of, 391
legislative oversight, 342–47
legislative rules, 247–68
legislative staff, growth in, 57
legislative support, 332–33
legislative weaknesses, 337–41
legislators
  characteristics of, 27–28
  female, 28–29
  preferences of, 232
  recruitments of, 26
legislature and executive, relations between, 201–3
legislatures
  as modest policy actor, 347
  new, 4
  as representative of people, 27–28
  strong, 352
Leninist legacy, 309
level of cohesion, 161
Liberal Democratic Party (LDP), 178, 186–93, 314–20
  breakup of, 315
Limongi, Fernando, 131–32
lobbying, legislative, 341
local activists, role of, 85
locked-in processes, 122, 134, 137

logrolling, 7, 270, 303
Lovenduski, Joni, 83, 90, 92, 101
lower chambers dominant, 375
Lower House, 181
Luebbert, Gregory, 205

MacArthur, Douglas, 184
Madison, James, 307–8
Maduro, Lídice Aparecida Pontes, 123–24
Mahtesian, Charles, 39
majoritarianism, 166
  systems, 180
  voting rules, 353
majority party, importance of, 8
malapportionment, 189
Maltzman, Forrest, 230, 241
manipulation of voting, 269, 276
Marsh, Michael, 84–86
Marshall, 369
martial law, 330
mass franchise, 203
mass media, influence of, 98
mass membership party, 186
Masuyama, Mikitaka, 254–56
Matthews, Donald, 48–49, 52
Mayhew, David R., 5–6, 30, 224
McCain, Tom, 157
McCarty, Nolan, 231
McCubbins, Mathew, 13, 228, 229–30, 236–37, 241, 249, 251–52, 254–56, 257, 263
  study of, 3–22
McKelvey, Richard D., 277
mechanisms, alternative, 163–68
Meciar, Valdimir, 365
media, 129, 311
median agenda, 281
Medium-Sized District System (MDS), 178–98, 325
  adoption of, 182
  defects of, 191
  defined, 178
  origins of, 180
  prewar, 189

membership
  stability, 374
  turnover, 16–17, 32
Mendes, Candido, 127
menu of choices, 251–57
  See also agenda-setting process; amendments, regulating
methods for comparison, 101
Michaux, Mickey, 152
military intervention, 128
Miller v. Johnson (1995), 155
minority cabinets, 202
minority constituencies, representation of, 162
minority interests in legislatures, 149–77, 156–63
minority-majority districts, 149
  See also redistricting
minority party, treatment of, 224
mixed systems, 167–68
modeling, commitment to, 389
modeling issues, 391–92
models, 3, 389–91
Moncrief, Gary, 25
Moreira, Maria Terezinha V., 123
mores, Congressional, 33
Morris, Robert, 295, 307
motivation, legislator, 25–26
Movimento Democrático Brasileiro (MDB), 120, 123–24, 126
multipartisan politics, in São Paulo, 124
multiple goals, 395

National Assembly, 255, 332
National Political Aptitude Test, 13
national political culture, 85
Netherlands, 91, 217–20
neutrality, of bureaucrats, 321
newcomers, Congressional, 14
New Institutionalism, 6
new legislatures, design of, 15–17
Nokken, Timothy, 13
non-preferential list-PR systems, 221
nonstrategic voting, 271–73
normative approach, 104

Norris, Pippa, 83, 90, 92, 101
Norway, 90–91
number of candidates in a district, 185
Nunes, Edson, 128–29

object of study, change in, 14
observation, unit of, 9
observational equivalence, 4, 9–13, 392–93
O'Connor, Justice Sandra Day, 154–55
oil crisis, 316
one-party dominance, 314–28
one person one vote, 155
opportunity structures, 88, 99
order of voting, 275
organizational approach, 133
organizations, legislative, 7–8
  design of, 4
Ostrom, Elinor, 303

Parahyba, Maria Antonieta de A. G., 123–24
Park Chan Wook, 390
Park Chung Hee, 330
parliamentary clubs, 367, 371
  configuration of, 373–74
  See also parties
parliamentary democracy, 4
parliamentary government, 201
parliamentary responsiveness, 100
parliamentary system and strong legislatures, 354
participants, 303
parties, 354
  consequences for, 186–87
  development of, 310–11
  divided, 201–23
  explanation of, 233
  influence, 12
  legislative, 367
  organizations, 12
  as unitary actors, 396
  See also political parties
partisan advantage, 151
partisan agenda model, 252, 255, 261

partisan dynamics, 320–26
party
  affiliations, 13
  campaign restrictions, 185
  cohesiveness, 225
  consequences, 169
  control, 357
  defined, 180
  difficulties, 188
  discipline, 203–6, 335
  discipline, decline of, 323–24
  effects, 231, 232–41
  effects, significant, 12
  independence, 6
  indiscipline, 216–17
  influence, 229–32, 240, 258–59
  leadership, 226
  polarization, 225, 227, 240
  and preferences, 11–13
  preferences, 257
  strategies, 99
  strength, 225
  switchers, 231
  switching, 258–59
  systems, impact of, 85
  theory, 228
  unity, 203
party-as-unitary-actor, 202, 206
party-centered campaigns, 192
pattern of voting, 230
patterns of behavior of women legislators, 55
Patzelt, Werner, 4, 25
pension benefits, 63
People's Welfare Tax, 321
perquisites, 37
personality-dominated political party, 333
personal preferences, 257
personal support organizations, 185
Pita, Nilda Agueda Martinez, 123
pivotal-politics thesis, 226–27, 233–36
  limitations of, 233–35
plenary agenda, 252
plumping, 164
plurality elections, 166–67

point of order, 300
Poland, 352–83
  party system, 359–64
  transition period, 359
polarization, 225, 240
policy
  choices, stability in, 9–10
  consensus, within the party, 324
  expertise, 315–20
  instability, 247
  making, 375–78
  responsiveness, 158
  vacuum, 354
policy-oriented inspection, 343
political careers, women's, 95–96
political clout, internal, 160
political cover, 229
political culture, 332–33
political cultures, differences in, 81
political elites, 80, 89
political entrepreneurs, 98
political environment, 329
political finance, reforms of, 325
Political Fund Regulation Law, 186
political leadership, 100
political parties, 333–36
  creation of, 121
  development of, in Brazil, 119–21
  as gatekeepers, 49
  importance of, in recruitment, 50
  recruitment role, 54
political reform, 191–93
political socialization process, 123–27
political subdivisions, 155
politicians
  incumbent, 314–28
  and interest groups, 319
politics
  of coalition, 202
  of commonality, 153
  of difference, 153
  intraparty, 202, 205
politics-dominated inspection, 343
Polsby, Nelson W., 17, 27, 32–33, 37–39, 130–31

Polsby's institutionalization indicators, 133, 137
pool of candidates, 53
Poole, Keith T., 231
Portugal, 89
position taking, 5
positive theories, 224–44, 391
post-election purpose, 63
prefectural districts, 181
preferential list-PR systems, 221
presidential system, 166, 201, 331, 355
 and strong legislatures, 354
President of Congress, powers of, 294
Presidium, 369
prestige of political position, 128
Price, H. Douglas, 17
primaries, effect of, 86
primary data sources, 53
prior experience, decline in, 131
Privy Council, 181
problem fixing, 5
procedures, standard operating, 37
professionalization, 15, 37–38, 102–3
 defined, 59
 German, 93
 increase in, 58
 legislative, 56–61
 measuring, 59
 state legislative, 67
 in state legislatures, 47
 See also careerism
professional staff, 58
progressive ambition, 48, 54
Project Vote Smart, 232
property right claim, 57
proportional list-PR systems, 221
proportional representation, 28–29, 166–67, 180, 325
proportional representation districts, 178
proportionality of electoral results, 187–89
proposal powers of committees, 389
provisory measures, 130
pure majority rule legislative institution, 300
pure-proportionality, 187–89
"quality" of candidate, 52
questionnaire data, lack of, 100

races, types of, 50
racial divides, 170
racial redistricting, 163
 consequences of, 156
 partisan implications of, 155–56
racial representation, measuring, 159–63
Ragin, Charles C., 101
Ramsay, David, 302
Randolph, Peyton, 294
Rasch, Bjørn Eric, 389, 393
rational actor approach, 50–53
rational choice approach, 4, 5–9, 30, 129–32, 133, 180
rational choice theory, 388
rationality, 390
Rayburn, Sam, 33
recall votes, 39
reconsolidation, 363
recruitment, 47–56, 49–50
 influence of gender on, 96
 patterns, 50
 planned, 127–29
 research in Europe, 80
 research needs, 55
 role of the party, 54
recruitment and retention
 of legislators in Brazil, 119–45
 in U.S. legislatures, 46–79
 in Western European parliaments, 80–118
redemocratization, 129
redistricting, 150–52
 principles of, 150
 See also gerrymandering; racial redistricting
reelection, 5, 8, 30, 371, 374
referenda, 39
reform, political, 191–93
reforms, recent, 168–69
regime changes, frequent, 330
regionalism, 334

reneging, by coalition partner, 209
representation, 47, 303
  geographical, 305
  by population, 304
  proportional, 28–29
  struggle over, 304–5
representational role of legislatures, 36
representational theory, 102
República Velha, 119
reputation of members, role of, 6
reputational hits, 212
research
  comparative legislation, 17–18
  Congressional, 4
  on European recruitment and retention, 82–96
  further, 192
  future directions of, 168
  literature on recruitment and retention, 122
  methods, 100–101
  questions, 97–100
  questions in European comparative recruitment, 83
  recent, 229–30, 241
  sources, 138–40
resources, legislative, 6, 37
responsibility
  collective cabinet, 208–12
  delegation of, 235
responsiveness, 102, 160
restitution, 311
restrictions, 7
restrictive rule model, 260–61
restructuring, committee, 372–73
retention of legislators, 56–61
retention pattern, 125
retirement from public office, 63
reunification, Eastern German recruitment after, 94
Rhee, Syngman, 330
Roberts, Geoffrey, 92–93
Rodino, Peter, 161
Roh Tae Woo, 330
Rohde, David, 225–26, 236–41, 388

roll call votes, 4
  and party, 11
  uniformity of, 11
  use of, 161
Rosenthal, Alan, 57, 58–59
Rosenthal, Howard, 231
Rule, Wilma, 167
rules
  constitutional, 249
  endogenous, 248–51
  exogenous, 248
  of order, 300
  of procedure, 247–68
rules and procedures of the First Federal Congress, 305–6
runoff elections, 152
Russia, 355

Sala, Brian, 16
salary, 58
  cuts, 39
  legislatures, 28–29
sanctions, 211, 216
  reversing, 216
Santos, André Marenco dos, 131
scandals
  Japanese, 322
  Korean, 345–46
scare-off tactics, 68
Schlesinger, Joseph A., 28, 51
seat bonus, 187–89
Second Republic, 330
Sejm, 274, 355, 368–70
  history of, 356–57
  institutional structure, 367–74
selectorate, 98
selectors' preferences, 85
self-reporting, problems of, 138
Seligman, Lester, 50
semi-proportional representation, 164
seniority, 17, 57
seniority principle, 131, 132
  difficulty in establishing, 122
seniority rules, 33, 60, 186
"Sequential" choice theory, 7

sequential elimination process, 273
session length, 37, 58
Shaw v. Reno (1993), 154–55
Shepsle, Kenneth A., 6–7, 30, 251–52
"shirking" of duties in the last term, 64
side payments, 257–58, 260
sincere voting, 271–73
Sinclair, Barbara, 12–13, 226, 228, 229
single-country approach, 82
single-member districts, 152–53, 178, 325
single nontransferable vote (SNTV), 179–93, 181–82, 325
  and Japanese electoral systems, 180
  and parties, 189–91
single transferable vote, 167, 221
Sixth Republic, 329–48
skill, in voting processes, 269
slating groups, 166, 169
Slovak Federal Republic, 365
Small Constitution, 360, 362
small district system, 178, 182
small Parliament, 358
Smith, Robert C., 157
Smith, Steven S., 230, 241, 390, 391, 393
snap vote, 340
Snyder, James M., 12, 13, 230, 231–32
social background variables, 83
  of parliamentarians, 87
social choice, 6, 353
social dilemmas, 293–302
socioeconomic status, in candidates, 85
sociological approach, 48–49
sociological systems theory, 6
sociopolitical systems, 27–29
Solidarity, 359–60, 378
Solidarity alliance, 370
sources of legitimacy, 201
Spain, 88–89
spatial modeling, 6
special consideration for minorities, 153–55
special interest groups, 39–40

special investigations, 344–46
specialization
  gains from, 8
  of members, 130, 134
  of Sejm committees, 369
sponsorship
  of candidates, 98
  of legislation, 162
Squire, Peverill, 59–60, 151
stability
  of minority governments, 205
  in policy choices, 9–10
staff
  number of, 37
  reductions, 39
  resources, 369–70
staggered terms, 153
standing committees, 129, 295, 297, 369
  evolution of, 16
state
  dominance, 295
  legislative studies, 57–59
  research, 54–55
state delegations, breakdown of, 305
statistical analysis, European, 101
status quo points, 253
status quo, voted on last, 279
Stewart, Charles, 13, 231–32
strategic elites, 395–96
strategic voting, 270, 271–73, 277
strategy in voting processes, 269
strict quorum rule, 306
structural functionalism, 6
structure induced equilibrium (SIE), 298
stylized facts, 13–14
subgovernments, ascendancy of, 11
subordination of legislature to executive, 341
substantive representation, 158–59
successive procedure, 271–76
suffrage
  requirements, 181
  universal manhood, 182–83
supermajority rules, 235, 301–2

Swain, Carol, 160–61
Sweden, 90
Switzerland, 92
system
  non-preferential list-PR, 221
  preferential list-PR, 221
  proportional list-PR, 221
  single nontransferable vote, 221
systems theory, 6, 388
system-theory approach, 5

Tallon, Robin, 161
tax policy, 318
temporal rigidity, 166
term limits, 39, 64–66, 135, 168–69
  effects of, 67
  movement, 40
  movement, history of, 64
  phenomenon, 47
theoretical frameworks, 102–3
theory
  exchange, 388
  game, 6
  rational choice, 388
  social choice, 6
  systems, 388
theory-driven requirements, 390
Third Republic, 330
three-way interplay, 7
time, legislative lack of, 249–51
total model, 83
traditional districting practices, 154–55
transitional governance in the United States, 291–313
transition governments, 308–11
transition period
  in Czechoslovakia, 359
  in Poland, 359
triad elite model, 316
trust of interest groups, 325
turnout, 163
turnover, 125
  decline in, 58
  effects of, 33
  membership, 32

turnover rates
  decline of, 56
  in U.S. legislatures, 56

unified actor, 206
unitary actor, 206
United Kingdom, 89–90
unit of observation, 9
unit rule, 300–302, 304, 306
units of analysis, 46
universal manhood suffrage, 182–83
urgent review process, 130
utility maximization, expected, 5

Valentine, Tim, 161
value-added tax, 318
Van Houweling, Robert, 63
Vargas, Getúlio, 119, 120
varguista populism, 120
velvet revolution, 364
vest pocket votes, 259
veto power
  of committees, 389
  use of, 340
Vianna, Maria Lúcia Teixeira Werneck, 123–24
vote dilution, 155
vote trading, 270
voting behavior, 241, 257–59
voting order, 275, 276, 278
voting procedures, 270

Wahlke, John, 49
Walesa, Lech, 360, 362
Weingast, Barry, 6, 30, 387
welfare provision, 316
Welsh, Helga A., 309–11
Weßels, Bernhard, 92–93
whip model, 259–60
whipping, 212–17
Williams, Hugh, 297
Wilson, James, 307
Wilson, Rick K., 231, 353–55, 389, 390, 393

women
    electoral success of, 92
    in European Parliament, 95
    in state legislatures, 55–56
women's benefits from proportional
    representation, 167
Women's Caucus, 161
working conditions, 58
workload of legislators, 295

Wythe, George, 299

Yamagata, Aritomo, Prime Minister,
    181–82
Yeltsin, Boris, 355

Zeman, Milos, 365, 377
zig zag career, 134–37